D1520562

Making North Carolina Literate

Making North Carolina Literate

The University of North Carolina at Greensboro, from Normal School to Metropolitan University

Allen W. Trelease

Carolina Academic Press
Durham, North Carolina

ISBN 0-89089-523-6
LCCN 2003107423

CAROLINA ACADEMIC PRESS
700 Kent Street
Durham, NC 27701
Phone (919) 489-7486
Fax (919) 493-5668
www.cap-press.com

Printed in the United States of America

To the Shade of
Charles Duncan McIver

Contents

Part V
Woman's College, 1950–1963

Part VI
University of North Carolina at Greensboro, 1963–1979

Part VII
University of North Carolina at Greensboro, 1979–1994

Maps and Illustrations

State Normal and Industrial School–1893

Buildings and Construction Dates

1. Main Building, 1892
2. Brick Dormitory, 1892
3. Guilford Hall, 1892
4. Dr. McIver's Home
5. Heating Plant/Laundry
6. Barn

Main Building

North Carolina College for Women–1928

Major Additions and Construction Dates

1. Spencer Hall, 1904
2. Forney Building, 1905
3. McIver Building, 1908
4. Quadrangle Dorms, 1919 to 1923
5. Curry Building, 1926
6. Aycock Auditorium, 1927

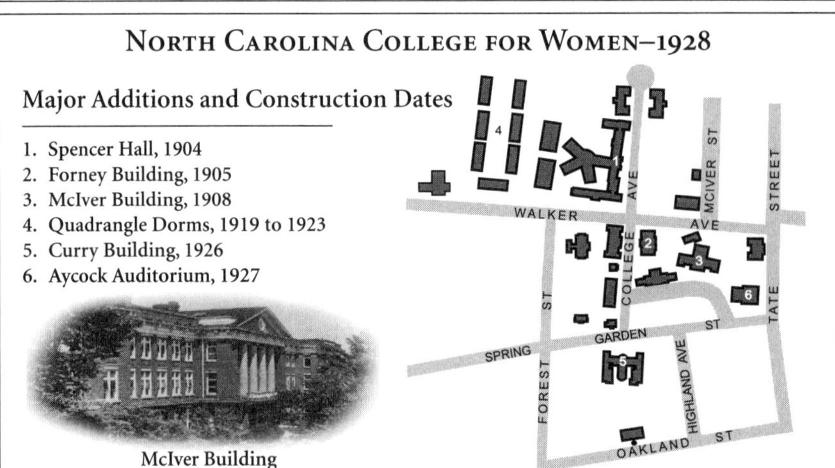

McIver Building

Woman's College of the Univ. of North Carolina–1954

Major Additions and Construction Dates

1. Completed Dining Hall, 1939
2. Petty Science Building, 1940
3. Jackson Library, 1950
4. Elliott Hall, 1953
5. Gove Health Center, 1954
6. Coleman Gym, 1952

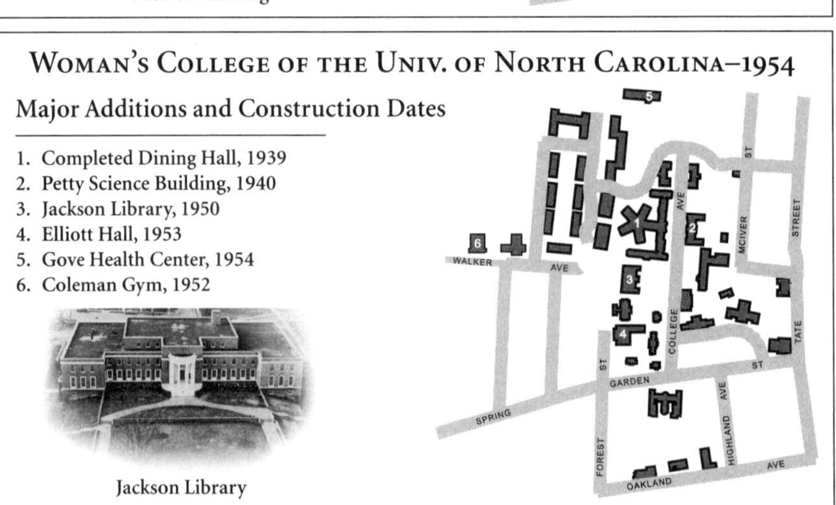

Jackson Library

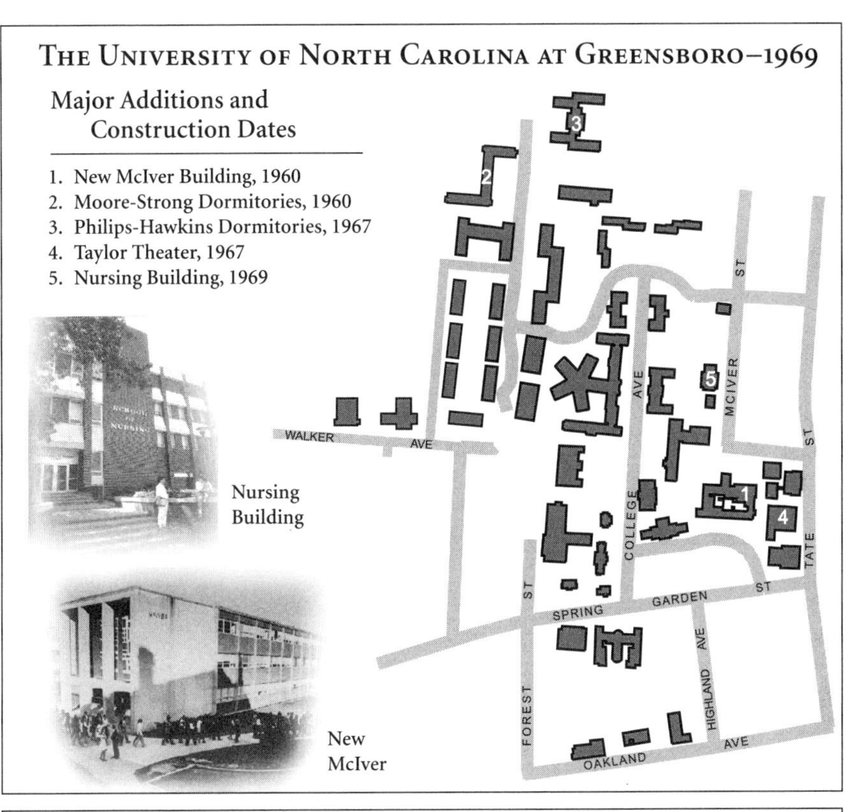

Nursing Building

New McIver

The University of North Carolina at Greensboro–1994

Major Additions and Construction Dates

1. McNutt Learning Resources Center, 1970
2. Life Sciences Building, 1971 & 1978
3. Jackson Library Tower, 1974
4. Mossman Building, 1975
5. Business and Economics Building, 1979
6. Ferguson Building, 1983
7. Weatherspoon Art Gallery, 1989

Jackson Library Tower

Cartography and Design by Jason Teaster

Preface

Founded in 1892 as North Carolina's first state college for women, the State Normal and Industrial School quickly transcended its name and, arguably, its original mission. From the beginning, founder and first President Charles Duncan McIver and his colleagues strove to attain the status of a full-fledged college centering on the liberal arts. In 1897 it became a College in name and by 1919 in reality, taking the new title North Carolina College for Women (NCCW). Two years after that, with accreditation, it established its own college of arts and sciences and the beginnings of a graduate program. Under McIver's successor Julius I. Foust, it set out to become the women's university of North Carolina, as nearly parallel as possible to the male university at Chapel Hill.

That dream evaporated in 1931 when as a Depression measure the legislature united the Greensboro and Chapel Hill campuses under a common board of trustees along with the state agricultural and mechanical college at Raleigh. Most graduate programs were concentrated at the Chapel Hill campus. The institution now became the Woman's College of the University of North Carolina (or familiarly, WC). So it remained until 1963, when all three campuses became fully coeducational. Thereafter it would be the University of North Carolina at Greensboro (UNCG). Starting with three campuses in the '30s, the University of North Carolina (UNC) system has come since 1972 to embrace sixteen campuses.

As one of the original three, UNCG nourished early hopes of achieving parity with Chapel Hill and Raleigh. But these hopes quickly faded as UNCG continued to occupy an uneasy third place in the hierarchy, with campuses at Charlotte and elsewhere nipping at its heels. The University of North Carolina at Chapel Hill and North Carolina State University in Raleigh are officially designated research universities; UNCG is a doctoral university—a research university in waiting. Their funding is determined accordingly.

UNCG occupies another, unofficial category: along with NC State and UNC-Charlotte it is a metropolitan university. That designation is relatively new yet widely recognized around the country; there is in fact a national organization to which UNCG belongs. Many of its members aspired to be research universities, and traditionalists in search of that standing have sometimes found it demeaning. Yet metropolitan universities and their mission are both honorable and essential. They have been called the land-grant universities of the twenty-first century, occupying the second line of modern higher education, after the community colleges. They commonly accept students from around the world and offer graduate and undergraduate programs of national if not international reputation. They are defined, however, by their urban locale and the fact that they draw most of their students from the surrounding region. They provide specialized programs of regional interest but also highly competitive programs in the professions as well as the arts and sciences. That is the niche that UNCG came to occupy after 1963.[1]

* * *

This book arose, as so many university histories do, from the centennial observance of 1991 and 1992. The author assembled at that time a pictorial history of the university entitled *Changing Assignments*. Although that title has enough felicity that I have wished I could use it again, the term is not fully accurate. Despite the institution's many name changes, it has experienced only two real changes of mission. The first of these, from normal school to liberal arts college for women, represented a mission creep that took almost thirty years to accomplish. The second change, from woman's college to coeducational university in the early '60s, was far more abrupt.

It had not occurred to me before taking up this assignment that the institution's history fell logically into periods of about fifteen years. They form the primary divisions of this book. They reflect the two mission changes, to be sure, but for the most part they follow changes of administration. This produces a top-down organization that is not altogether fashionable in an era of bottom-up social history. But top-down governance is the law in the UNC system. Power proceeds from the legislature and governor to the UNC trustees (or board of governors since 1972) to the president and general administration in Chapel Hill to the trustees, chancellors, and other administrators on each campus. The structure was analogous to this on each campus prior to the consolidations that began in the '30s. Chancellors are not absolute on their campuses but they have great power to set policy and priorities. They determine in large measure who is hired or fired and how the available moneys are spent. Academic and student affairs are at a farther remove, but even they reflect the imprint of the chancellor in office. Within each division of the book, then, separate chapters deal with administration and the campus or physical plant, with academic affairs, and with student and alumni affairs.

* * *

One of the recurrent themes in the book is that of underfunding; it appeared most seriously in physical maintenance—of buildings, grounds, and equipment. Every college or university feels budgetary pain, and the degree is very difficult to measure objectively from one to another; different missions or curricula vary widely in cost. North Carolina outdid itself in the late nineteenth and early twentieth centuries, establishing more institutions of higher education—segregated for whites, blacks, and Indians—than it could readily support. Only gradually have a growing population and the increasing proportion of people who attend college raised enrollments sufficiently to justify all these institutions. All of them were underfunded in some measure. At the Normal/NCCW/WC/UNCG, a feeling of financial neglect was ingrained from the earliest days and shaped a recurrent perception of itself as a "redheaded stepchild." That term dated from Woman's College days, but the identity problem it reflected was magnified after 1963 as the new university failed to attain the greater funding and status that its supporters felt it deserved. In the 1980s UNCG launched a systematic study of other institutions around the country having similar missions, and so clearly documented its case that the legislature provided compensatory funding. That helped if it did not end the problem.

Of the other themes or topics dealt with in these pages—among them changing patterns of administration, faculty organization and status, curriculum, student identity and activity, and alumni relations—nearly all are variants of higher education patterns across the United States (and the South) since the 1890s.

With only one serious exception—in the 1950s—the institution was led by a succession of able and dedicated presidents or chancellors—none of whom escaped controversy. Most served longer than a decade; Julius I. Foust presided for twenty-eight years and would have welcomed a twenty-ninth.

* * *

The school was built in 1892 on a cornfield at the outskirts of Greensboro, a town of little over 3,000 people. Both entities grew—the school/college/university to 12,000 and the city to 200,000 by the early 1990s. The campus soon found itself surrounded and landlocked. Although the city of Greensboro remained supportive over the years, neighborhood relations grew testy in the 1960s as enrollments mushroomed and the new university pushed for additional space. It was needed as much for parking lots as for buildings because the great majority of new students were commuters whose cars filled the streets and blocked driveways.

* * *

Woman's College admitted its first black students in 1956. As elsewhere in the desegregating South, the transition caused greater palpitations among administrators and the surrounding community than among the faculty and students involved. Black students were at first segregated in the dormitories but that soon disappeared by popular demand. They had other grievances and were not shy in voicing them; some were vocal participants in the protest movements of the '60s and early '70s.

Students of both races took part. They picketed neighboring businesses that did not admit black students as customers; they participated in downtown sit-ins and protest marches; and they staged campus rallies in behalf of black cafeteria workers and the black students' organization. They demonstrated against the Vietnam war. Most of this activity created anxiety in high places but none of it was violent owing to generally good judgment on the part of student leaders and administrators alike.

In the Normal/NCCW/WC years, the college enjoyed a healthy and quite typical women's student culture. Some of that disappeared with increasing enrollment and most of it succumbed to the demolition derby that came with coeducation and student protest in the '60s and early '70s. Even the early student generations won incremental progress in pushing back parietal regulations on and off campus, until by the 1980s hardly any were left.

University status after 1963 brought not only male students but the much larger and more consequential influx of commuter students. Among these were adults, many of whom could attend class only at night. While they were welcomed, campus administrators of the 1980s and '90s believed it essential to attract more young males and to recapitulate so far as possible the traditional undergraduate environment seen at, say, Chapel Hill. To that end they introduced fraternities and sororities and—over no little faculty and alumni opposition—athletic scholarships and membership in the NCAA's Division I. These policies were executed in exemplary fashion, yet they failed to produce the desired results; the campus remained two-thirds female and more than two-thirds commuter.

Woman's College alumnae, like those at many another institution, developed a fierce loyalty to their Alma Mater. They did not joyfully embrace coeducation and university status, but for the most part their loyalty survived the transition. There had always been an ambivalence in the relationship between the alumni association and the college or university. Most at issue were the allocation of alumni financial contributions, control of alumni publications and the campus Alumni House, and the dual allegiance of the woman who served at once as campus alumni director and the association's executive secretary. These issues were forced to a crisis in the late '80s, resulting in the temporary alienation of many alumni and the creation of a rather more self-sufficient Alumni Association.

* * *

Over a century the curriculum evolved in keeping with the nation and region. Well before the college achieved university status, it developed nationally recognized programs in education, home economics, music, theater, physical education for women, and some of the liberal arts. The English department, for instance, offered a writing program of some renown and attracted a faculty equally renowned. All these survived the university revolution of the '60s. And thereafter as academic fields multiplied and the students grew more diverse, the curriculum gained equally in complexity. Doctoral programs emerged in English, psychology, and a variety of professional fields ranging from music to what used to be called home economics and physical education.

* * *

For decades after 1892, faculty and students at the Normal/NCCW/WC interacted socially as well as academically. They each formed communities of their own but also a larger one together. This gradually broke down by the 1960s as enrollments grew, as students rebelled against the old tradition of *in loco parentis*, and as faculty members were pushed more and more toward research and publication as a condition of appointment, promotion, tenure, and salary. In an increasingly competitive national environment, that pressure had its rationale: no matter how sparkling one's classroom performance, committee service, or out-of-class student relations, they brought little outside recognition. Research and publication, on the other hand, did command attention, enhancing the reputation of both the individual and the university. By this calculus good researchers came to be more valuable than good teachers and they were rewarded accordingly—especially as good scholarship was said to bespeak an active mind that produced good teaching as well. In fact, there was little real evidence that classroom teaching suffered in this process. Younger faculty members, fresh from graduate school, were already imbued with the new ethic and found it confirmed on their arrival. Older members, however, were less mobile, had been hired with different expectations, and faced greater difficulty adapting to the new order; their professional status and income suffered accordingly.

The old faculty community also faded. As one's allegiance passed imperceptibly from the institution to one's own discipline, and from campus teaching and service to research, people reapportioned their time and energies. It became harder to staff committees and to assemble a respectable quorum in faculty meetings. Even the campus chapter of the American Association of University Professors expired in the 1990s, a victim of the new professional imperative.

A further reason for community breakdown lay in a growing recourse to temporary and part-time teachers. Some of these were highly experienced professionals who came to campus to teach specialized courses in their fields as a sideline, but the majority were relatively young people—mostly women—with master's degrees or even Ph.D.s who could not find full-time, tenure-track teaching jobs. Some were tied to the Greensboro area by marriage or other obligations. Most of them taught freshman and sophomore classes where they may well have interacted better and taught more effectively than their tenured elders. But like their counterparts around the country, they suffered low pay and second-class status.

* * *

In sum, the Normal/NCCW/WC/UNCG has become a different place. This is attributable partly to its own name and mission changes, to be sure, but also to the sea changes that American higher education has experienced since 1892.

Acknowledgments

Although the university approached me to undertake this work at the time of the 1992 centennial, it has played no part in the execution beyond answering my questions and affording me full access to the records not still in use. There has been no suggestion of censorship or any pressure beyond gently worded queries as to my progress over the years. I happily acknowledge the university's gift of a semester's research leave and its support of publication costs.

The vast majority of my research took place in the UNCG archives, located in the special collections department of Jackson Library. They are also the source of all photographs used in the book. The archives are a priceless resource, embracing among other things the manuscript records of every president or chancellor since the 1890s; the Alumni Association records; complete files of the *Alumni News* and the student newspaper, the *Carolinian*; and transcripts of the nearly 200 Centennial Oral History interviews. Records of some subordinate offices are incomplete but those of the president or chancellor provide by far the most valuable information concerning the institution as a whole. So far as institutional guidance is concerned, little of consequence transpired without crossing the president or chancellor's desk. The only records truly conspicuous by their absence are President Foust's papers for the year 1930 and the last years' records of the chancellor's advisory committee in the 1950s. We no longer have any clue as to what happened to the former; we suspect that the latter occupy some uncharted corner of the Greensboro landfill.

Given the archives' importance, my greatest debt is of course to those associated with them during the past decade: Emilie Mills and her successor William Finley as heads of the special collections department, and above all chief archivist Betty Carter and her staff at different times: Ella Ross, Janis Holder, Carolyn Shankle, Linda Jacobson, and Hermann Trojanowski. I am also obligated to my graduate research assistants Kelly Harden and Cheryl Junk, and to Jason Teaster who prepared the campus maps.

A substantial number of people have read parts of the manuscript or provided information on request, saving me from gaffes great and small. They include Richard Bardolph, Robert M. Calhoon, Betty Carter, Joseph E. Johnson,

William A. Link, Ernest A. Lumsden, Roland Nelson, Donald J. Reichard, Ann P. Saab, Terry G. Seaks, David H. Shelton, Kendon Smith, James H. Thompson, and H. Herbert Wells.

Many university historians refrain from treating recent events, partly to avoid the controversy that is certain to ensue. Casting aside such wholesome discretion, I made the decision to continue to the most recent stopping point available to me consistent with my overall organization—the resignation of Chancellor William Moran in 1994. I think this decision is readily defensible, given the university's growth and maturation during his fifteen years at the helm. But I have necessarily treated a host of subjects that generate controversy, personal and substantive, to this day. The line between history and journalism can be thin. A few of my informants preferred an anonymity that I gladly promised in return for information that was otherwise unobtainable. I hope they will recognize here my gratitude for that help.

Allen W. Trelease
Greensboro, N.C.
May, 2003

Part I
The Normal, 1891–1906

Chapter 1

Birth

The Civil War left the South poor and backward. Although North Carolina suffered little physical damage, it was no exception. In 1880, when white illiteracy ran at about 9 percent nationally, it was nearly a third in North Carolina, making it the most illiterate state in the Union.[1] The following decade brought little change. In 1890 only 57 percent of the state's school-age children attended school, compared with a national average of 69 percent. Its per pupil education expenditure was $3.36 per year, lowest in the nation save for South Carolina; the national figure was $17.62. The average school term was 60.3 days, lowest in the country, compared with 135.7 days nationally. Within this short term, North Carolina teachers averaged less than $24 per month in pay, about half the national average.[2]

Two-thirds of the state's teachers were men, usually young. They necessarily held other jobs and often saw teaching as a way station to another, more stable career. Few had any training beyond the public schools in which they taught. "It is the simple truth," remarked the state superintendent of public instruction in 1890, that many of the state's teachers were persons "whose geography does not extend much further than their localities and horizons; whose science is the multiplication table and simple arithmetic; and whose language, history and belles lettres are about comprised in Webster's Spelling-book." Teaching was a part-time trade and its practitioners were in effect political appointees, subject to the whims of local school boards.[3]

But reform was in the air. Everywhere the most potent agent for change was a growing market economy generated by railroads and centered in the towns. Educational reform, initially in the form of graded schools, reflected this modernization and was meant to hasten it. Wilmington and Greensboro had already established the state's first graded schools in 1868 and 1870. The new urban systems emphasized professionalism and better-trained teachers. "Graded school fever," says James Leloudis, the leading historian of this process, "consumed townsfolk throughout the new North Carolina."[4]

The public school movement was the first manifestation in North Carolina of Progressivism, the great national reform impulse. It assumed in the 1880s the dimensions of a holy crusade. Like other crusades, it was single-minded: true believers saw education as the foundation of human progress.[5] The movement lasted a full generation. It quickly embraced not only the establishment of graded schools but the training of those who would teach in them. The state Normal and Industrial School for women at Greensboro (chartered in 1891) was at once one of the crusade's most conspicuous achievements and one of its most potent weapons.

Spearheading the reforms were men like Charles Duncan McIver, Edwin Alderman, James Y. Joyner, and M.C.S. Noble, who met as students at the University of North Carolina in Chapel Hill. That institution became in effect a nursery of educational reform about 1880. All these men were too young to remember the Old South or much of the Civil War that ended it but they were all too aware of the shambles left behind. Repelled by the South's backwardness, these undergraduate idealists were fired by zeal to bring it into the modern world. Their conversion to the new education gospel came at the summer normal school first offered by the university in 1877. On graduation most of these men became school teachers and (very quickly) administrators. All benefited by the dynamic growth of this new profession, as well as the inestimable advantage of their gender.[6]

McIver, generally acknowledged as first among these equals, was born in 1860 near what is now Sanford. His was a typical farm upbringing in a family once prosperous but later sharing the general poverty. At college he showed the energy, leadership, humor, and formidable story-telling abilities that marked his later career. Graduating in 1881, he went first to Durham to organize a public school system, then to Winston in 1884 as school principal. After marriage to fellow-teacher Lula Martin in 1885, they went to Raleigh as teachers at Peace Institute for girls.

Alderman, graduating from UNC in 1882, soon became superintendent of schools in Goldsboro; Joyner succeeded him there in 1889. (In fact Goldsboro, with one of the first graded school systems, became something of a nursery too, of state public school administrators and future Normal professors.) Within half a dozen years of their graduation McIver and Alderman in particular were acknowledged leaders of public education in North Carolina.

It was McIver in 1886 who first broached the idea of creating a state teachers' college. This came in conversation with Alderman as they attended the North Carolina Teachers' Assembly in Black Mountain, near Asheville. Together they drew up a memorial calling for such an institution, to be coeducational. Although the Teachers' Assembly enthusiastically recommended the proposal, it failed to win over the next two legislatures in 1887 and 1889. But the latter session did agree to fund state Superintendent Sidney M. Finger's backup request for two educators to offer week-long teachers' institutes in each county. This would offer some professional training to a great many teachers, but at least as important, the two educators, properly chosen, might light a groundfire to influence the next legislature in favor of a teachers' college.

McIver and Aldermen were the chosen instruments. Meeting at the Chapel Hill commencement reunion that spring, they stayed up all night laying plans. For the next three years they traveled all over the state, at considerable cost to their young families and themselves. Joined sometimes by Joyner and others, they addressed thousands of the state's teachers and further thousands of curious citizens. Each institute ended with a plug for the proposed normal school. As Raleigh editor Josephus Daniels, a friend and supporter, put it, McIver and Alderman were traveling evangelists preaching the gospel of education; any specific pedagogical benefits from the institutes were almost incidental.

The two men usually traveled and worked independently, but when they took the stump together the contrast was striking. There was always something of the burly country boy about McIver. At first terrified to speak in public, he quickly identified with rural audiences, who appreciated his Lincolnian fund of rustic humor and anecdotes. (In later years there would sometimes be trouble getting him to stop.) By contrast, the handsome, urbane Alderman, from Wilmington, sporting handlebar moustaches, impressed audiences with his erudition but sometimes talked over their heads.

Their crusade converted multitudes. The Farmers' Alliance and a number of women's groups added their own calls for a normal and vocational institution for women. J.L.M. Curry, the well-known educational reformer and secretary of the Peabody Educational Fund, appeared before the legislature in 1891 to plead for a normal college. Governor Daniel G. Fowle echoed the demand. "It is almost getting fashionable now to be for public education," McIver quipped privately.[7]

Although the memorial asked for a coeducational institution, the proponents put special emphasis on its availability to women. Nationally, women comprised a larger and larger proportion of the teaching force, but in North Carolina they confronted a severe obstacle.[8] There was no state institution of higher education for white women, and the private denominational colleges were too expensive for many. (The state's primitive institutions for blacks and Indians were coeducational, but not Chapel Hill or the new Agricultural and Mechanical College for whites in Raleigh.) In 1893 McIver would congratulate the Normal's first graduates on their having attended the only state institution open to them unless they had become criminal, insane, or otherwise afflicted.[9]

McIver in particular was directed to women's education by the experiences of his wife and younger sister, who had had only limited opportunities.[10] (His sister Elizabeth, in fact, would attend the Normal as a student and would spend many years thereafter as a faculty member.) So he became a champion not only of public schools and teacher education, but particularly of higher education for women. He pursued this theme throughout his life. "Educate a man," he would declare, with variations, "and you educate an individual; educate a woman and you educate a family."[11] McIver almost certainly shared the dominant view that woman's primary role was in the home as wife and mother, but he strove mightily to convince the public that she deserved other options—before, after, or without marriage. He himself was married to an intelligent, independent woman who had with the greatest reluctance put aside for family a professional life of her own in either medicine or the law.[12]

When the so-called "farmers' legislature" (dominated by the Farmers' Alliance) assembled early in 1891, McIver, Alderman, and Superintendent Finger were back with a new normal school bill. Having failed narrowly in 1889, it now sailed through easily.[13] The only substantive difference was that the earlier measure had provided for coeducation and the present one was for women alone. Based on the reported legislative debate and other coverage in the Raleigh *News & Observer* during the session, the change received little public attention. Finger publicly expressed a hope in June that the Normal would someday become coeducational but neither he nor anyone else pressed the matter seriously. Certainly not McIver. Several years later he attacked a proposal for undergraduate coeducation at the university and the A&M college because it threatened to undercut the Normal.[14] In fact, McIver was much less interested in coeducation than he was in women's education and preserving the Normal, once created.

In the South generally, women's education was an easier sell than coeducation. Unlike the West and Midwest, where virtually all state colleges and universities were coeducational, it was exceptional in the South. Few if any of North Carolina's private colleges for whites were coeducational. Some people thought that the Normal bill's coeducational feature was responsible for its defeat in 1889, and the Teachers' Alliance abandoned coeducation in its later appeals.[15] Since the teachers' college campaign was part of a bigger crusade for universal education; since universal education was dependent on educating women; and since the most likely means of educating women was apparently jeopardized by coeducation, coeducation was jettisoned.[16]

The charter act of February 18, 1891 (An Act to Establish a Normal and Industrial School for White Girls) put the institution under a nine-man board of directors representing each of the state's congressional districts. Members would be chosen initially by the legislature and subsequently by the state board of education. The popularly elected superintendent of public instruction would serve ex officio as chairman. This organization lasted with little change until the 1930s.

Students, the charter continued, were to be drawn so far as feasible from every county proportionate to its white population. Tuition was free to those who promised to teach, and graduates would automatically receive teaching certificates. However, as the school's name implied, its stated purpose extended beyond teacher training, to instructing girls in "drawing, telegraphy, type-writing, stenography and such other industrial arts as may be suitable to their sex and conducive to their support and usefulness."[17]

* * *

One of the board's first duties was to locate the school. Localities around the state were in effect invited to bid for the site by furnishing buildings or raising money to construct them. The state's appropriation for support during the next biennium was a spare $10,000 a year.[18] As was common around the country, the process strongly resembled an auction although the prize was not specifically promised to the highest bidder. McIver said several years later that after passage of the charter he had agreed with university officials to try to locate in Chapel Hill, in order to share faculty in some measure, but the idea was vetoed as impractical.[19] The board then advertised for bids from any towns willing to offer a site and sufficient money for buildings. Only four communities put forth offers meriting serious consideration: Graham, Durham, Thomasville, and Greensboro. During four days in June the board heard representatives of the towns, inspected the sites they had to offer, and made a decision. Durham offered $22,000 and a site valued at $10,000. Graham and Thomasville each proffered $20,000 and a site. (Thomasville offered the campus and buildings of a defunct college.) Greensboro, the last visited, offered $25,000 and a site, yet to be determined. The board wired this information to the other three towns, prompting both Graham and Durham to raise their bids to $30,000 and a site. That news in turn was relayed to Greensboro.

Meanwhile Greensboro residents led by D.W.C. Benbow held a public meeting at which over fifty men made individual pledges totaling the original $25,000 offer. On hearing from Graham and Durham they met again and in a few minutes raised another $5,871. These pledges were made on the understanding that a municipal referendum would be held, asking Greensboro voters to assume the burden through a $30,000 bond issue. Without further ado the Normal board closed the bidding and accepted Greensboro's offer. This news brought a chorus of steam whistles, bells, and cheers around town. Incredibly, when the bond referendum was held in July, it carried unanimously, 771 to 0.[20]

The board clearly favored Greensboro from the outset, given a favorable offer. The other towns received only perfunctory visits. Major attractions were Greensboro's relatively central location and the convergence of railroad lines from six directions—accounting for the nickname Gate City that it adopted in this period. The area was regarded as healthy, and it was already something of an educational center, with Guilford College (Quaker), Greensboro Female College (Methodist), and Bennett College (Methodist, for blacks) already present. There were besides Edgeworth Female Seminary and a good public school system by the lights of the day. (A new Agricultural and Mechanical College for the Colored Race, chartered by the same 1891 legislature, located in Greensboro soon afterward.) Dr. Benbow in particular was a zealous and persistent lobbyist for both education and the city of Greensboro over many years. The town's leading hotel keeper, he was instrumental in attracting several of these institutions to the city and was supportive of them all.[21] Most of the losers in the contest took their loss in good part, but a Thomasville representative growled that the Normal girls were now condemned to spend unnecessary dollars clothing themselves in Greensboro, a town (population 3,300) "noted for its style, fashion and costly female dress."[22]

On June 12, before leaving Greensboro, the board elected McIver—the odds-on favorite—as president of the new school. He was at this point only 31 years old and only ten years removed from his own undergraduate diploma. He and Alderman had both been interested in the job, but carefully avoided campaigning against each other. Alderman loyally accepted a professorship of English and History, which he recognized as a consolation prize.[23] He left after a year, to become the first professor of pedagogy at Chapel Hill. Within the next dozen years he would become successively president of the University of North Carolina, Tulane University, and the University of Virginia. McIver would spend the rest of his short life at the Normal, but not without enticements to go elsewhere.

Their salaries would not begin until school opened over a year later. Meanwhile both men were busy holding institutes until almost that time. Responsibility for choosing the site and putting up the buildings fell largely on the board chairman, Finger.

It took much longer to settle on a specific location than it had taken to choose Greensboro. The board's site committee turned down a number of tracts around town, favoring among other things proximity to a railroad. (This was for advertising as well as utilitarian reasons: train passengers might be attracted by the sight of the buildings.) The final decision in November 1891 favored a ten-acre tract at what was then the southwest corner of the city, nearly a mile from its center, along Spring Garden Street. This choice was also influenced by the presence of mineral springs on the premises and across the street. (The thoroughfare, originally White Street, had reportedly been renamed earlier as a result of the many springs along its way.)[24] The Normal property was bounded on the south by Spring Garden Street and on the other sides (in terms of later development) by College Avenue on the west, an extension of Walker Avenue on the north, and a line behind Aycock Auditorium and Brown music building on the east. It was donated to the school by two Raleigh real estate speculators and philanthropists, Richard Stanhope Pullen (likewise donor of Raleigh's Pullen Park and the adjoining campus of the A&M College) and Robert T. Gray.[25]

The board found very quickly that more space was needed. In 1892, when the main buildings were nearing completion, it purchased from Pullen and Gray three and a half acres more, extending the property west to what became Forest Street.[26]

* * *

Construction began immediately, late in 1891. The plans called for two large brick buildings facing Spring Garden Street, one to house the school's academic functions and the other its students. Greensboro architects Epps and Hackett designed both structures and contractor Thomas Woodroffe built them. They followed the Romanesque Revival style recently popularized by architect Henry Hobson Richardson. Main Building (called Administration after the construction of McIver Building in 1908 and then Foust after 1960) contains three floors. The first held in the early years the president's office and six large classrooms. The second contained four classrooms, the library, a small gymnasium, and a 55 × 85-foot auditorium/chapel. The third floor would sometimes be used for academic purposes, but much of the time only for storage. Wings at both ends, called for in the original plans, were delayed by inadequate funds until 1895. They supplied six more classrooms and laboratories. The building, by 1980 the only surviving nineteenth-century structure on campus, was added that year to the National Register of Historic Places. Virtually unchanged since 1895 on the exterior, it has been extensively remodeled over the years inside.[27]

The next-door dormitory, on the site of the later McIver classroom building, was also of three stories. It was referred to originally as the matron's hall or the living building, but most often as Brick Dormitory. As with Main Building, inadequate funds postponed completion for several years. It contained a kitchen and a dining room that accommodated 150 students. A wing added in stages to the rear provided more student rooms and larger cooking and dining facilities. Within a dozen years the L-shaped wing would almost dwarf the original building.[28]

The art of estimating student enrollment—calculating the proportion of those admitted who will actually appear and those presently attending who will return—nowadays assumes the status of a science, in good years. It had not reached that state in 1892 and as a result the college was confronted even before its opening with the likelihood of more students than it could accommodate. Accordingly the board approved a second dormitory across College Avenue on the additional land just purchased, where the Alumnae House was later built. A very tight budget (the money had to be borrowed) mandated frame construction.[29] The resulting two-story Midway (or Guilford) Dormitory would also be added to in coming years and, as it happened, would long outlast its more imposing brick cousin.

In addition, given the dearth of housing nearby, the board built a president's home next door, on the corner of College Avenue and Spring Garden Street. It was a plain, two-story, ten-room, frame structure. McIver would live there (paying $15 monthly rent) throughout his presidency, as did his widow until her death in 1944. In the early years, campus visitors frequently stayed in the house overnight, and the McIvers even took in a few faculty roomers; Mrs. McIver continued to rent rooms after her husband's death in 1906.[30]

* * *

The neighborhood developed quickly. New homes sprang up along the east, west, and south sides of campus, attracted in large part by the school. In fact the institution encouraged the process, seeking nearby homes in which to house the overflow of students from the dormitories.[31] Walker Avenue was soon extended past the campus, also at the school's request, inviting similar residential development to the north if not interdicted quickly.[32] By 1895, McIver and the board awoke to the prospect of becoming landlocked. When they approached Pullen and Gray once more for additional land to the north, they were offered a full 112 acres for $12,000. This far exceeded the board's intent but, like Jefferson's Louisiana Purchase, it was too good a bargain to pass up; real estate prices were sure to climb.[33]

McIver lost no time in devising uses for the new tract, which was largely wooded. It could be at once an outdoor biology laboratory, a private park for student exercise and recreation, and paradoxically, an outlet for an expanded campus sewer system.[34] The land drains northward toward North Buffalo Creek, then rural. In 1897 he created a farm on the western side of the tract, to supply the school with milk, pork, and produce and to serve as a teaching laboratory in horticulture.

To run the farm and to beautify the campus generally, McIver hired Thomas L. Brown, an English horticulturist then working at Biltmore, the Vanderbilt estate near Asheville. Brown remained only three years, but in that time the appearance of the campus improved remarkably. Ditches were filled and drainage improved; much of the red mud was planted with shrubs, trees, and grass; walks and drives were laid out, graded, and graveled. A stone retaining wall (using dressed granite blocks mysteriously found on the premises) was built in front of Main Building to permit a circular carriage return, and a small fountain was installed in the center. As Walker Avenue was extended through campus at a level below grade, College Avenue now spanned it with a small wooden bridge.[35]

The farm started out ambitiously under Brown's supervision. McIver was never far from the operation and bought much of the livestock himself. The Normal already had a small barn or stable for its draft animals on College Avenue; it gave way to a substantial dairy barn near the later site of Shaw Dormitory.[36] The farm lost money in its early years, leading in 1900 to Brown's replacement and a reduction in the livestock herd.[37] It was making money by 1904, however, and remained a college enterprise until after World War II.

Brown's walks and drives extended into the recently acquired woods behind campus. The new park was originally to be named for Zebulon Vance, the state's recently deceased elder statesman.[38] But when philanthropist George Foster Peabody in 1901 gave the school $10,000, McIver earmarked half to develop the park and renamed it Peabody Park. (When the benefactor asked not to be commemorated in this fashion, McIver and the board with deliberate ambiguity named it for his famous relative, also named George Peabody, whose education fund was aiding the college even more generously.)[39] On the heels of the Peabody gift, and no doubt on McIver's prompting, Kitty Dees, a former student who had gone to work for landscape architect Warren H. Manning in Boston, persuaded him to visit the school and make a campus plan, charging only his expenses—something Manning had done for other institutions.[40] His plan included Peabody Park and by the fall of 1902 it contained five miles of graded drives and walkways.[41] For years to come it served as a resource for natural science classes, a theater for student ceremonies and dramatic productions, the scene of the students' mandatory walking period, and a favorite place to study or daydream.

Manning's plan called for campus development primarily northward along both sides of College Avenue, crossing Walker Avenue and terminating at the park.[42] One element of the plan was a fence along the east, north, and west sides of campus. Built in 1902, seven feet high, of wrought iron topped with barbed wire, it was intended to protect students from intruders, primarily in the park. But men and animals always managed to find their way under, through, or around it. The fence proved more expensive to maintain than it was worth, and soon fell into disrepair.[43]

Two new campus buildings appeared along College Avenue in 1902. The Students' Building replaced the former stable or barn on College Avenue at Walker. More ornate on the outside than its predecessors, with towers and turrets, it evoked correspondingly greater esthetic criticism in later years. This early student union held meeting rooms for the literary societies and other student organizations, music practice rooms, and classrooms for the domestic science and manual training departments. The Students' Building was financed by a long fund-raising campaign among students, alumnae, and others, with perhaps the largest gift being the other half of George Foster Peabody's $10,000 donation. The state was poor, money was scarce, and the building was pressed into service years before there were funds to complete it.[44]

The other building, a practice school for education students, stood diagonally across the corner, in the newly acquired tract. In writing to J.L.M. Curry, for whom it would soon be named, McIver called it the best public school building in the state.[45] However that may be, it was in process of replacement when it burned down twenty-four years later.

* * *

McIver's first tasks as president were to recruit the faculty and students. He did this in 1891–92 while still occupied with the teachers' institutes. J.L.M. Curry advised him at the outset to recruit bona fide, trained teachers. "Confederate soldiers... daughters of the Hon. Mr. A and the Rev. Mr. B will be urged upon you [so strongly that] it will require courage to resist, but *you must do it....*"[46] University of North Carolina President George T. Winston urged him to hire more women than men; he could get more people of better quality for the same money. "Besides, it is a woman's school, and it should emphasize the *woman idea.*"[47] McIver listened. Except for Alderman and two other men, he chose a faculty of professional women, most if not all unmarried. He made it a point to announce in the first annual catalog that all except two were natives of the South and two-thirds were native North Carolinians.[48] Many had attended leading northern universities, however, and McIver took the first of many northern trips to recruit faculty.

He received advice on students too. His old friend M.C.S. Noble urged him to recruit as diversified a student body as possible: daughters of the wealthy along with poor girls who planned to teach. The school should aim to be the best in the South for training women, not just for those who couldn't afford to go elsewhere. The kind of girls who came the first year, Noble said, would influence the kind who came for years afterward.[49]

* * *

College presidents of McIver's generation did everything. With only the tiniest staff they dealt daily and personally with trustees, faculty, students and their parents, prospective donors, state and local government, and the general public. Their purview included admissions, curriculum, legislative relations, fund raising, academic and social regulations, student discipline, buildings and grounds, purchasing supplies (including livestock for the college farm and rugs for the dormitories), campus security, and setting the proper moral tone in chapel and elsewhere. Many taught classes. They were often on the road, seeking funds, faculty, and students. "The old American college," says one scholar, "was the lengthened shadow of the president." The duties were so varied, he adds, that it clearly was not a profession for which one could be trained. In large part it was (as it remains) a public relations job.[50]

McIver fit this description to a tee. In the first place, he operated with the most minimal staff. As late as 1903 he wrote to another college president that his office force consisted of the bursar who collected and disbursed money and kept the books, the college secretary, a stenographer, a registrar, and a young woman who sold supplies for about an hour a day. He added that until a college secretary was appointed two years earlier he had performed most of her duties too. It was essential, he advised, that a president avoid bogging himself down in routine details that could be delegated.[51] Bureaucracy came to the Normal, even in McIver's time, but the college remained very small for many years.

The new "college secretary and general assistant to the president" was Laura Coit, an 1896 alumna turned faculty member, who was appointed to the post in 1901. She not only assumed many routine duties but came to advise McIver about a variety of matters, even faculty teaching assignments. Her presence freed him to travel more frequently, and she assumed increasing responsibility for directing campus activities in his absence. Coit's initiatives ranged from chapel talks admonishing the students about deportment to canceling classes on the death of J.L.M. Curry. She reported to the chief in writing almost daily, including news of his family as well as the college. In fact, she almost became a member of the family.

In 1900, before Coit's appointment, the board had granted McIver a summer leave and named a professor as dean of the faculty to officiate during his absence.[52] This position became permanent in 1902 with the appointment of Julius I. Foust as dean. The dean customarily dealt with academic matters during McIver's absence, leaving operational details to Coit.[53]

* * *

Despite this assistance, McIver seemed constantly in motion. One student recalled that he drove himself hard and loved doing it. He would dash into morning chapel exercises, out of breath and perspiring, vigorously waving a palm leaf fan that he used in all but the coldest weather. In times of crisis, she said, he exuded strength.[54] Josephus Daniels called him a "steam engine in breeches"—a phrase applied at the time to Theodore Roosevelt. McIver was increasingly occupied with public relations and fund raising—traveling, speaking, and writing to wealthy or influential people in behalf of public education generally and the Normal in particular. He constantly invited dignitaries and potential donors to campus. Some gave money, some lobbied the legislature, some simply conferred prestige by their presence, but nearly all addressed the student body. One early alumna recalled that the long-suffering girls were subjected in chapel to the banalities of every passing politician.[55]

When McIver prevailed on the education committee of the legislature to visit in 1897, he set the elocution department to work beforehand devising entertainments. The students restaged an earlier event called County Fair in which girls from around the state performed skits representing their home counties. Yadkin County girls, for instance, displayed corn shucks and a large bottle topped with a banner proclaiming, "Yadkin furnishes corn in all its forms." The girls then held a mock legislative session ending with approval of a $100,000 appropriation to the Normal.[56]

When the real legislative sessions came up, in odd-numbered years, McIver lobbied industriously for the school alongside his counterparts from Chapel Hill and the A&M. He appeared before committees, corresponded with legislators, and mobilized public support in the hinterland. He took to this activity easily and effectively, given his training in the teachers' institutes.

Politically, McIver was a lifelong Democrat but he made it a high priority to get along with governors, legislators, board members, and others who were of different persuasions. North Carolina in the 1890s was unique among the southern states in that a coalition of Republicans and Populists (called Fusionists) won control of the 1895 and 1897 legislatures and a Republican, Daniel L. Russell, was elected governor in 1896. These developments were reflected on the Normal's board of directors, especially as the board's president was the popularly elected superintendent of public instruction. From 1897 to 1901 this was Populist Charles H. Mebane. McIver recognized in Mebane a fellow public school crusader and they became fast friends. Mebane in fact remained on the board many years after his term as superintendent had expired. Owing partly to the state's usual one-party status, partly to McIver's diplomacy, and partly to the nonpartisan appeal of his cause, party politics seldom affected the Normal's operations or funding. Both of the Fusionist legislatures, in fact, treated the institution very well. The initial $10,000 appropriation gradually rose to $25,000 in 1897 and $100,000 a decade after that.[57] In 1899 Furnifold Simmons and other Democratic party leaders infuriated McIver by promising a moratorium on increased appropriations for higher education that year as a means of enlarging support for their current (and successful) campaign to disfranchise blacks.[58] McIver seems to have accepted segregation and disfranchisement without qualms, but white supremacy as an issue was never high on his agenda. As a result, Simmons—who came soon to dominate North Carolina politics—was never McIver's politician of choice.

McIver sought private donations as avidly as he did legislative appropriations. Large philanthropic foundations like the Peabody Fund were now facts of life and objects of intense courtship in higher education. The foundations not only gave money, they helped to transform colleges and universities by requiring them to improve their academic standards and business practices in return.[59] McIver avidly courted Andrew Carnegie, Robert C. Ogden, Wallace Buttrick, and other foundation leaders. For him one of the most obvious sources of money was the Peabody Education Fund. Governor Russell and Superintendents Finger and Mebane all joined him in courting its agent, J.L.M. Curry. It responded with an initial gift of $5000 in 1892 and varying amounts almost every year through 1911, for a total of over $50,000.[60] Besides George Foster Peabody's gift, McIver with student and other help generated smaller gifts as well, as in the Students' Building campaign.

Commencement was for McIver a God-given opportunity to show off the campus and students to the public and those in power. The governor almost always came; other celebrities often came from a distance. In 1894 McIver made friends in Washington with William Jennings Bryan and secured him as commencement speaker; this was two years before the Great Commoner's Cross of Gold speech that won him the Democratic presidential nomination. Bryan made a hit at the Normal, even while discussing free silver. McIver frankly admitted that he had planned this as an advertising event, and credited it with the hundred student applications that came in soon afterward.[61] Next year he captured as speaker Columbia University President Nicholas Murray Butler, and in 1897 an old Raleigh friend, Walter Hines Page, now with the *Atlantic Monthly*. Page's Forgotten Man speech, delivered at the Normal commencement that year, won national attention with its call for universal education and the overthrow of reactionary politicians and preachers in the South.[62] One of the early alumnae recalled that McIver was always excited at commencement time, leading longtime college retainer Zeke Robinson to remark, "Dr. McIver sho' do like a rally-do-round."[63]

* * *

Like many college presidents of his era, McIver also taught. Sometimes it was in his listed field of pedagogy or education, but he frequently taught a civics class as well, designed as a course in community service. He took students to visit Cone Mills near Greensboro, Reynolds Tobacco in Winston, and other neighboring businesses in order to let them learn about North Carolina industry; yet somehow these tours often resulted in corporate donations to the Normal as well.[64] McIver loved to talk—a sharp reversal of his youthful reticence. Both in class and in chapel, he kept the students after the appointed hour so frequently that faculty members tried to avoid having their own classes scheduled in the following periods.[65]

McIver's abilities and his dedication to the school were so transparent that students and faculty alike responded to him with admiration if not awe, and often with affection. A sense of community permeated the entire institution, enhanced no doubt by its relative geographic isolation in the early years, but owing in large measure to his leadership. Yet the admiration was tempered. Although McIver was sometimes open to persuasion, he was self-confident to a degree often perceived as overbearing and dogmatic. When crossed he could react explosively, but the anger was usually shortlived. Student opinion of him ranged from adoration to active dislike; faculty members were more favorable, or perhaps more circumspect. As future Chancellor Walter C. Jackson (who had known McIver) put it, everybody admired McIver but some did not necessarily like him all the time.[66]

The students quickly developed a fierce loyalty to the school, which usually extended to McIver personally. In the absence of athletics and other modern accoutrements of school spirit, they became ardent supporters of McIver in his relations with the outside world, especially the legislature. In 1893, when news arrived that the lawmakers had increased the annual appropriation to $12,500, the students staged a celebration to welcome him back from Raleigh. With bells, horns, pans, drums, and other noisemakers they marched forth toward the railroad station to meet him. Halfway there they unexpectedly encountered McIver coming toward them in a carriage. He alighted and all marched back to campus together, making a joyful noise. On demand, he ended the occasion with a short speech. Similar celebrations, with torchlight processions and other variations, occurred biennially for some years to come.[67]

For his part, McIver went out of his way to know the students individually. Beginning on the opening day in 1892, he met them on their arrival at the railroad station each fall and arranged their transportation to campus. Male faculty members would join in this activity for decades.[68] When a homesick student headed homeward without permission, McIver went to the railroad station personally to check on her whereabouts.[69] He often visited the dormitories, and even distributed the mail for a few weeks the first year to associate names with faces. He kept a list of students in his pocket and tried to speak to each of them at least once during the year.[70] Similarly, he made it a point to know about their homes and families, often amazing them with his knowledge of their backgrounds. He even lent money personally to students who could not otherwise return to school.[71]

* * *

Founding the Normal was a milestone in the public school crusade, but by no means its culmination. The charter actually required faculty members to continue holding teachers' institutes around the state during the summers, without extra pay.[72] From the beginning, McIver preached the public school gospel to the students. He never tired of telling them that they, like the faculty, were pioneers in higher education for women;[73] they had a duty to serve their state in return for its giving them the blessings of an education. In fact, "Service" became the motto and watchword of the institution and remains so to the present day. Walter Hines Page and a multitude of visiting speakers reinforced the message and provided additional inspiration. So did the faculty, teaching both by precept and example.

Thus McIver enlisted the students as crusaders or, in his own metaphor, as missionaries on "civilization's march . . . from savagery to the millenium." As historian Pamela Dean observes, he was adept at using traditional evangelical language to promote change.[74] The girls were encouraged to learn public speaking, to run meetings, to acquire the social graces that would make them effective in the civic world as well as in polite society. By educating women to be both schoolteachers and advocates, Dean continues, McIver recast them as potentially powerful public figures, and this in turn had broad implications for women's coming role in society.[75] He used every possible forum to deliver his message, but most common were his regular chapel appearances in an age when missing daily chapel brought condign punishment.[76]

One of his most effective missionary devices was the Woman's Association for the Betterment of Public School Houses, founded in 1902 to advance the cause in North Carolina. Women faculty and students were encouraged to join and most did so. Collectively they became effective lobbyists for every educational cause, including country schoolhouses and higher appropriations for the Normal.[77] One faculty member, Viola Boddie, recalled traveling around the state in an open buggy, pulled by a mule, observing rustic schools with spaces between the logs wide enough to "throw a cat through if not a dog." By 1925, she noted with satisfaction, these structures had been replaced by brick buildings.[78]

A broader agency of interest to McIver was the Southern Education Board, formed in 1901 by Robert C. Ogden, George Foster Peabody, and other northern philanthropists to supplement the existing Peabody and other foundations. Both McIver and Alderman became agents for this fund, which was active in every southern state.[79]

* * *

For years there would be debate over the Normal's mission and character. It was, in fact, part of a national debate about normal school curricula: how broad should teacher training be? The Normal's charter called for instruction in education and such "industrial arts" as drawing, typewriting, stenography, and telegraphy, but it said nothing about the liberal arts or general education. J.L.M. Curry told McIver at the outset that his fund would give money only to teacher-training institutions, but he had no objection to their including basic education and some vocational training.[80] He obviously approved the Normal's curriculum, as on a number of occasions he granted it money, asked the legislature to give it larger appropriations and, in 1897, suggested that it upgrade its name from School to College.[81]

From the beginning, McIver, the board of directors, and the faculty agreed that they had to provide a broad liberal arts background in order to turn out competent teachers. Accordingly, the first catalog announced courses in history, literature, mathematics, science, languages, art, and music in addition to pedagogy.[82] As early as 1897, a supporter referred to the school approvingly (but privately) as a woman's university in the making.[83] Meanwhile, the board in its first annual report said the school's purpose was to give "such education as will add to the efficiency of the average woman's work in whatever walk of life her lot may be cast."[84] In broad outline, that remained its mission for the next seventy years.[85]

Not all approved. Proponents of a normal school, pure and simple, criticized the curriculum almost immediately. Eugene C. Harrell, editor of the *North Carolina Teacher*, urged the legislature to withhold appropriations until the school conformed to a vocational interpretation of its charter. Not content with this attack on the school's direction, Harrell accused McIver of profligate spending. The charge had no basis and was easily refuted.[86]

But Harrell's call for an end to state support was taken up more broadly in 1894 by the state's private colleges and the churches that sponsored them, particularly the Baptists and Methodists. They attacked state support for higher education in general, not only because it undercut them in the competition for students, but also from a conviction that higher education involved moral training and was therefore the rightful province of the churches and the schools they established. This opposition was first expressed in the 1880s, when the legislature began voting small appropriations for the university; it mushroomed after the establishment of the Normal. Taking McIver's own argument about the centrality of women in molding society, many feared that a religiously neutral woman's college would generate a society of infidels. There also were objections to taking teacher certification from local school boards and handing it to a central agency such as the Normal. (Under the charter all of its graduates received teaching certificates.) This objection came closest to the traditionalists' fundamental criticism of all progressive reforms: their tendency to centralize and standardize. The legislature in 1901 met this criticism by requiring all teacher candidates, including Normal graduates, to pass the same exam, administered by local officials. McIver did not object.[87]

In a larger sense, the university, the A&M college, and now the Normal unquestionably posed a threat to the private institutions, especially during the economic depression of the 1890s; enrollments at the state institutions rose rapidly in these years while those at Wake Forest and other private colleges fell. But McIver and his allies predicted accurately that the new public school system would soon produce more students than all the existing colleges could handle. The state aid controversy peaked in 1897, but did not disappear altogether until the early 1920s, when the state was irretrievably committed to supporting higher education.[88]

In fact, the state went on to establish a number of regional, coeducational normal schools, culminating with East Carolina Teachers Training School at Greenville in 1907. It was now McIver's turn to resent newcomers. Fearing their effect on both enrollments and legislative appropriations at the existing institutions, he opposed them all, and particularly East Carolina—to no avail.[89]

In the Harrell and sectarian controversies the students again rallied in support of their school. (McIver seldom left their reaction wholly to chance.) In 1893 they organized a boycott of Harrell's *North Carolina Teacher*, and one student returned a scholarship she had received from the magazine.[90] The legislative appropriation increases of 1895 and 1897 and the change to college status in the midst of these attacks were all the more occasions for jubilation.[91]

McIver quickly won state, regional, and even national acclaim. In 1905 he was president of the Southern Education Association and an active candidate for the national presidency. Losing the post narrowly that year, he was widely expected to win it soon.[92] Other positions he found less tempting. As early as 1896 people urged him to seek the Democratic gubernatorial nomination or, alternatively, the university presidency. McIver seemingly had no trouble turning down both requests, preferring to stay on at the Normal.[93] (As it turned out, the Democratic nominee for governor in 1896 lost and Alderman took the UNC presidency.) But opportunities continued to offer. When Alderman left for Tulane in 1900 and when the University of Tennessee presidency was offered in 1904, he gave the same answer.[94] He did seriously consider an offer from the Peabody Education Fund in 1904 to become its general agent, succeeding the deceased J.L.M. Curry. But he dismissed the prospect in the crisis that arose on campus when Brick Dormitory burned.[95]

McIver was always hard-pressed financially, and his refusals exacted a toll. Josephus Daniels later revealed that McIver had borrowed money from him two or three times, small debts which the editor wrote off. On one occasion McIver came in for advice, saying he was in debt and barely able to support his family. A Rockingham County industrialist had offered him a position at several times his current salary, and McIver was sorely tempted. Daniels gave the reassurance McIver seemingly sought, that his present work was too important to leave. But reassurance didn't pay the bills.[96]

Chapter 2

Academic Affairs

The original, or charter faculty (as they were called in later years) numbered only fifteen.[1] Except for Miriam Bitting, the school physician, all lacked doctorates or even master's degrees; some lacked even the baccalaureate. But this was not unusual at the time, and nearly all were people of ability and accomplishment. Especially in the case of the women, they were well educated by the standards of their time, place, and gender.

Clearly first among the faculty was Edwin Alderman, whose $2000 salary approached McIver's $2250 and was at least double that of any other member. In his single year at the Normal his eloquence attracted not only students but local townspeople, who so crowded his classes that attendance had to be limited.[2]

Edward J. Forney, largely self-trained, would serve the institution for over forty years as treasurer and professor of business. McIver first met him in 1891, working as a shorthand writer and typist in Sidney Finger's office in Raleigh. He was, in fact, one of the first people in the South doing this work. Perceiving Forney's abilities, McIver commandeered his services, first in helping with the massive correspondence required to organize the school, and then permanently. He was hired as secretary to the president, treasurer of the school, and professor of "Book-keeping, Stenography, Typewriting and Telegraphy." Forney quickly trained a student to take over as McIver's secretary and no student ever showed an interest in telegraphy, but with colleagues he handled the rest, ultimately as head of the commercial department. Over the years Forney with his long wiry frame and sharp tongue became a campus institution, always demanding, frequently sarcastic, but at base deeply concerned for his students, who dubbed him the "wisecracker extraordinary." Whether he had taught Greek philosophy or bricklaying, one wrote, he would be a master teacher. Forney turned out a host of appreciative alumnae as secretaries, accountants, court reporters, and civil servants. In fact, he opened up to them careers outside of teaching which had never before been available to women. As college treasurer, he made sure the books always balanced. As a public accountant off campus, he set up budget accounting systems for the state and a number of Greensboro businesses, and was for many years city auditor.[3]

The third male in the group was Clarence R. Brown, teaching what was called vocal culture. (Instrumental music came later.) A native of Rochester, N.Y., he studied in Paris and came to the Normal from Winston, where he had been director of music in the public schools. Brown, who died in 1905, also taught students privately, making as much money (according to McIver) as he did at the college.[4]

Lula McIver reportedly insisted on hiring a woman physician, something very rare even in women's colleges. Dr. Miriam Bitting, the choice, was a native Virginian educated at the Woman's Medical College of Philadelphia. She was only the second woman physician in North Carolina. Leaving after a year to marry, she was succeeded by Dr. Anna Gove of New Hampshire, a graduate of a woman's medical school in New York later annexed by Cornell University. Bitting and Gove were objects of great curiosity among North Carolinians of both genders. A male physician reportedly visited Greensboro specifically to see Gove, whom he called the "female lady doctress;" he later sent his daughter to the school. In addition to her work as college physician, Gove headed the department of health (including for a time physical education) and in the early years taught classes in physiology and hygiene. Both as physician and teacher she encountered some early parental opposition. Some wrote to McIver asking that if their daughters became sick to call in a male physician; McIver did so, but found that Dr. Gove quickly won the confidence of the girls. As to physiology, one mother wrote her, "Please don't teach Mary so much about her insides. It ain't decent." Gove would leave the school many times over the years—for further study, to teach at Vassar and assume Dr. Bitting's private practice for two years, to serve in France during and after World War I, and to take a world tour. She always returned and continued to work part time after her retirement in 1936.[5]

It seems likely, as Pamela Dean remarks, that a number of the new faculty members knew each other and met McIver through the small network of young professional women seeking such positions as he had to offer. This was true of the new science teacher, Dixie Lee Bryant, who had been a fellow-student with Anna Gove at the Massachusetts Institute of Technology. Bryant was a Tennessean and an MIT graduate, who in 1904 would become the first Normal faculty member to earn a Ph.D. This was at the University of Erlangen, Germany, where she was the first woman to win that degree. As the only scientist in residence at the Normal the first year, she was called upon to teach geography, physics, zoology, geology, and chemistry. Relief came in the second year, in the person of Mary Petty. The two created primitive science laboratories, using what money and materials they could find. Falling out with McIver over her teaching assignments and salary, Bryant left the college in 1905.[6]

Viola Boddie was hired to teach Latin and French. A native North Carolinian, she had studied at Peabody Teachers College in Nashville and, at age 25, had several years of teaching experience. A strikingly attractive young woman, stylishly dressed, she turned down a succession of beaus, leading students to speculate that she was in love with McIver. Spending the rest of her career at the school, Miss Boddie became renowned as one "under whom the indolent found no comfort." In the early years she attracted the girls by her youth and appearance, then (as happens) lost them as she grew older and her discipline seemed more arbitrary.[7]

Another longtime member was Gertrude Mendenhall in mathematics (and initially, German). She belonged to the leading Quaker family in North Carolina, with roots near Greensboro. After attending what later became Guilford College, she went on to Wellesley. Following graduation, she taught at Raleigh's Peace Institute, meeting the McIvers, then returned to Guilford in 1888 as one of its original collegiate faculty members. Her sister, Mary Mendenhall Hobbs, a notable woman in her own right, was married to Guilford's first collegiate president. Gertrude Mendenhall would remain at the Normal as head of the math department until her death in 1926.[8]

During the next five years the faculty almost doubled. A number of the newcomers were recruited locally, some from the Normal's own graduates. Among the women particularly, as Pamela Dean notes, these "homegrown recruits" tended to come less from rural backgrounds than from the newly urbanizing New South. They were daughters of merchants, lawyers, judges, physicians, and ministers. Seldom wealthy, their families nonetheless provided educational opportunities and supported their efforts to translate these into careers. Most of the women, in Dean's words, "chose career over motherhood and self-support over domesticity." Many, like Gove and Bryant, would continue their studies for years, attending summer sessions and taking leaves of absence. They may well have "suggested exciting new possibilities to young women who had never before been far from their rural and small-town homes."[9]

Interestingly, the men, less than a quarter of the faculty, obtained college educations closer to home. In the prevailing culture they, unlike the women, could advance professionally with only bachelor's degrees. Like McIver and Alderman, their doctorates would mostly be honorary. In fact, the only earned doctorates at the Normal during the next twenty years (apart from the physicians) would belong to Dixie Lee Bryant, her science successor Eugene W. Gudger, and Virginia Ragsdale in mathematics.[10]

Three of the newcomers in 1893 would later win a measure of regional and even national notoriety. With Alderman's resignation, history and English were divided into two departments. His and McIver's friend James Y. Joyner replaced him at the Normal as he had at Goldsboro, now to teach English. A popular teacher, Joyner was active with other faculty members in giving teachers' institutes, and was elected both to the Greensboro city council and the board of Greensboro's Agricultural and Mechanical college for blacks—the later A&T State University. In 1902 Joyner left to become the state's superintendent of public instruction, where his efforts in the educational crusade would be crucial; in fact, he became in large measure the father of the state's high school system. As superintendent he was also chairman of the Normal's board of directors, remaining so until 1919. Joyner was elected in 1909 president of the National Education Association.[11]

Philander P. Claxton was a Tennessean who graduated from the state univerity at Knoxville and did graduate work at Johns Hopkins and in Germany. He came to the Normal from Asheville, where he had been superintendent of schools. As professor of pedagogy Claxton was instrumental in establishing the practice school, which some thought should have been named for him instead of J.L.M. Curry. Claxton was an extremely popular teacher, not entirely for academic reasons: some of the girls thought him the most handsome man they had ever seen. He too left in 1902, to work with the Southern Education Board. In 1911 Claxton became an unusually activist U.S. Commissioner of Education.[12]

The third newcomer in 1893, Mrs. Lucy Owen Robertson, had grown up in Hillsborough and attended its prestigious Nash and Kollock's Select School for Young Ladies. She began teaching at Greensboro Female College in 1875, several years before her husband's death. Robertson came to the Normal as professor of history partially (like Joyner in English) to replace Alderman. She returned to Greensboro College in 1900 to become lady principal and, two years later, president. She was not only its sole female president to date, but reportedly the first woman president of any college in the South.[13]

Mary Petty and her sister Annie, who came in 1893 and 1895, respectively, as science teacher and librarian, were daughters of a building contractor and manufacturer from nearby Archdale. As Quakers they were friends of Gertrude Mendenhall; Mary attended Wellesley with Mendenhall and joined her on the first Guilford College faculty. Many years later she would become the first woman member of its board of trustees. She remained at the Normal for the rest of her career, teaching chemistry as soon as it became differentiated. Among the early faculty, Mary Petty was one of the most avid in pursuit of graduate study, at Bryn Mawr (for a year), Harvard, Columbia, Cornell, and the University of California.[14]

Annie Petty was a recent Guilford College graduate in 1895 when she took over a library that consisted of one room in Main Building. This not keeping her busy, she also managed the campus post office, operated the textbook exchange, rang the bells between classes, and served as the school's information bureau. Underpaid and undervalued, she took a year off in 1898 to study at the Drexel Institute Library School in Philadelphia and returned as the first trained librarian in North Carolina. In 1904 she helped organize the state library association and later the state library commission. Petty had ample opportunity to confirm the reputation of librarianship as the worst paid profession in the country. She finally left the college in 1921 to join the state library commission, where she pioneered in North Carolina's use of bookmobiles.[15]

Coming to the faculty in 1896 was Mary Settle Sharpe, one of the few married women to serve the college during its first quarter century. Born in 1863, she was the daughter of Judge Thomas Settle, Jr., a leader of the North Carolina Republican party during Reconstruction, its gubernatorial candidate against Zebulon Vance in 1876, and later a justice of the state supreme court. As a girl she attended the Salem Academy in Salem and St. Mary's School in Raleigh. Like most of the early faculty, Mrs. Sharpe taught some of everything before institutional growth brought specialization. Her subjects included history and physical education (of which she was sometimes director), but her main interest was in reading and elocution, which included debate and drama. She directed many plays, and most particularly the massive May Day fetes of 1912 and 1916, based on themes from Renaissance England. In 1920, newly enfranchised under the nineteenth amendment, Mrs. Sharpe resigned from the faculty to accept the Republican nomination for superintendent of public instruction—a forlorn race in the Democratic Solid South of that day. Mrs. Sharpe had six children, two of them Normal students.[16]

An area of domestic science that McIver wanted to develop was dressmaking. To do this work he hired in 1903 Jessie Young Phillips from the Georgia State Normal and Industrial College in Milledgeville. Married to something of a ne'er do well, Mrs. Phillips was a strong-minded woman and feminist who provided the main support for her family—sewing, teaching, and taking in boarders. She was also widely known as a fashion stylist, and brought an assistant with her. Mrs. Phillips left the Normal after only a year, possibly for health reasons, but clearly impressed her students and colleagues with her abilities and spirit. She died two years later at the home of her son, the prominent southern historian Ulrich B. Phillips, then at the University of Wisconsin.[17]

Several of the Normal girls dedicated the rest of their lives to the college. Preeminent among these was Laura Hill Coit, identified with the school from her entrance as a student in 1894 until her retirement in 1937. After graduation in 1896 she too taught a variety of unrelated subjects until becoming in 1901 secretary of the college and McIver's woman Friday. The position embraced a multitude of tasks in the early years, and was hers for over three decades. Besides keeping the faculty minutes and serving as secretary and general trouble shooter for the president, she served at one time or another as registrar, admissions director, placement officer, director of religious activities, and always (as other functions split off with growth and greater specialization) financial aid director in charge of loans, scholarships, and student jobs. Even in the presence of a senior faculy member as dean, it was she who ran the college on a daily basis during McIver's many absences. Moreover, she helped to organize the Alumnae Association and served for years in effect as alumnae secretary before that post was created. Coit's ability to remember student names was legendary and her following among the alumnae was enormous.[18]

Minnie Lou Jamison, one of the original students, began teaching domestic science as an upperclassman before her graduation in 1896. She then joined the faculty, remaining forty years. Miss Jamison was a pioneer in home economics extension work around the state. For several years beginning in 1915, she published bulletins, gave lectures, organized women's clubs, and helped her students to set up home economics programs in the high schools. In 1897 she began an even longer parallel career with the college in student affairs: as dormitory resident and counselor, assistant lady principal, and during her last twelve years after 1924 as, in effect, dean of freshmen. Her warm disposition, motherly concern, sense of humor, and "liberal attitude toward changing conventions" enabled her to maintain rapport with succeeding classes of eighteen-year-olds.[19]

When Mrs. Robertson returned to Greensboro Female College in 1900, she was replaced by William Cunningham Smith, who quickly became one of the college's favorite teachers and most dependable leaders. A native of Greensboro, his father was the city's first superintendent of schools. Smith himself graduated from UNC in 1896, staying on for four more years as instructor in history, English, and pedagogy. He came to the Normal as professor of history, but when Joyner left in 1902, Smith became head of the English department as well. That arrangement lasted until a new history head arrived in 1909; Smith remained head of the English department until 1940. In time he would also serve successively as dean of the college, dean of the faculty, and (in the 1920s) dean of the college of liberal arts and sciences. Smith was characterized universally as a courteous, dignified man of scholarly demeanor, possessed also of a sly wit. His scholarship took the form of wide reading and careful preparation of his lectures rather than original research. Devoutly religious, he directed chapel exercises for many years, conducted a popular men's Bible class at First Presbyterian Church, and lectured around the state on English literature and the Bible. From the time of his arrival, Smith took a leading part in efforts to liberalize the curriculum and raise the college's academic level to the point of accreditation and beyond. His alma mater accorded him an honorary doctorate in 1920.[20]

Claxton's replacement in 1902 was Julius I. Foust, since 1895 the superintendent of schools in Goldsboro. He came not only as professor of pedagogy and superintendent of the practice school, but as dean of the college, a post that Joyner had held at least intermittently. Foust chaired faculty meetings and performed other services in McIver's absence, all the while depending on Laura Coit to make the place run on a daily basis. A native of next-door Alamance County, Foust had graduated from UNC in 1890. He was a full-fledged member of the education crusade, not only as a school teacher and administrator but as a participant in many of the summer institutes. Among other things, he taught psychology, then part of the education curriculum. An early student later characterized him as tall, lanky, countrified, and much given to jokes and puns.[21] The camera portrayed him as very boyish and handsome in appearance, though he seems never to have equalled Claxton's matinee idol status. As McIver's soon-to-be successor, Foust would guide the institution longer than anyone in its history.

When Dixie Lee Bryant left in 1901 for three years of graduate study in Europe her replacement was the young ornithologist T. Gilbert Pearson. A Quaker, Pearson had attended Guilford College and the university at Chapel Hill, then returned to Guilford as its first biology instructor. At the Normal he was captivated by the miniature wilderness of Peabody Park and took his students there on field trips. With McIver's encouragement he also began a museum of native birds. In short order Pearson organized on campus the North Carolina Audubon Society, wrote a well-received book on birds, gave speeches and lobbied the legislature successfully in behalf of a bird protection law, and showered the press with articles on bird identification and protection. Pearson's energy and enthusiasm captivated both students and faculty colleagues, who accompanied him on after-hours nature walks through the park. He even enlisted McIver to help raise funds for his work. When Bryant returned in 1904, the college had grown sufficiently that McIver was delighted to be able to retain Pearson. But several months into the fall term he left to become a full-time agent for the new national Audubon Society.[22] He would later serve many years as its president.

Bryant's final departure in 1905 brought a replacement not only as head of the science work but as the faculty's only Ph.D. Eugene W. Gudger was a native of Waynesville in the North Carolina mountains, who came to the Normal with a freshly-minted doctorate from Johns Hopkins. He was a marine biologist, in time a leading ichthyologist, whose research interests drew him permanently to the American Museum of Natural History in 1919. Meanwhile Gudger was a demanding but popular teacher and a regular researcher at marine laboratories in Beaufort and elsewhere.[23]

* * *

Faculty ranks and departmental organization were just coming into use nationally in the 1890s.[24] The Normal would not formally adopt the modern ranks of professor, associate professor, assistant professor, and instructor until 1921, after its accreditation and reincarnation as the North Carolina College for Women. Although the title professor soon came to be used informally, it was apparently confined at first to males.[25] Officially, the first teachers were designated only as faculty, assistants, and tutors—the last being advanced students. Each subject area or department had one ranking faculty member except for business education with two. The four assistants and seven tutors were distributed among the departments.[26] Departments were thus small, and department heads would not be so designated until 1901.

With no faculty ranks, there could be no salary scale by ranks; there would be none before the 1930s. Salaries at the Normal were low by national standards but competitive regionally. Women were unblushingly paid far less than men with the same qualifications and for the same work. As elsewhere, the most common justification was that the men were usually married with families, while the women were usually unmarried without families. In fact, single men without dependents were still paid more than single women who had dependent relatives. The national market forced women to accept lower pay if they wanted to work. As UNC president George T. Winston advised McIver in 1891, he could get the brightest and best educated women for $1000, "women whose talents and learning would command $3000, if they were men."[27] Dr. Miriam Bitting, the Normal's highest paid woman in 1892, received $1000, half of Alderman's salary. Five years later the average male's salary (not including McIver's) was $1537, compared with the average woman's $625. The disparity would last many years. When women at the Normal asked for more, as they occasionally did, they met with mixed results at best. Librarian Annie Petty was a frequent petitioner; in 1897 she received a pitiful $275, and won only modest relief thereafter. Dixie Lee Bryant, with her recent doctorate, departed the college in 1905 in a salary dispute with McIver.[28]

Male faculty members, like Forney and Joyner, lived with their families in houses within easy walking distance of campus. Some of the single women, like Mendenhall and Gove, initially rented rooms in the McIver house or in private homes nearby. In a few years they would build or buy houses of their own in the neighborhood. Assistants, or junior faculty women, lived by economic necessity in the dormitories where they paid the same board as students—in 1905 about $10 per month compared with $20 in private homes. These women also had supervisory duties as dormitory residents.[29]

Outside the major research universities, very few faculty in the 1890s were much engaged in scholarly research. Teaching loads were heavy, commonly fifteen to twenty hours per week, and teachers were expected to spend a significant amount of time in social as well as academic contact with students. This left the summer for those inclined toward research. Most were not; it was seldom expected or even rewarded when performed. Normal school faculties in particular seldom had the opportunity; they were heavily involved in conducting summer teachers' institutes or other outreach activity.[30]

All this was true at the North Carolina Normal. Both the teaching and social loads were heavy during the academic year. After spring commencement nearly all the faculty scattered in every direction, but mostly northward. Some taught in summer schools, or attended them in pursuit of advanced knowledge and degrees. By 1896 seven members had gone to Europe for study and travel. Some (McIver included) heeded the charter mandate by traveling the state conducting teachers' institutes. Many simply vacationed, traveling or visiting family. Faculty members were also frequent attenders of professional meetings, regional and national.[31]

McIver never saw faculty research as central to the mission of the Normal. He valued its positive impact on the college's reputation in the few cases where it existed, however, and therefore publicized Bryant's studies in Germany, sought funds for Pearson's ornithological work, and encouraged Gudger's research at Beaufort.[32] It would be many years before either the faculty or the administration saw research as a high priority.

* * *

In establishing the curriculum McIver, the board of directors, and the faculty determined to base the vocational programs on a broad liberal arts background.[33] Preferring a women's institution on the order of Chapel Hill, they lacked both the money and qualified students for such an enterprise in 1892. Nor did they fully agree with Bryn Mawr's militantly feminist president M. Carey Thomas that women's higher education should be identical to that of men.[34] The result was a combination of elements from the contemporary normal school and the liberal arts college. McIver confided privately in 1901 that he aspired to build "a great institution for women," combining "industrial and normal features... with the work of a high class college like Vassar or Smith."[35] That surely was his original objective, and it came close to the idea of a woman's university by the standards of the time and place. But it would not have been politic at any time to say that he wanted to create a female Chapel Hill.

* * *

Into the twentieth century, American colleges often ignored their published admission requirements. Many were colleges in name only. Public institutions in particular were under great pressure to take deserving young people with few prior educational opportunities. The remedial or preparatory work they offered to accommodate these students was gradually phased out as public high schools spread, and colleges restricted their admissions to high school graduates. A further selection of the best among these graduates did not come until the 1920s.[36]

In North Carolina the school system was so spotty that McIver admitted some applicants in 1892 with almost no formal schooling at all and others who had already graduated from private colleges, institutes, and seminaries. Eighty had already taught school. The minimum age he accepted was 16, the average 19 2/3. Given such divergent academic backgrounds, students took placement exams on arrival and were assigned to different levels and subjects accordingly. Some were admitted as sophomores, juniors, or seniors. This explains the existence of a first graduating class in 1893; all but one of its members had already graduated from another college.[37]

Progress had to be incremental. McIver defined freshman work in 1892 as beginning where the best country (not city) public schools left off.[38] Entrance and graduation requirements could rise only in company with the number and quality of high schools, and as funding permitted the expansion of the faculty and curriculum. For a decade the academic program was largely at the secondary level, and many entering students failed to match even that standard. In 1901, 110 of the 392 students were classified as sub-freshmen. As late as 1911, thirty percent of the students reportedly were taking some high school work.[39] In 1897 the legislature legally conferred the title College on the Normal, reflecting the improvements already achieved, but it would take nearly thirty years to achieve full accreditation.[40]

As Elisabeth Bowles points out in her history of the college, each county was to have student representation in proportion to its white school population. If there were too many applicants from one county, its school superintendent or another qualified official was to give an examination prepared by McIver, who then read the papers and made the appointment. If a county did not fill its quota, vacancies could be filled by applicants from other counties.[41] In some cases McIver, traveling around the state giving teachers' institutes, administered the exams himself. He was constantly in correspondence with prospective students, local officials, and the teachers, principals, ministers, family members, and friends giving references.

One of his requirements was a literacy test, in the form of a short letter written by the girl herself requesting admission. Many of these letters are preserved, describing often in poignant terms the writers' straitened circumstances and near-desperation to attend the school. Ethel Wicker, for example, identified herself as eighteen years old; having taught several schools, she had amassed $70 in savings. She saw the Normal as her only means of finishing her education. "I am not able to go to an expensive school. The N & I school is a great blessing for poor girls." Another applicant, Ethel Finlator, was a teacher at the Oxford Orphan Asylum and an orphan herself. She wrote that she could afford to come for only three months, but hoped to learn enough shorthand in that time to teach it to the "helpless ones" in the home who might never be able to attend the Normal.[42]

There were other stated requirements but, in truth, few girls meeting the minimum age were turned down as long as room could be found for them. The

1892–1893 catalog declared the school open to any girl who had taken all the public schooling that her community offered. "To make the requirements for admission lower than this is unnecessary, and to make them higher would exclude many worthy and ambitious young women" for whom the institution had been created. McIver reaffirmed the same policy as late as 1906.[43]

From the beginning he was swamped with applicants. It was positively embarrassing, he wrote privately in 1894, to have to decide between them.[44] For years to come, far more girls applied—often twice as many—as could be accepted. The assumption throughout was that virtually all of them had a perfect right to attend. That in turn provided the basis for perennial appeals to Raleigh for appropriations to create more dormitory space.

Under Dean Foust the faculty gradually upgraded the curriculum after 1902, dropping high school work, adding advanced courses, and raising entrance requirements as high school development permitted. In effect, the Normal (and other colleges) began to accredit high schools; graduates of those it approved were admitted without examination, while those from other schools had to take entrance exams and preparatory work.[45] This was a milestone, but some students continued to need preparatory work until it was dropped in 1916.

The first graduating class, of 1893, consisted of ten students who had entered the previous fall with advanced standing. Agreeable to the charter, they received diplomas that carried a lifetime teaching certificate in the North Carolina public schools. The diplomas were not baccalaureate degrees, however, as McIver and the faculty withheld that degree until they could obtain enough college-level students to justify it.[46] That time came in 1902—ten years after the opening—when the college offered a fifth year of baccalaureate work to any previous graduates who cared to return and complete it. Seven did so, receiving the first bachelors' degrees in May 1903. The class of 1909 was the first to receive bachelor's degrees without anyone requiring a fifth year, and the old diploma disappeared.

By waiting this long, the college avoided a problem that perplexed some other institutions. Unwilling to apply such a masculine designation as "bachelor" to women graduates, they were awarding instead such degrees as maid of science and mistress of English. These compunctions had largely disappeared by 1903.[47]

* * *

President Charles W. Eliot introduced at Harvard in 1869 a system of almost totally free electives: students could take virtually any course that was offered. The elective system spread widely around the country, but found its least lodgment in the South, where a highly prescribed curriculum continued in favor.[48] This was emphatically true at the Normal in its first years, when a small faculty if nothing else prevented curricular proliferation. The original curriculum was modeled partly on those of familiar men's colleges and partly on the Mississippi Industrial Institute and College, the South's first public college for women.[49]

At the beginning in 1892, the work was divided into three departments: normal, business, and domestic science. The normal, listed as the leading department, included not only McIver's own pedagogy courses but also those in English, history, math, science, foreign language, art, music, and physical culture. Some of these subjects were sure to be controversial as normal school offerings; McIver may have hoped they would be less so under the pedagogical umbrella. Others were clearly vocational in nature, however, despite their labels: art included mechanical drawing while vocal music (the only kind taught at first) aimed at training future teachers to teach group singing.[50]

Students specialized in one of three curricular programs, corresponding to the three departments. One could take all of her courses in a single area, an elective option in itself, but this was clearly a divergent path that fewer than 10 percent of the students chose to follow. Some who could not afford more than one year at the school, but expected to teach, were given a special course in methods. Otherwise, every freshman regardless of major took the same eight courses in algebra, English, general and English history, Latin, physical geography and botany, drawing, vocal music, and physical culture, except that domestic science students substituted sewing for drawing. Sophomores took nine identical courses, except for one prescribed substitution each in the domestic science and commercial programs. Divergences by field increased in the junior and senior years, but the stipulated program betrayed only one possible elective, between geology or zoology, and that may have been an option of the teacher rather than the students.[51] Taking the curriculum as a whole, it was distinctly more than a vocational program.

By modern collegiate (but not high school) standards, course loads were heavy. The standard student program included 22–27 class meetings per week divided among six to eight courses. Study time was curtailed by the dormitory lights-out rule from 10 p.m. to 6 a.m., designed to ensure enough sleep. Dixie Lee Bryant many years later recalled that the lecture method prevailed in most disciplines, but she and the other science teachers used laboratories as well.[52] Pearson in particular popularized the park as an outdoor laboratory. The Normal thus followed current national practice, substituting lectures and laboratories for the old recitation method.[53] Students of Dr. Bitting remembered that when she dissected a cat in her physiology class, two students fainted, a third became ill, and a fourth remarked on the beauty of the lungs as well as the fact that the cat was pregnant with two kittens. Some of the faculty, Joyner for one, appeared to emphasize the amassing of factual information, with the ability to regurgitate it upon demand, more than encouraging students to think for themselves.[54]

* * *

Professional teacher training has usually included some practice teaching. In the late nineteenth century, this typically occurred in a practice school attached to the college or university. The Normal opened its practice and observation school in 1893 under the direction of the newly arrived Philander P. Claxton. There were ten pupils at first, aged five to eight, none of whom had attended school before; among them were McIver's own children Annie and Charlie. The school was located temporarily in Midway, the frame dormitory on the site of the later Alumni House. It took McIver nearly a decade to raise enough funds for a separate building; in the meantime he added on to Midway as the enrollments increased. In 1898, when the school was incorporated into the Greensboro public school system, it had about 200 pupils.[55] The new building, named for J.L.M. Curry, opened in 1902, just as Foust was replacing Claxton as principal.

In 1898 Claxton urged the Normal to institute a summer session for the majority of the state's public school teachers who desperately needed professional training and could never come otherwise.[56] Seeing competing summer schools to the east at Chapel Hill and Wake Forest, McIver attempted to promote a Normal summer session in the mountains, at the resort of Blowing Rock. It did not materialize, perhaps because of a typhoid epidemic at the college in 1899.[57] Instead, he inaugurated on campus in May 1902 a month-long session called the May School. About thirty teachers attended in the first year.[58] (Some people referred to them irreverently as Maypops.) By 1906 this had expanded to two sessions of two months each, beginning about April 1 and September 15, respectively—timed to avoid conflict with the customary public school term running from from mid-November to the end of March.[59] Not until 1912 did the full summer term materialize as Claxton had proposed.

Pedagogy or education at first included subjects like music that would later be differentiated. Students and some parents quickly demanded that instrumental music be provided in addition to vocal culture. This was almost certain to antagonize the private colleges, who already offered such work. Nor could it be justified easily as a part of teacher training, since the schools were not yet offering it. McIver delayed his approval, therefore, until 1899 when the sectarian controversy had abated. Even then the initial piano instruction was given off campus and without academic credit.[60] A year later, Charles J. Brockmann and his sister Laura joined the faculty, he organizing a small orchestra and she teaching piano, still on an extracurricular basis. In the absence of any clear legislative authorization for a music department, the Brockmanns were forced to earn their keep through student fees.[61]

The business or commercial department provided vocational training "for those women who are thrown upon their own resources, but who do not care to teach."[62] Forney's courses in stenography and typing reflected technological innovations that were at that time transforming office work and helping usher women into the clerical labor force.[63] In addition to these courses and others in bookkeeping the department offered correspondence work in shorthand—the institution's first extension courses. Students entering the program sufficiently prepared could finish in a year if they cared to do so. The year-long commercial program would remain an identifiable part of the college curriculum until 1967.

McIver prefaced his description of the domestic science department by noting that "the natural and proper position in life for the average woman is at the head of her own household." This department aimed to prepare students for that destiny, with courses in cooking, sewing, cutting and fitting, care of the sick, and household economy. Some of the faculty (but not McIver) questioned the academic legitimacy of such courses and challenged department members to justify the science part of their title. Student majors were required to take some of their courses in other departments. As time passed, the department (like the home economics field nationally) expanded and did become more scientific. And as home economics increasingly came to the high schools, the Normal trained their teachers.[64]

Physical education (then called physical culture) was under the direction of the resident physician, who also taught physiology and hygiene. Some of the hygiene instruction came in the course of daily rounds in the dormitories, which Drs. Bitting and Gove conducted both morning and evening. A junior faculty member was in charge of the gymnasium, which for a few years occupied a room in Main Building—always intended to be temporary. Following national patterns, activities were limited to gymnastics and calisthenics. Students were taught exercises they could use later in the schools. But benefits appeared more immediately according to a report several months into the program: "many chests increased in girth, shoulders straightened, arms became stronger, and the general bearing [was] much improved." There were of course no showers, and students were "encouraged to take a cold sponge bath after exercising."[65]

In 1900 even that room was taken away, in expectation of a new gymnasium that fate then interdicted through a typhoid fever epidemic; the funds were needed elsewhere. For several years physical culture virtually disappeared from the curriculum although Mary Settle Sharpe sandwiched some into her expression classes. Taking its place were a walking period, already instituted as early as 1897, and intramural athletics.[66]

For over a decade the library, like the gymnasium, was confined to Main Building. It usually had a room of its own, but for a year or two was banished to the rear of the auditorium.[67] When Annie Petty arrived in 1895 it again had its own room, but as this was the most convenient place to receive visitors, it also served as a reception room and the meeting place of the faculty and the board of directors. At such times the librarian and students had to vacate the premises. Obviously the collection was small: it consisted in 1895 of several hundred books donated or paid for by the McIvers, the faculty, and the students, as well as duplicates from the student literary society libraries in Chapel Hill. The book budget was less than $50 a year.[68] In 1900, when the library moved to a larger room (the former gymnasium), it had grown to about 3000 volumes.[69]

Andrew Carnegie, the Scots-born industrialist, was gaining renown as a donor of library buildings to communities and colleges, especially colleges offering technical or practical education. In 1901 McIver asked Carnegie for money to build a library for the Normal. Almost simultaneously he joined Greensboro Mayor W.H. Osborn in an appeal for a building to serve the city. Both requests were successful. The college library opened in 1905, directly across College Avenue from the Students Building—the modern Forney Building. The collection at that time numbered about 5000 volumes.[70]

* * *

The college could not have operated without its support staff of cooks, maids, janitors, and handymen—as many as forty-two in 1894–95.[71] Nearly all were African Americans, many of them living in a small segregated neighborhood several blocks west of campus.[72] Amanda Rhodes (or Rhoads) and William Peoples were among those whom students encountered most often and remembered longest. In the style of the place and time, only thirty years removed from slavery, they were known to students as Aunt Amanda (or Mandy) and Uncle William. Both spent many years at the college, he as a general handyman whose large-wheeled pushcart became something of a trademark. Their son William Rhodes went on to attend the Boston Conservatory of Music and years later gave a recital of his compositions in Aycock Auditorium.[73] "Uncle Henderson" Faribault served as head cook for several years, assisted and later succeeded by his son Edmund.[74] By far the most prominent of the maintenance staff was Ezekiel Robinson, who came to the Normal from Peace Institute shortly after the McIvers and remained until his retirement in 1946. Only 25 at his arrival, he outlived the "Uncle" convention and was always known as Zeke Robinson, the last name recognized almost as readily as the first. In the early years he drove the college hack, rang the bell, got the mail, carried water, lit fires, planted trees, waited table at state dinners, and performed a multitude of other services for the school and the McIvers. As the institution expanded he became head janitor and presidential chauffeur. Robinson too had a musical son, who became an orchestra leader in New York.[75]

Chapter 3

The Students

The school opening, originally scheduled for September 28, 1892, had to be postponed to October 5 because the physical facilities were not ready; they were hardly so on October 5.[1] Nonetheless McIver went to the railroad station downtown that day to greet the arriving students, help them into carriages, and send them to campus. He still had no firm idea how many would come. As the last train arrived, with just one coach, he boarded and asked all the Normal girls to remain seated until everyone else got off. When no one got up, he threw up his arms in mock despair and asked, "What will I do with all of you?" There were 176 instead of the 125 he expected.[2] The total would reach 223 by the end of the year.

McIver said he could have gotten 300–400 if there had been room for them in the dormitories.[3] Almost every year McIver and the board, sometimes seconded by legislative committees, called for additional dormitory construction. The existing buildings were enlarged but space never equaled demand.

Nearby houses absorbed the spillover in two ways. The college by 1902 was renting a few private houses in the neighborhood as auxiliary dormitories. Other students boarded in private homes: in 1894 as many as 150 out of a total enrollment of 391, and in 1902 about 80. Most of these homes were located within a block or two of campus, reflecting the rapid development of the surrounding neighborhood. In fact, the school's demand for student rooms surely stimulated that development. Most of these students ate in the college dining hall, but a few kept house for themselves.

All of this made McIver uncomfortable. He felt as accountable for students living off campus as for those in the dormitories. (Indeed, many parents refused to let their daughters attend the school at all in the absence of dormitory space.) One of his most difficult problems, he reported, was finding satisfactory accommodations for the off-campus students. They were restricted to a list of approved homes that excluded any containing young men and non-student boarders. Even in the homes McIver did approve, parietal control surely fell short of that in the dorms; every boarding house must have seemed like a land mine, waiting for some incident or scandal to set it off. None ever did.[4]

Causing almost no parietal problems was the small number of Greensboro students who lived at home—46 in 1904.[5]

* * *

McIver made it a point every year to emphasize how representative the Normal's students were, economically and geographically, hence how valuable the institution was to the state. In 1896–97, the 412 students hailed from 81 of the state's 96 counties. Eighty-nine of the 412 were fatherless; of the remainder, 139 were the daughters of farmers, 48 of merchants, 18 of lawyers, 18 of physicians, 10 of clergymen, and so on. He was also careful to ask every year how many would have attended no other institution in North Carolina if they had not come to the Normal; in 1896–97 the proportion was two-thirds. About one-third that year were paying their own expenses, without parental help. Clearly the school satisfied a real need, but the constituency changed subtly in the early years. Older girls who had already graduated from another college, had taught school previously, and were paying their own expenses diminished in number. But the average age long remained about 19.[6]

The Normal's charges were very low by the standards even of that day and place. Tuition was only $40 a year and even it was waived for those—a large majority—who promised to teach in the state's schools for two years after graduation. Three-fifths of the dorm spaces were reserved for non-tuition students. Board, room, and fees totaled $88 in the first year, with those boarding off campus paying slightly more. (There were a few optional fees; a single bed cost $2.) By law, the board bill could not exceed actual cost; at the end of the first year $1.63 was refunded to each student. At least a few students paid part of their costs in farm produce or merchandise.[7] The father of one student (Fodie Buie, McIver's soon-to-be secretary) actually sold a small farm to raise her $88 expenses.[8] Student expenses rose surprisingly little in the early years; in 1915 they still totalled less than $200.[9]

During the first three decades about a third of the students paid their own way, with loans or earnings from teaching and other work. A few people donated small scholarships, but McIver's preference in student aid was interest-free loans. From the beginning, the student literary societies, alumnae, and others contributed money to loan funds. Many students took advantage of them, and the repayment rate was high.[10] McIver not only lent money personally but launched a drive to raise the loan fund to $100,000.[11] At least twenty students had campus jobs in the early years, most often in the dining room.[12]

These students were usually the first girls in their families to attend college. While cousins and neighbors chose wage labor in the textile mills to escape the hardships of farm life, Pamela Dean remarks, these young women and their families put their faith in education as a means of attaining self-support and a better life. Meeting female faculty members not too distant from themselves in age or origin, they seem to have identified easily with them. Together they created "an institutional culture." Dean regards them as heralds of both a "New Woman" and a new middle class South.[13]

* * *

The campus they encountered must have demoralized some of the girls who were leaving home for the first time. The buildings were planted in the middle of what had only just been a cornfield; in fact, a few ragged cornstalks were almost the only relief from the general red mud. The only trees grew near Forest street and at the lower edge of the front campus, where a marshy stream paralleled Spring Garden street. No streets were paved and only a few boardwalks between the buildings kept students out of the mud.[14]

The buildings themselves were not entirely completed. Scaffolding was still up, carpenters and plasterers were still at work, and for some time students had to sweep up construction debris daily. Rooms were only half furnished and girls were occasionally crowded four to a room instead of the planned three. The buildings at first were heated by stoves and open fireplaces and were lit by kerosene lamps which the girls had to clean and fill daily. Water had to be carried in buckets or pitchers from a well behind Brick Dorm or from the nearby springs. Sanitary facilities consisted of outdoor privies behind the dorms. Sponge baths were the only kind available, using water that sometimes in midwinter had a crust of ice in dormitory wash basins. Seeing all this, some of the girls wept, others laughed, but all adapted. Some came from homes with no better amenities.[15] McIver himself protested in 1894 that the Normal (and the university) possessed the only state buildings he knew which lacked the "ordinary conveniences of civilization.... Neither... can compare with our penitentiary for the ordinary comforts of life as to its bathing arrangements, etc."[16] In 1897 a legislative committee called for a quick remedy to what it saw as inadequate paint, plaster, heating, sanitary facilities, and furnishings at the Normal.[17]

Improvements came gradually. City water—and with it steam heat—arrived in the first year but for reasons not explained wells continued to supply drinking water until the college was rocked by the typhoid epidemic in 1899.[18] Gas lights, hot water, and indoor bathrooms (too few) came in 1895 and 1896.[19] Students and faculty members contributed to campus beautification. The first graduating class in 1893 gave back the $1.63 per capita refund on their board bill, which was used to buy grass seed for the front campus. Mrs. McIver planted flowers there, and trees began to appear as well on the barren front slope. Some were planted by students over the years as class trees.[20]

* * *

The doctrine of *in loco parentis* was very much in force. All members of the faculty were involved in the familial nurture of the students, from the male professors who met them at the train to (especially) the women faculty who doubled as dormitory residents. One of these, Viola Boddie, recalled that they made it a point to say goodnight to every girl every night and to make sure that she was safe within the fold. Sometimes they even made fires in the students' rooms on cold mornings if the maid did not appear.[21]

McIver's chief reliance in these matters was Miss Sue May Kirkland, who bore the daunting title "lady principal and referee in matters social and domestic." The oldest of the faculty, Miss Kirkland bore only limited resemblance to the others. She was born in 1843 into a prominent Hillsborough family that would be hit hard by the war just as she reached maturity. Closely related to Judge Thomas Ruffin, the state's most renowned jurist, she was reared in his home[22] and attended the same finishing school as Mrs. Robertson, the history professor. There, in the words of a biographer, she experienced "the best in culture and correct deportment" that the time and place afforded. Forced to make her own way in the world as an adult, she taught music for a time at Peace Institute where she met the McIvers.

Miss Kirkland filled a genuine need for the upstart Normal. One of the board members suggested at the outset that the school hire "a governess of good administrative ability and *high social* position," presumably in hopes of attracting students from upperclass families.[23] Miss Kirkland filled this role to perfection, reigning for more than twenty years as arbiter of student manners and behavior. She ranks as one of the most colorful figures in the institution's history. Regal in bearing, coiffed to perfection by her personal maid, she wore fine jewelry and long rustling silk skirts that gave ample notice of her impending presence. She regularly used her own silver service in the dining hall.

Students compared Miss Kirkland with Queen Victoria. They quickly found that "a suggestion from Miss Kirkland was equivalent to a command. Two frequent reminders were: 'Ladies never hurry,' and 'Where are your gloves? No lady goes shopping or to church without them.'" As for church, "regular attendance was arranged for and expected." The severity of this presence was often moderated by a gracious manner, acts of kindness, a warm smile, and a keen sense of humor. Once, when Miss Boddie spied two students sitting unchaperoned in the parlor with two young men, she reported this to Miss Kirkland, recalling that when they were girls this would not have been tolerated. Miss Kirkland responded with a twinkle, "Yes, and see what it did for us." One of the Normal's original students, Phoebe Pegram, who had come from a backwoods farm and claimed only five days of prior schooling, recalled that many a night Miss Kirkland sent her maid to summon Phoebe in order to help her with her lessons. "She taught me how to read, talk, and many other things. Sunday mornings she would have me go by her room to see that I was properly dressed. She never in any way criticized the home-made hat or dress. She told me instead such things as always to button my gloves, to walk straight, and to come right back after church."[24]

Her wards found it difficult to be neutral about Miss Kirkland. She variously evoked awe, admiration, love, terror, ridicule, and hatred.[25] In the words of a former student and later faculty member, she provided a valuable model of taste, poise, and propriety in an institution that drew its students from all walks of life.[26]

One of Miss Kirkland's command posts was at the head table in the dining hall. Here students and most of the women faculty came together regularly. Meals were served family style and faculty members were usually distributed around the hall, one to a table, where they could direct the conversation suitably and monitor table manners. The meals were plain but nourishing, if short on vegetables. (Everything had to fit within a board bill of $8 a month per student.) According to student Mary Wiley, a typical Sunday dinner in 1892 consisted of broiled chicken, cold boiled ham, bread, rice, sweet potatoes, pickle, corn bread, cake, apple float, and water.[27]

* * *

One or two rooms in Brick Dormitory were the school's earliest approach to an infirmary. When they were not available, students who were not seriously ill remained in their own rooms under the care of their roommates pending the school physician's twice-daily rounds. Dr. Gove's office was on the second floor of Main Building, behind the auditorium. Students waiting to see her sat on the stage.[28] A separate infirmary was constructed in the summer of 1895 in her absence. To her mortification and in disregard of her prepared plans, it took the form of a small brick house ill suited to the purpose; nevertheless it served until 1912.[29]

In predominantly rural North Carolina, many children reached college age without contracting such childhood diseases as measles, mumps, and chicken pox. When they appeared at the Normal, careful quarantining was required to prevent an epidemic. McIver credited the new infirmary with limiting a measles outbreak in 1896 to 40-odd students out of 200 who had never had the disease before; as it was, one student died.[30] Another hazard lay in the fact that Greensboro had no hospital at the time. Where surgery was indicated, students were sent home. Emergency surgery was performed on campus; an amputation and an abdominal operation were conducted under these circumstances.[31]

* * *

Student literary societies were a well-established part of American college life by 1890. They played important educational and social roles in student life, sponsoring debates, dramatic presentations, and visiting speakers as well as a variety of social events. Besides providing necessary social relief from classroom routines, they were effective promoters of leadership and citizenship skills. Often there were two societies, paired against each other, the members chosen frequently by the college authorities.[32]

The Normal's founding fathers were quite familiar with the Dialectic and Philanthropic societies at Chapel Hill. As early as March 1891, the board of directors planned to include society meeting rooms in the new buildings.[33] McIver was not yet president, but he certainly endorsed the society idea. Aside from their other contributions, societies could (under proper regulations) promote social equality. At the outset, therefore, he encouraged the students to organize two societies on their own. He or someone else named two students, requesting them to make as nearly equal a division of the others as possible, based on ability and talent. They did so, and the societies were born in the spring of 1893. During the second year, with the benefit of advice on and off campus, they chose the classical names Adelphian and Cornelian. Society colors and rituals followed. Despite the directors' early plan for meeting rooms, none were provided and the societies met in classrooms until the Students' Building opened in 1902.[34]

Virtually all students joined the societies. The emphasis on equality was preserved, with talents and abilities as evenly distributed as possible. Each year a joint committee drew up a list of the new freshman class according to that principle, and a third party then assigned individuals to each organization. The society invitations and initiations became times of great suspense in student life. When the invitations went out, freshmen wept tears of joy or regret over the assignments they received. Then, after mild forms of hazing were introduced, they trembled at initiation time over the prospect of having to ride the Cornelian goat, who was paraded around campus beforehand, or climb the Adelphian greasy pole. No description of these terrors has survived.[35]

McIver emphasized democracy in various ways. He noted in 1902, for instance, that each year at least one of the student marshals (chosen by the societies) had worked her way through school.[36] He absolutely forbade secret societies that savored of exclusivity. When fourteen girls tried to organize a Greek letter sorority in 1896, they were curtly ordered to disband; such affiliation was inappropriate to missionaries in the public education crusade. Paradoxically, the societies were themselves as secretive as any sorority; McIver himself suggested the secrecy, by one account.[37] Each member's affiliation was open knowledge, but alumnae went to their graves refusing to divulge almost everything else: their officers (in the early years), secret passwords, and other mysteries. The democratic selection process made this secrecy acceptable.

The societies met twice monthly. Members read papers on literary or other topics, but as Pamela Dean reports, plays and debates, both mock and serious, were the most popular. Debate topics ranged from whether "the consecrated spinster gets more pleasure out of life than her married sister," to "the State and not the church should educate her children." The Adelphians' very first debate revolved around coeducation. Plays were sometimes written for the occasion, sometimes adapted from existing works. All these activities, Dean adds, contributed to McIver's goal of training shy girls to appear in public and, perchance, to influence public opinion as he had learned to do himself. Until 1906, these productions appeared most often in classrooms or, in the case of major events, in the auditorium. Inter-society debates came in 1902.[38] Once a year, the societies staged elaborate banquets (within the scope of a narrow budget) with decorations, costumed waitresses, and scripted toasts and responses. The girls were training for social as well as educational leadership.[39]

The school's first dramatic production was the County Fair in 1894, conceived by McIver and resurrected three years later for a legislative committee.[40] This may not have been produced by the societies, but they were responsible for most of the dramatic activity in succeeding years. In general, girls played all the parts, including males, wearing jackets and long skirts to simulate trousers. But even in the early years, male faculty appeared on stage. P.P. Claxton, the students' *beau ideal*, even appeared once in a kilt.[41]

The societies were responsible jointly for the first student publication, the quarterly *State Normal Magazine*, beginning in 1897. With an editorial board drawn equally from the two societies, it was at once a literary magazine, student newspaper, and alumnae journal. It carried campus news, student and faculty writings (including some by McIver), notable articles from the current press, the remarks of visiting speakers as transcribed by Forney's stenography students, and news from other campuses. As Pamela Dean notes, being on the magazine staff was both prestigious and demanding. The editors in particular were student leaders who could also be found as class officers, athletes, and student marshals.[42] In 1902, the Normal's tenth anniversary, the societies collaborated in producing the *Decennial*, a retrospective yearbook with the usual information on all the previous classes. There was no true yearbook until 1909.

* * *

Women's colleges were only beginning to experiment with student self-government in the 1890s. The general pattern was for administrators to charge student leaders with enforcing rules made by the authorities themselves. But, as Mabel Newcomer long ago pointed out in her history of women's higher education, that limited authority often carried with it some informal voice in the rule-making as well, if only because unacceptable rules went unenforced.[43]

All this was true at the Normal, where the nearest approach to student government before 1910 consisted of the student marshals, nominated each spring by the two literary societies. Five juniors were chosen from each society for the coming year, plus a chief marshal who alternated annually between the societies. These elections were then confirmed by the board of directors in order to convey official standing. Marshals were ostensibly chosen on the basis of scholarship and character but, perhaps subversively, they tended also to be among the most popular and attractive girls on campus. Again, some were girls who had to work their way through school.

The marshals not only represented the student body at public functions, but were responsible for helping McIver and the faculty to enforce school regulations. It was they (and especially the chief marshal) who most often represented the students in dealings with the administration, whenever these matters were not transacted directly in chapel or mass meetings. Normal students were indeed consulted in advance about some regulations. They sometimes protested them in mass meetings or elsewhere, and even got them changed on rare occasions. But there was no organized agency to convey student opinion on a regular basis. Initiatives almost always came from above.

McIver often referred the correction of minor offenses like excessive noise, passing notes in chapel, or abusing library books to the marshals, the literary societies, and the student magazine, which dutifully produced admonitory editorials. The few serious offenses he handled personally with the student or her family. In general, the students were deferential to his authority and McIver for his part was firm but forgiving in the face of persuasive penitence.[44]

* * *

The early students, faculty, and administrators could hardly avoid establishing traditions. Many lasted well beyond the Normal period, and some to the present day. The college and university seal bearing the likeness of Minerva, the Roman goddess of wisdom, traces back to the diplomas of 1894, but lacked consistency or formal adoption until 1963.[45]

Student class organization began with the seniors in the first year, and the other classes soon followed.[46] Unlike the other student organizations, in which the faculty had a hand, class organization was almost exclusively a student prerogative. The classes sponsored a variety of activities, social and athletic, and class offices provided many opportunities for leadership during a four-year student life. Class identification, as Pamela Dean points out, became very important symbolically. The first senior class adopted gold and white as its colors and the daisy as its flower. These were taken over by the whole student body before the seniors graduated in 1893.[47] Gold and white remained the college and university colors until joined by blue in 1987. Succeeding classes, beginning with that of 1898, distinguished between school and class colors by adopting four different pairs of colors, always including white, for themselves. These rotated among classes for many decades: green and white, red and white, blue and white, and lavender and white.[48] The classes also adopted their own hats, songs, and other identifying symbols.

Tree Day and Class Day became important rituals from an early date. Tree Day, beginning in 1895, was a freshman class ceremony. Likely copied from similar rituals at Smith, Vassar, and other women's colleges, it was also adapted to the clear need for arboreal beautification at the Normal. Every year, the freshmen gathered at a stipulated time and place on campus and, amidst great ceremony, planted a young tree. The class revisited the spot annually in similar rituals of dedication to class, college, and tree. The class of 1905, having substituted ivy for a tree and then seen the ivy die, held a memorial service.

Finally, in the Class Day ceremony at graduation, the seniors once again gathered at their tree. Beginning in 1900 they marched in double file, bound together by long chains of daisies, carried on their outside shoulders. (The daisy chain was also adopted from Vassar or another woman's college. In the early years at the Normal daisies may have been in short supply; ropes of vines, other greenery, and even ribbons were sometimes substituted.) At the tree class members read their class poems, histories, and prophecies, sang their class song, and capped off the occasion by burying their class records (and sometimes textbooks) beneath the tree. Then, with great seriousness, they passed the spade on to the junior class.[49]

* * *

Though a public institution, the Normal was anything but secular. Everywhere in the United States, but particularly in the South, religion was a pervasive part of higher education in public as well as private institutions. The Supreme Court itself declared in 1892 that the United States was "a Christian nation."[50] At the Normal, Protestant Christianity exuded from every pore. As Pamela Dean remarks, the atmosphere was best described as non-sectarian. McIver was a Presbyterian; the faculty were diversely Protestant with few exceptions. In hiring faculty McIver was careful to ask about religious interest and affiliation.[51] The great majority of students were Methodist, Baptist, and Presbyterian, reflecting the state in which they lived. The student roster always contained a scattering of other Protestant denominations as well as Catholics and Jews. All were expected to attend the church (or temple) of their choice regularly; sometimes they accompanied faculty members to churches downtown. Sunday afternoons contained two hours in which students were supposed to be in their rooms reading the Bible and meditating.[52] Miss Kirkland said grace before meals; there were often vesper services after supper; faculty members organized voluntary Bible study classes; and a campus YWCA chapter, organized in December 1892, was soon sponsoring a widely-attended Sunday school and mid-week prayer meetings. Every graduate received a Bible at commencement, the governor himself often making the presentation.[53]

Above all, there was the compulsory chapel service, held at 8:45 each morning. McIver expected faculty members to attend as well. As Dean describes, he and they sat on the elevated stage of the auditorium, facing the students. He liked to start with a rousing rendition of "The Old North State," followed by the latest news, instructions, admonitions, and perchance a rebuke for some recent misdemeanor. "Young ladies," he would sometimes say, "I want to remind you to keep off the grass. If one of you walk on it, the other 600 have the same privilege." Or, "Be sure to turn off the heat before raising your windows. We cannot heat Guilford County." Or, "It is a mark of civilization to close a door once you have gone through it."[54] More broadly, he urged them to be "lifters not leaners" in helping to create the New South. Chapel exercises, as Dean says, combined secular with religious activity. There were hymns and readings of Bible verses. The emphasis in and out of chapel was on a broad, ecumenical Christianity transcending denominations. Even the Jewish students were required to attend, given the important secular information transmitted, though their own religious beliefs and practices were never denigrated. Early Jewish students would remain fervent lifelong supporters of the Normal. One, Etta Spier, served on the faculty and led the Alumnae Association.[55]

* * *

Individual faculty members took major parts in all of these organizations and activities. In fact, they played a vital role in almost every aspect of student life. There was constant social interaction, as students and faculty invited each other to parties, picnics, and other social events. The McIvers hosted picnics for the senior class at the Guilford Battleground Park. Many if not most of the faculty invited their classes to their homes for dinner, charades, candy-making, or other events. Some faculty had a standing open house for students on Sunday afternoons or evenings. Students reciprocated with events of their own, sometimes involving the expenditure of considerable time in preparation. Individual students invited favorite female faculty members to join them in the soon-to-be-mandatory afternoon walking period. Numbers of faculty lived amongst the students as dormitory residents and ate with them in the dining hall. Alumnae remembered fondly for decades afterward the warm faculty friendships they had formed.[56]

All this contributed, as Pamela Dean finds, to a unified college community binding administrators, faculty, and students together in a common culture. The lives of nearly all revolved primarily around the campus.[57] More than this, she argues, the extracurriculum was an integral part of the curriculum. The lessons taught in social life would be at least as important as those of the classroom in turning out progressive New Women. "At parties and picnics, spreads and at homes, walks down town and theatrical performances, the students would learn to negotiate the intricate rituals of 'polite society.'" And "the carefully decorated classrooms," preparatory to student parties, "were stages on which the young women rehearsed for their future roles in society." Understanding these rituals, she continues, would be essential to them as teachers as well as wives of upwardly mobile husbands.[58]

McIver emphasized repeatedly to the girls that the state was not educating them as a charitable venture. It expected a return on its investment. That return would most often take the form of classroom teaching, but alumnae in whatever walk of life were expected to render service to society. Although this message was not unique to the Normal, it was the central thrust of McIver's and the school's continuing educational and societal crusade.[59]

Not surprisingly, these messages provided a fertile seedbed for feminism, shared by students and faculty. Governor Daniel L. Russell drew resounding applause at the 1897 commencement when he attacked the legal subordination of married women to their husbands.[60] Student editorials and essays repeatedly touched upon such themes as female accomplishments and unequal pay. A 1901 editorial by Daphne Carraway, soon to be chief marshal, attacked long skirts as "the white woman's burden."[61] Woman suffrage was not yet the hot issue in North Carolina or the Normal that it would become a few years later.

* * *

McIver made much of the fact that the original student regulations were made in consultation with the students themselves, who approved them in an early mass meeting. He was surely right in saying that the original students, many of them already college graduates and school teachers paying their own way, could be relied on to behave properly. But beyond the setting of hours for waking, study, and lights out, it is not clear where student-set rules ended and management rules took over. Among the latter there were the physician's daily room inspections, the faculty residents' nightly bedchecks, daily chapel with its own rules, and a variety of mealtime regulations.

Then there were the social regulations. Although girls of that generation were used to being kept on a short leash, Miss Kirkland's limits and strictures evoked at least occasional anger. Students were not to leave campus without her permission; overnight trips even to go home were severely limited and required parental permission in writing. As the campus boundaries were not well marked at first, this allowed some leeway that girls were happy to exploit. At first only a path and an unpaved roadway led into town, so most were drawn by convenience to take the Tally-ho, the school's horse-drawn hack operated by Zeke Robinson. These trips were limited to either Friday or Saturday, when the hack went back and forth every thirty minutes. Students were required to wear hats and gloves as well as the long skirts and petticoats then in vogue. None left without getting permission and a personal inspection beforehand from Miss Kirkland. In fact, gloves were a necessity even crossing campus to the dining hall.[62] In 1902 material progress came in the form of a streetcar along Tate and Spring Garden Streets, taking passengers either downtown or to Lindley Park in the opposite direction.[63]

Something of a crisis erupted on April Fools Day, 1897 when a number of students smoked cigarettes as part of a broader protest against college rules. McIver extracted written confessions from thirty-two girls, admitting that they had at some time smoked. The offenders were campused for the remainder of the term and their liberties otherwise curtailed. Cigarettes were still a novelty at this time. A little later, when they were not, smoking could bring expulsion.[64]

Severity was sometimes tempered with lenience. McIver once went so far as to make tickets available to any girls who cared to attend a weekend baseball game in Chapel Hill.[65] Such occasions were rare, however, and subject to careful chaperoning. County Fair week was a perennial headache, he said, with students demanding and sometimes getting a day off from classes to attend.[66] When a traveling circus set up on a vacant lot across the street it created havoc on campus, he reported later, with circus personnel and others invading college buildings. He threatened a court injunction to prevent a repetition.[67]

Any socialization with the opposite sex required prior approval. "Visits from gentlemen must be restricted to holiday occasions and those stated times when the young ladies will announce that they are 'At Home' to their friends generally."[68] Miss Kirkland's chosen place for this was a parlor across the hall from her apartment. As Pamela Dean remarks, they were not necessarily under her eye, but there was the imminent possibility of being so. To limit off-campus meetings, Dean continues, "a web of restrictions" surrounded the girls whenever they left campus. Even the weekend trips to town were usually chaperoned by a faculty member or a senior.[69] Of course there were a few girls who did not conform. Mary Wiley in her diary noted disapprovingly that several girls went walking off campus every evening with men, leaving them when they got back in sight of the school. Temptations were there, if not for Mary: she had already remarked the newfound popularity of Moore's Mineral Springs among Greensboro boys when the Normal was built across the street. Ostensibly there for the health-giving waters, they seemed to spend their time watching nearby Brick Dormitory.[70]

* * *

With the temporary abandonment of physical education in 1900, physical activity was limited to extracurricular athletics and a mandatory walking period, recently adopted from other women's colleges. For over twenty years, students would have to spend about forty-five minutes every afternoon before dinner either walking or playing sports. The walking gravitated largely to Peabody Park, which underwent a new round of landscaping in 1902. For some girls the requirement was hateful; others welcomed it as a social occasion. "We make a regular engagement with our chum . . . clasp arms, saunter, and listen laddies! We talk love."[71]

Sports were confined at first to meager and poorly maintained outdoor facilities constructed in 1900 to replace the gymnasium: a small athletic field (screened from the public gaze by shrubbery) and four tennis courts. That year also saw the birth of the student Athletic Association. It actively recruited members and within two years a quarter of the student body was involved. Some girls played tennis but basketball—now less than ten years old as a sport—was clearly the game of choice. Class teams formed, class cheers were composed, and class rivalries deepened.[72] Nearly all this activity was intramural, but there is evidence from this early period that Normal teams occasionally played basketball and tennis against nearby Guilford and Greensboro Colleges.[73]

McIver made sure that the students were given as much cultural exposure as the school could afford. He and Alderman had found a sad deficiency among the rural teachers they met at the teachers' institutes. What was later called the Entertainment Course began modestly in 1893–94 with a series of lectures by local notables and readings from Shakespeare by a traveling actor. Music was introduced the second year, and in 1895 the Normal, Greensboro Female College, and the Greensboro YMCA joined to sponsor a Combined Entertainment Course of eight performances, a pattern that continued more or less faithfully for years.[74] From the beginning, Greensboro residents and the students of nearby colleges patronized the series, even if some Normal students did not.[75]

* * *

The Normal had been established primarily to train teachers, and it did. Three-fourths of the alumnae became teachers, at least for the two years required to work off their free tuition. By 1907, about 3500 former students had taught some 300,000 North Carolina children, or about half of the white school population.[76] In the process they "redefined teaching as women's work.... 'Normal Girls' became the foot soldiers of the graded school movement." But the college's imprint was deeper still. Thousands of alumnae would pursue the gospel of public service that they learned at the Normal. They lobbied the legislature and won seats on county school boards even before gaining the right to vote themselves.[77]

Teaching and civic activism did not preclude marriage, which most of them entered in their twenties. The marriage rate among the classes of 1893 to 1911 was 68 percent, somewhere between northern alumnae and those from other southern schools, where the rate was highest.[78] By 1905 Normal alumnae lived in twenty-five or thirty states from Maine to California.[79]

The Alumnae Association was organized at McIver's request at the first commencement in 1893. His main purpose was apparently to have graduates maintain a loan fund for needy students. For some years the association was a loose confederation of county chapters, held together by the indefatigable Laura Coit.[80]

* * *

Three traumatic events tested the mettle of everyone at the Normal. The first was a typhoid fever epidemic in the winter of 1899–1900 that killed fourteen or fifteen people, nearly all of them students. When indoor plumbing was installed in the school buildings in 1895, it was impossible to connect with the city sewage system as it then existed. The Normal thus got permission (over some citizen objections) to run its own sewer into the woods north of campus, just acquired partly for that reason. There it drained into an open stream flowing toward North Buffalo Creek and ultimately the Greensboro water supply. Although it proved unrelated to the typhoid outbreak, untreated sewage thus ran through the soon-to-be-created Peabody Park, where students conducted nature studies and took their daily walking period.[81]

The epidemic was traced to a well used for drinking water in the dining hall and a leaking sewer connection 125 feet distant. Equally responsible with the faulty connection was the college's decision to continue using the well for drinking water after city water was available and in use for other purposes.[82] Perhaps the college's own contribution to the city water supply, just noted, accounted for its reluctance to complete the link.

The fever appeared on campus in early November 1899 and was at first mistaken for malaria, which was already prevalent. Once typhoid was diagnosed and the number of cases escalated to nearly fifty, McIver closed the school until after Christmas. Many students were too sick to go home and the campus became an emergency hospital. Most of the maintenance staff fled, but Greensboro physicians, faculty, friends and relatives of students, and townspeople stepped in to serve as doctors, nurses, maids, cooks, and scrubwomen. Anna Gove, the college physician, deserved particular commendation. McIver's twelve-year-old son Charlie contracted the disease but eventually recovered. Among the fatalities was Fannie Turner, in charge of housekeeping, who succumbed while nursing sick students.[83]

Once public health officials located the cause, the college readily adopted their recommendations. McIver, rising to the occasion, said he would make the college a health resort.[84] The leaky sewer was replaced while ignoring the open one through the woods. All campus wells were filled and the college now relied entirely on city water, which it further treated. Buildings were disinfected. Every mattress was burned and double beds were replaced with singles. Taken together, the medical expenses and remedial measures cost at least $16,000. Funds earmarked for a new gymnasium were diverted to these ends and the college incurred debts that took nearly a decade to repay. McIver received some abuse for supposedly letting the disaster happen, but most people around the state, including relatives of the deceased, were immensely supportive.[85] When school reopened on January 30, about three-quarters of the students returned. In short order, enrollments were back to capacity.

* * *

The second crisis arose from the burning of Brick Dormitory on the night of January 20–21, 1904. The entire building was consumed, including the massive kitchen-dining room wing where the fire apparently started, and part of which was only a few months old. The nearby power plant and laundry building also burned. Almost miraculously, there was no panic, no lives lost, nor anyone seriously injured as over 300 residents of the largest dormitory on campus were rousted from bed and forced to evacuate in the middle of a frigid night. Virtually all of their clothing and other possessions were lost.

The absence of fatalities was attributable to previous fire drills and, more immediately, to faculty resident Minnie Jamison and several students who spread the alarm. One, Josephine Scott, ran outside in her nightgown to ring the college bell, which stood nearby, until everyone was out. To the rescue came luckier students, faculty, townspeople, and others around the state with offers of money, clothing, and spare rooms.

Again McIver closed the school to regroup, this time for about five weeks. The Students' Building, in use for the past two years but still not completed, was pressed into service as an emergency dormitory for many of the displaced. Sheets were hung to form impromptu rooms. The students, ever adaptable when the cause was good, spent the rest of the academic year there with little or no complaint. A temporary shed was set up on the tennis courts (the future site of Mary Foust Dormitory) to serve as kitchen and dining hall. Still, there were too few accommodations for all of the students, and over 100 did not return that year.[86]

McIver was out of town at the time of the fire, and only learned of it several hours later when the carriage driver taking him home from the railroad station told him, "Boss, yer school got burnt up last night."[87] On reaching campus and learning there were no casualties, he called a student assembly where he found an auditorium full of bedraggled girls, some in nightclothes, some in borrowed garb of imprecise fit. He asked all to join in singing "Praise God from whom all blessings flow."[88]

That hymn set the tone for the weeks and months to follow. McIver seemingly lived for crises like this. It was now that he turned down an offer he might well have taken otherwise, to succeed the late J.L.M. Curry as general agent of the Peabody Fund.[89] He repeatedly proclaimed the fire a blessing in disguise. He told an alumna who came to commiserate, "It's a good thing. We need a new dormitory, more space, more land." The front campus, he said, should be reserved for academic buildings; he wanted to put a science building on the burned-out site. Dormitories belonged in back, across Walker Avenue. Furthermore, he said, the campus should acquire all the property eastward to Tate Street, to make room for additional buildings that would soon be needed. Still further, he wrote P.P. Claxton, "no more cheap buildings will be erected on these grounds."[90]

The state promised $80,000 to build a new dormitory and within three days of the fire McIver and the faculty were planning its features.[91] The result: a very long building (492 feet) divided into fireproof sections, with only two stories, and primarily two-student rooms. Brick Dorm had had four floors and rooms with up to four students. The new building would also house the dining hall. Construction began in April along College Avenue beyond Walker where new dormitories were henceforth to be; by heroic effort the building was in service in October. At McIver's suggestion it was named for Cornelia Phillips Spencer, an outspoken champion of the university and its traditions in Chapel Hill, where she lived most of her life. Never a feminist or even a particular champion of women's education, she nevertheless exemplified for McIver and his contemporaries what a North Carolina woman could achieve with her pen. Spencer Hall, with its great length and multiple verandas, has been a campus landmark ever since. In 1948, architect Walter Gropius proclaimed it the finest piece of architecture on campus.[92]

A year after the fire McIver estimated its costs at $108,000, but thought he had appropriations in hand to pay it off with careful management. The new library was then underway and the college seemed never better.[93]

* * *

The third crisis was the sudden and premature passing of McIver himself. No later president or chancellor could have as profound an influence over the institution as its founder. His death came as a total surprise, except in retrospect. A driven man, he surely worked himself to death. A prodigious eater, overweight, careless of diet, and not given to exercise, he likely ate himself to death as well.[94]

William Jennings Bryan had come to the state in September 1906 on a political campaign trip, the first visit since his commencement appearance in 1894. McIver went to Raleigh to welcome him and then to accompany him to Greensboro on Bryan's special train. Before leaving Raleigh on September 17, McIver gulped down two dinners at the Yarborough House hotel, then raced for the train. At Durham, where the train stopped to let Bryan give a speech, McIver complained of indigestion and chest pains. A reporter helped him stretch out on a seat. In a few minutes he was dead. Bryan, riding in the observation car, rushed forward to pay his respects, and was led away in tears. As crowds had gathered to see him at stations ahead, Bryan stopped only to deliver the news and brief eulogies of McIver, then bade the train move on. The speech that he was to have given in Greensboro became a memorial tribute. The ensuing funeral was said to have been the largest-attended in Greensboro history.[95]

Part II
The Normal Grows Up, 1906–1919

Chapter 4

Administration and Student Affairs

As dean of the college, Julius Foust was clearly in line to succeed McIver temporarily. The permanent succession was another matter. When the board of directors met in November 1906, there was a solid consensus in favor of James Y. Joyner, who was board president by virtue of his elective post as superintendent of public instruction. But Joyner (like McIver on comparable occasions) felt an obligation to continue his present work, pushing public school reforms through the coming legislature. On his refusal Foust continued serving for the remainder of the academic year.[1] Some board members hoped Joyner would change his mind after the legislative session, and in fact he indicated in the spring of 1907 that he was reconsidering. Learning of this, Foust quickly announced his own candidacy. Clearly, each man had hoped the post would fall to him by acclamation. The two had been close friends but Foust now wrote Joyner accusing him of ambivalence if not duplicity. Faced with Foust's resolute stance, Joyner backed down. Further, he may have sensed some new opposition at the Normal by virtue of his helping engineer through the recent legislature the charter for the East Carolina Teachers' College—a measure distinctly unpopular in Greensboro. In any event, the board, delighted at having avoided a fight, now unanimously elected Foust as president. The two men remained friends and worked together harmoniously until Joyner's retirement from office in 1919. In fact, Foust served as manager of Joyner's successful campaign for president of the National Education Association in 1909.[2]

Five years McIver's junior, Foust was a native of next-door Alamance County and an 1890 graduate of the state university. He had served most of the intervening years as superintendent of schools in Wilson and Goldsboro before coming to the Normal in 1902 as professor of education. His doctorate like McIver's was an honorary one from their alma mater, received in 1910. McIver said of him in 1906, "He is not an eloquent speaker but is interesting and his judgment is always sound."[3] In contrast to McIver in appearance, Foust was tall, thin, and looked almost boyish in 1906. At first diffident (in his own later estimation) about his ability to fill McIver's shoes, he quickly developed an authoritative (if not authoritarian) persona of his own. Stern, even self-righteous, he could be forgiving after perceiving that he had made his desired point. He was capable of great personal and financial sacrifice in behalf of family, friends, faculty, or students whom he regarded as deserving. Like McIver, Foust made an effort in the early years to learn the name of every student. He conferred personally in those years with students in academic trouble. In 1912 he turned down a gubernatorial appointment to a child labor committee, citing his need to help students arrange their midyear programs.[4] Foust lacked McIver's gregariousness and speaking facility; his sometimes shambling chapel performances were tedious in the extreme. But he possessed enviable political skills and a wry sense of humor not always seen or appreciated by students. Everyone saw him as honest and wholly devoted to the college. In the end he served it twice as long as McIver and with fewer outside distractions. Where McIver was developing a national reputation with seemingly unlimited prospects, Foust operated within a narrower sphere and seems never to have been tempted to leave the college. He deferred to the faculty in setting curricular policy, but as the college grew in size and academic standing he was clearly the leader.

* * *

As early as 1899, Walter Clark, the respected but frequently contrarian state supreme court justice, recommended that the Normal's board like those of the university and the A&M college include representatives of its alumnae—in this case, obviously, women. When the idea resurfaced in 1913 Foust favored it in principle.[5] Alumnae pressure mounted as the equal rights movement gained strength nationally and alumnae trustees appeared at other women's colleges. In 1916 the *Alumnae News* carried an approving editorial by Annie McIver Young '05, McIver's daughter, and a session of the Alumnae Association backed the demand unanimously.[6] They prevailed the next year with the appointment of Minnie McIver Brown, another relative and former student. She would serve usefully for many years on the board, its executive committee, and later the consolidated university board.[7]

Although Foust lacked McIver's fund-raising connections out of state, he was equally adept in lobbying the legislature. The college constantly struggled to expand as the state's high schools turned out more and more graduates seeking admission. McIver and his colleagues had created a rising tide of public support for education, including higher education. The Normal's strongest card was the schools' obvious need for more teachers. Between 1907 and 1919, as the Normal's enrollments rose from 545 to 784, an increase of 44 percent, its annual appropriation increased by 74 percent, from $95,000 to $165,000. In fact, the 1907 appropriation equalled that of the university with its enrollment of 788.[8] Foust's achievements in the still balmier decade of the 1920s led to his lasting reputation as The Builder. And during his administration the college progressed academically fully as much as it did materially.

Students maintained much the same relationship with Foust as they had with McIver. They continued to stage the biennial dramatic production for visiting legislators and welcomed him back enthusiastically from his increasingly successful trips to Raleigh. He in turn valued and sought their own lobbying efforts. Foust and the faculty continued to entertain student groups on occasions ranging from formal parties with receiving lines to hayrides out to the Guilford Battleground. They reciprocated with parties of their own, including some on his birthday.[9]

* * *

Although Foust lived past 80, his health was never robust and he was forced to take brief leaves of absence over the years to recuperate. In addition, he spent most of the academic year 1918–1919 doing war work with the Federal Bureau for Vocational Education in Atlanta.[10] Even without these absences, the college's growth required the increasing delegation of responsibilities to others. For the most part, Foust recognized this fact and made the appropriate changes, but he did not yield graciously to what he perceived as faculty threats to his control.[11] These accordingly were rare.

The office of dean of the faculty, Foust's own launching pad to the presidency, was held sometimes formally, sometimes informally by William Cunningham Smith of the English department from 1907 until the college's reorganization in 1922. Smith's chief function was to fill in for the president during his absence; college Secretary Laura Coit continued to perform most of the routine administrative duties whether Foust was present or absent. Smith was always more interested in academic policy than other aspects of administration, and in 1911 education professor Junius A. Matheson was appointed to the additional position of dean of the college. After Matheson left for health reasons he was replaced in 1915 by history department head Walter Clinton Jackson. It was Jackson who took over Foust's administrative duties when he left for Atlanta in 1918.[12]

Another administrative post from the earliest years—off and on—was that of registrar. In 1909 Mary Taylor Moore began a thirty-nine-year tenure in the post. Like Coit, Moore '03 was an alumna who devoted her life to the college. She returned a year after graduation to teach Latin. As registrar she became active nationally and the system she developed in running her office was widely emulated. A gracious but strong-minded woman, Moore was a major player in lifting the college to national recognition academically in the 1920s.[13]

* * *

Until 1917 the capital improvement budget was too low to permit much campus planning. But Foust continued to call on Warren Manning of Boston occasionally as landscape planner. Manning favored extending College Avenue southward across Spring Garden Street to the railroad, creating the impressive vista for travelers that the board had contemplated when they located the campus in the first place.[14] For some years the property across Spring Garden was not for sale, however, and when the college did acquire much of it in 1918, priorities had shifted. Instead of presenting its best face to the railroad, the college surrendered to utility and constructed a new power plant there, in 1924. College Avenue was never extended to the railroad and the scenic panorama from the tracks quickly gave way to public and private buildings of every description a full generation before mass rail travel itself faded away. The college's front door continued to be Spring Garden Street.

Surrounded by actual or threatened development on three sides, the college was constantly on the lookout to buy adjacent real estate. Since before McIver's death, attention centered on expanding eastward to what would soon be McIver and Tate Streets and southward across Spring Garden to the railroad.[15] Foust acquired much of this land in separate parcels between 1908 and 1918—in the case of the eleven-acre Teague property across Spring Garden Street by creative financing through the Alumnae Association.[16] At the same time, the college felt it had no forseeable use for the northernmost part of the 1895 purchase, now separated by the extension of West Market Street. It sold these nine acres in 1907, using the proceeds to finance some of the purchases nearer at hand.[17]

* * *

Larger appropriations permitted the construction of greater classroom and dormitory space. McIver had seen the Brick Dormitory fire as freeing space for a new classroom building. The project now went forward, bearing his name. Foust and Manning envisioned the McIver Memorial Building as a large edifice with a central core and two wings, bigger overall than next-door Main. For the time being they had to content themselves with the central core, completed in 1908. The new building housed the science departments in particular; most of the others remained with the administrators in Main. (After the advent of McIver Building, Main gradually came to be called Administration Building.)

A new colonnaded south wing of Spencer Dormitory, completed in 1907, housed about seventy-five additional students. It also contained a makeshift gymnasium in the basement, interspersed with load-bearing columns making hazardous almost any activity except calisthenics. Two small dormitories, named Woman's and Kirkland (for the Noble Women of the Confederacy and Sue May Kirkland, respectively), were added behind Spencer in 1912 and 1914. Until 1917, at least, the college continued to rent houses and rooms in the neighborhood as adjunct dormitories. In addition, some overflow students rented rooms themselves in private homes; about fifty did so in 1917.[18] The 1909 legislature made it possible finally to complete the Students' Building, including a 900-seat auditorium on the second floor. This was soon outgrown but not replaced until Aycock Auditorium was built in 1927. A new and larger infirmary came in 1912, on the later site of Elliott University Center's north wing. It too served in part as an overflow dormitory.[19] The small brick house on College Avenue previously serving as infirmary became variously a dormitory and a music building.

* * *

Immediately after McIver's death a fund-raising campaign was launched to erect a statue in his memory. As it turned out, twin statues were erected in 1912, the work of sculptor Frederick W. Ruckstuhl. The original was placed on the State Capitol grounds in Raleigh, the duplicate on the Normal campus in front of the new McIver Memorial Building.[20] They were not entirely pleasing to those who had known the subject. The face, taken from a death mask, occasioned little controversy but the body rather understated McIver's actual girth and its stance was reportedly untypical of him. Ruckstuhl explained that he had been given conflicting evidence on these matters, so he resolved them idealistically, or in favor of "reasonable elegance." Foust replied diplomatically that everyone was coming to like the statue more and more as time passed.[21]

Appropriately, the statue was dedicated in 1912 on Founder's Day, an annual event first celebrated in 1909. It soon came to be scheduled on or about October 5, the anniversary of the school's first opening in 1892. As the purpose was primarily to commemorate McIver, the day typically featured speeches about him and his work by visiting dignitaries, administrators, faculty, and students, as well as a ceremonial decoration of his grave. It was a college holiday, and both faculty and students were expected to attend the main exercises. But as early as 1913 outside speakers were occasionally invited to come and address other topics.[22]

* * *

Peabody Park continued to serve as the favorite venue for the daily walking period as well as biology field trips. But it achieved new uses as well. In about 1908 an outdoor theater was created along one of the streams. A wooden platform served as a stage while spectators sat or stretched out on the sloping ground opposite. The theater usually hosted student dramatic productions, but professional productions were occasionally held there as well as certain commencement exercises. The college's ambitious May Day festivals of 1912 and 1916 featured events in the theater and a number of other places in the park and campus.[23]

McIver erected a summer house in the park, where student groups sometimes gathered for meetings and recreation. (It was said to have been constructed from logs salvaged from the original Guilford Court House, near the Revolutionary battleground, but that lineage rested more on faith than evidence.) During World War I, students helped build what they called the YWCA Hut in the park, just beyond the end of College Avenue. A substantial building with four large fireplaces, it more than supplanted the summer house and served for years as a student union supplementary to the Students' Building.

* * *

Like McIver before him, Foust was a buyer and seller of cows, and now milking machinery as well. In 1913 the dairy barn (on the later site of the dormitory quadrangle) was regarded as too close to the new Woman's Dormitory and a new barn was built farther west, near Dairy (later Aycock) Street.[24] In 1910 the farm produced more milk than the students could consume and the college sold the surplus.[25] But seven years later rising enrollments had overtaken it and Foust began looking for another farm farther away. For several years he had the use of an additional one southeast of Greensboro.[26]In charge of the farms from 1917 onward was superintendent of buildings and grounds James M. Sink. His long service in that post made him a campus institution by the time of his retirement in 1953.[27]

* * *

As the enrollment rose from 461 in 1906 to 784 in 1919, male faculty members continued to meet incoming students in the fall at the railway station downtown. They still came from all over the state, but when a county or region fell short, as the mountains often did, Foust made a special effort to recruit applicants there; for political reasons the college must never appear to be only regional. The number of students who had previously graduated from another college—high in the first years—dropped off to zero by 1912. But as late as 1915–16, the last year such statistics were recorded, sixty-eight (10 percent) of the students had themselves taught school before entering the Normal. In a period of gradual urbanization, farmers' daughters fell from a third in 1906 to a quarter in 1915. (They had never been much over a third.) Those paying their own way declined from 29 to 23 percent. The average age remained nineteen to twenty.[28]

In 1896 the Board permitted McIver to admit out-of-state students, charging $60 instead of the usual $40 tuition.[29] If any came they were too few to merit inclusion in the statistical tables that were published annually before 1916. Foreign students, on the other hand, evoked special attention. A Brazilian girl came in 1907, a Cuban in 1912, and two Serbian girls in 1919, admitted amidst much fanfare at student request and student expense, paid by subscription.[30]

* * *

Student tuition remained at the original $40 per year, with remission to those promising to teach in the state's schools for two years after graduation. (In 1919 prospective social workers were put on the same footing.)[31] At the same time, increasing general prosperity led to rising student expenses for a variety of extracurricular projects: class assessments, class pins, the annual, senior class gifts to the college, and other accoutrements of middle class college life beyond the dreams of the spartan Nineties. Many students were hard pressed to keep pace. Economic distinctions were sufficiently apparent by 1910 to evoke an editorial in the *State Normal Magazine* condemning snobbery.[32]

Although a few small scholarships were offered by such agencies as the United Daughters of the Confederacy, the college continued to regard loan funds as the preferred form of financial aid. They were self-replenishing and students benefited, said Foust, from paying part of their own expenses.[33] Following McIver's death the Alumnae Association launched a drive to create a McIver Loan Fund in his memory. Pledges and cash exceeded $18,000 by 1909.[34] Between a quarter and a third of the students borrowed from the various loan funds. The number working in the dining hall, the principal campus job, rose to about thirty-five; there were vastly more applicants than positions available. A few girls worked at the campus post office, newly created in the Administration Building basement in 1909.[35]

* * *

Sue May Kirkland remained as lady principal until her death in 1914, surely one of the last years that her regal, Victorian regime could have been accepted without open revolt. Students remained awestruck or hostile, depending on the individuals. Jane Summerell, '10, later a mainstay of the English department, long remembered how impressed she was as a student passing by Miss Kirkland in the dining hall: "I rarely raise my cup of tea to my lips now without thinking of how Miss Kirkland held her cup... the grace and gentility of it."[36] Even Foust and the faculty joked about her aristocratic airs, sometimes to her face, counting on Kirkland's proven sense of humor. Writing her in the summer of 1910, when she and virtually all the faculty were away, Foust noted the recent arrival of a freight shipment in her name, including a horse-drawn carriage without the horses. As time passed and no horses arrived, Foust facetiously offered her the use of the college mule team.[37]

Miss Kirkland's death brought a reexamination of her office. Lady principals were going out of fashion around the country and being recast as deans of women. Foust spent years reformulating her position and searching for a suitable successor. In the meantime, he appointed Emma King, an English instructor since 1909, as acting lady principal; a year later, in 1915, she took the title director or dean of dormitories and held it for nearly a decade. The year 1914 brought a new student government organization placing greater responsibility on the students for their own supervision.[38]

* * *

The growth of student government was incremental. From the beginning McIver sought help from the student marshals in enforcing rules that he and the students had agreed upon, usually at his initiative. The marshals themselves were nominated by the literary societies but appointed by the college board of directors. As Normal students learned of advances in student self-government around the country, they demanded a larger voice themselves.[39] A member of the class of 1910 remembered many years later in the riotous '70s, "I don't think we agitated much about anything. We studied."[40] Yet it was student agitation in her senior year that led to the creation of an elected Students' Council the following fall. A *State Normal Magazine* editorial in May 1910 called attention to earlier student government achievements at Bryn Mawr and declared: "The day of the timid, blushing, fainting maiden has gone; while our present day girl, although no less a real woman, is independent, resourceful, self-reliant." When she goes to college she expects to be treated like an adult, "not like the inmate of some prison." The resulting council was merely advisory, replacing the student marshals in that capacity. But it was elected, consisting of three representatives from each class and the chief marshal as ex officio president.[41]

This reform did not generate an outpouring of student interest. Rather, the magazine deplored the dearth of qualified students willing to undertake leadership roles. And those who were elected to student offices, it noted, were too often the best looking and best dressed.[42] Yet some in the next student generation found the advisory council inadequate and pushed for greater student power to make and enforce their own rules. They found great encouragement in the woman suffrage movement swirling about them and, closer home, from political scientist Harriet Elliott, their militant faculty confidante.[43] A cautious Foust agreed to their proposals in 1914, and they took effect that fall.[44] The new self-government association (SGA) consisted primarily of four elected officers together with the presidents of the respective dormitories. They were closely watched by an advisory board consisting of Foust and his fellow administrators.[45] The first president was Gladys Avery (Tillett), later prominent with Elliott in the state and national Democratic party.

Not surprisingly, the SGA turned early to the modification of student social regulations. Its mandate was ill-defined and Foust was reluctant to commit himself contractually to an experiment he and some older faculty members regarded as suspect. But he did permit Rosa Blakeney, the second president, to go north with Dean Emma King and report back from colleges with longer student government experience.[46] Despite occasional friction, he and the SGA leaders worked well together—some virtually idolized him—and it soon became an established part of the college.[47]

This relationship owed everything to the fact that the students who created student government were evolutionists rather than revolutionists. They did little more at first than codify the regulations they had inherited.[48] A student editorialist remarked rather acidly in 1917 that in three years of supposed self-government, small opportunity had been given them to fall by the wayside. But she did welcome two changes: the privilege of attending a motion picture without faculty chaperonage and the freedom to take the walking period at any time of the day. Agitation for modest reforms continued. When students became restless (in Foust's phrase) with class attendance regulations in 1918, they were withdrawn on an experimental basis.[49] Student judicial officers, for their part, could be severe when they found flagrant violations of the regulations. In 1919 the college followed their recommendation to expel a student who had left campus without permission to meet boys.[50]

* * *

The literary societies also evolved. College enrollment grew so large by 1918 that the existing Adelphian and Cornelian societies could no longer accommodate everyone. A third was formed in 1918, named Dikean (pronounced Deekian) after a Greek word for honesty or justice.[51] Hitherto, virtually every fact about the societies had been secret except the identity of their members. This imposed restraints that many found both burdensome and unnecessary. When a substantial number of students called for complete openness, a compromise was reached by 1918 that left secret only the ritual and initiation ceremonies.[52]

More important, the societies lost their near-monopoly control of the extracurriculum. The marshals, nominated by the societies and appointed by the board of directors, had originally been the core of student government, such as it was. Now, with an elected student government in place, the marshals were relegated to a largely honorific role as ushers at public assemblies and attendance-takers at chapel.[53] The respective classes—freshman to senior—also grew in importance at the expense of the societies. They were the primary intramural athletic units and drew corresponding student loyalty. The senior class sponsored the massive May Day pageants in 1912 and 1916. And a Red Cross drive in 1919 was conducted through the classes because "class spirit was strongest."[54]

Similarly, many of the activities previously carried on within and between the societies, like debate and drama, now spun off into separate clubs. Students increasingly focussed on these smaller groups that attracted persons with similar interests regardless of society affiliation. They included the Athletic Association, an Art Club, a Bird Club, a Miscellany Club (devoted to studying public issues), a Dramatic Club, a Debating Club, and a Consumers' League. Symbolic of the drift was a complaint in 1913 that the societies' traditional meeting time was preempted increasingly by entertainments.[55] By the 1920s the societies themselves would be reduced to little more than sponsors of entertainment.

Student publications showed the same centrifugal pull. The *State Normal Magazine* began in 1897 as a project of the two societies; so did the *Decennial*, the single-shot "annual" of 1902. But the magazine became progressively more independent of the societies and when a real annual (called the *Carolinian*) appeared in 1909 it was under the aegis of the senior class.[56] The administration and faculty retained considerable control of both. Faculty members were not impressed with the quality of the annual, and only reluctantly approved its continuing publication. In 1914 Foust called the magazine editor on the carpet for an editorial she had written, telling her sharply that she didn't have the right attitude. The editorial was not published.[57]

* * *

Elizabethan May Day pageants were all the rage in America between 1910 and our entry into World War I. Women's colleges in particular staged these outdoor events, featuring colorful processions, dramatic presentations, and old English folk dancing.[58] The Normal fell into step with a vengeance. It put on two of these productions, in 1912 and 1916, under the direction of Mary Settle Sharpe, the professor in charge of drama. Each required a massive outpouring of time and energy from students, faculty, and Curry School children; virtually all were involved in some capacity. Each event was correspondingly noteworthy, both in the photographic record and the memories evoked. Some of the work had to be contracted out: bows and arrows were made by students at Hampton Institute in Virginia. Preliminary parades or processions made their way downtown to advertise the attractions to be staged later at various campus venues. The dramatic presentations including Shakespearian plays were staged in Peabody Park. Maypole dances were held on the athletic field, the later site of Petty Science Building. Altogether, 3,000 spectators attended the five-hour first pageant, paying $1.50 apiece ($1.00 for children). The second production was larger than the first, but attendance figures were not given. In both cases the weather cooperated beautifully, and Foust was not amused when a disgruntled faculty member hoped aloud that rain would fall on the 1912 pageant.[59]

* * *

The mandatory, non-sectarian chapel services came to be held at mid-day, Monday through Friday—after 1909 in the new Students' Building auditorium. As the only occasions other than SGA meetings when all students were present, they continued to serve as the occasions for public announcements and exhortations as well as devotions.[60] In addition, individual students and faculty continued to conduct non-denominational prayer meetings and Bible study classes which were said to reach almost every student. Most of the work of campus ministry was left to the YWCA; denominational ministries, coming into existence in other parts of the country, would wait here for a later day.[61] The Normal YWCA unit affiliated with the national organization in 1911, and a year later a resident YWCA secretary arrived. Until then the work was borne entirely by students and their faculty advisers. The college not only hired and paid the secretary but quite openly endorsed the Y and its work. By the same token, the Y served the college; until formation of the SGA in 1914 it published the annual student handbook.[62] By 1910, as a fund-raising device, it operated a small campus store.

No doubt the Y's greatest material achievement was to build, during World War I, The Hut. This edifice drew its inspiration from similar buildings of the day, restricted by wartime financial and manpower constraints. In the summer of 1918 the girls received permission to build one of their own near the entrance to Peabody Park at the end of College Avenue. The construction was planned and supervised gratis by a local contractor, but up to a dozen students (dubbed carpenterettes) furnished all but the heaviest and most skilled labor. Alumnae, students, and the college shared the minimal costs. The resulting structure was a framed, board and batten building of 40 by 80 feet with four large fireplaces—one for each class. An object of immense student pride, it served for about thirty years as an informal student union and headquarters of the campus YWCA.[63]

The relative absence of religious bias at the college was evidenced by Jewish student Laura Weill's virtual sweep of the major campus offices prior to her graduation in 1910: editor of the *State Normal Magazine* and the annual *Carolinian*, senior class president, marshal—and member of her class's championship basketball team. Later marrying into a wealthy Greensboro textile family, Laura Weill Cone remained for many years a major presence at the college—an influential alumna and a trustee of the later consolidated university.[64]

Weill capped her student performance by writing just before graduation what has ever since been the college/university song. It emanated from a contest sponsored by the alumnae over a year earlier, which had drawn no satisfactory response despite the promised prize of $10 in gold.[65] Weill used a tune she had found in an anthology of college songs. First performed at her 1910 commencement, the song quickly found its way into the student handbook and was all but officially adopted by the college.[66] Only minor verbal changes were required with the advent of coeducation and university status many years later.

Weill's lyrics appealed partly because they emphasized what was by then a traditional obligation at the Normal to render service to society: "Deep graven on each heart/Our motto, "Service," will remain,/And service we will do. . . ."[67] This obligation in fact underlay the entire Progressive reform impulse of the day: to improve society through individual and collective action—or service. Many colleges and universities enlisted in the cause and some, particularly state-supported ones, took Service as a motto.[68] The Normal owed its life to this impulse and, not surprisingly, virtually all of its administrators, faculty, and students were devoted Progressives. Their causes (beyond education) ranged from the good roads movement to the fight against hookworm. Service surely came naturally to them as a motto. According to one of Weill's classmates, their Class of 1910 adopted Service as its motto, then willed it to the college at graduation. It too found its way into the student handbook that fall and was incorporated into the canon. As Foust remarked many years later, both motto and song seemed appropriate and were adopted without any formal action.[69]

Unanticipated forms of service were called for during World War I. Not only did students observe the standard meatless, wheatless days, but they took classes in food conservation, donated clothing and other possessions to the War Relief Fund, knitted, and made surgical dressings. Responding to President Woodrow Wilson's appeal to everyone to raise as much food as possible, the Normal (like Vassar and other colleges) secured the use of a farm outside Greensboro and called for student volunteers to help work it. The ten who responded—called farmerettes—performed all but the heaviest labor, producing 1100 bushels of wheat and 3000 bushels of corn; they also raised and canned 3000 to 4000 gallons of tomatoes and beans. The students as a whole took over the campus groundskeeping, freeing the regular crew for farm work. And there were the carpenterettes who built the YWCA Hut.[70]

Woman suffrage was another cause championed at the Normal. The issue seems to have surfaced first in 1909 when the Adelphian Society held a debate on the subject. The negative won, as it did in a student poll at Wellesley in 1911.[71] Interest and support picked up to the point that in 1915 some 250 students staged a suffrage parade during the walking period, complete with drums, cornets, and combs with tissue paper. It ended with militant speeches in front of Spencer Dormitory.[72] As Gladys Avery Tillett, '15, remembered, all of her senior class favored suffrage, stimulated in large measure by history and political science instructor Harriet Elliott. Elliott herself recalled that Tillett organized the first women's college suffrage group in the South. When Governor Locke Craig opined in a speech at the 1915 commencement that women in North Carolina did not really want the vote, the silence was deafening. Foust and the faculty appear to have proceeded in step with the students on this issue.[73] At the same time, Normal alumnae were taking a leading role in the statewide suffrage campaign.[74]

The first woman commencement speaker in the college's history, in 1917, was Helen Guthrie Miller, first vice president of the National American Woman's Suffrage Association.[75] The second, in 1919, was its former president, Anna Howard Shaw. But Shaw had already spoken on campus twice before; her triumph was so complete that the college named its newest dormitory for her. Meanwhile, in 1918, 575 of the nearly 800 students signed a petition supporting the woman suffrage amendment.[76] Although the amendment was ratified and went into effect in 1920, North Carolina itself did not ratify until 1971.

* * *

Most alumnae continued to marry after graduation. The rate rose from 63 percent among the classes of 1893–96 to 72 percent for those of 1916–20.[77] Nearly all—90 to 95 percent—taught in the state's schools. As some of the freshmen had already taught school before entering the Normal, so too there were students who dropped out for financial or other reasons after as little as a year in order to teach. By 1917, Foust estimated that the college had supplied the state with over 6,000 teachers.[78] Other careers continued to open up as well. He reported in 1915 that the college had sent out twenty missionaries, two doctors (with two others on the way), two lawyers, a chemist, at least sixty nurses, and "a host of stenographers." By 1919, fifty or sixty alumnae worked in federal government agencies in Washington.[79]

The Alumnae Association at first limited its membership to graduates, despite McIver's clear desire that all former students be eligible.[80] Thus arose a pervasive and perplexing issue on almost every campus: Is an alumni association an agency of the institution or of the alumni themselves? Or if both, how should control be allocated? At the Normal, for the time being, the issue was resolved in favor of organizing a separate and parallel organization for former students. But this was so clearly inefficient that the two were merged in 1907.[81] That solved the original membership dispute but it left open the question of relative control—an issue that never entirely disappeared before reaching crisis proportions in the late 1980s.

In the summer of 1907 the newly unified association sent out two field secretaries (at joint college-association expense) to organize county chapters and raise money for the student loan funds. Five years later the *Alumnae News* first appeared, on a quarterly basis, with Julia Dameron, an instructor in English and Latin, as editor. Laura Coit, who had been serving for years as both alumnae secretary and college secretary, found herself spread too thin and resigned the alumnae position in 1919. Ethel Bollinger, '13, took her place that year as the first full-time alumnae secretary; she also edited the *Alumnae News*.[82]

In this period the alumnae gradually achieved the numbers and political strength (even without the vote) that they had lacked in the earliest years. They were correspondingly more helpful to their alma mater in its own ascent to full collegiate status.

Chapter 5

Academic Affairs

The faculty almost doubled between 1907 and 1919—from forty-nine to ninety.[1] More frequently than McIver, Foust used the services of commercial teachers' agencies in recruiting new faculty. He continued McIver's political or public relations preference for southerners with some northern education,[2] but as northerners often came with better credentials, the faculty continued to be a geographical mix, with northern collegiate or postgraduate degrees the rule. One who overcame her northern origin was Illinoisan Harriet Elliott. Knowing Foust's preference, Elliott made a special appeal in 1913 citing not only her master's degree work in history and political science with William A. Dunning and other luminaries at Columbia University, but also her mother's Louisiana birth and consequent family visits South. "I assure you I have strong southern interests."[3]

Foust was also quite frank in his preference for church-going Protestants and, in certain positions, for either men or women. He wanted men to head the physics and economics/sociology departments while preferring women as assistants in French, German, and Latin. As junior women faculty often served as dormitory residents, they must be single. Further, given the South's overwhelmingly Protestant affiliation, "I do not think it best to have a Catholic, especially one who will come in as close touch with the students as the dietitian and supervisor of the kitchen." Twenty-six students worked in the dining hall, he explained.[4] These prohibitions were not absolute, however. In 1918–19 two faculty members, including the temporary resident physician, were Jewish and one was Catholic. The principal commencement speaker in 1914 was Rabbi Stephen S. Wise of New York; Foust characterized his speech as one of the best ever given in the state.

Columbia University with its Teachers College was a popular recruiting ground for the Normal; five of the nine newcomers in 1914, for instance, had Columbia degrees. The number of Ph.D.s had grown to five in 1918–19, two women and three men. Although some of the faculty pursued graduate study during the summers or taught at various summer schools, many spent the off-season simply vacationing.[5] For several years some junior faculty, at least, continued to switch from one discipline to another as college teaching needs dictated.[6]

The faculty community, while growing, continued much as it had under

McIver. Foust, at least in his early years, regularly played tennis with several women faculty members.[7] Apart from individual socializing, groups of faculty gave parties, as in 1910 when the new faculty entertained their colleagues with a colonial-era party featuring period costumes and dancing the minuet. A few days later they repeated the performance at a freshman tea.[8]

Although stern in his treatment of errant, inadequate, or discontented faculty and students, Foust sometimes went far out of his way to assist persons in need. In 1915 he personally took ailing education Professor Robert Merritt to Baltimore for diagnosis of his illness. When it turned out to be tuberculosis Foust granted him a leave of absence for the remainder of the academic year with half salary. Next year the board, on Joyner's prompting, offered Merritt the position of business manager if he were able to assume its duties.[9] Such consideration was by no means automatic at the time.

There were even harder decisions to make. Dean and English professor William C. Smith wrote Foust in April 1919: "Miss [Ethel D.] Kanton's case is little less than tragic. In all respects save one she is ideal. Scholarly, faithful, painstaking, loyal, wholly devoted to her work, attractive in person and disposition—no finer woman has ever served us. But she is deaf, and I question whether she understands one half of what is said to her or whether the students understand what she in turn says to them. This...is her first teaching position and she is eager to make good, pitifully eager and earnest beyond all saying." But, he concluded, good people were applying for her place and the department would benefit by replacing her.[10] Kanton was not reappointed.

* * *

Nationally, faculty salaries peaked in terms of buying power in 1913, then began a decline that lasted until well into the 1920s. Salaries at the Normal remained below national averages—much below, Foust told legislators in 1911.[11] Like many a southern administrator while recruiting, he made plentiful reference to the region's lower cost of living. Until 1918, when wartime inflation forced a general salary increase of about 20 percent,[12] raises were by no means automatic. They came most often to those who asked for them. As Foust made no bones about gender preference in hiring, he had few qualms about gender discrimination in salaries. In general, he remarked in 1918, the college paid women faculty members from $1000 to $1500 a year, and men from $1700 to $2500. The practice was so general that he apparently felt no need to amplify, although he remarked a few months later that, in the abstract, women should be paid equally with men for equal work.[13]

Those women faculty who did not live in the dormitories continued to rent rooms in private homes nearby; they often ate in the dining hall. Occasionally several joined to rent a house, but this was complicated by their tendency to scatter in the summertime. When the number of women desiring such accommodations outgrew the neighborhood's ability to absorb them, the college itself in 1917 rented two houses and sublet them to female faculty.[14]

The turnover was high among the junior women faculty. Every year a few asked and received leaves of absence without pay to pursue their studies in the North or in Europe. Every year some chose to leave permanently; a number took positions as high school teachers in the North.

There was no such thing as faculty tenure. Faculty members, like administrators, were appointed by the year but normally all but the most junior could expect routine reappointment.[15] Where this was not forthcoming Foust asked for resignations to avoid the blighting effect of outright dismissal. He even became a master at suggesting and receiving without actually asking for faculty resignations.

The first notable case was that of William C.A. Hammel, professor of physics and manual arts since 1903, who was forced to resign in 1916 (after a year's notice) on the ground that his courses lacked academic rigor.[16] At least in part, the controversy had a curricular basis. McIver had introduced the manual arts program owing to its inclusion in the public school curriculum; his aim was to supply the schools with whatever teachers they required.[17] Although manual or industrial arts was a favorite of Progressive educators in that era, many faculty members at the Normal (including Foust) increasingly questioned its standards and relevance to the college's rising academic aspirations. In response those under attack stoutly defended both the program and themselves. Hammel was thus at the center of a policy dispute that became personal and correspondingly bitter. By 1919 it led to the additional departures of vocational arts teachers Alma Long, Julia Raines, and Melville Fort, the last a charter member of the faculty since 1892. Criticism of them seemed more to involve the college's changing role than personal competency. For years to come, art would be treated as an adjunct to the education program. Hammel himself soon became Greensboro superintendent of schools.[18]

The same curricular shift likely explains the termination of an agriculture/rural economics program. McIver had hired Thomas L. Brown in 1897 not only to serve as grounds director but to teach horticulture. The effort was shortlived but ten years later, with agriculture instruction coming to the public schools, Foust reintroduced it at the Normal.[19] In 1911 he hired Ernest E. Balcomb, then secretary of the National Committee on Agricultural Education, to head the effort. The aim was to provide information and skills (such as dairying, gardening, poultry raising, and orchard management) that would be useful to rural housewives and prospective rural high school teachers. By 1913 agriculture courses were included in both the education and home economics programs, and were taken by nearly every student.[20] Balcomb was eager, energetic, professionally active, and apparently competent in every way. He took full part in the college's new extension activities. But the agriculture program seems to have withered on the vine. The number of courses offered (both required and elective) gradually declined and Balcomb seems to have felt increasingly out of place. He departed for California in 1919 and the program was abandoned.[21]

A very different case was that of Christine Reincken, the professor of German, who was ostensibly forced out by public hysteria during World War I. A native of Germany but resident in the United States since childhood, Reincken came to the Normal in 1913.[22] By all accounts she had the respect of both faculty and students; but she was officially an enemy alien. In March 1918 Davidson and Lafayette Colleges held a debate on the Normal campus on the question whether enemy aliens in the United States should be interned until the end of the war; the affirmative won. Meanwhile, in February, a Greensboro College music professor, also German, resigned after a GC student's family withdrew her from the school in protest at his presence on the faculty. Less than a week after that event was reported in the *Greensboro Daily News*, Reincken wrote to Foust, affirming her loyalty to the United States and the Allied cause, but offering to resign if the welfare of the Normal required it. For whatever reason, professional or political, Foust offered little support. Apparently on his advice, she submitted her resignation, hoping that in the end it would be refused. As late as June, he assured her that there had been no criticism of her or of the Normal on her account by students, their families, or anyone else. Yet in July he advised her (for her own good, he assured her) to take a leave of absence from any public work until war's end. Reincken expressed disappointment with this response, but accepted the verdict and never returned. Her successor that year, Caroline Schoch, was equally German in heritage but born in the United States. It is possible, in light of the Lindeman case several years later, that Foust was displeased with Reincken on other grounds and took this opportunity to get rid of her. The best that can be said of him and the college in this case is that German language instruction was never interrupted.[23]

* * *

By 1909 Foust found the faculty too large to consult any longer on a frequent and informal basis. At his bidding the board created a smaller faculty council consisting of the the department heads (professors) and, soon afterward, those in the new rank of associate. Omitted were the assistants, or junior faculty. The faculty council was now the college's legislative body, within limits set by the board and the president. Foust appointed the members of all committees and was himself an ex officio member of each. Nationally, as Laurence Veysey pointed out, presidents used such bodies to sound out faculty opinion, detect discontent, and give the most important faculty members a sense of participation.[24]

* * *

Student admissions in this period were still governed by the transitional status of the state's new high schools. Some had ten grades, some eleven, and some rural areas still lacked a high school altogether. The Normal's policy was to admit only those who had completed the highest grade of their local schools.[25] This produced in 1911 a freshman class of 135, almost half of whom were graduates of the Normal's own preparatory or high school remedial program. There were two sequential preparatory classes that year, totaling 164 students of the college's total enrollment of 568.[26] High schools varied so in quality that the Normal appointed a visitor (an alumna with high school teaching experience) to guide the college in accrediting them.[27] Entrance examinations were offered to applicants who had not graduated from an accredited high school. Further, placement exams were given to those who felt they could enter certain subjects at an advanced level. The minimum age was normally sixteen.[28] In general, Foust was lenient in readmitting students who had done badly in their studies the previous year.

Some faculty were delighted with the quality of their students, but others were not. Biologist Eugene Gudger wrote Foust in 1917: "I doubt if even you... realize what a tremendous abyss separates the average high school in N.C. from the Freshman work in our College. The ignorance and helplessness of our Freshmen students is literally appalling. To some of them our class rooms must seem like the inquiring rooms of the Spanish Inquisition."[29]

The level of work offered continued to rise. As the faculty grew, more courses were offered. Electives were increasingly available, especially for juniors and seniors. New subjects were introduced such as economics, political science, sociology, and nursing. The old departments were broadened or redefined and new ones were added. Beginning in 1909, there were five baccalaureate programs: Bachelor of Education, of Arts, of Science, of Music, and of Science in Home Economics. All required some liberal arts work, reaffirming the original commitment to a socially progressive vocational curriculum based on a solid liberal arts foundation.[30]

Teaching loads averaged about fifteen hours a week of classroom time for each instructor. The school week of five and a half days ended Saturday at noon.[31]

* * *

Foust always looked back on the years 1917 to 1921 as the turning point in the college's history. He was thinking partly of the higher appropriations that began then, but also of the full collegiate status and accreditation that came in those years. There had always been faculty debate, largely unrecorded, over the institution's mission. It surfaced most openly in the Hammel and vocational arts controversy, when proponents of the liberal arts won a clearcut victory. Foust was on that side, and many faculty credited him personally with the college's rise to accreditation. He himself gave major credit to Dean William C. Smith and the faculty.[32] All of them were responsible, and all were following the path that McIver had charted from the beginning.

Given these aspirations and achievements, the name Normal and Industrial College seemed anachronistic. Furthermore, alumnae seeking to pursue graduate study faced aggravating barriers in justifying their increasingly college-level Normal degrees to academic personnel out of state. After several years of discussion the Alumnae Association formally requested in 1916 that the legislature bestow a new name. The students followed suit. There was less agreement as to what the new name should be. The clear favorite among alumnae was McIver College, but the current students (who no longer remembered McIver) favored North Carolina State College.[33] (The Agricultural and Mechanical College in Raleigh had not yet taken that name.) Foust and the board remained neutral for a time, hoping for a consensus. Finally, in 1919, with students and alumnae still divided, the board voted five to four (with the minority scattered) in favor of North Carolina College for Women. That pleased the legislature, and so the name would be until statewide consolidation of higher education came in 1931.[34]

This seemed to Foust and the faculty the appropriate time to grant for the first time what was by now a perennial senior class request—to be allowed to wear caps and gowns at commencement.[35] In addition to the distinction they conferred, caps and gowns were great equalizers, dispensing with the need to wear expensive dresses.

The culminating step was accreditation by the relatively new Southern Association of Colleges and Secondary Schools (SACS). This came in 1921, and led quickly to a reorganization of the college.[36]

* * *

The history department brought to campus in this period two persons who would play vital roles in the college's history for the next forty years. The first, Walter Clinton Jackson, came in 1909 as head of the department. A native Georgian educated at Mercer University, his most recent position was principal of the Greensboro High School. Jackson's eventual doctorate, like those of McIver,

Foust, and W.C. Smith, was honorary, conferred by his alma mater in 1926. His professional field was American history and particularly race relations—the South's perennial hot topic throughout his lifetime. Jackson's publications, including *A Boy's Life of Booker T. Washington*, were minimal but he was professionally active and a frequent speaker in his field, working always toward interracial understanding and cooperation. Though he never felt free openly to challenge segregation or white supremacy, Jackson was clearly anxious to ameliorate their effects. He served as chairman of local, state, and southern Commissions on Interracial Cooperation, and was for years a member and sometimes chairman of the board of trustees of Bennett College, the liberal arts college for African-American women in Greensboro. Although he worked always in the southern professional and political mainstream, Jackson was a racial liberal by the standards of his time.[37]

At the Normal, Jackson offered courses in American history. He claimed later to have given one of the first college courses in the South—and perhaps in the nation—on race relations. His popularity as a classroom teacher became legendary—particularly in the later biographical course that he entitled Representative Americans.[38] As dean of the college after 1915 Jackson substituted for Foust during the president's nearly yearlong absence in Atlanta. In time he became vice president and, after Foust's retirement, his successor.

The second person was Harriet Elliott, who came in 1913 as an assistant in history. Twenty-nine years old, a native of Carbondale, Illinois with a freshly minted Columbia master's degree, she too proved a dynamic teacher whose impact on her students was at least equal to Jackson's. Elliott's primary interest was in political science—both academic and applied, as she would soon demonstrate—and before long her teaching centered in that area. But she also helped pioneer in her first few years at the Normal the teaching of economics and sociology.[39]

Elliott plunged immediately into the woman suffrage movement, taking most of the student body with her. She attended meetings and gave speeches all over the state, joining a women's professional and political network that nourished her, and vice versa, for the remainder of her life. It was continually replenished by generations of the college's alumnae. One particular friend that Elliott made at Columbia was suffrage leader Anna Howard Shaw. At Elliott's behest Shaw visited the Normal three times, giving the commencement address on the final occasion, in 1919. Elliott was also involved in the establishment of student government at the Normal, an event that not coincidentally came during the height of the woman suffrage movement in 1914.[40] Despite many offers to go elsewhere, Elliott remained at the college for the rest of her life, becoming dean of women under Jackson in 1935.[41]

Soon after his own arrival Jackson set out to broaden the curriculum to include the hitherto neglected disciplines of economics, sociology, and political science. He thought of history joining them to form a new social science division. This concept turned out to be highly controversial among a faculty that had recently seen history itself as an adjunct to the English department. Only with difficulty over a period of several years was Jackson able to incorporate introductory courses in these new disciplines. Economics and sociology were finally organized into a separate department in 1917.[42]

* * *

In scholarly production no one could match biologist Eugene Gudger's research and writings on marine life, ranging from embryology to the spotted sting ray and the whale shark. Not a splashy teacher, Gudger was a demanding one who provided a thorough laboratory training that alumnae remembered appreciatively for decades. One recalled that her freshman class in 1913–14 staged a mock evolution trial that prefigured the famous Scopes trial in Tennessee a decade later, except that in this case the evolutionists won. Both the facts and methods of their case, she said, rested on Gudger's biology laboratory.[43]

Gudger was a personal friend of Foust, whom he sometimes addressed in his letters as Dear Chief. But that did not prevent his expressing his mind freely to the chief on matters curricular and personal, and complaining of underpayment and a teaching load of twenty-six hours a week in 1917.[44] Eventually Gudger succumbed to the physical and emotional strain as well as the pull of research opportunities elsewhere, and in 1919 accepted a position with the American Museum of Natural History in New York. He remained there for the rest of his long life, but he always retained an affectionate concern for the college, corresponding with successive administrators and visiting the campus regularly on trips back to his family home in the North Carolina mountains. Foust made little effort to retain him, and one suspects that Gudger was a mite too independent for his taste.[45]

The college made a short curricular excursion into the related field of nursing. In 1907 Mary L. Wyche, once an infirmary nurse at the Normal and now president of the state nursing association, asked the institution to introduce a preparatory nursing program. Nursing, she said, should become more professional. Current training consisted of a hospital apprenticeship under doctors and nurses who were often overworked. Even good doctors and nurses were not always good teachers, she noted, and their students lacked the general education that should precede specialized training. All this the Normal could provide in abundance as background to the specialized year-long program that Wyche advocated. Foust was persuaded, but when the first course opened in the fall of 1912, only one student enrolled, and it folded. The course was revived during World War I and continued for a number of years in the biology department without ever attaining great popularity.[46]

* * *

The education department was plagued with sickness and changing leadership during much of this period. Junius A. Matheson, recent superintendent of schools in Durham, came in 1907 to replace Foust as professor, department head, and principal of Curry School. A Davidson College graduate, Matheson was a capable educator and administrator, and in 1911 Foust named him dean of the college. But three years later, having contracted tuberculosis, he was forced to resign from the faculty. His successor as principal of Curry, Robert A. Merritt, contracted the disease himself and had to drop out in 1915.[47] Stability returned in the persons of James A. Highsmith and John H. Cook, who arrived in 1916 and 1918, respectively. Cook served many years as head (and in the 1920s, dean) of education. Highsmith replaced Merritt as principal of the training school, and in the 1920s organized the psychology department.

Foust continued the two two-month courses for public school teachers that McIver initiated, beginning each year in early April and mid-September. Some forty students attended in the spring of 1907. But in 1912 he reverted to P.P. Claxton's original idea of a full summer session. Still intended primarily for teachers, it emphasized pedagogy and home economics. The faculty consisted mostly of department heads who volunteered their services the first year; modest compensation was offered thereafter. Most of the summer students were nontraditional by modern definition. Virtually all were teachers in the lower grades, and as late as 1920 over half had less than a high school education themselves. About 200 enrolled for the eight-week term in 1912, with another 200 or so taking an attached two-week teachers' institute.[48] The experiment was successful, and enrollments increased each year except during World War I.[49]

Another milestone came in 1914, in the form of male students. They first enrolled that year in the summer institute, and continued to do so thereafter.[50]

Curry School grew in proportion to the expansion of public education and of the college itself. It was in effect a neighborhood school within the Greensboro school system from 1898 until 1913, when city dissatisfaction with its unavoidably divergent mission as a trainer of teachers led to a partial separation. Central to the parting was the college's desire to train high school teachers at Curry. As the state's high school system expanded, demand grew correspondingly for high school teachers, and the Normal needed to respond. But Greensboro, for its part, did not yet need a second white high school. Under the new agreement Curry was considered an adjunct to the city system, which continued to support it jointly with the college. But city parents could send their children there or not, as they wished. Beginning in 1913, Curry added each year a new grade from eighth to eleventh, which was then the state's standard senior year. It produced its first high school graduating class in 1917.[51]

This expansion came to an abrupt if temporary halt the next year. Enrollment in the new high school grades fell off so sharply that they were discontinued in 1918. This may have resulted from wartime conditions but the program, planned under the direction of Matheson and Merritt, had to have suffered from their illnesses and the chaos of revolving chairs that followed. Foust seemed to ascribe the failure to the incapacity of John A. Lesh, who came the headship in 1915. On his departure three years later Foust hired A.P. Kephart as a professor specializing in secondary education, and the college's prospective high school teachers were sent out to observe in Greensboro High School.[52]

* * *

As with education and several other fields, the growth of domestic science at the Normal reflected its expansion in the public schools, which generated both student interest and a need for more teachers. Domestic science had its own degree program after 1911. Both nationally and locally, it continued to encounter criticism from those who charged that it lacked intellectual content. Home economists (to use the term coming into increasing use nationally) responded by placing more and more emphasis on science.[53] Foust echoed the criticism and steered the Normal's own program in that direction. Biologist Eugene Gudger offered a course in household bacteriology for domestic science majors, though his opinion of their abilities and motivation was not high.[54] Several years of experimentation[55] ended in 1918 when Blanche E. Shaffer, another Columbia University alumna, arrived to take over the home economics department.[56]

This reshuffling occurred as the federal government was beginning to subsidize vocational higher education, including home economics. Although the Normal offered the only home economics program in the state, the all-male Agricultural and Mechanical College in Raleigh was the designated recipient of North Carolina's funds. As a result, Foust secured only part of the home economics money—and that with difficulty.[57]

Much of the federal aid was earmarked for university extension work, which the University of Wisconsin had pioneered in 1906.[58] Foust won foundation money to support such work at the Normal in 1910. Its first fruit was a well-received pamphlet on foods by Minnie Jamison.[59] Other booklets followed, dealing with English, history, mathematics, and Latin as well as domestic science topics.[60] Increasingly, faculty members went out into the state to give talks, hold classes, and conduct demonstrations on a host of subjects related to household and family. These members included science teachers like Mary Petty and Eugene Gudger as well as vocational and home economics faculty.[61] When federal money became available in 1915, Jamison was the Normal's representative in the field.

In 1914 the college established its first home management house for domestic science students. It was located on the newly acquired property along Lithia (later Tate) Street, the future site of Brown Music Building and Taylor Theater. The aim was to have every student spend two weeks living in the house and participating in its management before her graduation.[62] In 1916 the college removed the house but successive replacements were established on other sites.[63]

* * *

Foust inherited a music program divided into two separate departments, vocal and instrumental. Clarence Brown, the original vocal head, was replaced on his death in 1906 by a young Columbia man, Hermann H. Hoexter.[64] The Brockmanns, Charles and his sister Laura, remained in charge of the instrumental program, still extracurricular and largely self-supporting. This arrangement satisfied no one, but Foust delayed action, perhaps because he did not trust the leadership abilities of any of the individuals involved.

Although the two departments were united in 1910, the music program still lacked unity or coherence until the advent of Wade R. Brown as music head in 1912.[65] A large, burly man with a goatee, Brown had served for ten years as director of music at Meredith, the Baptist women's college in Raleigh. He would remain at the Normal for twenty-five years. One alumna remembered him affectionately as stern and paternal—a perfectionist who was ready to shout at a student one moment and pat her on the back the next. By October he had organized a 125-voice chorus. An organist, he soon began giving recitals, at first in a local church and then on campus when the college acquired a pipe organ in 1913. Oratorios and operas followed, starting with the Messiah. One year the Philadelphia Orchestra with Eugene Ormandy came to do the Messiah. Before long, Brown and his wife began taking the senior music majors to New York each year to visit the city's cultural attractions.[66]

At the outset, virtually without precedent, Foust let Brown accompany him to New York to hire new faculty members. Others followed, including Alleine Minor in piano, one of Brown's students at Meredith. She remained for forty-three years.[67] The curriculum gradually expanded in company with music instruction in the public schools. Voice and piano continued to be the most popular, but violin, organ, and public school music (or music education) were also introduced, the last becoming a major field in 1919.[68]

* * *

The year 1907 brought a new gymnasium of sorts in the basement of South Spencer Dormitory, and with it the return of physical education instruction after a lapse of several years. (Following national patterns, the original name physical culture now gave way to physical training, and in 1917 to physical education.) As elsewhere, physical education was still closely related to hygiene, and maintaining or improving the health of each student was a central purpose of the program.[69] Postural examinations, and perhaps photographs, of every incoming student were made from an early date. Photographs were certainly taken in later years, but not in the nude nor were the subjects identifiable—a matter that piqued national interest in 1995 after some old pictures of Ivy League students turned up in the Smithsonian. Students at the Normal who "failed" the posture test were required to take a remedial course.[70]

Physical education gained a professional director for the first time in 1907. All students were required to take the subject, which continued for a time to emphasize calisthenics and gymnastics. But, again following national practice, dance and sports took an increasingly large part in the program, making for greater student interest. As in other departments, much of the emphasis was on training prospective teachers in the evolving curriculum of the public schools. Students in 1907 were required for the first time to wear a prescribed uniform, consisting of long serge bloomers, a long-sleeved blouse, tie, and stockings—all in black. Department members encouraged girls in the strongest terms to participate in intramural sports and related activities as an adjunct to the formal program and as a substitute for the still-mandatory walking period. They also lobbied assiduously for a better gymnasium and playing fields.[71]

Foust himself called repeatedly for a real gymnasium, uninterrupted by steel columns as in Spencer. Just as repeatedly the legislature refused to provide the necessary money, reflecting a widespread view that physical education was not entirely seemly for women, and in any case was a recreational activity not meriting taxpayer support. The faculty themselves were divided over physical education, Anna Gove remarked—a few favoring, some openly disapproving, and the majority merely tolerating it.[72]

To the two original sports, tennis and basketball, were added field hockey in 1909 and baseball in 1910. Class teams dominated the activity, playing outdoors on the site of the later Petty Science Building and Mary Foust Dormitory. In 1909 the college held the first of many annual field days. These were major springtime events, with classes canceled for the day and all students expected to attend if not participate. In 1915 a faculty-student baseball game was added. Indoor activities were also introduced, leading in 1911 to the first annual Gym Meet. Another popular activity, picked up in 1910, was camping or hiking. As sponsored by the student Athletic Association, it typically consisted of a late afternoon hike to nearby Lindley Park. The students cooked snacks over a fire, then waited for Zeke Robinson to bring their supper from campus. After the meal they sang class songs until time for the hike back to campus, about 8 or 9 p.m. All of this was well chaperoned.[73]

Virtually all of the athletic events were intramural. Earlier intercollegiate matches with Guilford and Greensboro Colleges were clearly exceptional. By 1912 some students were asking for more intercollegiate competition. A *State Normal Magazine* editorial decried the lack of college spirit, as distinguished from class or society spirit, of which there was a great deal. The writer suggested an annual intercollegiate debate rather than athletics as a remedy, but a few months later the Cornelian Society staged a debate on whether the Normal should participate in intercollegiate athletics. The affirmative won. The argument was renewed in 1915, with an editorialist calling for intercollegiate sports as an antidote not only for lack of school spirit but student provincialism and the college's supposedly dubious reputation as well: "The average citizen of North Carolina and neighboring states thinks of our College, if he knows of its existence, as a small, cheap apology for a normal school to which men who cannot afford a good college send their daughters." If our hockey, basketball, and tennis teams were playing with well-known regional colleges, she concluded, people would begin to notice and respect us.[74]

When student government president Adelaide Van Noppen finally persuaded Foust in 1919 to try intercollegiate athletics as a one-year experiment, physical education director Fay Davenport voiced her firm opposition on both financial and philosophical grounds.[75] In fact, the student desire ran counter to a growing conviction of women physical educators around the country that intercollegiate competition was harmful to women. Repelled by the exploitation and physical strain they saw in men's athletics, they embraced instead a philosophy of moderation that limited sports to presumably less stressful intramural competition, open to girls of all ability levels.[76] For many years to come, the only "varsity teams" at the college would be fictive assemblages of the best players from the respective intramural teams.

Meanwhile, when the first physical training director failed to work out, Foust turned in 1908 to Amy Morris Homans, the *grande dame* of American physical education for women. Homans was director of the Boston Normal School of Gymnastics, which she presently moved to Wellesley College. Homans had once taught in North Carolina and over the years she developed a friendship for the college and for Foust (whom she persisted for a time in calling Frost). She was at the same time a surrogate mother to her students, taking great care to place them in satisfactory jobs and continuing to counsel them thereafter. She was quite frank in telling Foust of their relative strengths and what salaries and working conditions they were entitled to. He in turn came to accept her candidates without the usual requirement of preliminary interviews.[77] These women seem to have been entirely satisfactory, but for various reasons—primarily low salary, too little help (the director had only one assistant until 1919) and inadequate facilities—they did not stay long.[78] As in education and music, the musical chairs eventually ended with the arrival in 1920 of someone who received greater support, stayed, and left her mark—Mary Channing Coleman.

Part III
North Carolina College for Women, 1919–1932
Woman's College, 1932–1934

Chapter 6

Campus and Administration

The college mushroomed in the 1920s, far exceeding anything seen before, or for many years afterward. Following national trends, enrollments more than doubled, from 784 in 1919 to 1,888 in 1929. By the latter year, NCCW claimed to be the second largest woman's college in the country. To accommodate the student influx twenty-one buildings (or the equivalent in major additions) were constructed between 1920 and 1928. The turning point in state financing had come in 1917, but building activity was delayed by the war.

President Foust decided in 1920 to part company with Warren Manning, the occasional campus planner since McIver's time, on the curious ground that Manning was more interested in the larger picture than in specific details. His replacement was Thomas W. Sears of Philadelphia, who seems not have been asked for large pictures.[1] Nevertheless, there was a rationale for the placement of the buildings that appeared in the next decade. New residence halls were concentrated in the northwest half of campus, from Spencer Dormitory west and north. Except for physical education with its unique spatial requirements, academic buildings were placed in the southeast half along Spring Garden, College Avenue, and finally McIver and Tate Streets. The dining halls were located near the center.

Foust himself came to be called The Builder. The boom began in 1919–20 with a dormitory, named for Anna Howard Shaw. Six others followed by 1923, forming the dormitory quadrangle: Gray, Hinshaw, Bailey, Cotten, Jamison, and Coit. (The empty north end was not filled until 1939.) Two more dormitories were built in 1927, facing each other on College Avenue north of Spencer: New Guilford (as distinguished from Old Guilford or Midway) and Mary Foust (named for President Foust's daughter, an alumna, who had recently died in childbirth). All conformed to the standard female dormitory plan of that era: spartan residential rooms with relatively lavish first-floor parlors for entertaining visitors.[2]

More students also necessitated more dining halls. The existing one extending back from Spencer Dormitory was badly overcrowded and a second was built nearby in 1921. Continuing growth brought two more matching structures in 1924 and 1927, all of them forming a four-spoke arrangement radiating from a common core. One of the four served as kitchen. (As with the dormitory quadrangle, space left for a fifth "spoke" was not filled until 1939.)

There was also a great deal of academic construction, though it failed to keep up with student enrollments. Massive long-planned east and west wings of the McIver Building came separately in 1920 and 1922, as funding permitted, opening up much more classroom space. By the end of the decade, Main (now Administration) Building was devoted almost entirely to administration, and accordingly was treated to an extensive interior remodeling.[3] The library was enlarged in 1923, tripling its capacity. A handsome brick music building—later named for Wade Brown—came in 1925, the first campus building to be located on Tate Street. The same year saw the construction of Rosenthal Gymnasium, something for which McIver and Foust had made perennial appeals for thirty-odd years. It was located along Walker Avenue, west of the dormitories, on land that had recently been the domain of the college dairy herd.

In 1926, just as a new and much improved education and Curry School Building neared completion on Spring Garden Street, the old one on College Avenue burned to the ground. (There was insurance but the fire was convincingly attributed to faulty electric wiring and poor original construction.)[4] The portico framing the front entrance survived the fire and was allowed to remain in place for well over a decade; students referred to it as "the ruins." Next-door, at the corner of Walker Avenue and McIver Street, a home economics building was completed in 1928.

In 1927 Aycock Auditorium made its appearance at the corner of Spring Garden and Tate Streets. It was a major production. The original purpose was to replace the 800-seat auditorium on the second floor of the Students Building, which by 1927 could hold less than half of the student body—to say nothing of friends, relatives, and townspeople. But drama teacher W. Raymond Taylor persuaded Foust to make the building a performing theater as well. (Anticipating some of the public reaction he would receive, Foust half-jokingly referred to Taylor's proposed backstage paraphernalia as the devil's workshop.) Taylor and his English department colleague Alonzo Hall traveled through Europe looking for appropriate details to include in the structure. Once completed, Aycock reportedly had the largest capacity of any building in Greensboro except the tobacco warehouses.[5] Accordingly, it served the community almost as much as the college. The Greensboro Civic Music Society, organized in 1927, made full use of it from the beginning.[6] Regular chapel services moved to Aycock and it was the scene of commencement exercises for the next thirty years.

From the earliest days the college had dependend on a power plant located on Walker Avenue behind the library and McIver Building. The original structure burned with Brick Dormitory in 1904 and was rebuilt on the same site. As the destination of perpetual coal deliveries by wagon and truck, churning the long-unpaved streets and annoying the neighbors, it was badly located. It was also dirty, noisy, and by the 1920s antiquated and inefficient.[7] The most practical site for a power plant was along the railroad, whence the coal supplies came. There, a large new Romanesque building went up in 1924; as power plants go, it was and remains a handsome structure. Despite Foust's effort to have the old building razed and replaced with something more fitting, it remained in place for another forty years—devoted first to the campus laundry (already sharing the building) and then, of all things, the campus TV station.

The president acquired a campus residence in 1923, for the first time since McIver's death. Mrs. McIver still occupied the boxlike frame house at the corner of College Avenue and Spring Garden, while Foust until now had lived in his own house just off campus, next to the Methodist Church. The new brick residence, on Spring Garden at the corner of Forest, was built atop one of the many springs that gave the main thoroughfare its name.

Almost all of these buildings were the work of Greensboro architect Harry Barton, who was responsible as well for the county courthouse and a variety of other public buildings around town. The power plant was Romanesque in style; most of the others were more or less Georgian, but all belonged to the then-popular classical revival style, featuring red brick with white trim. The campus never acquired a Gothic building.[8]

Corresponding to the above-ground development, campus roads and walkways now emerged from the mud. College Avenue was paved in 1928, bringing a new concrete bridge over Walker. And when the drive in front of Administration Building was paved in 1929, a new fountain was installed to replace the long-gone original near its front entrance.[9]

The surrounding neighborhood saw comparable changes. As part of a city-wide campaign, nearly all the streets around campus were paved between 1924 and 1926, with the blessings of the college and partly at its expense. West Market Street was extended past campus on the north and Aycock (hitherto Dairy) Street was extended northward to Market on the west. Commercial development, lacking in the neighborhood before 1920, quickly followed. In fact, Foust spent time in 1924 vainly trying to prevent the construction of gasoline stations on Tate and Spring Garden Streets. The latter location, across from the planned Aycock Auditorium, was the site of Moore's Springs, which were now abandoned, having lost their therapeutic appeal.[10]

Paving assessments even affected the college farm. By 1917 the campus farm had proved too small and the land it did occupy was needed more for other purposes. The dormitory quadrangle was carved out of its eastern end, and there were plans for physical education including a golf course in the remainder. For several years the college had the use of an additional farm southeast of Greensboro, apparently for raising fodder and other field crops. But when that property was incorporated into the city with resultant paving assessments, Foust in 1923 purchased a 250-acre farm about eight miles west, near what would soon become the Greensboro airport.[11] The campus barn was demolished. Some people acquainted with Frederick Jackson Turner's frontier thesis in American history referred jokingly to the westward movement of the college barn, from College Avenue to the dormitory quadrangle to Dairy/Aycock Street and now to western Guilford County.

Peabody Park continued for a time to be a focal point of student life, both academic and social, collective and solitary. Successive wooden stages were built for dramatic and other activities, with audiences of up to 3,000 continuing to sit or lie on the ground opposite.[12] Park Night, a major addition to student community life in this decade, was held there.

* * *

Everyone saw the 1921 accreditation by the Southern Association of Colleges and Secondary Schools as a milestone of major proportions. "We are standing on the brink of a great tomorrow," proclaimed an editorial in the *Carolinian*, the new student newspaper. Foust himself predicted that before long "we shall develop at this place the greatest College for Women South of New York City." Still further, when the 1923 legislature declined to appropriate money for a requested women's dormitory at Chapel Hill, he saw the refusal as an opening for NCCW to become "the university for the women of North Carolina."[13] Years later he reaffirmed that his ideal, "whether the faculty endorsed [it] or not," had been to make the college the equivalent for the women of North Carolina to what the university was for men.[14] That dream, he came to recognize, would never be accepted in Chapel Hill, which sought increasingly to become coeducational. But meanwhile, he did everything in his power to continue upgrading the college, including the introduction of graduate work on a modest scale.

Perhaps the most striking changes, coming in 1922, involved reorganization of the college, both faculty and administration. Although Foust was the prime mover and principal author of the plan adopted, he gave major credit to Dean of the Faculty William C. Smith and his curriculum committee for selling and implementing it. The plan adopted the by-then standard academic ranks of professor, associate professor, assistant professor, and instructor. The faculty council would still consist of the two highest ranks but greater emphasis was placed on their having the Ph.D. (At the time, the faculty contained only six earned doctorates apart from the college physician.) The dean of the college now became vice president. As further befitted an aspiring university, the institution was now divided into a college of liberal arts and sciences and schools of education, home economics, and music, each with its dean. Within the liberal arts college were three divisions: languages and literature, social science, and mathematics and pure science. Three other divisions—summer session, extension, and graduate studies—filled out the new bureaucracy. The president chaired a new advisory cabinet consisting of the vice president, the deans, most of the division heads, and (soon afterward) two elected faculty members. If all this seemed a trifle ambitious for an institution with 114 faculty and 1000 students, the growth already underway seemed to justify optimism.[15]

Most of the new administrative appointments were predictable. Walter C. Jackson was translated from dean of the college to vice president. He also became chairman of the social science division for which he had long been fighting, while remaining head of the history department. William C. Smith moved from dean of the faculty to dean of the new college of liberal arts and sciences, while remaining head of English. The current heads of education, home economics, and music became deans: John H. Cook, Blanche E. Shaffer, and Wade R. Brown, respectively. These appointments occasioned little controversy. But in picking chairmen of the literature and science divisions, a number of senior professors, many of them women, were passed over in favor of Winfield S. Barney and John P. Givler, the relatively new heads of romance languages and biology.

When the board took up the reorganization plan, alumna member Minnie McIver Brown queried why the new cabinet contained only one woman—home economics Dean Blanche Shaffer. Foust seems to have replied that no other women were sufficiently qualified, and went on to question the ability of the older faculty women generally to function effectively in the new era. Mrs. Brown was not persuaded and Foust later apologized for his remarks, paying tribute to the services these women had performed for the college and the state. Others also expressed misgivings about the gender imbalance in the cabinet. It was likely to allay this concern that an elective faculty member was added; the person chosen was Dr. Virginia Ragsdale in mathematics.[16] And when Gertrude Mendenhall, the popular and respected head of mathematics and a charter member of the faculty, appears to have expressed the same concern, a very solicitous Foust added her to the cabinet as well. But the chairmanship of the math and science division, held open for a time, went not to Mendenhall or chemistry head Mary Petty but to the new man Givler. The issue did not go away soon. In 1924 Foust referred only half-facetiously to a male-female power struggle among the faculty.[17]

There was clearly some faculty opposition to the college reorganization as a whole, Foust conceded, despite what he reported as a unanimous vote in the faculty council.[18] One dissenter was Harriet Elliott, who confided years later that she had never regretted her opposition. Apart from the feminist concern that she shared, she believed that the college was not yet big enough to sustain such an elaborate bureaucracy or to assume the ambitious role it was claiming. In hindsight at least, she apparently felt it was setting itself up for a battle with Chapel Hill that it could not win. Equally strong-minded as Foust, Elliott became (if she was not already) one of his most vocal critics.[19] Her abilities, services, and popularity secured her regular reappointment, promotion, and salary increases; she was one of the highest paid members of the faculty. But Foust certainly knew of her opposition. In 1928, while informing her of the latest salary increase, he called her on the carpet for criticizing administrators and faculty members behind their backs, especially while talking with students. He even advised her to rent an apartment off campus rather than continue to spread disaffection in off-hours campus conversation. It may well have been Elliott whom Foust suspected in 1926 of trying to influence appointments to the board of directors.[20]

Foust made it a point to avoid such efforts himself, thinking it unseemly to influence the choice of his own superiors. Board members were still chosen by the state board of education although its choices were usually those of the sitting governor. But like McIver, Foust cultivated assiduously and successfully those persons who were chosen. When university consolidation terminated the old board, Foust could recall no case of a divided vote, except as one member desired to be recorded in 1932 as opposing a relaxation of the ban on student smoking. It would be only a slight exaggeration to say that Foust dominated the board; he certainly had its respect.[21]

In 1921 Minnie McIver Brown was joined on the board by two additional women, one of them a former student: Katharine Smith Reynolds Johnson, the remarried widow of tobacco baron R.J. Reynolds. In 1929 the superintendent of public instruction gave way to the governor as *ex officio* chairman of the board, bringing the college into conformity with the university and the Agriculture and Engineering College in Raleigh.[22] But the boards of all three institutions disappeared entirely in 1932 with university consolidation.

* * *

Laurence Veysey, historian of the American university, characterized successful academic presidents of Foust's generation as ruling firmly without being autocratic; as appearing conciliatory while ready to make tough decisions—alone if necessary. This required consulting with everyone whose opinion counted or who might make trouble if overlooked. The best administrators were also gamblers in institutional futures, said Veysey, advancing bold proposals for expansion in advance of guaranteed resources. Sometimes they won, and sometimes they lost.[23]

Foust personified this description. Evidence of his successes lay at every hand in the academic and material growth of the college. If his successes were paralleled on other campuses in an era of economic prosperity and collegiate expansion, it is also true that his greatest gamble, trying to forge a women's university parallel to Chapel Hill, was brought down similarly by forces larger than he: the Great Depression and the accompanying university consolidation.

Foust was sometimes guilty of micromanagement, leaving subordinates underinformed.[24] Like McIver he overworked himself, and though the consequences were less dire, he was in poor health intermittently throughout the 1920s. Short summer vacations afforded little relief since he found it impossible to forget his work. After a stroke in April 1923 he took a six-month medical leave, leaving Jackson in charge. Two years later (also like McIver) he let board member Joe Rosenthal help subsidize a European vacation with his brother Thomas Foust, the Greensboro schools superintendent. (He had to come home early when his daughter Mary died.) In the fall of 1927 he interrupted medical treatment in Baltimore to return to the college, then broke down and spent several months in successive hospitals or sanatoria in Salisbury and Richmond. The diagnosis was usually exhaustion or overwork. Meanwhile, Mrs. Foust suffered a breakdown that required constant nursing care and, after 1929, hospitalization. She died in 1931. Apart from all the medical expenses, Foust was financially strapped with family obligations. At different times he helped to support his mother, a brother, and three widowed sisters with their children. In 1927 he probably organized and certainly joined a subscription campaign to assist Josephine Hege, an honor graduate and later faculty member of the college, to pursue graduate work at Yale.[25]

During these troubles Foust received a great deal of support from Clora McNeill, his secretary for some years past and an alumna from the class of 1913. Her support was limited to the office at first, but after Mrs. Foust's death she moved into the presidential residence and took over household management as well; two other women, one of them a niece who was a student at the college, were also in residence. In August 1932, a year after his wife's death, Foust and McNeill were married. She remained as his part-time secretary for at least a year afterward.[26] There resides in the university archives a double desk that they reportedly shared, face to face. The new Mrs. Foust long outlived her husband and remained his staunchest champion.

* * *

The state's higher education boom in the 1920s rested on unprecedented legislative appropriations, particularly in 1921 and 1923. These did not come unbidden; recalling the days of McIver, higher education leaders proclaimed a New Crusade. A year or more of groundwork culminated in six weeks of intensive lobbying in Raleigh and around the state in early 1921, orchestrated by Foust and UNC President Harry Woodburn Chase. Railroads ran special trains to carry those wanting to attend and speak at the appropriation committee hearings. At home, Laura Coit mobilized the faculty, students, and alumnae. The college's share of the large biennial appropriation was almost $1,500,000. Further recalling McIver, Foust returned home from Raleigh amid the cheers of the student body. He received a similar welcome in 1923 when the legislature voted $2,100,000.[27] It was the state's expenditures for higher education, along with comparable support for schools and roads, that gave North Carolina its reputation as the most progressive state in the South. As it turned out, the state overextended itself and appropriations fell off somewhat during the rest of the decade—even before the cuts of the Great Depression.

That overextension led in 1927 to a major change in state fiscal policy. The legislature required the state to operate henceforth on a balanced budget. To manage the process an advisory budget commission was created, headed by the governor. Since the revenues for any coming biennium could never be predicted with certainty, the legislature had to make educated guesses in voting appropriations. Sometimes revenues fell short of the estimates; on those occasions the commission was empowered to reduce appropriations correspondingly. Thus the college, and every state agency, had to stand ready to return part of its previous appropriation.[28] This would be a source of perennial anxiety, if not anguish, in the years to come.

Foust's private fund raising was minimal compared with McIver's. Small gifts for scholarships and other purposes came in from time to time, often unsolicited, particularly from the Weil family of Goldsboro (including Joe Rosenthal) and the Cone family of Greensboro. Foust made strong appeals to the Rockefeller-supported General Education Board and others for money to complete the new Curry Building and an alumnae building in 1926, with very modest results.[29]

By 1923 Foust and the local newspapers recognized the need for a campus publicity office or news bureau. Alumnae secretary Clara Byrd agreed to do the work part-time, but her time proved insufficient. In 1924 Foust hired J. Arthur Dunn of the English department. For nearly a decade he sent out a newsletter to the state's press reporting campus events. This won general approval, but Dunn too was part-time and felt the pressure of two jobs.[30] Not until 1935 did the college acquire a full-time public relations director.

* * *

Until the college reorganization in 1922, faculty members were reappointed annually by the board on Foust's recommendation. In that year, following national trends, annual appointments became permanent after three years. But the concession meant little; persons with more than three years' service could still be terminated if the president and board had a special reason to do so. Foust exercised this power twice in 1924, in one case terminating an associate professor of biology with seven years' service because she did not fit into the new regime that J.P. Givler was establishing in the department.[31]

Thus Foust retained immense power over faculty members. He often came across as autocratic, and there was an undercurrent of opposition among some faculty, such as Harriet Elliott, but it remained muted. In general, faculty members regarded him as fair, respectful of academic freedom (a relatively new concept in the '20s) and completely devoted to the institution. Apart from major directional changes, he left the curriculum and teaching to the faculty; his micromanagement never extended to the classroom unless an instructor were regarded as overstepping his professional bounds.[32] Though sometimes critical of older faculty members who had given their lives to the college but were now being bypassed by new developments in their fields, he nevertheless leaned over backward to protect them. He found places for domestic science teacher Minnie Jamison, for instance, as dormitory resident, *de facto* dean of freshmen, and college social director—roles that she performed admirably for many years.[33]

Foust's adherence to academic freedom must be understood in the light of his time and his own antecedents. When a romance languages professor divorced and remarried after his French wife left him to return to France, Foust advised him to leave the college and start life anew someplace else; his courtship of the second wife before the first marriage was dissolved had caused embarrassment to the college, Foust said.[34] When another member of that department persisted in living apart from her husband, Foust advised her also to leave. "I do not believe that this college, which should be placing before the young women of the state the highest ideals, should have as members of the faculty married women who are not living with their husbands." Although he sympathized with her situation, he said, he could not go around and explain to everyone all the circumstances connected with her married life.[35] In both cases, Foust had nothing but praise for the individual faculty members and their service.

Foust remained guilty of age and religious discrimination, though perhaps less than in previous years. He once explained to a department head that since North Carolina was largely Protestant in affiliation, it was normally best to hire Protestant faculty members. But he had no objection to hiring a Catholic in this case if she had good judgment; besides, it was only for a semester.[36] Yet in writing to a longtime Jewish friend and supporter of the college, he lamented the trouble that Catholics and Jews had in securing teaching jobs in the state.[37] The college continued to enroll Catholic and Jewish students without any apparent discrimination.

Foust had no difficulty with political activity by faculty women during and after the suffrage movement. Elliott and others were active not only in the League of Women Voters but also the state Democratic Party. But he expressed strong misgivings when education Dean John Cook, the chairman of the state teachers' association, sought to organize the teachers politically.[38]

Two serious cases arose in the 1920s involving off-campus activity by members of the faculty. The first involved Eduard C. Lindeman, head of the new sociology and economics department from 1920 to 1922. A sociologist himself, Lindeman was professionally active and a frequent participant in national and regional conferences. In 1920 he served as secretary and newsletter editor of the American Country Life Association; its headquarters were at the college. Next year, when he was considered for state commissioner of public welfare, Foust gave him a high recommendation and pledged to keep him at the college if at all possible.[39] But Lindeman soon fell from grace after he reportedly told a local church group that education was more important than religion.[40] Like other administrators, Foust was bothered primarily by the public relations impact of such remarks. And there were apparently comparable events on campus as well. Foust came to regard Lindeman as a loose cannon—a bad influence on the students and a bad representative of the college.[41]

All of this was prelude to Lindeman's confrontation with the Ku Klux Klan in February 1922. Foust later recalled this as the touchiest problem he had ever faced as president. The Lindemans permitted their live-in African-American cook to hold a birthday party in her basement room, despite prior telephone calls warning them not to do so. Subsequent gossip had the Lindemans themselves hosting a Negro gathering. That evoked a written notice to Foust from the local Klan, accusing Lindeman of entertaining Negroes as well as of socialism, religious infidelity, and unspecified classroom indiscretions. Foust was warned to terminate Lindeman without delay.[42]

As soon as garbled reports began to circulate, Lindeman went to Foust, suggesting a plain public statement of the facts. But Foust—ever fearful of public controversy—counselled silence, hoping the storm would blow over.[43] At one point he did declare publicly that the college would not be intimidated by outside organizations. Lindeman agreed rather reluctantly to remain silent in public but he discussed the matter widely with friends, who expressed their indignation and support. The story did not die, and Foust's worst fears were about to be realized when one of the local newspapers prepared to take it up. He went downtown and persuaded the editors to squelch the story. He was livid at what he regarded as Lindeman's loose tongue. Long since convinced of the man's poor judgment if not instability, Foust wanted badly to see him go. His main concern now, he admitted later, was to engineer Lindeman's departure without appearing to violate academic freedom and cave in to the KKK.

Once again, Foust proved his mastery at that kind of engineering. Lindeman resigned in April—on his own volition, he thought and both men averred. But Foust now had to combat suggestions from board members and other friends that the college refuse to accept the resignation lest it seem to have surrendered to the Klan. Lindeman again cooperated in his own ouster. He sent *The Survey* magazine (which had just carried a short item about his case) an account of the affair quite favorable to Foust and the college while reaffirming his resignation.

His academic freedom was not violated, he insisted. At Foust's bidding the board accepted the resignation while denying any Klan influence. No doubt also at his bidding, it refused to adopt a draft resolution (reportedly in W. C. Jackson's hand) containing a ringing endorsement of academic freedom.[44]

It was a near repeat of the Christine Reincken case a few years earlier. Scorning the Klan as he had the anti-German hysteria of 1918, Foust nevertheless found himself in agreement with the hooded brotherhood on the most visible issue at hand, Lindeman's departure, and for essentially the same reason, Lindeman's indiscretions. Yet he was able to maneuver Lindeman out while keeping him reasonably happy and appearing all the while to defy the Klan. Lindeman subsequently held a succession of academic and other positions around the country, seemingly none of them for very long.[45]

The second case, in 1925, involved first-year economics professor Albert S. Keister and the evolution controversy then raging in the South. Though an economist, Keister had done work in sociology and was teaching an extension class in sociology in Charlotte. During an informal round-table discussion after class, a student asked him how one could square the theory of evolution with the Bible. Kiester replied that it required one to discard a literal interpretation of certain passages in Genesis, which reflected efforts by a pre-scientific age to explain the origin of life and were thus mythological. One of the students, busy writing down Keister's remarks, turned out to be the wife of a Presbyterian minister. She turned over her notes to her husband, who laid the matter before the local ministerial association. It formally condemned Keister for teaching subversive doctrines that "sapped the very foundations of Christianity." Within a few days the incident was front page news, replete with exaggerations of Keister's actual remarks. In response to these reports a number of individuals and civic groups demanded Keister's sacking by the college. Anticipating what was surely Foust's most vivid nightmare, some suggested that appropriations to NCCW be withheld until that event took place.

In one sense Foust faced greater pressure in this case than he had with Lindeman; this time some members of the board echoed the cry for dismissal. But the cases differed in two important respects. To begin with, Foust admired Keister—in general and for his dignified silence during this ordeal. Keister was hardly an infidel; he taught a men's Bible class in Foust's own Presbyterian congregation and students regarded him as a positive influence. Had it been otherwise, Foust said, he would himself have asked for Keister's resignation; he had done so many times. Secondly, Foust was in his element dealing with board members behind closed doors. He reportedly sat up all night with one member, pressing for Keister's retention. In the end Keister did remain, and in later years he served on the Greensboro City Council, as a hearing officer and arbitrator for the National Labor Relations Board, and as president of the Southern Economics Association.[46]

Foust also made a more general plea to the board for academic freedom as he understood it. That principle was not "a license to employ infidels, or people who would in any way create disrespect for the Bible," he explained. But no one, lay or clerical, had the right to tell others how to interpret Scripture. "We cannot build at this place a great college based upon fear, nor can we grow a great democracy in North Carolina based upon timidity." If the NCCW faculty were to be discharged *en masse*, he said, rebuilding the college would require hiring men and women similar to those previously in service. Higher education required tolerance of different views.[47]

The public Foust was less stalwart than the private Foust, however. As soon as Keister's Charlotte remarks hit the press, state legislator David Poole introduced a resolution formally rebuking any state-supported teacher who taught the doctrine of evolution. Foust refused to speak out against the Poole resolution; so did the presidents of the other state colleges. It was UNC President Harry Woodburn Chase, a relative newcomer to the state, who stepped forward courageously to fight the measure. Amidst bitter controversy the House ultimately defeated the resolution, 67 to 46. Foust, who privately criticized Chase at the time for talking too much in public, later expressed regrets for his own "inability" to join him. But when the issue returned to the legislature two years later, Foust was no more visible.[48]

Chapter 7

Academic Affairs

As student enrollment more than doubled between 1919 and 1929, the number of faculty grew correspondingly from 73 to 150. Columbia University remained the main recruiting ground; the *Carolinian* reported in 1923 that two-thirds of the faculty had done work at Columbia. The new emphasis on the Ph.D. produced increasing numbers with that degree but scholarly interest and activity grew very slowly. Biology head J.P. Givler told Foust boldly in 1924 that the college suffered both from poor student preparation and low faculty scholarship.[1]

Foust surely agreed in some measure with this estimate but his hiring and firing priorities continued to reflect as much the religious and social prejudices (he would have said political realities) of the time and place as a desire to enhance faculty scholarship. It is not surprising that in seeking to replace Lindeman while that controversy yet raged in 1922, he should express a preference for a sociologist with not only the Ph.D. but a southern background; he also preferred that it be a young man.[2] Actually, as the college grew and his own health brought occasional absences, his personal involvement in hiring new faculty members diminished. As early as 1924 he admitted making appointments on the recommendation of the deans and department heads, without always having personal knowledge of the individuals.[3]

Nationally, women increased their proportion of college and university faculty members from a quarter to nearly a third during the 1920s.[4] NCCW differed sharply in this respect; in 1929 as in 1919, women faculty outnumbered men by about three to one, with the preponderance declining very slightly during the decade. But the college was firmly in step with its peers in relegating the great majority of its women to the lower ranks. The number of Ph.D.s in the faculty increased from four to twenty during the decade; of these, women accounted for one in 1919 and six in 1929.[5] Alumnae from this period remember primarily women faculty members, nearly all without the Ph.D., who were devoted to their students as well as their academic fields, and were often superlative teachers.[6]

Faculty salaries around the country peaked in terms of purchasing power in 1913, then suffered from inflation during and after World War I. Although dollar amounts rose in those years salaries did not reach their prewar purchasing levels until the late 1920s. Through most of the decade faculty members were often characterized as living in genteel poverty. At NCCW, Foust lamented in 1920 a faculty turnover of more than 25 percent, owing largely to salaries below even the modest national norms.[7] As women were kept in lower ranks nationally, they also received lower pay. But even high rank brought women lower salaries than men in the same ranks. Dean W.C. Smith told Foust in 1919 that the older women faculty were underpaid, given the services they rendered. One of these was Martha Winfield in his own English department—the namesake of a later dormitory. Winfield asked to borrow $50, $25, or even $10 from the Alumnae Fund in 1920 to tide her over at Columbia University that summer; she said she would have to continue borrowing money to live on when she returned home.[8] In 1921 Foust reported unblushingly to a fellow college president that male department heads were receiving $3600 to $4300 per year; women department heads received $2400 to $2600, about equal to male assistants. Taken as a whole, male faculty members in 1920–21 received an average salary of $3024, women $1806; in 1929–30 the figures were $3700 and $2329.[9] Foust and other administrators attributed the gender differential to the law of supply and demand; the college, said Smith, was competing for first-rate men with the men's colleges, the best women's colleges, and the business world. He added that practically all the faculty were below what he regarded as an acceptable minimum.[10]

One incidental result of student government—by which students took more responsibility for policing dormitory life—was to decrease the number of women faculty serving as dormitory residents.[11] They were thrown on the real estate market and found it increasingly difficult to find housing near campus. Not only the college but Greensboro itself was growing rapidly, and the wartime stoppage of construction had created a backlog. Foust wanted to build an apartment house for faculty members, but lacked the funds and continued to rent nearby houses, subletting rooms to women faculty. A few of the senior women, such as Anna Gove and Gertrude Mendenhall, bought houses of their own close by, but this was beyond the reach of most. The housing shortage also affected the new male faculty members with families. When several of them threatened in 1920 to leave if it were not addressed, Foust took drastic action. Securing the financial backing of a wealthy board member, he purchased seven partially prefabricated houses from the Aladdin Company. In about six weeks they were in place along McIver and West Market Streets. Three of them were reserved for women faculty.[12]

This helped to alleviate the problem, but it was not enough. In 1923, as student applications far exceeded the existing student housing capacity, students were allowed more freely than ever before to live off campus if they wanted to. Now students would be competing with faculty for off-campus housing.[13]

* * *

Teaching loads often remained at fifteen hours (five courses) per semester, though twelve hours (four courses) and even nine were becoming more common. The student course load was fifteen hours.[14] At the same time the student-faculty ratio (14.4 to 1 in 1928–29) was reportedly one of the lowest in the country; most classes were small.[15]

This did not translate to an active research program. Faculty members were still subject to social obligations and what one scholar calls petty formalities that combined to impede research. More important, there was no money to support it. When Eugene Gudger asked for a large enough biology staff to enable him to engage in research, should he return from his current unpaid leave in 1920, Foust replied that however desirable that might be, he could not afford it at a time when some faculty members were in actual want. "This college…has not reached the point where it can maintain Research Departments." So Gudger did not return.[16] Foust was not actively hostile to faculty research, but neither he nor the legislature assigned it a high priority. Foust did find money to pay faculty members' expenses to attend professional meetings, however—a maximum of one person per department to one meeting a year. E.C. Lindeman helped make himself *persona non grata* by persistently protesting this limitation.[17]

At the same time Foust favored the adoption of sabbatical leaves and retirement pensions. Both were coming into vogue nationally. The Carnegie Foundation and its offshoot, the Teachers Insurance and Annuities Association (TIAA) had begun to provide retirement benefits for faculties at a growing number of institutions including the University of North Carolina, but not yet NCCW. The absence of such benefits surely influenced Foust's considerate treatment of some of the older faculty who had given their lives to the college and had now passed their prime or were no longer congruent with the college's new orientation. They were kept on the payroll with lighter loads.[18] Retirement benefits would soon come, but sabbaticals had a steeper hill to climb in North Carolina.

* * *

Lest there be no misunderstanding about the institution's new identity and mission, the 1921–22 catalog announced that "The College of Liberal Arts and Sciences is the center of the North Carolina College for Women, out of which the professional schools have grown and around which they are grouped. Its instruction is foundational for the work of the professional schools." Two years of liberal arts training were required before specialization could begin.[19]

The college had already adopted a new curriculum in 1918, reducing the number of degrees from five to three: bachelor of arts, bachelor of science, and bachelor of music. It adopted the distribution or group system in the freshman and sophomore years, with electives occupying the last two—a nationally popular compromise between the two earlier models of a prescribed curriculum like the Normal's and completely free electives as pioneered at Harvard by President Eliot. This program remained in place in 1929, but NCCW's unprecedented growth in appropriations and faculty permitted a much greater variety of course offerings than before.[20] Only in 1930 did the college replace its old numerical grading system with letter grades—by then almost universal around the country.[21]

Nearly all of the students became public school teachers after graduation. Those planning to teach in the lower grades majored in education while prospective high school teachers ordinarily majored in the fields they planned to teach, with a minor in education.[22] Accordingly, education was always among the top majors. At a time when the bachelor of science degrees were limited to home economics and music, about three quarters of the students graduated with the A.B.[23]

* * *

The new social sciences division under Walter C. Jackson embraced two departments, history and political science, and sociology and economics. With an eye to the advent of woman suffrage in 1920, Jackson expanded the occasional civics course into a separate field of political science under Harriet Elliott. He recommended in 1922 that political science be made a separate department. Almost fifty years would pass before that happened, but Elliott enjoyed virtual autonomy.[24] Her courses in American and international government heavily emphasized current events and intensive newspaper reading. The classes were popular and former students testified decades later to Elliott's lasting impact on their attitudes toward public affairs and public service.[25] She herself remained active locally and nationally in the League of Women Voters and in the antiwar movement that culminated in the Kellogg-Briand peace pact of 1928. Reflecting their appeal to students, these activities were featured frequently in the *Carolinian*.

The history department, like others, grew rapidly in these years. Some of the newcomers would remain with the college for many years; one who came in 1922 but stayed only a year was the historian of Populism John D. Hicks.[26]

The dominant figures in sociology and economics, respectively, were department head Glenn R. Johnson (Lindeman's successor) and Albert Keister. Johnson began at once to expand the sociology offerings, including a course on race relations.

Although most of these people compiled impressive service records on and off campus, and both Benjamin B. Kendrick in history and Keister in economics served as presidents of their respective southern regional professional organizations, they were not known primarily as scholars. Even Kendrick, who coauthored two well-known textbooks in the 1930s, engaged in banking and real estate as much as scholarship.[27]

* * *

When Mary Settle Sharpe departed in 1920 to make her doomed race for superintendent of public instruction, her field of elocution or expression was assigned to the English department and translated into speech and drama. After a year's lapse the position went to W. Raymond Taylor, a North Carolinian and former student of George Pierce Baker at Harvard.[28] Foust apparently had misgivings about the legitimacy of drama as a part of the curriculum and Taylor's original assignment was to teach speech; but once on the scene he was allowed to shift his main focus to his first love, the theater. Over the next thirty-nine years "Teacher" Taylor became a campus institution. Within the English department he organized the first courses in drama, for many years teaching them and an occasional speech course alone.

Hitherto drama had been an extracurricular activity, with often minimal faculty supervision. Taylor brought it under faculty control and more nearly into the curriculum. He united various student dramatic groups into two complementary organizations: the Masqueraders, an honorary society, and the Playlikers, with sole authority to produce plays. (The equivalent organization at Chapel Hill, dating from the same period, was called the Playmakers.) The Playlikers went on tour, in the late '20s winning second place in a national play festival. At home, they made do until the advent of Aycock Auditorium in 1927 with the cramped quarters and antiquated facilities of the Students' Building auditorium.[29]

As early as 1922 Taylor had girls dressing in male attire when they played male roles. (These garments could not be borrowed; Taylor purchased several men's suits for the purpose.) By 1924 he reintroduced male faculty members into student productions, and by 1927 men from the community as well. He even had girls smoking on stage at a time when it was otherwise forbidden. During the '20s Taylor developed an outside business manufacturing theatrical equipment; the business flourished and Taylor continued to operate it with family members for the rest of his life.[30]

* * *

Art was taught under various rubrics from the earliest days of the college. It was usually vocational in nature, in some cases allied to education and in others to domestic science or home economics. Much of it was jettisoned in the struggle for collegiate status in the late Teens.[31] What remained was confined to home economics and to art education at Curry School. The dominant art figure at Curry for many years was McIver's younger sister, Elizabeth McIver Weatherspoon. Lizzie McIver studied under her brother's auspices at Peace Institute in Raleigh, then followed him to the Normal in 1892 as one of the original students. Staying only a year, she taught school in Greensboro until marrying James Weatherspoon of Sanford in 1900. After his death in 1904 and her brother's in 1906, she came to Curry School as supervisor of the first grade. Taking a year off in 1910 to study at Columbia, she returned to Curry as supervisor of art education, and remained there for the rest of her life. A popular teacher, she was professionally active at the state and regional levels and was called one of the pioneer art educators in the state.[32]

Although the college produced its first art education graduate in 1920, there was not even a course in art appreciation for general student election. Weatherspoon urged that a woman's college of NCCW's size ought to have a full-fledged art department,[33] but that was not to come for another decade. More than likely, Foust (as many administrators around the country) did not take esthetic or creative subjects like art very seriously.[34]

* * *

Spanish was added to the curriculum in 1916 and combined with French in the romance languages department. By 1919 only the English department had higher enrollments. Registrar Mary Taylor Moore estimated that four-fifths of the students took French, many of them expecting to teach it.[35] Winfield S. Barney arrived in 1919 as department head; one of his first requests, soon granted, was for a department office instead of merely a teacher's desk—a mark of prestige apparently lacking hitherto.[36] Like the social scientists, the colleagues Barney recruited were primarily teachers, professionally active but not much engaged in scholarship.[37]

Unlike romance languages, Latin and German were small departments, hurting for students. In the case of German, this was a national phenomenon attributable to World War I and the resultant abandonment of German instruction in the public schools. Caroline Schoch, coming in the wake of the Reincken affair in 1918, spent the next thirty years at the college, keeping the flame alive. Unbowed by the difficulties surrounding her subject, she was a dynamic teacher and a champion of Germanic culture if not politics.[38]

As late as 1914, Latin was required for the A.B. degree and some 45 percent of the students took it. But by 1919 the requirement had fallen victim to the elective system and total enrollments were down to fifty-four.[39] The department declined correspondingly. Its head since 1892, the redoubtable Viola Boddie, blamed the college's new academic directions and the competition of chic new fields of inferior merit. Others blamed the same national trends including the elective system—and Miss Boddie's own fearsome disposition. Students frequently left her classroom in tears, stung by her sarcastic appraisals of their work, or lack thereof. Neither Foust nor Dean W. C. Smith knew quite what to do. Foust had felt it necessary to relieve Miss Boddie from dormitory residence duties in 1918, but firing a charter member of the faculty was not an option.[40] Smith and Barney (the division head) recommended hiring a new faculty member ("a first-rate man") to supplement Miss Boddie and doubtless replace her in the fullness of time, but it was not done.[41] When the school of education, presumably attempting an end run, hired Marie Denneen, a Latin teacher, in 1926, Miss Boddie blocked effectively by refusing to sanction college credit for Denneen's courses. Foust thought she had intimidated education Dean John Cook, and it is not entirely clear that she had not intimidated him too.[42]

* * *

A far different personality was Gertrude Mendenhall, the mathematics head and also a charter member of the faculty. Foust had apparently spoken disparagingly of her and the other senior women faculty at the time of the college reorganization. When almost simultaneously math was dropped as a requirement for all freshmen and enrollments fell in consequence, Mendenhall concluded that her usefulness to the college was about over. She was a sympathetic figure among the faculty, including Foust himself, and he rushed to reassure her. Not only did she get a position on the new faculty cabinet, but a stream of personal kindnesses from Foust, including a reminder that math enrollments had been rising ever since the original drop occurred. Mendenhall was in poor health and likely suffering from depression. She died in 1926.[43] Another mainstay of this small department was Virginia Ragsdale, one of the few women Ph.D.s (Bryn Mawr), who in the pre-pension, pre-social security year of 1928 resigned to care for an invalid mother. A third was Cornelia Strong, who came in 1905 and remained until retirement in 1948. In 1931 Strong introduced the first course in astronomy.[44] Mendenhall's successor as department head, after a two-year hiatus, was Helen Barton, who too became a faculty leader of many years' standing.

John Paul Givler arrived in 1920 as head of the biology department, succeeding Eugene Gudger. Finding its enrollments flagging, he cast the blame successively on Gudger, the smallness of his department, and its inadequate facilities.[45] Dean Smith inclined to blame the chronic unpopularity of science in women's colleges. Despite his disadvantages, Givler secured a 50 percent staff increase in 1922 and unquestionably built up the department qualitatively as well. In terms of its research activity, however, an informed visitor in 1931 ranked the department well behind others around the country to which it would like to be compared.[46]

Chemistry and physics showed even less progress in these years. Mary M. Petty remained head of chemistry. She was joined in 1922 by Florence Schaeffer, who in turn served many years, eventually replacing Petty as head.

Foust had always been disappointed in the physics department. W.C.A. Hammel, whom he forced out in 1916 for lack of academic rigor, was replaced by a succession of short-term appointees whom he found no more satisfactory. The two-man department offered only two basic courses and suffered from deplorable facilities.[47] A new head, Calvin N. Warfield, came in 1929. In company with John A. Tiedeman after 1931, he produced the desired results, introducing more experimental work into the program. According to their successor, Anna Joyce Reardon, the department by 1932 had a highly acceptable undergraduate program.[48]

The psychology department made its debut in the 1920s. A few courses in educational psychology had been taught from the beginning by McIver, Claxton, Foust, and Robert Merritt in the education department. When Merritt contracted tuberculosis and had to retire in 1916, he recruited as his successor James A. Highsmith, then principal of the high school at Pomona, a mill village just west of Greensboro. For Highsmith as for Merritt the position was a dual one: teacher of psychology and principal of Curry School.[49] By 1924, Highsmith headed a small psychology department within the new school of education. That year he called Foust's attention to the recent growth of psychology as an experimental science and suggested that it be expanded, reoriented toward greater research, and incorporated into the College of Liberal Arts and Sciences. This was done, effective in the fall of 1925.[50] Within the next few years the department added more advanced courses, and in 1931 hired Key L. Barkley, an experimental psychologist. Many years later Barkley recalled the paucity of laboratory equipment he found, but also his success in acquiring more, even in the depths of the Depression.[51] In Foust's eyes, the department actually overachieved; he complained in 1932 that it offered more courses than an undergraduate psychology department ought to have in depression times.[52]

* * *

Teacher education was transformed nationally in the '20s from a short-term normal school program to one occupying four years of college work. Accordingly, teacher education students accounted for a substantial portion of the growing college and university population.[53]

This was true at NCCW, where over 90 percent of alumnae went into teaching.[54] In 1919 North Carolina adopted statewide certification, basing it on college work.[55]By 1925, campus enrollments in education outstripped those in any other field; at 846 they reportedly outnumbered those at any school of education south of the Mason-Dixon line and west to California. Well over a third of juniors and seniors were education majors, and that did not include the many who planned to teach high school and majored in their own subject areas. Just over half of the education graduates went into elementary school teaching, Dean John H. Cook reported, and NCCW was practically the only place in the state where they could get a four-year college education with training school experience. As a result, its graduates commanded the best jobs and salaries available. There was greater competition in the training of high school teachers. Cook was frank to admit that too many students went into teaching, often because society offered them few other alternatives.[56]

Cook was another Columbia Ph.D., who arrived at the college in 1918, having served as assistant superintendent of public instruction in his native Ohio.[57] Within a year he determined that while the state needed over 2200 women elementary school teachers per year, it required only about 80 new women high school teachers per year. As NCCW by this calculation was turning out too many of the latter and far too few of the former, he advocated special measures to produce more grade school teachers. Obliquely or not, he added a new dimension to the vocational versus academic debate then raging on campus: professional education training (primarily for the grade school teachers) versus liberal arts training (for the high school teachers).[58] In 1924 Foust (himself a former education professor) told Cook that he had often heard students say that once they had taken Highsmith's educational psychology course, they found little else of importance to them in the school of education. By 1928 Foust was proposing that no one should be allowed to major in education as an undergraduate; those planning to teach history should major in history, etc. Cook disagreed, of course, arguing that it would be passing strange for a college whose chief mission was to produce teachers to prevent its students from majoring in education.[59] Foust did not press the issue.

Although the two men were sometimes at odds on questions like this, they maintained a mutual respect. On Cook's death in 1941, Foust wrote privately from retirement that he regarded him as having been the strongest professional educator in the state, and the only one who could compare with the best faculty members in other departments of the college. Meanwhile students protested, as they would for generations afterward, that mounting education requirements deprived them of free electives they held in greater esteem.[60]

Curry School's first high school graduating class in 1917 proved to be its last in over a decade. Interrupted during World War I, the high school resumed, two grades at a time, in 1926 and 1927. (As with the state as a whole, the four high school grades ran from eight through eleven; there was no twelfth grade.) The resumption owed much to a grant from the Rockefeller-funded General Education Board.[61] In the meantime, prospective high school teachers sometimes did practice teaching at Greensboro and Pomona High Schools and sometimes did none at all. Even without a high school, the existing Curry building was seriously overcrowded by 1921, accounting for the construction of the new building on Spring Garden Street in 1926—even as the old one burned down. Curry continued as an adjunct to the Greensboro city system, drawing children from the surrounding area and receiving a partial subsidy from the city.[62] In December 1928 the enrollment was 402—284 in the elementary grades and 118 in high school.[63]

As the summer school was designed primarily to accommodate teachers, Dean Cook served also as summer school director. Growing patronage from regular college students as well as teachers warranted the addition of a second session in 1923. Enrollments grew from 380 in 1919 to almost 2000 in 1926. Men reappeared in 1923 after an apparent absence.[64] Twenty-eight of them came in 1928, living in private houses.

In the early years some of the summer work offered was below college level, to serve a grade school teacher corps many of whom had not graduated from high school. (As late as 1931, only 12 per cent of the nation's elementary school teachers had a bachelor's degree.) Beginning in 1921, however, a high school diploma was required for entrance and the number of high school teachers in attendance was growing. By 1925 over a hundred summer students already had college degrees; many were working on graduate degrees.[65]

* * *

Although Wade Brown greatly expanded the music program that he had found in 1912, it remained largely a piano, voice, and organ conservatory, with little other instrumental work. His efforts to rectify this situation in the early '20s did not bear fruit, perhaps again because Foust's priorities lay elsewhere than in the creative arts.[66] The pipe organ that Brown had previously installed in the Students' Building auditorium was overhauled, enlarged, and reinstalled in the recital hall of the new (1925) music building, later named for him. Efforts to acquire a second organ for Aycock Auditorium (1927) also fell afoul of different priorities, to say nothing of the Depression.[67] The completion of Aycock, the largest auditorium in the city, did enable Brown to help organize the Greensboro Civic Music Association in 1927. In cooperation with the college it would provide fine concert series for many years.[68]

Brown's most heralded accomplishment was to organize, in emulation of other states, a high school music contest designed to stimulate interest in music in the public schools. The first contest, in May 1920, featured only thirteen pianists from as many schools. (At the time piano was the only instrument taught in the schools.) The contest quickly had its desired effect. The number of contestants and instruments (including choral groups) grew so rapidly that by 1929 it was necessary to hold district elimination contests around the state prior to the final competition at the college. Students from 166 schools participated in that year's events.[69]

* * *

Edward J. Forney's commercial program was a conspicuous surviver of the vocational slaughter of the late Teens. From the beginning it had been a one-year program rather carefully separated from the rest of the college. Thus it did not appear to threaten the college's rising academic aspirations. There was a growing demand for secretaries around the state and the program thrived, though enrollments were limited to fewer than 100 students through the 1920s. Foust long toyed with the idea of creating a four-year program with greater academic content, and that came to pass in 1932.[70] At the same time, the one-year program continued, and would assume major proportions during the Depression.

* * *

Home economics also grew rapidly around the country in the '20s, nourished by federal appropriations inaugurated in the previous decade. It became increasingly scientific and specialized as well. But since the science was applied, critics from the liberal arts who previously accused the field of lacking intellectual content proceeded now to attack it as too narrowly technical.[71] Peace was kept locally by the requirement that all students get a two-year liberal arts foundation before going on to their majors. Inevitably at a college where more than 90 percent of the graduates became teachers, much of the home economics curriculum was aimed at turning out home economics teachers. Much of the remainder was aimed at turning out better homemakers and mothers. Still other students became home demonstration agents, although State College in Raleigh claimed most of that training.[72]

A new home management house was built on McIver Street in 1922. With it came a child development program, the first children to be studied being babies up for adoption and supplied by the Greensboro welfare department. They lived in the new house and were cared for by rotating shifts of six to eight college students. When the home economics building was completed next door in 1928, a nursery school was established there to serve as the new child development laboratory. The children now were those of faculty members and others from the community, taken on a first come, first served basis.[73]

Another innovation made possible by the new building was the home economics cafeteria. For decades after its opening in 1929 it served lunch (primarily) and dinner to faculty members, town students, Curry and nursery school students, and campus visitors. It too was a laboratory, for students in the newly-accredited dietetics program.[74]

* * *

The 1905 library building was already overcrowded by 1910.[75] The major expansion of 1923 tripled the building's capacity, well beyond the current collection of 20,000 volumes.[76] But a rapidly growing faculty and student body translated into a rapidly growing library collection as well; it reached 60,000 in 1930. Students had long enjoyed open stack privileges but books were being stolen at such a rate that the privilege was revoked in 1925.[77]

Annie Petty's departure in 1920 came as the college entered its new era. Foust had malnourished both her and the library for years, and he may well have thought new male leadership was in order. (A chancellor of the University of Nebraska informed the woman he had just appointed acting librarian that he would hire a man "as soon as the University could pay a fitting salary.")[78] Charles B. Shaw, a member of the English department, took a year's leave in 1919 to study library science in New York. Hardly had Petty signified her intention to leave than Foust recruited Shaw as her successor. He held the job seven years before departing to become librarian at Swarthmore.[79] Shaw's successor was Charles H. Stone of George Peabody College.

With Foust's reluctant approval Stone immediately began setting up an academic department of library science with an undergraduate major and minor primarily to train school librarians. The Southern Association of Colleges and Secondary Schools (SACS) had just established standards for school librarians, and the new program was designed to provide the necessary personnel. It was the first such program in the state and one of the first in the South, opening in 1928 and graduating twenty students in 1930. By 1932 it was fully accredited by SACS and the American Library Association.[80]

* * *

Foust was unwilling to establish a graduate program without consulting beforehand with the university, which was temporarily without a president. His preliminary thinking ran toward professional training in areas popular with women, leaving everything else to the university—for men and women students alike. He seems to have had no trouble getting incoming UNC President Harry Woodburn Chase to agree to that limited role, but relations between the two institutions in this matter as others were fraught with sensitivity.[81]

In 1920 the Faculty Council approved granting the A.M. degree. Master's degree candidates were permitted to work in all the liberal arts departments as well as education.[82] In fact, the major focus of the program was to train high school teachers and school administrators. The college established a graduate division as part of the reorganization in 1922, and that year the first master's degree was awarded—to May Meador, class of 1917, who used it to move from grade school to high school teaching.[83]

The graduate program grew very slowly; despite the addition of the M.S. degree in 1924,[84] only six master's degrees were awarded in the 1920s. One in education went in 1930 to Eugene Davis Owen, who thus became the first male graduate of the institution.[85]

* * *

College reorganization also brought new emphasis to extension work. A separate extension division was organized in 1921 under the direction of college librarian Charles B. Shaw. The effort was aimed primarily at helping school teachers around the state, either to secure a college degree or to upgrade their certification. Classes were offered at night and on Saturdays. There was also a speakers' bureau through which faculty members gave talks to a variety of civic and other groups. Home economics was a conspicuous contributor to the program, but many disciplines were involved. (Albert Keister's ill-fated sociology class in Charlotte fell within this program.) The division issued bulletins or pamphlets on a variety of subjects; the first, by J. A. Highsmith, dealt with mental tests.[86] Over 600 students were enrolled in extension courses in 1927–28.[87]

* * *

In 1920 the federal government made money available to colleges and universities to teach public health. To get some of this money Foust reorganized the health department under Dr. Anna Gove, who had just returned to the college from war work.[88] By 1924 the department included both physical education and the infirmary staff. It was attached to the College of Liberal Arts and Sciences on a basis comparable to the divisions of languages, science, and social science.[89]

For practical purposes, physical education had been autonomous since its own resurrection in 1907. Its director, Fay Davenport, departed in 1921, to be replaced by Mary Channing Coleman, whom Foust had hired as her assistant a year earlier. Under Coleman physical education achieved a stature hitherto unimagined.[90] She was a product of Amy Morris Homans's famous physical education program at Wellesley College, followed by work at Columbia University. In birth as well as manner Coleman belonged to the First Families of Virginia. A descendant of Pocahontas and two signers of the Declaration of Independence, she was tall, slim, well dressed, well traveled, highly cultivated, and not to be trifled with. She resembled her mentor Homans in counseling and placing her graduates—all of them, even during the Depression. It was understood that all took the jobs she found for them. From her promotion to director of physical education at NCCW in 1921 until her death in 1947 Coleman built up a department of national renown—one of the leading places in the country to train women physical education teachers. Very active professionally, she rose through the ranks in her field to become president of the American Physical Education Association in 1933.[91]

Part of Coleman's legacy lay in the physical plant she was able to build. Like the campus as a whole, physical education benefited from the prosperity and the broader horizons of the '20s. The first structure was a 50 × 90-foot outdoor gymnasium—little more than a floor and a roof supported by posts—that superseded the basement gym in Spencer in 1922. Although it served for more than forty years, it was quickly overshadowed by next-door Rosenthal Gymnasium, completed in 1925. With its swimming pool, basketball court, and other amenities Rosenthal was praised as one of the best facilities of its kind in the country. A story, familiar with variations to every administrator, goes that when Coleman was told she could have either a swimming pool or a gymnasium but not both, she chose the swimming pool on the ground that a gym was so obviously needed it would have to follow shortly. That was what happened. New playing fields and tennis courts came at the same time, replacing the former dairy farm.[92]

The curriculum advanced correspondingly. Activities newly offered for credit in this decade included hiking, swimming, soccer, and folk dancing. New extracurricular activities included track and horseback riding—the latter offered in conjunction with a riding school in nearby Sedgefield. Hitherto physical education had been purely a service program, required of all students. But when the state legislature mandated its inclusion in the public schools, the college responded in 1923 with a physical education major, designed primarily to train teachers.[93] Physical education was everywhere on the defensive academically, and Coleman was determined not to be found wanting. She picked her majors carefully, weeding out those interested only in sports along with any others she regarded as academically unfit. Like majors in other fields, they did most of their practice teaching at Curry and went primarily into teaching after graduation.[94]

Hiking and camping assumed new dimensions in these years. Rather than merely walk to Lindley Park to eat, sing, and then walk back to campus, students began in 1922 to make overnight trips to a succession of camps that the college rented in the countryside. Neither Coleman's nor Gove's influence was great enough to persuade Foust to spend college funds to buy a camp. Coleman resorted to alternative revenue sources, therefore, and the student Athletic Association began raising money by selling gym suits to their fellow students. In 1929 they had amassed enough capital to buy a camp five miles south of town; in a campus contest in 1932 it was named Camp Ahutforfun. It was replaced in 1943 by another of the same name near the Guilford Battleground.[95]

Intramural athletics continued to thrive, partly because of improving facilities, partly because they could be substituted for the walking period, called more accurately after 1920 the recreation period. It lasted for forty-five minutes, Tuesday through Saturday, and could be taken at any time of day but most of the sports were held between 5 and 6 p.m. Competition was mainly between classes at first, but with the proliferation of dormitories it developed between them as well. The favorite sports were field hockey, tennis, basketball, and softball.[96] With Rosenthal Gymnasium in place, the indoor Gym Meet was revived after a lapse, in 1927.

Mary Channing Coleman was emphatically among those physical educators who disapproved of intercollegiate sports for women. She brought Foust, who had previously wavered on the question, around to her point of view. But the ban was not absolute, and mixed-team competition (each team composed of players from two or more institutions) became a popular national substitute. In 1928 NCCW hosted the first intercollegiate Play Day in North Carolina, with mixed teams from seven schools playing a variety of sports. It became an annual event.[97]

Chapter 8

Students and Alumnae

At the very time Foust and the faculty were building what they hoped would be the woman's University of North Carolina, women's colleges were beginning to lose popularity nationally. Many of the increasingly liberated women of the 1920s found single-sex college life boring and protested the monastic regulations of their mothers' day. The automobile removed some of the sting of separation, however, and there was no mass exodus to coeducation. The trend was unmistakably present at NCCW, where what Pamela Dean calls a peer-based student culture emerged in place of the faculty-student culture of the early days.[1]

One of Foust's major challenges was accommodating to the new and assertive student culture while retaining the confidence of parents, faculty, alumnae, and legislators. He did so with surprising ease, acknowledging in 1924 that students not only expected but probably deserved many liberties denied them in previous years.[2] "The day of the policeman has passed," he admonished the new dean of students that year; "the Social Directors should be able to lead for they cannot drive." He advised her to listen to the students respectfully and steer a prudent middle course between them and faculty members who might be resistant to change.[3] Students of the '20s, he said on a number of occasions, held as wholesome values as those in the past, but they were now more honest, independent, and self-reliant than ever before. He claimed in 1933 to have vetoed a student judicial board action only once, and in that case the students reversed themselves before he had to take action.[4]

Old-timers on the faculty took differing views of the New Women in their midst. Viola Boddie, the belle of the faculty in the '90s, decried the growth of materialism in the intervening years and the concomitant loss of respect for education and those who imparted it. Laura Coit, ever sunny, believed on the other hand that economic prosperity had improved student outlook as well as opportunity. Similarly, Walter C. Jackson called the students of 1929 more self-reliant, knowledgeable, and properly demanding of their teachers than when he came to campus twenty years earlier.[5] Although Harriet Elliott blamed Foust for failing to make the academic and social adjustments necessary to accommodate the mushrooming enrollments, Foust himself thought that students and faculty had adjusted admirably from what he called the earlier family life on campus to the new community life. But even he conceded in 1924 that student social life had been neglected.[6]

Students themselves were sometimes alarmed at the changes. As early as 1924 letters and editorials in the *Carolinian* newspaper lamented student apathy. An editorial of 1929 asserted that many students came to the college because they had to; they didn't expect to enjoy it. But some arrived with enthusiasm only to have it wear off under the "indifference of the mob." The editorial lamented the lack of school spirit and called for rejuvenation through intercollegiate competition—not in athletics, which was beyond expectation, but in debate, dramatics, singing, and other activities.[7]

As enrollments grew, Foust's personal contacts were confined more and more to the opposite poles of student life: leaders and offenders. Proportionately more students found him remote and somewhat forbidding, but he remained reasonably popular—a father figure at home and the college's champion in the outside world. He was always graceful in acknowledging the birthday presents or parties, the get-well telegrams, and the welcome-home celebrations during legislative years. He continued to hammer home the Service message in semiweekly chapel talks that students rather dreaded at the time but looked back on with a kind of fierce pride in later years.[8]

* * *

Nationally, college students in the 1920s came increasingly from urban, middle-class backgrounds.[9] This was true even in rural and small-town North Carolina; although farming remained the largest parental occupation of NCCW students into the 1930s, farmers now numbered less than a quarter of the total. Students continued to come from all over the state, with special attention given to applicants from underrepresented areas. By 1921 the college was accepting, within its physical capacity, virtually all applicants from the state's accredited high schools. And as applications exceeded capacity until late in the decade, it did practically no recruiting. The minimum age continued to be sixteen, and the vast majority were Methodist, Baptist, and Presbyterian in that order.[10]

Out-of-state students rose gradually in number from 17 in 1920 to nearly 150 in 1929. Half of the total in 1928 were from South Carolina and Virginia, but many came from the North. The college did not recruit out of state either, but as it grew in size, quality, and reputation out-of-staters found it an acceptable alternative to the much more expensive private women's colleges. Not only were out-of-staters chosen more selectively, but the northern girls in particular were apt to be good students and they usually had finished twelfth grade at a time when southern high schools stopped at the eleventh. Foust, the faculty, and most of the students welcomed the out-of-staters as a leavening agent.[11] A handful of foreign students also attended during the decade, from Serbia, France, and China.

In terms of academic standing, 75 percent of the freshmen in 1928 came from the upper half of their high school classes.[12] Though the preparatory program had been phased out, some of the freshman and sophomore work continued to duplicate material given in the better high schools. In 1926, seventy-one freshmen dropped out after a new rule was invoked requiring them to pass at least six of their first fifteen hours of work.[13]

A large majority of the students—70 percent in 1928—were candidates for the A.B. degree within the College of Liberal Arts.[14] Whether in that program or others, most were preparing to teach.

* * *

Despite the campus building boom, enrollment growth surpassed dormitory growth. In 1923, more students than ever before were allowed to live in rooms off campus. This decision was calculated. As applications mounted well beyond the capacity of the dormitories, Foust insisted on taking as many qualified students as possible, expecting the legislature to vote correspondingly larger appropriations—as it did—for new dorms. Apart from a common administrator's desire to see his enterprise grow, Foust believed that the state had an obligation to educate all of its young, lest an unacceptable aristocracy of learning develop.[15] Accordingly, the college approved about 125 rooms in the neighborhood and students began renting them, taking their meals in the dining halls. Meanwhile the college continued to reject hundreds of other applicants, showing the same pain McIver and Foust had felt from the beginning.[16]

The college long was remiss in its treatment of town students. By 1928 they had the use of a bare, dirty, and uninviting room in the basement of Students' Building. As it had no lockers, they had to carry all their books around with them all day.[17] When they protested their second-class status, college officials encouraged them in 1929 to form a Day Students' Association. Organization quickly brought greater respect and a larger share of elective student offices. It also brought a new and more attractive study hall. But it never brought full integration into the student body—a problem for commuting students in every generation.[18] Campus parking, a transcendent problem in later years, first arose in 1929 when the eighteen commuting students who then had cars complained that faculty members monopolized too many spaces.[19]

* * *

Meals were still served family-style for the most part, with students receiving new table assignments at three-month intervals. Each table was headed by a hostess, either a faculty member or upperclassman, who was charged with maintaining decorum. The rules gradually loosened. Cafeteria-style breakfasts were introduced by 1929 and became standard at both breakfast and lunch in 1932. Students preferred this arrangement, at least in part because they could eat with whomever they wished. It was popular with Foust because it cut labor costs.[20]

* * *

Dr. Anna Gove, the college physician, was given to wanderlust. Throughout her service at the college there were leaves of absence, including service in France during World War I. In some of these cases her return was by no means certain either to her or Foust, but she always did return. Sometimes he replaced her with a full-time staff physician; sometimes he called upon Greensboro physician W. P. Beall, who had helped out in emergencies from the college's beginning.[21] In time the college grew large enough to hire a second physician. Dr. Ruth Collings came aboard as Gove's assistant in 1925. Eventually succeeding her, Collings too would spend the rest of her career at the college.

The first generation or so of college health programs in America focused on sanitation and disease prevention. After World War I they concentrated more on the prevention and correction of individual students' health problems. According to Collings, NCCW was one of the first colleges in the nation to perform tuberculin testing and group X-raying. She also took pride in the fact that only four students had died during her first twenty-one years at the college; two of them were from accidents.[22] The most severe challenges to the infirmary in these years were flu outbreaks in 1919–20 and 1928–29, both of which passed without major incident. Foust opined privately in 1932 that if Gove and Collings were to give half of their time to the college and the other half to private practice, both they and the college would benefit; that did not happen, and he seems not to have shared this opinion with them.[23]

* * *

Student tuition and fees remained low. Most students continued to take the teaching or service pledge and avoided the modest $45 annual tuition. For them the remaining fees amounted to $260 in 1919 and $324 a decade later. These figures amounted to well over half the total cost of educating each student; the state paid the remainder.[24]

Kathleen Pettit Hawkins, a graduate of the one-year commercial program, joined the staff as financial aid officer in 1920, initially assisting Laura Coit. She remained for 47 years, cajoling donors for additional loan funds and diplomatically dunning recipients for repayment after graduation. Her success rate was impressive.[25] Scholarships, by comparison with loans, were few. But several funds were established, beginning in the 1920s, by the Weil family of Goldsboro, who sent daughters to the college and assisted it in a variety of ways. Most notable was the Weil graduate fellowship, awarded to an alumna who intended to pursue graduate work.[26]

Campus jobs were still available to needy students, but the college removed the great majority of them in 1923 when it began to hire non-student dining room help. Forty-eight part-time students—the usual complement—were estimated to cost almost twice as much as twelve full-time African-American men doing the same work. The change drew vigorous protests on both economic and racial grounds, but it lasted until 1932, when cafeteria meals were instituted at breakfast and lunch and students were restored to the remaining jobs. This was a Depression measure that no doubt enabled some students to return who could not otherwise do so. On that occasion over 300 students applied for the 58 available jobs.[27]

Meanwhile the remaining jobs—126 of them in 1926—were scattered over campus, in the library, bookstore, laundry, telephone switchboard, and science laboratories. Many students worked off campus as part-time baby sitters, store clerks, and in other capacities.[28]

* * *

Given the growing numbers of both faculty and students, it was impossible for them to fraternize as much as they had in previous years. But the change was gradual. The faculty-student baseball game, for instance, persisted for decades. (President Foust played first base in 1919, when the faculty team [consisting of both males and females] beat the students 17 to 5.) The faculty often entertained groups of students in their homes or at such places as the YWCA Hut. The Dikean Society in 1922 held a minstrel show featuring both faculty and student performers.[29] Harriet Elliott annually took her government classes to Washington, Wade Brown and Raymond Taylor their music and drama classes to New York. Others continued to take students to church with them—sometimes varied churches, for educational purposes. Male faculty members continued to meet incoming students at the depot in the fall.[30] Nevertheless, *Carolinian* editorials in the late '20s and early '30s decried the distance that had developed—often a physical distance as the automobile enabled faculty members to live farther away from campus. Too many did not even know their students' names. The editors sometimes blamed the students as well for the problem, growing from a reluctance to cultivate faculty members lest they be perceived as currying favor.[31]

* * *

Emma King remained for a time as director of dormitories and *de facto* dean of students, but even with an assistant she could not keep up with the burgeoning student body. In the early 1920s Foust hired a succession of social directors and counselors with different titles, but none met his requirements and all were shortlived. In 1924 he dropped King as well and hired Mrs. Sue Stone Durand in the office now called for the first time dean of students.[32] Durand herself lasted only four years, her disciplinary actions evoking student hostility and making her *persona non grata* with alumnae, board members, and ultimately Foust himself. Some of her unpopularity transferred to him, but the problem extended beyond the personalities involved, as he recognized. In this time of rapidly growing student enrollments and student assertiveness everywhere, almost every institution had trouble defining the limits of student freedom.[33] Failing to find a proper replacement for Durand in 1928, Foust divided the responsibilities between Minnie Jamison, who became in effect dean of freshmen, and Lillian Killingsworth, in charge of upperclassmen. (An accompanying decision to segregate freshmen in separate dormitories was very unpopular with them and the upperclassmen alike.)[34] Jamison was ever-popular with students and Killingsworth was not, but the arrangement worked well enough that Foust retained it for the remaining six years of his presidency.[35]

Student counselling—academic, social, and spiritual—was a matter of active concern nationally during the '20s. NCCW followed the trend in establishing academic advisory boards as well as an orientation week for freshmen in 1928—the year they were moved into separate dormitories.[36] That year Foust also hired economist Chase Going Woodhouse as director of vocational guidance and placement. She soon coupled this position with the directorship of a new Institute of Women's Professional Relations—a clearing house for women's work outside the home, sponsored by the American Association of University Women. Woodhouse was a leading and productive member of the faculty, departing when Foust left the presidency and her job was abolished in favor of a new counseling system in 1934. She moved to Connecticut College and was elected to two terms in Congress from that state in the 1940s.[37] Although she and Harriet Elliott were both feminists and Democratic party activists, they seem not to have been friendly. Elliott perhaps saw Woodhouse as a rival, and certainly as a Foust loyalist. She doubtless played a part in Woodhouse's ouster, and even rejoiced quietly when Woodhouse was defeated for re-election in one of her congressional races.[38]

* * *

The New Woman of the 1920s, unlike her immediate predecessors in the suffrage movement, was concerned almost entirely with campus issues, especially social ones. Although this new creature came unmistakably to the South and to NCCW, her appearance was slightly delayed and the campus regulations restraining her were slightly tighter than in other parts of the country.[39] Almost everywhere student government—from its beginnings in the Teens until the wholesale abolition of social regulations in the early '70s—occupied itself primarily with enforcing these regulations and trying incrementally to relax them.

Contact with males at the Normal had been so limited when Harriet Elliott arrived in 1913 that she characterized the campus as a "no man's land." Students seeking greater freedom in the '20s found firm allies in her and Minnie Jamison. Elliott helped student leaders in 1921 to revise student government and moderate the rules. Jamison helped introduce the first dance on campus in 1930, a year after Bryn Mawr—considered the northern laggard in this respect—fell in line.[40]

The revision of 1921 made student government (SGA) at once more representative and more cumbersome. The previous governing body had consisted primarily of four elected officers (president, vice president, secretary, and treasurer) and the dormitory presidents. The new organization, patterned after the federal government, contained the same elected officers, a senate composed of the dormitory presidents, and a house of representatives elected by all the students. A further revision in 1930 adhered even more closely to the federal system with executive, legislative, and judicial branches. That arrangement lasted with only slight changes until 1971.[41]

Meanwhile, curbs on student behavior became so irksome that students turned increasingly to passive resistance, ignoring regulations and boycotting SGA elections. In 1927 only 75 of the 1000 sophomores, juniors, and seniors showed up for the mass meeting called to elect officers. Next year, following Dean Durand's ouster, the *Carolinian* reported that the great majority of students were violating the honor code with impunity while openly pitying the SGA officers who were supposed to enforce it.[42]

Faced with rebellion on this scale, administrators and student leaders in 1929 held an unprecedented meeting—nowadays it would be called a retreat—before the beginning of the fall semester. About fifteen administrators (including Foust and Dean Killingsworth) and thirty-five students met over a period of several days at Camp Yonahlossee in the mountains near Blowing Rock. The students included the SGA officers, class presidents, editors of the student publications, and representatives of the YWCA and the Day Students' Association. All of the current student regulations were reviewed and many were liberalized or abolished. When the meeting ended the *Carolinian* hailed it as a milestone in college history, marking the first time in their memory when administrators and students had a chance to hear and understand each other. The fall leadership conference became an annual event.[43]

One manifestation of the Spirit of Yonahlasee was the first male-female dance in campus history. On earlier occasions the *Carolinian* had noted acidly that while the state of North Carolina sanctioned social dancing in a variety of ways, NCCW had not gotten the message. Instead, the only event in the year to which students could invite male guests was a dull and expensive junior-senior banquet. In the spring of 1930 the banquet gave way to a junior-senior dance.[44]

The stream thus begun grew to a torrent. Before long, men not only attended annual dances sponsored by the former literary societies, but weekly tea dances held in the gymnasium. All were well chaperoned. By 1932, selected juniors and seniors were attending weekend dances out of town, also well chaperoned.[45] Noting their absence, Foust could not help lamenting the lost weekends involved; too many students, he thought, socialized too much and studied too little.[46]

Drinking was much less a problem. National prohibition was in force, the campus ban on liquor was absolute, and violation was a shipping offense.[47]

Another cause for suspension was what Foust variously called "night riding" or "indiscreet automobiling." Girls were forbidden to ride about in cars, or even possess them without special permission, regardless of whom they rode with or at what hour. Foust regarded this in part as a safety measure, especially after several girls drove into a telephone pole with serious injuries resulting.[48]

Owing to the widespread perception that smoking was unladylike, anti-smoking regulations were much stricter on women's campuses than men's. Girls resented the double standard and made freedom to smoke a *cause celebre* on many campuses in the '20s.[49] NCCW was among the last in the region to maintain the ban. In 1931 more than a thousand students petitioned for its abolition and the student judicial board pronounced it impossible to enforce any longer. Foust polled parents and board members, sent Dean Killingsworth to reconnoitre nearby colleges, and ended by doing as most of them were doing: allowing students to smoke in their own rooms. Only about 300 students (of 1710) registered their intent to do so; some of the remainder were no doubt influenced in this Depression year by the college's refusal to extend student loans to smokers. The rationale: they were less employable and the college needed to collect these debts after graduation. Some parents, board members, and others vehemently opposed the relaxation. Interestingly, nothing in the discussion or apparently the decision of this issue reflected the fact that North Carolina was a tobacco state, increasingly dependent on tobacco revenues.[50]

* * *

Despite the constant push to relax burdensome regulations, tradition remained strong. The school year was studded with ceremonies, old and occasionally new, dedicated to preserving inherited ties, symbols, and values. Even with larger enrollments and less intimate student-faculty relations, the college was small enough to engender a continuing sense of student community and sisterhood—something rapidly disappearing outside the South.[51]

May Day was one of the most enduring traditions. The May Day pageants of 1912 and 1916 were so successful that there was talk of making them quadrennial events—once in the college life of each student. World War I brought a reevaluation, and there was no pageant in 1920. In 1921 and 1922, May Day returned more modestly, coupled with Field Day and featuring athletics and folk dances. After another hiatus it was restored by the senior class in 1926 and became an annual event thereafter.[52] Although these ceremonies never rivalled the first two in size, they continued to feature traditional folk dancing and the crowning of a May Queen, one of the seniors elected by her classmates. Students from each class participated, as well as Curry School children in bit parts. The ceremonies were held in different campus locales over the years, but the outdoor theater in Peabody Park was a favorite site in the early years.[53]

Slightly newer than May Day and carrying a heavier spiritual content was Park Night, an allegorical masque celebrating the college's dedication to Service. In fact, a character named Service was analagous to the May Queen as the masque's central figure. She and her attendants were also elected, in this case by all the students. Harriet Elliott inspired and initially directed the event but it was written and performed by the students themselves from its debut preceding commencement in 1919. The performance was intended, and appears for years to have succeeded, as an inspirational, even quasi-religious call to duty on the part of the student body—no mean achievement in the worldly 1920s. Park Night finally disappeared in 1935, when graduating seniors decided to commemorate the individual achievements of their leading classmates.[54]

Another event heavily overlain with allegory was the annual nuptial ceremony between the freshman and junior classes. Also dating from about 1919, this celebration of interclass solidarity pushed big sister-little sister ties to the utmost. Participants from both classes dressed as in a formal wedding with freshmen playing the bride and her attendants while juniors took the male roles dressed in black tuxedos. A faculty member acted as the minister.[55] It is interesting that Foust was able to accept this annual case of ceremonial cross-dressing as well as the regular appearance of students in male attire in dramatic presentations, but he became quite disturbed at students appearing on campus in riding habits ("male attire") after the introduction of horseback riding classes.[56]

The daisy chain, fashioned since 1900 by the sophomores for their senior sisters at commencement, endured for many decades. Distinctive class jackets saw their debut in the late '20s. Colored in correspondence with the rotating class colors (green, red, blue, and lavender), they were purchased and worn by nearly every student from her sophomore year onward.[57]

* * *

The old literary societies were rapidly losing their academic or intellectual content and becoming social clubs. One of the last steps in that direction was their abandonment in 1922 of the traditional inter-society debates. The reason: too much pressure on the too-few students who participated.[58] The decision left a gap and there were suggestions that the college embrace intercollegiate debating, if only to generate school spirit. Foust apparently disapproved initially but came around after the faculty cabinet approved the idea in 1929. (The Spirit of Yonahlasee, again.) The idea proved to be stillborn, nevertheless—owing again to too little student interest.[59]

Since every student was assigned impartially to one of the societies, they avoided the status hierarchy associated with fraternities and sororities on other campuses. But like all organizations, they were dominated by a small minority of activists. As college enrollments mounted, a fourth society was added in 1923, the Aletheian, named for the Greek goddess of Truth. In 1930 each of the four was divided into two chapters to accommodate still further numbers. For a time, inter-society athletics threatened to supplant those between classes, but by the 1930s the societies were limited almost entirely to sponsoring parties and dances. They continued to elect the honorific student marshals.[60]

Freshman hazing—distinguished from the half-humorous, half-scary threats of the early days—appeared on campus in 1923, again associated with new students' admission into the societies. Foust secured an agreement in 1925 to channel the activity into a week of acceptable pranks including revival of the old stories about riding the goat, climbing the greasy pole, and dancing with the skeleton. In addition, freshmen were conscripted into housecleaning duties and required to sing the words of a laundry list to the tune of Home Sweet Home or some other song.[61] But by 1931 freshmen were being asked to accost male strangers off campus and to cross streets and proceed down steep embankments in long lines while blindfolded. At this point Minnie Jamison urged that the revels be reined in again and confined to a single day.[62] Perhaps they were for the time being, but this genie, once out of the bottle, proved hard to keep confined.

* * *

The *State Normal Magazine* disappeared in 1919 with the State Normal itself. In its wake came a trio of student publications. First was the *Carolinian*, a weekly newspaper that began publication in May 1919 and continues into the new millenium. The idea for the paper appears to have originated with students in Alonzo Hall's creative writing class during World War I; wartime restrictions delayed its appearance for a year.[63] There was some initial uncertainty about the title, which had recently belonged to the campus yearbook. But that publication reappeared under a new name and *Carolinian* stuck with the newspaper.[64]

Although Hall helped the early staff to get the paper on its feet and their successors would sometimes call on administrators and faculty for advice on particular matters, the paper operated by its own choice without a faculty advisory board. Indeed, its appearance, quality, and tone perennially attested the editors' freedom; there was no censorship. Financing came from the student affairs budget and advertising. For several years the paper tended to be more critical of students than of the administration and faculty. But that changed in the mid-'20s, leading up to the crisis preceding Camp Yonahlasee.[65]

Another successor to the *State Normal Magazine* was the literary magazine *Coraddi*, which has also continued to date. Appearing in October 1919, it took its name from the three student societies then in existence: Cornelian, Adelphian, and Dikean. Like all student publications, its quality varied; it reflected the talents and sweat of a small minority of the student body. In the 1920s it drew on the work of others as well as students, and did not yet benefit from the superb writing faculty whom the English department assembled in later decades. In the early '30s, according to a former editor, it was a question of getting submissions, not choosing among them.[66]

The student yearbook reappeared in 1920 as *Pine Needles*. Originally issued by the senior class, it passed by 1929 to the Student Government Association. True to its type, *Pine Needles* featured campus scenes as well as pictures of the students individually and in a host of organizational groupings. Although the publication won respectable mention nationally in 1924, inadequate student support kept it in financial jeopardy much of the time.[67]

* * *

Historian Paula Fass, in her study of student life in the 1920s, found a pervasive secularism—a growing indifference if not actual hostility to religion. As an example she pointed to students at North Carolina's Trinity College, which became Duke University in this decade. Almost everywhere compulsory chapel came under attack.[68]

Students at NCCW, noting widespread faculty absenteeism at the noon services each day, pushed for optional student attendance themselves. Increasingly they took to passive resistance by not showing up, by walking out after attendance was taken, or by talking or reading during the services. When attendance was made optional on an experimental basis in 1926 and put on the honor system in 1930, turnouts were embarrassingly low and the experiments were terminated.[69] Ultimately, mandatory attendance was preserved by other concessions.

At least one modification was dictated by increasing enrollments that outstripped the capacity of the Students' Building auditorium. In 1923 students were divided into two groups, each attending twice a week Monday through Thursday, with Friday optional. Music was introduced in 1924, Dean Wade Brown organizing a chapel choir and his colleague George Thompson playing organ preludes. Students asked and were allowed to lead the services themselves periodically. When Aycock Auditorium opened in 1927 with a capacity large enough to hold all of the students, services were reduced to twice a week, on Tuesdays and Fridays. Still held at noon, they lasted thirty minutes and students were required to attend both days.[70] The rationale for mandatory attendance was secular as well as religious. This was the only occasion on which all students gathered together for announcements and exhortations.

The programs too were a combination of the religious and secular. Faculty chapel committees struggled mightily to present programs that would be of interest to students as well as faculty. They ranged from devotional exercises conducted by faculty, students, and visiting clergymen to talks by Amy Morris Homans about physical education, Julius Foust about his lobbying efforts in Raleigh, and Louise Alexander (a Greensboro attorney and future faculty member) about her work with the police department. Tuskegee's George Washington Carver spoke in 1933. Musical programs included faculty recitals, group singing, and performances by outside groups like the A&T College glee club from across town.

The Depression occasioned a further advance of secularism: in 1930 the college stopped handing out Bibles to the seniors at commencement. They had been paid for out of student fees, which were now cut back as far as possible.[71]

The shift toward secularism was also reflected in the changing emphases (and waning influence) of the YWCA.[72] Every year a number of NCCW students met their counterparts from other institutions at two-week summer conferences in the Y's Blue Ridge center near Asheville. These meetings introduced many southern students for the first time to interracial gatherings, interracial cooperation, and eventually integration. In fact, the student YWCA (much more than the YMCA) was a leading force for racial and social reform in the '20s and later.[73]

At NCCW, the campus YWCA fell into step early in the '20s under the leadership of campus secretary Lois McDonald. She introduced students to the living and working conditions of mill workers in Greensboro and Atlanta. She helped organize a meeting with a dean at one of the local black colleges. But the number of students interested in these matters, or other YWCA activity, was small. The *Carolinian* carried two isolated editorials in 1926, one calling for legal and political equality for blacks, leaving social equality to individual judgment, and the other attacking lynching as "the indisputable proof of Southern hysteria" on the race question. Far more editorials portrayed and attacked a pervasive student apathy on almost all subjects except men. The campus Y seriously considered dissolving in 1923, a year before McDonald's departure. In the course of the decade it declined in influence, with student government assuming what formerly had been the Y's hegemony over student publications and traditions. The Y continued, however, to operate the Hut and to hold Sunday evening vesper services.[74]

That interracial experiments did not advance farther was doubtless comforting to Foust. Never a fanatic on any issue, he felt acute discomfort at the approach of anything likely to involve the college in controversy—and no button was hotter than race relations. Foust did not object overly to students attending interracial meetings when conducted elsewhere, but he put his foot down when they asked to hold one on campus. He also refused black institutions like Bennett College the use of the new Aycock Auditorium, pleading the high number of requests.[75] On an exceptional basis only, he did permit blacks to attend concerts in Aycock during Grand Opera week in 1929. When W C. Jackson interceded in behalf of the A&T State College library across town to let their students occasionally borrow books from the library, Foust agreed. But at the same time he asked Dr. Gove to report what danger from disease NCCW students might incur as a result of such use.[76]

* * *

Aycock Auditorium facilitated expansion of the concert-lecture program that McIver had begun. Beginning in 1913 students were charged a $1 annual concert-lecture fee. The proceeds, plus box office receipts, paid for three good concerts and four to six lectures a year, Wade Brown later recalled. Before Aycock's completion some of the larger concerts had to be held in theaters downtown. With the auditorium in place, the Greensboro Civic Music Association sponsored all or most of its concerts there, aided by student fees.[77] In 1929 the San Carlo Opera Company presented five different operas in as many evenings. As the *Carolinian* pointed out, prior to Aycock Greensboro seldom saw a full opera, for lack of a hall large enough to accommodate it.[78] In charge of the lecture committee during the '20s and '30s was English professor Leonard Hurley. Over the years it brought such personages as Cornelia Otis Skinner, Thomas Mann, Eve Curie, Bertrand Russell, Robert Frost, and Eleanor Roosevelt.[79]

* * *

Many feminists found it ironic and not a little frustrating in the wake of their suffrage victory to see more women college students than ever before set their sights on marriage and domesticity after graduation. Marriage rates among northeastern women's college graduates in the '20s indicate that that mission was accomplished to an unprecedented degree.[80] But locally, if the results of a 1948 student's survey (with the cooperation of the Alumnae Association) are correct, the trend among Normal/NCCW graduates was by no means as clear. Studying half of the alumnae classes spaced evenly between 1908 and 1934, she found a stable marriage rate of 68 to 72 percent over the period, with the highest rate of 72 percent arising from the classes of 1916–1920.[81]

A career usually preceded marriage, and increasingly coexisted with it. The vast majority of graduates continued to go into teaching. In 1920 and surely later, over a third of the public school teachers in North Carolina were Normal/NCCW graduates.[82] In early 1926, 88 percent of the previous year's graduating class were then teaching, about a third of them in high schools. And by 1929, 95 percent of all alumnae to that date were either present or former teachers.[83] A few went on to graduate school and, sometimes, careers in college teaching. Ten alumnae from the classes of 1919 to 1929 ultimately attained doctorates, in all but one case more than a decade after graduation.[84]

A minority of graduates continued to go into other fields. One of the most prominent student radicals of her day turned up in 1924 as chief probation officer for Judge Ben Lindsey's pioneering Juvenile and Family Court in Denver. More prominent was Harriet Morehead Berry, '97 who as executive secretary of the North Carolina Good Roads Association led the way in creating a statewide highway system in the 1920s. She was thus a major contributor to the state's modernization program that gained national attention in that decade.[85]

* * *

Frederick Rudolph, historian of the American college and university, describes the rise of alumni in the early 20th century in ecclesiastical terms. Alumni developed an almost religious devotion to their alma maters, erecting campus shrines (alumni houses), sponsoring filiopietistic histories, and investing high priests (alumni secretaries) with authority to superintendent their efforts. Regional clubs were organized and publications were issued to propagate the faith. Almsgiving became a science with annual giving and reunion fundraising campaigns.[86]

At NCCW, Ethel Bollinger, taking office in 1919 as the first full-time alumnae secretary, played the designated role. She traveled the state organizing local clubs and raising money for the student loan funds, launched plans to build a campus alumnae house, and edited the *Alumnae News*.[87] On her resignation in 1922 to get married, her place went to Clara Booth Byrd '13, an assistant to E.J. Forney in the commercial department and the treasurer's office. Byrd's headquarters, like Bollinger's, consisted at first of a desk in one of the college offices. The *Alumnae News* was essentially a newsletter, devoted more to college than alumnae affairs. In the next quarter century Byrd went far to transform the association in the manner and direction described by Rudolph. One of her first major efforts was a successful alumnae lobbying campaign with the state legislature in 1923 for higher appropriations.[88]

The Alumnae Association chose the secretary and paid her office expenses while the college paid her salary. Although the state budget commission questioned this arrangement in 1921 (as it did on other campuses, holding that this official was not properly a state employee) the arrangement continued, with the college formally recognizing her as a member of the faculty. Foust hoped ultimately to make the association self-supporting, but that was impossible when its only dependable source of income was annual dues from a small and impecunious membership.[89] Although the association continued to grow in the 1920s, the alumnae house would have to wait until New Deal relief funds became available in the next decade. Financial independence was still a dream at the dawn of the next century.

Chapter 9

Depression, Consolidation, Coeducation

It was a rare American whose life was not affected, even dominated by the Great Depression. In North Carolina as elsewhere, the worst may have passed by 1935 but the effects lasted a full decade after the 1929 stock market crash. The 1931 legislature attacked the crisis on a broad front, reorganizing state government and slashing expenditures. Higher education took its share of hits. The college's annual appropriation fell from $465,000 in 1928–29 to $161,195 in 1933–34, the worst year—a drop of 65 percent.[1] Legislators also mandated a 10 percent salary reduction for all state employees, including university and college faculty. Still deeper cuts came in 1933, when faculty salaries were reduced by another 32 percent.[2] Nationally, prices fell even more than salaries and the professoriat, paradoxically, was better off on balance in 1935 than it had been in 1929. But in North Carolina faculty at the three state institutions suffered almost triple the national average salary cut of 15 percent. As late as 1942, some of these cuts had not yet been fully restored.[3] Adding further injury were three Greensboro bank failures by 1933 in which nearly every faculty member lost money.[4]

By far the worst sufferers were those who lost their jobs altogether—chiefly junior faculty. Facing a 20 percent budget cutback as early as 1930, Foust released about twenty-five faculty members—some 17 percent of the total. These terminations had a more chilling effect on faculty morale than the subsequent salary cuts.[5] A faculty daughter recalled many years later that hearing of these cases was like learning of deaths; nobody else was hiring and there was often no place to go.[6] And reflecting the severance of workers farther down the scale, students were pressed into service as groundskeepers in 1930, as they had been during World War I.[7]

Student enrollments in the same period dropped 31 percent, several times the national average of 8 percent.[8] The human side of this loss was brought home in a letter from Mildred Pearson, a farm girl near Clinton who sadly withdrew her application in 1931 despite a longstanding wish to attend NCCW. Her earnings of $75 from raising chickens and $40 from picking huckleberries were swallowed up in a local bank failure. So were her father's savings. And when they took the year's tobacco crop to market it brought only three to seven cents a pound.[9] Foust's correspondence in these years is full of letters from parents seeking financial aid, some leeway in making payments, or sorrowfully withdrawing their daughters. Foust helped them as far as he could, even creating a loan fund himself in memory of his daughter Mary. But his efforts to raise money for the fund met with only indifferent success.[10] In 1931 he declined a father's request to pay his daughter's tuition in apples, but several months later the state permitted him to accept produce.[11] Ironically, given the terrible economic conditions, free tuition in return for the promise to teach after graduation disappeared in 1933. As the numbers of alumnae grew, it became a bookkeeping nightmare to determine whether recipients had kept their promise.[12] Hard times, moreover, so reduced the number of available teaching jobs than many graduates could not redeem the pledge if they *had* been bound to it.

As enrollments fell the college closed three dormitories and the others were not fully occupied. Spring vacation was canceled one year; few had bus or train fare to go home.[13]

* * *

The Depression hastened a movement already underway in many states to bring the multiplying public colleges and universities under some common control. Elected officials were eager to remove what they perceived as unnecessary duplication and the consequent waste of scarce taxpayer dollars.[14] Proposals of this nature had been made in North Carolina at least as early as 1919, but not until the Depression did they gain traction. In 1930, following a recommendation of the Brookings Institution, Governor O. Max Gardner proposed to bring the university in Chapel Hill, State College in Raleigh, and NCCW under a common president and board of trustees. (He thus omitted the three state teachers' colleges for whites and the six institutions for blacks and Indians.) The 1931 legislature passed the enabling bill with little opposition as part of its broader reorganization of state government. Most of the opposition, in fact, developed on the three campuses only after the law had passed, and centered on the details of implementation.[15]

Consolidation was intended to minimize a competition that had existed among the three institutions from the beginning. The most sensitive areas involved curricular overlap and the admission of women. Although the Normal/NCCW was the assigned destination for virtually all white women, the other two campuses managed to break the gender barrier just as NCCW had in the case of summer and graduate students. In fact, Chapel Hill had been admitting a few specialized women students ever since President Edwin Alderman's day in 1897. It got its first women's dormitory in 1925 and by 1930 had 205 women in attendance.[16] Competition reached the point that a treaty of sorts was negotiated between the three powers in 1925. Under it the university would not admit freshman and sophomore women unless they were entering programs not offered in Greensboro, while NCCW limited its graduate programs to those traditionally associated with women.[17] This agreement was no more effective than the near-contemporary Kellogg-Briand treaty outlawing war . State College, for its part, was accused of introducing liberal arts work and in 1927 it organized a school of education open to women students. Although Foust developed a close relationship with UNC President Harry Woodburn Chase, he continued to distrust the university and its ambitions.[18]

When consolidation was proposed in 1930, State College President Eugene C. Brooks came out against it, a position he held to consistently. Chase left Chapel Hill that year for the University of Illinois; his successor Frank Porter Graham, initially reluctant, soon came to support the idea. Foust's first reaction was also negative, but during the next few years he shifted back and forth, depending on the changing prospects for NCCW. Early in 1931 he polled the alumnae, got a mixed response, then testified favorably before the legislature. He shared the view of some alumnae that consolidation offered the best chance of holding off coeducation at the other campuses and thereby preserving the college's identity.[19] But consolidation sounded the death knell for NCCW becoming the state's university for women. In fact, Foust now began revising history by downplaying, even denying his past hopes in that direction and the progress already achieved in creating a graduate program.[20]

By late 1932 he was even less sanguine. Outside experts found few monetary savings to be expected from consolidation although they believed it would make the state's higher education system more efficient. (That remained the verdict after a decade's experience.)[21] The legislature had empowered itself to elect a new consolidated board of trustees—a full 100 members, at least ten of them to be women—to supersede the three existing boards on 1 July 1932. Not surprisingly given their own antecedents, legislators chose a majority of Chapel Hill graduates. In 1934 eleven trustees were women, five of them Normal/NCCW alumnae. Given the impossibility of transacting business in a body so large, the board elected a twelve-member executive committee whose recommendations it normally followed. Two women, including Laura Weill Cone, served on that panel.[22]

The North Carolina College for Women now became the Woman's College of the University of North Carolina—WC for short. In November 1932 the new board elected Frank Porter Graham president of the consolidated university. Foust, Brooks, and Graham's successor at Chapel Hill were to be vice presidents.[23] Needless to say, consolidation did not end competition among the three campuses; it merely shifted the main arena from the legislature to the board of trustees.

Graham was surely the best man for the job of president. His own feet were planted firmly in Chapel Hill, but he went out of his way to treat the three campuses equitably—within the master plan. Graham paid his first official visit to Woman's College and spoke to the faculty in May 1933.[24] He returned many times in his seventeen-year tenure as president—even playing in faculty-student softball games. Contrary to Foust's view during the stresses and strains of consolidation, Graham was a genuinely principled man who came to be idolized by generations of Tarheels from all three campuses and well beyond.[25]

Yet the entire male power structure in the state—from the legislature through the UNC board to the new general administration headquartered in Chapel Hill—was oriented toward Chapel Hill and State College, in that order. After ten years of consolidation, the institutional affiliation of board members to that time was estimated to have been: Chapel Hill 62 percent, State College 16 percent, Woman's College 8 percent, while 14 percent were unaffiliated.[26] With three layers of male authority to penetrate instead of the previous one in Raleigh, Woman's College seemed likely to be a distant third in the university pecking order. Such was the widespread apprehension of alumnae and others associated with the college then and later.[27] The WC faculty at first supported consolidation. But resentment gathered as the process unrolled.[28]

Implementation plans called for the preservation of each institution's present identity while concentrating advanced programs on a single campus. Accordingly, Chapel Hill (amidst great controversy) gave up its engineering school in favor of State College, which surrendered its business school in return. Woman's College gave up its fledgling library science program to Chapel Hill but retained its near-monopoly of freshman and sophomore women. Elementary education was confined to the Greensboro campus at the undergraduate level while secondary education was permitted at both Chapel Hill and WC. Most graduate work was concentrated at Chapel Hill; WC theoretically retained graduate work in home economics and business education (or secretarial science). In fact, it offered no graduate work in any field for several years after 1932; by 1939, one master's degree had been awarded in each of the two fields. All of this was called the "allocation of functions," a phrase that would reverberate through the system for decades.[29]

* * *

Another allocation decision grew out of WC's one-year brush with coeducation in 1932–33. Foust appears to have favored coeducation as a theoretical matter for many years, though he did not parade the opinion.[30] More importantly, he regarded it as inevitable, given national trends and the creeping coeducation on all three state campuses during the '20s. Consolidation's promise to continue WC's near-monopoly of female students carried little weight with those watching the erosion of the 1925 agreement. Foust doubted in 1932 that public opinion in North Carolina was quite ready for coeducation at its major state colleges.[31] But the Depression offered an opportunity to test the waters. If the experiment worked it might well carve out a secure niche for his institution in the coming era.

Not only were WC enrollments declining in 1932, but many Greensboro boys similarly found it impossible to leave home that fall. When Greensboro High School Principal Charles Phillips conveyed their concerns and queries about attending WC on an emergency basis, Foust jumped at the opportunity.[32] Eighty men registered as day students, living at home, and spent the next academic year as Woman's College "coeds." Some were transfers from other colleges but a majority were freshmen.[33] Psychology professor Key L. Barkley, only a year on campus himself, served as *de facto* dean of men. The boys attended classes with the girls, including a physical education class in ballroom dancing. They took male parts in student plays.[34] Organizing a basketball team, they called themselves the Tom Cats and (unlike the girls) played intercollegiate teams from nearby colleges. The girls not only took the development in stride but turned out in large numbers to cheer on the team.[35]

The experiment worked well and Foust clearly anticipated continuing it indefinitely.[36] But that was not to be; the board of trustees found that it exceeded WC's allocated functions, and in June 1933 voted unanimously to terminate male enrollments.[37] On receiving a telegram to that effect, Foust wrote an angry letter to Graham protesting the double standard of allowing coeducation at Chapel Hill and State but not at Greensboro. As would happen a number of times, he withheld the letter and sent a more submissive reply next day. A later unsent letter accused board members of failing to recognize that their obligations extended equally to all three campuses.[38]

* * *

Meanwhile, Graham patiently worked out the details of consolidation with faculty committees and administrators at the three institutions. Effective in the fall of 1933, summer sessions and graduate work were each to be under a single head in Chapel Hill. Existing academic schools on each campus were reduced to departments. At WC, actually, music remained a school; education and home economics were restored to that status in 1948 and 1949, respectively.[39]

Foust, accustomed to authority, sharply criticized Graham for bypassing him in the reorganization process in favor of faculty committees to whose meetings he was not invited. The differences grew personal. A loyal Clora Foust wrote her stepson, "I think Frank Graham grows more contemptible with every act of his life."[40] Foust also resented the important roles played by historian Benjamin B. Kendrick, whom he had regarded as a confidant, and Harriet Elliott, whom he recognized as his chief faculty enemy.[41] Both had been appointed to an all-university council guiding the consolidation process.

Elliott was only the most visible of Foust's opponents. Other faculty members made it known to Graham and the trustees that they favored Foust's early retirement.[42] Similar forces were at work at State College, and a trustee committee decided in the spring of 1934 to ask for the resignations of both Foust and Brooks. Very little notice was provided, and it was left to Graham to convey the message. When he gently suggested retirement to Foust, not mentioning the faculty letters or trustee recommendation, Foust bristled. He had no choice but to comply although he had hoped to carry on another year until he was 70, then the normal retirement age. Graham had a similar session with Brooks in Raleigh.[43] Foust was deeply hurt by these developments; he and his wife remained bitter for years about what they regarded as Graham's shabby behavior.[44]

In return for a continuing half-salary Foust agreed to write a history of the college. Not particularly enthusiastic about the project, he nevertheless set to work in the fall of 1934 collecting materials, and eventually completed over 200 pages, carrying events into the 1920s. Ill health prevented its completion, but Foust's draft and the notes and correspondence he collected remain valuable sources for later historians of the college.[45]

When Graham systematically polled faculty, staff, students, and alumnae concerning Foust's successor, Walter Clinton Jackson was the practically unanimous choice. (After prayer, head janitor Zeke Robinson pronounced him the choice of the Almighty as well.)[46] Long second in command to Foust, Jackson had left the college in 1932 to become dean of a new school of public administration at Chapel Hill. When he returned to Greensboro in 1934 it was as dean of administration, the new—many thought demeaning—title for the chief executive at each campus. Despite its general unpopularity the designation remained until replaced by "chancellor" in 1945.[47]

* * *

The merits of consolidation—for the state and for each campus—were argued for over thirty years, until further combination in the 1960s and 1970s raised the number of campuses to sixteen and rendered the earlier debates obsolete. The official position both at general administration and on each campus was favorable once the initial wrinkles were ironed out: consolidation removed the worst cases of duplication and rendered the system more efficient if not more economical. This was the position of David Lockmiller, whose history of consolidation appeared in 1942. It was also the view of Louis Round Wilson, whose history of the university under consolidation was published by general administration itself in 1964.[48]

Competition among the three campuses gained intensity as each grew in size and tried to maximize its own allocated functions. Although these battles were fought out primarily before the board of trustees, individual campuses continued to lobby the legislature at appropriations time.

As the process evolved, Woman's College faculty like those on the other campuses were ambivalent. On the one hand, university affiliation brought some increase in prestige, especially outside the state. On the other, the college's relative lack of political clout became painfully apparent. When Chapel Hill's renowned sociologist Howard Odum grumbled to Jackson in 1937 about his campus's relegation to second-class status after (if not because of) consolidation, Jackson ticked off a list of all the university officers from president to dean of library science, pointing out that every one was located in Chapel Hill and drawn from that campus.[49] During the remainder of the 1930s financial support for the three institutions rose in rough parity; the average appropriation per student was $173 at Chapel Hill (with its graduate programs), $143 at Woman's College, and $136 at State.[50] Jackson sometimes claimed that consolidation had brought higher enrollments and appropriations as well as a Phi Beta Kappa chapter to WC, but candor compelled the admission that these might well have come anyway.[51] The same was true of curricular expansion. In the competitive fray that followed, there were good years and bad, and the Woman's College would do about as well comparatively as it had before consolidation.

Part IV
Woman's College, 1934–1950

Chapter 10

Administration and the Campus

Consolidation brought reorganization to every campus. At first it was unclear how much authority the system president would exercise on each campus; Graham visited each of them frequently. As it turned out, he was no micromanager. While providing general direction and retaining ultimate control of the most important matters, he gradually gave the institutions more autonomy.[1] The deans of administration were normally his conduits to each campus. Contrary to Foust's perception in his own case, Graham did not operate behind Dean Jackson's back. (The weakest campus executive, ironically, was understood to be the dean of administration at Chapel Hill, whom proximity placed directly under the president's eye.) In 1944 the trustees created visiting committees that began coming to the three campuses on a regular basis, investigating conditions and listening to administrators, faculty, and students who had information or complaints to relay. These visits became in time an important safety valve.[2]

In keeping with national developments in the 1930s, Graham granted more power to the respective faculties than they had previously enjoyed. Some matters that once were settled quickly by executive order on each campus now had to wait for committee recommendations, followed sometimes by final settlement in Chapel Hill. In 1937 Jackson told an alumnae group, at least semi-seriously, that he had no authority whatever; he could not even employ a janitor.[3] By this he surely meant that important matters, including personnel and budget decisions, had to be approved in Chapel Hill. This was usually done *pro forma*.

Reorganization assumed major proportions at WC. The institution was formally identified now as an undergraduate liberal arts college; its vocational and graduate programs were regarded as subordinate. This had been true for at least fifteen years, but the new designation signalled an end to the university-style aspirations that had underlain the reorganization of 1922.

The details this time were worked out by a faculty committee appointed by Graham, who promulgated its recommendations in January 1935. The college of liberal arts and sciences disappeared along with its multi-disciplinary subdivisions. Dean William C. Smith had already resigned in 1934, while remaining head of the English department. Owing to a special appeal by Jackson, music remained a school and Wade Brown its dean but education and home economics reverted to departments for over a decade.[4] The college business manager became assistant controller, reporting to a system controller in Chapel Hill.[5] Claude Teague, a former superintendent of schools in Sanford, served as business manager/assistant controller at WC from 1931 until 1943, when he took the same position at Chapel Hill. His successor, John C. Lockhart, was another former schools superintendent, as well as president of the state education association and a leader in getting legislative approval of a twelfth year of high school around the state. Lockhart remained in this college post until his retirement in 1957.[6] Subordinate to him until his own retirement in 1953 was the veteran James M. Sink, superintendent of buildings and grounds since 1917.

Edward J. Forney carried on as treasurer until 1940—a forty-eight-year tenure—although health problems forced him to step down as head of the commercial department several years earlier.[7] George M. Joyce, his successor in both positions for many years, carried the title auditor rather than treasurer.

Laura Coit persisted valiantly as college secretary and woman-of-all-tasks until 1937 when her health broke down under the strain. Requiring extensive medical and even institutional care, she became frantic in the realization that she lacked any resources with which to pay for it. She had spent her life giving away whatever she could manage from her meager salary to those who seemed less fortunate. Now, unable to work and too young at 62 to receive retirement benefits, she was stranded. Jackson, Foust, and others meditated raising a private subscription for her support, but were able ultimately to negotiate a continuance of her salary. She was officially retired in 1939 and died in 1944.[8]

The office of secretary was abolished and its functions transferred to the registrar's office. One of these functions had been admissions, which was assigned to Mildred Newton, another longtime employee. With the death of Registrar Mary Taylor Moore in 1948, admissions became a separate office, still under Newton.[9]

A new dean of women appeared in 1934, in the person of Geneva Drinkwater of Carleton College. When she left after a single year Jackson induced an apparently reluctant Harriet Elliott to take the position.[10] Once characterized by Foust as a "rank politician," Elliott had won the confidence of President Graham and likely played a part in Jackson's return as dean of administration. The two worked well together—as they always had—Elliott becoming Jackson's virtual *alter ego* in the administration of the college. In fact, she made her presence felt more deeply than anyone in the history of the institution up to that time who was not its chief executive. Drinkwater, then Elliott acquired an official campus residence—one of the Aladdin houses erected on McIver Street to accommodate faculty members after World War I.[11]

* * *

Not only did the faculty on each campus receive a greater voice in decision-making, the UNC system was possibly near the vanguard in this respect.[12] The major responsibility lay with Graham but locally Jackson too was by nature less authoritarian than Foust.

The faculty council was broadened to include assistant professors; instructors could attend but lacked a vote. The spearhead of the new democracy, as Jackson termed it, was the faculty advisory committee, replacing Foust's administrator-dominated cabinet. As created by the faculty council in 1934, this committee included (besides Jackson) the dean of women and the assistant controller *ex officio*, four elected faculty members and two appointed by Jackson. As most committee votes turned out in practice to be unanimous the distinction between appointed and elected members faded and in 1945, at Jackson's request, all six faculty positions became elective. In 1949 he went a step further and removed the three *ex officio* members (including himself) leaving nine elective members who chose their own chairman; until then, Jackson had presided except when Graham was in town. By the late '40s, membership was esteemed so highly that rival slates of candidates ran against each other in faculty elections.

From the beginning, Jackson consulted the advisory committee on every issue of importance, from the budget through personnel decisions (including hiring, promotion, and salaries) to the creation of new programs and departments. It interviewed candidates for faculty appointment and nominated honorary degree recipients. After ten years Jackson reported that neither he nor Graham had ever overruled the committee.[13] Jackson's deference was so great that he sometimes refused to indicate his own opinion on an issue before hearing from the committee. Jackson was not without opinions of his own, and made them known as he felt appropriate, but he bent over backward not to dominate the committee.[14]

For some years Jackson appointed the other faculty committees, following earlier practice under McIver and Foust. The most important of these, the curriculum committee, in 1935 was given veto power over all new courses proposed by the respective departments. Ten years later it got even broader responsibility for curricular policy and was reorganized to consist of a representative chosen by each of the twenty-odd departments; the new committee then elected its own steering committee which in turn chose the overall chairman. Jackson readily accepted these changes, if indeed he did not initiate them.[15]

Yet the new democracy was not absolute. The very unanimity of the advisory committee over more than a decade makes its freedom a little suspect. And at bottom all committees could only advise: their opinions and recommendations went to the faculty, to Jackson, to Graham, or to some combination thereof. Under law, power in the UNC system from the beginning descended from the trustees and the president downward to the deans of administration or chancellors, and from them to subordinate officials and faculties. In 1946, anticipating in spirit the federal Taft-Hartley Act of the next year, the trustees refused to recognize any collective bargaining unit (or union) among university employees. In 1959 the legislature went further, forbidding all state employees to join labor unions; that has remained the law since.[16]

From the beginning Jackson exercised his powers impartially and with good humor. He was very popular with both faculty and students. The latter flocked continuously to the course in American biography that he taught (with dramatic embellishment) even during his two-year absence in Chapel Hill, his first several years as dean of administration, and again after stepping down as chancellor in 1950. Ever courtly and avuncular, he loved to stop and chat with students and faculty members on campus or in his office. He had a standing offer to entering freshmen to come and see him, if only to say "Hello." They did so in large numbers. His informal management style sometimes led to laxity about details, as leaving the terms of faculty appointments to oral agreement rather than putting them on paper. A few persons thought him too much under the thumb of Harriet Elliott, but their relationship was more nearly a partnership with Jackson clearly the senior partner.[17]

Jackson retained his lifelong concern to improve southern race relations. Aside from his continuing organizational ties to that movement, he served from 1938 to 1953 as chairman of the board of trustees of Bennett College, the African-American woman's college across town. In granting him an honorary doctorate in 1949, Bennett called him a "pioneer in the field of better race relations."[18]

Conscious that he would turn 70 in 1949, Jackson tried to retire in 1948 but was persuaded by Graham to remain another year. He then made formal announcement of his departure in 1949 and was feted by students who presented him with a fishing pole to use during his coming leisure hours. As it turned out, Graham himself left office in 1949 to accept a U.S. Senate appointment. Little was done to identify a new chancellor and Jackson was pressured into staying yet another year. He said, only half-facetiously, that he felt like a boy forced to stay after school because of someone else's (Graham's) misbehavior.[19]

Jackson's popularity was well-nigh universal. The trustee visiting committee of 1948 reported that "visiting Woman's College is like coming into a big happy family; there is no sign of dissension."[20] In truth, as Jackson himself had been saying for three years, he was tired. He was torn between leaving a new building program and other fresh initiatives to someone who could see them through to completion, or staying on to make as much headway as possible himself. For lack of a clear alternative under the circumstances, he took the latter course and before the year was out suffered some of the same effects of overwork and fatigue that had plagued McIver and Foust.[21] He gratefully turned over the office to a new chancellor in 1950.

* * *

Prior to becoming dean of women in the fall of 1935, Harriet Elliott had taken a six-month leave of absence to work for the women's division of the Democratic National Committee, heading an educational program on the aims of the New Deal. Always a political activist, she would take other assignments from time to time, in the process winning the friendship of administration leaders, and particularly of Eleanor Roosevelt who twice visited campus at her behest. Early in 1940 she joined Mrs. Roosevelt in conducting a Washington conference on women's unemployment. Becoming known as a consumer advocate, Elliott served for a year and a half in 1940–41 as the consumer adviser (and only woman) on the National Defense Advisory Commission. She resigned shortly before Pearl Harbor, reportedly in frustration over the lack of White House interest in consumer affairs. But in 1942 she was called on again as an adviser in the creation of the WAVES, the women's naval auxiliary. Soon after that she was drafted by Treasury Secretary Henry Morgenthau to form a women's division in the Treasury's War Bond program. In 1945 she was one of the United States delegation to the London conference that created the United Nations Educational, Scientific, and Cultural Organization (UNESCO).[22]

Some of these positions were part-time or of short duration; others required extensive leaves of absence. As a result, many wartime WC students saw little of Elliott. She reported having turned down many offers to leave permanently for jobs with higher pay and greater national prestige, explaining that her primary vocation remained education and service to the college where she had spent most of her life.[23] In February 1947, one day after returning from the funeral of former Governor O. Max Gardner, Elliott suffered a cerebral hemorrhage from which she never revovered. She died in August, at age 63.

Her successor as dean of women was Katherine Taylor, NCCW Class of 1928. Outstanding as a student, Taylor had gone on to earn a master's degree at Radcliffe, then returned to the college in 1929 to teach French. She remained for the rest of her career, except for two wartime years with the WAVES. Much of the time she served also as a student counselor, and was the senior counselor in point of service when Elliott died. Where Elliott was once described as short and round in appearance, Taylor was tall and strikingly attractive. In other respects she was a disciple of Elliott's, maintaining the counseling system that she had helped Elliott to put in place in the '30s. And like Elliott, she was popular with the students, both in the classroom and as dean.

* * *

For nearly a decade English professor Arthur Dunn had sent out a regular newsletter to the state press reporting campus events, but everyone agreed that public relations required more time than he was able to spend.[24] In 1935 Jackson created a public relations department, recruiting former Greensboro High School principal Charles W. Phillips to head it. Charlie Phillips belonged to a family of educators prominent in the state. A born diplomat, fully imbued with the gospel of service, he became a campus institution over the next twenty-seven years before retiring to serve six terms in the legislature. His original appointment included the placement bureau as well as public relations.[25] Following that precedent his assignments multiplied, eventually eclipsing his continuing title of public relations director. They included extension, alumnae relations, student recruiting, financial aid, fund raising, summer school, campus television, organizer of the Greensboro Evening College, and director of WC's Parkway Playhouse in the mountains.[26]

Phillips was not a journalist, however, and the original need for a news bureau continued. It came in 1937, under his general direction but headed soon by Virginia Terrell Lathrop, a professional journalist since her 1923 graduation from NCCW. By 1940 Lathrop had ten part-time student helpers, financed by the New Deal's National Youth Administration. A perceptive and articulate woman, she too had a long connection with the college, as news director, active alumna, and eventually university trustee.[27] Lathrop gave way in 1941 to her classmate and former *Carolinian* editor Nell Craig, who remained for four years. In 1947 the post went to Albert A. Wilkinson, a former editor of the Duke University alumni magazine and associate editor of the Durham *Herald*. The genial Wilkinson (Mr. Wilkie) remained at the college for twenty years, ruefully spending much of his time behind a camera because the budget long forbade hiring a photographer. By the mid-1950s the news bureau was compiling files on individual students, faculty members, campus buildings, and campus history, in addition to covering newsworthy campus stories and sending them to newspapers and radio and television stations around the state. Wilkinson did all this with a handful of part-time student helpers (one of them future novelist Doris Waugh Betts); he worked a six or seven-day week.[28]

* * *

By 1944 there was a feeling around campus that the college was nearing a crossroads. After a severe dip during the Depression, enrollment pressures were again exceeding the college's capacity. It continued nonetheless to recruit junior class transfer students from other institutions, regarding them as a healthy counterbalance to upperclassmen who flunked out or transferred away. Moreover, these applicants were eagerly courted by Chapel Hill and State as well, and many would surely go there if WC had no space for them. Most important of all: if WC were forced to reject more and more freshman applicants for lack of space, there would surely be pressure for full coeducation at the other two campuses, making the Woman's College redundant. Hence the faculty in April 1944 voted all but unanimously to endorse expansion.[29]

That would have to wait until after the war, of course, but it was not immediately forthcoming even then. The 1945 legislature ignored Woman's College expansion as it rushed to help Chapel Hill and State cope with a deluge of returning veterans armed with the GI Bill. Further, in a case of very unlucky timing, WC's enrollment actually dropped slightly at this time as high schools around the state added a twelfth grade. While the other two campuses experienced a postwar building boom, therefore, WC did not. What seemed a crossroads in 1944 looked like a crisis in 1946.[30]

Harriet Elliott had cherished high hopes for consolidation. But she now shared a palpable undercurrent of fear at the college. Chapel Hill and State not only continued to expand and to recruit women but they were invading curricular areas belonging to WC in the allocation of functions. Jackson reported his own view that Chapel Hill faculty scorned WC as academically inferior and therefore fair game.[31] Fearing that the college could never win a political battle with its rivals, he and Elliott continued perforce to pray that the state would heed President Graham's reiterated goal of preserving the institution in its traditional mission. Jackson fed information and arguments to the Greensboro press, which ran supportive editorials.[32]

Others were more venturesome. Perceiving the national and even regional trend away from single-sex colleges, they embraced coeducation as the college's surest salvation. Among these was Julius Foust. He continued to favor coeducation until his death in 1946, while expressing the view privately to avoid embarrassing his successors in authority. Foust returned by 1940 to the entering wedge position he had adopted in 1932: enroll as day students any qualified Greensboro boys who were still asking the college for admission. In making this suggestion he knowingly imitated the ongoing and ultimately successful efforts of Chapel Hill to admit local women.[33]

Support for coeducation grew further amid the postwar enrollment pressures. A woman's college, some argued, denied higher educational opportunities to half of the population—that half which had just fought the nation's wars. They called for maximizing the university's capacity by making it—or at least the Woman's College—coeducational. Many in Greensboro saw coeducation at WC as a boon to the city. In this camp, reportedly—in even greater secrecy than Foust, given her constituency—was alumnae secretary Clara Byrd.[34]

The alumnae as a whole were opposed. Laura Weill Cone, still a university trustee, spoke for many if not most alumnae in arguing that there would always be a need for single-sex colleges, even if most students chose coeducation. Were WC to lose its historic identity, she predicted, it would sink to a level of perpetual mediocrity in competition with Chapel Hill and State College.

President Graham and the leaders of all three campuses, including Jackson and Elliott, also opposed coeducation, effectively killing it formally.[35] But the issue remained on a back burner for the next fifteen years and creeping coeducation proceeded apace on every campus.

* * *

Not since McIver's time had the college seriously gone after private funds to supplement the state appropriation. In 1935 Graham asked the college (and perhaps the other campuses) to consider the matter, identifying areas particularly eligible for private funding.[36] Yet this was clearly not a high priority for either Graham or Jackson. Jackson told alumnae in 1938 that while the university at Chapel Hill might seek endowments similar to a private institution, the Woman's College ought to hold back; he and Graham both feared that successful fund raising might induce legislators to cut back the state appropriation. Fund raising was left almost entirely to the Alumnae Association, whose annual appeal brought only modest returns.[37]

After the war Jackson returned to the issue, wondering out loud whether to follow other colleges in establishing fund-raising offices. Despite a formal request from the Alumnae Association, he never did so, pleading first an absence of funds to support the effort and then (when funds were promised) an inability to find the right person to head it. Instead he followed the course of least resistance and handed fund raising over to Charlie Phillips, who was already overburdened. From 1946 to 1950, when Jackson left office, the college received only $68,000 from private sources.[38]

There were, however, three special fund-raising activities on campus, one of them originating with Jackson personally. He had long felt a need for a non-denominational chapel on campus. As this could not be built with state funds, he launched a special fund in 1942, using an initial $10,000 gift from industrialist J. Spencer Love.[39] Other contributions, all of them small and insufficient to launch the project, filtered in until 1961. By that time the fund was encountering legal problems. A succession of North Carolina attorneys general ruled that such a chapel, even funded privately, violated constitutional provisions separating church and state. In 1992, after fifty years of compounding interest, the fund amounted to some $800,000—still unspent.[40]

Meanwhile, in the same year of 1942 the new Weatherspoon Art Gallery on campus organized a Gallery Association designed in part to help support the enterprise financially. Four years later the Home Economics Foundation—a formal endowment—was established for a comparable purpose. The first of its kind on campus, it started small and was generating only $6,000 annual income by the early 1960s.[41]

For its lifeblood the college relied as always on legislative appropriations. Despite consolidation, everyone on campus plus alumnae made the traditional biennial effort to lobby legislators in behalf of the college. The process bore a strong resemblance to that in the 1920s and earlier.[42] In this contest WC was not strikingly successful. As Charlie Phillips was quoted as saying, "When it comes to getting money in Raleigh, we women have a hard time."[43] Appropriations fell off drastically during the Depression; the war years saw a restoration to the level of 1929 and a little beyond.[44]

* * *

Low revenues were reflected in minimal building and campus expansion. What there was, was financed in large measure by the federal government through a variety of New Deal relief programs. The prime example at WC was the Alumnae House. This building was the product of a long, often agonizing process which began as early as 1916, when alumnae asked for a place to stay (other than student dormitories) during their campus visits. In 1919 Ethel Bollinger, the first full-time alumnae secretary, made plans for such a building, that could also serve as the association's headquarters and a home for unmarried faculty.[45] A site was chosen on the newly-acquired Teague field, across Spring Garden Street. Fund raising proved to be slow in an alumnae body consisting mostly of underpaid schoolteachers, and it was decided to build the structure in stages. The first stage, a tea house, opened in 1924 with hopes that it would generate revenue toward completion of the whole.[46] The tea house barely cleared expenses, however, and Bollinger's successor Clara Byrd persuaded Foust and the alumnae board to build instead on the site of the aging Guilford or Midway dormitory on College Avenue, when funds were available. And in the absence of an adequate student union and a faculty club the new structure should serve those two purposes as well. In 1926 the short-lived tea house was therefore incorporated into the new Curry education building.[47]

By the early 1930s about $53,000 had been collected for the Alumnae House. Most of it was invested in Greensboro city bonds which presently lost much of their value as the city was forced into default. Yet it was the Depression, paradoxically, that opened the way to federal government money that finally brought the building to completion. Julius Foust and Clara Byrd handled most of the details, Foust continuing at alumnae request after his retirement in 1934. It was Byrd who chose a model: Homewood on the Johns Hopkins University campus, erected by Charles Carroll of Carrollton about 1800 and supposedly one of the best surviving examples in America of eighteenth-century Georgian architecture. Old Guilford was razed and, with money from the Public Works Administration, the new Homewood rose in its place, reaching completion early in

1937. (Homewood served as prototype for only the exterior; the alumnae designed their own interior.) Virtually every aspect of the building's construction, from money raising to ultimate use, was a matter of controversy among the alumnae. But the building quickly became what Byrd intended, an activity center for students and faculty as well as alumnae. Over the years it has hosted alumnae meetings, faculty meetings, fund raising phonothons, and wedding receptions. At different times it has housed a variety of administrative offices including the chancellor's, and always the Alumnae Association and a limited number of overnight visitors. The Alumnae House represented Foust's last active contribution to the college and, appropriately, his funeral was held there in 1946.[48]

Federal money helped finance a number of other campus buildings and projects in the '30s: a log field house near the athletic fields at Walker Avenue and Aycock Street (1934); Weil and Winfield residence halls at the north end of the quadrangle (1939); an additional dining hall wing (1939); a new science building (1940, ultimately named for Mary Petty); and a variety of smaller projects ranging from building renovations to creating a campus lake.[49] The new, relatively fireproof, science building was especially important. Chemistry in particular had been endangering the old McIver Building and its many inhabitants for over thirty years. Except for the log house, these buildings conformed more or less to the red-brick Georgian architecture that had dominated the campus since the early 1920s. With World War II in the offing, further building would have to wait for nearly a decade.

When new construction did come, the campus had just experienced a remarkable physical change in preparation: the closing of Walker Avenue. As Greensboro expanded to the west, Walker had become a major thoroughfare into town. Traffic mounted yearly. At the same time a growing college contributed more and more students who lived in residence halls north of the street while attending classroom buildings south of it. None was ever killed or seriously injured, but the prospect was a matter of concern to students and college authorities as early as 1938.[50] More bridges or underpasses might have solved this problem, but the street also offered too-easy access for unwanted intruders. Most important to the college, it wanted the right of way for its own expansion; it was an ideal location for a much-desired new library and an addition to the home economics building. In 1944 Jackson incorporated this issue as part of his postwar planning.[51]

The campaign reached its climax in 1946 and 1947, when the college believed itself in crisis. Its future existence, claimed Jackson in public meetings and other forums, required the closure of this divisive thoroughfare. Until that happened, he said, the university trustees were holding up further campus construction. Many Greensboro residents, including the city council, were reluctant, arguing that the city needed more, not fewer through streets to the west; closing Walker would only add congestion to Market, Spring Garden, and other remaining streets. In the end the council agreed to the proposal in 1947, unwilling to wound or offend the college it had learned to love since assisting at its birth over a half century earlier. But there were hard feelings, particularly among residents who had to drive longer distances between home and downtown. It was the first significant town-and-gown disagreement in the college's history. The street closure occurred in September 1948 and work soon began on the new library and home economics buildings, both straddling the former thoroughfare. The College Avenue bridge, in its different forms a campus landmark since early in college history, was demolished in October 1950.[52]

* * *

Ironically, against the background of impending doom right after the war, the college now entered a period that some would look back on nostalgically as its Golden Age. In company with campuses nationwide, it saw a new spurt of growth in the late 1940s. After intensive lobbying by Jackson, the alumnae, and students, the 1947 legislature voted a permanent improvements appropriation of $3,177,000 and a maintenance budget of $983,000—both far in excess of previous years. The amounts in 1949 were even larger, representing in Graham's words the largest per capita appropriation to any college or university in the South.[53] Enrollments also began to rise again, reaching 2,500 in 1950. Higher appropriations and enrollments brought higher campus morale. Once again pride was expressed in being one of the largest—and best—women's colleges in the land.

Jackson in 1945 had submitted an ambitious building program; the first parts of it were funded in 1947. His plans included the new library and home economics buildings, two additional residence halls, a student union, a new classroom building, a second gymnasium, a new infirmary, and a new laundry. The last named was the first to be constructed, near the railroad and alongside the power plant. (The old laundry building, once itself the power plant, had risen from the ashes of the 1904 fire and was now regarded as an eyesore and firetrap. Although many preferred to demolish it, it soon became—of all things—the campus TV station.)[54]

Only after this program was well started did the trustees' visiting committee in 1948 call for the creation of a long-range landscape and architectural plan for the campus.[55] (Although campus plans went back to McIver and Thomas Brown, this generation of college officials like others before and after seem to have believed they were first on the ground.) Landscape architect Edward W. Waugh of State College in Raleigh produced a plan in 1949. Among other things it called for the demolition of the Students' Building, which Jackson described as poorly built in the first place and now deteriorating badly. A new student union was expected to replace it.[56]

Foremost in Jackson's building program was the new library—later named for him. The existing Carnegie Library had been tripled in size as part of Foust's massive building campaign of the early 1920s. Then, in 1932, much of the building was destroyed by fire. (Since the book stacks were fireproof, most of the collection survived, often with considerable water damage.) The Students' Building, across the street, served as a temporary library during the year it took to restore and once again enlarge the building. It reopened in September 1933. Financial straits limited the expansion and before long the building was again overcrowded. By 1939 Librarian Guy R. Lyle was calling for a new building.[57] The war nullified all such projects, and by the late 1940s growing student enrollments and library acquisitions rendered the situation desperate. The building that actually emerged in 1950 resulted from years of planning. Once completed it became a showplace for college librarians and their architects. Charles M. Adams, by then WC librarian, became an authority on college library construction and wrote for professional journals on the subject.[58]

Construction had hardly begun when the building stimulated the first public debate over campus architecture in the college's history—published in the *Alumnae News*. Two recent alumnae, Bonnie Angelo and Marie Belk, wrote to the trustee building committee remonstrating against what they saw as the outmoded Georgian architecture provided by the Winston-Salem firm Northup and O'Brien. With a new building program in the offing, they said, the college should do better than copy stale models from the past; a Georgian exterior inherently limits the functioning of a modern building. (Architect Walter Gropius, who visited campus while the building was still in the planning stage, agreed with this position.) Committee chairman Laura Cone replied that one must conform to what is already in place. Some campus buildings, she said, were of little value, but others were worthy of emulation. Supreme in that respect was the Alumnae House. The committee decided that succeeding buildings should conform to that example. Modern architecture, Cone added authoritatively, was still experimental; further, it would create disharmony in the middle of campus. The result was a building as nearly as possible modern on the inside and traditional on the outside.[59] There was little sentiment for architectural diversity as an end in itself. Mendenhall and Ragsdale dormitories, added in 1950, also conformed to the Georgian norm.

No doubt Harriet Elliott echoed the common view when she termed the Students' Building not only a firetrap, but ugly to boot. Ugly or not, the old building (scraped together through years of student and alumnae frugality) was now decrepit, combustible, and in need of replacement.[60] By 1949, when it was demolished, only the first floor remained in use.[61] The new student union, intended to replace it, had to wait several more years. As a kind of downpayment the college built the Soda Shop next door to the doomed building in 1948.

The McIvers had regularly rented space in their ten-room house at the corner of College Avenue and Spring Garden Street to faculty and students not otherwise provided for. When Lula Martin McIver died in December 1944, the house became an auxiliary dormitory, primarily for student war veterans who were not subject (or amenable) to the usual undergraduate discipline.[62]

* * *

Peabody Park deteriorated after the disappearance in the '20s of the mandatory student walking period which had centered there, and of Park Night in 1935. Students, faculty, and neighbors used the wooded area less and less, and over the years it became less parklike. Despite efforts by the Botany Club and even New Deal relief agencies to plant new vegetation, create nature trails, and beautify the grounds, they became trashy. Even the college maintenance crew inadvertently mowed down new plantings around the perimeter.[63]

As early as 1922 the college considered replacing the crowded campus farm with a nine-hole golf course.[64] The farm relocated next year and the golf course materialized gradually over the next decade, reaching completion with the help of federal money in 1934. A log caddy or field house replaced the old barn. But maintenance of the course proved expensive and it was underused by students and faculty alike.[65]

In 1941 the college pre-empted much of its acreage with a small lake and grassy amphitheater—also paid for with New Deal relief funds.[66] The dam was just off Market Street where the Gray Drive campus entrance was later built. For over a decade the three-acre lake was used for instructional and recreational boating. The amphitheater was the site of May Day festivities.[67]

The college farm, now located west of the city, continued to provide milk for the students during the school year, its produce being sold to local dairies in the summer. With the advent of World War II, labor became scarce and the college resorted to employing forty to fifty German prisoners of war, who were bused daily from Winston-Salem. When they returned home in 1945 the labor shortage recurred.[68]

As early as 1931 Foust had been advised to sell the farm as a money loser. He resisted, distrusting the quality and quantity of milk obtainable from local dairies.[69] Jackson adhered to the same policy. But in 1945 the farm was again operating at a loss and satisfactory milk supplies were clearly available commercially at less cost. The 250-acre farm was sold at auction late that year, therefore, bringing $76,000. The proceeds were used to fund a variety of campus projects including the Soda Shop.[70]

Chapter 11

The Faculty

The years embracing the college's fiftieth anniversary brought retirement and death to many of its longtime faculty members. In addition to Julius Foust, Harriet Elliott, Laura Coit, and registrar Mary Taylor Moore, already mentioned, Latin professor Viola Boddie passed away in 1940, former English department head and liberal arts dean William C. Smith in 1943. Physical education's Mary Channing Coleman died suddenly in 1947, just as she was planning retirement. Three of the earliest faculty—Minnie Jamison, Anna Gove, and E.J. Forney (as well as his wife)—died within a week of each other in January 1948. Chemist Mary Petty, who had come in 1893, survived until 1958, the last of her generation.

As student enrollments grew, so did the faculty. From 160 in 1929, it climbed to 241 in 1951. Much of the increase in student hours was absorbed by part-time faculty, who rose in number from two to twenty-five in that period. At the same time, administrators grew from nine to fifteen. The ratio of students to faculty remained low—11.5 in the fall of 1947.[1]

There was still a strong preponderance of women in the faculty—70 percent in both 1934 and 1949. Although the percentage of women with doctorates doubled to 16 percent in these years, women were still clustered disproportionately in the lower ranks. By comparison, over a third of the male faculty in both years had doctorates and most men were in the top two ranks. That disparity diminished somewhat. Under Jackson the number of women full professors almost doubled to 25 while males in that rank rose only from 25 to 27.[2] Harriet Elliott approved and surely contributed to that trend. "Since women have no opportunity for academic positions in men's colleges and almost no chance for promotion in universities," she wrote Jackson in 1945, "I think it is important for women's colleges to give careful consideration to women."[3] Students likely knew little about academic ranks, but they were clearly impressed by the female role models they saw on the faculty.[4]

As in earlier years at this women's college, female faculty encountered a variety of gender barriers. Unlike the men, nearly all were unmarried. The enduring anti-nepotism rule almost guaranteed that qualified faculty wives were limited to part-time or temporary service—or work as librarians, who were not regarded for this purpose as part of the faculty.[5] (There were a few exceptions. Psychologist Elizabeth Duffy kept her job after marrying English professor John

Bridgers.) Jackson in 1941 passed over an apparently qualified woman candidate for principal of Curry School because incoming education head Franklin McNutt believed that a man could better control the high school boys.[6] Department heads sometimes continued to prefer male candidates without feeling it necessary to explain why.[7]

Women still received less pay for similar responsibilities, although this inequity receded as the most talented or persevering were promoted to higher ranks and salaries.[8] Divorce was still a problem for job aspirants, though no longer insurmountable: a counselor candidate was turned down for that reason in 1943 but (after due consideration) at least two separated or divorced women were hired as teachers in the 1930s and '40s. And there was a dress code for women faculty: a junior member was admonished by the dean of women's office in 1947 for wearing slacks on campus.[9]

Racial and religious discrimination also persisted. Blacks were not yet considered for faculty employment. Jews were considered and even hired although a committee head felt that the "Jewish appearance" of one candidate's family merited special mention. When a Jewish candidate from southern California was hired in 1949, Jackson required special background information, citing trustee concern about communism.[10] Although communism was not a raging issue in North Carolina during the McCarthy era, the university trustees began requiring faculty members to take a loyalty oath in the late 1940s. Jackson was rather relaxed in his enforcement of it.[11]

* * *

The college had never had a salary scale before Jackson took over; Foust had in fact opposed the idea as robbing the most deserving in order to reward anyone who happened to fit the predetermined scale. Nor was there a regular review of faculty members to determine eligibility for promotion and salary increases. They tended to go to those most persistent in asking for them. Jackson tried to rectify the inevitable inequities but absent a regular review they persisted. The college did adopt a salary scale, however, in the wake of the general 32 per cent salary cut in 1933. The scale almost duplicated that in effect at Chapel Hill: professors were to receive a minimum of $2550, associate professors $2040, assistant professors $1530, and instructors $1330. It was too expensive to implement fully for several years, but the legislature helped considerably with a 20 per cent increase in 1935; another 10 per cent came in 1937.[12]

For years thereafter, the college attempted with little success to match the salaries paid at Chapel Hill. The chief reason for the shortfall, said Jackson, was the low pay of women, which he was attempting to rectify. Virtually every department head complained that the college was underpaying its best personnel and losing them to other institutions with higher salaries, chiefly in the North. Similarly, low salaries made it very difficult to fill existing vacancies. These protests reached a climax in 1944 when the trustees' visiting committee uncharacteristically exploded in indignation against those higher up in authority—the full board, the legislature, or both—accusing them of shortchanging the Woman's College because it *was* a woman's college.[13] Even some department heads complained of making less money than they had many years earlier.[14] The visiting committee's anger, coupled with even more insistent appeals by Jackson, brought more salary money in 1945 though not the desired parity with Chapel Hill.[15] Even two 20 per cent increases in 1947 and 1949, pretty much across the board, left too little to finance many merited promotions .[16]

As early as 1920 President Foust voiced interest in the Carnegie Foundation's retirement pension program for college teachers, recently incorporated as the Teachers' Insurance and Annuities Association (TIAA).[17] Despite his continuing interest, the college had no retirement system in operation until several years after he left office in 1934. However, the university trustees mandated a partial plan for all three branches that year which permitted faculty members to go on part-time service and pay at age 65. It required them to do so at 70, subject to annual reappointment at the pleasure of the institution. For administrators, including department heads, these ages were 63 and 68, respectively.[18] This came just in time for the oldest members of the faculty, some of whom could not or had not saved enough money to support themselves in retirement. In addition to Foust himself, Viola Boddie, Mary Petty, E.J. Forney, and Elizabeth McIver Weatherspoon went on part-time basis the first year. They were soon joined by Anna Gove and Minnie Jamison.[19] Jamison was counselor of the Students' Building (seemingly a sinecure) from her semi-retirement in 1936 until her death in 1948. Dr. Gove continued to work part-time in the infirmary. Forney gave up his teaching activities but remained part-time treasurer of the college. Petty acted as college social director, arranging parties and receptions. Foust busied himself with his college history.

A genuine retirement plan for all state employees came only in 1941. Specific retirement ages and other details would vary over the years, but they tended to favor 65 as the minimum and 70 as the maximum age, subject to special conditions. The plan, authored in large part by WC education head John H. Cook, was designed primarily for public school teachers and other state employees. It provided for matching contributions by the state and the individual. Although it represented a great improvement over existing practice, its benefits at first did not match those at many (largely private) colleges and universities using TIAA. Further, like Social Security, it largely bypassed persons who had not had an opportunity to contribute to the plan over a long period. In 1946 the UNC trustees invited private donations to relieve the worst sufferers. At WC, $31,500 was donated anonymously—by Laura Cone in large part. Chancellor Jackson became the principal beneficiary of this money on his own retirement in 1950.[20]

There was perennial discussion of other faculty amenities, or their absence. For some time until 1941, most members enjoyed private offices; that benefit gradually eroded as the faculty grew in size.[21] Department heads (who did have private offices) noticed that virtually all of the campus secretaries were assigned to the top administrators; they themselves were required to pen or peck out their own correspondence except as student labor might offer relief for a few hours a week.[22]

Although many faculty continued to live within easy walking distance of campus, the advent of the automobile enabled others to move farther away, primarily to newer neighborhoods farther north and west along Market Street and what would become Friendly Avenue.[23] Unmarried persons, nearly all women, faced the greatest problem, as housing was increasingly scarce adjacent to campus. In 1938 the college considered building a faculty apartment building on or adjacent to campus, but it was not done. One-third of the faculty, again nearly all women, shared apartments or houses for varying periods of time.[24]

During Foust's later years faculty members were in effect hired by department heads, though the president made the official appointments. This continued under Jackson, with the major addition of an intermediate faculty role in screening candidates once they had been identified by the department heads. Senior appointments were reviewed by small special committees and then by the new advisory committee, which also passed on promotion and salary recommendations.[25]

Once hired, faculty members were subject to an evolving tenure system. Until 1936 all new appointments regardless of rank were for one year, with no written provision for reappointment. Administrative procedures were so informal that Jackson learned the university's regulations on the subject only through specific inquiry of President Graham two years after taking office. On learning, he proceeded to modify them for WC: instructors continued to serve on one-year appointments; assistant and associate professors, after initial one-year terms, could be reappointed for three years and five years, respectively; and full professors received permanent appointments.[26] Even with this clarification, the terms of appointment in individual cases were not always written down, leading to misunderstandings. And Jackson was even known to grant tenure to individuals well before their stipulated probationary periods had ended.[27]

Faculty members organized a campus chapter of the American Association of University Professors in 1938. They seem not to have been responding to any particular problem or dispute. Jackson explained next year that, while the university trustees had not formally adopted national AAUP tenure guidelines, all three campuses were expected in general to follow them.[28] Despite the AAUP's adoption in 1940 of a seven-year maximum probation period for untenured faculty, none was established at WC. Nor was there any clear set of guidelines governing promotions. Codifying such matters was not high on his priority list, or that of President Graham.[29]

Although the doctorate was an important qualification for senior rank in the faculty, it was not yet essential and the proportion of Ph.D.s grew slowly. The sources of the doctorates were more widely scattered than in earlier years: of the twenty-three listed in 1936, four each came from Columbia (the old favorite), Johns Hopkins, and the University of North Carolina. But the master's degrees still came predominantly from Columbia.[30]

The primary criteria for promotion, tenure, and salary increases were teaching and service, on and off campus. Teaching loads were normally twelve hours (four courses—often different courses) per semester; but many persons, particularly during the war and in small departments like classics or German, taught more.[31]

From the beginning, faculty members had rendered service beyond the campus. They taught extension courses and gave talks to community groups. Mereb Mossman, new to the sociology department in 1937, had lived and taught in China; Jackson asked her to talk about China, which she did frequently to civic organizations in the wake of the Japanese invasion of that country. Many faculty members performed such services in addition to their committee work and extracurricular activities on campus advising student groups, chaperoning dances, and attending dormitory open houses. Male faculty still met incoming freshmen at the railway station and served as volunteer ushers in the auditorium. During World War II, when servicemen were stationed in town, they took turns patrolling the campus at night. Faculty and students alike were more or less expected to attend the lecture and concert series.[32]

From the earliest days, many faculty were active in their respective professional organizations. A few gained national attention; Mary Channing Coleman, for instance, served in the 1930s as president of the American Physical Education Association. B.B. Kendrick was president in 1941 of the Southern Historical Association, a level of distinction matched by a number of his colleagues in different fields. Although professional activity was noted and appreciated in the 1930s and '40s, faculty members were lucky to get any reimbursement for their expenses in simply attending professional meetings; officers did better.

Research and publication continued to be rewarded in the hope that the college might attract a more scholarly faculty, gaining a name for itself in the process. Jackson told the faculty in 1936 that "our fundamental task is to teach," and he urged them to take the task seriously, making time for students well beyond the classroom. (A generation earlier that admonition would not have been regarded as necessary, but faculty members were now developing broader interests, professional and personal.) At the same time, Jackson noted the frequently close correlation between research and effective teaching, and he pledged to do all in his power to further faculty scholarship.[33] In fact, he could do little, as there were no funds budgeted to support faculty research. In 1944 he listed thirteen members who had published what he termed important work in the past ten years. (He was generous: a number of these works were textbooks, some of them co-authored, and some of the persons mentioned had served only briefly at the college.)[34]

Department heads varied in their enthusiasm for faculty research. Biology head J.P. Givler was always turning out lights, and forbade one of his faculty to do laboratory research at night if it required using electricity.[35] One of those who *was* interested in research was physics head Calvin Warfield. Jackson advised him in 1945 that the college could never offer him the research opportunities he desired; Jackson's efforts to procure Warfield a part-time teaching and research position at Chapel Hill were unavailing.[36]

Psychologist Elizabeth Duffy was responsible for several college firsts in the matter of research support. A 1925 NCCW graduate, she returned to the college in 1937 with a Ph.D. from Johns Hopkins and eight years' teaching experience at Sarah Lawrence. Her faculty appointment was more than routine. As a bright young woman with high prospects, she was promised some released teaching time to do research. In 1942 she received a half-time release and in 1947 a full year.[37] The college for many years had granted leaves for further study, always without pay, but these were apparently its first research leaves.

Actual sabbatical leaves were recommended by a tri-campus faculty committee in 1946, but none were instituted. The state advisory budget commission repeatedly turned down modest requests for appropriations in aid of research at both Chapel Hill and WC.[38] The college's solution, beginning in 1947, was to hire limited numbers of substitute teachers at lower pay than the regulars, allowing the latter to pocket the difference as a research subsidy. This was presumably the arrangement Duffy made that year.[39]

Jackson was well aware that the college did not attract the nation's best candidates. Its status as a woman's college, its location in the South, and its relatively low salaries made it unattractive to those persons, especially males, who were in greatest demand. In order to boost its prestige Jackson secured permission in 1937 to recruit three prominent scholars—at up to $4,500 apiece—in English, elementary education, and science. The science position was the first filled, going to psychology. But Jackson subverted his original intent by bestowing it on two relatively junior people, one of them Elizabeth Duffy. He hoped this longer-term investment might confer the same result.[40] More in keeping with Jackson's plan, poet Allen Tate and his wife, novelist Caroline Gordon, were hired in 1938 to fill positions in English. Unfortunately, Tate and Gordon departed for Princeton after only a year and a half—to Jackson's mortification.[41] The third position, in education, apparently went unfilled.

As the trustees' visiting committee noted, there was still much of the old faculty-as-family atmosphere. For many years the first faculty meeting in the fall had been an informal dinner meeting at which Foust or Jackson or (in later years) department heads introduced the new members. Subsequent meetings during the year were heavily attended and, under Jackson, discussion was free. Faculty committees wielded considerable power and members considered it an honor to be appointed or elected to them.[42] Faculty members continued to socialize frequently with students and to chaperone their dances.

Faculty and staff members of both sexes served in the armed forces and performed a variety of civilian activities during the war. Twenty-eight were absent on government service in 1945.[43] One of the servicewomen was Katherine Taylor, a lieutenant in the WAVES, who returned at war's end. Civic activity was not limited to the war years. English professor Alonzo C. Hall served in the late 1940s as chairman of the Greensboro Housing Authority, a service later commemorated in the high-rise Alonzo Hall Towers housing project.

* * *

Faculty and students alike took pride in the institution. Some thought it academically superior to Chapel Hill and the other neighboring men's colleges.[44] It ranked behind—but they believed not far behind—the private women's colleges of the Northeast. Such claims are hard to validate. A rough comparison in 1931 of the numbers of courses offered in various fields and the numbers of instructors teaching them at NCCW, Chapel Hill, State College, Winthrop College (the South Carolina woman's college), and Smith College in Massachusetts—all supposedly similar in enrollment—gave a strong quantitative edge to Smith, both in numbers of courses and of instructors. NCCW came in third behind Chapel Hill.[45]

Students recognized the devotion of their teachers, who spent vast amounts of time in their offices grading essays, term papers, and exams and making themselves accessible. Essay examinations were the rule. There being no graduate program to speak of, there were no graduate assistants.[46] Lecture courses prevailed until the junior and senior years, when students met in smaller seminar classes in their major fields. But most classes were kept under forty students.

As early as 1921 the faculty endorsed a student request to create an honors society recognizing student scholarship. The board of directors apparently saw this as a violation of the long-standing rule against sororities.[47] Not until 1930 was that obstacle overcome and a local honor society formed. People looked to this group as a possible precursor to a Phi Beta Kappa chapter, and it closely followed Phi Beta Kappa's eligibility requirements. Four years later, after consolidation, the chapter-in-waiting was recognized as a branch of Chapel Hill's Phi Beta Kappa chapter. Finally, in 1956 the college acquired its own chapter, only the fifth in the state.[48]

In 1946 the college permitted students for the first time to graduate with honors: cum laude, magna cum laude, summa cum laude.[49] Next year it adopted an honors program for the best students. (It was hardly in the vanguard: honors programs had originated in the early 1920s and by 1944 nearly three-quarters of the institutions approved by the American Association of Universities had adopted them.) The program was highly selective; only six students were enrolled during the first year.[50]

* * *

Prior to consolidation the Normal/NCCW conferred no honorary degrees. This abstention was fairly typical of women's colleges, which prior to the 1950s granted fewer than 25 percent of the national total. Women correspondingly received only a small proportion of those conferred.[51] When Woman's College did begin awarding honorary doctorates in 1939—apparently after nudging by President Graham—the recipients were all women. And as if to make up for lost time, it was soon granting them two and three at a time. The total reached twenty-three in 1950, the year that Graham himself became the first man so honored.[52]

The first recipient, in 1939, was Judge Florence E. Allen of the United States Circuit Court of Appeals in Cleveland. Although she was a jurist of some distinction, she was not a North Carolinian and had no prior connection with the college. Many if not most of the later honorees, like Laura Weill Cone (1942) and Judge Susie Sharp (1950)—both alumnae—did have at least one of those associations. Graham, who had left the university to accept a United States Senate appointment in 1949, had the unique distinction of receiving an honorary degree from all three campuses in 1950—of course orchestrated beforehand.[53] If there was any intent to influence the ensuing Democratic senatorial primary in which Graham was a candidate, it failed. Tragically (in the eyes of almost everyone in the university) Graham went down to defeat in a campaign marked by race- and red-baiting.[54]

* * *

As early as 1928 President Foust had asked the faculty to consider moving the academic calendar from the semester to the quarter system, in use at Chapel Hill and State. Jackson also raised the point several times, but the idea engendered more enthusiasm from students than from the faculty, who faced the necessity of revising their course programs in return for a doubtful advantage. Although the discrepancy between campuses caused some complications in scheduling summer school and graduate work, the college never made the change.[55] In 1953 Chapel Hill and State themselves moved back to the semester system.

* * *

Under consolidation, President Graham visualized WC as a liberal arts college with a few traditional women's professional programs attached. As Jackson and most of the faculty subscribed to the same view, the college posed few problems for Graham.[56] Once new departments of art, classical civilization, philosophy, and geography were established in the mid-1930s (some of them requested by Foust earlier) there was little change in the undergraduate curriculum beyond the adding of new courses in existing fields.[57]

In terms of student majors, the three largest departments between 1939 and 1946 were secretarial administration, home economics, and education. In fact, regardless of major, most students continued to prepare for teaching careers and pursued them after graduation. Except during World War II they had little alternative besides matrimony.[58] Harriet Elliott was among those who advocated vocational courses training students for jobs they could realistically expect to attain in peacetime. With the existing social prejudices, she advised Jackson in 1942, the college would only prepare women for the breadlines if it guided them into fields like engineering. Beyond the standard liberal arts background, the vocational areas she recommended most strongly that year were nursing, childcare, radio, and secretarial training.[59]

The most significant curricular developments in the Jackson years lay in graduate study. Several master's degrees had been awarded in each of the years immediately preceding consolidation, but for several years afterward the college catalog omitted all mention of graduate work. A master's degree program in home economics, authorized in 1928, was not actually instituted until 1934. It was followed soon by business education, which meant secretarial training. These programs were exceedingly small: by 1939 only two persons had received degrees. Like many of the undergraduate programs, they emphasized teacher training in their respective fields. Accordingly, they were practical rather than research-oriented.[60]

The college would have offered more graduate work, given the chance. Hearing that the all-university graduate school would not award students the WC master's degree in home economics unless they came to Chapel Hill for graduate courses in supporting fields like chemistry, the college vainly sought permission in 1936 to offer such courses itself.[61] Jackson was repeatedly combatting what he regarded as invasive efforts by Chapel Hill administrators to undercut the college's allocation of functions, or to confine certain graduate instruction to faculty from that campus even when it was offered in Greensboro.[62]

Graduate programs did in fact expand in the 1940s. The university in 1942 authorized each campus to establish a branch of the graduate school under its own associate dean, and in 1945 to create its own graduate faculty. At WC the expansion was spearheaded by Franklin H. McNutt who arrived in 1941 as head of education and soon became associate dean of graduate studies as well. A master's program in elementary education came immediately in 1942. The successful bachelor of fine arts program initiated in 1946 led to a comparable master's program in 1949, with majors available in writing, music composition, painting and graphic arts, and dance. In 1951 the master of education was broadened to include concentration in art, English, home economics, music, physical education, and secretarial science.[63] Graduate enrollments rose sharply, with education accounting for the great majority. In fact, most of the students were public school teachers or principals, taking their courses in the evenings, on Saturdays, and in summer school. Twenty master's degrees were awarded in 1950, rising to 105 in 1954.[64]

Chapter 12

The Library and Liberal Arts

College Librarian Charles H. Stone came to the campus in 1927, set up a library science program that graduated twenty students in 1930 and won full accreditation two years later. When university consolidation almost immediately closed down the program in favor of the larger operation at Chapel Hill, it is not surprising that Stone chose to move on. In 1935 he left for William and Mary to establish a library science program there.[1] His successor in 1936, Guy R. Lyle of Antioch College, was a productive scholar as well as administrator who was already making a name for himself nationally. The author of a widely-used periodicals bibliography when he came, Lyle in 1944 produced what became the standard work on college library administration. He left that year to become library director at Louisiana State University.[2]

After another year's hiatus, Charles M. Adams of Columbia University arrived in 1945 to begin what would be a twenty-four-year tenure as head librarian. He began almost immediately to plan and preside over the construction of a new library building. In the process he became a recognized authority on the subject at a time when academic library construction was booming nationwide. Later Adams would lead the library into the university era with its attendant multiplication of the faculty, the student body, the number and diversity of graduate and undergraduate programs, and the corresponding expansion of library holdings. At the same time he was active professionally at the regional and national levels, serving in 1950–51 as president of the Association of College and Research Librarians.[3]

Initially, Adams was in charge of a staff of about twelve professional librarians plus many assistants—all women except perhaps for janitors.[4] (Nationally, librarianship like elementary school teaching remained all but exclusively female, with salaries correspondingly low.) Like his immediate predecessors, Adams held faculty rank as a full professor. The professional librarians under him who had grown in numbers and qualifications over the years were of uncertain status. They were not regarded as teaching faculty with the perquisites and voting privileges pertaining thereto; yet they were above the clerical staff. When Guy Lyle asked for clarification of the matter in 1936, Jackson and the advisory committee offered little support beyond inviting the librarians to attend faculty meetings on a non-voting basis.[5] The issue was clearly controversial among the teaching faculty. Five years later Lyle raised the question again, asserting that "the best colleges and universities throughout the country" were now according faculty status to their librarians.[6] But when a committee of librarians presumably appointed by him failed to agree on specific recommendations, nothing happened. Although Adams raised the matter again periodically, it was not resolved until the 1970s.[7]

The library's book purchase budget sank to $5000 in the Depression biennium of 1935–37, but rose to $23,000 by 1948. In the interval the collection almost doubled in size from 70,000 to 134,000 volumes.[8] It was recognized at least locally as a good undergraduate library, but it could not compete with the northeastern women's colleges. In 1947 the library held only 79 per cent of the periodicals that the Southern Association of Colleges and Secondary Schools regarded as desirable for an undergraduate library; that percentage would decrease in the 1950s. In 1931 and presumably later, the library staff selected the books and periodicals to be ordered, acting largely on the requests of faculty members.[9]

The library developed in this period a college collection that eventually grew into the university archives. It was conceived at the time of the fiftieth anniversary in 1942 and came into being two years later when materials in the general collection relating to the college's history were withdrawn and reclassified. Work proceeded slowly and concentrated mostly on printed materials.[10] Only later did the library begin to receive manuscript papers and records that would convert the collection into the university archives.

* * *

William Cunningham Smith served as head of the English department from 1902 until his retirement in 1940. Nearly all of that time he had doubled as dean of the college (1905–15), dean of the faculty (1915–22), or dean of the college of liberal arts and sciences (1922–34). President Foust repeatedly credited Smith more than any other person with spearheading the institution's development from normal school to liberal arts college with full academic accreditation. Smith was also a superb classroom teacher and representative of the college in his frequent forays off campus (into the 1920s, at least) to give scholarly and inspirational talks to civic and educational groups around the state. Students, colleagues, and others characterized him as courtly, good-humored, quiet (even shy), serene, and dignified. His correspondence betrays a puckish sense of humor as well.[11]

It is clear at the same time that the English department was falling behind recent developments in the field and increasingly needed new leadership. In 1941 Winfield H. Rogers of Western Reserve University arrived as department head, but he remained only four years.[12] His successor from 1945 to 1960 was Leonard B. Hurley, an insider who had come to the college in 1921. Another newcomer who left his mark in the classroom and on the college was Marc Friedlaender, who came from Tulane in 1937.[13]

In time, what most set the English department apart was its writing program. Although the students had asked as early as 1930 for more courses in writing, and John Crowe Ransom was recruited to teach in the 1935 summer session, the program really got underway with the arrival in 1938 of poet and critic Allen Tate and his wife, novelist Caroline Gordon—Jackson's first distinguished professors. Each was to teach only six hours a week, at $2400 apiece per year.[14] Although Gordon thought Greensboro to be "frightful" and her students stupid, they included (as she later recalled) Margaret Coit, later Pulitzer Prize-winning biographer of John C. Calhoun; lexicographer Sheila Corley; poet Eleanor Ross Taylor; and (off campus) Taylor's brother and husband, respectively: writers James Ross and Peter Taylor, who himself later taught in the program.[15] Tate and Gordon's departure for Princeton after a year and a half unquestionably set the program back and the college cast about with mixed success to find suitable replacements. Their first notable successor, Hiram Haydn, likewise served only a year and a half before leaving early in 1944 to become executive secretary of Phi Beta Kappa and editor of its journal *American Scholar*.[16] Peter Taylor, recently out of military service, came in 1946 and remained off and on for the next six years, publishing his first two books while at the college. He would return for four years in the '60s, and (like Tate) was a frequent visitor at other times.[17] Another catch, engineered by Taylor, was poet and critic Randall Jarrell, who came in 1947 and remained (with occasional absences) for the rest of his life.

What attracted these writers to Greensboro and the college? Robert Watson, a later director of the program, identified it half-facetiously as boredom—an atmosphere of quiet in which to pursue one's thoughts. In the same vein, Jarrell referred to the college as "Sleeping Beauty."[18] Taylor and Watson recognized another precondition at least as important: a receptive administration that offered a light teaching load, few interruptions such as committee assignments, and a living (but hardly princely) wage to writers who could not subsist on royalties alone. A third factor was the faculty companionship or critical mass that began to form with Jarrell's arrival in 1947; Watson and others soon came aboard, forming a small and congenial community. They also formed close friendships with a few others on the faculty such as Marc Friedlaender, French professor Malcolm Hooke, and classicist Frank Laine. And the students, while driving them sometimes to scorn and sarcasm, were frequently adoring and occasionally precocious.[19]

In 1943 the English department sponsored a modest Writing Forum with Hiram Haydn in charge. Next year, under Winfield Rogers and Marc Friedlaender, it blossomed into an annual interdisciplinary Arts Forum featuring writing, music composition, art, and dance. Soon a three-day event, the forum brought to campus leading figures in each field to give readings, recitals, or exhibitions of their own work and to evaluate that of students. In 1946 the forum became regional and in 1947 national, ultimately drawing students and their teachers from over sixty colleges and universities. In the writing field, Lionel Trilling led the panel of critics in 1946 and Flannery O'Connor was one of the student participants in 1947. In other fields, participants included architect Walter Gropius, dancers Martha Graham and Jose Limon, and composer Howard Hanson. For over a decade after 1945 Marc Friedlaender remained the forum's guiding spirit. The interdisciplinary cooperation that faculty members achieved in arranging the forum contributed mightily to the ensuing BFA and MFA programs in those same fields.[20]

The forum was so successful that the social science departments—at Chancellor Jackson's suggestion—created one of their own in 1948. It was soon named for Harriet Elliott, who died during the planning stage. Eugene Pfaff of the history department headed the planning committee. For more than a decade the Harriet Elliott Social Science Forum followed the same format as the Arts Forum and it appears to have been equally successful. After the first event it moved to the fall semester, leaving spring to the arts.[21]

Until the 1950s speech and drama remained part of the English department. W. Raymond Taylor had come to the college in 1921 to teach speech but his first love was theater, and speech fell by the wayside. He returned to the subject in 1935, however, asking for the appointment of two speech specialists. The need, he said, was obvious among the students: "Nasality, lisping, harshness, weak and thin voice texture, lack of breath control, sameness and monotony of tone, drawling and stuttering, exaggerated and disagreeable sectional accents, nervous rapidity, faulty enunciation and pronunciation, [and] affected elocution are the rule rather than the exception." The authorities found his case compelling and speech courses were added to the curriculum in 1936.[22]

Taylor pursued his theater interests. The Playlikers, whom he had formed in the '20s, became a combination student and community theater company. Its members were drawn from both areas, the community providing a larger number of willing male actors than the faculty alone could provide. By 1939 they were mounting at least one play per month before audiences averaging at least 2000 people.[23]

Although Taylor found this pace excessive and cut back somewhat, he instituted a summer repertory program in 1946. Like the school-year productions, it was staged in Aycock Auditorium. Next year he made an even greater leap, moving the summer program to the town of Burnsville in the mountains, adjacent to Mount Mitchell and in time the Blue Ridge Parkway. It was rare at the time for academic institutions to sponsor such enterprises.[24] WC proceeded to offer other courses there too as part of its extension program, calling the whole operation the Burnsville School of Fine Arts. It was another manifestation of the arts collaboration on campus. The Burnsville community, who had extended the invitation, offered a building—an old high school gym. It was hastily remodeled and eventually named the Parkway Playhouse. In 1948 President Graham secured a $10,000 Carnegie Foundation grant for the project. For a few years, until dormitories became available, students and other participants roomed with townspeople. Local residents also supplied volunteer labor, took parts in the plays, and at first even supplied food for the cafeteria. With the college staging several plays over six to eight weeks each summer, the playhouse provided a significant tourist attraction and a boost for the local economy. And with small additional subsidies it also cleared expenses and occasionally earned a little money for the college.[25] One of the mainstays of the Playlikers was journalist and amateur thespian William C. (Mutt) Burton of the *Greensboro Daily News*, who followed the program into summer repertory and then the mountains. All told, he acted in WC/UNCG productions for fifty years.[26]

Unfortunately, Taylor's position at the college began to crumble in the late 1940s, just as the Burnsville project was getting underway. He had acquired three badly needed associates in the drama division, but soon found himself temperamentally or philosophically incompatible with two of them. The Playlikers operation began to disintegrate. Audiences fell off drastically and the organization started losing money. These conditions spread in some measure to the Burnsville operation. Critics charged Taylor and the Playlikers with sloppy business practices. Taylor himself admitted that student interest in dramatics had fallen to the lowest level in his memory. Conditions reached such a pass in 1949 that the faculty advisory committee called for a new director of dramatics.[27] Jackson, conscious of his own imminent departure, left the problem in the lap of his successor.

* * *

Art had always been taught at the college, chiefly as a vocational adjunct to education and home economics. In 1935 it finally came into its own as a separate department. (Two hundred American colleges and universities had already taken this step by 1932.)[28] Elizabeth McIver Weatherspoon was a charter member of the department but in no position professionally or physically to take leadership. (She would die in 1939 after years of heroic effort to meet her classes despite debilitating illness.) The headship went to Gregory Ivy, a watercolorist of some repute and a champion of contemporary art. Ivy remained for twenty-five years, minus time off for service in World War II, contributing importantly to the development of the college as well as his department.[29] The 1935–36 catalog lists a faculty of four, including Ivy and Weatherspoon, and twenty-one courses. Then as later, they heavily emphasized studio and vocational work, from painting and sculpture to costume design and house planning and furnishing. By 1950 there were over 125 art majors, half of them in the bachelor of fine arts program. In that fifteen-year period, WC graduates virtually monopolized the supervisory positions in public school art around the state.[30] The department quickly acquired a good reputation in the South and beyond.[31]

The department was initially scattered in four campus buildings. It moved in 1940 to McIver Building, replacing the science departments which now had a building of their own. McIver Building had not been designed for art, and the department's quarters became a source of discontent for decades. Nevertheless it opened up space for a small gallery that was named for the recently deceased Mrs. Weatherspoon. In 1942 a Friends organization, soon named the Weatherspoon Gallery Association, was formed to support acquisitions; these were not paid for by the state. For financial reasons in part, the gallery from the beginning specialized in twentieth-century American art, though not to the exclusion of other periods and places. In 1950 it received a substantial gift of works by Matisse, Picasso, and other French and American artists from the Cone sisters of Baltimore (Claribel and Etta), kin to the Cone textile family of Greensboro. Reflecting that local interest, the gallery developed in the '40s an annual International Textile Exhibition.[32]

Art participated fully in the interdisciplinary programs of the 1940s and later. As early as 1938 it began conducting summer courses at the coastal town of Beaufort in conjunction with the college's marine biology program, already in operation there. That effort was interrupted by World War II, but afterwards art joined in the Burnsville Fine Arts School at the opposite end of the state as well as the BFA and MFA programs on campus.[33]

* * *

In the heady expansionist year of 1923, amid dreams of a women's university, Foust and Jackson (as department head) brought in a trio of male historians—all southerners and two of them with degrees from Columbia University, the college's great training ground. They served the college well for a generation. Perhaps the ablest of them, Benjamin B. Kendrick, succeeded to the headship of history and political science when Jackson departed for Chapel Hill in 1932. He served very capably until incapacitated by a stroke in 1943. Administrators and faculty colleagues repeatedly appointed or elected Kendrick to such influential bodies as the advisory committee and the three-campus faculty council making plans for consolidation. He was also prominent in history professional organizations, regional and national.[34] Kendrick's departure was followed in 1945 by the death of Alex M. Arnett, the second member of the trio, almost as well known for his publications in southern history. After four years under an interim leadership committee headed by the third veteran, Clarence D. Johns, the department persuaded Johns finally to step in as head. But his service was cut short by his own untimely death in 1950.[35]

Johns wrote Jackson in 1946 that the department had already begun to slip academically before Kendrick's stroke. Members had gone on leave and their courses were suspended or handed off to substitutes. Students also complained of too few courses in fields of emerging interest like Asia. The number of prospective majors fell off—some transferring to Chapel Hill to take the desired courses. (The same phenomenon was observable in other fields too as Chapel Hill spread its welcoming arms wider; cynics said the main target of opportunity there was men.) Johns and the department may well have reflected the crisis mentality that permeated the campus between 1944 and 1947. His request to hire a distinguished professor from the outside, on the order of Allen Tate, was not granted.[36]

At least until the creative writing program got fully underway in the late '40s, the history department liked to think of itself as the most productive in the college from a scholarly standpoint.[37] Although Kendrick, Arnett, and others had written books, the department's productivity would by no means have passed muster a generation later. It did contain a number of popular, even superb teachers, however, starting with Deans Jackson and Elliott, who each continued for a time to teach a class. Eugene Pfaff, Bernice Draper, and Vera Largent in European history and a 1944 recruit, Richard Bardolph in American, were popular teachers who more than pulled their weight inside and outside the department. Bardolph in particular would publish and assume leadership in later years.

The most popular instructor on campus in these years was Louise Alexander in political science. She came in 1935 to replace Harriet Elliott, who had gone on leave prior to her appointment as dean of women. Alexander had first come to Greensboro in 1911 with a degree from Presbyterian College in Charlotte, some graduate work at the University of Tennessee, and three years' teaching experience at Lees-McRae Institute in the mountains. Failing to secure a faculty position at the Normal, she settled for Greensboro High School, remaining there until 1919. Alexander was an avid suffragist and after that a lifelong political activist. She and Elliott (who arrived in 1913) became close friends and comrades in the suffrage wars, the League of Women Voters (of which Alexander served for a time as state president), and the Democratic party. (The two had dinner together on election night for thirty years, turning on the radio afterward to hear the returns.) In what turned out eventually to be only a temporary career change, Alexander entered law school at Chapel

Hill in 1919 and returned to Greensboro a year later as the city's first woman attorney. From 1923 until her arrival on campus she was clerk of the municipal court.[38]

By all accounts Alexander was a passionate instructor (and an easy grader) whose classes regularly overflowed. To the admiring student body she was known as Miss Alex. (Nevertheless her fervent classroom espousal of the Democratic party inadvertently created a few Republicans.) In time she took over Jackson's American biography course and even outdid him in the classroom.[39] Not surprisingly, she was also a popular off-campus speaker. In 1949 Alexander became the first recipient of the O. Max Gardner award, recently endowed by the late governor to honor the consolidated university faculty member "who in the past academic year has made the greatest contribution to the human race." One may query whether Miss Alexander's accomplishments really met that demanding standard, but there was no gainsaying the honor to her or to the college. It was conferred specifically for her teaching record.[40]

* * *

Although one or two departments offered courses that more or less resembled philosophy, there was no philosophy department until Jackson pushed for one in 1935. Even then, the one-man department floundered for the next fourteen years under ineffectual and (during the war) absentee direction, to the increasing resentment of students.[41] Although a member of the economics department offered a philosophy course for several years, it was 1949 before the college secured both the funding and an acceptable candidate to reactivate the department. This time, in Warren Ashby it found a person it could live with. He remained until his death in 1985. A native Virginian, Ashby received his doctorate at Yale, spent five years in the Methodist ministry, then taught philosophy at Chapel Hill for three years before accepting the call from WC.[42]

* * *

By 1935, the Latin department had declined so far in clientele that it was, in Jackson's words, almost extinct. Viola Boddie, the lovely, fashionable, and totally enviable Victorian belle who helped to open the college in 1892 had become a hyper-sensitive and contentious old woman, out of touch with the few teen-age girls who dared to cross her doorstep forty years later. The streak of sarcasm noted from the beginning had been honed to perfection over the years. Yet Miss Boddie was only partly responsible for the decline in Latin; it had parallels across the country. In 1935 she agreed to a partial retirement under the university's new regulations; a faculty committee recommended that she be limited to one course. At the same time President Graham himself urged the college to go ahead with its desire to create a new department of classical civilization. The plan was to offer courses in Greek, archaeology, and perhaps ancient history as well as Latin. Dr. Charlton C. Jernigan of Duke University was hired to head the new department.[43]

Jernigan was young, dynamic, and male; enrollments rose dramatically. Soon carrying the burden alone, he was offering courses by 1942 in mythology, Greek and Latin literature in translation, and comparative world literature—all in addition to Greek and Latin language courses. Jernigan had added Greek at the outset and twelve years later claimed up to 175 students in those courses. "Baby Greek," the elementary course, he boasted, had one of the largest enrollments in the nation. A student Classical Club in 1947 numbered fifty. In 1949 Jernigan departed for Florida State University, to be replaced by Frank Laine, a freshly minted Ph.D. from Vanderbilt.[44] Like Warren Ashby, he would create a small but successful department and spend the rest of his life at the institution.

* * *

Geography, like art and philosophy, was for years homeless. In the absence of any geography department the school of education sought in the 1920s to create one there. Foust thought it belonged elsewhere, and at length lodged it in the biology department. There it remained even after he hired a full-time geographer in 1931. That man, Dr. Charles Crittenden, was offered some hope of a separate department, but the faculty could agree neither where to house the field nor what to emphasize within it. Crittenden was caught in the middle and, fairly or not, was asked to leave in 1937.[45]

His successor that year, Edna Arundel, came as an instructor on a temporary one-year appointment while the college wrestled with the problem of what to do with geography. The decision in 1938 was to create a department of geography and geology offering courses in both fields.[46] But implementation was put off, presumably for financial reasons, until 1942. Meanwhile, geography was treated as an interim department and Arundel remained on one-year reappointments as interim head. Although she produced general satisfaction, she lacked the Ph.D., on which she was working as opportunity offered. In 1942, with a Yale doctorate in hand, she was promoted to assistant professor and geography became a full-fledged department. In 1940 she acquired a colleague, permitting the geography offerings to expand, but there was no mention of geology.[47] Arundel remained at the college for over twenty years.

* * *

The department of sociology and economics divided into its two constituent parts in 1936. Glenn Johnson remained sociology head while Albert Keister became head of economics. In the case of sociology, both enrollments and majors rose sharply after 1937 with the advent of courses in social work. Johnson claimed nearly 100 majors in 1946, many or most of whom were expected to enter that field. The department also claimed in the early '40s the largest percentage of majors who went on to graduate work.[48]

Of the four sociologists in 1946, two were women who had come in the '30s, stayed for the remainder of their lives, and made their mark. Lyda Gordon Shivers was a Mississippian who arrived in 1933 with both a law degree and a freshly minted doctorate in sociology from Chapel Hill. Her fields were criminology and the family. The second newcomer, Mereb Mossman, was a graduate of Morningside College in Iowa, which her father had headed as president. She received her master's at the University of Chicago and subsequently taught for several years at Ginling College for women in Nanking, China. In 1937 she returned to the United States, intending to finish her doctorate at Chicago. Instead she applied for and received a position at WC teaching social work. It was she who introduced those courses that year. Mossman's probity and discretion won her steady advancement, and as early as 1948 Jackson was ready to nominate her for the university's prestigious O. Max Gardner award, behind Louise Alexander. Three years later Jackson's successor picked her for the new position of academic dean—a position she held for twenty years. Mossman's impact on the institution can only be compared with that of Harriet Elliott.[49]

* * *

J.P. Givler continued to head the biology department until his retirement in 1949. Perhaps its greatest accomplishment in these years was to acquire in 1940—with chemistry and physics—a new science building. Givler had long regarded the cramped and antiquated quarters in McIver Building as an embarrassment that seriously retarded the department's development.[50]

Biology maintained a summer marine laboratory in the coastal town of Beaufort. Archie D. Shaftesbury, a marine biologist with a doctorate from Johns Hopkins, had come to the college in 1924 and soon began taking small numbers of advanced students to Beaufort in the summers for work and study. Shaftesbury chose Beaufort because the nearby waters were unusually rich in both northern and Gulf Stream marine species. (The United States Bureau of Fisheries had a research laboratory there and Duke University would soon follow suit.) After several years of trying, Shaftesbury and the department persuaded Jackson to upgrade the college's activity there. In 1935, armed with a small federal grant and a plot of land donated by the town, the college erected a modest frame laboratory building. (It bore a strong resemblance to the typical one-room rural North Carolina schoolhouse.) The laboratory was more a teaching than a research facility. Lacking a dormitory, students rented rooms in town. Beginning in 1938, the art department also offered courses there, giving rise to the name Beaufort Summer School. Suspended during the war, the enterprise resumed in 1946 but moved in 1951 to the mountains at Burnsville. The marine lab closed down and the property was disposed of.[51]

This closure was probably attributable to Shaftesbury himself. Although biology remained one of the most popular majors, its zoology enrollments fell off drastically in the late 1930s and it became in effect a department of botany. Givler blamed Shaftesbury, whose students had long regarded him as too demanding—even those who had a crush on him. He became increasingly subject to rages and vituperative outbursts, causing students to leave class in tears. His enrollments fell off accordingly, on campus and at Beaufort.[52]

* * *

Mary Petty, who had led the chemistry department since its founding at the turn of the century, stepped down in 1934 under the new retirement regulations. Her successor, Florence L. Schaeffer (who had come to the college in 1922) held the position for another thirty years. The department gradually expanded, reflecting the growth of both the field and the college. Schaeffer's own abilities propelled her into a position of considerable faculty leadership in the 1930s and afterward.[53]

The two male physics professors, Calvin Warfield and John Tiedeman, were called into military service during the war and never returned. Anna Joyce Reardon, with a recent Ph.D. from St. Louis University, arrived in 1941 on a one-year appointment, stepped almost immediately into the headship, and never left. Reardon had done research in photography, and when she offered an elective course in the subject she was swamped with students. In conjunction with a flight instructor at the Greensboro airport, she also offered an aviation course that garnered both students and publicity.[54]

In general, neither chemistry nor physics was heavily elected at a time when women found few career opportunities in science. The few who did major in these fields were headed primarily for high school teaching jobs. Even there, they faced abundant male competition and favoritism. Nevertheless Schaeffer complained of being seriously shorthanded in the face of rising chemistry enrollments in 1946.[55]

* * *

For some years the new science building had room only for biology, chemistry, and physics. Psychology, left in the McIver building, expanded into much of the space they vacated in 1940. The department grew to seven full-time members by 1950 under its founding head, J.A. Highsmith. Experimental psychologist Key L. Barkley and college business manager Claude Teague managed through creative acquisition strategies in the lean '30s to garner enough equipment that Highsmith could boast in 1945 of its comparing favorably with almost any undergraduate college in the country. Barkley's departure in 1947 for North Carolina State cost the college an important and colorful figure: a superb teacher, champion of student freedoms, and onetime dean of men. Highsmith was even more prominent on campus and off, heading the curriculum committee for a decade and also for a time the all-university general policies committee. He retired in 1953.[56]

Chapter 13

The Professional Schools

John H. Cook, who had led education since 1918 as department head, dean, and again head, died suddenly in January 1941. This came just before the legislature enacted the state employees' retirement law that he had played a large part in creating. His successor, Franklin H. McNutt of the University of Cincinnati, found a faction-ridden department of dubious academic standing. A number of its members were getting on in years, and with one exception (Eugenia Hunter) McNutt regarded their educational "rejuvenation" as a "task of first magnitude."[1] The factionalism continued and McNutt resigned as head in 1946, taking Jackson by surprise.[2] The position was still vacant when education was raised again to school level in 1948. Appointed dean in 1949 was Charles E. Prall, a Chicago Ph.D. and former dean of education at the University of Pittsburgh.[3]

Franklin McNutt stayed on in 1946 in the new position of associate dean of the graduate school—in effect WC's graduate dean. His appointment sprang in part from education's newly prominent role in the college's graduate program, rapidly overshadowing the small existing programs in home economics and secretarial training. That was surely also a factor in boosting the department back to school status in 1948.

By the 1930s professional educators and public school officials were winning their battle to require North Carolina teachers to have at least a bachelor's degree. Thereafter, in the state as nationally, emphasis shifted to graduate training, particularly for school administrators. Under the original UNC allocation of functions all graduate work in education was centered at Chapel Hill. But with salary and career advancements increasingly tied to the acquisition of a master's degree, Chapel Hill could no longer meet the demand. The university's first answer was to have that campus offer a few extension courses around the state. Some were held on or adjacent to the Raleigh and Greensboro campuses, leading inevitably to requests that they be allowed to offer the courses themselves. The next step at Woman's College was permission to develop its own master's program in elementary education. The college fought hard for this program, which went into effect in 1942. But since it was not permitted to offer graduate work in necessary related fields, students still had to take part of their work at

Chapel Hill. WC's request for a comparable master's program in secondary education was not granted.[4]

Curry School remained small, its student body limited pretty much to faculty children and others living in the vicinity. It added a kindergarten in 1935 and the twelfth year of high school in 1946. The graduating class that year numbered only twenty-two, most of whom went on to college.[5] Enrollments remained so low, in fact, that many WC students continued to do their practice teaching in the public schools.[6] Curry's chief service to the college lay in its availability as a laboratory for new ideas and methods.

The low enrollments derived primarily from the size of the building. Jackson reported in 1944 that the school had a long waiting list and every year it had to reject scores of applicants living outside its small district. It was still part of the Greensboro city school system, which (in the college's view) shortchanged it financially. McNutt characterized Curry as lagging behind the state's better schools in every important particular—except quality of instruction.[7]

* * *

The college's one-year commercial program was sometimes regarded as a stepchild; through the 1920s it was limited to 80 students. But during the Depression this program was as close as many North Carolina girls ever got to a college education. It also helped the college itself at a time of sagging enrollments.[8] In those circumstances, it accepted virtually every applicant and in 1936 enrollments reached 267. As this was more than the program could easily handle, and as applications for the four-year secretarial program began to rise, the college again limited the one-year enrollments to about 100.[9] Jackson and others tended to view the one-year program much as they had the high school remedial work offered before 1910. But the program, though short, was intensive and despite some misgivings it continued to turn out capable secretaries and other office workers until 1967.[10] After E. J. Forney's retirement in 1935 the commercial department was under George M. Joyce, his eventual successor also as the college's chief financial officer.

At the same time a new department of secretarial administration (later called business education) took over the four-year program initiated in 1932. It included the same liberal arts foundation that was common to all of the college's majors, and culminated in a bachelor of science degree. Graduate work, authorized in 1937, was first taught only in summer school but beginning in 1941 the department offered a full-time graduate program—the only one in the South Atlantic states. By that time the department had grown from four to eleven members and was turning out more graduating seniors than any department in the college—20 to 25 percent of the total. Its head after 1943 was Vance Littlejohn, who had come to campus in 1938. Over half of the department's alumnae became secretaries; the remainder were high school and junior college teachers of the subject and a variety of business employees from personnel directors to office managers. Employers sought them out because this was one of the few programs in the field that offered a liberal arts base.[11]

* * *

Dean Blanche Shaffer of the school of home economics resigned in 1933 to get married.[12] As her departure coincided with university consolidation, her successor that year, Margaret M. Edwards, came as department head, and so she remained until her own retirement in 1951. Although school status was restored at President Graham's suggestion in 1949 and Edwards seems to have compiled an impressive number of accomplishments, she was nearing retirement age and the title of dean was reserved for her successor.[13]

Edwards had first come to North Carolina in 1926 as state supervisor of home economics. Like Shaffer she lacked the doctorate in a field where it was neither widely available nor regarded as necessary. During her tenure at WC she led in planning the major addition to the home economics building, matching the new library and facing it across College Avenue. (Unlike librarian Charles Adams she would not remain long enough to occupy the new building herself.) Edwards also presided over the creation in 1946 of the Home Economics Foundation, the college's first such fund-raising entity.[14]

By 1936 the department was divided into seven specialized areas: general home economics, clothing and textiles, teacher education, food and nutrition, home relations and child development, housing, and institutional economics. Of these, teacher education long remained the most popular among students looking for paying jobs after graduation. A masters' program had been authorized in the '20s but it lagged for a decade, then picked up markedly in the '40s when almost forty theses were written.[15]

Home economics never had a problem placing its graduates. In 1941, about two-thirds of them went into teaching. The remainder were dietitians, textile analysts, dress designers, interior designers, and holders of a host of other occupations.[16]

* * *

Unlike education and home economics, music retained its school status (hence its dean) after consolidation. Wade Brown left that post in 1936 and retired the next year. His successor, H. Hugh Altvater, had been dean of the school of fine arts at Southwestern Methodist College in Kansas.[17]

The school had been primarily a voice, piano, and organ conservatory, emphasizing more the imparting of musical culture to prospective teachers than turning out professional musicians. But during the late '30s and '40s, as economic conditions improved, the public schools began (or in some cases resumed) offering instrumental instruction beyond piano. Under Altvater the school anticipated this development, adding new faculty members to teach instrumental music, both wind and string. In the process its orientation became more professional, but still based on the college's liberal arts foundation.[18] Accordingly, Altvater in 1936 recruited Herbert Hazelman of the Greensboro public schools to organize a college band. With interruptions, Hazelman served as part-time band director for years, always keeping his "day job" at Greensboro High School.[19] Altvater also set to work organizing a string orchestra, and in 1938 hired George Dickieson to take on that activity. It gave concerts on campus and around the state.

All of this was prelude to forming in 1939 the Greensboro Orchestra, forerunner of the later Greensboro Symphony. Altvater served as its conductor for twelve years. The thirty-five or so players were drawn from every quarter: faculty and students from WC, Greensboro College, and the Greensboro schools as well as other townspeople. As the years passed the orchestra gained both quality and quantity.[20]

Less dear to Altvater's heart was the annual high school music contest that he inherited from Wade Brown. (In 1937—Brown's last year as director, and following a national trend—the name was changed from Contest to Festival.) Altvater recognized its importance in stimulating high school music instruction, however, and the festival continued to grow under his supervision. By 1940 there were 8,000 representatives from 350 schools.[21] That number, including forty brass bands, created musical indigestion on campus, in the words of business manager Claude Teague, and stricter requirements next year cut the number in half. Even so, management chores continually diverted Altvater and his faculty from their more immediate tasks.[22] After 1951, when his health broke down, the college turned over its sponsorship to the state Musical Educators Association.

The music school received national accreditation in 1938. Faculty and former students of that period agreed that the program was rigorous and well respected. It was not large; the number of graduates seldom reached twenty. A large proportion of them went into teaching.[23] A small master's program in composition came in 1949.

* * *

Following earlier national practice, health and physical education at WC were joined in a single department until 1935. The separation that year, at physical education's behest, followed years of increasing friction as the two fields grew more professionalized and farther apart.[24] Thereafter, the health department consisted of the infirmary staff and those teaching the hygiene courses. Following Anna Gove's retirement in 1936, her successor as college physician, Ruth Collings, headed the department.

Mary Channing Coleman continued to lead physical education as head of the new department. (She had recently completed a year as president of the American Physical Education Association.) By her own testimony, her most valuable colleague was Ethel L. Martus, who had arrived in 1931 with a new master's degree from Wellesley, one of the capitals of physical education training for women. By the early '40s, Coleman was looking toward retirement and began grooming Martus as her successor. That event came a year earlier than anticipated, with Coleman's sudden death in October 1947.[25] Martus was fully up to the task, building further the department's national prominence in women's physical education.

The program grew with the college. By 1940 students could choose from twenty-nine different activity courses. Golf was first offered in 1937, boating and canoeing in 1942 with the completion of the campus lake. By the late 1940s physical education graduates were getting jobs in dance, recreation, and corrective work as well as the traditional teaching. The curriculum was adjusted accordingly. There was never any problem placing these girls.[26]

Graduate work in physical education began, perhaps unlikely, in the field of dance. In 1945 Coleman hired Virginia Moomaw of Iowa State to develop a program in dance. She did so, almost immediately offering the department's first graduate course. Next year, dance became part of the new interdisciplinary bachelor of fine arts program. It also participated in the comparable master of fine arts degree program, established in 1949. Although organized dance activity went back many years at the college—and was part of the summer programs at Beaufort and Burnsville—Moomaw brought it to a degree of excellence and curricular acceptance hitherto unequaled. Under her guidance WC's dance program was hailed as one of the best in the country.[27]

* * *

The college's summer school was another victim of consolidation. Previously a successful twelve-week session (the largest in the state at one point) it was told to cut back to six weeks for several years in the '30s. There was even a proposal in 1936 to concentrate all summer work at Chapel Hill. That was not done and the twelve-week ban was lifted. But when the college tried to return to its prior basis, it had lost so much competitive ground that it was forced to retreat again to six weeks. Also responsible was the prohibition of all graduate work except in home economics, and even there supporting work had to be taken at Chapel Hill. Although secretarial administration was soon added, most public school teachers had to look elsewhere for their required upgrading. Added attractions such as the Beaufort summer session did not change the picture appreciably. By 1944, Jackson reported, summer enrollments had fallen so low as to make the session's future problematic.[28]

At that point the picture brightened remarkably. Jackson reported in 1945 the best summer session in years, and in 1946 the best he had ever known, generously crediting its director, Charlie Phillips. More responsible was the university's agreement to expand graduate work once again at Raleigh and Greensboro. Spearheaded by graduate school head Franklin McNutt, master's work in elementary education was gradually followed by programs in other fields. In a complaint that would echo on every campus, McNutt lamented the longstanding requirement that summer session pay its own way, without any state appropriation.[29]

* * *

Consolidation also diverted most of the college's extension work to Chapel Hill. But here too the limitations were relaxed a decade later, particularly with the advent of more graduate work.[30] Beginning in 1943, the college began offering summer extension courses as far away as Asheville, aimed primarily if not wholly at public school teachers. The Parkway Playhouse and its adjunct, the Burnsville school of fine arts, beginning in 1947, were operated by the extension division and aimed at both graduate and undergraduate students. These were summer programs, but by the late '40s, most extension courses were held in evenings or on Saturdays during the school year. Largely graduate courses in education aimed at public school teachers, they were offered on campus and in towns throughout the northwest quadrant of the state. Like summer school, these operations had to pay for themselves and the college basically broke even on them. Also like summer school, they were in the capable hands of Charlie Phillips.[31]

In 1946, McNutt, Phillips, and the Greensboro Chamber of Commerce helped to create a Greensboro Evening College. Reflecting developments around the country, it offered both high school and college level courses to interested adults, many of them veterans. The courses ranged from broadly cultural to narrowly vocational. They were taught on the WC campus by faculty members from WC and, to a lesser degree, other local colleges. The program was one of four in the state in 1949–50, and some students commuted from other towns. The enrollments were small, averaging from forty to seventy-five per quarter in the late '40s. For a time the college offered a similar program in Burnsville, unrelated to the fine arts school.[32] Jackson supported the program enthusiastically but insisted that it be administratively independent of WC; many of the students were men and he was highly concerned not to introduce coeducation through the back door at a time when his predecessor and others were advocating it for the college.[33]

The evening college program represented a preliminary step toward the later community college system and WC's own emergence as a metropolitan university. It did not last long at WC, however. Jackson's successor, Edward Kidder Graham, found the program lacking in academic rigor compared with the college's regular offerings and he terminated WC's connection in 1952.[34] Its place was taken by Guilford College.

Chapter 14

Students and Alumnae

As mentioned earlier, the Depression caused a drastic downturn in student enrollment—by one third, from the previous high of 1,888 in 1929 to 1,266 in 1933. Three dormitories closed and others were not fully occupied. The college now stepped up its previously minimal recruiting activity. With little money for advertising, Laura Coit and Dean Jackson increased the number of letters (and later brochures) going out to selected high school students.[1] When Charlie Phillips arrived in 1935, his first assignment was to fill the two dormitories still empty. He and Jackson traveled the state promoting the college. They hired students to go out similarly in the summers of 1935 and 1936. Phillips continued for years to make a circuit of the most promising high schools; by the time he retired in 1962 he had visited 97 of the state's 100 counties.[2]

Better times brought higher enrollments. As early as 1937 they reached a new high of (coincidentally) 1,937. Amidst the renewed luxury of surplus applications that year the faculty, apparently for the first time, formed an admissions committee to screen applicants, taking over a role played hitherto by administrators.[3] In 1939 enrollments reached a plateau of about 2,250 where they remained for a decade. In 1942 WC overtook the Texas State College for Women to become the largest residential woman's college in the country. (Hunter College in New York City, composed of day students, was over three times as large.) Thereafter they traded that distinction back and forth, depending on their respective dormitory construction.

In fact, WC's own enrollment plateau was the product of limited dormitory space as more and more qualified applicants were turned down. The college had abandoned Foust's earlier policy of allowing large numbers of students to live in approved housing off campus; they were under too little supervision, Dean Harriet Elliott explained.[4]

Students continued to come from all over the state, excepting only three or four counties at the eastern and western extremities. During the Depression Greensboro and Guilford County contributed a disproportionately large share of enrollments—22 percent in 1932–33—including that year both girls and boys who in other times would have attended colleges out of town. By the late 1940s Guilford's representation was down to 13 percent.[5]

A few of these lived on campus, but most were town students—220 of them in 1949.[6] Many of the town students participated only minimally in college life. They attended class, socialized and played bridge in a room set aside for them in the Administration Building, then went home. Others made it a point to participate and derived much from the experience. In an effort to expand their number the college in 1942 assigned each town student to the residence hall of her choice, with the right to take part in all its programs. The experiment seems to have had little impact.[7]

Before the Depression, out-of-state students had arrived in gradually increasing numbers. Largely unbidden hitherto, they now were courted as a means of filling the dormitories. Their numbers rose to 262 (including three foreign students) in 1938–39. The largest contributor states in order were New Jersey, New York, South Carolina, Massachusetts, and Connecticut.[8]

Even before in-state applications began to recover, some in Raleigh and elsewhere grew alarmed at the thought of hard-pressed North Carolina taxpayers subsidizing out-of-state students. When old friend and supporter Josephus Daniels asked Foust in 1931 about their cost to the state, Foust parried by remarking, "I guess you and I never hoped to live to see the day when nearly all other parts of the country would look to North Carolina for the higher education of the[ir] boys and girls. It is the best advertisement we have."[9] But his and other educators' defense of outside students as a leavening agent was not universally persuasive then or later.

Low tuition was in fact a chief attraction for the northern girls in particular. Northeastern states, where private colleges and universities had reigned supreme, were slow in creating comparable state institutions. Tuition at both public and private institutions was higher than in North Carolina.[10] In 1939, as in-state applications were rising again, the legislature increased the tuition premium for out-of-state students from $50 per year to $125. Despite that increase, WC's out-of-state enrollment rose to 323 in 1942.[11] This led the state budget commission to fix a quota of about 300 out-of-state students at WC and the university trustees to impose a limit of 10 percent on all three campuses. Although that would have cut WC to about 225, it reported 284 out-of-state students in 1948. Across the country, the average out-of-state enrollment in public institutions was about 10 percent.[12]

Mereb Mossman, coming to the faculty in 1937, described the students in her early years as lower to upper middle class. Many were the first of their families to attend college, but she could remember no one from a truly deprived background.[13]

Until World War II, married students were few and far between, and lived off campus. The war hastened many marriages as boyfriends were about to be sent off on military duty. The great majority of these war brides remained as students, and the college temporarily lifted its ban on married women in the dormitories. In 1948, when a campus poll found 25 such students remaining, the *Carolinian* protested the college's reinstatement of the old rule. If officials feared that these women might engage too freely in discussions of marital life, the editorial concluded, segregation was more acceptable than expulsion.[14]

War's end brought an influx of female veterans—ex-WAVES and WACS along with a few nurses—armed with the GI Bill. Jackson announced in November 1946 that the college had so far accepted every veteran who had applied—fifty-four at that time. At least some of them were also segregated, perhaps at their own request, in the McIver house, which served as an overflow dormitory after Mrs. McIver's death in 1944.[15]

* * *

After 1939 students ate in four dining halls (North, West, South, and Spencer) all radiating from a central hub behind Spencer Dormitory. After 1932 breakfast and lunch were served cafeteria style and students could eat with whomever they wished. Dinner remained a formal meal, with white tablecloths and food served by fellow students working to pay their expenses. (During World War II and for a time afterward, all students were required to take turns performing this service.) For this meal there were year-long table assignments, largely self-selected, and a moderate dress code. Students sang blessing beforehand and heard announcements afterward. Alumnae reported many years later that the food was plentiful, nourishing, and reasonably appetizing. After 1935 faculty counselors were required to eat all three meals with the students; Dean Elliott invoked that rule (to the counselors' initial consternation) in order to quell food fights and other improprieties that developed as previous rules had been relaxed.[16]

* * *

Students of the 1930s, especially, made sacrifices to attend college. At NCCW/WC, a year's expenses for in-state students (including tuition, room, board, and fees) had been $369 in 1929. They dropped only to $339 in 1932 and remained there with very minor changes into the 1940s.[17] The college had never been able to offer much scholarship aid and some of that disappeared through legislative action in 1933. Financial aid continued to come primarily through loans and jobs. In a piece of good news, student loan funds increased dramatically when the university was permitted to share in the state's escheat revenues. Accordingly, Jackson reported in 1939 that 230 students were borrowing money from the college; he had no way of knowing how many might be doing so from other sources.[18]

New Deal relief agencies helped by increasing the number of student jobs. The National Youth Administration in particular helped over half a million students nationwide to stay in school. It provided small direct grants to students as well as work-study programs through colleges and universities.[19] The NYA seems to have supported about half of the student workers at WC. In 1935, Charlie Phillips reported that nearly 200 were receiving NYA money for a wide variety of campus jobs including work in the library, the mail room, the dining hall, and at the switchboard; some served as part-time departmental secretaries. In 1937, about 400 students (one-fifth of the total) were working at jobs on and off campus, half of them paid by the NYA. As late as 1940, some 500 girls had jobs on and off campus, many of them paid by the NYA. The largest group of all that year, paid by the college, were the 175 working in the dining hall.[20]

Prosperity returned to college and country with World War II. In 1943 Edna Forney, E.J.'s daughter and assistant in the treasurer's office, reported that students were paying off their loans and spending money as never before. But the college always needed student help to keep the wheels turning. During the war the general labor shortage forced every student into her share of dining hall service.[21] Even after the war the college's loan funds lay idle for lack of applicants and it had to raise student wages to get the necessary help. In 1949 about 300 girls had jobs, half of them in the dining hall.[22]

* * *

As a byproduct of consolidation, the college adopted a far-ranging, integrated academic and social advising system for students, patterned on plans previously advanced at Smith, Wellesley, and other women's colleges.[23] Harriet Elliott, who helped formulate the WC program, took charge at its inception in 1935 and made it a model for many other campuses. What seems to have made this program more successful than others was that WC managed in significant measure to surmount the common rivalry between the counselors and the academic faculty. But that achievement was by no means complete; Elliott and her successor Katherine Taylor tried for years to gain academic status for the majority of counselors who were not members of the teaching faculty.[24]

Elliott's plan called for uniting what had been separate academic and social guidance programs (the latter under Chase Going Woodhouse, who left in 1934 with the advent of the new regime) and then decentralizing the whole effort among an expanded group of both academic and social counselors. There were fifteen residence hall counselors by 1944.[25] The purpose of uniting academic and social counseling was to head off what Elliott termed lopsided student development in either direction. Decentralization was meant to prevent a student from being evaluated and perhaps misdirected for life by a single person in a single office. This operation would be under four main faculty advisers, called class chairmen. In time, one was permanently assigned to the freshman class while the others each took over a sophomore class and continued with it to graduation. The four, all members of the teaching faculty, were in charge of both academic and social advising to the members of their respective classes. Under them were several other faculty academic advisers who dealt primarily with freshmen and sophomores. In the junior and senior years academic advising was taken over primarily by the heads of students' major departments.[26]

The residence halls—Elliott rejected the term "dormitory" as too passive—were extensively refurbished and made more homelike, thanks largely to the time, effort, and perhaps money of Laura Cone. More than ever before, they became miniature communities within the larger college fold. Each developed its own social and even academic program, following general guidelines. Maternal housemothers gave way to college-educated counselors, often relatively young. Required to live and take their meals with the students, the counselors too were to be both academic and social advisers. Several (like Katherine Taylor, Elliott's eventual successor) were members of the faculty.[27] Under their direction, students organized residence hall concerts and discussion groups as well as dances, receptions, and parties.[28] By 1943 Elliott (and later Taylor) was asking that all the counselors be given faculty status with salaries to match. Some of the best, Elliott noted, were leaving for other places where they could achieve greater professional satisfaction and financial security. Several became deans of women at other institutions.[29]

All this bore a striking resemblance to the early days when women faculty members had shared life with the students in both dormitory and dining hall. Though she did not draw that parallel specifically, Elliott (and her contemporaries around the country) were trying in effect to recreate through decentralization and closer personal attention an academic community that had fallen victim by the 1920s to surging institutional growth, of faculty as well as students.[30] In the same spirit, Jackson continued to appoint half a dozen male faculty members to welcome incoming freshmen at the train and bus stations every fall—a tradition going back to McIver. (With the end of wartime gas rationing, however, more and more students came directly to their dormitories by car, bypassing the welcoming committee.)[31] Elliott also retained the fall pre-school conference of administrators and student leaders that had originated at Camp Yonahlassee in 1929.

Elliott sought continually to improve the counseling system. By the mid-1940s she believed that two groups of students in particular were being neglected: town students, who needed better integration into college life, and the small minority who needed psychiatric help. Moreover, the job of class chairman had become so onerous that it was hard to find faculty members willing to take it on.[32] But with occasional modifications before and after her premature death in 1947, her system remained in place until the early 1960s.

Unlike the old days, Elliott's system was coupled with greater student freedom and a relaxation of parietal regulations— though not enough to alarm parents and legislators. Elliott continually preached the doctrine of "responsible freedom," which she thought vital in the progress to maturity. In return for greater freedom students had a corresponding responsibility to ensure its continuance through self-discipline. That responsibility included taking a major part both in making and enforcing the regulations that remained. The honor system was dusted off and returned to a place of central importance. Recreational outlets were added on campus. Moreover, students felt less compulsion to leave campus on weekends, as scheduled social activities (in the residence halls and campuswide) were increased at those times and men came more often to visit the girls instead of vice versa. All of these events were chaperoned by faculty and counselors to the fullest extent possible within the college budget.[33]

By all accounts Elliott's system was a resounding success with both students and faculty. Student rebelliousness diminished. Heretofore, students had been critical of faculty inattention outside the classroom; with some notable exceptions, they said, faculty had not seemed much interested in them or indeed in the college community. A 1935 *Carolinian* editorial writer gave as two examples the poor faculty attendance at chapel exercises and student musical concerts. These complaints now fell off abruptly, and students gave particular credit to Chancellor Jackson and Dean Elliott for setting the new tone. (Both were extraordinarily popular; students referred to Elliott familiarly, but presumably not to her face, as Aunt Het.) When another *Carolinian* writer returned to the subject of faculty-student relations a decade later, she blamed the students primarily for the distance that she perceived as remaining. The problem would never disappear entirely; the *Carolinian* noted in 1949 that departments were less likely than before to entertain their senior majors, something the students clearly appreciated.[34]

As always, the single women faculty (with fewer home ties and perhaps living nearer to campus) were most apt to carry on the old tradition of close social involvement with their students. It was they primarily (but not exclusively) who invited students to their homes for waffles on Sunday or took them to the Moravian Easter sunrise service in Winston-Salem. Occasionally these contacts led to close friendships. Students periodically invited faculty members to eat with them in the dining hall and to attend dormitory open-houses and other social events. During the war a few married male faculty members were even permitted to escort students to dances, well chaperoned. The degree of camaraderie of course depended on the individuals involved. One alumna from the '40s recalled student-faculty relations as friendly but formal. That was surely true of the residence hall teas at which the girls were required to wear hats, gloves, and heels.[35]

Elliott's concern with a lack of psychological counseling was well founded. When psychologist Key Barkley arrived on campus in 1931, there was no such help available. When it got out that he had had professional experience as a psychotherapist, students (in small numbers) began beating a path to his door. He gave them confidential advice and felt that he accomplished some good. At the same time he pushed for the hiring of a staff member assigned to that duty; in time an outside professional was hired to perform this service part-time, but not to Elliott's entire satisfaction. Meanwhile, when she got wind of Barkley's extracurricular counseling, she summoned him to her office for questioning. When he indicated that he had given advice on a variety of issues including homosexuality, she threw up her hands and leaned back in her chair crying, "Oh, my God!" She reported the interview to Jackson, leading to another summons. When Jackson failed to persuade Barkley to discontinue what he firmly believed was a necessary service, Jackson finally relented, observing, "Well, I guess as I've been counseling all these years without training, you ought to be allowed to counsel with training." Homosexuality, Barkley believed, was a response of normally charged girls to a lack of heterosexual outlets, and would "go poof" when those outlets appeared—presumably after graduation.[36]

* * *

Although student government changed little in form from the federal-style plan adopted in 1930, its spirit improved markedly under Elliott's program of responsible freedom. Students were given a greater voice in setting and enforcing parietal regulations, which accordingly were relaxed. The results were more favorable than unfavorable.[37] Like the counseling system, judicial enforcement was decentralized, with judicial boards in each hall responsible to a campus board.[38] Students, and board members in particular, took these responsibilities very seriously. The honor code had fallen into disregard by the late 1920s. Its rejuvenation began under Foust in early 1934, a year and a half before Elliott became dean; but like the counseling system, it subsequently flourished under her leadership. By 1942, students were pledging to report infractions by others as well as abiding by the code themselves. That year they asked and received permission to take exams without proctors on hand. In practice, the system worked very well in the academic arena, less well in the social. A student who would not think of cheating on an exam might readily omit to sign out on a date, indicating where she was going and with whom.[39]

Part of the work of student government continued to be done in mass meetings, held two or three times a year in Aycock Auditorium. As with chapel, attendance was mandatory and students sat by class in assigned seats.[40] Otherwise, the rate of participation in student government (as other activities) ebbed and flowed. Little over half of the students turned out for the 1938 SGA presidential election, and in 1941 writers to the *Carolinian* bemoaned what they described as a prevailing apathy and lack of school spirit. Only a week after the paper applied that criticism to the SGA elections, nine of the ten presidential candidates withdrew in favor of Mary Eppes, who won by default. That experience seems to have energized students into new activity and, a year later in 1942, Mary Jo Rendleman triumphed in a record turnout of 1,750—77 percent of the student body; for the remainder of the decade turnouts ran from 79 to 93 percent.[41] Nevertheless, succeeding generations of administrators and student leaders would deplore the willingness of most students to let a few take the lion's share of responsibilities.[42]

* * *

In 1937, a *Carolinian* writer found student regulations at WC to be quite comparable to those reported in a national campus survey. By general consensus, they were markedly relaxed from those of previous years—and those currently in force at Greensboro College and other nearby campuses.[43] Nevertheless, it still took several pages to enumerate them in the *Student Handbook*. One of the first reforms of the Jackson-Elliott regime was to institute a class cut system, permitting a limited number of absences from each class; hitherto there had been almost no excused cuts, to the perennial anger of students.[44]

The purpose of the social regulations was to recreate as nearly as possible the environment and limitations that girls had known at home. The college was still expected by society to act *in loco parentis*. For freshmen this meant no dates on weeknights, fewer weekends away, longer evening study hours, and an earlier lights-out than upperclassmen enjoyed. (This was a major reason why freshmen were housed separately.) Students signed themselves in and out for dates, an obligation honored frequently in the breach; first-floor windows were not unknown as points of ingress and egress. Trips downtown had to be made in groups of at least two. The major smoking war had been won in 1931, but there were still residual skirmishes over where the privilege might be allowed on campus. (Jackson reinforced his reputation for camaraderie by remarking, "When I remember that the mother of George Washington smoked a pipe and that the wife of Andrew Jackson smoked cigars, I think that you young ladies are not so very modern. You haven't even caught up.")[45] Alcohol consumption on campus was still a shipping offense, and not a serious problem.

The dress code was largely unwritten but well understood and seldom transgressed. It meant no hair curlers, gym suits, blue jeans, or even slacks on campus—unless covered by an overcoat. Until the '40s it meant no appearance downtown without hats, hose, and gloves. This apparel continued to be required at such campus events as residence hall teas. Apart from these occasions, appearance improved markedly on weekends, when men appeared in strength on campus. But even they had to meet certain standards; one alumna recalled her residence hall counselor turning away boys without neckties.[46] At one wartime event held to boost war bond sales, Harriet Elliott appeared as a student in a staged classroom skit wearing slacks—a gross violation of the regulations. It brought down the house.[47]

* * *

One of Elliott's greatest priorities was to provide acceptable social outlets on campus. Movies were shown every Saturday night in Aycock Auditorium.[48] Informal dances—illegal until 1929—were held seemingly every weekend. Each class and each of the old literary societies annually sponsored formal dances—eight of them by 1949.[49] The College Tavern (non-alcoholic) opened in 1935 in West dining hall, operated by home economics students; it was quickly filled to capacity, especially on weekends with students and their dates. So popular was it that a competing New Tavern was established in the early '40s in Students' Building under the same management. In 1949 the Soda Shop took their place with its own small building on College Avenue—the later Faculty Center. The YWCA Hut, at the end of College Avenue, remained a focus of extracurricular meetings as well as social occasions.[50]

Off-campus opportunities also increased in number, except as limited by Depression and war. Beginning in 1938, Greater University Day brought students from all three campuses together at either Chapel Hill or State. (WC would host such occasions too in the 1950s after construction of the student union.) These events featured the State-Carolina football game, a dance, and other festivities. Football tickets were also made available at WC on other weekends for a nominal price, and chartered buses lined up on Walker Avenue to take the students off to Chapel Hill or Raleigh.[51]

In Greensboro, the favorite student resort was Tate Street, still the eastern edge of campus. The commercial neighborhood clustering around the intersection with Walker Avenue was known generically as The Corner. Nearby were at least two restaurants, a drug store, a bakery, a grocery store, one or more gas stations, and beginning in 1939 or 1940 a movie theater. Some of these places employed boys on bikes to deliver sandwiches and drinks to the residence halls. (One restaurateur sometimes put bourbon in the cokes and sent them to campus if he knew the recipients well enough.) The number of establishments grew over the years, especially after the war when a post office and a sandwich shop named The Corner were added.[52]

On the other side of campus, at Spring Garden and Forest, the Yum Yum was perennially popular. In the '30s it added hot dogs to the growing number of ice cream flavors that had drawn students since 1921.[53] Near the western edge of town, where Walker Avenue met Market Street, was the Boar & Castle drive-in. Students also walked or rode the streetcar downtown to shop, see a movie, or have dinner at, perchance, the Lotus Chinese restaurant on Greene Street.[54]

For two months in the fall of 1941 the United States Army sent several thousand men to train in and near Greensboro. That was followed in 1943 by the establishment across town of a training camp, later designated as the Overseas Replacement Depot (ORD). There many other thousands of young men were sent for brief periods before being shipped overseas. It took no time at all for these men to find the Woman's College. Initially, the imaginations of WC administrators and faculty ran riot over the potentialities for disorder posed by these deployments. The first reaction was to raise the walls. Students in 1941 were in effect campused over weekends; at such times they could not even walk on Walker Avenue, and were advised to use the College Avenue bridge to reach classes. Male faculty members were drafted to patrol the campus, and shrubbery around the residence halls was pruned back to about three feet so as to limit untoward activity.

The sense of alarm soon abated. Before long the college was going out of its way to entertain soldiers, in limited numbers, at campus dances and other activities. They were heavily chaperoned by faculty members and even by army MPs called in by a nervous Jackson. In time, the college not only permitted but sent girls to comparable events on the base and downtown. Although some weekends saw more men on campus than women, experience showed that the severest precautions were unnecessary and they were soon relaxed. The faculty patrols continued but they never found much to report. Many or most girls looked forward to these visits; eligible males were in short supply. Others, perhaps with boyfriends in service elsewhere, felt pressured into performing this patriotic social duty. Individual soldiers were stationed so briefly in Greensboro that their contacts with students were by necessity very temporary.[55]

* * *

Following earlier patterns, three-quarters of the 1,964 students who responded to a religious affiliation survey in 1939–40 listed themselves as Methodist, Baptist, or Presbyterian; Episcopalians were a strong fourth. There were 47 Jews and 35 Catholics.[56] By 1932 the four leading denominations each had a campus representative working with students. Nationally, such representatives largely replaced the YWCA secretaries who had orchestrated campus religious activity until the '20s.[57] At the college, after eight years without a YWCA secretary, Foust in 1932 hired Lucy Crisp in that capacity. Under Jackson she and her successors served as campus directors of religious activities, working with the denominational representatives but concerned with all of the students.[58]

In 1934 Jackson initiated a series of visiting religious speakers which he called the University Sermons. Although they were generally of high quality, student attendance was embarrassingly low—about 100 students, usually—and the series was on the verge of abandonment when the four student classes picked it up as class projects. Under their sponsorship it endured for at least a decade. Each of the four speakers in a given year remained for three days, meeting with and speaking to students.[59]

One of their assignments was chapel service. Mandatory half-hour chapel services continued to be held at noon on Tuesdays and Fridays until 1936, when they were confined to Tuesdays and rechristened as convocations or assemblies.[60] Until then, the services evoked perennial if not perpetual editorial comment in the *Carolinian*. Some editorials criticized the programs that were offered but a majority assailed the students for poor deportment. (Often they could not hear; an amplifying system rectified that problem in 1939.) In defending mandatory services Jackson recurred to the argument of his predecessors: apart from the infrequent SGA mass meetings, these were the only opportunities to unify the student body by bringing them all together. Many students accepted that argument but still pushed (successfully) for a limited number of cuts, as they had gotten in the classroom.[61]

The programs continued to be mixed, some of them religious and others not. Student opinion rather favored the non-religious topics. Speakers included the governor, high university officials, and such celebrities as Eleanor Roosevelt (Harriet Elliott's friend) as well as eminent clerics. One regular speaker was Charlotte Hawkins Brown, the founder and leader of Palmer Institute, a preparatory school for blacks in nearby Sedalia.[62]

* * *

Although the college maintained its official commitment to Service and students were still reminded of it, one gets the impression that the pervasive growth of secularism around them diluted that message much as it did the chapel services. Depression and war added mightily to the outside distractions.[63] That the service impulse had not died out was evidenced in 1948 when (reportedly after twelve years of effort) students organized the Golden Chain fraternity, honoring campus service. Their hope to form a chapter of the national Mortar Board fraternity was never realized, but Golden Chain continues on campus to the present day.[64]

Service sometimes took the form of social or political activism. The transcendent off-campus student issue in the 1930s was the peace movement. Spurred by the rise of aggressive foreign dictatorships and disillusion over the results of World War I, the peace movement became what two scholars call the first student mass movement in American history.[65] Although they remark that most campuses were not affected, WC was. Harriet Elliott had supported a similar movement back in the '20s. With Jackson's blessing and hers, 1,200 students and over 100 faculty participated in a nationwide peace strike on April 22, 1936.[66] The movement gradually subsided thereafter and evaporated altogether with Pearl Harbor.

Students soon turned to a different issue of greater immediate relevance to them as southerners: race relations. Wilmina Rowland, who arrived in 1937 as campus religious activities director, was cut from the same cloth as Lois McDonald, the YWCA secretary who had introduced girls to social activism in the early '20s. Rowland turned immediately to interracial activities. Students began taking sociology courses on race relations and the YWCA chapter became active again in behalf of racial understanding. Rowland invited to campus black leaders who spoke and ate meals with students; the latter activity was particularly perilous in the segregation era.[67] In 1946, after Rowland's departure, several students helped operate a kindergarten for neighboring black children at the Episcopalian St. Mary's House, just off campus, but Jackson persuaded them to discontinue the operation when neighbors complained.[68]

Jackson was far more sympathetic than Foust to the claims of blacks for greater equality. He continued to preside at meetings of the Guilford County interracial commission; as a native Georgian, he said he felt relatively free to express egalitarian views without being run out of town as a Communist. But he faced the same legal and political constraints as Foust in leading the college; it could not appear too far in advance of public opinion. Student activists regarded him as hopelessly conservative and felt, correctly, that they were scaring him to death. Only after meditation did Jackson in 1935 give his approval to singer Marian Anderson performing in Aycock Auditorium.[69]

A more difficult question arose when blacks asked to attend Civic Music Association concerts in Aycock. Particularly interested was Charlotte Hawkins Brown of the nearby Palmer Institute, who made music an important part of her school's curriculum. When she asked in 1935 for permission to buy fifty tickets for her students, Jackson regarded the matter as sensitive enough to consult the advisory committee and then request a personal conference with her before answering. After the conference he wrote offering her a block of seats at one side of the mezzanine, or lower balcony. After a couple weeks of meditation and consultation herself, Brown politely declined the offer. She recognized that any appearance by her students would have to be segregated under state law, but as she had initiated the request she did not want fellow blacks to conclude that she had requested segregation.

Jackson's response indicated that they understood each other perfectly, and equally regretted the positions they were in. Two years later Brown swallowed her pride and asked for fifty tickets on the terms Jackson had previously offered. She declared her continuing hatred for segregation but concluded that the musical opportunities these concerts brought to her students were worth the sacrifice to their pride and hers; she could not afford to send them to New York. Brown absolved Jackson and the WC faculty of any responsibility for segregation, but could not forbear mentioning that hundreds of whites from WC and other local colleges freely attended concerts at her Palmer Institute chapel where segregation was not observed.[70] The subsequent appearance of blacks in Aycock (where there were no segregated washrooms) caused some adverse comment in the press and therefore great misgivings on campus. The general disposition thereafter seems to have been to hold these occasions to a minimum.[71]

When Jackson refused to rescind an interracial meeting scheduled without his knowledge in the Alumnae House in 1947, he felt obliged to justify himself to the university administration and trustees. Rather chastened by the experience, he directed campus personnel in future to clear all such invitations with him in advance. When an interracial student group asked to meet on campus in 1949, he refused, citing past criticism from trustees and others.[72] He did organize in 1948 a faculty committee on race relations to deal with this issue that seemed to recur with increasing frequency.[73]

In 1949 a student confessed in a creative writing class paper that she had developed a romantic attachment with a fellow dining hall employee—a black male student from A&T College across town. Her instructor reported it to campus authorities, no doubt Dean Katherine Taylor and perhaps Jackson as well. They advised her to drop out of school at the end of the year, promising in return not to report the reason. She did so.[74]

Meanwhile, on a different key, World War II channeled students into patriotic activity reminiscent of the first war a generation earlier. A few followed Katherine Taylor (then a French teacher) into the female military services. Most remained in school but devoted extracurricular time to knitting clothing, rolling bandages, and contributing money to such causes as Bundles for Britain and Japanese-American victims of the West Coast relocation program. Some regularly visited the ORD base hospital to cheer up sick and wounded servicemen. Many gave and raised money for war bond drives. As in earlier war and depression years, students did campus grounds work and all of them helped out in the dining hall. Much of this activity was orchestrated by a campus War Service League.[75]

* * *

The former literary societies had already lost most of their functions to special-interest clubs and other college agencies. Students were still assigned to the societies, pretty much by lot. They had grown so large (even with division and subdivision) that *esprit de corps* was difficult to maintain. They were reduced primarily to sponsoring annual dances and electing student marshals. Students called increasingly for their abolition but tradition kept them alive until 1953.[76] After a lapse of fifty years alumnae from this period sometimes could not recall which society they had belonged to.

The societies' greatest contribution to college history in these years may have been the evolution of freshman hazing into Rat Day. Even limited to one day, hazing was always apt to get out of hand, leading to periodic calls for reform from both administrators and the *Carolinian.*[77] In 1940, when the name Rat Day may first have come into use, upperclassmen still required freshmen to perform a variety of housekeeping tasks that now included scrubbing the McIver statue with toothbrushes. There were other, more embarrassing assignments: writing ardent love letters to males they may or may not have known; salaaming to upperclassmen while shouting, "Praise Allah!"; stopping automobiles to get drivers' autographs; or standing on a tabletop while reading aloud Dorothy Dix's newspaper advice to the lovelorn. By 1943 freshmen were required, on bended knee, to propose marriage to selected male faculty members and visiting soldiers. Over the years male faculty members came to regard these events as unavoidable rites of passage for themselves.[78]

* * *

This generation of students passed on virtually all of the traditions they had inherited from the 1920s, with the notable exception of Park Night, which expired in 1935. Seniors and sophomores, juniors and freshmen still regarded each other as sister classes; the juniors and freshmen still performed their symbolic wedding ceremony each fall.[79] Sophomores still looked forward to buying their distinctively colored class jackets, which they wore for the remainder of their college careers.[80] At the last mass meeting of the year, the seniors ceremonially vacated their privileged seats in the first rows of the auditorium while singing their class song, and each of the other classes moved into the seats just left by their predecessors; for the freshmen that meant moving downstairs from the balcony.[81] As commencement approached, the sophomores continued to pick thousands of daisies in the countryside and fashion them into chains through which the graduating seniors marched to the Class Day ceremonies.[82] Commencement ceremonies were held in Aycock Auditorium. The governor usually attended, marched in the academic procession, and handed out the diplomas.[83]

* * *

One student institution that experienced a transformation in these years was the Junior Shop. In 1920 or earlier, President Foust gave the junior class the privilege of operating a small shop on campus for the sale of sundries to the students. It was located at different times in the Students' Building and the basement of the Administration Building. The juniors used its proceeds to finance class projects, particularly the junior-senior banquet—later dance. They started out selling such items as camera film, hair nets, picture postcards, memory books, and college rings. Over the years the inventory multiplied along with the student clientele. In 1931 the shop installed tables and chairs and was selling sandwiches and cold drinks. By the mid-1940s it was jammed beyond capacity and turning an annual profit of up to $12,000. This was more money than the junior class needed—or so Jackson argued—and the college took over the operation itself in 1945. Renamed the Soda Shop, it moved in 1949 into a new building on College Avenue where Little Guilford (the 1895 infirmary) had just been demolished to make room for it. A few years later it moved into the new student union. Under college auspices profits from the shop were used to finance student scholarships.[84]

* * *

The *Carolinian*, *Pine Needles*, and *Coraddi*—the student newspaper, yearbook, and literary magazine that evolved from the *State Normal Magazine* in 1919 and 1920—all continued publication through these years. During the '30s *Coraddi* came to be written and edited entirely by students, and in 1938 was one of three publications receiving the national Scholastic Press Association's highest rating. In the '40s *Coraddi* benefited from the emerging writing program in the English department and became the mouthpiece for the campus's annual Arts Forum. It published a number of student writers from WC and other institutions who were then unknown but became quite famous in later years, among them Heather Ross Miller, Robert Agee, James Dickey, Flannery O'Connor, Doris Betts, and Sylvia Wilkinson.[85]

* * *

Intramural athletics continued to thrive for a time under the direction of the student Athletic Association. Competition heretofore had been primarily between classes. In 1933 the annual spring Field Day was expanded into Sports Day, with competition now between the four student societies, giving them an additional lease on life.[86]

The program underwent a major change in 1941, when the Athletic Association became the Recreation Association. This shift had national origins and signified a new campaign to recruit girls whose recreational interests lay outside of athletics. Thus broadened, the recreational program operated through four new leagues (instead of the societies) based on the residence halls and named for four popular campus figures who had little if any connection with sports: Harriet Elliott, Louise Alexander, Charles W. Phillips, and the ubiquitous Key L. Barkley. Under these new auspices several hundred students participated each year in the culminating activity that was still called Sports Day. In 1943 it featured thirty different activities, ranging from softball and tennis to hopscotch and bridge— striking testimony to the push for inclusiveness. The motto was "A game for every girl and a girl for every game."[87] For those truly athletically inclined, there was also Gym Day, held annually in March; but even it included different forms of dancing.[88]

The expansion of organized recreational activity accompanied (if it was not caused by) a national decline of women's interest in athletics.[89] Conforming to this trend, the *Carolinian*, which had focused heavily on intramural sports into the 1940s, cut back its coverage markedly over the next decade or so. Boredom with sports may have derived from a growing preoccupation with femininity in these years; but it was surely attributable as well to the widespread exclusion of women from competitive intercollegiate athletics. College girls increasingly protested these restrictions, and as interest in intramurals began to flag in the mid-1940s some institutions experimented with low-key intercollegiate matches. Until then intercollegiate Play Days at WC had emphasized competition between mixed teams. In March 1944, however, the *Carolinian* was happy to report victories by the WC basketball team over teams from Guilford and Greensboro Colleges at the recent Winter Sports Play Day in Rosenthal Gym. In the next few years intercollegiate competition extended to field hockey, golf, and perhaps other sports. Except for individual golfers who began to compete nationally it was apparently confined to teams within the state.[90]

* * *

Teaching remained the primary occupation for alumnae—60 percent in 1941.[91] The Depression ended many of the previous alternatives; indeed it ended many teaching jobs. World War II, on the other hand, ushered in a short-term bonanza for women job-seekers; the number of alumnae teachers fell below half in 1946 for perhaps the first time. Yet opportunities outside of teaching receded as the veterans returned. Between 1948 and 1952, the number of graduating seniors qualifying for teacher certification climbed back from 47 percent to 74 percent.[92] One lasting result of the war nationally was a reduction in the bias against married women working outside the home. Henceforth marriage did not end as many teaching and other jobs as it had in previous years.[93]

* * *

The Alumnae Association suffered multiple stresses during the 1930s and '40s. They arose first from differences over the design of the Alumnae House, then over its uses. The latter mainly involved how far it should be opened to students and the general public. In the absence of a student union, student organizations took up quarters there freely but Alumnae Secretary Clara Byrd was fearful of parties leading to spilled drinks and feet on the new furniture.[94] Well before the building's 1937 dedication these differences ripened into a personal and factional controversy that continued off and on for over a decade. Byrd was accused, with reason, of being domineering and inflexible, and as early as 1933 a number of articulate opponents including Laura Weill Cone and Gladys Avery Tillett began efforts to remove her from office. On the other hand, Byrd's unquestioned abilities and dedication continued for years to win her the support of many—probably most—active alumnae. The controversy became so endless and petty that even so ardent a feminist as Harriet Elliott referred to them privately as mere "quarrels of women."[95]

Neither Foust nor Jackson was party to the dispute and like Elliott they tried hard to stay clear of it. But it was a matter of legitimate concern. As on most campuses, the Alumnae Association bore an ambivalent relationship to the institution; it was at once an autonomous organization of the alumnae and a branch of the college. In 1935 the college continued to pay the salaries of Byrd and a secretary, while the association paid for office and travel expenses and published the *Alumnae News* out of its annual dues revenue. That amounted to only $1,300 in 1934–35, a year when dues were uncommonly hard to collect. In 1940 there were only 581 paid members out of a potential total of 19,000 living persons who had attended the school. That membership nevertheless represented about 10 percent of those living who had finished four years and graduated —close to the southern if not national average.[96]

Jackson was sufficiently concerned about the college-alumnae relationship to make a trip in 1936 to the Florida State College for Women to investigate its alumnae organization and operations.[97] In 1939, amidst the continuing factional controversy, he took the issue to the university trustees. On his recommendation they ruled that the Alumnae Association be confirmed in its power to select its executive secretary, but that she no longer be considered a member of the college faculty. The trustees retained the right to ratify the selection and the college continued to pay most of the association's expenses. The college's share in 1946–47 was about $8,700.[98] The question of ultimate authority over the association and its secretary was left unresolved.

The alumnae warfare abated in the mid-'40s and Clara Byrd indicated that she would step down as soon as retirement benefits became available in 1947.[99] Her decision had not been publicized in advance and the new association president, Betty Brown Jester, was stunned to learn that she had inherited both the presidency and the job of interim executive secretary. Jester, '31, had spent twenty years on campus as manager of the bookstore and was well aware of the preceding turmoil. She performed so well that the alumnae board elected her to replace Byrd on a continuing basis and she resigned the presidency.[100] Under Jester's management the factionalism disappeared and the Alumnae Association thrived. In 1949 she reported the existence of 62 chapters, 14 of them outside the state. Active membership in 1950 exceeded 2,600.[101] Jester was to have serious problems in a few years, but they would not be with her fellow alumnae.

Charles Duncan McIver, President, 1892–1906

The Faculty in 1893

First row, l. to r.: Viola Boddie (Latin), Florence Stone (French). *Second row*: Edith A. McIntyre (Domestic Science), Mary Petty (Science), Anna M. Gove (physician), McIver, Lucy H. Robertson (History and Reading). *Third row*: Edward J. Forney (Commercial Department), Maude Broadaway (Physical Culture), James Y. Joyner (English and Mathematics), Melville V. Fort (Industrial Arts), Philander P. Claxton (Pedagogy and German). *Fourth row*: Sue May Kirkland (Lady Principal), Dixie Lee Bryant (Science), Gertrude Mendenhall (Mathematics). *Absent*: Clarence R. Brown (Music).

Presidents and Chancellors

Julius I. Foust,
1906–1934

Walter C. Jackson,
1934–1950

Edward Kidder Graham,
1950–1956

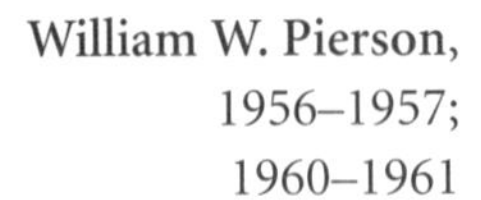

William W. Pierson,
1956–1957;
1960–1961

Presidents and Chancellors

Gordon Blackwell,
1957–1960

Otis Singletary,
1961–1966

Presidents and Chancellors

James S. Ferguson,
1966–1979

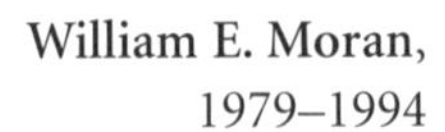

William E. Moran,
1979–1994

Aerial Views of Campus

1927

1995

"Ah, Ma Petite! Eeet Weel Last Another Two Years!"

William Sanders, *Greensboro Daily News*

Underfunding: The Perennial Issue - 1959
(Actually, 1959 was a very good year for the college.)

DEDICATED TO

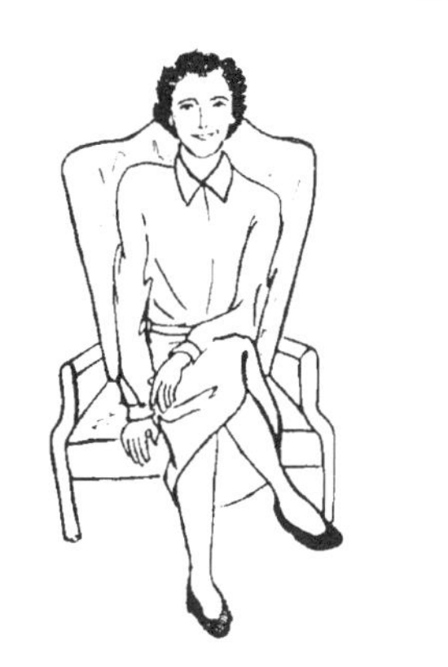

and

Trilby Boerner and Norma Cofer,
Oh College Dear, To You

Top: **Chancellor Jackson** and **Dean Katherine Taylor**, on his retirement in 1950. *Bottom*: **Dean Taylor and Chancellor Graham**, caricatured in 1953.

Other Administrators Who Made Their Marks

Harriet Elliott,
Dean of Students

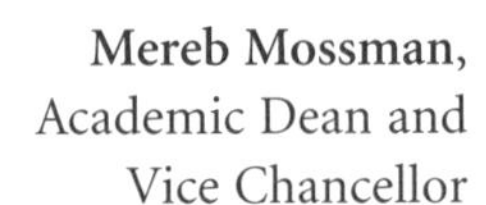

Mereb Mossman,
Academic Dean and
Vice Chancellor

Stanley Jones,
Academic Vice Chancellor

Other Administrators Who Made Their Marks

James Allen,
Dean and Vice Chancellor
for Student Affairs

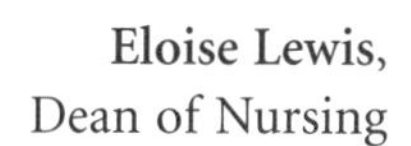

Eloise Lewis,
Dean of Nursing

Robert Miller,
Dean of Arts and Sciences

Top: The McIver Statue on Founder's Day (*left*) and at Halloween (*right*).
Bottom: The Rock

Part V
Woman's College, 1950–1963

Chapter 15

Administration: The Revolving Door

Although the Jackson period had been marked by depression, war, and seemingly serious threats to the college's future, many faculty and alumnae came to look back on it as a time of stability, democracy, and general contentment. Despite the years of administrative turbulence that followed, some would even extend the reputed Golden Age to the early 1960s when coeducation and university status ended the old order forever. In 1950, however, most of the college community was ready to move on with new policies under new leadership. Jackson himself had been trying to retire for two years.

As early as Julius Foust's retirement in 1934, a few women suggested that the time had come for the Woman's College to be headed by a woman. Some of them approached Harriet Elliott, who demurred in favor of Jackson, her longtime ally. But she too felt that after Jackson it might be time for a woman—a younger one than she.[1] When Jackson announced his desire to step down in 1948, alumnae groups recommended a female successor if possible. President Frank Graham was ready to go along—but not the students. They voted 1,576 to 78 by secret ballot in favor of a male chancellor; men carried more weight politically, they explained. When Jackson did finally step down in 1950, some alumnae continued to hope for a woman chancellor. The name of Elliott's successor, Dean Katherine Taylor, was mentioned.[2] It was not to be.

The succession that did occur could hardly have brought a more dramatic change. The courtly, grandfatherly, almost universally beloved Jackson gave way to a brash young man who proceeded almost immediately to split the college down the middle and provoke animosities that survived for a generation. Edward Kidder Graham, Jr., was himself the son of a young and popular University of North Carolina president who had died in the devastating influenza epidemic of 1918. He was also a cousin of Frank Porter Graham. The young Graham had already lost his mother and was only seven years old when his father died. Formally adopted by the university board of trustees, he was raised by a maternal aunt and uncle in Chapel Hill and graduated from the university in 1933. He received a Ph.D. in history from Cornell University in 1938 and stayed on as assistant to the president and later secretary of the university. In 1947 he moved to Washington University in St. Louis, becoming dean of the faculties in 1948.[3] Thirty-nine years old in 1950, bright, seemingly personable, and possessed of an ideal family and professional pedigree, Graham appeared ideally suited to lead the Woman's College into the postwar era. So believed the alumnae, faculty, and trustee committees who reviewed his candidacy.

Harold W. Dodds, the former president of Princeton University, wrote a wise book on academic presidents not long after Graham's time at WC. Speaking of succession, he said the most difficult president to follow is one who, long in service, has become the idol of his constituents. The successor of such a man should treat his memory respectfully and be ready for a period of testing. New presidents should be innovators, continued Dodds, but recognize that successful leadership consists not only in advancing new ideas but in getting them accepted. "Healthy turmoil" may generate new ideas but it can degenerate into chaos. The president who wants to succeed stops short of precipitating open rebellion.[4]

Graham violated these maxims, spectacularly. He concluded that his predecessor had long since passed his prime and that many of the older faculty were also over the hill. These views got out. Jackson continued on campus for two years, teaching his popular course on American biography. But reportedly feeling affronted by Graham on a number of occasions, he resigned abruptly in 1952. Graham bent over backward thereafter to appease Jackson, with the college awarding him an honorary degree in 1955. He died in 1957.[5]

Some of Graham's policies were progressive and won general approval. It was his management style and personal behavior that engendered hostility. Where Jackson had been too lax in observing bureaucratic routines, Graham observed them to a fault. He thought Jackson had ceded too much power to the faculty advisory committee, particularly in personnel matters. Increasingly he bypassed and then supplanted the committee. He was accused of bringing in new deans and department heads without approval of the faculties involved.[6] In effect, Graham was returning to the early management style of Julius Foust, and no leader is more hated or feared than one who threatens liberties previously granted.[7] Most important, perhaps, in his personal relationships he had a genius for antagonizing people unnecessarily, both by word and deed.

Graham hit the ground running. He redoubled Jackson's efforts to upgrade the scholarly level of the faculty. In the process he was quoted in the fall of 1950 as saying that the existing faculty contained a good deal of dead wood who needed clearing out. He then proceeded unilaterally to codify the informal tenure system that Jackson had conducted partly by word of mouth. The purpose was laudable, even necessary, but his pronouncements were couched in authoritarian terms that seemed to confirm the worst faculty fears. (In practice, Graham adhered to the same national AAUP guidelines that Jackson had followed; his innovation lay mainly in reducing it all to writing.)[8] He also antagonized faculty with a schoolmasterish notice requiring them to get his permission if they planned to be absent from class; there was no indication that absenteeism had been a problem.[9]

The tenure regulations exhibited one of the most substantial criticisms of Graham—that he failed to consult adequately with the faculty before making decisions. (Of course, Jackson had set a very high standard in that regard.) Soon after his arrival he began meeting regularly with the deans and department heads, largely substituting them for the elected advisory committee. And by 1954 he felt so uncomfortable with many of the department heads that he eliminated them too from his administrative council.

Graham soon discovered that the advisory committee was the focal point of faculty opposition to his leadership. Early in 1951 he consulted it about creating an academic deanship and appointing sociology professor Mereb Mossman. The position was not entirely new to the college; Foust had held a comparable post under McIver, and both Jackson and W.C. Smith under Foust. There had been talk of appointing an academic dean in the 1940s. But the committee, already reflecting distrust of Graham, withheld its approval. It objected both to the creation of a buffer between him and the faculty and to placing Mossman in that position. The committee recognized her abilities and had no objection to her serving as his administrative assistant but it noted that she lacked the doctorate, which seemed requisite for an academic dean at a time when the college was increasing its emphasis on faculty scholarship. Graham's response was to poll the faculty. When it voted by secret ballot 93 to 44 to sustain him he went ahead to create the position of dean of instruction and named Mossman to fill it. At the same time he promoted Katherine Taylor from dean of women to dean of students with additional responsibilities.[10] In 1955 a new faculty instrument of government or constitution replaced the advisory committee with an elected academic policies committee over which Graham himself presided.[11]

* * *

The issue that generated the greatest furor and precipitated Graham's eventual downfall was his proposal to reform the general education requirements. "General education" had been the leading focus of curricular attention around the country since 1945, when a Harvard faculty committee issued a widely publicized report, *General Education in a Free Society*. It called for the substitution of broad interdisciplinary liberal arts courses for the introductory departmental courses that had long filled college students' first two years. Harvard adopted the plan by stages and it was in full operation in 1951. Other institutions adopted variations of it. Attractive in principle, interdisciplinary courses proved exceedingly hard to implement or sustain. They required faculty members who were trained as specialists in their own fields to become generalists, cooperating systematically with specialists from other fields. Many found this not only difficult but professionally unrewarding at a time when knowledge was proliferating and scholarship in every field was becoming more and more specialized. One achieved promotion and tenure through research and publication much more than through interdisciplinary teaching assignments. Harvard was among the first to find that truly interdisciplinary instruction faced an uphill climb.[12]

Woman's College had taken up the issue by the spring of 1950 —under Jackson—with Mereb Mossman heading an exploratory faculty committee. (It was this assignment that put her on the road to the academic deanship under Graham.) Apart from their challenge to specialization, interdisciplinary courses everywhere threatened the vested interest of each department in its own introductory courses and the student clientele it was hoped they attracted. Romance languages head W.S. Barney quoted the late Viola Boddie about the danger of the big fishes devouring the little fishes whenever departments were asked to work in tandem.[13]

Graham made general education one of his first orders of business. He created a new steering committee and wisely retained Mossman as its chairman. The committee continued in operation for three years, garnering a $3,000 Carnegie Foundation grant in 1951. Outside experts like Harvard's David Owen were brought in as consultants. Nearly half of the faculty were drawn into the study as members of subcommittees.[14]

At first all went well. "It would take a genius to fumble this," Graham boasted to a friend in 1951; "I'm no genius."[15] He proved wrong on the first count. The study dragged on until late in 1953, when general agreement on principles finally brought up the question of implementation—creating actual interdisciplinary courses. Under Jackson the curriculum committee, composed of a representative from each department, had had exclusive power to pass on new courses. Finding little enthusiasm on that committee for interdisciplinary courses, Graham decided to bypass it using one appointed by himself and composed of his supporters. This brought a major confrontation in January 1954 when the faculty approved 88 to 63 a resolution upholding the curriculum committee's sole right to make course recommendations unless otherwise directed by the faculty.[16]

Although UNC President Gordon Gray upheld Graham,[17] new course proposals were not forthcoming and Graham chose not to press the matter.[18] Interdisciplinary courses were already going out of fashion nationally and the issue was losing its edge. (Like most curricular innovations they would come back another day.) He later confided to a faculty member that he had never been especially committed to general education.[19] Rather, he had used a currently popular issue to stamp himself as an innovator. And like many administrators—especially new ones—he saw self-study as a beneficial exercise both for the faculty and himself; the specific impetus was secondary.[20] In this case the experiment backfired with severe consequences for all concerned. The January vote proved to be the beginning of Graham's long downward slide.

* * *

General education receded from view but controversy flared as never before, with Graham himself now the focal point. Local newspapers quickly caught wind of the dispute and pursued it through public statements and surreptitious leaks from both sides.[21] Administrators, faculty, staff, and ultimately students avidly opened the papers each day to see who had just said what about whom. A growing majority of the faculty opposed Graham but a substantial minority remained supportive. Those who sought neutrality found it increasingly difficult. In general, junior faculty were most likely to see Graham as a welcome innovator. Certain departments, notably physical education, tended to side with him while others, particularly in the arts and sciences, did not. But there were many exceptions. Members of the two factions ate lunch at separate tables in the home ec cafeteria. Personal animosities became so deep that some people took them to their graves. A faculty daughter, Janice Hooke Moore, recalled that her father, curriculum committee chairman Malcolm Hooke, and his erstwhile close friend Marc Friedlaender in English were never reconciled after the latter supported Graham. The same was true of Friedlaender and poet Randall Jarrell in the same department.[22]

From the beginning the split was more personal than policy-driven. The general education debate had clearly evoked academic provincialism and turf warfare. But many of Graham's opponents claimed convincingly to support general education reform at the same time they were repulsed by his tactics and, most of all, his abrasive personality. Graham brought an air of informality that offended some older faculty members. He called them by their first names—unprecedented in this locale. He smoked his pipe in faculty meetings. He slouched in his chair, sometimes with his legs over the arms and sometimes on the table or atop his desk. More disturbing were his arrogance, sarcasm, and open disdain for those who did not agree with him. (Some attributed his cockiness to his short stature and hard childhood.) Graham did possess the necessary social graces; he could be charming, but these traits were not always in requisition. He could socialize amiably with faculty members of an evening, then turn on them the next morning. He took to applying sarcastic nicknames and characterizations behind the backs of faculty members, who quickly learned of them. Sometimes he spoke in this vein to students. Even supporters found these habits hard to take.

Additional charges of excessive drinking and womanizing are harder to substantiate. Almost from the beginning Graham's chief academic confidante was not Mossman, who possessed ample judgment and similar academic views but a sober personal demeanor wholly unlike Graham's; rather it was the quick, personable, and attractive Katherine Taylor. They became so close, in fact, with Graham paying frequent late afternoon visits to Taylor's campus home for drinks and after-hours gossip that rumors got afloat of an extramarital affair. (Elizabeth McFadyen Graham was a gracious lady, slightly older than her husband and very popular with the faculty; they had three children.) These cocktail-hour visits were likely chaperoned; Taylor shared her house with counselor, later Elliott Hall director Elvira Prondecki. It was Prondecki whom Graham married after divorcing his wife several years after leaving campus. But Taylor's reputation suffered, probably unjustly, in this politically charged atmosphere and for many years afterward.[23]

* * *

Frank Porter Graham left the UNC presidency in 1949 for the United States Senate, to be succeeded early in 1950 by Gordon Gray. The son of an R.J. Reynolds Tobacco Company executive, Gray was a lawyer and businessman who had most recently served as Harry Truman's secretary of the army. Unlike the people-oriented Frank Graham, Gray was an efficiency expert, meticulous to a fault. He brought considerable order to university administration, but as a disciplinarian accustomed to the military chain of command he generated fear where "Dr. Frank" had inspired something akin to worship. Gray found little satisfaction in the job and decided in 1955 to leave it.[24]

Meanwhile, it was Gray who appointed Edward Kidder Graham chancellor of the Woman's College. The younger Graham cultivated Gray and they got along well. When Graham found himself confronted by a fractious faculty, Gray unhesitatingly came to his aid. He visited campus in February 1954, a month after the pivotal vote on general education, and spoke to the faculty. Conceding that blame for the situation likely rested with both sides, he nevertheless advised faculty members in only slightly muted terms to shape up or ship out. The conflict was clearly so deep, however, that Gray returned early in March for two days of conferences with faculty members who wished to see him. There were so many that he had to come back later for a third day.[25]

University administrators and trustees were baffled. Their first inclination was to support the chancellor, but evidence kept arriving from credible sources that in large measure he had brought his troubles on himself. Perhaps the best appraisal came from Virginia Terrell Lathrop—alumna, former head of the campus news bureau, and now a university trustee. Admiring Graham's mental endowments and ideas, she nevertheless doubted from her own acquaintance with him whether he possessed the "humility and kindness" requisite to carry them out. His "immature, impulsive, self-confident manner" tended to antagonize people. "Most often Ed's troubles have arisen not from what he did but from the way he did it.... He has a wonderful wife who has been an asset to him on the campus, and from whom he could learn much in relationships with people." Lathrop considered talking to him about these problems, but "it is difficult to talk with Ed. He doesn't listen well." When they did talk later the main effect was to drive her unreservedly into the opposition camp.[26]

Although the decibel level fell off in the spring of 1954, the controversy would not die. Faculty members met in pro- and anti-Graham caucuses before elections and other important votes.[27] (The antis continued to meet in the home ec cafeteria. When its management, firmly in the Graham camp, arranged the tables to permit only four persons to eat together, the antis sometimes pushed tables back together and sometimes went elsewhere.)[28] Organization worked; the antis kept control of the important elective committees.[29] Rather like a brushfire, the conflagration flared up in certain quarters while remaining subdued in others. Members of the music faculty divided into hostile factions following the sudden death of Dean Hugh Altvater in 1952 and his replacement after a lapse of two years by G. Welton Marquis, who quickly established himself as a Graham in miniature. The quarrel had roots in his curricular and personnel policies—he summarily demoted veteran choral director George Thompson and student orchestra conductor George Dickieson, who also led the Greensboro Orchestra—but it also had ties to the larger college-wide factionalism.[30] Infighting appeared as well in home economics, biology, and English. In the last case, W. Raymond Taylor, who had built the drama program since 1921, was replaced by a newcomer and relegated to teaching speech and English until his retirement in 1960. Graham was also blamed for killing off the Burnsville fine arts school in the mountains.[31] These actions and accusations generated tremendous bitterness within the faculty.

Graham continued to get along famously with Deans Taylor, Marquis, and Katherine Roberts of home economics who offered unquestioning support. But by the spring of 1955 he had turned his sarcasm on Mereb Mossman, who was trying with diminishing success to balance her loyalties to him and the faculty. In March the two agreed, at whose instigation is not clear, that she would step down as dean of instruction at the end of the 1955–56 academic year, more than a year hence. Ever-dutiful, Mossman absorbed his sallies and seems never to have shared her frustrations with others. But by December they were hardly on speaking terms.[32]

* * *

One of Graham's strongest constituencies was the student body. Rather like the junior faculty, students welcomed his new ideas and his breezy style. They had no vested interest to protect, no rebellion to mount—the era of student rebellion was still a decade away. They did not threaten him and were never treated to his sarcasm. Without in any sense repudiating Jackson (to whose class they continued to flock) students identified readily with Graham and he with them. To use a later term, he was cool. They applauded his creation in 1951 of a student committee to meet with him regularly on matters of common interest. The *Carolinian* in 1952 carried an open letter from three students (claiming to speak for all) praising him for his availability and honesty with them whenever they wanted a hearing. If they did "takeoffs" on his energetic style, these were intended as a form of applause.[33]

Faculty members for the most part avoided discussing with students the growing conflict over Graham. Until it became public knowledge after the faculty vote in January 1954, most students knew little or nothing about it. Their initial reaction was to rally behind the chancellor. The student legislature in February gave him a unanimous vote of confidence.[34] The *Carolinian* in an editorial entitled "The Rotten Road Downhill" deplored the introduction of personalities into the controversy and praised Graham for his refusal publicly to answer in kind. Thereafter the paper avoided the conflict like a hot potato except occasionally to deplore its continuation.[35] In May 1956, however, shortly before its outcome was announced, incoming SGA President Sadye Dunn pushed through the legislature a resolution commending Graham for his administrative leadership and judgment. It received 37 votes to 4 opposed and 13 abstentions.[36]

* * *

Student support followed Graham into a wholly different kind of controversy that garnered the college a brief notoriety off campus and even nationally. *Coraddi*, the student literary magazine, published in its Fall 1954 issue a pen and ink drawing— a nearly frontal view—of a nude male. Graham appears to have waited for the student legislature to react first. When it voted narrowly to reprimand the *Coraddi* staff, then abruptly reversed itself, he quickly stepped in with a formal censure of his own, charging the staff with irresponsible behavior. The *Carolinian* backed the chancellor, as did an informal student poll, but the *Coraddi* staff protested the censure by resigning in a body. So did novelist Lettie Hamlett Rogers of the English department who resigned from the faculty. A dozen or so faculty members, including several in English and art, wrote Graham formally protesting his action. On the other hand, the trustees' visiting committee and others off campus supported him for his refusal to tolerate what one of them called a simple case of indecent exposure.[37]

Some faculty members thought that Graham chose to humiliate the students publicly, instead of delivering a closed-door lecture, in order to pander to off-campus critics.[38] He himself admitted to no second thoughts. Unhappiness about the issue, he wrote privately a month later, was limited pretty much to "excitable aesthetes and a few other [absolutist] disciples of freedom.... So be it." He regretted that circumstances had forced him to take a position seemingly opposed to free speech, but he noted that no one had been punished or any prior censorship imposed on the student press.[39] Lee Hall, the student who drew the picture, graduated and in time became president of the Rhode Island School of Design.[40]

* * *

A substantial proportion of the faculty as well as alumnae leaders reached the conclusion in 1955 that the college would never prosper until Graham departed. Accordingly, alumnae president and UNC trustee Emily Harris Preyer with others prevailed on the trustees' visiting committee to investigate Graham's leadership as the centerpiece of its annual campus inspection in October. When the committee, chaired by Robert M. Hanes of Winston-Salem, arrived it found a long list of faculty members and others ready if not eager to talk with it. So fearful were many of identification and retribution that the committee, after meeting on campus in the morning with Graham, Taylor, and members of the supportive physical education department, moved after lunch to the Presbyterian Church of the Covenant several blocks away to interview the remainder.[41]

The visiting committee's report was not released until the next meeting of the full board of trustees in late February 1956. At that time the board endorsed the committee's call for a full investigation of the conflict at WC.[42] Entrusted with launching this inquiry was William Friday, newly named acting president of the university. Only 35 years old, Friday was already a seasoned UNC administrator, having worked closely with both Frank Graham and Gordon Gray. Friday's biographer, William Link, credits his handling of the Woman's College crisis as the leading factor in his appointment soon afterward as continuing president.[43] He remained as UNC president for the next thirty years.

Friday quickly appointed a blue-ribbon panel to begin hearings on campus March 8. It consisted of university Vice President William D. Carmichael as chairman, acting Provost William M. Whyburn, and graduate school Dean William W. Pierson.[44] Graham left town during the proceedings, which were held in the Pecky Cypress Room of the Alumnae House. Some 132 persons talked to the committee individually and in groups; the hearings occupied five full days. The testimony remained confidential and the more than 600-page transcript was later destroyed.[45]

When Graham was shown an edited version of the testimony he chose to interpret the troubles as springing from differences in educational philosophy and administrative procedure rather than his own transgressions. The committee report assigned blame to both sides, but plainly it felt Graham's period of usefulness to the college had ended. Friday and Carmichael persuaded him, if the testimony alone had not, that he must leave. He promptly submitted his resignation, effective at the end of the school year in June.[46] Graham quickly landed a job as dean of liberal arts at Boston University. But he stayed there no longer than at WC, and spent even less time at five other institutions—seemingly in positions of less and less authority—before retiring in 1972. He died in 1976 at age 65. At the University of North Carolina at Greensboro, flags flew at half-staff. Even after the passage of twenty years some bitterness remained, but also a sense of sadness over a life of such promise unfulfilled.[47]

* * *

The Carmichael committee recommended a temporary acting chancellor to start the healing process before bringing in (and possibly contaminating) a permanent successor. Friday's choice was William Whatley Pierson, dean of the university graduate school and a member of the committee. Those two assignments left him familiar with the campus and where the land mines were apt to be buried. Pierson was 66 years old, an Alabamian with a Columbia Ph.D. who had come to Chapel Hill in 1915 to teach Latin American history. Having headed the graduate school since 1930, he was a seasoned administrator with an established record of conciliation. That was his primary assignment at WC, and he performed it well in the eyes of all observers.[48] As early as October Pierson and a variety of persons on campus assured the trustee visiting committee that factionalism had abated everywhere except in music.[49] Nevertheless, new faculty members in the early 1960s were quite aware of continuing factionalism. For at least a decade after Graham's departure those identified with him were routinely defeated in faculty elections.[50] Pierson's first tour of duty—there would be two—occupied the single year 1956–57. For reasons emphatically not of Pierson's choosing it proved a momentous year: the college admitted its first black students.

Except for Katherine Taylor, who spent the rest of her career at the college, some of Graham's most zealous partisans such as Deans Katherine Roberts and Welton Marquis and drama head Michael Casey left with him or soon afterward. Mereb Mossman reconsidered her resignation and remained as academic dean (under different titles) until 1971.[51] In fact, given the revolving chancellorship, racial desegregation, coeducation, and university status that dominated the campus in those years, people joked that succeeding chief executives in effect served under Mereb Mossman, who provided a focal point of institutional stability. In March 1956, just as she was apparently on the way out as dean of instruction, she won the university's coveted O. Max Gardner award, first granted to Louise Alexander several years earlier.[52]

Mossman was a workaholic who kept long hours and mastered virtually every detail of the college's operation. Her door was always open to faculty members and she got to know them all. Department heads and others who worked with her closely credited her with the proverbial iron fist in the velvet glove. Never confrontational, always smiling, and seemingly unflappable, she was nevertheless a master of the polite negative. Except for her notable reluctance to delegate, they regarded her as a model administrator. Mossman had been baptized in fire under Graham and was unfailingly loyal to every succeeding chancellor. Gordon Blackwell, who raised her to dean of the college in 1958, described her as his right arm. Seldom an originator of ideas herself, she joined those who sought to enlarge the institution in both size and mission and to improve its academic quality. She was in these years perhaps the major contributor to those ends.[53]

There was, however, a strikingly discordant note that rose from Mossman's female colleagues. They argued with considerable passion that Mossman systematically discriminated against women in hiring, promotion, and salaries. Some felt so strongly that they tried in vain to prevent the new administration building from being named for her after her retirement. Mossman's defenders either denied the charge or argued (with some merit) that the candidate pool from which the college needed to choose in its efforts to upgrade itself was primarily male.[54] That was Mossman's own view; she would herself argue in public against what was later called the glass ceiling for women.[55]

* * *

Edward Kidder Graham was hardly gone before President William Friday organized a search effort to find a permanent successor. Trustees, alumnae, faculty, and students were consulted on a scale never seen before.[56] The product of this search was sociologist Gordon W. Blackwell, 45, a South Carolinian with degrees from Furman, UNC, and Harvard. (At Chapel Hill he was a student of W.C. Jackson's.)[57] Since 1944 he had been Howard Odum's successor as director of the university's Institute for Research in Social Science, a major southern liberal think tank.[58]

Blackwell soon launched the familiar self-study, his equivalent to Graham's general education initiative, with a similar propensity to expend faculty time. But Blackwell's personality was more akin to Pierson's than Graham's. He got along well with faculty and students, stirring up neither the hatred nor the adulation that Graham had evoked. Well aware of the recent schism, Blackwell was careful to follow in Pierson's footsteps. (He scored points with students by wearing a breast-pocket handkerchief proclaiming, "I like girls.")[59] In 1960 Blackwell received a presidential bid from Florida State University, which had recently made the transition from the state's women's college. Blackwell found the offer too good to resist, especially as it came at a time when Chapel Hill was rebuffing a number of WC efforts to expand its curricular offerings.[60] He remained at Florida State for five years, then returned permanently to his alma mater Furman as president in 1965.

Blackwell left on short notice, and the college again found itself in need of an acting chancellor to serve while a new search was launched. By popular demand, W. W. Pierson came out of retirement in Chapel Hill to fill the role during the academic year 1960–61.[61] Pierson was now 70 years old and past his prime, but few complained. At the end of the year he went back into retirement. He died in 1966.

It was William Friday who first suggested the next chancellor, Otis A. Singletary of the University of Texas, following a visit Singletary had made to him on other business. A native Mississippian, Singletary was only 39, an American historian, and currently an assistant to the president at Texas.[62] When the search committee contacted one of his former teachers for information about him, the response was, "Otis Singletary is a very ambitious man who's on his way up fast."[63] (As fate would have it, Singletary later brought that same former teacher, James S. Ferguson, to campus as dean of the graduate school, and before long Ferguson succeeded Singletary as chancellor.) There was a feeling at the time, no doubt rendered clearer in hindsight, that Singletary saw WC as a good place to begin his climb up the presidential ladder. That certainly was his own view in retrospect.[64] He did not stay long, but he made his mark and left good memories.

Young, attractive, and verging on flamboyance, Singletary had much the same impact on students that Graham had had. (They also compared him with John F. Kennedy, whose presidency came at the same time.) His political antennae were far more sensitive than Graham's, and despite occasional spats he got along much better with the faculty. A man of strong opinions, he yet was open to persuasion.[65] The campus Phi Beta Kappa chapter thought so highly of Singletary that it elected him an honorary member; though his schedule prevented a personal appearance at his induction, he went on eventually to become the society's national president. Like Jackson in his early years, he found time to teach a course in the history department while chancellor.[66]

* * *

Subordinate administrators were relatively unaffected by the top-level turnovers. Franklin H. McNutt, assistant dean of the graduate school (who had hitherto reported to Pierson as the overall UNC dean) expressed a desire to step down in 1956 but was persuaded to continue temporarily while the whole university graduate school arrangement underwent reorganization.[67] In 1958, a year after each campus acquired its own dean, a successor was found in Junius A.

Davis. Davis departed in 1961 and a year later Singletary brought in James S. Ferguson from his alma mater, Millsaps College in Mississippi.

Although Mary Taylor Moore had been something of a leader in the registrar field, her death in 1948 brought in younger people with newer methods and technologies. Rollin E. Godfrey, who arrived in 1953, introduced IBM computers and punchcards.[68] His successor in 1960 was Hoyt Price, who remained for twenty-seven years.

College business manager John C. Lockhart retired in 1957, to be replaced by Wendell Murray who similarly updated procedures.[69] Murray himself died suddenly in 1961, to be succeeded the next year by Henry Ferguson. He too remained in place for many years afterward.

Reporting to the business manager, veteran buildings and grounds superintendent James M. Sink retired in 1953 after forty-three years with the college. His assistant, Nestus Gurley, would serve many years as his successor. (Gurley's son of the same name delivered newspapers to the home of Randall Jarrell who commemorated him in a poem, also of the same name.)

Until his retirement in 1962 Charlie Phillips continued to do the work of two or three, winning the plaudits of all, even during the divisive Graham days. Three of the Greensboro civic clubs even endorsed him for chancellor after Graham's departure. Phillips was the chief student recruiter well into the 1950s, visiting high schools and speaking to student groups throughout the state and beyond. Between these and talks to assorted educational and alumnae groups, he met with sixty-six organizations and logged 5,000 miles between September and December 1951. Graham put him in charge of a short-lived fund-raising program in 1955.[70] In 1957 Blackwell hired Sadye Dunn, recent alumna and SGA president, to take over Phillips' recruiting duties. All the while, Phillips remained in charge of public relations and extension work.

Under Phillips, A.A. Wilkinson continued to head the news bureau throughout these years. Except for student help, he did the work alone until 1956. Wilkinson's job was in some jeopardy at that time; at least one well-placed trustee blamed him for much of the bad publicity the college received during the recent Graham controversy. His fault seems to have lain in failing to spin the story more favorably to the college.[71] Even with a second person aboard, the bureau failed to provide as much publicity as many trustees and faculty members—especially in the performing arts—felt necessary.[72]

* * *

Contrary to the feeling of impending doom that pervaded the college at the end of the war, postwar legislatures treated it well. The perennial complaint of underfunding was hard to demonstrate on a comparative basis in these years.

Chancellor Graham did not try. He boasted to the advisory budget commission in 1954 that WC was virtually the only state-supported woman's college in the nation to increase in size and support since 1940.[73] But he paid for that candor next year when the commission threatened to cut the college budget by $90,000 for the coming biennium. Graham responded in the old McIver-Foust fashion, calling on the students to lobby for the college with their legislators at home.[74] Whether that was the reason, WC in 1955 received the third largest per capita funding of any publicly supported campus in the state: $569 per student.[75] (In efforts to save racial segregation the small minority institutions at Elizabeth City and Pembroke were highest.) Chancellor Blackwell continued the tactic, and in 1959 WC remained near the top in appropriation per student. The justification for this generosity, not widely accepted at other campuses, was that it cost more to properly fund a woman's college.[76]

In 1951 President Gordon Gray encouraged the three campuses to develop their own fund-raising programs. Chancellor Graham's belated effort to comply in 1955 fell victim to the turmoil over his own leadership.[77] Gordon Blackwell also recognized the need for outside funds and was active in raising them, but it was left to Otis Singletary to inaugurate a formal development program in 1962. Meanwhile, the Alumnae Association organized an ongoing campaign in 1951, but its annual gift to the college in the '50s never exceeded $2,500 and was usually less.[78]

Even without a development office to solicit and coordinate gifts, the late 1950s and early '60s brought larger donations than ever before, aimed at a variety of programs or causes. The college's first endowed professorship fund was started in 1957, to create a Mary Frances Stone chair in home economics. By 1961 there were two others, a Burlington Industries chair in textiles (home economics) and a Kathleen Price Bryan professorship in financial affairs. In each case the endowments were too small to fund the chair alone; except for the Bryan fund, which was used at first to hire temporary outside lecturers, the funds supplemented existing salaries.[79] Substantial scholarship funds also began to come in, from Greensboro's Jefferson Standard Life Insurance Company and the R.J. Reynolds Tobacco Company in Winston-Salem.

The Home Economics Foundation, established in 1946, claimed an endowment fifteen years later of about $166,000.[80] Joining it and the earlier Weatherspoon gallery support group, new endowment funds were gradually added, including the Friends of the Library in 1959. The total college endowment in 1963 amounted to just over $500,000.[81]

* * *

Beginning in 1957, general administration in Chapel Hill became more interested in long-range planning at all three campuses. WC again hired Edward

Waugh of Raleigh, who had prepared a campus plan in 1949. He presented a new one in 1961.[82] In the meantime, a faculty buildings and grounds committee was created in 1957 to advise on such elements as landscaping and the location and design of buildings, roads, and walkways. The committee took its responsibilities seriously, and was quite active.[83]

The most striking part of the Waugh report in 1961 was its assertion that the college was becoming landlocked and would need to expand. This was hardly news but it focused attention on a matter little discussed in recent years. The campus embraced 130 acres, about the same as in the early 1920s. Much of it was undeveloped in the form of Peabody Park and a small golf course. These were always subject to incursions, but even if the college were willing to build and pave them into oblivion, it would still need more land eventually. Demographic projections (later borne out in practice) pointed to ever-increasing enrollments in the years ahead.

By 1958 the college already had its eyes on adjacent properties along McIver Street to the east, Walker Avenue to the west, and across Spring Garden Street to the south. All had been developed for many years and would be expensive. But the college met little response in Raleigh when it asked for money to buy them.[84] The quest for additional land became increasingly urgent in the years to come.

In 1949, College Avenue was a dead-end street carrying traffic from Spring Garden to a turn-around between Mary Foust and Guilford dormitories. It carried traffic in both directions and was chronically congested. Edward Waugh's campus plan that year called for closing it off altogether to vehicular traffic. The proposal met near-universal opposition, most notably from the fire department. So campus officials went back to the drawing board and came up with a solution that proceeded in the opposite direction: make College Avenue a thoroughfare, extending all the way north to Market Street; that intersection would then become the main entrance to campus. This proposal would have opened most of Peabody Park to development and, in fact, plans were prepared for an arts building at the corner of Market Street and College Avenue. For several years Chancellor Graham and the trustee building committee pushed hard for this proposal. But in 1957, when the legislature finally appropriated the necessary funds, campus authorities backed away and settled for an arrangement that would endure through the 1990s: extend College Avenue a little farther to North Drive (running perpendicularly from McIver Street to the west campus) and except for the first block (adjacent to Administration Building and the Alumnae House) make it one-directional away from Spring Garden. Since a Market Street entrance to campus was still deemed necessary owing to the city's development north and westward, they built it farther west as an extension of Gray Drive, near the dormitory quadrangle.[85]

Thus Peabody Park was spared major assault while it continued to suffer nibbling at the edges. The park had been allowed to deteriorate since the 1930s and was little used. But there were some—both students and faculty—who continued to value the wooded area as a refuge from nearby campus and urban development.[86] Most of the nibbling took the form of residence hall construction. The Mendenhall and Ragsdale twin dormitories were built in 1950 on Gray Drive, across from the 1920s quadrangle and north of the dining halls. A new health center, named for Anna Gove, followed next door in 1953. Across Gray Drive and north of the quadrangle came the conjoined Moore and Strong Dormitories in 1960. In 1963 came Grogan and Reynolds Halls on North Drive. (Development of that street had already forced the razing of the YWCA Hut, now supplanted by the new student union.) Still more construction in this area followed through the 1990s.

A three-acre campus lake had been built in 1941 at the western edge of the park, along Market Street. Although students enjoyed boating there, it soon appeared that the two small creeks feeding the pond provided too little water to maintain it dependably. Stagnant water brought mosquitoes and complaints from the neighbors. The college decided in 1954 to drain the lake and restore the golf course that had occupied the space earlier. The nine-hole course reopened formally in 1957. The new Market Street campus entrance replaced the former dam.[87]

* * *

The 1953 health center was a much-updated replacement of the old infirmary. That 1912 structure continued to serve as an office building.[88] In fact, its next tenant in the '50s was the U.S. Department of Commerce, which rented it to use in case of an enemy attack during the Cold War. That interest flagged within a few years and the college slated the building for demolition, which occurred in 1966. Until then it was used for faculty offices.[89]

Nationally, the 1950s saw the advent of modern campus architecture; diversity began to replace unified design.[90] At WC, the harbinger of the new era was Coleman Gymnasium, completed in 1952. Following more or less in step were the student union and the health center in 1953, a child care center in 1954, a new McIver Building and the Moore-Strong Dormitories in 1960, and the Reynolds and Grogan Dormitories in 1963. All except Coleman were of red brick and bore at least that relationship to the buildings already in place. They were the work of Northup and O'Brien of Winston-Salem, who had designed the campus buildings since World War II. Coleman was also brick but of lighter hue—designed by Greensboro architect Edward Lowenstein and physical education head Ethel Martus. As the first (and arguably the most distinguished) modern building on campus, it bore the brunt of traditionalist criticism.[91] Chancellor Gordon Blackwell attributed the campus's traditional appearance to conservative trustees and administrators at the state level. Nevertheless, the ice had been broken.[92]

A number of the early buildings seemed inadequate to changing needs; some indeed were dangerous. Heading the demolition list was the old Students' Building, first occupied in 1902. Built on a shoestring, it had become so dilapidated and was regarded as such a fire hazard that much of it had been closed off well before its final demise; moreover, architectural tastes had so changed in fifty years that with its towers and turrets it was regarded as ugly. Conversely, there was an urgent need for a modern student union with space for dances, informal gatherings, and offices for student organizations. Students were forced to scrounge space in classrooms, residence halls, the gymnasium, the YWCA Hut, and the Alumnae House. By 1941, money for a new student union had been pledged collectively by the state, the federal WPA, and the Cone family, but Pearl Harbor put all such projects on ice for the duration. The long-deferred result was the demolition of the old building in 1949 and the construction nearby of the new, which opened in 1953. Elliott Hall was named appropriately for the dean of women who had advocated it for more than a decade before her death in 1947.[93] Early in the 1960s Elliott Hall added a small cafeteria which appropriated both the name and function of the existing soda shop.[94] The next-door soda shop building was then transformed into a faculty center.

The old McIver house, used as an auxiliary dormitory since Mrs. McIver's death in 1944, was unattractive by any standard and only marginally serviceable. Few tears were shed when it came down in 1952.[95] The resulting space at College Avenue and Spring Garden Street—the college's main entrance—was then attractively landscaped.

Far more controversial was Chancellor Blackwell's proposal in the late '50s to replace the 1892 Administration (former Main) Building, arguing that its frame interior made it a fire hazard. Although outside consultants seconded the motion, money was not forthcoming. In 1961 it received yet another remodeling for administrative use, and soon afterward was formally named for Julius I. Foust.[96]

The largest actual demolition-construction project—and in retrospect the most controversial—involved the massive McIver Building. In 1955 it housed eleven departments, over seventy faculty members, and classrooms holding up to 1600 students at a time. It had been constructed in three stages between 1908 and the early '20s. As early as 1928 the central core of the building, then only twenty years old but housing chemistry and the other science departments, was condemned by sciences head J.P. Givler as both obsolete and a fire hazard. He referred to the electric wiring as "a patchwork of peril."[97] A 1932 fire, emanating from chemistry, was fortunately caught early. The worst hazards were averted with the completion of the Petty Science Building in 1940, but McIver was still regarded as a firetrap. State engineers advised that while the timber frame and brick veneer were sound, it would cost more to fireproof the building than to replace it altogether. (The latter finding was in dispute; the state budget office reported in 1956 that a complete renovation would cost about $750,000 and a new building about $1 million.) Beginning in 1950, the college sought appropriations for a new building.[98]

What really focused attention was the partial collapse of a plaster ceiling in one of the classrooms in 1956. Faulty plastering in the building had gained attention as early as 1913. The 1956 collapse occurred between classes and no one was hurt, but from that time on the building was doomed. Chancellor Pierson removed all classes from it that fall. The next legislature provided minimal financing for a new building, and in 1958 old McIver came down. A new McIver opened in 1960.[99]

Controversy came aplenty with the new building. A box-like contemporary building in red brick and gray stone, it featured an abstract lighted mural over the main entrance that offended traditionalists. At the same time, occupants compared its spartan concrete block interior to a penitentiary. Randall Jarrell called it the Thunderbird Motel. Now, when it was too late, critics waxed nostalgic over the solid, massive, traditional McIver Building that was no more.[100] By 1962 the new building was already overcrowded and an annex providing room for the art department and the Weatherspoon Gallery was added in 1967.[101]

The McIver statue long adorned the front lawn of the old McIver Building. It did not harmonize with the new building, so people said, and in 1960 it was moved to the front lawn of Jackson Library, more nearly in the center of campus.[102]

* * *

Modern air conditioning appealed to the state's advisory budget commission even less than modern architecture. It did not reach campus until 1960, and even then appropriations were niggardly. Funds for the new McIver Building permitted air conditioning only in the second and third floors, leaving the first and the partial basement for a later day. The English department, occupying most of the first floor, long remembered this "temporary delay" that lasted for over a decade.[103] As it happened, the upper floors of McIver pushed in ahead of the library, which had been asking this boon for several years. Everyone conceded the library a high priority. But when it was constructed in 1950 air conditioning was regarded as a luxury beyond the reach of the North Carolina budget if not its public morality. Everyone reported the building as intolerable in hot weather and allegedly for that reason students avoided it like the plague. Funds finally became available in 1963.[104] Administrative offices, which are generally found at the cutting edge in these respects, also acquired air conditioning in the early 1960s. But the chancellor's residence, thoroughly remodeled for the Blackwells in 1957, did not acquire this amenity until the advent of the Singletarys in 1961.[105]

Chapter 16

The Faculty, Curriculum, and Library

The 1950s brought more than the usual tension between older and younger faculty members. To hear the latter tell it, many of their seniors had grown comfortable in the routines of earlier years and resented newcomers who threatened to rock the boat. Guiltiest by far in seniors' eyes was Chancellor Graham, but he managed to antagonize junior faculty members too and the tension outlasted him. One point of contention was the push for interdisciplinary courses in general education. Older faculty also felt threatened by the continually greater emphasis on research and publication; new colleagues often had doctorates in hand or in the offing and were hired in large part because of their scholarly potential. Part of the tension was also gender-based; the older faculty were predominantly female while the latter were more evenly divided.[1]

A 1952 statistical survey of the faculties on the three UNC campuses showed that 68 percent of those at WC were female, compared with 10 percent at Chapel Hill and even fewer at State. By 1960, the proportion of females at WC had fallen to 61 percent. (In the upper two ranks, where males figured most heavily, the percentage of women declined from 61 to 54 between 1951 and 1962; in fact, their actual numbers stood still at 51 while men accounted for the total increase.)[2] This decline matched a national trend beginning about 1940, even in women's colleges. It was less precipitous at WC than at Smith, Wellesley, Bryn Mawr, and Vassar.[3]

In fact, WC's lag could be seen as evidence of inferiority, since the most prestigious institutions were most guilty of discrimination. It was regarded as a sign of progress, as historian Margaret Rossiter trenchantly remarks, to get rid of the old girls, raise salaries, reduce teaching loads, hire more Ph.D.s, rename the school a state university, and urge the new faculty to get on with their research. There was little recognition at the time that these policies were discriminatory, she adds. Even when women's colleges practiced them, protests were in vain. WC, under Dean Mereb Mossman, was by no means the only institution where a woman helped preside over the operation. (Dean Marjorie Hope Nicolson of Smith College boasted that Smith was the best woman's college of its time because it had the most men on the faculty.) The fundamental injustice lay in the broader societal discrimination that reduced the number of women who could even aspire to professional careers.[4]

Among the barriers were antinepotism rules, denying employment to faculty wives. WC supposedly had such an unwritten policy. If so, it was frequently violated; several married couples taught in the same departments—she always in lower rank.[5] The great exception was Elizabeth Duffy, a full professor of psychology at a time when her husband, John E. Bridgers in English, was an associate professor. Other faculty wives secured positions at other local colleges.

In later years some of the young men with Ph.D.s would become quite emotional in their tributes to the spinster ladies who mentored them and whose vocation had been undergraduate classroom teaching, often of a high order.[6] Otis Singletary recalled that he had learned at WC to appreciate the value of strong, capable women in higher education (he mentioned Mereb Mossman specifically) before the woman's movement made such an understanding mandatory.[7] Not always included in these tributes were the librarians—all women except for their director. They continued to socialize with the teaching faculty, who respected their services but regarded them as inferior in status.

In 1953, only 7 percent of the faculty were part-time employees. A decade later the proportion was 10 percent. Nearly all were instructors and teaching assistants who served also as residence hall counselors. Only four of the seventeen in 1960 were men.[8]

* * *

The 1952 UNC faculties survey showed that a quarter of the WC faculty held the doctorate, compared with half at Chapel Hill where most of the graduate work was concentrated. But WC faculty compared quite closely to those at the other two campuses in both membership and office-holding in local, regional, and national professional organizations. They were only slightly behind in numbers of published works or other measurable evidences of creative activity.[9] In that same year of 1952, eight younger faculty members received prestigious research and study grants: four Ford fellowships, three Fulbrights, and a Carnegie internship.[10] Faculty with doctorates rose from 25 percent in 1952 to 44 percent in 1962. (In the latter year WC exceeded the national averages for public colleges.) The doctorates were earned all over the country; the top three institutions were UNC, Yale, and the University of Illinois.[11]

Nationally, World War II, the Cold War, and Sputnik vastly increased the emphasis on faculty research. It was spurred by unprecedented financial support from the federal government and private foundations. Until the mid-1960s most of this money went to research universities for work in the sciences, especially that with military applications.[12] Women's colleges received very little.

At WC, faculty members from the 1950s recall a continued emphasis on classroom teaching with much less pressure to publish than they experienced in later decades.[13] Some confessed that they would never have been hired under the standards of later years. On the other hand, some remember (and the record confirms) an emphasis on hiring faculty members with research potential. With this came a correspondingly greater interest in research among younger faculty than had been true in earlier decades. Junior members even organized a discussion group in the early '50s to share ideas, research findings, and teaching techniques. The principal founder of this group was Warren Ashby, the relatively new head of the philosophy department.[14] People differed as to whether classroom teaching benefited or suffered from the new emphasis.

Foremost among the sponsors of research activity was Chancellor Edward Kidder Graham—helping to explain his popularity among young faculty members already leaning in that direction. "I am trying to shove some of our better biddies off the nest for a little while on leaves of absence for study—temporary loss for a long-term gain, both for us and for them," he confided in 1951 to John Gardner of the Carnegie Foundation. He wrote a year later that he could not conceive of a first-rate teaching division in which creative work was either neglected or left to chance.[15] Accordingly, Graham sought outside funds and offered reduced teaching loads to promising individuals. He bragged repeatedly about faculty members who won prestigious awards.[16] The library recognized by 1953 that one of its functions was to support faculty research. In his first annual report as head of the biology department that year, Victor Cutter announced that most faculty positions nationally were filled on the basis of research productivity rather than teaching ability; he accepted that priority without question.[17]

The momentum did not stop with Graham's ouster. Acting Chancellor W. W. Pierson was instrumental in creating a campus research council in 1957. Armed with an annual $10,000 state appropriation, it began handing out small grants in aid of faculty research.[18] The faculty were asked that year for the first time to list all their publications during the past twelve months.[19] The *Carolinian* reported in 1958 that in the past three years the faculty had written or co-authored ten books and fifty articles in professional journals; the history department alone was responsible for a large proportion.[20] Nevertheless, so few faculty members applied for the grants that the graduate dean had to make an annual appeal to drum up interest in them. Book publication was confined in large measure to a handful of persons in the departments of history and English.[21] The legislature never agreed to regular sabbatical leaves, but in 1958 Chancellor Gordon Blackwell began granting faculty leaves of absence on a competitive basis, awarding full pay for a semester or half pay for a year.[22]

Graham conceded in 1953 that "many of the faculty are distressed over my insistence upon research or other evidence of creative activity as a requirement for promotion...."[23] Five years later, after his departure, so many faculty still felt threatened that Blackwell thought it necessary to reassure them. His new faculty leave program, originally planned to facilitate research, was broadened to include those "whose primary function is undergraduate teaching" and who wanted to study elsewhere to enhance their classroom effectiveness.[24]

By 1959 Mereb Mossman was voicing the argument that all defenders of faculty research have made in succeeding decades: active scholars make the best teachers. Although the college continued to regard teaching as pre-eminent, she said, it sought to recruit faculty members who would excel in both areas. She was constantly alert to promote scholarly activity among those already on hand.[25]

It was not until 1963 that students began publicly to question the college's research priorities. "It is a shame," wrote two students in a letter to the *Carolinian*, "that more of the faculty are not able to find time between their contributions to professional journals, the books they are writing, the research projects they are conducting, the Ph.D.'s they are trying so hard to get, and the classes they teach to find a little bit of time to take an interest in 'their' students...."[26] Although faculty members continued to spend much more time socializing with students than would be true in later decades, cynics could say that the institution clearly was getting ready for its university debut.[27]

Among the rewards offered for scholarly activity (beyond grants and leaves) were reduced teaching loads (generally from twelve down to nine hours per week), relief from heavy committee assignments, and favorable class schedules.[28] (Reimbursement for travel expenses to professional meetings—something the faculty had actively pursued since McIver's day—was perennially pitiful; it averaged $7 per faculty member in 1957–58.) In what was surely the most important inducement to research activity, it increasingly governed decisions on promotion, tenure, and salary.[29]

Chancellor Graham began his downward slide at a memorable faculty council meeting in October 1950, when he delivered his ukase codifying and modifying the informal promotion, tenure, and salary practices of the Jackson administration. Without consulting the advisory committee or anyone else, he simply announced these policies, based on his prior experiences at Cornell and Washington Universities.[30] The substance was less startling than the method, for the new regulations continued to adhere to national AAUP guidelines. They prevailed until 1959 when, at the bidding of President William Friday, the trustees adopted university-wide regulations on academic freedom, tenure, and due process. These too adhered generally to AAUP guidelines and caused little change in practice at WC. It was still rather informal by later standards, with no written contracts and new faculty members being informed of the regulations only when they thought to ask. The elected academic policies committee advised the chancellor on departmental promotion and tenure recommendations, and an elected due process committee (mandated by the new regulations) heard individual faculty appeals.[31]

Informality led to at least the perception of unfairness; Dean Mossman was repeatedly suspected of playing favorites in recommending promotion, tenure, and salary increases to the chancellor—especially in favor of men.[32] Subsequently Graham required an annual review of all faculty members and issued (this time after consultation) a set of criteria for appointment and promotion to each rank. Predictably, it gave first priority to teaching ability, but second came professional attainments headed by research "with or without publication." This annual review far exceeded the procedures of earlier years. With the accompanying criteria it long survived Graham.[33]

* * *

Nationally, faculty salaries in the 1950s began rising faster than the consumer price index—for a change. At WC the increase from 1955 to 1961 ranged from 26 percent for full professors to 46 percent for instructors.[34] But this increase followed an alarming exodus of faculty members to other institutions offering them up to twice their WC salaries. Thirty-nine left in 1956 alone, before dropping off in the wake of a new salary scale—and a more stable political environment on campus.[35] Despite the impressive gains after 1955, national norms also rose; the college's rankings in the AAUP's annual salary grading program in 1962–63 remained only D, D, C, and B respectively for the ranks from professor to instructor. Unlike research faculty at Chapel Hill and Raleigh, few at WC received salary supplements from outside sources.[36] As usual here and elsewhere, market conditions forced proportionately higher salaries for new and recent hires than for older faculty members who had been recruited many years earlier.

Chancellor Graham's strong preference before 1956 had been to use the sparse available funds for merit increases rather than across-the-board raises. The latter, in his words, would reward the fourth team at the expense of the first; only through merit increases could the college retain its best and brightest. Most faculty members, on the other hand, lined up on the opposite side in what was becoming a perennial debate.[37]

Although a state retirement program was in place, benefits were so low that faculty members dreaded the prospect of stepping down at the stipulated age of 65. On reaching that age they routinely asked and were usually granted permission to continue on annual appointments for another three years; then the process commonly ended.[38] Even with this relaxation, the end result was sometimes traumatic for the individuals involved and the entire subject evoked anxiety, controversy, and bitterness.[39]

* * *

The student-teacher ratio in the 1950s was about 15 to 1—favorable by national standards.[40] The standard teaching load remained four courses, or twelve hours a week, although research scholars and those active in campus service might teach only nine hours. On the other hand, a few, often in smaller departments, were required to teach fifteen or more hours in order to cover the minimal curricular requirements. In their cases smaller enrollments partially compensated for the large number of preparations. Teaching loads and how to compute them were particularly sensitive in chemistry and the other sciences, where instructors taught laboratory sessions in addition to their lecture classes. Chemistry head Florence Schaeffer insisted that a twelve-hour load plus mandatory lab sections was alienating her faculty and turning away possible recruits. Chancellor Graham's insistence on the twelve-hour rule in turn alienated him from his academic dean, Mereb Mossman.[41] By late 1956, Chancellor Pierson reported that the average full or associate professor was teaching nine hours and the average assistant professor and instructor twelve hours a week. Classes were still held six days a week, though faculty and students alike gained skill in avoiding Saturday classes.[42]

* * *

Otis Singletary recalled many years later that the faculty during his tenure had been a strong one, well aware of its power over the curriculum and the academic process in general, and responsible in exercising it.[43] This strength had not developed overnight; Chancellor Jackson in particular nurtured faculty government during his sixteen years at the helm. Even Edward Kidder Graham advanced the process; at his urging a committee drew up an Instrument of Government or constitution for the faculty, which it adopted almost unanimously in 1955.[44] Under it Jackson's advisory committee gave way to a weaker academic policies committee presided over by the chancellor. The curriculum committee (formerly with one member from each department) was trimmed down to more manageable size. Both were elective. A Faculty Handbook appeared in 1961, containing the Instrument and other documents relating to faculty status and governance. The campus AAUP chapter in 1962 claimed sixty-three active members in a faculty of 236.[45] At its instance in 1959 Chancellor Blackwell appointed a faculty welfare committee to deal with medical insurance and any other matters of faculty concern.[46] In fact, the greater part of faculty government took place in committees. In 1961, with fifty-nine standing and twelve *ad hoc* committees, members were complaining of overwork. It was increasingly difficult to balance these responsibilities with the demand for research productivity.[47]

There still remained evidences of the old faculty community. For many members, the college remained the main if not the only social outlet. Faculty and committee meetings were held in the evening and were well attended.[48] The home ec cafeteria remained a place for socializing as well as political caucuses. As the opening of the fall semester still brought a faculty banquet at which new members were introduced, the end of the school year was marked by a faculty picnic to which spouses and children were invited.[49]

* * *

Student enrollment ranged from about 2400 in the early 1950s to nearly 3600 in 1962–63. Student recruitment was still confined pretty much to visiting the state's high schools on their annual College Days.[50] When Edward Kidder Graham arrived in 1950, admissions standards were hardly more selective than the high schools were in deciding whom to graduate. The college's problem, Graham confided to an off-campus friend, was to devise the best it could for both the gifted students (of whom there were many) "and for those who, by comparison, are the academically halt, lame, and blind."[51]

All this changed with the admission of the first black students in 1956. That event came almost simultaneously on all three campuses as the result of a court order at Chapel Hill. To protect the campuses against a feared inundation of poorly prepared African Americans—a payoff for centuries of academic neglect in that quarter—admissions policies were suddenly tightened and centralized. That year for the first time, freshman applicants were required to take qualifying examinations; the College Entrance Examination Board's Scholastic Aptitude Test was prescribed in 1958. Each chancellor appointed a faculty admissions policies committee, which in turn sent representatives to a similar all-university committee. Although the joint committee set minimum test scores for admission to any campus, each retained a great deal of latitude in setting its own standards. WC continued to factor in high school grades with the SAT scores. In the early 1960s it significantly increased admission standards; a sharp enrollment rise came in spite of these increases.[52] When some faculty proposed raising the standards even higher, Chancellor Blackwell and Dean Mossman objected that that would invite Chapel Hill to become fully coeducational by admitting freshman and sophomore women whom WC rejected.[53]

Use of the SAT made possible more precise comparisons with other institutions. The college noted that its incoming freshmen in 1958 exceeded by about twenty points the national average for public and private colleges.[54] They ranked quite closely with those at Chapel Hill and State. In a 1954 alumnae poll almost 80 percent of the respondents ranked the college excellent, while nearly all the remainder called it good. Over 60 percent said they would send a daughter to WC and most of the others refrained only because of unwillingness to dictate such a matter.[55]

Yet some on campus complained that academic standards were falling below the other two institutions. Registrar Rollin Godfrey pointed out in 1956 that Chapel Hill and State required a C average for graduation while WC in effect permitted a D+ average. They also included in a student's final average any grades for courses failed, while WC did not. The faculty adopted his call to rectify these deficiencies.[56] There was also a widespread impression that the college suffered from grade inflation.[57] A faculty study of the grades handed out in the fall of 1956 found "a shocking lack of standards" across the college and between departments. There is no evidence that this report led to any marked changes in policy or practice.[58] Charges of grade inflation would occasionally surface in the future as they had in the past.

Student evaluation of teaching began modestly in 1953 at students' initiative but with the blessings of Chancellor Graham. It followed almost three years of study, occasioned by faculty trepidation that was unwarranted by later experience.[59]

* * *

In the course of Graham's aborted general education initiative, outside consultants were invited to visit campus, make appraisals, and offer suggestions. One of them praised the advisory system devised by Harriet Elliott, the concern taken with the academic and social progress of each student, the friendly relations between students and faculty, and the general happiness of students with the college. He criticized the existing required courses in most disciplines as, in effect, introductory courses for departmental majors; they lacked the integrative feature of general education as he understood it.[60] Students themselves spoke highly of student-faculty relations. They were less generous about the advising system, claiming in particular that faculty academic advisers were frequently ill-informed about the regulations. They echoed the criticism of introductory courses and called for greater access to free electives outside their majors.[61]

In 1962–63 student academic requirements were virtually unchanged from the 1940s. In what remained a demanding if traditional program, bachelor of arts students were required to take twelve hours of English (writing and literature); six hours of modern European history; six additional social science hours drawn from history, government, economics, sociology, or geography; twelve hours in math and natural science (biology, chemistry, physics, psychology, or geography) including at least six of a laboratory science; twelve hours in a single foreign language (French, German, Greek, Latin, Russian, or Spanish); a three-hour health course; and four semester activity courses in physical education. Bachelor of science requirements varied according to field, but they too included large dollops of English, history, foreign language, and laboratory science.[62] Although the outside visiting committee connected with the 1962 reaccreditation suggested that the college might want to revisit the subject of more integrative general education courses, it did not do so. A faculty curricular study in 1963–64 recommended only modest adjustments.[63]

Student enrollments were not surprisingly heaviest in the departments with required courses for underclassmen: English, history, and physical education. Student majors and the degrees they received were another matter. In the liberal arts, English attracted the largest number of majors, but it was usually a poor fourth to elementary education, business education (or secretarial administration), and home economics.[64]

* * *

Nationally, the 1950s and '60s were a period of tremendous expansion in graduate programs—more, eventually, than the nation could absorb.[65] Woman's College and its successor were no exception to the trend. It already had in place by 1950 master's programs in home economics, business education, elementary education, and musical composition, as well as the interdisciplinary master of fine arts. By 1960, physical education, music education, and an M.Ed. in English had followed suit. Close to a hundred persons were receiving master's degrees annually by the early '60s—a fifth of the total degrees awarded.[66] All the degrees were professional and nearly all the recipients were teachers, prospective teachers, or administrators in the public schools. In the late '50s the graduate offerings were still an appendage to the undergraduate program. Nearly all were given on Saturdays and in summer session. Faculty members taught them on an overtime basis, receiving extra compensation. By 1960 efforts were afoot to make the program more residential and integrate it better into the total curriculum.[67] Moreover, many people saw the limitation to professional degrees as a serious handicap to the college's overall graduate program. Within the UNC allocation of functions, graduate work in the liberal arts and sciences belonged only to Chapel Hill. When growing demand brought the lifting of that restriction in 1962, it evoked cheers at WC and opened the door to a variety of master's programs in the arts and sciences.[68]

The first doctoral program was approved in 1960 in child development, within home economics. Its initial recipient, Nance White, won the distinction of being the first and only person to receive a Woman's College doctorate—in 1963, just before the institution was transformed into the University of North Carolina at Greensboro.[69]

* * *

Graduate programs were especially dependent on holdings in the library. Measured by the number of books per student as well as library purchase and binding expenditures per student, WC remained far behind the leading northeastern women's colleges in the early 1950s.[70] But rising enrollments and appropriations in the plush '50s brought improvements. The collection grew from 143,000 to 222,000 volumes between 1953 and 1963. (The Smith College collection in 1960 was over 400,000.)[71] Nevertheless the number of periodical holdings (while rising) sank from 79 percent of those recommended by the Southeastern Association of Colleges and Secondary Schools in 1947 to 68 percent of its higher standards in 1955.[72] An outside consultant gave a generally positive appraisal of library holdings for the proposed doctorate in child development in 1958—as long as students had easy access to the collections at Chapel Hill and Raleigh.[73]

The library gradually developed or acquired a number of specialized collections. One was the Amy Morris Homans collection of over 2000 books and pamphlets on women's physical education. It was acquired from Wellesley College in 1958 after Wellesley gave up the graduate program in physical education that Homans had founded. The acquisition owed much to the long connection between physical educationists at the two institutions.[74]

The college collection (mostly college records) grew slowly following its creation in the '40s. Progress consisted mostly of collecting and providing better storage for records from the college's early days. Some of these had been warehoused in campus basements and others were acquired from private sources such as the McIver family.[75] Library director Charles M. Adams took a real interest in the collection, getting state archives personnel to come and inventory the materials already on hand and draw up policies for the acquisition and preservation of those yet to come. It was apparently the first such campus records schedule in the United States. When it went into effect in 1962, the college collection became the college archives.[76] Growth remained slow; not only were campus offices slow to turn over their old records, a library staff barely large enough to handle the daily routine did not prod them. Despite repeated efforts, Adams could get no more than part-time help to accession and arrange the records that did come in. As late as 1975, the archives contained almost no institutional records more recent than the Jackson administration, in office when the collection began.[77]

Closed stacks were the rule on American campuses before World War II; library authorities feared lost or stolen books, property damage, and other erratic behavior if students were allowed free access to the stacks. That policy changed rapidly after the war, as enrollments rose and pedagogical methods increasingly emphasized student reading. Library staffs could not keep up with the increased usage.[78] At WC, the number of volumes checked out annually rose from 50,000 to 77,000 between 1950 and 1960. It joined the open-stacks movement in 1956, rather late.[79] Some of the preceding apprehensions, particularly of mis-shelved and stolen books, were well-founded and led to security measures in later years, but the library never returned to closed stacks.

Under director Charles Adams, the library staff in 1961 consisted of nineteen persons, all female, ten of them professional librarians.[80] They continued to have an amorphous faculty status without the normally attendant academic rank or privileges.[81]

Harvard started the first Friends of the Library organization in 1925. They proliferated thereafter as agencies to raise funds for rare books and other special collections that ordinary funding sources did not reach.[82] Threatened with a book budget cut in 1955, Charles Adams proposed creating a friends organization at WC. Revolving college leadership helped delay its birth until 1959.[83]

Chapter 17

Departments and Schools

Leonard B. Hurley presided over an increasingly prominent and often fractious English department from 1945 until his retirement in 1960. On the faculty since 1921, Hurley was conservative both in demeanor and policy. He was prominent among the faculty leaders who opposed and ultimately deposed Chancellor Graham. English more than most departments was rent internally by that controversy, with Graham partisans Marc Friedlaender and one or two others pitted against a majority including Hurley and Randall Jarrell. Friedlaender left in 1957, later joining Hiram Haydn to found the Atheneum Press. Within the department, Hurley was respectful and notably tolerant of the prickly personalities around him—some of them being teachers, writers, and campus leaders of the first magnitude. Nonetheless, there was a feeling among younger members as well as Chancellor Blackwell by the late '50s that the department needed fresh leadership.[1] Despite plenty of advance notice of Hurley's retirement, new leadership had to wait until the arrival in 1961 of Joseph A. Bryant of Duke University.

Although the writing program remained one of the department's best-known features, it was the theater program that experienced the greatest changes in this period. Drama acquired separate department status in 1953—a development that involved the removal of W. Raymond Taylor from its leadership. (He continued to teach until his retirement in 1960.) Although Taylor was virtually the father of theatrical arts at the college, the program had faltered in recent years. An English actor/director, Giles Playfair, served as acting head of dramatics in 1953–54, to be succeeded for two years by director and playwright Michael Casey.[2] It was left to his successor in 1956, Herman Middleton, to build up the department—something to which Middleton devoted the remainder of his career. He admired Taylor's previous work, developed a close friendship with him, and was instrumental in having the new campus theater named for Taylor in 1967.[3]

Middleton introduced Broadway musical comedy in 1957 with a performance of "Oklahoma." Opera soon followed, in conjunction with the school of music. Children's theater productions started in 1958. Middleton took students on three USO-sponsored tours to entertain American servicemen and women overseas in 1959, 1962, and 1966. WC theater troupes also toured the state frequently. By 1960 Middleton could boast that one-seventh of the student body was participating in play production. That year he organized a Theatre Angels support group.[4]

From the beginning, the new department offered courses in radio and television production, with cinema following a year later. In 1960 speech courses were separated from the English department and added to what now became the department of drama and speech. Speech pathology and audiology were soon transferred from the school of education. By 1963 the departmental major contained three tracks: drama, speech, and speech correction.[5]

University-wide television materialized in January 1955 in the form of WUNC-TV—the first university-sponsored television network in the country. Broadcasts emanated from studios on each of the three campuses. Each produced about a third of the programs—informational, cultural, athletic, and even religious. For a time the university extension office offered both credit and non-credit TV courses, with popular teachers on each campus appearing before the cameras. Programming gradually became more sophisticated and additional transmitters made it possible by the early 1970s for WUNC broadcasts to be viewed all over the state. Color broadcasts began in 1968.[6] At WC, the TV station was first located in one of the most improbable places on campus: the old power plant/laundry structure behind the McIver Building.

Like the theater program in general, the college's three-year-old summer Burnsville School of Fine Arts in the mountains was suffering from lagging receipts and other ailments when Chancellor Graham arrived in 1950. Some complained that under W. R. Taylor dramatics tended to overshadow the other elements in the school's curriculum. Part of Taylor's general demotion, therefore, included transfer of the school's leadership in 1952 from him to Gregory Ivy, head of the art department. The curriculum in 1953 and 1954 included art, dance, drama, music, and writing. But matters continued to go badly and in 1954 the school was moved back to Beaufort on the coast, where the college had maintained marine biology and arts programs in the 1930s and early '40s. The school continued to lose money and Graham decided to terminate it in 1955. A decade later, under a new chancellor, the college (now university) would return to Burnsville.[7]

* * *

Ever since its establishment in 1935, the art department had been scattered around campus in makeshift quarters. The fledgling Weatherspoon Gallery was subject to all these inconveniences plus danger from fire. Its collection program was stymied and other museums hesitated to lend their own objects for display. Some consolidation into the old McIver Building occurred in the 1950s, but when it had to be evacuated in 1956 the problem was compounded. Plans for the new McIver Building were cut back in size for financial reasons, and as completed in 1960 it provided less than half the space needed by the department.[8] This was the last straw for Gregory Ivy, who had waged annual battles for adequate quarters ever since his arrival as head in 1935. He resigned in 1961, remarking that this was probably the only art department in the country that taught graduate classes on gymnasium balconies. Although chancellors and trustee visiting committees had repeatedly seconded his appeals, Ivy felt they had not done enough to overcome opposition or indifference farther up the line.[9] The worst of the problem disappeared only in 1967 with the completion of a new wing on the McIver Building devoted entirely to art.

Despite his handicaps Ivy built up one of the largest and best art departments in the Southeast.[10] It was primarily a studio department, with some leavening in art history and appreciation. One-third of its students came from out of state—a tribute to the department and also (he said) to the poverty of art preparation in North Carolina high schools.[11] In the '50s the department asked but did not receive elevation to school status. This also rankled Ivy, who regarded his department as the best known nationally in the college. Although the Weatherspoon collection boasted only 200-odd items, it gained sufficient standing by 1959 to acquire its first full-time curator, James E. Tucker.[12]

* * *

The music program was also aimed primarily at performance, with additional courses in music appreciation and history. Its graduates went primarily into teaching and amateur playing. The school continued to be active in outreach programs helping the public schools locally and statewide to train musical performers.[13] To the original master's degree in composition (1949) others were added in the early '60s in music education, theory, and most instrumental and vocal areas. By 1963 the school was sponsoring a chorale, a choir, a glee club, a band, a chamber orchestra, and an opera theater. All presented concerts on and off campus.[14] Most of these accomplishments were attributable to the leadership of Dean Lee Rigsby, who arrived in 1959.

Dean Hugh Altvater had been a popular and effective leader, and the school enjoyed a good reputation prior to his untimely death in 1952.[15] That event led to nearly a decade of discontinuity and mismanagement that went far to destroy the school's reputation. In the first place, it took two years to hire a successor—G. Welton Marquis of Northern Illinois State Teachers College. His tactless leadership—featuring summary reassignments, demotions, and consequent resignations—managed within a year to alienate most of the faculty. The discord reached the newspapers and undermined the remainder of his three-year tenure. Marquis was a Graham loyalist in the larger campus warfare and in 1957, a year after Graham's departure, Marquis also left; some of his own music loyalists in turn followed him.[16] Two more years were consumed in finding the next dean, Rigsby, of Florida State University. In his own six-year tenure Rigsby went far to restore faculty and student morale as well as the school's off-campus reputation.[17]

The college continued to sponsor the Greensboro Orchestra as a joint venture with the community. When failing health forced Altvater to step down as conductor in 1951, that position went to concertmaster George Dickieson of the music faculty. Under his leadership the orchestra grew to ninety members. Until the early 1960s concerts were held in Aycock Auditorium and the college charged no admission fees. A Greensboro Symphony Society was formed in 1959 to broaden community support for the orchestra. With the cooperation of Rigsby and the college, the society gradually took greater control, choosing the conductor after 1963. The orchestra became financially independent of the college (now university) in 1967. Faculty members and students continued to play in the orchestra for many years to come.[18]

* * *

The history and political science department suffered from twelve years of interim and short-term leaders following Benjamin Kendrick's incapacitating stroke in 1943. For a time American history grew at the expense of the European and other fields. Chancellor Graham, himself a historian by training, noted these problems on his arrival in 1950.[19] His preference, only partially shared by the department, was to bring in as head a senior scholar from outside. At least two well-known historians—J.H. Hexter and Goldwin Smith—were interested but proved elusive.[20] Not until 1955 did the department secure a new head in the person of Richard N. Current, an increasingly noted and upwardly mobile American historian at the University of Illinois.[21] Meanwhile political scientist Louise Alexander served as acting head. Current remained only five years, answering a call from the University of Wisconsin in 1960. (By this time he had moved frequently enough to become known informally in the profession as "Alternating Current;" he returned to UNCG in 1966 for the remainder of his career.) His successor as head, Richard Bardolph (the leading "inside" candidate in the early '50s) had been at the college since 1944 and came to provide a greater longevity in leadership than the department had known for many years.[22]

After the retirement in 1957 of Louise Alexander, four years passed before the arrival of another full-time political scientist, Margaret Hunt. Even after her arrival, historians (including Chancellor Singletary on at least one occasion) taught political science courses. They even introduced the political science major in 1959.[23]

* * *

The romance languages department had always cut a low profile, despite its dozen or more members and its substantial enrollments. Since the 1920s it had offered majors in French and Spanish, as well as beginning and intermediate courses in Italian. Winfield S. Barney, the head since 1919, retired in 1953. Meta Helena Miller, a department member since 1922, replaced him as head until her own retirement in 1962. Chancellor Graham took a dim view of the department's academic standing (a view shared by some students) but neither he nor his immediate successors did much by way of remediation.[24] Miller conceded before her retirement that she still regarded herself primarily as a caretaker. One of the candidates to succeed her found the department lacking in direction and outdated methodologically, yet highly receptive to innovation.[25] The new head in 1962 was Charles D. Blend of Ohio State University.

After witnessing a second war with Germany, Caroline Schoch, the intrepid head (and recently sole member) of the German department, retired in 1948. Her successor was William R. Barrett, a 29-year-old South Carolinian with an impending Ph.D. from Chapel Hill. By 1953 Barrett, with the assistance of his wife who taught part-time, could point to enrollments more than double those he inherited.[26] Nevertheless the German major was dropped that year for lack of student interest. The Barretts left in 1954, to be replaced on a year-to-year basis by an older man, Dr. Ernst Breisacher, who retired in 1960.[27] That impending event prompted Mereb Mossman in 1959 to float the idea of combining romance languages and German into a single department of modern languages. When romance languages objected, she dropped the idea and hired a new German professor—Anne F. Baecker of the University of Cincinnati. At Baecker's urging the German major was restored in 1962. That year also saw the department title change to German and Russian—a Russian course having been added in 1959 under the impact of the USSR's Sputnik launch. The department had grown to two persons—sometimes two and a half—and enrollments were up correspondingly.[28]

Sputnik also led to the creation of interdisciplinary international studies programs around the country. WC's came in 1962. Its two original focal points were Asia and Latin America. The language departments were involved, as were history and the social sciences.[29]

With cooperation from the language departments, the college also adopted a junior year abroad program by 1961, permitting approved students to study in France, Spain, Switzerland, Germany, or Mexico.[30]

* * *

Warren Ashby arrived in 1949 as head (and sole member) of the philosophy department. An idealist and social activist, he devoted his career to the college/university, the Greensboro community, and a number of wider causes. His campus activities (apart from building up the philosophy department) included development of the honors council, a residential college, and a department of religious studies, each of which he headed for a time. Off campus, he was a conspicuous advocate of racial desegregation in Greensboro at a time when this was neither popular nor safe. In the mid-1960s, he spent two years in India working for the American Friends Service Committee. Parts of many other years were devoted to researching and writing a biography of UNC President Frank Porter Graham, one of the liberal heroes of his generation in North Carolina.[31]

Ashby was also an early and ardent supporter of Chancellor Edward Kidder Graham and his general education proposals; he apparently suffered for years in consequence.[32] One possible casualty was the philosophy major, which Ashby requested perennially. Opponents confidentially voiced lack of confidence in him as a philosopher as well as the proposed major's partial reliance on cognate courses in other departments. He finally prevailed in 1962 after the department added a second member, Robert Rosthal. Ashby was promoted to full professor in 1959 and received both teaching and service awards in later years.[33]

Meanwhile, in answer to student demand Ashby (an ordained Methodist minister) was permitted to offer two courses in the philosophy of religion and the history of Christian thought. By 1956 these courses accounted for nearly two-thirds of the departmental enrollment, reflecting a national religious revival of sorts, shown on campuses not only in proliferating religion courses but also departments of religious studies.[34] The latter development had to wait a number of years locally, but when it came, Ashby was at its center.

* * *

Biology remained the largest science department on campus. J. P. Givler retired as head in 1949, not to be replaced until 1952. His successor, Victor Cutter, Jr., was heir to a United Fruit Company fortune and was offered by his father early in life a seat on the New York Stock Exchange. He elected instead to attend graduate school in biology at Cornell, where he met Edward Kidder Graham. Like other new department heads under Graham, his assignment was to encourage research activity in a faculty that had not hitherto seen this as a priority.[35] His own field was cancer research and, ironically, he was suddenly diagnosed with the disease himself and died from it in 1962, a decade after his arrival.[36] By that time the department numbered twelve members, nine of them with the doctorate.

* * *

James Highsmith, founder of the psychology department, retired in 1953. Elizabeth Duffy, the department's (if not the college's) primary research scholar, expressed interest in succeeding him and was recommended by a number of outside consultants. But personal opposition inside and outside the department led to the appointment a year later of Kendon Smith, a Minnesotan coming from Pennsylvania State University.[37] Smith regarded the department as a whole as professionally weak, and spent several years replacing junior members as humanely as possible.[38]

Smith quickly concluded that the college needed at least one staff psychologist to counsel students. There was none, although as he pointed out to Chancellor Graham, most colleges around the country retained close to two full-time psychologists per thousand students; Chapel Hill and State both had active psychological clinics. Such a facility would also be invaluable as a laboratory for students in clinical psychology, a newly opening vocational area for women. For budgetary reasons all he could get, beginning in 1955, was a Greensboro psychiatrist coming to campus one day a week, assisted by a member of Smith's department. After a few years, as enrollments grew and needs increased, the psychiatrist came more often.[39]

* * *

The sociology department suffered considerable losses in the 1950s; Mereb Mossman became academic dean, two other popular teachers (one of them the later-prominent Guy Johnson) departed to accept higher salaries elsewhere, and department head Glenn Johnson retired in 1954. Student enrollments and majors slumped temporarily but climbed back to unprecedented heights by the end of the decade.[40] Two young women joined the department in 1960 and 1961, Elaine Burgess specializing in race relations and Harriet Kupferer in anthropology. Both believed that the department, under Mossman's influence, was too much oriented toward her vocational social work field and too little to the academic and theoretical concerns of modern sociology. They convinced Chancellor Otis Singletary, another young Turk. Under pressure from above and below, therefore, Lyda Gordon Shivers (department head since 1954) gradually made the desired changes. In 1961 the department formally broadened its title to sociology and anthropology.[41]

* * *

Tension between the liberal arts faculty and those teaching in professional or vocational fields was as old as the college. Whether it occurred within departments or (more often) between the liberal arts departments and the professional schools, it surfaced whenever institutional directions or priorities were at issue. It constantly arose in faculty elections. The complainants, more often than not, were the professional schools or departments, who were in the minority and frequently saw themselves as step-children.

Home economics entered the '50s with morale at low ebb. Outgoing department head Margaret Edwards appears to have left in 1951 under duress, primarily from members of her own faculty. The department had attained a measure of national recognition along with school status in 1949 but Edwards was not promoted to dean. When Graham, who engineered her ouster, tried to make amends by offering to name the new home economics building for her (especially as she had led in planning it) Edwards rejected the idea and severed all ties with the college.[42]

Her successor, Katherine Roberts, now dean, was recruited in 1952 from the Mayo Clinic, apparently without consulting the home ec faculty—most of whom Graham held in low regard.[43] With his full support, Roberts set out to build up the school academically and promote research. Although it already included two faculty members who were engaged heavily if not primarily in research, very few of them held the doctorate—only three out of twenty-five as late as 1958. (Until recently the doctorate had not been regarded as necessary nor was it widely available in home economics.) A stronger graduate program required not only a stronger faculty but the availability of graduate work in cognate areas. In nutrition, for instance, it depended on graduate courses in chemistry, which the college did not offer. All this required funding at a level beyond what the state was providing. And hopes of raising money through the Home Economics Foundation were jeopardized by the turmoil now raging around Graham.[44]

A capable scholar and administrator, Roberts attributed her difficulties partly to that turmoil and partly to lack of faculty support for home economics in general. Regarding Graham as her strongest supporter, she became his; her faculty remained divided. One of their concerns, never fully addressed, was to give department status and some autonomy to the six instructional areas within the school. Her faculty did agree with Roberts that—despite school status and a new state-of-the-art building—they were still second-class citizens in a liberal arts college. When Graham was forced out in 1956, Roberts left also, seeing little prospect of support professionally or personally in his absence.[45]

With Acting Chancellor Pierson unwilling to make long-range commitments, Gordon Blackwell faced the necessity of appointing a new dean. In 1958 he conferred the mantle upon Naomi Albanese, a dynamic young assistant professor at Ohio State University—only three years past her doctorate.[46] (Again, there seems to have been minimal consultation among the home ec faculty.) Albanese went to work raising money, recruiting faculty with doctorates, and upgrading the curriculum. Owing to her own personality and also to growing support for higher education throughout the country, she succeeded far beyond the level of her predecessors. The school (like the college) began to receive larger appropriations, and more research money came from the agricultural extension office at State College. Albanese carefully cultivated business leaders, who responded not only with donations to the school but consulting assignments and even corporate board memberships for herself. In fact, she was something of a pioneer for women in both respects. She opened doors in the business world as well as higher education for a great many of her women graduates. At her instance Burlington Industries endowed a professorship in textiles in 1959–60. Also in 1959, the school organized an Institute of Child and Family Development (financed by a reinvigorated Home Economics Foundation) to sponsor research in that field. The doctoral program in child development came at the same time.[47]

Albanese also cultivated her own faculty, treating them as family and making herself part of their families. She remembered birthdays (theirs and their children's), attended weddings, baptisms, even Eagle Scout award ceremonies. If this did not win over everyone, it came very close. She was an intense person with a strong personality and occasionally a sharp temper.[48]

Administrators developed a healthy regard for Dean Albanese, even if they continued to suspect her academic standards and those of the home economics faculty. Some of the skepticism came from Chapel Hill (both the campus and general administration) which seldom rejoiced in extending any graduate programs to Raleigh and Greensboro. (Chancellor Blackwell assigned that attitude as one of his reasons for leaving for Florida State after three years.) But the criticism did not always emanate from Chapel Hill. WC graduate Dean J.A. Davis was very critical of the home ec faculty's research activity and scholarly attainments. He reported to Blackwell that "on every contact I have had with [one new faculty member, that individual] has proved... unable to talk in sentences or to have any clear cut, self-directed purposes and goals." Davis agreed with authorities in Chapel Hill that the new doctoral program rested more on future promise than on present capacity. "As long as we accept such [master's thesis topics] as 'Storage Requirements for Bathrooms'... or 'Information on Home Furniture for Potential Television Programs...' we cannot demonstrate that the graduate faculty in home economics knows how to direct or evaluate graduate level research." When Davis took his comments and suggestions for improvement to Albanese, he found her hostile.[49]

Otis Singletary, arriving in 1961 when the doctoral program was a *fait accompli*, echoed Davis's skepticism that either the home ec faculty or the college's science departments could support it without additional reinforcement. He was ready to see the school of home economics move to State College, and Dean Albanese with it.[50] As it happened, she long outlasted him.

How much of this criticism sprang from liberal arts bias against professional training is debatable. When SACS sent its interdisciplinary evaluation committee to the college for its accreditation study in 1962, the committee reported faculty morale in home economics as high and praised Albanese for her achievements. Although it still found the number of Ph.D.'s—six at that time—as too low, the committee nevertheless recommended the creation of additional doctoral programs in home ec education, nutrition, and textiles.[51]

A laboratory for the program in child development, and a main drawing card for its doctoral program, was the nursery school, founded in 1929 and housed after 1954 in a modern new building on McIver Street. The children were three and four-year-olds. (Older children were studied primarily at Curry School.) In its new quarters the nursery school became so popular with townspeople that long waiting lists developed. The American Home Economics Association publicized it nationally. Beginning in 1957, other preschool programs were created as well, housed in various locations on campus.[52]

On completion of the new home economics building in 1951, the cafeteria relocated there, with increased business.[53] Although it was operated as a laboratory for the foods and nutrition students, the cafeteria became a virtual faculty club as well, with departments, committees, and political caucuses holding meetings there over lunch.

As the number of American women attending college after World War II rose, so did the numbers majoring in home economics. Their proportion of the total female enrollment shrank, however, as women acquired more and more vocational options.[54] At WC, about 60 percent of their course work was in the liberal arts and 40 percent in home economics—a reversal of the national averages. The school graduated fifty bachelor's and seven master's candidates in 1961.[55]

* * *

The college's minimal nursing program of World War I—itself the successor to a false start in 1912—did not survive the 1920s. The shortage of nurses in World War II inspired yet another start. In 1942 the faculty approved a bachelor of science in nursing (BSN) program, to be carried out with cooperating hospitals. The college was to provide two and a half years of liberal arts and science training, followed by another two and a half years in an approved hospital nursing school. (It was later changed to two years at WC and three at a hospital.) At the end the student received both the BSN and RN degrees. The program got off to a slow start and was still floundering when Chancellor Jackson left office in 1950.[56] Edward Kidder Graham regarded it as academically deficient and would have phased it out, but outside pressures made that inadvisable. There was a critical shortage of nurses nationwide, to which the university responded in the early '50s with a new school of nursing at Chapel Hill. At the same time, Moses Cone Hospital was under construction in Greensboro. It needed nurses and would cooperate with Woman's College or any other institution in the area that would help it to train them.[57]

But this was a moving target. Nurses came increasingly to be trained in shorter periods. The BSN program expired in 1962,[58] unable to compete with a two-year associate degree program established in 1957, involving two years at the college and three months at Cone Hospital. With up to thirty-two graduates per year, that program operated until 1967 when a full baccalaureate nursing school opened at UNCG.[59]

* * *

The college entered the 1950s, as it had the '40s, with both a four-year baccalaureate program in business education (or secretarial administration) and a one-year commercial program that also turned out secretaries. They were offered by separate departments. Outside consultants urged in 1954 that the programs be merged. But the matter got sidetracked during the Graham controversy and it was decided at least for the time being to keep them separate.[60] The business education department under Vance Littlejohn continued to offer a master's degree although the relative dearth of doctorates among its faculty caused concern.[61]

The short commercial program—dating from the college's founding and a mainstay during the Depression—enrolled about 200 students annually during the '50s. All came from North Carolina and virtually all remained in the state after graduation.[62] Except for the college-wide health and physical education requirements, the curriculum was confined to typing, shorthand, accounting, business correspondence, and training in the use of office machines. Even more than the four-year program, its thin intellectual content worried many faculty and administrators.[63]Furthermore, enrollments fell off sharply in the early 1960s owing to competition from the new, lower-cost community colleges, technical institutes, and private business colleges. In 1967, faced with only 111 students, the institution (now UNCG) decided to terminate the program. That action was clearly indicated, and administrators likened it to the concurrent termination of the two-year nursing program. But it came with no little sorrow given the program's long history and its body of devoted alumnae.[64]

* * *

The college's best foundation for graduate work in the early 1950s may well have been in physical education. Mary Channing Coleman and Ethel Martus had built one of the leading PE training programs for women in the country. Doctoral degrees in physical education were still rare, but Martus (who often regretted not having gotten one herself) began recruiting actual and incipient Ph.D.s as fast as she could, beginning with Rosemary McGee in 1954. Meanwhile, she set out to offer graduate work in the department. Following approval of the MFA degree in dance in 1949, she secured a master of education in PE in 1951 and (after long effort) a master of science in 1959. By that year some sixty students had already earned one of these degrees in the department; virtually all of them secured college teaching jobs after graduation. The master's program soon was well known and students came from around the world. In 1962 Martus and the PE department at Chapel Hill proposed a joint Ph.D. program. Rebuffed by general administration, she pushed for one at WC intended primarily for women which also failed despite Singletary's strong backing. But she (and UNCG) did secure a doctoral program through the back door in 1966—a doctor of education in physical education. The Ph.D. would take longer.

In 1954 Martus began pushing for school status. This also took many years to achieve, owing partly to the shifting chancellorship, partly to the political strength on campus of the liberal arts, partly to controversy over placement of the health department, and partly to opposition in Chapel Hill.

The health matter became particularly acute. That department in 1954 included college physician Ruth Collings as well as Alice Schriver, who taught certain health courses required of physical education majors. (In the public schools physical education teachers often taught health as well, hence the requirement.) Physical education students found these courses inadequate, which led to a long curricular-turned-personal controversy between Martus and Schriver. Martus saw her proposal for school status as a perfect solution to the problem. Citing a national trend toward combining health and physical education instruction into a single administrative entity, she asked that health be incorporated into the new school, presumably under her leadership. (Ironically, this would reverse her predecessor's action in 1935, when in the interest of greater autonomy for physical education, Coleman led it out of a combined department with health.) In 1954–55 the health department at WC was still independent and seeking closer ties with the science departments, not physical education. The matter remained unresolved until Collings' retirement in 1963, when Chancellor Singletary combined the two departments under Martus' leadership. Although this represented a political triumph for her, school status still had to wait.[65]

Despite her emphasis on graduate programs, Martus was not a research scholar nor did she push her faculty in that direction. A number chose to take the path on their own, receiving her blessing, and became well known. Martus herself continued to stress the traditional college goals of teaching excellence and active service in one's professional organizations. The department did in fact contain some excellent and popular teachers, such as Virginia Moomaw in dance and Ellen Griffin, who attracted 400 students a year to her golf classes. Later faculty recruits sometimes accused their elders of mothering the students. That solicitude explains the perpetuation of the Old Girl professional and job network that traced back through Martus and Coleman to Amy Morris Homans at Wellesley College.[66]

The department's programs were advanced considerably with the opening in 1952 of a second gymnasium: the modernistic building conceived by Mary Channing Coleman and ultimately named for her.

At a greater distance, the lake at the college's Camp Ahutforfun (the second of that name, purchased in 1943 near the Guilford battleground) became polluted and unusable. In 1956 the college bought Piney Lake, a larger and finer spread several miles south of town. (The property totaled forty acres, the lake itself four. The college borrowed the necessary $70,000, which it gradually repaid out of student and user fees.) After more than forty years, its affiliation with the institution has lasted longer than all its predecessors combined. From the beginning, Piney Lake with its buildings and grounds was used as a laboratory for recreation majors. It also served as an outdoor classroom and recreational facility for other students from WC, Curry School, and the community. Classes were taught in water biology, arts and crafts, sports, and camping. In 1962 it averaged sixty campers per week.[67]

* * *

No professional field received more criticism from the liberal arts than did education. It was a national phenomenon, reaching major proportions after the formation in 1952 of NCATE: the National Council for Accreditation of Teacher Education. The liberal arts attack was expressed most articulately by historian Arthur Bestor in a book entitled *Educational Wastelands* (1953). At issue were the quality of professional standards in teacher training, particularly the curriculum. Critics said professional educators overemphasized their own (often vapid) methods courses at the expense of the academic subjects that prospective teachers would be expected to teach. There was merit to the complaints, but also an element of self-interest on both sides of the ensuing debate.[68]

At WC, such concerns were evident as early as the 1930s, when the faculty limited students (the great majority of them prospective teachers) in the number of education hours they could take and required them to major in subject fields. Except for an interdepartmental concentration in elementary education introduced in the '40s, there was no education major.[69] Students voiced the same criticisms over the years, protesting the methods courses they were required to take for teacher certification. A *Carolinian* editorial of 1953 dismissed the education curriculum as a collection of "redundant, skimpy courses" with little relevance to the problems teachers would actually experience in the classroom.[70]

As certification requirements were set by the state, the college had only a limited ability to respond to the criticisms. Chancellor Graham himself lashed out publicly at the national education establishment in 1952, calling for a review of state requirements.[71] Even education Dean Charles Prall was concerned to maximize the academic and minimize the methods courses in the curriculum. The limitations of the 1930s remained in place.[72] On Prall's retirement in 1958, his successor Kenneth Howe created a faculty Teacher Education Council, interdisciplinary in composition, to manage the program.[73] As in other professional fields, the doctoral degree was not a standard requirement in earlier years. In 1958 there were only two Ph.D.s in the education faculty. Dean Howe increased the number to twelve by the time he stepped down in 1966.[74]

National accreditation also began to intrude on the college's teacher training arrangements. NCATE first reached WC in 1962. Its visiting team appeared more interested in the program's organization than its content. It criticized the college-wide diffusion of control, preferring centralization in the school of education. This opinion pleased few outside the school of education. Chancellor Singletary noted that NCATE had refused to accredit Yale University and queried whether it was not in fact abasing national education standards. The college received only provisional accreditation in 1962. Singletary and the faculty considered thumbing their noses at NCATE but feared to penalize alumnae, who could expect a harder time finding teaching jobs in other states after graduating from a non-accredited institution. So Singletary orchestrated a reorganization of the Teacher Education Council and a few other modifications without fundamentally changing the program. This proved sufficient and in 1964 NCATE granted full accreditation.[75]

Nearly every member of the education faculty had some role at Curry School, usually supervising student teachers. WC student enrollment increases in the 1950s were so great as to overwhelm Curry's capacity to absorb the practice teachers. More and more were sent out to the public schools. By 1966, they were going to other counties, even as far as Charlotte. Many Curry pupils and their parents (often WC faculty members) found the small classes and the individual attention they received there invaluable. But at the secondary level Curry was so small and its offerings so limited that students often transferred to the other high schools for both curricular and extracurricular enrichment.[76]

Curry's problems were legion. It had always been intended not only as a practice teaching facility but as a laboratory for research and experimentation in child development, curriculum, teaching methods, and school administration. It fell short in each of these particulars. It did not in the '50s attract the quality of faculty that its laboratory function required. And the physical plant had so deteriorated that one of the deanship candidates in 1958 proclaimed it the worst he had ever seen.[77] By Spring 1959 rumors were flying that the college would close Curry altogether. Although administrators scurried to scotch the rumors, serious discussions in fact were held that year about closing the high school. The decision was to retain it and try to raise its academic standards, emphasizing the liberal arts and college preparatory work. Although that decision was reaffirmed in 1962 for another three years, Dean Howe dissented concerning the high school. He regarded the Curry program and faculty as no better than average; if it could not soon rise above the level of the other Greensboro schools he favored closing the entire school. On the other hand, thanks to the passage of a state bond referendum in 1959, the physical plant was greatly improved. The repairs and additions included the construction in 1961 of Park Gymnasium next door to the Curry Building.[78]

* * *

Summer school was always closely related to education, as most of the summer school students were public school teachers. The college offered two six-week terms each summer, with the vast majority of enrollments taking place in the first term. Total enrollments in the late '50s and early '60s were about a thousand, roughly two-thirds of them graduate students.[79] Further, graduate Dean Davis reported in 1960, almost two thirds of the instructional hours taken by graduate students in the course of a calendar year were taken in the summer. The summer session was still required to be self-supporting, with the result that faculty were paid less than they received for equivalent work during the school year.[80]

Much of the college's graduate work was also taken in the form of extension courses—on and off campus, some via television. It too was geared largely to teachers.[81] The extension department operated the summer Burnsville Fine Arts School until the college dropped it in 1954. It hosted a multitude of academic, civic, and athletic meetings on campus, ranging from Girls' State and the High School Music Contest to the North Carolina Coaches' Clinic and a regional High School Debating Contest.[82] The department remained underfunded and undermanned. Heading it (along with development) was the indefatigable Charlie Phillips until his retirement in 1962, after twenty-seven years of service. His successor Clarence Shipton was a member of the education and Curry faculties. Shipton would make his largest splash after 1964 as dean of men.

Chapter 18

Students and Alumnae

Woman's College shared fully in the surge of college enrollments after World War II. Student numbers rose 60 percent between 1945 and 1962—to 3,575. They could have risen higher: the limiting factor was still dormitory space. Despite the existence by 1962 of nineteen residence halls, many students continued to be crowded by threes into rooms intended for two. Only for graduate students did the college return to the neighborhood overflow policy of McIver and Foust—allowing students to rent rooms off campus.

There were two interesting demographic trends in this period. Out-of-state students increased from about 10 percent to 15 percent of the total enrollment, reflecting a relaxation of the university-wide limit. At the same time, students hailing from Guilford and the eight nearest counties rose from a quarter to a third of the total enrollment.[1] Except for graduate students, most of them lived on campus. Commuters—the day or town students—represented fewer than 10 percent of the total; in 1960 they numbered 203. They continued to have a campus room for study and socializing, after 1954 in Elliott Hall.[2] Foreign students were so few—five to seven per year—that Chancellor Blackwell tried in 1959 to recruit more.[3]

Transfer students, both in and out, became a matter of great interest and concern. In the coeducational Depression year of 1932 the college counted 101 students of both genders who had transferred at least temporarily from other institutions, many for economic reasons.[4] Better times brought a decrease until the 1950s, when they rose again along with overall enrollment. There were slightly over 100 transfer students in 1962. Many or most were graduates of junior colleges, the leading contributor being Mars Hill in the mountains near Asheville. About 15 percent of WC graduates in the early '50s had come as transfer students.[5]

Those students replaced others who transferred out. The latter began to cause anxiety in the 1940s, particularly if they were transferring to Chapel Hill. Until 1963, that campus could accept only a few women at the freshman and sophomore levels: local girls and those whose academic programs were not offered at WC. But the junior and senior years were a different matter. Substantial numbers of WC students transferred after the sophomore year if their grades were good enough. Some had come to WC as freshmen intending to transfer after two years. The attraction was partly academic but mostly masculine, according to both anecdotal evidence and an informal survey of departing students in 1963.[6]

The college was sufficiently concerned to keep records, which showed that the exodus was being exaggerated. In the mid-'50s, at least, WC had a higher retention rate between the sophomore and junior years than either Chapel Hill or State.[7] Moreover, 49.6 percent of the freshmen admitted in 1955 continued to graduation in 1959, a percentage normal for WC in that period and about ten points higher than the national average. The largest mortality was that following the freshman year, and it was primarily for academic reasons. Most end-of-the-year sophomores who left did so primarily to transfer elsewhere, but they amounted to only about 20 percent of their original freshman class. Chancellor Blackwell said in 1960 that junior transfers to Chapel Hill numbered about seventy-five per year, a level he did not find bothersome. The problem lay less in the numbers who were leaving than in their high academic quality.[8]

The great majority of students now came from urban middle class backgrounds. Almost half of the parents of entering freshmen in 1952 had themselves attended college.[9] The homogeneous student community of earlier years was still present, if slightly more cosmopolitan.[10] Married students were no longer turned away as they had been before the war. About 10 percent of the seniors married before graduation, according to Dean Katherine Taylor in 1956; most of their husbands were in the military. In 1958 she counted sixty-five married undergraduates, about a third of them living in the residence halls. Most of the graduate students but only a few undergraduates were above the traditional college age.[11] Finally, it was regarded as safe for male graduate students to return in 1962, six years after racial desegregation caused their ouster.

* * *

Family-style meals had been the rule morning, noon, and evening until 1932 and most evenings thereafter. They disappeared in 1956; the student body had outgrown the dining halls and could no longer eat simultaneously. Given a choice between consecutive family sittings and a cafeteria format, the students voted for the latter, leaving them free to sit with whomever they pleased. The price they paid was waiting in long lines. The food service was still in college hands, serving traditional southern cooking to a generally appreciative clientele.[12]

* * *

When Dr. Ruth Collings retired in 1963, the health service consisted of three full-time physicians, a part-time psychiatrist, six nurses, a lab technician, and a secretary. The two most prevalent illnesses, Collings indicated in a parting statement, were now mental illness and mononucleosis—both of them little recognized if not unknown when she came aboard in 1925. A Greensboro psychiatrist now came to campus for ten hours a week and the other physicians spent at least half of their time dealing with emotional problems. As for mononucleosis, the infirmary now contained three to five students suffering from that disease at any given time.[13] In 1958 an outside consultant gave the health service high marks despite its spartan budget, calling special attention to the new Anna Gove infirmary building on Gray Drive.[14]

* * *

By the early 1960s, in-state students were paying $870 a year in expenses including tuition, room, and board; out-of-state girls paid $1295.[15] The traditional form of financial aid since McIver's day had been student loans, bearing no interest until after graduation. But students now regarded loans as a last resort, and in any case the college limited the amount they could borrow. In the early '50s, fewer than forty students per year took out loans. In 1959–60, after a federal student loan program had been instituted, the number rose to 142, averaging about $350 apiece.[16]

There were more scholarships than in earlier years but they were still too few and too small, leading many promising applicants to go elsewhere. Most of the scholarships, like the loans, covered little beyond tuition.[17]

Otis Singletary regarded scholarship money as the college's greatest single need and he directed the growing fund-raising efforts to that end. Greensboro's Jefferson Standard Life Insurance Company endowed four scholarships in 1961, each amounting to $750 per year.[18] The greatest windfall came next year when the Z. Smith Reynolds Foundation created the Katharine Smith Reynolds Scholarships, named for the Normal student who left school in 1900 and later married R.J. Reynolds. Under this grant eleven students would each receive $1,200 per year, renewable for four years.[19] Overall, the number of scholarships awarded rose from 195 in 1953 to 717 in 1963—or from 8 percent to 20 percent of the student enrollment.[20]

Loans and scholarships frequently went hand in hand with part-time jobs. The number of students working on campus rose from 584 in 1952–53 to 625 a decade later, but that represented a significant decrease in the proportion who were employed—from 24 percent down to 17 percent of the total enrollment. The drop was surely attributable in part to increased scholarship money and the triumph of the cafeteria dining system. Many more students applied for work than the college could employ. The jobs that were performed seemed almost infinite in variety, from office work to shifting scenery in the TV studio to lifeguarding at the swimming pool. Although the going wage for all campus work kept increasing in the face of inflation, it was usually well below any acceptable minimum, to use Katherine Taylor's phrase. At least a few students worked downtown, or at least off campus. They might get paid more, but higher lunch, clothing, and transportation costs could eat up the difference.[21]

* * *

Katherine Taylor remained through this period as dean of women or—after 1951—dean of students. Her responsibilities in the Graham years embraced student counseling, the residence halls, the dining halls, the health service, the student union, student organizations and their publications, religious activities, financial aid, and placement.[22] Graham entrusted her with a variety of academic tasks as well, such as chairing important faculty committees. As a result, he told President Gordon Gray in 1953, Taylor "is about as closely related to academic quality control as Dean Mossman or I."[23] As an active Graham lieutenant, she suffered some slings, arrows, and diminution of authority after his departure. But the diminution derived also from bureaucratic shifts required by the college's enrollment growth. Taylor was so clearly in command of her job that it seems never to have been in danger. She also had a large following among the students, although her notions of proper behavior and attire were not always as advanced as theirs.[24]

A new student union opened in March 1953, replacing the already-gone Students' Building. Named for Harriet Elliott, who had launched the battle to have it erected, it became the focal point of extracurricular activities by students, and often by faculty as well. It contained a ballroom (named for Laura Cone, a major donor to the building); a variety of meeting and recreation rooms; offices for student organizations; the campus bookstore; a dining room open to students, faculty, and the general public; and (after 1960) new quarters for the Soda Shop. Some of its rooms and hallways doubled as an art gallery. It housed the campus post office until 1959, when the college began delivering mail to the dormitories. Cone Ballroom was used for dances, but also for lectures, recitals, exhibits, banquets, and student meetings. In charge of the building and its activities was Elvira Prondecki, who had come to the college in 1945 as a residence hall counselor. (She, like Laura Anderton, had met Katherine Taylor in the WAVES. And it was Prondecki, a housemate of Dean Taylor's, who years later married former Chancellor Graham.)[25]

Harriet Elliott's counseling or advisory system continued through the 1950s under Taylor's direction. Helen Burns continued each year as freshman class chairman, or academic adviser. Other faculty members rotated as chairmen of the other classes, each following her designated class from the sophomore year through to graduation. Still other women served as residence hall counselors, charged with the "whole development" of each student, academic as well as social. But the '50s saw a gradual breakdown of the always-difficult integration between academic and social counseling. Sharing responsibility for the breakdown were mounting enrollments and the college's effort to upgrade itself academically. Under Elliott, some of the residence hall counselors were faculty members, but in the late '50s Dean Mossman made it clear that these women could no longer expect academic promotions as only part-time teachers. They all moved into full-time teaching, therefore, and the dormitory counselors who remained (and reported to Dean Taylor) had virtually no contact with the faculty. In fact, the college reverted to its earlier days: older women—some never married, others widows with grown children—served again as surrogate mothers to the students. They performed a vital role, but they reflected an unacknowledged retreat if not repeal of the Elliott plan.

By 1960, mounting enrollments and the retirement of Helen Burns seemed to mandate changes in academic advising too. Chancellor Blackwell appointed Laura Anderton of the biology department as associate dean of the college (under Mossman) in charge of all academic and vocational counseling. There was little effort to reintegrate academic and social counseling (or the academic and social life of students) beyond a general admonition for the two campus offices to cooperate.[26]

* * *

Student religious affiliations did not change markedly from earlier years. Methodists, Baptists, Presbyterians, and Episcopalians in that order led five successive annual polls in the 1950s. Thirteen denominational organizations existed on campus in 1958.[27] The four largest maintained nearby student centers as they had since the '30s. The college itself continued to operate a religious activities center, located after 1953 in Elliott Hall. Chancellor Blackwell felt that religion occupied a greater place in student life at WC than any other state institution he knew.[28] The evidence for this included four annual university sermons, weekly dormitory devotions, Sunday evening vespers, an annual inter-faith forum, and a Thanksgiving assembly, all attended by substantial numbers of students. In addition, according to Dean Taylor, about 1,200 students regularly attended church services in Greensboro. Depending on size, the churches sent buses or cars to pick up students on campus.[29]

The campus YWCA was moribund by 1958, following a national trend. Its functions were picked up by a new campus Inter-Faith Council. By 1959 the council was responsible for many of the campus activities just mentioned.[30]

Campus religious observance no longer included the mandatory chapel services. Since 1936 they had given way to student assemblies or mass meetings, still mandatory. They were primarily secular although the Inter-Faith Council sponsored some which it pointedly called chapel services.[31] In 1962, owing to burgeoning enrollments and the limited capacity of Aycock Auditorium, regular assemblies were restricted to one per semester; all students were expected to attend but upperclassmen were not checked.[32]

* * *

Student government changed very little following the reforms of the 1930s and '40s. "Student Government on this campus does what student governments at other colleges and universities claim to do—an[d] in that respect is unique," wrote Edward Kidder Graham in 1952. "The kids are so natural and unselfconscious about the way they run the largest woman's college in the country that they do not realize that they themselves are about as strong and sophisticated a department of political science as you would find anywhere." (No wonder the students backed Graham in return.) The visiting SACS accreditation team came to about the same conclusion a decade later.[33] SGA continued to sponsor an annual pre-school conference for student leaders, which by 1953 occupied two and a half days. Administrators, faculty members, and fellow students gave talks, made reports, and participated in panel discussions. Louise Alexander that year gave two of the talks, one of them entitled "The Elliott Influence (The W.C. Renaissance)." UNC President Gordon Gray also spoke.[34]

The heart of student government was the judicial system and the honor policy that it implemented. The girls even hosted an annual honor policy conference for high school students.[35] The honor code was so well respected as it applied to academic conduct that students were insulted if a faculty member remained in the classroom to proctor a test. Yet it remained difficult to enforce the social regulations, where the code also applied.[36]

Student government presidents were known and well regarded by the college administrators. They served in the chancellor's administrative council or cabinet; in 1960 that group changed its meeting time because the SGA president had a class conflict. At least two presidents in the '50s deserve mention. June Rainey's freshman class contributed money to create a scholarship for one of their number who was in financial need. Her identity was kept secret, and only at graduation in 1952 was it announced that their scholarship recipient was Rainey, the outgoing SGA president and the person they had just elected everlasting class president. A year after graduation she returned to campus as secretary to Chancellor Graham. She was among those who departed soon after he did in 1956. The SGA president in 1956–57 was Sadye Dunn. On her graduation the admissions office hired her as its field director, or head recruiter.[37] In 1962 Dunn became director of admissions, and in 1964 dean of women.

Although June Rainey had been elected SGA president in 1951 in what was hailed as a record 91 percent student turnout, critics occasionally called the process dull or farcical and urged the introduction of political parties *a la* Chapel Hill to spice it up. A political party was organized in 1952, but it met so much opposition that it declared its purpose to be educational only, and refused to nominate candidates.[38]

* * *

Students of the 1950s were not much interested in politics or public affairs at any level. At WC as elsewhere, college girls seemed most interested in finding a husband. Indeed many dropped out early to get married. Annual fashion shows were held on campus featuring bridal gowns and attendants' attire. Girls who sported engagement rings before graduation enjoyed particular esteem. The *Carolinian* ran articles early in 1952 tallying the numbers who had become engaged over the recent Christmas holidays. There were so many, one of these stories remarked, "that one would think half the campus had been majoring in marriage with a minor in diamond cutting." The story ended with a reminder to readers that this was leap year: "Good luck and good hunting!"[39] This preoccupation always existed in some degree, but it now exceeded anything since the 1920s. In fact, many '50s students were attracted to the Roaring '20s and avidly sought out the works of F. Scott Fitzgerald.

At WC as elsewhere, the signals depended on which students one heard or saw. In 1951, faculty members and students themselves decried what they variously termed apathy or low morale; the *Carolinian* reverted to this subject for years. And (to repeat) the infirmary noted a great increase in the number of students with emotional problems. Yet student government flourished, the honor system (at least for academic conduct) functioned well, and campus visitors were favorably impressed with the students they met. So were faculty members who recalled these years from a distance. The trustees' visiting committee in 1958 lauded (as it often had in the past) the "poise, ambition, leadership, and healthy, happy outlook of the students."[40]

Administrators tended for several years to downplay the charges of apathy or low morale. By the early '60s, however, they grew more concerned. Katherine Taylor lamented in 1962 that a world famous composer addressed only empty chairs in Cone Ballroom while the next night students hung from the rafters watching a fashion show. "Aycock [Auditorium] has not had a capacity audience for years," she said; and "not even Robert Frost can fill Cone Ballroom." On the other hand, the dean of women at Florida State, who came to campus and interviewed students as part of the SACS accreditation that year, sought to reassure Chancellor Singletary. She thought the students she had met were probably representative, and except for a few "beatnics" (whom she encountered on every campus) all seemed happy and proud of the college. Taylor herself noted that the National Student Association had recently attracted a standing room only audience.[41]

In fact, there were signs of a growing student concern with larger social issues—particularly race, the one closest to home. The college admitted its first two black students in 1956 and the numbers grew slowly thereafter; there were about thirty black undergraduates by 1963. Simultaneously, the civil rights movement came to Greensboro. On Monday, February 1, 1960, four students from the state Agricultural and Technical College for blacks, in Greensboro, staged a sit-in demonstration at the lunch counter in the Woolworth's store downtown. Without realizing it at the time, they launched one of the most effective components of the entire civil rights struggle. By Friday the original four had grown to over 300 students from several local campuses. The great majority were blacks but a conspicuous few were whites, including three from WC wearing their class jackets. (Some of WC's new black students were also present, but they did not stand out from the crowd and their collegiate identity got less attention.) As historian William Chafe has noted, the three white girls provoked headlines across the state.

Next day, an alarmed Chancellor Gordon Blackwell stepped in to contain the damage that he feared the demonstrations might cause the community, and particularly that these girls might cause the college. All three of the white students were conveniently from out of state: Washington, D.C., Florida, and London, England. For weeks afterward they were subjected to hate mail and phone calls, most of them intercepted by the college. Blackwell persuaded them not to return to the sit-ins. At the same time he convened a meeting of local college executives who persuaded the sit-in leaders to call a moratorium pending a resolution of their main demands. On February 9 Blackwell convoked a student assembly at WC. He told the students that the sit-ins were setting back the course of race relations in Greensboro and he dressed down the participants from WC. However well-meaning they may have been, he said, they brought discredit to the college. This speech too received great publicity. Governor Luther Hodges praised Blackwell as an example for all the state's college presidents to follow.

As to his personal views and motivations in the matter, Blackwell sent mixed signals. A year earlier, he remarked in a private letter that "I have never felt the urge to crusade against segregation.... Social status cannot be legislated." He participated actively and successfully in efforts to delay desegregation at Curry School. On the other hand, some of his associates (and the Woolworth store manager) claim that Blackwell quietly sympathized with the demonstrators, and prior to his departure for Florida in the summer of 1960 he placed no obstacles in the path of students who participated in the subsequent picketing of Woolworth's and other local establishments that continued to operate segregated lunch counters. On balance, historian Chafe is surely correct in counting Blackwell among those Greensboro community leaders who feared racial disorder more than they disliked racial discrimination.[42]

Although the lunch counters desegregated in July 1960, schools, buses, hospitals, theaters, restaurants, motels, and other businesses remained segregated. Blacks returned to the attack in the fall of 1962, the demonstrations led once again by students from A&T and Bennett, the black college for women. They numbered over two thousand on some occasions—six months before followers of Martin Luther King took to the streets of Birmingham. When these efforts proved unavailing, the students renewed and broadened them in May and June 1963. Their most visible and charismatic leader was A&T student body president Jesse Jackson. Many hundreds were arrested; in fact, they courted arrest in order to fill the jails and strain the city's capacity to hold them. That these demonstrations never became violent was testimony to the discipline maintained by both the students and the Greensboro police. Finally in June 1963, the city leaders capitulated and businesses proceeded to desegregate.[43]

WC's black students participated in these events downtown; white students were free to watch as long as they didn't wear their identifying jackets.[44] Some of them launched a smaller-scale operation of their own on Tate Street, adjacent to campus. In March 1962 the college's black students called the attention of student government leaders to the fact that the Cinema Theater and several restaurants, all of which catered to students, were closed to blacks. Meeting no response, they repeated the complaint a year later to Chancellor Otis Singletary. He, Katherine Taylor, and the SGA president met with some of the refractory businessmen but made no headway. Soon afterward, on May 15—coinciding with the demonstrations downtown—about two dozen students began picketing and launched a boycott of the Cinema Theater and the Town and College and Apple House Restaurants.[45] These efforts, coupled with those downtown, bore fruit that fall when the last Tate Street businesses desegregated.[46] Only a small minority of students were involved in these activities, but they represented something of an entering wedge to the later 1960s and '70s.

* * *

Meanwhile, student rebellion on campus failed to match the '20s, much less the years just ahead. The college remained firmly *in loco parentis* and the great majority of students accepted without serious question the social regulations they found on arrival. Where the sharpest edges could be avoided by cutting corners, they did so, like every college generation.[47] The dress code was little changed from the 1940s although hats and gloves were no longer required.

Slacks and shorts were prohibited almost everywhere on campus; but like gym suits and even pajamas, they were often hidden by raincoats. According to the 1957–58 *Student Handbook*, students were forbidden to take rides from strangers except to and from church. They could not go away overnight, or even downtown alone after 7:30 p.m. without special permission. Those attending formal dances had to be in their rooms by 12:30 a.m. Walking on campus after dark was restricted to the residence area and College Avenue. Freshmen were under even stricter regulations.[48] Although some faculty members thought these rules too restrictive, most of them remained in place for a few more years.[49]

An exception was the ban on resident students having cars on campus. That was lifted in 1959 for seniors, who were required to pay fifty cents for a parking permit—a figure that would boggle the minds of later generations. Cars were still a luxury, and four years later only 175 were registered.[50]

Nevertheless, parking was a problem. As early as 1952, when only the small minority of town students had cars, they complained of terrible parking conditions on campus. The places then in existence were apparently reserved for faculty.[51] Faculty members themselves soon began complaining of parking problems, but not until the mid-'60s did they have to register their cars and pay a fee too.[52]

President Foust had once regretted the weekend exodus of too many socially-minded upperclassmen. After two decades of depression, war, and perhaps the diversionary Elliott social program on campus, the phenomenon returned, big time. Busloads of WC students from every class departed for social mixers at Chapel Hill, particularly on football weekends. Many had dates already arranged, but others—particularly freshmen—did not; crowds of waiting boys picked out girls as they got off the buses. One alumna compared it to a cattle auction but said they loved it at the time. Meanwhile, to stem the tide, the college stepped up its home attractions, including weekly dances and other programs in Elliott Hall, free movies in Aycock Auditorium, and dances or open houses in the residence halls. These were not without effect: on some weekends the campus was crowded with boys.[53]

Greater (or Consolidated) University Day was a similar event but on a much grander scale. It was traditionally scheduled on the day of the State-Carolina football game in Chapel Hill or Raleigh. That morning at WC, buses lined up on campus to convey girls (1,200 of them in 1953) to the game and the related activities. A Consolidated University Queen was crowned at half-time. (WC had a natural advantage here but with some women enrolled on each campus, no monopoly.) Beginning in April 1953 with the opening of Elliott Hall, the new student union, WC hosted an annual Spring Consolidated University Day, with several hundred State and Carolina students in attendance.[54]

* * *

The student societies, dating back to the college's earliest days, were now on their last legs. Most of their functions had been taken over by other organizations. There remained in the early '50s four societies, each with about 600 members. According to a 1951 *Carolinian* editorial advocating their abolition, the peak attendance at a society meeting that year was about fifty. In an ensuing plebiscite, students narrowly voted to prolong their life; it was the freshmen who provided the margin of victory. But two years later the vote was reversed, with the blessing of the four society presidents. The Adelphian, Cornelian, Dikean, and Aletheian Societies were no more.[55]

The societies had previously chosen the student marshals, by now ceremonial ushers. These positions, twenty to thirty-two in number, were henceforth elected by the rising junior and senior classes.[56] The chief marshal continued to be elected by the student body as a whole. Her stated qualifications in 1952 had been scholarship, charm, and service. A decade later charm remained, but scholarship and service had given way to poise and leadership.[57]

* * *

Rat Day, the hazing activity heretofore sponsored by the societies, passed in 1953 under the aegis of the sophomore class. As hazing could become humdrum even to sophomores, the students in charge were always looking for avenues of revitalization.[58] Even so, the late '50s saw increasing student calls for abolition of the "ridiculous, useless, infantile" activity, even if it was traditional. A modified program in 1960 emphasized campus beautification and ended with an evening party at which the rat ears and bibs that freshmen had worn all day were consigned to a bonfire. Freed of the most humiliating and occasionally dangerous activities of earlier years, Rat Day survived well into the 1960s, when traditions came to be scrapped *because* they were traditions.[59]

Jacket Day also survived. Nearly every sophomore purchased a jacket, decked out in her year's class color, and continued to wear it for the remainder of her college career. Wherever they went, these wool blazers marked the WC girls and conveyed, they thought, a considerable cachet. Jacket Day itself, when the garments arrived and were distributed, was a ceremonial occasion of the first importance. The entire class paraded through the dining hall, clad in the new jackets, singing their class song. Ring Day, in the junior year, similarly marked the arrival of class rings. They too were important to many students, but were less conspicuous and evoked fewer memories among older alumnae.[60]

The sister class relationship—freshmen with juniors and sophomores with seniors—was still valued. Sister classes shared projects and socialized together. On Class Day preceding commencement, seniors continued to march through the twin daisy chains that their sophomore sisters had painstakingly picked in the fields and woven into strands the day before. (The college apparently contracted with farmers over the years to raise daisies for this purpose.) This tradition too lasted well into the 1960s—until the arrival of men.[61]

May Day, by contrast, expired a decade earlier. A generation that still cherished tradition if it were not too burdensome eventually found May Day a drag. It was a senior class project consuming large amounts of time, energy, and even money at a time of year (near commencement) when seniors were busy with other matters. In 1954 they voted to abolish it. (Dean Mossman facetiously opposed the action because 1954 was a year of terrible drought, and May Day had perennially brought rain.) The May Pole disappeared but not the Queen. She would now be crowned at the junior-senior dance each spring.[62]

* * *

The student Recreation Association still offered intramural sports, featuring games between class and residence hall teams. But most students had lost interest and, compared with earlier decades, the *Carolinian* gave them very short shrift.

Interest was little greater in varsity sports. Many physical educators continued to oppose intercollegiate athletics for women in the 1950s, thinking them too strenuous and too open to commercial exploitation.[63] But the national trend was toward greater participation. Under Ethel Martus WC followed the trend. In fact, members of the physical education department produced some of the research supporting women's capacity to participate in competitive athletics. In 1953 the college hosted the National Women's Collegiate Golf Tournament.[64] Although WC had played a few basketball games against neighboring colleges in the 1940s and even earlier, they did not resume with any frequency until the college's last months as a women's institution in 1963. Early that year the WC basketball team won three out of four games against nearby colleges.[65]

* * *

Campus security had not been a compelling issue for many years. Although students walked around after dark without much sense of danger, Chancellor Graham was concerned enough in 1956 to call for better fencing and planting to ward off intruders on the north campus.[66] The campus police that year consisted of five uniformed officers, who had legal authority to make arrests on campus. That power was conferred by the county sheriff until 1963 when state law granted it directly to campus police around the state.[67]

* * *

The annual commencement exercises were held in Aycock Auditorium from its completion in 1927 through 1959. Efforts were made during the '50s to hold the ceremonies on the lawn in front of the library, but four straight years of rainfall on the appointed day drove the event back into Aycock. In 1960 it moved to the new Greensboro Coliseum where it has remained except for times of structural renovation.[68]

* * *

Among WC graduates in the 1950s, a fairly constant 90 percent married within ten years of graduation. But they waited longer within that period before tying the knot. More and more reported going on to graduate school—42 percent from the class of 1959. Much of that interest sprang from increasing educational requirements for public school teachers. Whereas earlier decades had seen the vast majority of alumnae go into teaching, the proportion of those graduating in the 1950s was only half, and still falling. Conversely, those who reported full-time employment of any kind ten years after graduation significantly increased—to over a third for the class of 1959—as did those combining employment with marriage and child-rearing. The leading alternative careers for these women in the 1950s were still secretarial work (9 percent), social work, and home demonstration work, together with science and journalism. Few yet entered law, medicine, or college teaching.[69]

The alumnae had seldom exercised much influence over the college's policies, procedures, or general welfare. When their leaders now sought to play a larger role the primary suggestion they received was to raise money—enjoined system-wide by President Gordon Gray in 1951. Accordingly they launched that year a systematic Annual Giving campaign. It was the college's first campus-wide fund-raising effort.[70]

The Alumnae Association continued in its ambiguous role as a joint child of the alumnae and the college. The college paid most of its bills but was far from lavish.[71] (A Winthrop College survey of southern colleges and universities in 1954 found that most of them controlled their alumni associations financially.)[72] In 1952 the association repealed its annual $3 membership fee, relying instead on the Annual Giving campaign to provide whatever support the college did not supply.[73] Many of the proceeds passed to the college itself. It was over the use of this contribution—$2,500 in 1952—that Chancellor Graham, with his facility in antagonizing others, managed to fall out with Executive Secretary Betty Brown Jester and other alumnae leaders.[74] The dispute deteriorated until 1954, when Graham demanded and received Jester's resignation, effective in June 1955.[75] She in turn played a major part in his own ouster as chancellor in 1956.[76]

Jester's successor was Barbara Parrish. Following graduation from WC in 1948, Parrish worked at Limestone College in South Carolina, after 1953 as dean of women. Apparently like her predecessors, she was nominated by the alumnae board, appointed by the chancellor, and confirmed by the university trustees; and like them she continued to serve both masters. As Graham himself pointed out, the practical solution appeared to lie in "harmonious and effective collaboration"—something that had usually existed before his time and would now resume—usually.[77] Parrish was very supportive of Graham during his last and her first year in office (1955–56) and continued to work harmoniously with most of the chancellors thereafter.[78]

Also like her predecessors, Parrish proved utterly devoted to the alumnae and the association. She had a phenomenal memory for names and faces. Although she was sometimes criticized for conservatism or resistance to change, she won the lasting support of most alumnae. By 1962 she had two secretarial assistants but with all her duties including editing the quarterly *Alumnae News* she was vastly overworked.[79]

Chapter 19

Desegregation, Coeducation, University Status

Complications from the revolving chancellorship paled by comparison with the organic changes that transformed the institution during the same years. No mission or name change since the founding could compare. In 1964 the college for white women had become a desegregated coeducational university.

Desegregation came first, in 1956. Walter Clinton Jackson had shown almost visible pain when forced to deny blacks' requests for access to campus facilities and meetings in the 1930s and '40s. Edward Kidder Graham, unlike his predecessor, was neither a specialist in race relations nor a visible champion of Negro rights. An organization man, he was even less ready to challenge established rules and mores. Yet his personal views were similar to Jackson's and, in the early stages of the civil rights revolution, he gradually achieved more latitude. When a university trustee in 1951 demanded the identities of faculty members who were rumored to favor desegregated meetings on campus, Graham wrote what he described to President Gordon Gray as an expurgated reply—after clearing it with Gray. Refusing to provide any names, he assured the trustee that no one on campus had violated state law or created any disorder. Beyond that, he was unwilling to engage in speech or thought control.[1] In a speech to the state PTA a few months later Graham reaffirmed his commitment to separate but equal educational facilities, but cautioned against those he called the segregationist "Fire Eaters of 1951." On the other hand, he was distinctly unhappy when historian Franklin Parker invited a black professor from the A&T College to talk to one of his classes.[2]

Perhaps the most visible racial issue on campus before 1956 arose from occasional requests by faculty and students at A&T and Bennett, the local women's college for blacks, to use the WC library. Jackson had allowed this; he and trustee Laura Cone defended librarian Charles Adams when he came under fire for permitting it. Graham's first reaction was to reprimand Adams for continuing the practice without his permission; his second reaction, after consulting President Gray, was to let it continue. Outside use (by blacks and whites alike) increased after the new library building opened. Tighter restrictions soon diminished the flow to the previous safe trickle. Although the subject was clearly sensitive, no one seems to have favored ending the use of the library by blacks altogether.[3]

In fact, students and faculty alike sought to sponsor more interracial events on campus during the '50s. Graham shared the inclination and walked the resulting tightrope with increasing assurance, expanding such events while avoiding any flagrant violations of state law and UNC regulations. The most liberal reading of the latter allowed the campus to host integrated professional meetings while barring interracial social gatherings or any to which the general public was admitted. Beginning in 1950, Graham invited faculty and students of both Bennett and A&T to attend the Harriet Elliott Social Science Forum. They could participate fully in the round table discussions, he told the two presidents, sitting wherever they pleased. But all meals and any events in Aycock Auditorium (which was regarded as public) would have to be segregated. For events in Aycock generally, including concerts by the North Carolina Symphony Orchestra, Graham set aside for blacks a bloc of the most desirable orchestra seats. He was not offended when most of these seats went begging; a black colleague told him that the best segregated seats were not appreciably better than the worst segregated seats.[4] A student activist of that period recalled many years later that Graham quietly let her conduct integrated student meetings on campus. When the student legislature in 1953 asked for a repeal of the ban on serving refreshments to blacks, a clearly sympathetic Graham forwarded their request to President Gray.[5] As Graham's departure coincided with the arrival of the first black students, his successors faced fewer of these problems.

A number of faculty members displayed a growing and increasingly vocal commitment to racial equality in the 1950s. For years some of them met regularly for lunch at the YMCA with faculty members from A&T. They also held biracial meetings at all of the local campuses. Foremost among these persons at WC was philosophy professor Warren Ashby. Others were Eugene Pfaff and Franklin Parker in history and Marc Friedlaender in English. Ashby held meetings at his home periodically with students from WC, Greensboro College, and Bennett College.[6] In 1955 Ashby publicly endorsed school desegregation in a letter to the *Greensboro Daily News*. During Greensboro's civil rights demonstrations in the '60s, he served on successive biracial committees seeking racial harmony in the city.[7]

Ashby also spearheaded a faculty council resolution in 1955 supporting desegregation of the UNC campuses. As watered down prior to passage (by 96 to 24) it emphasized obedience to federal court decisions on the subject and expressed confidence that campus desegregation would proceed satisfactorily. Student leaders had more than anticipated this move a week earlier by adopting (in their case unanimously) a resolution favoring equal admission policies regardless of race. Chancellor Graham publicly supported their right to speak out.[8]

These actions took place against a backdrop of United States Supreme Court decisions going back to 1938, banning racial segregation in higher education whenever facilities for blacks were not truly equal to those for whites. The Chapel Hill campus began admitting blacks to its graduate and professional schools in 1951 and to its undergraduate program in 1956, in each case after court orders requiring it—orders that applied to all three campuses. The university trustees did not as a group oppose the orders once given—nor did they rush to implement them. Desegregation on each campus proceeded at a snail's pace for years to come. As late as 1968, only 1.7 percent of the students at the university's traditionally white campuses were black.[9]

At WC, beginning with the graduate school orders of 1951, Chancellor Graham made sure that no one overtly discriminated against black applicants, though he required that any who met the normal admission requirements must receive his personal attention. Most of WC's graduate programs were paralleled at least theoretically by programs at the state's black campuses.[10] (North Carolina had exceeded every other southern state in establishing separate campuses for blacks. There were five of them: three teachers' colleges at Elizabeth City, Fayetteville, and Winston-Salem, a liberal arts college in Durham, and A&T, the agricultural and engineering college in Greensboro. Still further, there was a college for Native Americans at Pembroke.) Graham consulted Gordon Gray before breaking with precedent and admitting a Native American girl as an undergraduate in 1951.[11]

The *Carolinian* in 1952 proclaimed that segregation was legally, morally, and practically wrong—a position it adhered to thereafter.[12] When the trustee visiting committee asked student leaders that year how their fellow-students would react to black classmates, they said they would welcome them. In fact, most students seem to have been ambivalent, with no strong convictions either way.[13] When the time actually came to receive the first black students, the great majority were supportive.

As that prospect loomed at each campus, university authorities prepared for the worst eventualities they could conceive. To prevent an avalanche of ill-prepared black students, products of the state's inferior Jim Crow public education system, they centralized and tightened the admissions policies. In 1956, for the first time, applicants to each campus had to take qualifying examinations. Two years later the university settled upon the College Entrance Examination Board's Scholastic Aptitude Test.[14] Administrators refused to attribute the new policy solely to the prospect of black students, thereby evoking charges of evading the court decisions. In fact, there were other reasons. The post-World War II years saw a huge influx of college students, and universities all over the country adopted selective admissions tests to cope with the crowds.[15]

The second catastrophe to be guarded against was the introduction of black male students. For years the college had enrolled male graduate and summer school students, many of them school teachers and principals. But rather than see black males fraternizing with white female classmates at WC, the trustees forbade all new male enrollments in 1956. The ban remained in place until 1962.[16]

As fate would have it, Acting Chancellor William Whately Pierson was at the helm when WC's first two black students arrived in the fall of 1956. Originally from Alabama, Pierson was probably the only leader of the college since Foust or even McIver who personally favored racial segregation. At the pre-school conference with student leaders that year he advised sternly against "extremes of attitude and conduct, especially... undue cordiality and 'exaggerated humanitarianism'" toward the new students. Later he explained to a student convocation (in the presence of the black students) that the college had admitted them only under duress. Nevertheless he called for obedience to court decisions that he clearly opposed. The faculty as a whole were more receptive to the change and, with some exceptions, sought earnestly to implement it.[17]

The two students in question (selected from ten black applicants) were Elizabeth JoAnne Smart of Raleigh and Mrs. Bettye Ann Davis Tillman of Wadesboro. Despite Pierson's assurance that the two freshmen, aged 17 and 19, would be treated the same as all other students, they were housed by themselves in Shaw Dormitory, occupying the whole first floor of the building's east wing. They had a private bathroom. This segregated arrangement, reflecting some of the deepest anxieties of white southerners, echoed that for the first black students at Chapel Hill.[18]

There were apprehensions, probably originating off campus, that violent confrontations might occur with the new students' arrival. The Greensboro papers carried stories about them, but the *Carolinian* and the *Alumnae News* maintained a total blackout, failing for several years to mention the presence of African American students on campus.

There were no untoward events. For the first few days Smart and Tillman felt isolated, but other girls gradually befriended them; only a small minority were hostile. The same was true of faculty members. (A notable exception was admissions director Mildred Newton, who persistently referred to black applicants as "Supreme Court Models.") The early black students were seen, and saw themselves, as test cases; if they misbehaved or flunked out it would receive as much publicity as their original admission. They felt a corresponding responsibility to do well academically, to join in extracurricular activities and, in general, to be model citizens. They never felt totally included, as Claudette Graves, who came in 1957, later recalled, but they appreciated the times when they were. Although some of them brought dates to campus dances, they usually preferred to socialize at A&T, where most of their dates were enrolled.

Off campus, Jim Crow remained in full sway until several years after Smart and Tillman graduated in 1960. By that time WC had twenty African-American students; in the spring of 1963, WC's last semester, there were twenty-nine black undergraduates and thirty-four part-time black graduate students, the latter living off campus.[19] Bettye Tillman died eight years after graduation. JoAnne Smart Drane went on for a master's degree at Duke and became a public school official in Raleigh. In 1990 she was elected vice president of the UNCG Alumni Association and in 1996 to its board of trustees. Claudette Graves, later Claudette Burroughs-White, won election in the '90s to the Greensboro City Council.

The segregated arrangement in Shaw dormitory lasted only about three years. At that time overcrowded white students demanded and received equal access to the underused wing. As black students advanced to the sophomore and later classes, they moved to other dormitories, but individual rooms continued to be assigned by race for the next decade. That occasioned little protest on either side. In fact, self-segregation prevailed by mutual consent in the dining hall and at most social gatherings. It would even intensify in the more belligerent years ahead.[20]

Despite their having been selected carefully, and despite their eagerness to prove themselves academically, most of the black students suffered from poorer academic backgrounds and started at a disadvantage. Those entering from 1961 through 1964 posted SAT verbal and mathematical scores one-half and two-thirds, respectively, of the mean scores for all freshmen enrolling in the same period. As freshmen, their grade point averages were one-third of the class mean. Although their graduation rate by 1967 actually began to exceed that of white students, the problems of inferior preparation did not go away.[21] There were exceptions, however. Diane Oliver rose to managing editor of the *Carolinian*. On graduation in 1964 she received a prestigious scholarship in writing at the University of Iowa—where she died in a motorcycle accident.[22]

* * *

Since the 1930s, the trend in American higher education was toward coeducation. One after another, single-sex institutions began to admit students of the opposite gender. The trend accelerated in the '50s; by 1956–57, only 9.6 percent of all college women were attending women's colleges. To some degree coeducation was an economic response by colleges to falling enrollments in the '30s and early '40s. Conversely, it became a response to burgeoning applications, especially by males, after World War II. There were other reasons. Gender distinctions were diminishing in both professional and social life. Some opponents of single-sex education saw a parallel with racial segregation, now on its way out. Others, living in college towns, resented having to send their children to distant institutions because they were of the wrong gender—a view that resonated through the years in Greensboro. And increasing numbers of students, particularly women, simply preferred coeducation.[23]

At WC, the last motivation was partly responsible for the modest but worrisome stream of students—particularly good students—toward Chapel Hill.[24] The coeducational year of 1932–33 was a fluke and the 1940s debate over coeducation came to nothing. But male students had been attending summer school off and on since 1914 and taking graduate courses since the 1920s. In the mid-'50s they constituted 40 percent of the summer session enrollment and 24 percent of the master's degree recipients. Both of these opportunities were cut off abruptly for new applicants in 1956 in the panic accompanying racial desegregation. Only a year after that ban was lifted in 1962 (for graduate students only) men accounted for 32 percent of the graduate enrollment.[25]

Meanwhile, North Carolina faced the demographic challenge of the postwar era. A dramatic increase in the college-age population was expected soon. Moreover, the state already ranked forty-ninth out of fifty in sending its high school graduates on to college. How would it accommodate the coming flood and, if at all possible, raise its embarrassing national standing? Newly-elected Governor Terry Sanford in 1961 created a Commission on Education Beyond the High School, headed by Winston-Salem lawyer Irving E. Carlyle. UNC President William Friday was a member. The Carlyle Commission predicted a near doubling of college enrollments in the state by 1975, from the current 75,000 to 139,000. (That estimate proved far too modest; actual enrollments in 1975 topped 168,000, exclusive of the new community colleges and technical institutes.) Duke, Wake Forest, Davidson, and the other private institutions projected only an 11,000 increase in that period, leaving the state to handle the remainder.

The Carlyle Commission's report, issued in 1962, called for a major overhaul of the state's higher education system. Most of its recommendations, along with those of a supplemental UNC trustees' committee under Thomas J. Pearsall, were enacted into law by the 1963 legislature. They included the creation of a community college system and the elevation of existing state-supported two-year colleges in Charlotte, Asheville, and Wilmington to four-year institutions. Following California precedent, the legislature designated the three existing UNC branches as the University of North Carolina at Chapel Hill, at Greensboro, and at Raleigh. All three campuses were to be coeducational. Finally, lawmakers left the door open to add the upgraded campuses at Charlotte, Asheville, and Wilmington to the system. That followed in short order: UNC Charlotte was added in 1965, the other two in 1969. (State College alumni fought a strenuous and ultimately successful battle to avoid designation of their institution as the University of North Carolina at Raleigh; it would be North Carolina State University.) President William Friday was a driving force in reaching these agreements. He favored coeducation on every campus and went out of his way to persuade his reluctant predecessors Frank Graham and Gordon Gray.[26]

The reaction at WC was decidedly mixed. The institutional self-study report prepared for the SACS accreditation in 1962 affirmed that "the College... should continue to be a liberal arts college with professional programs"—the mission it had pursued since before the first accreditation in 1921. Coeducation was mentioned only in relation to readmitting male graduate students. However, coeducation had been a matter of idle speculation and occasional debate for decades. The deliberations of the Carlyle Commission brought it front and center. President Friday long recalled his icy reception when he visited campus in the spring of 1963 shortly after the legislature had done its work.[27]

Most alumnae opposed the change; the Alumnae Association trustees loyally endorsed university status but could not bring themselves to mention coeducation.[28] Students were divided; they formed Pink and Blue factions, alternately painting the McIver statue and decorating the campus in those colors. The *Carolinian* reported the division and ultimately supported the change.[29] The faculty were also divided, to some degree along generational lines with senior members least receptive.[30] Predictably under the circumstances, administrators favored the change—Chancellor Singletary and Dean Mossman clearly so, and Dean Taylor (an alumna) with clear misgivings. Singletary had arrived in 1961 with no strong convictions on the matter. He discovered quickly, as he confided to UNC Vice President Donald Anderson, that at that point "he could not even suggest coeducation at Greensboro and survive." Within a year, however, he concluded that coeducation was inevitable at the other branches and WC would have no choice but to adopt it too.[31]

Doubters took little consolation in the prospect of gaining male students in return for lost female enrollments. Most male applicants, they thought, were apt to be rejects from Chapel Hill and State. Perhaps inconsistently, they feared that most of the student leadership positions would fall to men. Similarly, women would gradually be eliminated from the faculty, except as low-level instructors teaching introductory courses. Coeducation would bring demands for fraternities, sororities, and football. And university status would likely drive undergraduate teaching into the background in favor of proliferating graduate programs. Some of these things in fact came to pass, and Katherine Taylor was not the last to suggest that the institution was moving from a first-rate college to a mediocre university.[32]

The strongest argument for the change was inevitability. Many had to agree with Singletary that WC's monopoly of women students (he called it a "protective tariff") was already fast-eroding and would soon disappear as all the other campuses in the system, old and new, embraced coeducation. (There were already more than two thousand women students at Chapel Hill in 1962, and State was building its first women's dormitory.) As they siphoned off a growing share of WC's traditional clientele, it could compensate only by recruiting men. There were hundreds of potential male applicants in the Greensboro area (as there had always been) who would apply here for economic or family reasons having nothing to do with academic ability.

A quite different motive—recalled by both Gordon Blackwell and Mereb Mossman many years later—sprang from the conviction that WC had always been treated as a "redheaded step-child" (the *Greensboro Daily News's* phrase) by legislators and UNC administrators oriented toward Chapel Hill and State. As Blackwell put it less delicately, "we felt that we were usually sucking on the hind tit" at appropriations time. Accordingly, some hoped that coeducation and coordinate university status would bring more equitable appropriations. Time would soon shatter this illusion.

In the end, it became clear that coeducation was in the air, was mandated from above, and was therefore unavoidable. Accordingly public opposition was minimal.

Infinitely more important in the long run was university status. Woman's College had been receptive to that idea since Julius Foust's dreams of a woman's university in the 1920s. By 1962, after a time in the wilderness, the educational demands generated by World War II had already propelled the college significantly and willingly toward university status in substance. The ratification by name, to The University of North Carolina at Greensboro, came in July 1963. But reflecting the prevailing concern with coeducation, male undergraduates were not admitted until Fall 1964, giving a year to prepare for the transition.[33]

Part VI
University of North Carolina at Greensboro, 1963–1979

Chapter 20

Administration and the Campus

Although Otis Singletary presided over the initial transition to coeducation and university status, that burden fell primarily on his designated heir-apparent James S. Ferguson. Singletary had come to campus in 1961 with his eyes trained upward, and most of his last two years as chancellor were spent in Washington. In November 1964 he left to become director of the Job Corps, part of Lyndon Johnson's Great Society program. He returned in January 1966 but resigned definitively that September to become vice president of the American Council on Education. By 1970, he was president of the University of Kentucky.[1]

Singletary's departures were by no means attributable to unpopularity on campus. The faculty's academic policies committee paid special tribute late in 1963 to his "vigorous, forthright, dedicated, and imaginative leadership" in the difficult transition process. Not only did he champion free discussion of important issues, they said, but he encouraged more faculty participation in academic policy-making.[2] As for the students, they gave him a thunderous standing ovation and serenaded him with "We love you, Otis!" when he announced his first departure in 1964. Two years later, at his final departure, student protests over social regulations had gained headway and some SGA leaders regarded him as overbearing.[3] Nonetheless, he was genuinely popular with the great majority in his two campus constituencies.

A primary reason for leaving, Singletary recalled later, was frustration over the limited role that UNC officials were prepared to accord the new university—echoing Blackwell's concern several years earlier. Looking for a new institutional focus to distinguish the campus from its compeers, Singletary urged (with strong campus support) that UNCG be made the center for performing arts within the university system. It soon became clear that that was not going to happen; he blamed it on the political power of Chapel Hill, but so far as any one campus was responsible, it was surely the new School of the Arts in Winston-Salem. Singletary was perceived as a fighter, and for that reason some faculty members doubly regretted his loss.[4]

James Ferguson by comparison was a gentle and courtly man, less confrontational and wholly devoted to the institution where he spent his remaining years. He was beloved as no other leader except Walter Clinton Jackson; the two Deep South natives shared significant personality traits.[5] Ferguson grew up in Mississippi, the son of a Methodist minister. He took his doctorate in history at Chapel Hill and was teaching at Mississippi's Millsaps College when Otis Singletary appeared there as a student. Years later, in 1962, when Ferguson was academic dean at Millsaps, Singletary brought him to WC as dean of the graduate school; before long he was grooming the new recruit as his own successor.[6] Ferguson filled in as acting chancellor during Singletary's absence in 1964–65. He generated such widespread approval that Singletary on his return engineered Ferguson's appointment to the new post of vice chancellor, handling many of the day-to-day administrative duties. On Singletary's final departure in November 1966, Ferguson stepped in again as acting chancellor. The following January, with overwhelming alumni, faculty, and student support, he was named to the post in his own right. President William Friday remarked years later that Ferguson was the only chancellor in his experience to have been recommended by faculty petition. Ferguson remained in place until 1979; the revolving chancellorship had come to an end.[7]

Although Ferguson kept well informed, he was a low-key administrator, widely accessible and willing to delegate. His secretary reported that he never once turned down a student seeking an appointment. One student activist (James Lancester, himself later a senior administrator in student affairs) recalled marching into Ferguson's office to protest what seemed unreasonable delays in the student registration process then going on; Ferguson dropped what he was doing, accompanied Lancaster back to the registration site, and relayed the student concerns to those in charge. Ferguson was never averse to making hard decisions, yet he always took pains (some thought excessively) to make sure that every voice was heard beforehand.[8] Ferguson initially followed Singletary's example in teaching a course regularly—they were both American historians. But he soon found that administrative duties were demanding so much of his attention that he had to give up teaching.[9]

The institution grew mightily during Ferguson's tenure—student enrollment more than doubled, from 4,249 in 1964 to 9,925 in 1979; graduate enrollments more than tripled. The faculty grew from 296 to 678 in the same time. The bureaucracy also grew, and there were more and more people to consult. From the beginning he rued the time spent in frequently unproductive meetings, and no doubt some of the social gatherings as well that enduring small-college conventions required him to attend. His greatest frustration, he reported, was the lack of time for long-range planning or simple reflection. As it was, he confessed to rising frequently at 4 a.m. and working until late at night.[10]

Faculty members correctly saw Ferguson as one of them in spirit. He had formerly been active in the American Association of University Professors, and as chancellor worked hard to secure better status, pay, and working conditions for the faculty. Students saw him, also correctly, as sympathetic with their aspirations for greater freedom—on campus and in society. He fully supported the civil rights revolution. In fact, his departure from Mississippi had come amid growing threats and harassment to himself and family arising from his liberal racial views.[11] Some of Ferguson's strongest supporters (at least in retrospect) were student rebels like Ada Fisher, a black woman who went on to become a medical doctor. "I absolutely adored him," she wrote at the time of his death, "for he allowed students such as me to thrive in an atmosphere of academic excellence and freedom."[12]

Ferguson was never in robust health. He had a kidney removed in 1976, by which time his wife Frances had contracted cancer. Even before her death in 1978 he decided to step down as chancellor and spend his last few professional years in the classroom. He did so in 1979 (at age 62) but continuing ill health—also cancer—led to his full retirement in 1983 and death in 1984.[13]

* * *

In the expansion of higher education after World War II, universities grew exponentially, both in number and in size. More students and faculty required, to some degree, more administrators to oversee them. The contemporaneous growth of outside funding, both public and private, had correspondingly longer strings attached: regulations to enforce and reports to fill out. Presidents and chancellors found themselves less the authoritarian "captains of erudition" described by Thorstein Veblen early in the century than the "captains of bureaucracy" seen by the University of California's Clark Kerr.[14]

UNCG, in its new incarnation, was clearly a product of the postwar boom, sharing in the escalating populations of students, faculty, and administrators. Faculty members credited Ferguson with holding bureaucracy to a minimum, but that was mostly in retrospect as they watched the phenomenon compound in later years. The most visible administrative changes lay in the adoption of a university organizational structure. The decade beginning in 1966 saw the creation of three new professional schools and a college of arts and sciences along with a multiplication of vice chancellors and deans. Although the idea of creating a college of arts and sciences went back at least as far as 1956, it was another twelve years before a dean was hired and the college was organized. (Institutional memory was so poor that no one in charge by 1968 seemed to have heard of its long-departed predecessor: Dean William Cunningham Smith's college of liberal arts and sciences in the 1920s.) The new college initially embraced fifteen liberal arts departments.[15]

The professional schools surviving from earlier days were music, education, and home economics. Nursing was added in 1966; business and economics in

1970; and health, physical education and recreation in 1971. Until the college's advent, the professional school deans and the liberal arts department heads were administratively on a par, all reporting to Mereb Mossman as dean of the faculty; thereafter, the department heads reported to their own dean and he to Mossman.[16]

In 1969 Mossman became vice chancellor for academic affairs—a title she held only briefly. Early in 1971, having provided a steady hand through twenty years of institutional turbulence, she stepped down and returned to full-time teaching. Since 1963, at least, there had been no stronger supporter of university status and the requisite changes pertaining thereto than Mereb Mossman. Her resignation was almost as momentous as the changing of chancellors, but it brought no change of direction.[17]

Her successor was Stanley L. Jones, a historian from the Chicago campus of the University of Illinois. He was if anything more popular with the faculty and fellow administrators, given Mossman's reputation for micromanagement and her widely believed bias against women faculty. Jones was readier to delegate and he encouraged broader faculty participation in governance.[18] Like Mossman, he shared Chancellor Ferguson's educational and institutional priorities; in a period of chronic financial shortage both gave top priority to academic excellence in fashioning the new university. Both were faculty-oriented. Given his Chicago background, Jones was more receptive than many on campus to making the institution an openly urban or metropolitan university, relying primarily on commuter students.[19] That is in fact what happened, and it was never clear what alternatives were available.

Although the deans were on a par administratively, some deference was paid to the dean of the college, who represented about as many faculty members and student enrollments as the others combined. Dean Robert L. Miller, a chemist also from the University of Illinois, Chicago, came to that post in 1968 and spent the next year organizing the college. (He played a key part in recruiting Jones soon afterward.) Miller's leadership was most apparent in campus curricular matters, applying mainly to underclassmen who had not yet chosen their majors. That role produced little if any strain since all of the deans shared a commitment to the liberal arts as a foundation for later specialization.[20] Within the college, Miller set up two advisory councils, both of which he chaired—one consisting of the department heads and the other elected by the college faculty. Mossman had hired a number of capable department heads over the years, and Miller worked well with most if not all of them.[21]

Arriving as dean of the new school of nursing in 1966 was Eloise Lewis. The new dean of the graduate school that year, succeeding Ferguson himself, was economics head John W. Kennedy. David Shelton became dean of business and economics in 1970. Ethel Martus Lawther, the head of physical education since

1947, became dean of the new school of health, physical education, and recreation.

By 1974, there were six vice chancellors in place. Five of them had been promoted from earlier deanships or equivalent: academic affairs, graduate studies, student affairs, business affairs, and development.[22] The sixth, the vice chancellor for administration, was created as an assistant chancellor with much the same routine administrative duties as Ferguson had exercised in Singletary's last year. He was also in charge of campus planning and soon became the university's compliance officer responding to federal civil rights mandates. Charles D. Hounshell, a former president of Birmingham-Southern College in Alabama, was appointed to this post in 1972.[23] John Kennedy was advanced in 1971 from dean to vice chancellor for graduate studies. Business manager Henry L. Ferguson became vice chancellor for business affairs.[24] Development director (or chief fund raiser) George W. Hamer in 1973 became vice chancellor for development.

Student affairs saw an almost constant shuffling of chairs in this period, occasioned only in part by the institution's changing size and mission. Katherine Taylor, successively dean of women and students since 1947, was clearly unenthusiastic about the transition to coeducation, and the new order generally. It was once again a tribute to her personal abilities and her popularity with alumnae and faculty (those who overlooked her fervent support of Chancellor Graham) that she remained on board as long as she did. She and Singletary did not mix well and in 1964 he created for her a new position beyond his daily purview as dean of student services. As such, she was in charge of Elliott Hall and the extracurriculum. It was clearly an artificial arrangement designed to give her meaningful work while removing her from the mainstream of university development.[25] He appointed a new dean of women and (for the first time) a dean of men, both reporting directly to him: admissions director (and relatively recent alumna) Sadye Dunn became dean of women in 1964 while extension director Clarence Shipton was in place as dean of men to greet the first male undergraduates that year.[26] Dunn left two years later, to be replaced successively by physical education professor Rosemary McGee and Shirley K. Flynn.

In 1968, as the student population grew in size, diversity, and also militancy, Ferguson re-created the office of dean of students. He appointed a man who had already engendered great good will among students, Rev. Thomas J.C. Smyth, the former rector of Greensboro's Holy Trinity Church and more recently the Episcopal campus chaplain at UNCG and Greensboro and Guilford Colleges. Smyth performed his role to near-perfection, only to succumb to a heart attack two years later. Ferguson in 1970 drew on another clergyman with similar credentials and student rapport, Rev. James H. Allen, currently the campus Presbyterian minister.[27]

Only after Katherine Taylor took early retirement in 1972 did Ferguson unite all student affairs under Jim Allen as vice chancellor. In 1975 Allen had three deans reporting to him. The deans of men and women gave way to deans for residence life (Shirley Flynn, in charge of both men's and women's dormitories); student services (Clarence Shipton, largely concerned with commuting students); and student development and programs (Clifford Lowery, essentially filling Taylor's old position).[28]

Despite deep and enduring faculty skepticism, much of the administrative proliferation was essential—the product of mushrooming student and faculty populations and a geometrical increase in government reporting requirements, especially relating to civil rights. Accordingly, the university's 1972 self-study report called for more intermediate-level administrators along with a variety of other support personnel across campus.[29] This call was heard in high places; by the time Ferguson stepped down as chancellor in 1979 there were, in addition to the six vice chancellors, three assistant vice chancellors, eleven deans, four assistant deans, and twenty-three persons with the title director.[30] Although Ferguson did not deserve all the credit he received in later years for holding down bureaucratic growth, he and some of his top lieutenants were genuinely overworked. Mereb Mossman, despite her attention to every detail and membership on every committee, worked with little more than an administrative assistant and a secretary. Stanley Jones in time took on two assistant vice chancellors as well, but there were times when Mossman, Jones, and their staffs had to work nights and weekends to turn out necessary paperwork.[31]

The news bureau was one of the oldest agencies on campus. When its longtime director, Albert A. Wilkinson, retired in 1967, outside consultants found it understaffed. It remained so, chronically. Wilkinson's successor, Wilson Davis, protested in 1975 that no relief had yet arrived—indeed, there had been no staff increase since 1956, when the student body was a small fraction of its present size. The bureau, he said, was stretched to capacity. For years he depended on part-time student photographers while his perennial requests for a professional photographer (relayed upward by Ferguson) were perennially ignored.[32]

Another of the twenty-three directors guided the office of institutional research. Such agencies were spreading rapidly on American campuses. They were credited with enhancing administrative efficiency, and private foundations increasingly demanded their presence on a campus before granting financial aid.[33] The SACS accreditation team had recommended one for WC as early as 1962, but funding did not appear until just before Singetary's departure in 1966. These offices appeared on all the UNC campuses at about the same time, aimed primarily at feeding data to general administration, which sent much of it to the federal government.[34] UNCG's first director, John W. Harris, was put to work immediately on sixteen projects including a comparative study of freshman academic performance among black and white students. For nearly a decade he and his successors had the assistance of only a half-time clerical worker and two student helpers. But with access to the administrative computer center after 1973 they produced an array of statistical studies relating to every aspect of the university.[35] The administrative computer center itself came into being in 1973, largely to cope with federal government reporting demands. It relied on secondhand, limited-capacity equipment that survived into the 1980s.[36] Later staff growth in institutional research came primarily in response to stepped-up queries from the federal government, which could not be ignored. Neither Ferguson nor Stanley Jones made much use of the office otherwise. Only later was it called on significantly for long-range planning and other campus-initiated issues.[37] Beginning in 1980 institutional research issued an annual *Fact Book*, a veritable *World Almanac* of data concerning the university's past and present.

* * *

Campus planning was becoming a way of life, nationally and throughout the UNC system. In 1966 the state mandated long-range plans for each campus.[38] UNCG's self-study report of 1972 called for a continuous planning process under a professional planner and a faculty advisory committee.[39] As it happened, that report coincided with a third round of UNC restructuring, resulting in a much larger sixteen-campus system. "Reconsolidation" (as it was called) now brought greater urgency to the planning process on every campus. At UNCG, Charles Hounshell arrived in 1972 as vice chancellor for administration with particular responsibility for planning.[40] A comprehensive plan was begun in 1974 but possibly for financial reasons it never got far. Planning under Ferguson was essentially ad hoc.[41]

Campus physical planning consisted essentially of two issues: expansion and construction. As every administrator since McIver had anticipated and dreaded, the campus was increasingly landlocked. By the 1960s residential, commercial, even industrial development penetrated what the institution had come to regard as its "natural boundaries:" Market Street on the north, Aycock Street on the west, the Southern Railway tracks on the south, and (less definitively) Tate Street on the east. It had tried to buy up properties within this area as they came on the market, but funds were almost never available. They did loosen, however, when Henry Ferguson demonstrated that UNCG (at 130 acres) had more students per acre than any other campus in the system.[42]

Campus expansion in the '60s created the first really serious town-and-gown controversy in the institution's history—far exceeding that when Walker Avenue closed in the late '40s. Most of the houses adjacent to campus had been built early in the century. Their occupants were often elderly, with limited incomes and low mobility. In addition, student parking in front of their homes, sometimes blocking driveways, had become a problem of major proportions. The university tried to inform residents of its expansion plans well in advance of taking action, but this public relations effort was seldom received in good humor.[43] Injury became insult in 1966 when the city (with obvious university backing) considered seeking federal funds for campus expansion under the guise of urban renewal. The region in question was an eight-block tract between Spring Garden and the railroad extending from Aycock Street to Joyner Street (a block east of Tate). Neighbors (some of them retired faculty members or their widows) were outraged at the exaggerated claim that two-thirds of their houses were substandard or blighted, thereby qualifying the area for redevelopment. They turned out en masse and hired lawyers to block the proposal. Under law, only the city had the power to create a redevelopment area. Bowing to the public uprising, it shelved the matter and no federal money was forthcoming. However the episode exacerbated neighborhood relations for a generation.[44] When most of these properties did gradually fall to the university in later years, a substantial proportion had to be acquired through condemnation. Some people, including Greensboro Mayor Carson Bain, even urged the university to move out of town altogether, relocating in the adjacent countryside where land was plentiful and cheap.[45]

Few took that advice seriously and the university continued its painstaking acquisition of real estate within the "natural boundaries." Gradually, more money became available. Attention in the '60s focused first on expanding eastward to McIver Street; this resulted in acquisition of the remaining property on its west side, and even some on the east side at Walker where the life sciences building was later built. Next came a big segment of the recent redevelopment area, bounded by Spring Garden, Tate, Highland Avenue, and the railroad, where lots and homes were picked up piecemeal over several years. The third area, acquired in the '70s, lay west of campus and mostly north of Spring Garden, where the new administration and business/economics buildings were built. A fourth area, only begun in the '70s, lay south of Spring Garden and westward to Aycock Street.[46]

One of the arguments used by neighbors fighting this expansion was that the university did not use all the space it already had. They referred to Peabody Park and the golf course. Both figured in the university's future plans, however. Peabody Park consisted of about twenty-three acres in 1965, following the earlier encroachments around its edges. Remaining were the lower courses of the two small creeks originating in the natural springs long since built or paved over along Spring Garden Street, as well as a few narrow, winding, unpaved driveways and pathways. Campus planners in the '60s proposed to retain the nucleus as a wooded park while continuing to build new dormitories around the periphery; these would occupy both park land and the adjoining residential properties being acquired along McIver and Market Streets.[47] Some of this construction took place but most of it proved unnecessary for the time being as subsequent enrollment growth consisted almost entirely of commuter students. Most of the park survived, then, subject to recurrent periods of interest by students and administrators. Steps were taken in 1970 to upgrade the pathways into walking trails. Student government sponsored a cleanup day in 1973 to revitalize the park.[48]

The nine-hole golf course, rebuilt in 1957, faced almost certain destruction in the '60s and early '70s. Coeducation would surely require a men's gymnasium and larger athletic fields that could come only at the expense of the golf course. Yet these things did not happen and the course survived (despite indifferent maintenance) into the 1990s.[49]

* * *

One of the most persistent headaches from the early '60s onward was the shortage of parking space. As student enrollment almost tripled to 9,900 in 1979, the increase came primarily from commuting students, driving to campus. Faculty and staff grew similarly and, living ever farther from campus, contributed similarly to the problem. The perennial quest for parking space was a major—perhaps *the* major—contributor to the university's perennial land hunger. For every campus constituency the allocation of existing parking space was a matter of urgent concern. When maintenance personnel—largely black—were at long last awarded equal access to faculty/staff parking spaces in the late 1960s, it had a rippling effect across campus, determining when others left home and where they parked because these workers came earliest in the morning and had first choice. Similarly, there was friction between students and faculty over the allocation of space. The beginning of every year if not semester required new estimates of what parking lots filled up at what times on what days of the week.

Parking had remained manageable as long as there were only a few hundred commuter students and seniors vying for space. In 1963 parking regulations were instituted for the first time. In return for a $1 annual fee, students, faculty, and staff were allowed to park on campus streets and a few small campus lots.[50] Under new legal rulings, however, dormitory residents were in effect guaranteed the right to have cars. The university could not interfere as long as they were parked off campus. Accordingly, the number of these vehicles increased exponentially, taking up curbside space throughout the neighborhood. These cars were often kept for weekend use only, and commonly sat untouched for days on end. As the commuter population mushroomed, they were forced to cruise farther and farther from campus to find parking places. The cumulative result was that, during daylight hours especially, curbside parking was virtually unobtainable for blocks on every side of campus. Would-be visitors were discouraged from attending campus meetings, concerts, or other events. Tate Street merchants complained that customers could not reach their establishments. Neighboring residents could not park in front of their own homes or even receive deliveries, much less invite friends to visit. Those with driveways sometimes found them blocked. Resentment escalated into outrage at this invasion of their lives. It was more than ironic that many of those who suffered most from this plague were the same people targeted to lose their homes when the university sought to address it through annexation to create parking lots. Either way, the college/university, once a magnet for neighborhood residents in search of recreation and mental stimulation, was increasingly regarded as the enemy.[51]

The parking problem was acute by 1965. Administrators, subscribing to the principle that every student should be guaranteed either a bed or a parking space, gave it high priority as they sought land for expansion. Around the country campus planners were recommending that, except for service vehicles, cars and trucks be kept at the perimeter. UNCG attempted to follow this principle. Most of the large city block bounded by Spring Garden, Tate, Highland, and the railroad was earmarked for parking; academic buildings would be confined to the strip nearest to Spring Garden Street, where the Graham and Cone Buildings were later placed.[52] The slow pace of property acquisition delayed completion of this 600-space lot until 1971. Officials investigated the feasibility of multitiered parking decks but their high cost delayed that kind of construction until the 1990s. Instead, as state funding permitted, new tracts were acquired (some only by lease) and converted into parking lots. Most were small and temporary, located at the south and west edges of campus where land was most available. Some neighboring churches lent their parking lots on weekdays.[53]

As state law required campus lots to be self-liquidating, the cost of parking permits kept rising. With completion of the large lot behind Graham building in 1971, the annual fee was raised to $16—an amount that many found extortionate.[54] It was quickly found that as the fee mounted, students and even faculty members chose to avoid it by taking their chances again on the streets, further exacerbating neighborhood relations. Some of the remoter parking lots even went unfilled.[55]

Nevertheless, the combined pressure of rising enrollments and rising car ownership was remorseless. Especially in the morning "prime time" hours when the greatest number of classes met, parking space was hard to find. Matters reached a crisis in 1974 when the university started leasing parking land and even offered to refund the $16 fee to any students who found it impossible to find parking spaces. Enrollments that year surpassed all expectations with commuters accounting for the entire increase. In 1975 they represented 62 percent of the student body, reversing the picture only seven years earlier when 62 percent lived in the dormitories. Commuters now approached 6,000 in a total enrollment of 9,500. Two years later, when the total campus population (students, faculty, and staff) exceeded 11,000, there were not yet 2,000 campus parking places.[56]

In 1978 the United States Supreme Court came to the rescue of UNCG's neighbors when it permitted cities to restrict parking on designated streets to the residents on those streets. Greensboro seized the opportunity.[57] For the residents involved it was a godsend; for the university it was a potential nightmare. It set out immediately to lease more off-campus lots, particularly for the dormitory students who had caused much of the curbside problem; it also had the city post four-hour time limits on some of the closest streets. Commuters responded by buying more permits and using the campus lots as never before, thereby averting another crisis. The university continued to acquire more land within its "natural boundaries" for both building and parking space, to serve the expanding numbers yet to come.[58]

It was an unhappy paradox that, at the very time campus expansion was fueling the bitterest relations in its history with the surrounding neighborhoods, the university desperately needed the political and financial support of the Greensboro community to achieve that expansion. It set out purposefully to court that support, sponsoring a survey in 1965 showing that the university had contributed over $9 million to the economy of Guilford County during the preceding academic year. It predicted an impact of nearly $15 million in 1969–70.[59] The Greensboro business community, as represented by the chamber of commerce, was fully cooperative.[60] Its support was reflected in the ill-fated urban redevelopment scheme and, more positively, in the legislative appropriations that funded the extraordinary campus growth over the next few years.

* * *

Landlocked campuses are almost forced to build densely and upward. In campus architecture, modernists by 1960 had won out nationally over Georgian and Gothic traditionalists. But for continuity's sake bows were still being made to existing buildings nearby—echoing prominent features or construction materials.[61] Woman's College had already made the transition, starting with Coleman Gymnasium. Although many of the new campus buildings continued to use the traditional red brick, all were modern in design and three of the five dormitories completed in 1963 and 1967 were high-rise. (No further dormitories were required for many years because commuters accounted for the subsequent enrollment increase.) UNCG now diverged from earlier practice by employing a succession of architects—almost as many as there were building projects. The resulting structures, while modern, varied largely in style and attractiveness.[62]

All told, eighteen buildings or major additions were completed between 1964 and 1979. They included a wing of the new McIver Building for the art department and Weatherspoon Gallery (1966), a music annex and a broadcasting/cinema building (1966), Phillips-Hawkins and Cone Dormitories (1967), Taylor Theater (1967), a new wing of Elliott Hall (1968), a nursing school building (1969), the McNutt Learning Resources Center (1970), the Frank Porter Graham classroom building (1970), the life sciences building (in two installments, 1971 and 1978), a tower annex to the library (1973), a new administration building (1975, named for Mereb Mossman), and a business and economics building (1979).

From a distance, the new library tower was the most visible building on campus. A nine-story concrete structure with plain walls on the east and west and textured many-windowed facades on the north and south, it diverged sharply from the Georgian structure to which it was attached. The plain sides came to serve a purpose the architect surely never contemplated: a rappelling venue for student athletes and Greensboro firemen.

Although administration buildings commonly are top campus priorities, it must be said that on this campus administrators had never lived in luxury. Until 1966 every president or chancellor since McIver had occupied the bay window office just left of the main entrance to the old Administration Building. Seeking additional space, Otis Singletary moved that year into what everyone supposed would be temporary quarters in the Pecky Cypress room in the basement of the Alumni House—scene of the Graham hearings a decade earlier—pending the construction of a new administration building. Dean Mossman took his former quarters.[63] Singletary departed campus almost immediately, but James Ferguson remained in the Alumni House for most of his years in office, until the construction of the Mossman Building in 1975. Even then, funding ran out temporarily, preventing its occupation by many other tenants until 1979. The new building was erected on recently acquired land at the northwest corner of Spring Garden and Forest Streets. Its most striking internal feature is a massive three-story lobby, around which the offices are grouped. Those most used by students and the public—admissions, academic advising, student affairs, registrar, cashier, and financial aid—were on the first floor. The chancellor was ensconced in a third-floor suite that made up for the years of denial.

The first reaction of some administrators to the prospect of a new administration building was to call again for demolition of the old.[64] But Foust Building, as it came to be called in the 1960s, was the only structure left that dated back to the founding; in the early years, except for the dormitories, it *was* the college. Countless alumnae and others valued it accordingly, and thoughts of scrapping it were finally discarded.[65] In 1980 it was added to the National Register of Historic Places. Much renovated inside, it continued to house a variety of administrative offices.

Three older structures dating from 1912–14 *were* torn down, however, in the 1960s: the Woman's and Kirkland Dormitories, behind the dining halls, and the old infirmary building. All were in poor condition and regarded as fire hazards. All had been superseded by new buildings and they conflicted with current planning. The infirmary made room for the new wing of Elliott Hall.

Campus growth was so rapid in the '60s and '70s that some of the new buildings were overcrowded from the beginning. As a result, auxiliary facilities were constantly in requisition to handle the overflow. Some schools or departments continued to have faculty or staff members scattered in four or five different buildings.[66]

And amidst all the new construction, the existing plant was falling into disrepair. Maintenance costs, unlike new construction, came out of the operational budget where they competed with academic affairs. Chancellor Ferguson admitted in 1970 that he sometimes knowingly stinted maintenance in the interest of boosting the academic program. That was a general impression during his administration; it helped solidify his popularity with faculty members who generally understood his dilemma and shared his priorities.[67]

The most serious deterioration involved the aging performing arts buildings. Dean Lawrence Hart in 1974 wrathfully characterized conditions in the music building as disgraceful. Rats invaded classrooms and practice rooms, which were also subject to periodic flooding. (This building like Aycock Auditorium was built over the stream draining the nearby mineral springs.) Damage to equipment, he said, threatened to consume most of the annual repair budget while damage to the walls, doors, and floors perforce went unnoticed.[68] The worst of these problems were alleviated but the building still needed major renovation.

Aycock suffered correspondingly, having had no comprehensive renovation since opening in 1927. When decade-long appeals for a special legislative appropriation bore fruit in 1973, the architect found that conditions were even worse than previously believed. The electrical system was so unsafe that the building was closed down altogether pending renovation. It reopened, much refurbished, in 1976.[69]

Related to maintenance were the matters of air conditioning and handicapped access, the latter required by recent legislation. When the new McIver Building opened in 1960 there were insufficient funds to air condition the entire building, so the first floor was left out on the theory that it needed the service least. The English, mathematics, and drama departments who occupied that floor were no worse off than denizens of nearly all the older buildings on campus including those most inhabited by students: the dormitories, dining halls, infirmary, and Elliott Hall. Temperatures on the second floor of the Gove infirmary were well over 100 degrees in the summer of 1968. It took years for these concerns to be satisfied.[70]

Under state law, all new construction came to include handicapped access. But even more than with air conditioning it took many years to retrofit the entire campus.[71]

Despite the new construction on campus, the physical deterioration of existing buildings reinforced the historic and deep-seated conviction that the institution was underfunded. The trustee visiting committee recalled in 1963 that it had perennially requested larger appropriations. Even when these appeals were supported by the full board, they were usually ignored in Raleigh. A year later, Chancellor Singletary was even more blunt: UNCG "must be competitively good and stand on its own merits. The future of this institution is hanging in the balance. And I am not interested in old plans for equal treatment. If the trustees do what has to be done, somewhere along the line the University at Greensboro will have to be given *preferential* treatment."[72] It did not happen, and he soon departed.

Funding at any campus depends on its mission. At UNCG, that mission (and with it, the student body) remained in transition. Primarily responsible for the uncertainty was North Carolina's third major university reorganization, in 1972.

Chapter 21

A New Identity

University consolidation was occurring nationwide. To some degree it pursued the same goals driving the first round during the Depression—economy and minimizing curricular overlap. But also, as the number of campuses and student enrollments multiplied, there was need for more centralized direction.[1] Special-purpose campuses like WC gave way to multi-purpose campuses like UNCG. Institutions were informally classified into different leagues according to their resources, prestige, and public or private status. Competition occurred less between leagues than among institutions within each league.[2]

North Carolina's third round of consolidation came in 1972, as sequel to a merger of 200-odd state government agencies into twenty-five. The guiding spirit was Governor Robert Scott, who wanted to make state government, including higher education, more efficient and more politically accountable. An N.C. State alumnus, he also wanted to reduce the traditional dominance of Chapel Hill within North Carolina's higher education establishment. President William Friday and the UNC leadership, with their partisans around the state, saw the governor's proposal as a threat to the university's survival. After a bitter and apparently losing political battle lasting several months they salvaged a partial victory. The plan adopted by the legislature late in 1971 incorporated all sixteen of the state-supported four-year institutions of higher education into one system as Scott wanted, but it was to be the UNC system, headed by a general administration and a new board of governors located in Chapel Hill. All but the School of the Arts were designated as universities. The new board of governors promptly re-elected Friday as president. Each institution was to have its own board of trustees, elected by and responsible to the board of governors. (The old visiting committees now disappeared.) The UNC system thus assumed much larger dimensions, diluting the power of Chapel Hill and every other individual campus.[3]

North Carolina did not need and could not easily afford fifteen state universities. True rationalization would have reduced their number, but each institution had its own constituency and was politically untouchable. The new dispensation by no means guaranteed equal or automatic funding. Now that all sixteen campuses were under the UNC umbrella, the perennial scramble for money centered more than ever before within its general administration and the board of governors to which it reported.

The UNCG trustees were fifteen in number, drawn from Greensboro and around the state. Some were alumnae; some were legislators; some were prominent lawyers and businessmen. In keeping with the times, there were sometimes more women on the board now than when it was a woman's college. Also in keeping with the times, the president of the student body was now an *ex officio* member.[4]

* * *

What was UNCG's mission to be, and in what league was it to fall? Over two hundred institutions around the country were experiencing similar metamorphoses. As a group they lacked the prestige or status of the flagship universities in their states—Chapel Hill and its equivalents. Upward mobility seemed to require emulating those role models, building up faculties (which was relatively easy to do in the current buyers' market) and placing more emphasis than before on research and graduate programs. Among all these institutions WC was almost unique in having attained a marginal university status with graduate, even a doctoral program in place before it achieved coeducation and formal designation as a university. But designation did not convey substance. Typically, these institutions were funded at a much lower level than the flagships and they found the going difficult.[5]

Many at UNCG hoped that university status would itself bring the necessary funding, and for a time morale soared.[6] But from the beginning there were the skeptics like Katherine Taylor who feared the new order would prove a recipe for mediocrity. In the words of a 1966 *Carolinian* editorial echoing her position, the school had "moved from a first rate college to a second rate university."[7] These criticisms were not altogether consistent. *Carolinian* editorials like other expressions of campus opinion had complained for decades that WC was the "redheaded stepchild" of the university system; it was hardly fair to pin the responsibility now on coeducation and university status. In fact, UNCG's first decade brought substantially increased student enrollments and per pupil funding. Enrollment grew from about 3,700 in 1963 to 9,500 in 1975, when it gradually leveled off, following a national pattern.

Not all this growth was expected or welcomed. An administrator recalled many years later that the only time he ever saw Jim Ferguson truly angry was when he learned of an unexpected enrollment surge in 1974, placing the university 2 percent beyond the number of students for which it had been budgeted; he could see resultant crises in the classrooms, dining halls, dormitories, and parking lots. The problem resulted from overestimating the number of current students expected to drop out; other institutions made the same mistake but not to the same degree. Since much of the budget was enrollment-driven, the flagging growth after 1975 brought flagging appropriations as well, slowing momentum in every respect.[8]

During Ferguson's administration, state funding for higher education in North Carolina increased by about two-thirds, but given the rising expectations on every hand there was still not enough money to go around.[9] In 1978–79, his last year, state appropriations accounted for 54 percent of the university's revenue; students provided another 38 percent, primarily through tuition, fees, and charges for room and board. Federal money had risen over the years, but in 1978–79 it was still only $1,243,000, or 3.2 percent of the institution's total revenue. (Ferguson estimated in 1976 that the cost of responding to federal reporting requirements amounted to $150,000 to $200,000 per year.) The remaining 5 percent of revenue came from a variety of public and private sources.[10]

Reconsolidation in 1972 brought a unified budget for the entire UNC system. More than ever before, priorities and allocations came to be set by general administration and the board of governors.[11] Once again UNCG administrators perceived inequities within the system; even before enrollments leveled off in 1975, money for new faculty positions virtually dried up. Ferguson protested in vain to his superiors, citing UNCG's high graduate enrollment compared with some more-favored campuses.[12] General administration classified Chapel Hill and State as "Major Research Universities" with UNCG by itself in a second "Other Doctoral" category—a confirmation of its relative status since the 1930s. Theoretically UNCG was above the remaining "Comprehensive" and "Baccalaureate" institutions. Yet by 1977 it had fallen to thirteenth among the sixteen campuses in appropriations per student.[13]

It was not illogical to blame reconsolidation for this state of affairs; even Chapel Hill and State felt some adverse effects. The new campuses at Charlotte, Asheville, and Wilmington needed continuing nurture. The former white teachers' colleges—Appalachian, Western Carolina, and East Carolina—had always lagged behind the UNC campuses at appropriations time and needed upgrading. Most of all, the black institutions (along with Pembroke, the Lumbee Indian college-turned-university) faced a tremendous climb to achieve parity with the white campuses; in their case, federal civil rights mandates required no less. Fairly or not, some at UNCG felt their campus to be the greatest loser by reconsolidation.[14]

The result was a longstanding identity crisis. A tendency had already developed among many faculty and alumnae to recall the later years of the Woman's College as a Golden Age. For them the sequel was profoundly depressing. Those too young or too recent for that memory were disappointed nonetheless at the signs of penury amidst a faculty and curriculum of genuine merit. In the absence of adequate funding people saw the institution as drifting without clear direction. Even students, whose collegiate memories are necessarily short, saw it as lacking in the normal campus amenities: football, fraternities, school spirit, and a rollicking social life. The *Carolinian* in 1969 called it a "suitcase college," acceptable academically but not socially. Indeed, what the editor most feared was rapidly coming to pass: a growing proportion of the students were commuters, often of mature years, who had lives off campus and were not much interested in school spirit.[15] The continuous flood of newcomers, faculty as well as students, had no tie to the Woman's College and only a mixed concern for traditional college life. As Chancellor Ferguson left office in 1979, and for years afterward, people were still debating how far the university should go in repudiating its Woman's College heritage. It would take many years to heal the wounds created by a revolution that people perceived so differently.[16]

When people sought scapegoats for UNCG's problems they looked primarily to the top: general administration in Chapel Hill and the legislature in Raleigh. They were reluctant to blame Ferguson, who more clearly than anyone else perceived the realities. But he was a southern gentleman, soft-spoken to a fault—unlike Leo Jenkins, the vocal chancellor at East Carolina who persuaded the legislature to create a second UNC medical school on his campus. When UNC Vice President Arnold King, speaking at UNCG, sought to compliment his hosts by declaring that, of all the constituent institutions, UNCG gave his colleagues the least trouble, it evoked bitter laughter in the audience.[17]

Administrators cast about for an alternative role or mission that might save the institution from the beckoning abyss of mediocrity. That of "urban university" received some attention in the early 1970s, then was abandoned. UNCG did not despise the idea of serving the needs of its host community, as its record then and later attests. Some of the professional schools were already active in that respect. But most of the faculty and administrators held out for what they regarded as more—a research university with a regional if not national reputation.[18] That status offered too much prestige to pass up as long as the faculty continued to develop.

By general agreement everywhere, the best university was the one whose faculty had the best record of publication and, increasingly, of attracting outside funding for research.[19] In fact, research activity and recognition did spread rapidly among the nation's campuses in the postwar era. By 1979, the ten leading institutions were producing only 20 percent of total academic research, a figure that was remarkably less than in previous years and was destined to decline still further.[20] Upward mobility was impossible without adequate funding, however. Some faculty members at UNCG departed for greener pastures, but the number was gratifyingly small; competition everywhere was fierce.

* * *

By the 1960s it was apparent that academic excellence, even in public institutions, required substantial private as well as public funding.[21] In 1962, WC's last year, Otis Singletary created a development office and named as its director George W. Hamer, at that time personnel manager for Greensboro's Cone Mills textile firm. Hamer's charge was to raise more money than ever before and in the process coordinate the activities already taking place around campus. The greatest windfall in his first year was the endowment for the Katharine Smith Reynolds Scholarships. Hamer retired in 1974, shortly after his elevation to vice chancellor. His successor, Charles W. Patterson, extended the alumni annual giving campaign well beyond the alumni and introduced telephone solicitation—the Phonothon.[22] Both men actively solicited area businesses and foundations as well as individual donors. Their success could be read in the figures. Annual gifts from all quarters climbed from $263,000 in 1962–63 to just over $1 million in 1978–79. The alumni contribution to these totals rose from $33,000 to $439,000.[23] In 1977–78, in fact, UNCG ranked thirteenth in the nation (among public institutions) in the percentage of alumni contributing to its annual fund. Yet the unpleasant fact remained that in 1978–79 gifts and endowment income accounted for only 2 percent of its total revenue.[24] The total endowment had a market value in 1979 of about $3.5 million—a great improvement over earlier years, yet infinitesimal in terms of the university's needs.[25]

Much of that endowment resided in the Excellence Fund, created under Hamer's leadership in 1966. It reached its goal of $1 million in 1973 but advanced no further during Ferguson's administration. Although UNCG resisted the designation as an urban university, the Excellence Fund was designed specifically to raise funds in the Piedmont Triad area: Greensboro, Winston-Salem, High Point, and their environs. Most of the money, in fact, came from businesses and individual donors in Greensboro. The proceeds were invested, with the income used primarily to supplement existing scholarship and faculty research funds as well as the salaries of outstanding faculty members whom the university wanted to attract or retain. (Although there was money enough now to endow one or more chairs completely from private funds, it reached more people as salary supplements.) In 1974, there were seven of these professorships, five of them named for the organizations donating the largest amounts of money: Burlington Industries, Jefferson Standard Life Insurance Company, North Carolina National Bank, Pilot Life Insurance Company, and the Wayne (later Elizabeth Rosenthal) Foundation representing the Weil and Rosenthal families of Goldsboro—longtime supporters of the Woman's College.[26] In addition, President Friday assigned three system-wide University Distinguished Professorships to UNCG in the '60s—the most prestigious of all.[27]

* * *

The university was utterly transformed by the enrollment changes it experienced in the 1960s and '70s. In little more than a decade a student body composed overwhelmingly of middle-class white girls came to embrace every gender, race, class, age group, and student category known to the state. Some of this was welcome and came easily; some of it was unbidden and came only with prodding and great pain.

Prior to 1972, the several UNC campuses maintained a common admissions policy and standards, with local variations. The reconsolidation that year ended any hope of uniformity and each of the sixteen institutions, through its faculty and trustees, established its own admissions policies. UNCG continued to accept or reject applicants on the basis of their high school grades and their scores in the national Scholastic Aptitude Test. Of the two, the high school record was regarded as the better predictor of performance in college.[28]

Statewide coeducation in 1963 and reconsolidation a decade later vastly increased the competition for students. Until the early '70s, UNCG followed its traditional recruiting practices. They were limited pretty much to visiting high schools around the state and informing their prospective graduates of the university's programs and attractions. This activity had migrated from Charlie Phillips's public relations office to the admissions office, where additional personnel markedly broadened the coverage. Increasingly, students, faculty, and alumni were enlisted to contact promising high school students. Efforts were also made to recruit outside the state, relying chiefly on alumni.[29] In the early 1970s the university began inviting to campus each spring about eighty outstanding high school seniors who were finalists for its competitive scholarships.[30]

Coeducation was the most visible change to the student body. Hardly any former woman's college became coeducational easily or overnight. Men were notoriously more reluctant than women to break this gender barrier. In addition, the university found itself swimming against a national tide. Since the 1970s, female college enrollments have surpassed male enrollments almost everywhere. Even at Chapel Hill, women began to outnumber men. At UNCG, only 66 male undergraduates enrolled in 1964, the first year they were eligible; graduate students brought the male total to 277.[31] (The first five bachelor's degrees awarded to men were granted in 1966.) Not until 1972 did male undergraduates outnumber male graduate students. By 1979, the male enrollment had climbed to 3,000 but it still represented only 30 percent of the total.[32]

Part of the problem in attracting men related to the curriculum. At the outset much of it was female-oriented by usual perceptions, stronger in the arts and humanities than in the sciences. But administrators and faculty worked hard to introduce or expand programs of interest to men—in the sciences and business administration, for instance.[33] More scholarship aid was made available to men. The athletic program was also expanded, but to nowhere near the degree seen later.

Out-of-state enrollment was limited by law to 15 percent. It remained at about that level until 1972 when the legislature doubled out-of-state tuition, causing a decline to less than 10 percent by 1975.[34] These students continued to be drawn primarily from the neighboring states of Virginia and South Carolina along with New York, New Jersey, Pennsylvania, and Maryland.[35] Also as in earlier years, they tended on average to be better students. Their high schools were often better and their entrance requirements were higher.[36]

Unlike North Carolina A&T University across town with its engineering and other technical programs, UNCG attracted few foreign students; there were forty-nine in 1977, haling from twenty-two countries.[37]

Within North Carolina, UNCG continued to attract students from all over the state. But an ever-larger proportion came from its home region. By 1979, Guilford and seven adjacent counties contributed 63 percent of the enrollment, compared with only 31 percent in 1960; the proportion from Guilford itself doubled in that time, to 42 percent.[38]

Thus commuters represented the second great element in transforming the student body. Their influx was so great that before long it surpassed coeducation in its impact on the university. Commuters accounted for all the enrollment growth after 1967, when the last dormitories for a generation were completed. They became the majority in 1971–72. For better or worse, UNCG was now primarily a commuter college with parking problems to match. The commuters were a diverse group, ranging from traditional-age freshmen to middle aged and even elderly people. Half of them were twenty-five or older, half were married, and most were male. Almost half were part-time students.[39]

Adult students therefore comprised a third overlapping addition to the student body. Colleges around the country found in the 1970s that growing adult enrollments more than compensated for a sagging population of eighteen to twenty-two-year-olds.[40] At UNCG, when the number of adult undergraduates reached 500 in 1972, the university opened a special counseling center for them. They came from diverse backgrounds and did not always meet the standard admissions requirements. Some took remedial work—hearkening back to the Normal days—but once established, they did better academically on average than the students who came with freshly minted high school diplomas. Adult students generally paid their own way and knew why they were there. Most had daytime jobs and, like the graduate students, needed evening classes. The adult student center put continuing pressure on departments to accommodate them.[41]

Graduate students were also adults and shared many of the same concerns. Their increase was even faster than that of the undergraduates. Where total student enrollments rose by 164 percent between 1963 and 1978, graduate enrollments grew by 478 percent, from 13 to 28 percent of the total enrollment.[42] The great majority of graduate students attended part-time, and in fact accounted for most of the part-time enrollment.[43]

Transfer students were another growing category, rising from 100 in 1963 to almost 900 by 1978. The vast majority were sophomores and juniors. After 1970, about two-thirds were women, corresponding to the overall student ratio. Although they came from a variety of institutions, a quarter of them were products of the state's new community college system.[44] (Several community colleges and technical institutes were established in the region, the closest being Guilford Technical Institute in nearby Jamestown.) At the same time, the university's retention rate increased: the number of outgoing transfers declined while incoming transfers increased. The result was an unprecedented growth of the junior and senior classes compared with freshmen and sophomores. Transfers to Chapel Hill—that troublesome issue of previous years—fell off sharply as that campus became coeducational in all four years and as UNCG expanded its own degree programs.[45]

A university's quality and prestige rest almost as much on the caliber of its students as on its faculty. At UNCG, distress over the failure to attract more men was, if anything, surpassed by distress over failing to attract more top-notch students. Indeed the university rejected proportionately twice as many male as female applicants in the early years, though the proportions gradually leveled off. Among incoming freshmen, males outscored females consistently in the Scholastic Aptitude Test math scores and about half the time in the verbal scores. However, applicants were accepted or rejected on the basis of high school records as well as SAT scores, and boys typically got poorer grades than girls.[46] The anecdotal evidence from both faculty members and alumnae (the feminine form used advisedly) found the early male students to have been inferior academically to the girls.[47]

Overall, the picture if disappointing was far from bleak. Three-quarters of UNCG's incoming freshmen were drawn from the top quarter of their high school classes. In the decade 1963–73, when national SAT scores sagged slightly, those of UNCG freshmen fell at the same rate but remained above the national average.[48] Incoming students in 1977 exceeded the average verbal and math scores for North Carolina, the South, and the nation. Within the UNC system, they consistently outscored the new students at all the campuses except Chapel Hill and State.[49] Those exceptions rankled, however.

The admissions office in 1979 made a study of North Carolina high school students who had taken the SATs, comparing those who enrolled at UNCG with those who were accepted but chose to go elsewhere. On average, those who enrolled scored lower on the SATs than those who chose not to come. Estimated parental income, which correlated well with SAT scores, was also higher for those who elected to go elsewhere. UNCG, in other words, was a second or third choice among many of its best applicants. A large proportion of those who did enroll came from the lower middle class. They commuted from home and they needed financial aid. The university had plenty of company in these respects. By 1980, over half of American colleges and universities admitted most if not all applicants who met their minimum qualifications; only 10 percent remained truly competitive.[50]

In fact, UNCG became from the outset a metropolitan university, before that term or category was widely recognized. Like other metropolitan universities it served a substantial urbanized area with a largely traditional curriculum; there was no general focus on urban affairs.[51] It provided a vital service for its region, furnishing educational, economic, and social mobility to thousands of persons who had little other access to a four-year college. This role was different from that of the Woman's College in its later years but not terribly different from the one that animated Charles Duncan McIver in the 1890s. UNCG delivered these blessings to infinitely more people than he could have imagined. Nevertheless, it was a role that disappointed, even mortified administrators, faculty members, alumnae, and students animated by the revolution of rising expectations, whose values derived from the traditional, selective university campus.

What UNCG seemed to lack in drawing power, according to some observers on and off campus, was not academic quality (except for some early shortages in subjects of interest to men) but rather the athletics and social atmosphere of the traditional campus.[52]

The evidence was mixed. In the mid-'70s UNCG also suffered from a widespread perception that it lacked academic standing compared with Chapel Hill, State, and perhaps other campuses. The admissions office was sufficiently alarmed to ask that faculty members write letters to promising high school seniors touting the academic programs and personnel of their departments.[53] In a 1978 survey of those applicants who were accepted but did not enroll, the two main reasons they gave for bypassing UNCG were academic—weakness not only in their prospective majors but overall: 30 and 21 percent, respectively. Trailing those reasons were inadequate athletic programs and social outlets: 18 and 16 percent. Surveys of entering students and of former students who dropped out provided similar results.[54] On the other hand, a survey of undergraduates in 1979—administrators were obviously worried about this matter—showed that 71 percent of students found campus social life no better than fair while 75 percent respected the academic environment. In response to the bottom-line question, How well do you like UNCG?, 19 percent were enthusiastic, 53 percent were favorable, 24 percent were more or less neutral, and 6 percent were hostile. Nearly three-quarters reported that, if starting over, they would go to UNCG again.[55]

How much the responses reflected curricular and vocational concerns peculiar to men does not appear; but except for technical fields like engineering, those concerns were rapidly being addressed. Whatever the causes of UNCG's enrollment and public relations problems, its identity crisis would preoccupy the institution for decades.

* * *

Another thorny issue arose from the university's anemic black enrollment, which amounted in 1970 to only 3.7 percent of the total. In this case UNCG found itself part of a much larger dispute between the UNC system and the federal government. The Civil Rights Act of 1964 had outlawed racial segregation across a broad spectrum of American life, including public education. Enforcement was entrusted to the Department of Health, Education, and Welfare and its Office of Civil Rights. In 1969 they turned from their original priority, the public schools, to higher education. After determining that the southern states had not yet advanced beyond token integration in their state universities, federal officals demanded early in 1970 that they move to desegregate these institutions just as actively as the courts were currently forcing them to do in their public schools. The proof of desegregation must lie not merely in nondiscriminatory admissions and hiring policies but in equal facilities and genuinely biracial student bodies and faculties.

North Carolina and its fellow respondents dragged their feet, promising only in general terms to recruit black students and faculty. There was little immediate change either in practice or results, and the Office of Civil Rights declared North Carolina and nine other states to be in violation of the law. Its ultimate sanction, if carried out, was to withdraw all federal funding from these universities, approaching $90 million in the case of the UNC system. When higher-ups in the Nixon administration appeared ready to drop the matter, the National Association for the Advancement of Colored People brought suit in federal court later in 1970 to make it enforce the law. This case and others growing from it dragged on for years amidst great controversy. In 1973 an appeals court upheld the NAACP, leading soon to racial enrollment quotas for individual institutions, including UNCG. Implementation remained slow and the NAACP returned to court, obtaining in 1977 another order declaring North Carolina and other states in violation of the law.

Almost alone on the UNCG faculty, philosophy professor Warren Ashby openly questioned the university's position. In 1971 he had come out reluctantly for a quota system as the only way to guarantee minority employment. Hardly anyone in authority favored such a course, however, and in an article Ashby wrote for the *Greensboro Daily News* in 1978 he offered little substantive advice;

indeed, there were few easy answers.[56] If, hypothetically, every state institution in North Carolina were allocated a student body reflecting the black proportion of the state's population—about 25 percent—it would have caused rebellion in the black community, which sought desperately to preserve the traditionally black campuses it had built up through generations of adversity. One of their greatest fears throughout the controversy was that in the interest of desegregation North Carolina would abolish one or more of those five institutions as some other states were doing. It never did. On the other hand, as those campuses kept their black identity, they necessarily preempted a large portion of the state's black college population, leaving fewer for the traditionally white campuses. In a time of falling college-age populations of both races, there were not enough young blacks to go around.

A major concern of federal officials was program duplication among the historically black and white institutions, particularly those in close proximity. They suggested closing down some of these programs and transferring others to different campuses. An example particularly relevant to UNCG involved nursing; it was suggested that UNCG's young and thriving nursing program be moved to historically black North Carolina A&T University across town, whose own nursing program was foundering. Whatever the abstract logic in this suggestion (and its parallels across the state) it threatened to destroy a valuable existing program without any guaranteed benefit in return. (This proved to be the experience of other states that bought peace with the government in this way; students refused to follow the programs to other campuses.) UNC officials, including President William Friday and the board of governors, regarded all such proposals as an unacceptable invasion of the university's right to establish its own educational programs.

North Carolina failed a major test in this regard when the UNC system decided in 1974 to create a school of veterinary medicine—something it had never had. Both A&T and North Carolina State University in Raleigh had supportive programs in agriculture and related sciences; both wanted this school badly. UNC officials would have advanced their and the state's credibility no end by setting up this new program at A&T, but the plum went to State. The justification was that State's supporting departments were stronger and it would cost too much to upgrade A&T—a tacit confirmation that the traditional discrimination was still thriving.

Negotiations dragged on while the university continued to upgrade the traditionally black campuses and distribute new programs more equitably. But these efforts were too modest to satisfy Carter administration officials in the late '70s, who threatened again to withdraw federal funding. In 1979 the university took to the courts itself to prevent that action and, just as important, to get the matter transferred to a federal court in North Carolina with a more amenable judge. The tactic succeeded and the funds were never withheld. Even more helpful to the university was the national election of 1980, bringing to power a Reagan administration much less interested in civil rights enforcement. In a 1981 agreement fostered by Senator Jesse Helms and seen everywhere as a victory for the university, it agreed to continue upgrading its black campuses and to strive for a non-binding black enrollment goal of 10.6 percent on the traditionally white campuses by 1986.

Progress did continue under this agreement, even if it failed to meet all the 1981 goals. The traditionally black and white campuses all survived without fundamental change—as demanded in effect by both races. By the late 1980s, the legislature was providing as much or more funding per student to the black institutions as to the white campuses with comparable missions. Black enrollments at the white institutions reached 8 percent overall in 1992, well behind the 10.6 percent goal but enough to rank North Carolina among the leading states in that respect. At the same time, white enrollments at the black institutions rose to 19 percent, well ahead of the 1981 goals. The last court case was dismissed in 1990, twenty years after the first was initiated.

The controversy was not only long but expensive; UNC Vice President Arnold King estimated that it cost the university well over $2 million in legal fees alone. One can never know how far the compromise results just cited would have materialized without the government's outside stimulus, but the record before 1970 gave little ground for optimism.[57]

* * *

Initially WC/UNCG, like the other traditionally white campuses, had continued after 1956 to admit any black applicants who met all the normal qualifications. It did not recruit them. In 1966 it began to participate in the national Upward Bound summer program for college-bound black high school students. In 1970, following the initial federal demands, it hired a part-time black admissions officer to recruit students, primarily at the traditionally black high schools around the state.[58] Those who enrolled that year received over 20 percent of the financial aid granted, based on relative need. But they represented only 3.7 percent of the total enrollment; black faculty members represented a comparably small proportion.[59]

Actually, UNC was only a little behind other institutions, including northern ones, in its rates of integration. Blacks scored well below whites in standardized tests and other accepted measurements of college-readiness. Most institutions, North and South, public and private, saw themselves as having to choose between academic standards and racial integration. Faced with that choice, they opted almost everywhere for academic standards. Affirmative action—the active recruitment of blacks—usually came only under pressure. But the pressure did come, and race became almost everywhere one of the selective criteria.[60]

Under the North Carolina desegregation plan of 1974 UNCG was required to attain a black enrollment of 550 by 1977. The original part-time black recruiter of 1970 became two full-time black recruiters by 1978. Substantial numbers of promising black high school students were brought to campus for visits every year.[61] The results were positive if not spectacular. Black enrollments rose from 109 in 1964 to 857 in 1977, or 8.6 percent of the total—well ahead of the quota. By 1979 black students numbered 894, or 9.8 percent. (A substantial minority of them were part-time graduate students.)[62] They more than held their own academically. Student retention rates are always of interest to administrators, but never more so than under the shadow of a court order. It was found by 1979 that despite lower SAT scores and predicted grade point averages, UNCG's black students remained in school and graduated at a slightly higher rate than whites.[63]

Part of the black enrollment came through a special services program—also instituted in 1970—and funded almost entirely by the federal government. It was aimed at disadvantaged and minority students who could not meet the regular admissions requirements but showed promise nonetheless. This program provided most if not all of the remedial work offered on campus—none of it given for academic credit—and was responsible in no small measure for the high black retention rate. Before long, the program embraced not only incoming students but those already on campus, many of them adult students, who needed the counseling and tutoring it provided.[64] With modifications the program remained in place through the 1990s.

Chancellor Ferguson fully supported desegregation and affirmative action. In 1965 he wrote an article for the *Carolinian* emphatically endorsing racial equality and the civil rights laws and decisions designed to bring it about. No president or chancellor in the institution's history had cared or dared to go so far.[65] Two years later he responded to requests from students of both races by ordering that dormitory room assignments, hitherto segregated, be assigned without regard to race. In 1968 he appointed a faculty committee under sociologist Elaine Burgess to study campus race relations and make recommendations for their improvement.

In its 1969 report the Burgess committee called for greater efforts to recruit black students, and to make them feel more comfortable once admitted. It had talked with black alumnae who said their most traumatic experiences had been dealing with the majority of white students who did not accept them as equals. Current black students found less to complain about in this respect, partly because they themselves had organized in 1967. What came to be called the Neo-Black Society was avowedly separatist, sponsoring parallel events for black students. The committee noted that there was only one black member of the faculty at that time, and recommended strong efforts to acquire more. Black students were angrily calling for a larger black presence in the curriculum as well, through black studies and other programs. The committee, like the faculty at large, divided over black studies but advocated nevertheless a larger representation of African-American culture in the curriculum.[66] The campus launched a special orientation program for minority students; it proved so successful that the federal court took it as the model for a general requirement.[67]

Nevertheless, the black student population, taken as a group, was less happy with campus life than was the white majority. Although 81 percent of students of both races reported in the 1979 survey that they had social contacts with students of both races, there remained a substantial measure of self-segregation. Blacks were less apt than whites to report equality of treatment.[68]

Black faculty proved even harder to recruit than black students. The reasons were similar: highly qualified black candidates were few in number and therefore in great demand. (Nationally, blacks earned only 447 of the 24,235 Ph.D.s awarded in 1974.)[69] They tended to be absorbed by the most prestigious institutions and those that were traditionally black. After 1970, affirmative action affected the recruitment of faculty as well as students, nationally and locally. To satisfy federal requirements, every tenure-track appointment had to be made through a public, nationwide search process that went far to guarantee equal access by minorities and women. These searches were costly, time-consuming, and often irritating compared with the "old boy network" of previous years. They did increase the numbers of women and blacks appointed to academic jobs, however, even if they could not flush out masses of minority applicants from minuscule candidate pools.[70]

In 1964, the UNCG faculty council actually defeated by a narrow margin a resolution endorsing "the merit employment of faculty and staff personnel at this institution without regard to race, color, creed, or sex."[71] The first black academic staff member, Odessa Patrick, had already come to the biology department years earlier in 1958 as a laboratory assistant; in 1969, with the rising concern for affirmative action, she was given faculty status as an instructor. Meanwhile, the first faculty appointment went in 1967 to Ernestine Small in the school of nursing, which led the campus in recruiting black faculty and students alike.[72] By 1969 there were six black faculty members, including Joseph S. Himes, a distinguished sociologist from the state's historically black North Carolina College in Durham, who soon was given one of the few endowed professorships. But despite considerable good-faith efforts, the number of black faculty remained stationary during the '70s.[73]

* * *

The university continued to depend on a maintenance staff who were predominantly black. They worked everywhere on campus, but in the largest numbers as groundskeepers, janitors, dormitory maids, kitchen and dining hall staff, and laundry workers until the campus laundry closed in 1975. Not until the early 1960s were blacks considered for clerical positions, and the numbers actually employed in that capacity grew very slowly. In 1972 there were only eleven black clerical employees in a total of 178.[74]

As the civil rights revolution moved onward, black employees became more aware of their rights and more assertive in demanding them. In the spring of 1969 the cafeteria workers organized a union and went out on strike, with major ramifications to be discussed later. Other campus workers resisted similar efforts from off campus to organize them, but they did form a grievance committee at the instance of the faculty committee on race relations. Both committees urged the university to make such grievance procedures permanent and to step up its hiring of black personnel beyond maintenance workers.[75]

Ferguson met the workers' committee and granted many of its requests, such as establishing a permanent grievance committee and desegregating the last segregated rest rooms. Henceforth all university employees had equal access to parking lots around campus that hitherto had been open only to faculty and administrators. Ferguson also agreed to establish a training program to help workers improve their skills, and to open up employment opportunities of all kinds to black workers.[76] In 1971 it was estimated that about 25 percent of the nonacademic employees were illiterate; at their request, the university offered literacy courses in off hours to the relatively small numbers of workers who turned out; they were taught by faculty of Guilford Technical Institute.[77]

In a similar vein, administrators in 1972 encouraged the campus office employees (predominantly white) to organize. Taking the name Academic and Administrative Staff Associates (AASA), they too got permission to take work-related courses on campus at university expense.[78]

* * *

Throughout the years UNCG and its predecessors had had only the most minimal contacts with A&T. The black institution was chartered by the same 1891 legislature that created the Normal. After a brief time in Raleigh it moved to the east side of Greensboro, about two miles from the Normal. Their main buildings bore a striking resemblance. There was a long history of A&T students working in the dining halls and elsewhere on the white campus. On a higher level, Charles Duncan McIver, Julius Foust, and Walter Clinton Jackson all had cordial professional relationships with longtime A&T President James B. Dudley and his successors. Foust, in fact, served for over a decade as an A&T trustee. But relations between the two colleges were more personal than institutional, and maintained always with an eye to the proprieties of the color line.

All that changed with the civil rights revolution. The relations that began in 1970—the year of the NAACP lawsuit—were conducted for years under the shadow not only of a court order but of a possible institutional merger. For people who favored that solution to segregation, and they were never very visible in North Carolina, proximity made these two institutions the most obvious candidates in the state. Merger was a subject of occasional idle conversation at UNCG, where few people either desired it or thought it a likely prospect. (One who raised the issue was Warren Ashby.) At A&T, the smaller school that would more nearly have lost its identity, it was a dark and hovering cloud that underlay every inter-campus discssion.[79]

Beginning in 1970, talk centered primarily around ways in which the two institutions could cooperate in academic programs. Consultations to this end went on for years, with administrators and faculty members coming together for campus meetings and off-campus weekend retreats. Starting in 1971, students at each institution registered in small numbers for courses on the other campus. Meanwhile, the three local private colleges, Guilford, Greensboro, and Bennett (a black women's college) already had a consortium permitting students enrolled at one to take courses offered by the others; they even had a shuttle bus service to facilitate the arrangement. In 1973 UNCG and A&T, with High Point College, joined the consortium.[80]

Faculty and program exchanges were harder to arrange and maintain. History department head Richard Bardolph worked out an exchange in 1970 with his opposite number at A&T; each taught a course at the other campus but the experiment lasted only a year.[81] In the field of social work, where the two institutions offered roughly parallel undergraduate programs, the federal government required that the programs be coordinated as the price of financial aid for which both had applied. The resultant plan took effect in 1972 and worked so well that the two departments began planning a joint master's degree program in the '80s.[82] From 1973 to 1976 the physics departments at both universities exchanged faculty members. The UNCG nursing school was responsible for all the contacts with their opposite numbers at A&T; the latter were afraid of absorption into UNCG's much stronger program.[83]

The fear was general. Throughout the mid-to later '70s, when President William Friday directed both universities to get together, identify program duplications, and either justify or suggest remedies for them, UNCG was the more forthcoming. Except for a few areas like social work, A&T administrators and faculty members were inclined to deny that duplications existed. Fearing that the call to eliminate duplication was a code formula for sacrificing their own programs, they pointed to the two institutions' differing missions as reason for maintaining a separate but equal status.

Not only did A&T feel under the gun as an institution, its faculty feared for their own careers. Their concern had some basis. Generations of discrimination had contributed to a widespread inferiority of programs, faculty training, and student preparation at black institutions. Other states were abolishing academic programs at these institutions, or abolishing the institutions altogether. Add to that a visceral suspicion of southern whites and their motives, and one sees a barrier to effective cooperation that most well-meaning whites did not altogether fathom. It would handicap relations with A&T for many years to come.[84]

Although UNCG initiated most of the contacts, it was under prodding from above. There was no desire to annex A&T or its programs, and cooperation required making that message clear. Indeed, UNCG was usually quite happy to agree that their respective programs were more complementary than duplicative. Vice Chancellor Stanley Jones, in charge of most of the negotiations with A&T, called for accentuating the differences as one of the best means to attack racial duality, rather than eliminating programs. Program elimination could easily cut both ways.[85]

UNCG did not formally enter the local college consortium until 1973, but it already had a student cross-registration program with Guilford, Greensboro, and Bennett Colleges as early as 1969.[86] When relations with A&T came to the fore in 1970, thoughts turned not only to making an equivalent arrangement with it, but also to having both of the state institutions join the existing consortium.[87] After those objectives were realized in 1971 and 1973, the program grew modestly in size; by 1980, 627 students were taking 888 courses on the six campuses. Many of the UNCG students taking courses at A&T were registered in ROTC courses, which UNCG did not offer; the remainder were disproportionately black students.[88] The early shuttle bus service continued to serve mainly the three private campuses that had established it. More students from UNCG and A&T would likely have used the program if they had not had to provide their own transportation.[89]

* * *

As noted earlier, UNCG derived more and more of its students as transfers from the community colleges and technical institutes. There was a general conviction at UNCG and other senior institutions that faculty members at the technical institutes in particular were not trained to offer college-level academic work, nor were their students necessarily capable of doing it satisfactorily. It would be dangerous to accept transfer credits automatically, as was done with the community colleges. The initial solution for UNCG and Randolph Technical Institute in Asheboro in 1970 was to have UNCG offer its own extension courses on that campus, for which students would receive UNCG credit. The teachers would be UNCG faculty or, more often, advanced graduate students; the courses involved were all at the introductory level. This plan was extended to Guilford Tech in 1971.[90] In 1972 the program with Randolph Tech was extended to the sophomore year, allowing some 200 students by 1977 to transfer to UNCG as juniors. A similar arrangement was made with Piedmont Technical Institute in Roxboro in 1975.[91]

But increasingly, Guilford and other technical institutes sought transfer credit for courses taught by their own faculties.[92] Guilford County had no community college and Guilford Tech's repeated quest for that status was long denied. In the meantime, UNCG continued to deny transfer credit for its courses.[93]

Chapter 22

The Faculty

As the student body mushroomed after 1963, so did the faculty—from 279 to 678.[1] It was discovered in 1976 that over half of the faculty had arrived in the past five years.[2]

From the 1960s onward, it was not hard in most fields to recruit good people with doctorates—in the offing if not in hand. The postwar student population surge carried through to the graduate schools, which multiplied in size and number as everyone looked forward to a strong market for college teachers in the years ahead. The volume of new Ph.D.s nearly tripled in the '60s. Institutions all over the country took advantage of the opportunity to upgrade their faculties with bright, young, well-trained recruits. In the '70s, however, supply overtook demand and a Ph.D. glut ensued. For the colleges and universities, and those individuals who managed to land full-time, tenure-track jobs, these were days of jubilee. For the rest who could secure only part-time work or none at all in their chosen fields, it was a nightmare.[3]

In 1963, 45 percent of the faculty members in American public universities possessed doctorates.[4] UNCG matched that number in its full-time faculty and by 1980 it had reached 70 percent.[5]

Women were earning 30 percent of the doctorates awarded by 1980. This represented an increase over previous decades, but past discrimination kept them at a somewhat smaller percentage of full-time college and university faculties. Furthermore, women were found disproportionately in the lower echelons: among the part-time faculty, in the lower and untenured ranks, and at community colleges and other institutions placing little emphasis on the doctorate and less on research.[6] When the rising woman's movement leveled its guns at these disparities the federal government responded in 1972 with legislation barring gender discrimination. But as new hires were primarily in the lower ranks, restricted to that 30 percent pool of women Ph.D.s, reaching gender parity was an uphill battle.

UNCG willingly followed the national trends but always at a somewhat higher level of female participation. In the fall of 1963, 56 percent of the full-time faculty were women.[7] But those senior women who (with Mereb Mossman) had helped guide WC through its final decades were retiring at a rapid pace in the new era. Through the 1960s Dean Mossman seemed in the eyes of many to be deliberately replacing them with men. Her professed aim was to build the graduate programs and enhance the institution's prestige; she may also have wanted to project a more visible male image in the faculty to attract male students. At any rate, from 1966 to 1970, 70 percent of the newly hired faculty were men—matching the proportion of male Ph.D. recipients. Of the twenty-eight persons hired or promoted to the highest rank of professor in those years, twenty-seven were men, as were twenty of the twenty-seven hired or promoted to associate professor.[8] Mossman was not blind to the controversy building over these figures and cited in justification the well-documented shortage of qualified women applicants. Given her primary goal of building the university academically, it is not clear that she could have done much otherwise. Nevertheless, she herself began in 1970 an affirmative action campaign to recruit more women, much as the university was doing with blacks. This effort continued under Stanley Jones, but highly qualified women were still in short supply.[9] As a result, in the fall of 1979, there were only 184 women, or 36 percent, in a full-time faculty of 516; even that figure exceeded the larger UNC system's 25 percent, however.[10]

At UNCG as nationally, a much larger proportion of male than female faculty held the Ph.D. Accordingly, they were found more heavily in the top two ranks of professor and associate professor, which carried with them the greatest prize of all: tenure.[11] Women had by no means disappeared from the higher echelons, but they were diminished. In 1978 three of the seven academic deans and two of the three assistant vice chancellors were women—but none of the vice chancellors themselves. Of the sixteen department heads in arts and sciences, only three were women.[12]

Although there was no formal provision for maternity leaves, women faculty customarily received them for a semester without pay. In 1977 Ferguson stipulated that such leaves would not be held to interrupt the continuous service that instructors had to serve prior to receiving promotion and tenure; rather, that service would be extended by the length of the leave.[13] The university made no provision for child care beyond the instructional facilities operated by the school of home economics, which were open to the public.

* * *

Faculty salaries around the country, measured against the consumer price index, rose markedly from the late 1950s into the early '70s, then slumped badly into the '80s.[14] In general, UNCG followed that pattern. In the '60s it was often below the average of institutions in its category, most of them longer-established, and scored low in the annual salary grading program recently started by the American Association of University Professors (AAUP). The deficiency turned up most often in the higher ranks; although UNCG had fewer people in these ranks proportionately, they were often paid less than their peers in the state and nationally. On the other hand, instructors and assistant professors—those most frequently recruited—were paid at very competitive rates. By the '70s, UNCG was usually earning grades of 2 (on a scale of 1 to 5, where 1 was highest) in the AAUP rankings.[15] In 1969–70, UNCG placed 28th among 31 state universities and other leading institutions in the South in average faculty compensation.[16]

There was a perennial concern that some of the best faculty would be enticed into leaving by the offer of higher salaries elsewhere; some were.[17] At the top, there was Excellence Fund money to pay premium salaries to a handful of well-known scholars who, it was hoped, would serve as a nucleus for others with the potential to become well known themselves.[18]

The gender differential was also a perennial concern at most institutions. Women were not only fewer in number but they continued to receive less pay than men—15 percent less nationally in 1978.[19] That this was now regarded as a national problem made it more conspicuous, but solutions were still hard to find. It flowed in part from the failure of women to earn the Ph.D. in the same ratio as men, or to get promoted to the higher-paying ranks for which that degree was the prerequisite. But the differential even applied to men and women in the same ranks and, presumably, doing similar work. Women more often favored disciplines, in the humanities for instance, where there was less competition from outside the academy and salaries were correspondingly lower. Willingly or unwillingly, they often went to institutions that favored teaching over research and paid lower salaries accordingly. Women of child-bearing and rearing age often dropped out temporarily, losing continuity and seniority. Even without the open discrimination of earlier years, these obstacles were hard to surmount.[20]

In 1964, when the issue had begun to get significant national attention, the AAUP encouraged its chapters to survey men's and women's salaries on their own campuses. Political science professor Margaret Hunt headed the investigation at UNCG. Her 1966 report found that gender differences among the full-time faculty did exist at UNCG, but not on the scale being reported nationally. Moreover, they were so scattered and there were so many exceptions that there was no evidence of deliberate discrimination. The committee found the problem to be minor, based on the full-time faculty which at that time comprised some 90 percent of the whole. But this and later studies that followed Mereb Mossman's hiring campaign found the discrepancies to be greatest in the higher ranks.[21] The 1972 SACS accreditation committee pointed to one department in which a female full professor—a former department head—with many years' service was earning $100 a year less than a new male assistant professor. Although Vice Chancellor Jones and Chancellor Ferguson were opposed to discrimination in principle, the problem continued.[22]

Faculty fringe benefits improved modestly during these years. Retirement was mandatory at age 65, but with approval from one's department head and dean annual reappointment could continue until age 70 and on a part-time basis until 72. After 1971 faculty members could choose between the state employees' retirement system (hitherto mandatory) and private plans such as TIAA.[23]

* * *

As universities and faculties expanded, so did faculty government. Many functions were dispersed among the constituent colleges, schools, and departments. Matters requiring central decision were entrusted to elected senates instead of the increasingly cumbersome assemblies of the full faculty. Faculties won the major voice in recruiting their new members and in setting student admissions policies; they were even given a larger voice in choosing administrators. These powers still resided formally in the trustees and administrators, but they were more inclined to consult. Paradoxically, their quest for faculty assistance ran counter to an even stronger faculty imperative, sprung from institutional growth and the administrators' own admonition to publish. By the '70s most faculty members had changed their primary allegiance from the institution to their own disciplines and departments. In fact, the higher an individual's visibility in his field, the less dependent he was on local administrators.[24] Many faculties outside the South embraced collective bargaining. This was never an option in the UNC system, where state law prevented any public employees from joining unions.

UNCG followed the pattern, sometimes with a time lag. Chancellor Ferguson's popularity with faculty members lay largely in his readiness to ask and listen to their advice before making significant decisions. This represented no sharp break from his predecessors, but it was more obvious in his case than it had been since the time of Jackson, who was equally popular. In 1963 as before, the faculty council consisted of virtually all the faculty and administrators. Voting privileges extended to all with the rank of assistant professor and higher, and to lecturers, instructors, professional librarians, and many part-time faculty after two years of service.[25]

Despite this largely inclusive franchise, it became increasingly difficult to get faculty members to attend the council meetings. As the institution grew, the routine governance issues usually dominating the agenda (and often involving only a few academic units) seemed less and less immediate to the majority of members. Ferguson himself conceded that the meetings had become "quite sterile." Save in the most exceptional circumstances, faculty members allowed other professional and personal obligations to take priority. The same was true of committee service, which younger members in particular tried to evade.[26]

General discontent with these conditions led to the call for a new governance system. An *ad hoc* committee under Margaret Hunt was appointed in 1970 to draw up a new instrument of government. The document, which took nearly four years to draft and implement, created at least on the surface a more inclusive system. In company with new tenure regulations that went into effect at about the same time, it confirmed librarians and instructors in a full faculty status with the same voting rights and access to tenure as the full-time teaching faculty. (On the other hand, the growing number of part-time faculty lost the partial franchise they had previously enjoyed.) Students and campus employees now received a token voice in the faculty council and committees. (This was the time when the clerical and physical plant employees were themselves organizing.) A continuing town meeting structure called the community forum was created to mediate town and gown relations, which had been none too cordial in recent years with the controversies over parking and campus expansion. As it turned out, the forum met only a few times and faded away through lack of interest.

Most important, the 1974 instrument left the faculty council much as it was before. The framers shrank from creating a senate with legislative powers, providing instead for an advisory body called the academic cabinet. It was composed of thirty-odd members elected primarily by the faculty, but also by the deans' council and the graduate and undergraduate student associations. The chancellor remained as chairman of the faculty council but there was now a vice chairman, elected by the faculty to serve as its spokesman.[27] The first to hold this office was Richard Bardolph of the history department.

The new document brought useful changes. The academic cabinet better represented a growing and increasingly diverse faculty than did the small academic policies committee it replaced. The new vice chairman was a visible and useful faculty spokesman. But the new instrument was more radical in appearance than substance. It left power in the hands of a faculty council whose members took less and less interest in its doings. The problems that had called it into being remained.

* * *

Administrators had historically served indefinite terms until they chose to resign or retire. Under Stanley Jones in the 1970s the deans were subjected to periodic reviews, though few if any were removed in consequence. Department heads too had enjoyed virtually unlimited tenure. As early as 1962, Chancellor Singletary, new on the scene, raised the possibility of rotating department heads every few years, but the reaction was tepid and he let the matter lie.[28] The heads at that time had great power over programs and personnel in their domains, and many were reluctant to give it up. Sometimes perceived as despots, they were more often than not accepted as benevolent. As it happened, a number of senior department heads chose to step down or retire during the '60s. This created openings for young and usually male replacements, often charged with creating new graduate programs.[29]

Within the college of arts and sciences, all department heads changed between 1960 and 1974. That proceeded partly from the calculus of time and partly from Dean Robert Miller's inauguration of periodic review. In time, heads came to be appointed to four-year terms, renewable once. Subsequently the practice spread to the professional schools. Moreover, the heads were gradually required to share power, usually through the medium of faculty committees. This extended to the most sensitive issues of program, promotion, tenure, and salary.[30]

* * *

The idea of the faculty as a community had been eroding for decades as it grew in size and diversity; there were few traces left in the 1970s. Members whose service spanned from the '40s to the '70s were most aware, and often most troubled, by the revolution that had occurred in this as every other aspect of the campus. In the 1940s the faculty was still an extended family. Older members recalled the faculty dinner, inherited from McIver's day, in the dining hall every September as the college opened for the new year. Department heads introduced their new members. Returning members stood and recounted what they had done during the summer. In 1963 the dinner gave way to a meeting and reception; department heads still introduced new members but no one was asked to describe his summer. Even the introduction of new members had become long and tedious by 1971 and was turned over to college and school meetings. Similarly, there was an annual faculty picnic until at least 1967, held at the university's Piney Lake. When this had gotten too big, some of the schools and departments continued with picnics of their own, but by the late '70s even the education faculty had become too large and diverse to enjoy such an occasion.[31]

Faculty-student relations saw a comparable decline. The self-study report of 1962 noted that faculty participation in extracurricular activities with students was increasingly limited to small groups with similar interests.[32] In the decade ahead the distance between them grew into positive estrangement. Students resented faculty preoccupation with research; the *Carolinian* reportedly declared that every hour spent on research was an hour that cheated students.[33] Student organizations found it harder and harder to secure the faculty advisers that each was required to have. Faculty members were so unwilling to commit time to this activity that the requirement was lifted.[34] SGA President Robie McFarland affirmed under questioning in 1971 that most students distrusted the faculty. They believed it was "out to get them," opposing almost automatically any reform they espoused. At the same time, faculty members found themselves repulsed by the new student counter-culture of the '60s and early '70s and the confrontational behavior of many activists.[35]

Such hostility should not be exaggerated. In the first place, it sprang more from group perceptions than from relations between individuals. The latter were usually friendly, if not as close or frequent as in earlier days when classes were smaller and different priorities were in order. Faculty members themselves often regretted the lack of personal contact with students, whether academic or social.[36] Student protest at UNCG did not reach the extremes seen in other parts of the country, and many faculty members did in fact sympathize with many of the student objectives. Some, for instance, contributed money in 1969 to support striking campus cafeteria workers whose cause had been taken up by the Student Government Association.[37] And students gained at least a token voice in university governance in the '70s, more than they had had before, and more than most of them cared to exercise.

* * *

Much of the student dissatisfaction of the 1960s sprang from the growing emphasis on faculty research.[38] Institutions aspiring to university status do emphasize research, though never ostensibly to the exclusion of teaching. Faculty members often are conflicted over the twin requirements;[39] there seems too little time in the day or week to do justice to both. The problem is greatest for younger faculty still working toward tenure—even those who relish research activity and signed on with full knowledge that it was required. Students are not the only ones neglected. Service activity, on and off campus, is also slighted because all too often it is not significantly rewarded. The difficulty in staffing faculty committees or finding faculty advisers to student organizations extends to community outreach work in all but the most applied fields.[40]

A standard defense of the research requirement is that it reinforces teaching; a productive scholar is more apt to have an inquiring, innovative mind and be a good classroom teacher. That argument clearly applies in graduate and even upper level undergraduate instruction, but is less relevant in the broad survey courses taken by freshmen and sophomores, where individual research is too specialized to show up. The most potent reason for "publish or perish" is that it is the recognized road to prestige in higher education, individual as well as institutional. A defender of the requirement, Lionel Lewis, argues that university professors are assumed to be producers of new knowledge, not just transmitters of received knowledge. Good scholars are rarer than good teachers; they reach more people, perform more valuable services, are in greater demand, and thus merit greater rewards. In sum, they perform much the same service for their institutions as successful athletes.[41]

As it is applied, the research emphasis tends to overshadow, even penalize other necessary activities. Although a great deal of it expands knowledge, much does not. In evaluating it, quantity is often confused with quality. Members of faculty promotion and tenure committees, drawn from across the university, cannot easily judge the merit of specialized research and publications in fields remote from their own. Administrators who make the final decisions have the same handicap. Thus promotion and tenure are often conferred on the basis of bulk, reinforced by glowing recommendations from departments that are interested in seeing their colleagues advance.[42]

UNCG was very much the aspiring university, and had been so since well before acquiring the name. Although it continued to support good classroom teaching, tangibly as well as verbally, the chief criterion in promotion, tenure, and salary decisions was research and publication.[43] Faculty members, especially untenured ones, had the same reservations on this matter as they had nationally.[44] In 1971, Charles Tisdale, an assistant professor of English, circulated a petition to amend the promotion criteria by specifying the primacy of teaching over research and service. It had the full support of the Student Government Association and gained the signatures of 43 percent of the faculty. Despite opposition by most administrators, department heads, and even the AAUP chapter, the faculty council adopted it that fall (in a secret ballot) by a vote of 174 to 111.[45] The amendment's principal effect was to trigger a flurry of efforts to measure effective teaching. In actual practice, the amendment made very little difference; despite a gesture in the direction of "distinguished teaching," publication remained the primary determinant of professional advancement. The *Carolinian* seethed at the loss of several popular teachers who were dropped in the very first year.[46]

The commitment to good teaching was not hollow; it was merely secondary. The Alumni Association began funding annual teaching excellence awards in 1964. Two were given each year, one to a full or associate professor and one to an assistant professor or instructor. Nominations were made by separate student and faculty committees, then reconciled by an administrative committee. Many or most of the recipients had been named by both the student and faculty committees. The awards carry a financial stipend and are considered a distinct honor by the university community as well as the recipients.[47] Yet twenty-seven of the thirty-one recipients through 1978 came from the college of arts and sciences. As members of the professional schools saw it, this was attributable primarily to the fact that professional school faculty had less exposure to the students as a whole and were less often nominated by the student committee. However that may be, from 1979 onward the professional schools were represented with great regularity.[48]

Students contributed to the cause in 1968 with a computerized teaching evaluation program, utilizing student questionnaires. It proved too ambitious for their resources and in 1971 they received faculty help.[49] In the wake of that year's Tisdale amendment and in the absence of any other credible device to measure teaching effectiveness, each school or department was encouraged to develop its own questionnaire. In time such surveys became mandatory. The results were distributed at first to the participating instructors only, and later to department heads as well. The survey became a useful if not infallible tool to evaluate faculty teaching. But unless the results (with other data available to department heads) were spectacularly good or bad, their effect was greater on salary levels than on promotion and tenure.[50]

* * *

Given the faculty research requirement, the university needed to make it possible. The teaching load in 1965 was still twelve hours a week for those teaching only undergraduates and (theoretically) nine hours for those with graduate students. Over the next few years the nine-hour load was extended to all who were engaged in research. These figures remained in place for many years, with some variation among departments and schools.[51]

The state continued to provide an annual research fund, which reached $30,000 a year by 1967. It was administered by a faculty research council and the dean of the graduate school. As the faculty grew, so did the demands on this fund. By December 1967, it was providing at least partial support for the projects of 102 faculty members. Beginning in 1971, additional summer research stipends were offered. And faculty members increasingly received grants from outside sources, exceeding $900,000 in 1966–67. In 1977 an office for sponsored programs was opened to help faculty members in making grant applications.[52]

Sabbatical leaves had long been forbidden as a matter of state policy. Instead the UNC system developed a program of "research assignments," in which faculty members could substitute research activity for classroom teaching during limited terms—one semester at full pay or a year at half pay. They differed from sabbaticals only in that they were not considered automatic; they were awarded or withheld on grounds of merit. In 1963, WC/UNCG was granting only two or three of these leaves a year, but Dean Mossman strove to increase funding for the program.[53] By 1978, a dozen faculty members were receiving these assignments with full or half pay and eight others got leaves without pay. A substantial majority of them every year went to faculty in the college of arts and sciences.[54]

Ever since McIver's day the institution encouraged faculty members to attend professional meetings, and they continued to do so. But it was largely at their own expense. The university received very little travel money and it was earmarked for those persons who were giving papers or otherwise on the program.[55]

* * *

Although academic tenure was frequently called in question nationally, there was no serious effort to repeal it within the UNC system. In fact, the reconsolidation of 1972 led to its codification and expansion throughout the system to institutions that had not hitherto enjoyed much academic freedom. UNCG's new regulations of 1976, based on national AAUP guidelines, brought no fundamental changes. Professional librarians now became eligible for tenure, a maximum probationary period of seven years now preceded tenure decisions, and (hitherto recommended but not required) department heads now had to consult their senior colleagues before making promotion, tenure, and salary recommendations.[56] The proportion of faculty members with tenure grew steadily, from 42 percent in 1973 (the first year reported) to 60 percent in 1982. Both figures lagged slightly behind national averages.[57]

* * *

Ultimate power in virtually all matters of university governance continued under law to lie with the Board of Governors, the local trustees, and the administrators they appointed. But UNCG's new instrument of government and tenure regulations, with other measures, significantly increased faculty powers to influence the process. It was, again, a paradox that this growing faculty voice coincided with increasing professional demands that diminished faculty interest and participation in the process. The campus AAUP chapter fell victim to the same condition. Boasting nearly half of the faculty as members in 1965, it provided a forum for discussing issues that were increasingly taken over by other groups. The chapter gradually declined in the '70s and '80s, and lapsed altogether in the '90s. James Ferguson had been an active AAUP member in Mississippi. As chancellor, he supported the local chapter, spoke frequently at its meetings, and subsidized members' expenses in attending national meetings. Had he tried instead to suppress the chapter, it might well have flourished in opposition to administration tyranny. But here as elsewhere, the AAUP did not prosper among faculties at once secure in their personal status, localized in their campus interests, and preoccupied with their competing professional obligations off campus. While it lasted, the AAUP chapter provided a link to the state and national organizations that intervened usefully at other, less favored institutions. At home, it gave solace and sometimes substantial aid to individuals who felt mistreated, particularly in promotion and tenure matters. The university continued to offer the primary avenues of appeal: a faculty committee on due process to hear promotion and tenure cases and a grievance committee to deal with lesser complaints.[58]

The broadest and most publicized threat to academic freedom was the statewide speaker ban law enacted by the legislature in 1963. This measure was passed almost without warning on the last day of the session as President William Friday raced to Raleigh to head it off. It forbade all colleges or universities receiving state funds to permit as a campus speaker any person who was a known communist or who had pleaded the Fifth Amendment in refusing to answer a question about communist affiliation. The university trustees condemned the measure, as did administrators and faculty on every campus. At UNCG Chancellor Singletary, the faculty, and the student body all issued denunciations. The law was generally understood as retaliation against the faculty and students at Chapel Hill, whom the Ku Klux Klan, Raleigh TV commentator Jesse Helms, and others regarded as aiding and abetting if not spearheading the civil rights movement in North Carolina; to them, civil rights and communism were peas in the same pod. The speaker ban controversy dragged on for five years. When the legislature refused to repeal the measure, it was the students who took to the courts, retaining Greensboro attorney McNeill Smith. In 1968 a federal appeals court upheld their position and declared the law unconstitutional. By that time it had been so discredited that there were few to lament its passing.[59]

* * *

Woman's College had confined its honorary degrees to female recipients, with only three exceptions: former UNC President Frank Porter Graham and former Chancellors Walter Clinton Jackson and William Whatley Pierson. With coeducation and university status, the institution began honoring men about as frequently as women.

There was no connection between honorary degree recipients and commencement speakers. The latter continued, as for many years past, to be chosen by the senior class. Their choices, as in the case of Senator Birch Bayh of Indiana in 1970, did not always please the older alumnae. But so far as the record shows, Chancellor Ferguson was stalwart in his defense of the seniors' right to choose whomever they wished.[60]

Chapter 23

Curriculum and the Library

From the beginning, the Normal/NCCW/Woman's College operated on the semester system despite suggestions that it follow Chapel Hill and State to the quarter system. They subsequently returned, and by 1965 over 80 percent of institutions nationwide were on the semester system, causing that perennial back-burner issue to subside.[1]

Taking its place were new issues: the early calendar, Saturday classes, and evening classes. At WC as generally, the traditional fall semester opened in September, broke for the Christmas holidays, then resumed for a short session in January. The Christmas interruption was widely regarded as disruptive and favor turned increasingly in the 1960s to an early calendar, with the fall semester opening late in August and finishing before Christmas; the spring semester would then start early in January and run until May. The change was particularly popular with students, who dreaded returning to campus after Christmas to face midyear exams. Faculties, on the other hand, found no compelling reason to change and dragged their feet, contributing to the growing student-faculty alienation of the period. But as there was no compelling argument against it either, continuing student pressure eventually led every other campus in the region to adopt the early calendar by 1971. UNCG fell in line in 1972.[2]

From its earliest days, the college had held classes from Monday morning through Saturday morning. As more and more students, often adults, had to balance family and employment with college responsibilities, Saturday classes became increasingly burdensome. They had few partisans among either faculty or students, and were abandoned in 1970 to widespread rejoicing.[3]

The addition of evening classes was equally if not more imperative. Graduate students—often fully employed business people or public school teachers and principals—had always been handicapped by the sparsity of evening classes. They were joined now by many undergraduates in a similar predicament. Pressure mounted steadily from them, from the business school and other units particularly dependent on employed and adult students, and from Dean of Men Clarence Shipton and others concerned to increase male enrollment. The university responded with great deliberation, emphasizing late afternoon classes at first. Indeed, undergraduate classes were not even permitted after 6 p.m. until

1971; there were concerns over campus security and interference with evening extracurricular events.[4]

Most faculty were lukewarm at best to giving up their free evenings. And on this issue student opinion was divided. Opposing the change were most undergraduates who had afternoon or evening jobs, or none at all. In the spring of 1975, more than a decade after the issue had first arisen regarding undergraduates, the number of classes meeting after 6 p.m. was still only about 70, compared with 650 or so in what everyone referred to as "prime time:" from 9 a.m. to noon.

But those more fully employed were a growing constituency and increasingly insistent. Under pressure from Stanley Jones the number of evening classes moved upward. Most responsive were the college of arts and sciences and the school of business and economics. By 1979, that school offered enough evening courses to enable an undergraduate to complete the degree requirements at night—something hitherto available only to graduate students.[5] The campus bookstore and various administrative offices also began keeping later hours to accommodate evening students.

* * *

The familial student advising system of Harriet Elliott had already broken down by 1963. Beginning the next year the faculty class chairmen were phased out and replaced by several faculty members drawn from different parts of the college and the professional schools. They worked for the associate dean, who in 1970 became the dean of academic advising. The front line of academic advising remained the growing battalions of faculty members across campus, each of whom was assigned half a dozen or more students who had expressed some interest in the adviser's field. But the broader that net extended the leakier it became; faculty members varied dramatically in their knowledge of the regulations and their devotion to this responsibility. The academic advising office responded to any problems that students cared to bring in, but far more important, it served as the advisers' adviser, the system coordinator, and court of appeals. Tommie Lou Smith of the business education/secretarial department replaced Laura Anderton as assoociate dean in 1963; Bert Goldman from the school of education replaced her as the first dean of academic advising in 1970.[6]

* * *

One of the academic concerns of the '60s and early '70s, here and elsewhere, was grade inflation. Student grades rose markedly almost everywhere; Phi Beta Kappa membership doubled. Graduate schools, faced with applicants boasting ever-better academic records, were forced to depend more on standardized tests, personal impressions, and family influence. Indeed, student gravitation toward graduate study (impelled by upward mobility and the Vietnam War draft) was a contributing factor. Some students were motivated to work harder, and at a time of widespread student rebellion, acquiescent faculty members may possibly have succumbed to pressure for higher grades. But other factors were at work too. More flexible curricular requirements permitted students to take more courses within their own range of interests and talents. Many campuses adopted the pass/not pass option, whereby students could take a limited number of courses for which they received only a grade of pass or not pass. A close relative was the option to drop a course without penalty at almost any time before the final exam. All these measures were adopted as ways to broaden intellectual horizons, and all tended to raise grade point averages.[7]

At UNCG, grade inflation reached its peak in about 1973, coinciding with the peak of its student movement. The percentage of students receiving unsatisfactory grade reports dropped from 38 percent in 1965 to 14 percent in 1973 before leveling off. Average course grades followed the same trajectory in reverse. Faculty members denied lowering their standards but all the other factors were in place. Forty-two percent of UNCG students were using the pass/not pass option in the spring of 1973—actually less than the national average. The inflation created enough alarm that within a few years the faculty tightened up the regulations that had contributed to it. Pass/not pass and easy withdrawal, adopted in 1970 and 1971, were severely modified in 1977 and pass/not pass disappeared altogether in 1980. These changes largely ended the problem.[8]

* * *

Another perennial concern was to provide incentive for truly superior students. Previously, Woman's College had had a vestigial honors program consisting of some independent work and a senior thesis. At Otis Singletary's urging, the college inaugurated a more ambitious program in 1962. As initially funded by the Ford Foundation, one of its purposes was to attract academically talented students into graduate work and, ultimately, college teaching. Honors sections of several introductory courses plus an interdisciplinary seminar for freshmen and sophomores quickly evolved into a four-year program still culminating in a senior honors thesis.[9] From the beginning, the program enrolled some 100 students each year; after a decade it neared 200. The number of faculty members involved had grown to forty-six, drawn from some twenty disciplines; English was particularly conspicuous. But as with all interdisciplinary programs, it was a perennial struggle to recruit faculty members for part-time service away from their home departments. That difficulty in turn limited course offerings and student enrollments. One alumna recalled that it was the honors program that kept her from transferring to Chapel Hill.[10]

Recognition for exceptional students was also a concern. Although teaching excellence awards for faculty were initiated in 1963, there was still no equivalent for students beyond graduation with honors. But beginning in 1971, student excellence awards were added for several students each year with outstanding academic and extracurricular records. They were conferred together with the teaching awards at the annual spring honors convocation.[11]

* * *

Education was still the most popular major, with elementary education alone accounting for 20–25 percent of the bachelor's degrees; those going into secondary education majored in their subject fields. At the same time, the master of education accounted for between a third and a half of all master's degrees.[12] Whether graduates or undergraduates, students divided significantly along gender lines in choosing majors. From 1970 to 1975, with males comprising under a third of the student body, they graduated with 21 percent of the liberal arts degrees. At the same time they made up 83 percent of the graduates in physics, 52 percent in chemistry, and 70 percent in business administration.[13]

* * *

As the century wore on, college curricula were increasingly driven by the market. Graduates by the '70s found jobs harder to find; 1975 was described as the worst year to graduate since the Depression. Faculty and administrators listened more and more to the demands of students and potential employers for "relevant" courses and programs, by which they usually meant vocational offerings. Nowhere was this truer than in the metropolitan universities that drew their clientele from the surrounding areas. New courses and programs multiplied, subject only to occasional pruning as fads changed and budgets shrank. Strict requirements gave way to a greater freedom of choice. There was no effort to retrieve the free elective system of the late nineteenth century, but when it came to general education for freshmen and sophomores, there was endless debate (as at Woman's College in the troubled days of Edward Kidder Graham) over the comparative virtues of interdisciplinary core courses versus introductory survey courses in each field. Since the faculty determined these matters, the latter alternative usually prevailed; they had themselves trained and were most comfortable in a single field. In general, freshmen and sophomores were given more freedom within the familiar distribution system. They could choose from an increasing number of introductory courses. Among upperclassmen, the drive for relevance meant greater specialization. That, in turn, led to more double majors or even specially crafted majors to suit the individual student; the older interdisciplinary concentrations like American Studies faced hard times or disappeared. Similarly, the proportion of seniors graduating with vocational majors increased at the expense of those in the liberal arts.[14]

Curricular change at UNCG came modestly in 1964 and then on a larger scale in 1972 at the recommendation of a faculty committee chaired by anthropology professor Harriet Kupferer. Mereb Mossman (now retired from administration) was an active presence on the committee, helping to steer it toward greater freedom of choice. No single course was any longer prescribed for graduation. Opponents of the plan in departments (like history) with a vested interest in the existing requirements referred to the arrangement as the "cafeteria plan."[15] From their perspective, the reservations were well grounded; history enrollments fell by 31 percent while those in psychology rose by at least 50 percent.[16]

In keeping with national trends, the two-course requirement in physical education was dropped in 1978, at the suggestion of the PE faculty. Activity courses were henceforth offered on a voluntary basis and for the first time carried academic credit, up to eight hours per student.[17]

At the same time, faculty and administrators explored curricular avenues to attract male students. A business school and a major in business administration were introduced together with pre-professional courses looking to careers in law, medicine, dentistry, pharmacy, and engineering.[18]

UNCG never offered ROTC courses, instead sending interested students to the program at neighboring A&T. This effort was stalled for some years, partly by the national student campaign of the '60s to remove all military courses from college campuses, but mostly because of lagging federal appropriations.[19] The arrangement with A&T finally got underway in 1974 but it was handicapped at the outset by faculty unwillingness to give academic credit for these courses; they equated them with the physical education activity courses that still carried no academic credit. This reluctance not only displeased the students involved, it offended A&T at a most inopportune time, when the federal government was pushing for the greatest possible cooperation with that institution. After considerable effort, the faculty was persuaded in 1977 to allow up to twelve hours of credit for ROTC courses taken at A&T.[20]

* * *

The greatest curricular developments of these years lay in the expansion of the graduate program. Just as rising college enrollments around the state brought coeducation, so rising demand for graduate programs meant they could no longer be concentrated in Chapel Hill. Most of the growth at UNCG occurred in the decade from 1962 to 1972, before program overproduction around the country discredited new proposals and caused funds to dry up.[21]

Prior to 1962, WC's last year, it had master's degree programs in seven fields—three in the professional schools and four in the arts—plus one doctoral program in home economics that soon would turn out its first graduate. That year the college was permitted to offer new master's programs in the arts and sciences. As UNCG took form over the next few years, master's programs were established in one discipline after another.[22]

Mereb Mossman looked forward to more doctoral programs as well and hired deans, department heads, and senior faculty with that end in mind. With encouragement from general administration in Chapel Hill, she provided most of the driving force, as did Stanley Jones after her, but some of the impetus came from the schools and departments themselves. Within the arts and sciences, enthusiasm for graduate programs, especially new doctorates, varied widely from one department to another. Richard Current had come to the history department in the 1950s, then left to join the top-rated graduate program at the University of Wisconsin. He returned to UNCG several years later, partly to escape the pressure so many graduate students placed on his own research activity; he was by no means enthusiastic about launching a history Ph.D. here. In the sciences, Mossman recruited four men as department heads in the 1960s with the expectation that they would develop graduate programs—master's wherever they did not presently exist and doctorates in the larger departments.

Psychology and English did develop Ph.D. programs; biology tried to follow but the money dried up. The window of opportunity proved to be very narrow and the remaining departments were either too small, too slow, or too little interested before the demand and the funding gave out. So few doctoral programs reached fruition that the few that did stood like isolated peaks. No matter how sound they were internally, they suffered from isolation; there were too few comparable programs in related fields. At the master's level this was not a problem. Some of the arts programs, which had been geared in WC days to training future public school teachers, now began turning out more practicing artists, musicians, and actors as well.[23] By 1979 there were eighty master's and twelve doctoral programs in existence, most in the latter in the professional schools. They awarded 617 degrees that year, 79 of them doctorates.[24]

The readiness to develop new graduate programs was matched by the graduate school's readiness to admit new students. If departments would not admit them as degree candidates, they were admitted as special or probationary students and showed up in class anyway. Graduate Dean John Kennedy confessed to Chancellor Ferguson in 1971 that "we have . . . absorbed unnumbered persons who would have been eligible to enter Chapel Hill only through the undergraduate division." Many of these students were interested in only one course, not a degree program, but were classified as graduate students because they had already earned a bachelor's degree somewhere. No wonder that in 1972 UNCG had a larger proportion of graduate students among its total enrollment (26.3 percent) than any institution in the state. As most of those who did desire degrees were part-time students, they sometimes took a long time to attain them.[25] The institution granted its first doctoral degree to a male in 1967 and to blacks, a man and woman, in 1971.[26]

Graduate programs seldom thrive without offering student financial aid in the form of fellowships or assistantships. Teaching assistantships are particularly important for doctoral programs, offering aspiring college professors the chance to earn money and gain teaching experience at the introductory level while pursuing the degree. But whether assistantships are awarded at the doctoral or master's level, whether they involve teaching, research assistance to faculty members, or other service, they are essential for any program to remain competitive; it is hard to recruit students without them. At UNCG the first such funds, totaling only $27,500, were allocated in 1963–64. By 1977–78 there were 470 graduate assistants receiving an average stipend of $2,040, or $959,000 total. Slightly over half of the money and positions were allocated to the college of arts and sciences.[27]

Assistantships were frequently enhanced by waivers on out-of-state tuition. Many states extend these waivers to out-of-state students who perform a special task such as teaching, letting them pay the lower in-state tuition rate; some states even forgive tuition altogether. Not only do these waivers make state institutions more competitive in the national market, they enhance the diversity of the student body—something at least as desirable among graduate students as undergraduates.

North Carolina was less generous than most. In 1972 it doubled out-of-state tuition and cut back sharply on waivers, though a limited number were retained in order to permit the recruiting of out-of-state students with "special talents." Statewide, these talents ranged from academic promise to athletic prowess. Like the other state institutions, UNCG suffered; its out-of-state enrollments—both graduate and undergraduate—fell sharply. Nevertheless, it was receiving by 1980 about $160,000 a year in tuition waivers to recruit promising out-of-state students. (It did not yet subsidize athletes.) Most of the waivers went to graduate assistants, but the money could not be averaged out among all who were eligible; some got waivers and some did not, based often and unavoidably on arbitrary grounds. It was bad for morale.[28]

* * *

Even into the computer age it is a truism that the heart of a college or university is its library. It is doubly true where graduate programs are involved.[29]

The WC library had long been a source of strength to the undergraduate program. Further growth was now essential, much of it during the inflation-racked '70s when universities were strapped for cash and frequently cut back library appropriations. Libraries had to become more selective, both in books and serials, thereby increasing their dependence on others with different specialties. Interlibrary loan services became important as never before.[30] In this process, UNCG was a net lender although it borrowed a great deal from Duke, Chapel Hill, and more distant facilities.

The library collection grew from 222,000 volumes in 1963 to 556,000 in 1979. Its budget in that time increased from $203,000 to $1,887,000 while the staff grew from twenty-one (eleven of them professionals) to sixty-five (twenty-two professionals).[31] In 1964 the library became a federal document depository. In 1966 it switched from the Dewey to the Library of Congress classification system. For years afterward, until the previous holdings were recatalogued, library users had to find books and serials classified according to one system or the other.[32] As the value of books mounted, so did the danger of theft. Following national precedent, the library began stationing guards at the front door in 1970. The collections were highly accessible to students, however; the stacks remained open and in 1971, at student request, library hours were extended until midnight, seven days a week.[33] The circulation system was fully automated in 1977.

By far the most visible development was the addition of the nine-story tower along with the renovation of the existing building in 1973–74. The 1950 Jackson Library was approaching capacity by 1965 when Director Charles Adams began planning for expansion. Given space limitations, the most efficient direction to move was upward. The resultant tower more than doubled the available floor space, and a quarter-century later it still dominates the campus.[34]

In 1969 Adams retired after twenty-four years as library director. His successor next year was James H. Thompson, a librarian and historian from the university at Chapel Hill. Like Adams he kept abreast of the field and won the widespread support of subordinates, faculty, and students alike. It was on his watch (with strong national momentum and after many years' lobbying by Adams) that the professional library staff received full faculty status in 1976. As was true nationally, the librarians like the faculty were progressively better trained and more professionally active than in earlier years. And as the library grew in size, separate departments and divisions evolved along with a more formal governance system.[35]

One of the new units was special collections, housing rare books, manuscripts, and the university archives. The archives had emerged from the old college collection in 1962, but for the next decade there was little money to develop them beyond the continued solicitation of old records. When Emilie Mills arrived in 1972 to head the new division, the archives consisted mostly of the

McIver, Foust, and Jackson papers, all sitting in cartons, unorganized. Although a precedent-setting official records schedule had been promulgated in 1962, campus administrators with few exceptions ignored it and held onto their old records. Mills gave top priority to processing the collections already on hand, starting with McIver. Some thought was given as early as 1967 to developing the small existing collection of private manuscripts, but with the official records in such parlous condition, there was little enthusiasm or money to reach farther.[36]

When consolidation shut down WC's library science program in 1933, instruction was concentrated at Chapel Hill. But before long, the demand for new school librarians outstripped Chapel Hill's capacity to produce them. WC was therefore permitted in 1939 to offer a sequence of courses designed to train that specialized group. It did so until 1946 when the program, as a stepchild in the department of education, fell by the wayside.[37] The revolving chancellorship seems to have delayed its resurrection until 1962. As it remained a program to train school librarians, it was still assigned to education. A master's degree was added in 1965 but the American Library Association refused to accredit it until 1982.[38]

* * *

The consolidated university opened a computation center at Chapel Hill in 1959. It was intended to serve all three campuses, and a seminar for interested faculty and students was held at WC in November of that year.[39] In 1967 UNCG opened its own computer center in the Petty science building. It came under the direction of Roscoe Allen, who had headed the old one-year commercial program, just terminated. One of his early assignments was to computerize the university personnel records, as required by the federal government in the ongoing civil rights litigation. The center's computer, like others of its generation, subsisted on IBM cards.[40]

As demands on the system grew, academic and administrative computing were divided into separate offices in 1973. Administrators used the existing campus computer while faculty and student tasks were handled by terminals connecting to the Triangle Universities Computation Center (TUCC), a central facility serving primarily Duke, Chapel Hill, and State. In keeping with national developments, more and more schools and departments at UNCG were turning to computer applications. By 1976 when Theodore Hildebrandt arrived to head academic computing, there were at least thirteen TUCC terminals distributed in three campus locations. That arrangement quickly fell short of the mounting needs and reached crisis proportions in 1977, when computer access had to be rationed. Faculty research (and professional advancement) suffered along with student instruction. Only after years of increasingly desperate requests for the necessary funding did UNCG acquire its first on-campus academic computer, in 1981. Meanwhile, with completion of the new business and economics building, the academic computer center moved there in 1979.[41]

Chapter 24

The Arts and Sciences

The mathematics department came into its own with the advent of the computer age. There had been a math department since the beginning of the college, and its mainstays—Gertrude Mendenhall, Virginia Ragsdale, Cornelia Strong, and Helen Barton—were for decades mainstays of the college as well; they are commemorated in the names of campus rooms and buildings. But the field changed vastly after their day. The first male head, Eldon E. Posey, arrived in 1965 and began to develop fields in applied mathematics, where most of the jobs for graduates were opening up. Statistics courses were introduced and, in 1972, a statistical consulting center for faculty and students in all fields. Also in keeping with the trend were courses and an eventual major in computer science.[1] The department attained master's degree programs in 1967 and '68 and began planning for a Ph.D., but members were divided on the issue and the doctorate fell victim to the national overflow.[2]

Such was the case in other fields as well. Bruce Eberhart came from Princeton in 1963 to head the biology department and to build graduate programs. The master's was instituted in 1965 and permission was received to plan for a Ph.D. in 1968. It never happened. There were already similar programs in the state, the department was divided on the issue, and the money ran out. Much of the opposition came from senior members of the department, bewildered if not alienated by the switch to university status.[3] The effort consumed valuable time and, in addition, research activity was virtually suspended for two years by dislocations attendant on moving into a new building in 1977. A department that had led the campus in pursuit of outside grants lost that momentum for nearly a decade.[4] Eberhart stepped down as head in 1979. His most lasting contribution may have lain in the planning for the new life sciences building—named for him following his premature death from cancer (like his predecessor Victor Cutter) in 1983.

As early as 1956 Chancellor Graham found the chemistry department sadly wanting in creative effort. Its longtime head, Florence Schaeffer, was a formidable campus leader but neither she nor her department was involved in significant research.[5] Schaeffer's retirement as head in 1964 afforded Dean Mossman an opportunity to turn the department around. The chosen instrument was Walter Puterbaugh, from Thiel College in Pennsylvania. With Mossman's blessing, Puterbaugh rapidly introduced ten other males into what had hitherto been an exclusively female department. In the next decade, with the help of a lessened teaching load, the desired creativity was well on its way. With it came a newfound atmosphere of collegiality attested in particular by the surviving female members; one called it "our Camelot period." A master's degree was instituted in 1967 and next year the department was accredited by the American Chemical Society. The department looked forward to a Ph.D. by the early '70s, but it did not come.[6] Puterbaugh too became a formidable campus presence, well beyond the chemistry department. He served in the '70s as vice chairman of the faculty council, the highest elective position in faculty government.

The physics department also needed upgrading. In 1964 it still consisted of only two persons. Longtime head Anna Reardon doubled for decades as campus audio-visual director and was clearly overworked. An official from general administration recommended broadening the department by recruiting a new head and two other persons with Ph.Ds.[7] Reardon's replacement in 1965 was C. Bob Clark, head of the physics department at Southern Methodist University. Over the next few years he too brought in several new, very capable men and, with them, a master's degree program in 1967.[8] Clark stepped down as head in 1975, to be replaced by Gaylord Hageseth, one of his first recruits. Like Puterbaugh, Clark was active in faculty government, also serving as vice chairman of the faculty council and later, chairman of the faculty senate.

The SACS accreditation team in 1972 found biology, chemistry, and physics all manned by capable people, primarily young and interested in both research and teaching. But all three departments were seriously underfunded—biology and chemistry at about half the national average.[9]

* * *

The greatest success story among the sciences was psychology. The department already included such active researchers as Elizabeth Duffy and department head Kendon Smith. It attracted many undergraduate majors and launched a master's program in 1964. The department doubled in size between 1962 and 1967. When it decided to go ahead for the Ph.D., Smith stepped down as head; he embraced the decision but not the administrative duties that were already mounting.[10] When Robert Eason of San Diego State College arrived to succeed him in 1967, his assignment was clear. The funding was not in sight, but he pushed ahead anyway, banking on its becoming available once the program was in place. The gamble paid off, though the program (launched in 1970) was never in clover. Like his three science compeers, Eason brought in capable new people—women as well as men. The department grew from eight to twenty-four. Most of the growth was concentrated in the decade 1967–77, after which the department reached a plateau and, in Eason's recollection, the *esprit de corps* began to wane. He stepped down as head in 1980.[11]

The department's original intention was to create a basic psychology Ph.D. from which special fields such as applied or clinical psychology might evolve. But the department had so much trouble placing its graduates in scarce academic positions during the 1970s and so much success placing them in clinical positions that the program (and the department) took a definite turn toward clinical psychology. It soon drew students from all over the country. Recalling its development after twenty years, Smith believed they had built it well but like other doctoral programs on campus it suffered from isolation; there were no doctoral programs in related departments like biology, sociology, or anthropology. By 1979 the program was fully accredited by the American Psychological Association.[12]

* * *

As it turned out, English was the first arts and sciences department to launch the Ph.D., in 1968. Despite the continued strength of its writing program, the department had seemed to be going stale before the arrival of Joseph A. Bryant as head in 1961.[13] Bryant had taught previously at Vanderbilt and Duke. The MFA writing program was already in place and the MA in English came in 1963. Yet next year Bryant found only three of the five full professors in the department qualified to direct master's theses, and two of those (poet Randall Jarrell and novelist Peter Taylor) would only direct graduate work in the writing program. The situation was a little better among the eight associate and assistant professors, most of them relative newcomers.[14]

Despite these lukewarm credentials, general administration in Chapel Hill urged the department to develop a Ph.D. program. It fell in line with little hesitation. According to the formal proposal the department drew up in 1965, if a doctoral program were not established soon, the existing faculty and library facilities would be wasted and current staff members would leave.[15] The latter concern was real enough; some department members, particularly in the writing program, were highly marketable. Even when Peter Taylor received an endowed professorship in 1966, he left almost immediately for the University of Virginia.[16] In fact, Bryant himself left for the University of Kentucky in 1968, the year the doctoral program started.

His successor was William G. Lane from the University of Colorado. The greatest influx of new faculty came in 1969–1972, making English with forty-two members the largest arts and sciences department. Much of its size arose from the multi-sectioned freshman composition course, required of all undergraduates. The diversity of programs—ranging from composition through English and American literature to the writing program—brought a corresponding diversity in personnel, but they were generally harmonious; the bitterness and factionalism of the '50s had disappeared.[17]

As with psychology, the doctoral program in English took forms that were not predicted, or perhaps predictable, at the beginning. Outside consultants seconded the call for a Ph.D. primarily to train college teachers of English.[18] That was the original focus, but the demand for English teachers soon faded. The department made a partial turn toward linguistics, which also waned. The third focus was on composition and rhetoric, in effect a return to the training of college teachers. Unlike psychology, which soon drew students from all over the country, the Ph.D. program in English remained small and relatively localized. In the early years particularly, many of the students were faculty members from other schools in the region; they commuted over varying distances. Like every other program on campus, it was run on a shoestring.[19]

The writing program remained a strong contender with the Ph.D. as the department's centerpiece. The two were mutually reinforcing; students in one often took courses in the other. The master of fine arts degree in writing dated from the '40s but the program remained small and relatively unpublicized until Peter Taylor and Robert Watson upgraded it in 1966.[20] Its faculty over the years represented something of a Who's Who of southern writing. Randall Jarrell was present, with short interruptions, from 1947 until his death in 1965. (That event, regarded as a suicide by many who knew him in his last months, was a major blow to the program.) Peter Taylor was in and out of the department several times in the 1940s, '50s, and '60s. Allen Tate remained a frequent visitor. Robert Watson came in 1953 and stayed; so did Fred Chappell in 1964 and Tom Kirby-Smith in 1967. Some New York *literati* in the 1960s regarded Greensboro as a "literary place." Accordingly, the MFA program attracted more and more students from all over the country—so much so that it suffered greatly by the doubling of out-of-state tuition in 1972.[21] Many of the students made names for themselves after graduation, as had been true from the beginning.

At the same time, scores of new and often better-funded writing programs sprang up around the country in the '70s and siphoned off the best applicants. By 1979 the situation was so dire that the writing faculty declared the MFA program no longer competitive and recommended its dissolution unless more money were forthcoming.[22] The incoming chancellor that year, William Moran, was so impressed with their case that he diverted more funds to the program, thus saving it.

One of its mainstays was the *Greensboro Review*, a magazine it launched when the program was restructured in 1966. The editors and, initially, most of the contributors were graduate students in the MFA program. (Undergraduates brought out a short-lived journal of their own, *The Catalyst*, in addition to their traditional outlet, *Coraddi.*) As faculty adviser Fred Chappell put it in 1968, the *Review* was already a source of pride to the program and department: "successful—but not solvent." Despite precarious finances and an irregular publication schedule, the *Review* survives into the new millenium. But only because, during the rebellious early '70s, it came under a greater measure of faculty oversight. In time, the *Review* attracted contributors from all over the country as well as new students to the MFA program.[23]

* * *

The communications age brought phenomenal growth to the various fields, old and new, that crowded under that title. UNCG's drama and speech department grew exponentially, partly as a result of new career opportunities in these fields and partly from changes in the graduation requirements allowing students more freedom to choose them.[24] In response to market demand, the department seemed continually to generate new bachelor's and master's programs. By the mid-1960s it offered Ed.D. degrees in two speech areas.[25] Herman Middleton continued to lead the department until 1974, when no one could longer dissuade him from stepping down.[26] His successor was John Lee Jellicorse from the University of Tennessee.

The department had had two separate divisions since 1960, when the English department gave up its speech courses. In 1977 it became the department of communication and theatre, with four divisions: theatre, broadcasting-cinema, speech communication, and communication disorders. As the department expanded, its constituent parts developed professional lives and associations of their own, increasingly different from each other and from the liberal arts model prevalent elsewhere in the college of arts and sciences. As early as 1972, when Middleton announced his desire to step down as head, there was speculation whether anyone could continue much longer to operate it as a single unit. People talked of dividing it into at least two departments.[27]

Jellicorse continued to operate it as heretofore—a *de facto* professional school within the college. But in 1978 the department formally requested school status and separation from the college. With its multiple degree programs and 513 majors, it far surpassed all the other departments, although its faculty of thirty-two was smaller than English. The much smaller social work department was later allowed to depart the college and join the school of home economics, but Dean Robert Miller and his successors regarded communication and theatre as too large to part with. As long as it refused alternative suggestions to break up into smaller departments, college opposition killed the proposal.[28]

The theatre division grew so fast that Taylor Theater—several years in the planning—was too small by the time it opened in 1967. For five years, beginning in 1963, the National Repertory Theatre came to campus every fall to rehearse and perform plays before taking them on national tour. In 1966 the university resumed operation of the Parkway Playhouse in Burnsville. A separate summer repertory theater was re-established on campus in 1973. Not until the mid-'70s was the program able to dispense altogether with faculty members and townspeople to take male roles.[29]

During WC/UNCG's thirteen-year absence from Burnsville, the Parkway Playhouse was operated by the University of Miami, Florida. UNCG's return in 1966 was sparked by a legislative appropriation of $25,000 to refurbish the buildings, which still belonged to the local board of education. Raymond Taylor accepted Middleton's invitation to come out of retirement and direct the first production, "Our Town," with which he had inaugurated the playhouse in 1947. Under UNCG auspices, forty-odd students operated the theater with faculty supervision each summer during a six or seven-week term. Tourists and summer residents accounted for about half of the clientele, making it a significant contributor to the local economy.[30]

* * *

With twenty-five members in 1977, the art department was one of the largest on campus. Gregory Ivy, who had built the department almost from scratch, departed in 1961, disgusted with its perennial lack of space and facilities. This was not remedied until 1967, with the completion of a wing to the new McIver Building. Art, with the Weatherspoon Gallery, would occupy all of that wing. Ivy's successor in 1963 was painter Gilbert F. Carpenter, who built upon what was already a departmental orientation toward studio art. Reflecting that focus, only four members possessed the doctorate in 1977. Perhaps the most famous member was sculptor Peter Agostini. But the department, like the writing program, constantly brought in noted persons as adjunct faculty or artists in residence. The program flourished, often in collaboration with equivalent programs in writing, music, and dance. Though small in size, it was seen, by Carpenter at least, as one of the four or five best art programs in the country; it attracted students nationwide. He stepped down as head in 1974 after it suffered what he regarded as a mortal blow—the diversion of its out-of-state scholarship money (tuition waivers) to the new Ph.D. program in psychology. Joan Gregory (one of the department's Ph.D.s) was promoted from within to succeed him. Her tenure coincided with the successive rounds of budget cuts that plagued most departments in the '70s.[31]

No longer department head, Carpenter retained his position as director of the Weatherspoon Gallery; James Tucker remained as curator. (According to a 1966 study, only 8 percent of all four-year colleges possessed an art museum.)[32]

From the beginning, the gallery had specialized in twentieth-century American art—the most accessible field for a gallery on a tight budget, and also the most sensible adjunct to a department teaching students to be contemporary artists. As there was no state appropriation for art acquisitions, the gallery continued to depend on its Friends organization, formed in 1942. One of the major donors, beginning in 1965, was the Dillard Paper Company of Greensboro which sponsored an annual Art on Paper exhibit at the gallery.[33] In 1979 Weatherspoon opened a branch in the newly-opened Greensboro Arts Center downtown.[34]

* * *

UNCG inherited for a time Woman's College's claim to be a regional if not national center for the arts: writing, drama, music, art, and dance. The annual arts forum had been renamed the arts festival in 1954 and spread out over a period of three weeks or so every spring. In 1963, when Governor Terry Sanford called for the creation of a state-supported arts conservatory, music Dean Lee Rigsby and others on campus pushed hard to have it located at UNCG. They even sent a student delegation to Raleigh to lobby the legislature. It was to no avail; the School of the Arts was established in Winston-Salem.[35] Before long, the campus arts festival itself expired after students took over its management (in the spirit of the '60s) and proved incapable of sustaining it.[36] The arts clearly were not the top priority with campus administrators in these years. With money always in short supply, preference went to the new graduate, and particularly doctoral, programs that were seen as the hallmark of an aspiring university.[37]

Further evidence lay in the failure of efforts in the '70s to establish the Unicorn Press at the university. Alan Brilliant, the proprietor of this small independent publishing firm in Santa Barbara, California wanted to relocate to Greensboro, which despite setbacks still had the lingering reputation as an arts center. Robert Watson, Gilbert Carpenter, and others on campus backed the project strongly, and local backers recruited enough outside support in 1972 to launch the press if it could locate within the library building. General administration in Chapel Hill discouraged the idea, partly because of the ambiguous legal relationship between a state university and a private business, and partly because it might compete with the state-sponsored UNC Press. Brilliant moved his operation to Greensboro in 1973 anyway, off campus and without university affiliation. The press was always marginal financially, and in 1979 he offered to give all the equipment to the university *gratis*. But the campus bureaucracy moved so slowly that Brilliant changed his mind and sold the equipment commercially.[38]

* * *

The philosophy department consisted of two people in 1963; there were three and one-half in 1969 when Warren Ashby stepped down as head. Outside consultants discouraged the idea of a master's degree program; the department was too small. Indeed Robert Rosthal, soon to be promoted as Ashby's successor, held that it was too small even to support its undergraduate major satisfactorily.[39] Although the department grew to nine by 1979, there was as yet no master's degree. Beginning in the mid-'70s, the department began sponsoring an annual philosophy symposium, drawing five to ten nationally prominent philosophers as speakers.[40]

Closely related to philosophy in its origins was the department of religious studies. Religion had been a vital part of the extracurriculum at the Normal but that emphasis gradually receded, reflecting the secularization of American society. And for many years it had not been a formal part of the curriculum; indeed, public institutions around the country carefully avoided it out of concern for the separation of church and state.[41] Nevertheless, Dean Jackson in 1938 approved a formal course on the life and teachings of Jesus, to be under a standing faculty committee in lieu of a formal department.[42] Over the following years several departments offered courses relating to religion, but requests to create a separate department of religious studies were not granted until 1971.[43]

The '70s were in fact the decade in which religious studies gained widespread academic acceptance around the country. Here as elsewhere, academic courses on the Bible and the Christian tradition were offered but were outnumbered by those concerning other religions past and present, often of a sociological or philosophical bent.[44] The first department head at UNCG was Benjamin Ladner, an assistant professor who had come to the philosophy department in 1969. An undergraduate major was established in 1975. By 1979 the department numbered eight.[45]

* * *

History, with its large survey courses, particularly in European history, was another service department helping to fill liberal arts distribution requirements for graduation. The department numbered twenty-three persons in 1977, all but one with the Ph.D.[46] Richard Bardolph, a faculty veteran since 1944, served as head from 1960 until stepping down in 1978. His successor was Ann P. Saab, a European historian who had come to the department in 1965. Beginning in 1963, Mereb Mossman conducted an intensive campaign to bring back Richard N. Current, the prominent and prolific American historian who had served as department head from 1955 to 1960, then departed for the University of Wisconsin. Current (in 1963 the Harmsworth visiting professor of American history at Oxford University and author of ten books to date) acquiesced following the tender of an endowed professorship in 1965. (His salary in 1967 was exceeded on campus only by that of the chancellor.)[47]

The department had already initiated a master's degree program, in 1963. Though Mossman avoided saying so publicly, she must have been disappointed at the reluctance of both Current and Bardolph to endorse a history Ph.D. They did not fight it—in fact, the department brought in new personnel to advance the cause, and plans were drawn up. But in the end departmental ambivalence, much of it over the absence of visible funding for library resources, caused the department to miss the narrow window of opportunity exploited by English and psychology. The clear absence of a market for additional Ph.D. programs and graduates in the '70s assuaged most lingering regrets for the loss within the department.[48]

* * *

History was the mother of most of the social science departments on campus. The last to leave the nest was political science. By 1966 there were twenty-five political science majors and Margaret Hunt, the lead political scientist in the combined department, was pushing for additional faculty members to permit a more diversified program. As it was, a substantial number of the prospective majors were transferring to Chapel Hill after the sophomore year. Bardolph not only seconded her call but urged that political science become a separate department. In fact, everyone involved regarded the connection as increasingly anomalous, given the development of political science as a discipline over the past generation, as well as UNCG's new university status.[49]

For budgetary reasons, presumably, it took four years to achieve the amicable separation, in 1970. Political science moved across the street to the new Frank Porter Graham Building, with the other social sciences. A year later, David Olson from the University of Georgia arrived as department head. He hit the ground running, recruiting new department members and organizing political candidates' forums a year in advance of the 1972 elections.[50] A master's degree was approved in 1976.

* * *

The two-person geography department remained for years a service department for students majoring in other fields. Longtime department head Edna Arundel retired in 1960. Her desire for a geography major was not secured until three years later, under her successor Craig Dozier; by that time the department had grown to three. Coeducation opened up new vistas and in 1979 the department was offering courses and concentrations in earth science, urban land management, and urban/regional planning.[51] Nevertheless, the number of majors was so small that the SACS accrediting committee in 1972 raised the question whether its departmental status should be revoked. That was not done, and geography would see better days ahead.[52]

* * *

The department of sociology and anthropology consisted of three fairly distinct groups by 1963: academic sociologists, anthropologists, and specialists in social work. As each grew in size and specialization, they were harder and harder to accommodate within a single department. Each had its own professional associations at the state, regional, and national levels; social work had accreditation concerns that the others did not face.

Anthropology had gradually taken on new personnel and offered more and more courses; it introduced an undergraduate major in 1968. Harriet Kupferer, the senior anthropologist, was initially reluctant to separate from sociology and face the world as a small department but when the separation came in 1974, she became head. Kupferer was a WC alumna, a faculty member since 1961, and recently acting head of the combined department.[53]

Social work followed in 1977, at first under a coordinating committee. In its case a precipitating cause of separation lay in its increasingly stringent professional accreditation requirements that did not mesh well with sociology's liberal arts orientation. (The initial accreditation in 1974 was renewed periodically thereafter.) Until the separation a substantial majority of the departmental majors actually specialized in social work, although the faculty were primarily academic sociologists.[54] Mereb Mossman returned to teaching social work in 1971. She was closely involved in planning the joint social work program with A&T that started the next year. Mossman retired in 1973 but continued to teach part-time until 1976, almost forty years after her first arrival at Woman's College. She died in 1990, aged 84.[55] The social work program was so professionally oriented that the department received permission in 1987 to leave the college and join the school of human environmental sciences, formerly home economics.

When Mossman returned in 1971, it was to a still-combined department that she herself had done much to build up as the university's chief academic officer. Joseph Himes, a distinguished black scholar, came from the historically black North Carolina College in Durham in 1969, soon to receive an endowed chair. Lyda Gordon Shivers stepped down as department head in 1968. Her successor after a four-year hiatus was Alvin H. Scaff from the University of Iowa. With him came the sociology M.A. The department decided against a Ph.D. for the time being, though an outside evaluator in 1970 pronounced the nine-person sociology faculty superior to many he knew of who were offering the Ph.D. That window of opportunity also closed very shortly.[56] On Scaff's retirement in 1978 his replacement, Daniel O. Price from the University of Texas, was a former director of the Institute for Research in Social Science at Chapel Hill, having succeeded Gordon Blackwell in that post in 1957.

* * *

The classical civilization department numbered three persons in 1977. A substantial part of its enrollment came from the lower-level classics in translation course, but it continued to offer majors in Greek and Latin. Along with religious studies, geography, and German, its small size drew the attention of the SACS accreditation team in 1972. They questioned whether classics and German should not be combined with romance languages into a single department. None of the departments in question desired that and they remained separate. Frank Laine, the long-time classics head, stepped down in 1978.[57]

Despite its larger size, the romance languages department continued to occupy a back row. Student enrollment in all the language departments fell off during the 1970s, owing largely to reductions in the foreign language requirements for graduation. The department numbered thirty persons in 1977, only seventeen of them with the doctorate.[58] It offered majors in French and Spanish, with courses in Italian as well. Department head Charles Blend left the university in 1966 after only four years, to be replaced next year by George McSpadden of George Washington University. Like other new department heads of this era, McSpadden sought to develop a Ph.D. program in at least one of the languages; but unlike most, he was discouraged by campus administrators, who either doubted the department's capacity to sustain such a program or the existence of a demand for it. However, master's degree programs in French and Spanish were initiated in 1968 and 1969.[59] McSpadden stepped down as head in 1975; his successor, after the lapse of two years, was Herbert S. Gochberg from the University of Wisconsin, Madison.

The German and Russian department had grown to six members in 1977, all of them possessing the doctorate. The department was stronger than ever before in the institution's history, as head Anne Baecker remarked in 1974, yet it suffered like all the language departments from declining enrollment. It survived in large measure by introducing a variety of literature courses in translation. As between its two languages, the great majority of students took German; in keeping with national trends, Russian enrollments almost disappeared in 1966, but they recovered after the arrival in 1973 of Joachim Baer, a Russian specialist. In 1976 the department added a major in Russian studies (not Russian language) to the existing German major, but it offered no master's degree.[60]

* * *

The launching of the Soviet satellite Sputnik in 1957 caused major reverberations on American campuses. Interest in things international grew dramatically, even if its staying power (as in the study of Russian) proved variable. WC/UNCG followed the trend with a variety of new activities and programs in the '60s and '70s: the junior year abroad; a summer study abroad program (initially with Guilford College); an interdisciplinary international studies program; Asian, Russian, and Latin American studies programs; an international house dormitory; and a self-instructional foreign language program. Most of these were created independently and had little coordination with each other. For the most part, they failed to receive major support from either administrators or the faculty. In an era of exceptionally tight funding like the '70s, the existing departments claimed first place at the table. Faculty members, no matter how interested they were personally in interdisciplinary programs, recognized or were advised by their department heads that such programs offered little outlet for scholarly publication, the gate to professional advancement. As a result, it was difficult to fund or staff them, especially after the novelty wore off. This discouraged large student enrollments, which further depressed funding and staffing; the problem was circular.[61]

* * *

By 1968 black students were arguing that black history and culture merited a much larger place in the curriculum.[62] Next year a faculty committee agreed, recommending that appropriate courses and faculty members be added in a number of departments. The history department quickly proposed a course in African-American history, to be taught by department head Richard Bardolph, who had published in that field. When the student Neo-Black society, which had spearheaded these demands, called for a black instructor, Bardolph and his opposite number at A&T, Frank White, agreed to trade courses on their respective campuses for an experimental year in 1970.[63] Next year the department hired an African-American specialist, a student of John Hope Franklin at the University of Chicago. But the new recruit, Loren Schweninger, was white; although he did not satisfy some black militants, he remained many years, teaching the survey, developing upper-level courses, and becoming a prominent scholar in the field. Other departments gradually added new black-oriented courses and faculty members of their own.

These events coincided with the university's concerted effort—under court order—to recruit more black students and faculty. They also coincided with demands by black students nationally and locally for the creation of black studies programs, not just individual courses scattered through the curriculum. Such programs multiplied around the country, peaking in 1971. David Riesman was probably right to suggest that white students had more to gain than blacks by the consciousness-raising they offered. (The same may have been true of men and the women's studies programs that burgeoned simultaneously.) Nevertheless, it was blacks almost entirely who enrolled in black studies programs; in Riesman's phrase, they served as "decompression chambers" for blacks seeking release from the "white studies" in which they were otherwise immersed. These programs did little to satisfy the vocational needs of most black students, and their enrollments nationwide began to sag.[64] It was a little paradoxical, then, that the black studies program at UNCG did not start until 1982.

The largest of the interdisciplinary programs was women's studies, inaugurated in 1973. By 1974, there were 112 women's studies programs on American campuses, with more to come. At UNCG as elsewhere it was a major problem to secure qualified faculty; all were borrowed on a part-time basis from existing departments. Some heads were cooperative in supplying personnel; others had to be coerced. Nevertheless, with the help of outside grants, the program soon acquired critical mass. By 1979 it was offering about fifteen courses, consisting of two core courses bearing the women's studies label and selected offerings from participating departments. There was no women's studies major but the program did offer a minor.[65]

* * *

Another form of interdisciplinary activity was represented by the residential colleges springing up at many larger institutions in the 1960s and '70s. Typically, a residence hall was taken over for the purpose, with students living and taking all or most of their courses in that building from faculty members lent by their respective departments or schools. As this arrangement did not comport well with the specialized studies taken in the junior and senior years, necessarily scattered around campus, residential colleges usually were confined to the first two years. They faced many of the same obstacles as the interdisciplinary programs just described. Yet many of them proved rewarding to those involved and have enjoyed long and useful lives.[66]

All this was true at UNCG, where a residential college was established in 1970 in Mary Foust Dormitory, at the end of College Avenue. Dean Robert Miller brought the idea with him when he arrived in 1968 to form the new college of arts and sciences. Another of RC's founding fathers and its first director was Warren Ashby, who had recently stepped down as head of the philosophy department. Murray Arndt of the English department, with his wife Frances, lived in the dormitory as resident master and counselor; in later years each would serve as director. The remaining faculty, drawn from most of the schools and the arts and sciences departments, came in to teach specially designed courses, often interdisciplinary and team-taught. The core curriculum resembled only in broad outline the one that most freshmen and sophomores in the college took; in fact, it remained more tightly structured than the one that came into general use in the early '70s. There were slightly over 100 students, more or less evenly divided between freshmen and sophomores. These arrangements persisted over the years, subject to changes mainly in personnel. (There was an effort in the second year to double the enrollment, calling into requisition the matching Guilford Dormitory across the street. That proved more than the program could digest, and it was cut back to the 100-plus students in Mary Foust.) In its first years the college was funded partly with outside money; when that dried up in the late '70s, it barely survived.[67]

Students enrolled in the residential college by invitation. The effort was to pick a representative group, academically, economically, ethnically, and by gender. Many of its alumni became campus leaders in their last two years; others were notable as non-establishment types. Unfortunately, the college was also tagged at the outset as a center of drug use. As Dean Miller recalled, it was the only dormitory on campus that tackled this problem directly, on a group basis.[68]

Chapter 25

The Professional Schools

No academic fields experienced more dramatic change than those called business. The term changed meaning in these years. In 1963 business education still meant for the most part secretarial training, an all but exclusively female preserve; by 1979 it meant primarily business administration, training men (and increasingly women) how to function as business executives. An early step in that direction came in 1964, when the department of economics added business administration to its name and mandate. The ensuing transformation engendered a tidal wave of growth that almost overwhelmed those responsible for guiding it. Western Electric, R. J. Reynolds, Burlington Industries, and other regional businesses began sending employees to take graduate work in the department, even before it developed any graduate degree programs.[1]

John W. Kennedy, who had served since 1956 as economics head, turned over the headship in 1967 to David Shelton. A Mississippian and (like Chancellors Singletary and Ferguson) a Millsaps graduate, Shelton had recently arrived from the University of Delaware. To him was entrusted the tasks of developing a program in business administration and then a school of business and economics; he became its first dean in 1970. In its initial year it managed to outstrip all the other professional schools in the number of credit hours taught. By 1974 the school consisted of four departments: economics, business administration, business and distributive education (including the former secretarial training), and accounting.

All were professional departments save economics, which maintained for a time a presence in the college of arts and sciences as well. That affiliation had little practical significance, but there was always an element of friction between economics and its sister departments in the business school. Traditionally, economics had attracted few majors at WC; it had been primarily a service department, offering lower level courses to satisfy graduation requirements in other fields. Coeducation brought male students to the department, but it also coincided with the women's movement; the number of economics majors climbed to forty-six in 1966, of whom twenty-eight were women.[2] It began offering a master of arts degree in 1969.

At the same time, the field of secretarial administration began to stagnate, largely because of competition from the new community colleges. (The old one-year commercial program, going back to the first years of the college, disappeared for this reason in 1967.) It was the new field of business administration that skyrocketed, providing the major reason for establishing the B&E school.[3]

For a number of years, WC/UNCG had ignored pleas from the community to offer courses in business administration, especially in the evening hours. Guilford College partially filled the gap, earning goodwill correspondingly.[4] Although Kennedy had appealed for permission to offer graduate classes in evenings and on Saturdays to accommodate businessmen, they did not materialize until Shelton's accession to the headship in 1967. Indeed, his advent signaled a shift in emphasis toward professional training.[5] Undergraduate full-time enrollment was already exploding; with the introduction of evening classes, the enrollment of part-time advanced students grew exponentially as well, despite the absence at first of a graduate degree program. The department was soon drowning in students while lacking in facilities to handle them.

Similarly, when the B&E school in 1970, its first year, introduced a master's degree program in business, it was responding to the insistent demands of local businessmen. The program was based initially on hope and prayer; Shelton confessed privately that it was "laughable" to suppose the school could yet mount a graduate program of quality. Nevertheless, there were ninety students the first year. As they poured in, academic standards gave way: essay examinations became fewer, faculty-student contacts rarer, student research papers almost out of the question, student advising ever more perfunctory. Faculty research was delayed by an absence of clerical help, poor computer facilities, and weak library holdings. For Shelton the only conceivable direction was up, "since 'down' did not exist."

For some years the business program relied heavily on part-time adjunct faculty from the local community as well as doctoral students from Duke, Chapel Hill, and State. Most persons across the nation who were qualified to teach full-time gravitated toward established programs that had been accredited. Moreover, those people were in such demand in the business world that it was nearly impossible to recruit them without paying salaries regarded as exorbitant elsewhere in the university. Yet there were successes. As early as 1967, Arthur Lee Svenson was recruited from New York University as Burlington Industries professor. In charge of the business program and chairman of the business administration department at its creation in 1972 was Dwight L. Gentry, recently associate dean of the business school at the University of Maryland; he was succeeded in 1975 by Joseph E. Johnson, an insurance specialist with advanced degrees from Georgia State. Both were among Shelton's early recruits.[6]

The faculty grew, but student enrollment seemed always to grow more. Class sizes mounted, creating a serious morale problem among the faculty already in place, including Shelton himself. They cast envious eyes on the school of education and other units that hired senior professors despite enrollment pressures much lower than those at B&E.

Why not limit enrollments? First, the university did not want to offend a vitally important constituency—the Greensboro business community—by rejecting qualified applicants for a program the community so obviously wanted. There was no equivalent program within commuting distance, and UNCG had no desire to stimulate another. Second, the university's budget was driven largely by student enrollment; to limit enrollments is to diminish one's bargaining power with general administration and the legislature. McIver had learned this in the 1890s. As countless departments had discovered since (and psychology was learning now with its Ph.D.), programs and facilities deeply desired must often be gained through initial privation and suffering. No administrator since McIver better articulated his unit's pain than David Shelton. It did not help either that the school was scattered in four campus buildings, all now quite venerable: Forney, Foust, Curry, and a house on McIver Street.[7]

The picture did brighten as the '70s drew to a close. The school numbered sixty-six faculty in 1977, of whom thirty-eight had the doctorate. As the national applicant pool consisted primarily of young people, with or without the terminal degree, and experienced applicants commanded impossible salaries, the faculty was disproportionately young and concentrated in the junior ranks. This was true in some measure of all four departments, but particularly of business administration and accounting. Shelton commended the energy and abilities they displayed in meeting consistently large classes.[8] A handsome new building came into service in 1980, and the next few years would bring more money, more faculty, and professional accreditation.

From the outset, UNCG departed from the traditional business school pattern (exemplified at Chapel Hill) of restricting graduate enrollments in business to full-time students; the greatest demand here and around the country was for programs accessible to employed persons after working hours. For them, as for schoolteachers, professional advancement depended on taking additional courses and degrees.[9] By 1972, the school had 800 majors, half of them graduate students; by 1977 it was 1600 majors, 400 of them graduate students. The MBA program alone numbered 350 students in 1978; most were part-time. The proportion of women in that program rose sharply, from fewer than 10 percent in 1975 to 30 percent in 1980.[10]

The department of business and distributive education came into being in 1972, chaired in its first year by faculty veteran Vance Littlejohn. He retired next year, to be succeeded by James W. Crews, head of the business education program at the University of Florida. In 1977, with eight members, the department offered bachelors' and masters' degree programs designed primarily to train high school teachers of such subjects as accounting, data processing, marketing, typing, and shorthand. In addition there were undergraduate programs in merchandising and office administration; the latter (formerly secretarial administration) became increasingly devoted to data processing and technology. As time passed, the department recruited more persons with the doctorate, but in the beginning it was heavily dependent (like business administration) on part-time faculty from the Greensboro business community. Shelton pronounced it in 1977 the best department of its kind in the state.[11]

For some years, accounting courses had been offered by both the economics and the business education departments. In the late '60s and '70s accounting experienced much the same growth as business administration, with the same problems. The creation of a separate department was delayed until 1972, apparently by the difficulty in hiring qualified faculty; even then, it was not fully independent of business administration until 1979.[12]

In 1974 the B&E school established a Center for Applied Research, designed to study state and local issues of concern to area businesses. Among the industries the center hoped to serve in this fashion were textiles, furniture, and insurance. (Its press release did not mention tobacco.) The subjects in contemplation included industrial growth, urbanization, labor and financial markets, and environmental protection. Although sponsored by the school of business and economics, the center expected to draw on faculty expertise from all over the university. G. Donald Jud of the economics faculty was placed in charge. One of the center's main projects was the publication, beginning in 1974, of a quarterly journal, the *North Carolina Review of Business and Economics*.[13]

* * *

All the professional schools grew, if not on the scale of the business school. As befitted units of an aspiring university, all developed graduate programs. Music, like art, was increasingly performance-oriented. This shift was attributable in large measure to two successive deans, Lee Rigsby who left in 1966 for Ohio State, and his successor Lawrence Hart from Iowa State. The school's traditional role, training music teachers for the public schools, remained strong, nevertheless; although the faculty consisted increasingly of performers, many or most of the student majors were still drawn to the education program. Rigsby appears to have pushed hard to increase the number of performance majors, partly in hopes of landing the state musical conservatory that ended up instead in Winston-Salem as part of the School of the Arts. UNCG also offered courses in music history, theory, and appreciation but they remained subordinate.[14]

By 1978 the music school offered a bachelor of arts in music; bachelor's and master's degrees in applied music; an MFA in composition; and an Ed.D. in music education, introduced in 1968.[15] It was also planning a performance-oriented doctor of musical arts degree, which came in the '80s. The number of majors had grown by 1978 to 320 undergraduates and 70 graduate students; 16

were in the doctoral program. There were forty-two full-time faculty and about twenty-five part-timers that year; only seventeen or so held the doctorate, which was uncommon in the performance fields.[16] Music budgets were as tight as everyone else's and some of the money for these developments came from private funds; a musical arts guild was formed for this purpose in 1972.[17]

Although a small music annex building was completed in 1966, growth continually outstripped the facilities; many of the music faculty (like others) were scattered around campus in a variety of makeshift quarters, including former private homes. There was a high faculty turnover.[18]

Coeducation vastly improved certain parts of the program. Male students were largely responsible for developing the brass, woodwind, and percussion sections, and until their arrival choral director Richard Cox had to scout the city for male voices as Herman Middleton did for male actors. Under Cox's direction the university chorale garnered a great deal of national, even international renown. It gave ten concerts on a trip to Romania in 1974.[19]

The music school still administered Greensboro's civic music program, including the Greensboro Symphony until 1967. When the symphony separated, George Dickieson of the music faculty formed a university orchestra and a smaller chamber orchestra for student players.[20] Faculty members and some students continued to play in the Greensboro Symphony, however. Some even performed with the Winston-Salem Symphony and other orchestras in the area.[21]

* * *

Naomi Albanese remained as dean of home economics until her retirement in 1982. She gained a high national visibility, serving as president of the American Home Economics Association in 1971–72. During that term the AHEA became the accrediting body for undergraduate programs in home economics; UNCG's program was the first to receive accreditation. Albanese served on the boards of a number of corporations including Duke Power, Jefferson-Pilot Life Insurance, and the Blue Bell textile firm; she also chaired the board of the Federal Reserve Bank of Richmond's Charlotte branch.[22]

In 1969, the full-time home economics faculty numbered forty-three, just over half of them with doctorates; that was still the proportion in 1978.[23] Almost half had received their last degree from UNCG, raising the specter of inbreeding in the minds of the 1972 AHEA accreditation team. While the team found much to praise and approved the program as a whole, they pronounced it underfunded. It survived through donations from private business, usually conveyed through the Home Economics Foundation. Dean Albanese was an indefatigable fund-raiser. Faculty research was limited in large part by the high school-teaching and home-making emphases prevalent when many of the faculty had arrived or done their own graduate work. But those who did engage in active research found significant support through the school's continuing land-grant affiliation with North Carolina State University.[24]

Undergraduate enrollments in home ec rose remarkably in the '60s, then dropped by almost 25 percent in the late '70s; but that loss was balanced by a rise in graduate students. Both graduate and undergraduate enrollments in home ec in 1980 were among the highest in the United States. With forty-seven faculty members in 1978, the UNCG program was by far the largest in the state. The students remained overwhelmingly female, although a few men entered the more professional and scientific fields as both graduate and undergraduate students.[25]

The school embraced six specialized areas that were organized into departments in 1975: child development and family relations, clothing and textiles, food and nutrition, housing, interior design, and home economics education. The education and home-making programs had long been the most popular with students, but with the opening up of alternative job opportunities for women in the '60s, enrollments and majors shifted toward more professional fields such as interior design and food/nutrition.[26]

Dean Albanese was eager to expand graduate work, and Mereb Mossman was eager to cooperate.[27] Chief attention went to the doctorate, originally limited to child development and awarded for the first time by WC at its final commencement in 1963. The school's request for a blanket doctoral program was approved in 1966. It was the only home economics Ph.D. in North Carolina. Outside consultants in 1978 commended both the baccalaureate and master's programs and rated the doctoral program as outstanding.[28]

Back in 1922, the college had erected its first home management house on McIver Street to provide hands-on training for future home-makers. As enrollments grew over the years, additional houses were acquired. But then, as home economics changed its emphasis from home-making to professionalism and science, the houses were phased out. By the mid-1980s, all had been sold or transferred to other uses.[29]

The nursery school, by contrast, remained and multiplied. By 1973, in response to both community and curricular demands, there were six separate facilities for as many ages and categories of children. Scattered around campus, they were under the direction of Mary Elizabeth Keister, a daughter of former economics head Albert Keister. Her own professional prominence won her in time an endowed chair and (like Albanese) the consolidated university's coveted O. Max Gardner award.[30]

The interior design program in earlier years had trained prospective high school teachers and extension workers; their primary concern was to make the home more beautiful and functional. Beginning in the '60s, the program increasingly trained professionals to design the interiors of public buildings. It always had as much in common with art as with home economics, and was chronically in tension between them. In 1936 Chancellor Jackson assigned interior design courses to the art department while allotting home furnishings to home economics.[31] That hardly solved the problem, and it took a fine eye to distinguish between the courses offered by each unit.

No matter where interior design resided, it was in danger of being treated (or at least perceiving itself) as a neglected stepchild. Clara Ridder, who came to the faculty in 1959, believed that Dean Albanese consistently undernourished the program because it was distant from her own interests and understanding. Whatever the cause, there was a widespread perception in the '60s that interior design was a feather-weight program, offering few courses and turning out graduates who were ashamed of their training. Art department head Gilbert Carpenter decried the standards of the home ec program while Albanese was characteristically defensive.[32]

One of Stanley Jones's tasks on his arrival in 1971 was to settle this problem. He consulted far and wide. A High Point furniture executive criticized home economics for being too traditional and art for being too *avant garde* to serve the needs of the interior design majors. Eventually, a weightier interior design baccalaureate program was set up in 1975—in home economics—requiring four full years plus summers. Mary Miller, a WC alumna and faculty member since 1967, became chairman of the new department. As in other fields with substantial competition in the business world, it was difficult to recruit and retain suitable new faculty; their frequent turnover led in turn to renewed student dissatisfaction and a retention rate in the major of less than 50 percent.[33]

* * *

UNCG entered the '60s with a two-year associate degree program in nursing, run in collaboration with Greensboro's Moses Cone Hospital. That program better belonged in the new community college system, and its director urged strongly that UNCG develop a four-year baccalaureate program.[34] Accordingly, Dr. Eloise Lewis was recruited in 1966 to organize a school of nursing; it opened a year later. Lewis, a native South Carolinian, had been in 1953 one of the original faculty of the UNC nursing school in Chapel Hill and had risen to assistant dean. She spent the rest of her career at UNCG, building its nursing school into a model of its kind. It received national accreditation in 1970, before the graduation of its first class. When successive classes did graduate, they compiled an enviable record in passing the mandatory state nursing exam. A master's program was initiated in 1976 and accredited in 1978—one of only two in the nation to receive initial accreditation for eight years. The faculty entered into scholarly activity as never before. Lewis quickly became a major presence on campus, in the community, and in the nursing profession at large. In 1976 she won the O. Max Gardner award and in 1978–80 served as president of the American Association of Colleges of Nursing; she was the first editor of its *Journal of Professional Nursing.*[35]

It was clear from the outset that Lewis ran a tight ship. The faculty she recruited, increasing from five in 1967 to forty-eight a decade later, were capable and intensely loyal. Their morale was high except as it was limited by the campus-wide standards for promotion and tenure. In a field where the doctorate was almost unknown, Lewis herself was for a decade or more the only nursing professor with that degree.[36] Others attained it with her encouragement. Whether from her ability or the nature of the field, she was more successful than others in recruiting capable black faculty at a time when they were in very short supply. Lewis possessed formidable bureaucratic and political skills. Given the choice of several temporary quarters for the new school, she chose the least desirable—the infirmary basement—as the most promising base from which to negotiate a new building. The tactic succeeded; the new building opened in 1969 on McIver Street.[37]

The school's reputation spread rapidly. It was soon receiving more student applications than it could accommodate. Upperclass and graduate majors exceeded 200 by the late '70s, with half that number graduating each year. These enrollments not only exceeded early projections; by 1973 they exceeded the capacity of the Greensboro hospitals to provide on-site clinical training. (The nursing schools at A&T and the new Guilford Technical Institute were also competing for places in the local hospitals.) Some students and supervising faculty members thus were forced to commute to health care institutions outside the city. Even then, limited clinical facilities restricted the number of students who could be admitted to what was clearly a superior program.[38]

* * *

In 1963, with the retirement of longtime college physician Ruth Collings, the health department was recombined with physical education and recreation. Under Ethel Martus the combined department was organized into four divisions: health education, physical education, dance, and recreation. There were two additional non-academic divisions devoted to intramural and intercollegiate athletics, financed by student fees. The department continued to pursue its earlier quests for school status and a Ph.D. program. Both encountered stiff resistance from Chapel Hill—the campus as well as general administration. When a doctorate did arrive in 1966 it took the form of an education degree with a specialization in physical education. The Ph.D. had to wait until 1987.[39]

School status came in 1971, with Lawther as dean until her retirement in 1974. Her successor, Margaret Mordy of Ohio State University, served only five years before her own retirement. In 1977 the school's faculty numbered fifty-six persons, twenty of them with the doctorate, a relatively recent degree in physical education.[40]

No part of the university was more immediately impacted by coeducation. The department had been for a generation one of the nation's prime training grounds for female physical educators. The introduction of male students required in some cases separate facilities and separate faculty members to teach and coach. The women in charge of the program had not been enthusiastic (to say the least) about the prospect of coeducation and they broke no speed records in preparing for it. They made the change nevertheless. Martus hired as her first male faculty member Frank Pleasants, a physiologist. Jim Swiggett soon followed as men's basketball coach.[41] Male students had to fit within the existing buildings; despite requests for a new, separate gymnasium, no new structures appeared for many years.

Most of the women faculty remained. Ellen Griffin, a 1940 WC graduate, had joined the faculty upon graduation and taught golf classes to crowds of appreciative students. She left in 1968 to found a private golf school south of Greensboro.[42] Celeste Ulrich (WC '46 and a faculty member since 1956) served in 1976–77 as president of the American Alliance for Health, Physical Education, and Recreation (AHPER); in 1979 she left to become dean at the University of Oregon. Others had national reputations as well; Gail Hennis served in the mid-'70s as president of the National Association for Sport and Physical Education, the largest of AHPER's seven divisions; Marie Riley followed her in that post in 1980.[43] Virginia Moomaw continued to head the well-known dance program.

The recreation division continued to hold classes at Piney Lake, south of town, while the university sponsored programs there for groups ranging from grade schoolers to Elderhostelers.[44]

* * *

Education Dean Kenneth Howe departed in 1966; his successor a year later was Robert M. O'Kane of Rutgers University. Although the recruitment of faculty members was by this time primarily a faculty responsibility, O'Kane managed in the next few years to hire so many people (like himself) with Harvard degrees as to evoke grumblings of a Harvard Mafia. Some of the newcomers were nationally or internationally recognized. Perhaps the most notable was Roland Nelson, coming in 1970 from the presidency of Marshall University in West Virginia. The emphasis, as never before, was on research. By 1977, in a faculty of sixty-five, forty-one held the doctorate. Yet, arguably the most prominent member of the education faculty was a native of piedmont North Carolina who joined the faculty in 1962—before O'Kane—with the rank of instructor pending the completion of her doctorate. Lois Edinger was already a recent president of the North Carolina Education Association; two years after her arrival she was installed as president of the National Education Association, serving during the year 1964–65. Almost a decade later, in 1973, she served as the first chairman of Greensboro's commission on the status of women.[45]

Edinger recalled the late '60s and early '70s as the school's golden age. Much of it resulted from federal appropriations for higher education that benefited many institutions in those years. For instance, UNCG operated a successful practice school at Camp Lejeune, the marine corps base on the North Carolina coast, from 1973 to 1976 when the funds dried up. UNCG soon began to have trouble placing its graduates as public school teachers, causing it to scale back its program.[46]

The school had awarded master's degrees since 1922; it acquired a doctor of education degree in 1966. About 90 percent of all the graduate work on campus that year was carried on in education. The proportion declined as other fields added programs; by 1979, education was responsible for about a third of the graduate degrees conferred, and almost half of the doctorates.[47] In line with national trends away from professional teacher training at the undergraduate level,[48] Dean O'Kane and some of his faculty sought increasingly to focus on the graduate programs.

Nevertheless, it was the graduate programs that garnered the greatest criticism in 1971–72 from NCATE, the national teacher education accrediting agency, and from the state department of public instruction. In large measure this criticism echoed the last evaluation in 1962. UNC Vice President Arnold King wrote Chancellor Ferguson that it was "real humiliating" to hear one of his constituent institutions dressed down as he had just heard state officials lambaste UNCG's teacher training program. NCATE, for its part, extended only a provisional three-year accreditation.

The focus of criticism in 1972 as in 1962 was the weakness (if not absence) of central control over campus teacher education programs. The interdisciplinary teacher education council, reshuffled when this question arose a decade earlier, was mainly advisory. In the secondary school program particularly, authority was vested largely in the schools and departments where prospective teachers majored. That arrangement reflected widespread convictions in higher education nationally, as well as long-standing policy at WC/UNCG. Only a tiny percentage of the nation's high school teachers had actually majored in education.[49] At WC/UNCG the faculty as a whole, leaning strongly to the liberal arts, had never been willing to surrender full control of teacher training to the school of education. On the other hand, teacher certification requirements came from the state, filtered through the school of education. As a result, there was widespread confusion on campus as to what the requirements were for any given program at any given time. Communication between the school of education and subject area departments was poor. No wonder that outside evaluation teams, like faculty members, found the situation baffling if not anarchical.[50]

Neither O'Kane nor the education faculty were targets of NCATE or state criticism; no doubt they agreed with most of it. So far as undergraduate training was concerned, they pointed out, the school was prevented from offering either a degree or a major. Some of them were reportedly ready to dispense with the undergraduate program altogether, but there was long-standing resentment at the old campus regulation limiting sharply the number of hours an undergraduate—even a prospective teacher—could take in the school of education. Furthermore, O'Kane declared, if teaching was a profession the preparatory training program ought to be centered in the professional school offering the instruction.[51]

Arts and science leaders responded that NCATE was controlled by schools of education nationally, and that the education faculty at UNCG may actually have prompted its criticisms.[52] However that may be, Vice Chancellor Jones and some of O'Kane's fellow deans laid many of the ills directly on his doorstep. NCATE had not questioned the teacher education council or its composition; it simply pointed to that body's ineffectiveness. O'Kane chaired the council, and in the eyes of Jones and others its weakness stemmed from his own failure of leadership. The consequences extended beyond the issue of program control to substantive curricular matters that the teacher education council had so far avoided. After a faculty study, Chancellor Ferguson early in 1974 appointed education professor Dwight Clark as coordinator of teacher education.[53] O'Kane stepped down as dean, to be replaced that fall by David Reilly, head of the school psychology program at UNC-Chapel Hill.

As Reilly recalled it some years later, not only was NCATE accreditation up in the air when he arrived and the coordination of teacher education removed from the dean's office, but faculty morale was low and "there was no sense of direction or purpose for the School or its programs." By the end of his first year, he continued, NCATE accreditation was secured and he had created a preliminary departmental organization within the school. In 1977, a study of teacher education programs throughout the UNC system gave UNCG's programs high marks. Yet Reilly had to concede that faculty morale remained low, with older members tuning out and others aligning into hostile factions; there was still no accepted sense of purpose or direction. Part of the problem sprang from departmentalization, which many faculty regarded as unnecessary and divisive.[54]

Stanley Jones, for his part, was tremendously impressed with Reilly's work, feeling that he hit the ground running and in the ensuing years built the school to new heights.[55] In 1976 Reilly hired two well-known school psychologists, Jack I. Bardon and William W. Purkey; indeed Bardon, who came from Rutgers that year, was sometimes referred to as the father of modern school psychology. Other senior appointments both preceded and followed these two, sometimes to the mortification of faculty members in the business school and other units not similarly favored. Unfortunately the factionalism noted by Reilly did not abate; it escalated, ending only with his own resignation in 1986.

Curry building was renovated in the early 1960s and again, more thoroughly, in the 1980s. That gratified the education faculty but it did not save Curry School. The high school in particular hung by a thread in 1962, when the college decided to give it another three years of probation. Curry was seen more and more as an elite institution, good perhaps for the younger children lucky enough to gain admission, but too constricted in its offerings for older students, many of whom transferred to the public high schools. Its operating costs per pupil were almost double those of the public schools. As early as the '50s, moreover, WC produced far more education students than Curry could absorb as practice teachers; from that time onward most got assignments in the public schools, which were after all the field for which they were training.[56]

Little of this was unique to UNCG; practice schools around the country were closing down for similar reasons. Outside consultants and an education faculty study in 1966 all recommended closure of at least the high school. O'Kane agreed and the high school closed in 1969. There had always been a hope, little realized in practice, that Curry could serve as a laboratory for educational innovation. That hope was now reaffirmed for the elementary school, containing kindergarten through grade six. But it closed too in 1970. A truly innovative, experimental school required a research-oriented faculty and the funds to support them. Those prerequisites did not exist in sufficient quantity. Furthermore, the school was too small to offer much opportunity for cooperative activity like team-teaching. Indeed, a number of the public schools were more innovative than Curry.

That Curry lasted as long as it did was attributable to the power of tradition and the vigorous support of its students and their families. (On one occasion in the early '60s, after Dean Howe had spoken favorably of closure, Curry students hanged him in effigy.) Despite its affiliation with the Greensboro school system, Curry was viewed as a quasi-private school. Most of its students were drawn from the upper middle class; about 40 percent were children of UNCG faculty. They had few learning problems. Over 90 percent were white. Of the 203 elementary school students remaining in 1970, only 22 lived in the Curry district; the rest were brought from all over the city and county. The successive closures caused great pain for most of the people concerned, yet it was hard to deny their necessity.[57]

* * *

Summer school had always been associated primarily with teacher education. But that was changing by the '70s when undergraduate enrollments rose as dramatically in summer school as in the regular terms. In 1964, for the first time in recent years, undergraduates outnumbered graduate students in the summer session.[58] The new majority fell into two main groups: those who needed to raise their grade point averages to stay in school, and those who were accelerating their programs. Total enrollments increased from 1,336 in 1964 to 6,094 in 1976, then leveled off in company with overall enrollments.[59] By 1974, only one-sixth of summer students lived on campus; the remainder were commuters.[60] As between the two six-week sessions, enrollments in the first always exceeded those in the second, reflecting a preference of both students and faculty. Summer sessions were supported primarily from student tuition and fees but the state also offered a supplement based on enrollment.[61]

* * *

One of the most important directions in higher education since the 1960s has been answering a growing demand by adults for further professional and vocational training—often technological. Metropolitan universities were ideally suited to meet this need.[62] Woman's College had long provided extension work around the state for students and practitioners in education, home economics, and other fields. UNCG continued that tradition, shifting its emphases to accommodate changing demand. Like summer school, the extension office was expected to pay its own way through student tuition and fees, with only slight help from the university. In 1964, Joseph Bryson was hired as director of extension; for several years he doubled as director of the summer session too. On his return to full-time teaching (in education), both positions went to Joseph E. Johnson of the business school in 1973 and in 1975 to Jean Eason (wife of psychology head Robert Eason and a long-time UNCG administrator). Following national usage, extension was renamed continuing education in 1974.[63]

The academic courses given off campus in the '60s were usually graduate-level versions of campus offerings, taught by members of the faculty over and above their normal course load. In 1970, the greatest demand for these courses lay in education, home economics, mathematics, and history.[64] An exception was the Parkway Playhouse program in the mountains, resumed by UNCG in 1966 and administered by the extension office. During the '70s the university offered fewer and fewer off-campus courses. The faculty, faced with increasing research responsibilities, were not as ready to take on the burden of overtime teaching and travel. Better roads and the opening of community colleges and technical institutes made it easier for students to commute to institutions reasonably near home where the offerings were more varied.

Rapidly taking the place of off-campus courses, therefore, were new extension programs at nearby technical institutes, which could not themselves offer academic work: Randolph Tech in Asheboro (where UNCG's first such program was launched in 1970), Piedmont Tech in Roxboro, and Guilford Tech in neighboring Jamestown. By the late '70s, UNCG was offering thirty courses a year for some 200 students at Randolph Tech alone. The instructors were quite often graduate students approved by their respective departments or schools.[65] These were undergraduate courses at the freshman and sophomore levels. Graduate students increasingly chose to commute to UNCG or other universities where evening courses were more and more available.

Chapter 26

Student Life: Gender, Residence, Race

Women students like the faculty were of mixed minds concerning coeducation. Some pointedly ostracized the first boys in their classes and on campus. Some regarded them as effeminate since (supposedly) they often majored in "female subjects" like music or interior design. When the town students first elected a male representative to student government, some of the girls walked out when he spoke and voted down any motions he offered. For some, the resentment endured; when the class of 1966 held its tenth reunion in 1976, the male student government president was hissed as he got up to make welcoming remarks.[1]

Yet his very presence in that capacity shows how limited the resentment was. In fact, what many people feared at the outset had come to pass: within a few years the girls were electing male students to leadership positions far beyond their proportion of the student population. In the twenty-five years beginning in 1970, all but five of the annual SGA presidents were men; much the same was true of other positions. The same deference appeared in classrooms, where girls spoke up less in the presence of boys.[2]

On American campuses, 1968 fell very late in the age of the panty raid, wherein male students stormed women's dormitories demanding items of intimate apparel. The male students at UNCG staged their first such raid in October 1968. It was carefully organized. Every participant was conscious that this was no ordinary panty raid; their masculinity had been challenged so often that its affirmation was now a point of honor. As the first male editor of the *Carolinian* pointed out a few days later, one could have criticized its tardiness except that earlier attempts would likely have been suicide missions, given the campus gender ratio. As it was, some of the raiders lost their own underwear in counterattacks on their own quarters by members of the female majority. There were not enough men to attack every woman's dorm, but they were encouraged to try again by residents of the neglected buildings. Campus and city police were equally sympathetic; having been tipped off in advance, they did little or nothing to interfere. Once it was over, the participants took some satisfaction in the operation; they had won respect.[3]

* * *

Most of the early male students were commuters, but one of the clearest needs arising from coeducation was to provide housing for those who were not. The conversion of an existing dormitory was ruled out for the time being; the university was turning away applicants for lack of housing, and girls were tripling up in any dorm with rooms large enough to permit it. For several years, beginning in 1965, the university rented an unused nurses' dormitory at Wesley Long Hospital, a mile from campus, as a women's dorm, and for the first time in decades some female students were permitted to live in university-approved housing off campus.[4]

The first few male students who did not live at home also had to find rooms or apartments off campus. Several occupied a converted firehouse at Mendenhall and Walker, a block from campus, that was billed as the "first men's dorm."[5] From 1965 to '67, as their number grew, men were housed in three small apartment buildings adjacent to campus, purchased by the university.

The housing shortage was greatly alleviated in 1967 with the completion of Phillips, Hawkins, and Cone dormitories. Phillips was turned over to the men, who nearly filled it by the second year. By 1978 men had taken over five of the dormitories, the women retaining fourteen. No further residence halls were constructed until 1990. To some degree, UNCG shared a nationwide student trend away from college dormitories, obviating a need for further construction, but virtually all the continuing enrollment increase consisted of commuters living off campus.[6]

* * *

Most institutions tended to regard commuting students as just like the dormitory students, except for their residence. It took years of experience to learn otherwise. Many if not most commuters were adults living multiple lives, with jobs to work, households to maintain, children to raise. They had little time or taste for traditional student interests outside the classroom; their greatest extracurricular concern was parking space.[7] At UNCG, the commuters ranged from recent high school graduates living with their parents to parents with college age children of their own. About half of them were 25 or older; half were married; almost half were part-time students.[8]

As a traditional student from the class of '67 recalled, the town students tended to be disconnected from the others, uninvolved in the dorm life that was central to her student experience. Outside of class many or most of them self-segregated in their own lounge in Elliott Hall. They held their own dances and parties. To the degree that younger commuters answered this description, they lost some of the opportunity to grow up free from daily parental oversight. As late as 1991, the divergence was still present if less extreme in the view of James

Lancaster, '72, a town student who was very active in student life, then stayed on for advanced degrees and many years' service as an administrator in the student affairs office.[9] But Lancaster's own experience was not unique; town students became increasingly active on campus. In 1978, in fact, they held every office in student government as well as the editorships of the *Carolinian*, *Coraddi*, and *Pine Needles*, and the directorship of WUAG, the student radio station. Clearly, they were assimilating.[10]

* * *

Given the South's long history of slavery and segregation, the hardest group to recruit and then assimilate were the black students. Like the first-generation white collegians who were coming to campus in increasing numbers, blacks often had little knowledge of higher education or collegiate life. Their experience with the white power structure in the ongoing civil rights revolution seemed to teach that success came sooner to those who demanded than to those who asked politely. They often shared if they did not spearhead the anger and the attraction to separatism and black power that animated many of their generation. Almost everywhere they demanded more black faculty members and a greater Afro-American presence in the curriculum; the latter desire soon resolved itself into demands for black studies programs. Demands escalated after the assassination of Martin Luther King, Jr. in 1968.[11] These currents, like the broader protest movements embracing students of every race, never reached the same level of magnitude at UNCG (or the South generally) as in other parts of the country, but they appeared nonetheless.

African-American enrollment at UNCG rose from 109 in 1964 to 894—or 9.8 percent of the total—in 1979. There was a high degree of segregation on campus, initially in separate dormitory rooms but also in campus social life. Although some, perhaps many, black and white students hit it off well together, the separation was largely voluntary on both sides. They had grown up on opposite sides of a great divide and often felt uneasy in each other's company. Most of the black students socialized together, often at the A&T campus across town. Some black graduate students charged in 1968 that they were being systematically discriminated against in grades, but an examination of transcripts seemed to refute the charge. A survey of thirty-one black students in 1975 revealed that about half found both the academic work and the social life harder than they had expected. Three-quarters felt they had personally encountered discrimination at UNCG, primarily from white students but occasionally from faculty, administrators, or staff members. Although they frequently found faculty members too distant or impersonal, they respected the university's academic standing and saw its diploma as a ticket to better jobs and life prospects after graduation.

All decried what they saw as an underemphasis on black culture in the curriculum. (Departments were adding courses of this nature but a distinct black studies program did not appear on campus until 1982.) Nevertheless, three-quarters of the students reported themselves at least relatively satisfied with their experience at UNCG and all planned to continue to graduation.[12] Their retention rate was good.

One who remained despite early misgivings was Ada Fisher, '70, the daughter of a Baptist minister in Durham. She concluded in time that the university needed her at least as much as she needed it. Fisher did well enough academically to graduate and to win admission to the University of Wisconsin medical school; meanwhile she served as sports editor of the *Carolinian*; participated actively in student government, winning SGA's "outstanding legislator" award in her senior year; led in creating a black students' organization (the Neo-Black Society); and took an active part in the campus protest movements of her time. In the process she developed an abiding respect and friendship for Chancellor Ferguson.[13] By 1971, UNCG had a variety of counseling and support services in place, aimed specifically at black students.[14]

One of the first black male students, arriving in 1965, recalled more difficulties from being male than being black; his overall impression was very positive. He also recalled that in May 1969, when racial violence erupted at A&T between students, passersby, and the National Guard, UNCG permitted its black students to go home for a week or so to avoid similar dangers; most if not all did so.[15]

Even as Ferguson in 1967 acquiesced in calls by students of both races to end segregation in the residence halls,[16] black students formed their own organization which they called the Neo-Black Society. By 1975, virtually all black students were members though relatively few were active. The NBS first met in student lounges in Elliott Hall. When the members asked for a permanent meeting place, they characterized the one they received as a storage room. Nonetheless, they moved in, decorated, and made it home.[17] The society's greatest undertaking was an annual Black Arts Festival but it also sponsored a Gospel Choir and other activities, especially social gatherings.[18]

The *Carolinian* offers a fascinating picture of changing race relations on campus during the civil rights revolution. Although black students first entered Woman's College in 1956, it took years for either the *Carolinian* or the *Alumnae News* to acknowledge their presence. The *Carolinian's* first mention came in April 1963, when some black students joined a larger number of white students to picket neighboring merchants who refused to serve blacks. Once the ice was broken, the paper gradually warmed to the subject, protesting the exclusion that fall of two black students from a biology field trip to the mountains because the place where the class stayed was segregated. A 1968 editorial went still farther, calling the university to task for the absence of black trustees, faculty, and clerical staff and for the neglect of black culture in the curriculum. By 1971 the *Carolinian* was devoting a regular column to the Neo-Black Society and its activities. When the society criticized that coverage as insufficient, the paper extended itself farther. It submitted, in fact, to considerable bullying from the society and its spokespersons.[19] So did student government in the view of many white students, including some sympathetic to blacks, who accepted this as a part of payback time.

All told, the Neo-Black Society was more sinned against than sinning. Efforts of the student legislature in 1973 to end its university funding provoked a major sit-in demonstration—of which more later.

* * *

More and more American college students combined their studies with full or part-time jobs; by 1979 the proportion was 51 percent. To some extent they were driven by a desire for the good life: better clothes, cars, electronic toys, and entertainment. But as Paul Loeb points out, economic pressures bore on almost everyone, especially the lower middle class who provided an ever-larger fraction of the college population. Both educational and living expenses rose during the inflation-ridden '60s and '70s. The proportion of students taking out loans to finance their education rose correspondingly.[20]

At UNCG, in-state tuition and fees rose from $400 in 1967 to $600 in 1978; at the same time, room and board charges almost doubled, from $665 to $1,298. Out-of-state tuition rose in that period from roughly double to quadruple the in-state rate, the largest increase coming in 1972.[21]

An important part of the institution's mission was always to help those applicants whose academic promise outstripped their financial resources. In 1964 Kathleen Hawkins was in charge of financial aid, as she had been since the 1920s. Her office consisted of a desk, her staff a student assistant, and her student records: a card file housed in something like a shoe box.[22] About 40 percent of all students received financial aid at that time and again in 1979, when enrollments, office, and personnel were much larger. This aid included loans and scholarships as well as the familiar campus jobs in the dining halls, library, science labs, and swimming pool.[23] The most prestigious awards were the Reynolds scholarships awarded annually, beginning in 1963 and opened to men in 1975. Even with foundation and federal government support, however, financial aid funds never met the need, causing the university to lose both qualified applicants and current students.[24]

* * *

WC students had been relatively content with the cafeteria food service introduced in the '50s. But complaints mounted as growing enrollments brought longer lines. In November 1963, nearly a hundred students protested delays in the conveyer mechanism that removed dirty dishes by leaving their trays on the floor.[25] Dissatisfaction extended to the choices and quality of food, and to the requirement that students pay a fixed charge for meals whether they ate all of them or not. The *Carolinian* in 1964 carried a comparative analysis of the food services at Chapel Hill and State, finding both of them superior to UNCG's. In response to this criticism the university gave up its own food service that summer and for the first time contracted with a national campus food service, ARA-Slater.[26]

The ARA relationship was not always happy. As early as December 1964, the firm precipitated a strike by its full-time black employees when it required them to perform the same work in less time or incur a pay cut. At 95 cents an hour, they received only a dime more than the minimum wage paid the part-time student workers. The latter divided, some backing the strikers and others not. Students also divided over whether the lines were as long and the food as bad as it had been the previous year. After a year's experience, a *Carolinian* editorial judged that ARA was better than what it had replaced, but not good enough to be mandatory; students should have a choice where to eat.

The paper and student government would return to this argument in the future and the university continued to negotiate more flexible arrangements with ARA.[27] In 1975 the south dining hall was remodeled as a fast food restaurant. Hamburgers, hot dogs, and French fries were cooked to order. The place quickly filled to capacity, selling 300 pounds of hamburger and 650 pounds of French fries daily. The dining hall service that fall served a record 3,900 students, with the major remaining complaint being long lines. UNCG seems to have been in the vanguard with some of these changes; ARA often sent its sales representatives from other regions to view the operation.[28]

* * *

The infirmary too encountered the complications of rising enrollment. Despite staff increases, doctors and nurses were both overworked and—by the standards of the Greensboro medical community—underpaid. Students complained of shoddy treatment; a *Carolinian* editorial on the subject was entitled "The House of Ill Repute."[29]

Following the retirement of longtime physician Ruth Collings in 1963, the infirmary limped along for several years under transient leadership.[30] An outside consultant in 1970 urged the recruitment of younger personnel with competitive salaries and faculty status, so they would not feel like second-class citizens.[31] The situation turned around that year with the hiring of William McRae from UNC Chapel Hill as director.[32] McRae found the whole operation old-fashioned and tradition-bound; one of his first acts was to drop the name infirmary in favor of health center. Changing its focus from inpatient to outpatient care, McRae worked overtime to train the nurses in basic diagnosis and treatment beyond what they had done before. He created a pharmacy, buying medicines wholesale at state contract prices, then re-selling them to students at cost. He closed the infirmary kitchen, saying he could fly in catered meals from the Waldorf Astoria for less money than the kitchen was costing, and relied instead on the ARA food service a few hundred yards away. He also created a small student-manned ambulance service, converting a university-owned station wagon.

McRae found the doctors and nurses alike unprepared either professionally or psychologically to cope with the sexual revolution and the drug abuse that had come into full view on campus. Students, for their part, were afraid to come in for advice or treatment of such matters for fear of being reported to the authorities or their parents. In 1971, having approached the UNC Board of Governors and gotten no response, McRae began on his own responsibility to advertise and dispense advice on birth control and pregnancy. In doing so, he braved opposition from members of his own staff as well as possible sanctions from his superiors. (When the student legislature in 1967 considered a measure widely referred to as the "pill bill," asking the infirmary to dispense oral contraceptives, there had been a good deal of stir; Ferguson vetoed the idea and the legislature voted it down.)[33] But staff resistance to McRae's initiatives gradually disappeared (partly through resignation or retirement) and the administration proved supportive.

To deal with the many students who distrusted the health service and the establishment generally, McRae formed a student peer-group counseling service, recruiting and training its members. In one of the health service rooms they manned telephones all night long, seven nights a week, listening and giving out advice. They also fitted out a padded room with psychedelic lights where they talked down students who came in on bad trips.

In recruiting new doctors McRae was never able to offer salaries competitive with the private sector, but the university offered attractive fringe benefits. He was aided immeasurably by the emergence in these years of student health as a worthwhile career for young physicians. As a result, he could obtain the part-time or temporary services of third-year residents from Cone Hospital as well as senior medical students from Chapel Hill and Wake Forest.

All these changes increased the proportion of students using the health service and improved their attitudes toward it. Younger doctors also facilitated cooperation with the growing athletic activities on campus. By the 1980s, as medical expenses and insurance costs mounted nationally, McRae found persons who registered for only a single course at UNCG in order to use its health service, paying only the blanket student fee.

McRae's work was recognized beyond the campus. President Friday named him to head an all-university student health advisory committee. He developed immunization programs that were adopted on the other campuses, and he was a leader in formulating university-wide policies to deal with AIDS.[34]

Student counseling—academic, vocational, social, and psychological—was divided into separate parts after 1964. The fields had become too diverse and specialized to keep under a single umbrella. Academic advising was the province of the faculty and a separate office. A social and vocational counseling center opened in 1964; by 1977 it merged with a psychological counseling service and resided in the health center.[35]

* * *

An ancient campus institution—the laundry—disappeared in 1975 in the wake of student protests over the costs and quality of its service. To fill the void, washers and dryers were installed in each dorm—but not in sufficient quantity, causing further protests.[36] The university's main reluctance about closing the laundry was that it cost the jobs of black employees, only some of whom it could place elsewhere on campus.[37]

* * *

Elliott Hall was built as a student union in the 1950s when the enrollment was about 2,400. Even with a new wing in 1968 it could not accommodate all of the organizations and activities generated by an enrollment of 10,000, which the university approached in the mid-'70s. Many found other campus homes, therefore, even as the building was rechristened in 1974 the Elliott University Center.[38]

One EUC resident was the campus bookstore. Like the laundry it incurred student criticism for its monopoly status and high prices. (It helped only slightly to know that the store's $75,000 annual profit went to fund scholarships.) When students tried to generate competition by having the university share faculty textbook orders with the Daedalus, an off-campus bookstore, they encountered "the magnificent delaying tactics" of university business manager Henry Ferguson.[39] When they made plans in 1973 to open a cooperative campus bookstore of their own, the university pronounced it illegal. In the end, the bookstore continued to operate pretty much as it had, with its profits going to the all-too-small scholarship funds.[40]

Chapter 27

Student Life: The Protests

It will seem perverse to preface a chapter on student protest with a discussion of student apathy. But activism was limited to a minority—often a small minority—of the student body. This was true everywhere, in the 1960s as before and after.[1] Interspersed among the scenes of insurrection, student apathy was a source of perennial concern among faculty as well as student leaders. The *Carolinian* carried an almost constant stream of scathing letters and editorials on the subject. A long list of students wrote a letter in 1966 calling UNCG a "rather mediocre marriage mill," too concerned with trivial regulations and not enough with the burning issues of the day. An editorial of the same year (it could have been any year) proclaimed that everything done on campus was the work of a tiny minority of talented, motivated people; the rest belonged in a finishing school.[2] At least a few good students transferred away for this reason. Randolph Bulgin of the English department spoke for many faculty when he told the students in a 1965 *Carolinian* piece that the great majority of them were passive, quiet, and mouse-like—part of their tradition as southern women. He told them to rise above it.[3]

Jim Allen, newly installed as dean of students in 1971, said the problem was less apathy than a lack of common identity among a heterogeneous student body in a new university that was itself seeking identity. By 1976 he and others found a better sense of community; there was greater student participation in extracurricular affairs. But they conceded that students by then were less motivated politically. The time of confrontation was over. Those who continued to seek change did it within the system. For most, social concerns had given way to vocational concerns. So far as student government was involved, that translated to apathy.[4] The SGA elections of 1978 and 1979 attracted only about 10 percent of the electorate. A constitutional referendum brought out 5 percent. If it afforded any solace, the phenomenon was national. Not only were students on all campuses preoccupied with academic and personal concerns, adult commuting students were particularly so. And as the new Chancellor William Moran pointed out to the *Carolinian* in 1979, the transitory nature of student life tended always to doom long-range planning, no matter how well conceived.[5]

* * *

In 1963 the Student Government Association was not very different in composition, outlook, or process from what it had been in the 1930s. Such was emphatically not the case a decade and a half later, in the wake of coeducation, commuters, and the nationwide protest movements. The old political order was well described by *Carolinian* editor Gail Wright in a series of editorials in 1965, just as it took its final bows. Student interest in campus politics, she observed, was minimal until just before the annual spring elections. Just over half the student body voted that year. As campaign platforms were often nearly identical, elections were largely personality contests in which candidates drew on their previous friendships and associations. Dormitory affiliations were very important. Freshmen were always the largest class, with the greatest voting potential. As they were not apt to know the candidates well, they depended heavily on the advice of their house presidents. Successful candidates normally had to present at least the image of ladylike campaigning. "A winning candidate is often chosen because she has nicer eyes, prettier hair, or a greater speaking voice and stage presence than her opposition." It was the freshman vote that elected Nancye Baker as SGA president that year.[6]

In 1978, by contrast, the new president, Ralph Wilkerson, was not only a black male but a first-year transfer student from Rockingham Community College. He attributed his victory—in a 10 percent voter turnout—to strenuous campaigning on the issues.[7]

Coeducation, in fact, soon brought the predominance of male leadership that many had feared beforehand. Anthony Thompson broke the ice modestly in 1965 with election as vice president of the town students' association.[8] Jack Pinnix became editor of the *Carolinian* in 1968. Lindsay Lamson was elected as SGA president in 1970. Except for Robie McFarland in 1971, men held the top post every year thereafter into the 1980s. They did not seize power; they were voted in by an overwhelmingly female electorate. Sometimes there were not even any female candidates for president. Fairly or not, a *Carolinian* editorial asserted in 1975 that the student senate was dominated by men with the initiative to speak up and be influential while most of the women sat back and let their minds be made up for them. Subsequent Editor Pamela Blackburn lamented that "today's UNC-G co-ed" might actually be "less liberated . . . than her grandmother was." Administrators and alumnae who studied, even agonized over the matter could find no ready solution; repealing coeducation was not an option. Again, for whatever consolation it offered, the phenomenon was nationwide.[9]

* * *

The new order at UNCG as elsewhere came in the late '60s. It did not come all at once. Simultaneous with the 1965 campus elections, some 175 students marched downtown to hear a speech by a representative of the Polish communist government. They thereby protested (without violating) the legislature's speaker ban law, enacted in 1963 to prevent communists from speaking on state-owned campuses. (The legislature followed this up in 1965 with a law against disruptive sit-ins and demonstrations on campuses.)[10] This march represented only the second student "demonstration," following the Tate Street desegregation picketing of 1963. Elaine Burgess, who taught a sociology course on race relations in the late '60s, recalled the advent of an "exciting, yeasty time" in those years. After a few years, she added, the atmosphere deteriorated for a time in the '70s, with widespread name-calling and shotgun charges of racism. None of this matched in intensity the events getting national publicity at some campuses farther north and west. But in both timing and intensity UNCG was quite typical of most campuses around the country.[11]

If one had to assign the transition to a single year, it would be 1967. That year SGA sponsored a series of topical forums to which President Jane Ann Ward invited faculty attention and attendance. The forums took up such topics as black power, Vietnam, student drug use, urban unrest, and community involvement.[12] As it happened, the November symposium on black power generated so much controversy as to overshadow all the others. It featured several outside speakers, some of them at the cutting edge of militancy. City and state police were alerted by the advance publicity and took no chances. Elliott Hall, the scene of the event, was patrolled by plain-clothesmen who quietly turned away several members of the Ku Klux Klan. State highway patrolmen, for their part, arrested one of the panelists for driving without a license.[13] When it was over, James Ferguson stood up courageously to a barrage of off-campus criticism for permitting this event; in return he won the hearty applause of both faculty and students. Summarizing all of these activities, Ward acknowledged the novelty of many but reaffirmed withal SGA's continuing adherence to Harriet Elliott's theme of "responsible freedom."[14]

In keeping with that spirit Ferguson created a chancellor's cabinet consisting of administrators and student leaders, designed to amplify the lines of communication between them. To the same end he revived the office of dean of students, appointing to that post the popular Episcopal campus minister, Thomas J.C. Smyth.[15] Smyth and his successor Jim Allen were usually successful in communicating with students and keeping the bridges in good repair. With Ferguson they defused a number of episodes that could have proved costly with different leadership.[16]

On the night following Martin Luther King's assassination in April 1968, a group of students stormed the chancellor's residence. Ferguson answered the door, in his pajamas. Asking time only to get a bathrobe, he listened sympathetically as they poured out their anger and frustration.[17] A few weeks later, students staged a sit-in on the library lawn. Both student and faculty speakers protested racial injustice and the Vietnam war. The event was entirely peaceful.[18] When alumnae or others off campus wrote him to protest such demonstrations, Ferguson not only defended students' right to speak and assemble, he praised their restraint and sense of responsibility.[19]

But Ferguson was quite capable of rejecting student demands that he felt went too far. When SGA in 1968 formally requested the university no longer to proceed against students accused of sexual immorality, leaving such matters to the criminal courts, Ferguson objected firmly. That policy, he said, would conflict with his own clear responsibilities as defined by the board of trustees.[20]

* * *

Much of the student protest at UNCG aimed to repudiate the Woman's College past. It showed up primarily in the abolition of a host of student traditions, some going back to McIver's day. Not surprisingly, coeducation rang the death knell for the daisy chain, apparently fashioned for the last time in 1968. Following in short order and without fanfare came the concept of sister classes, class colors, class jackets, class rings, and the junior show.[21] Even Rat Day, which might have appealed as much to sophomoric boys as girls, seems to have disappeared in 1970.[22] Older alumnae may well have wept tears and uttered anathemas at the young bolsheviks who had taken over their college.

The most important casualty was class organization, which disappeared in 1970. Freshmen, sophomores, juniors, and seniors continued to exist for academic purposes, but they were no longer organized entities. This had come gradually. Alumnae Secretary Barbara Parrish noted in 1962 that class organization at WC was not as cohesive as formerly. That did not bode well for the Alumnae Association, which had traditionally functioned through class organization. Accordingly, her discomfiture was vast when the student legislature finally dropped the shoe in 1970.[23] Class government had certainly become moribund, but as the sponsor of the abolition motion made clear, it proceeded as much from a desire to repudiate Woman's College traditions as from a zeal for efficiency.[24]

Possibly the most outspoken rejection of the past was that of student Peter Hanley, who wrote the *Carolinian* in May 1968 to protest the erection of a memorial arch on the site of the former McIver house at College Avenue and Spring Garden Street. The arch would contain—for a time—the old college bell, dear to the memories of older alumnae. Hanley lamented bitterly that the lasting legacy of that academic year would not be sit-ins, building takeovers, or the black power forum, but rather "putting up an execrable and shoddy monument to the nonexistent glories of the past, Charlie McIver's goddam bell." In a year when students on other campuses were getting bloodied as they fought to speak the truth, he continued, those at UNCG "are erecting a monument to a man who is chiefly remembered for having said, 'Educate a woman, and you educate a family.'"[25]

* * *

The greatest test of administration-student relations came in March 1969, when the cafeteria workers went out on strike against ARA Slater, the food service provider on campus. That event followed similar actions on the campuses at Chapel Hill and A&T. Virtually all these workers were black and were by general agreement grossly underpaid. A strike on one campus easily spread to others; this was particularly true of A&T and UNCG, two miles apart. Some of the UNCG food service workers were in fact A&T students. At both Chapel Hill and A&T students supported the strikers, staging sit-ins or boycotts in their behalf.[26]

When UNCG workers launched their own strike on March 26, the Neo-Black society and sympathetic white students began picketing the dining hall and urging student support of the strike. On the 27th the student legislature passed a resolution of support. That evening some 750 students met in Cone Ballroom and agreed to boycott the cafeteria. They set up food lines in Elliott Hall. The SGA even appropriated funds, drawn from student activity fees, to hire a lawyer in behalf of the strikers. Conditions worsened over the weekend that followed. Student militants from A&T came over to join the action and tensions soon developed along racial lines. Although most students supported the strike, the blacks from both campuses were clearly the most militant. Relations between them and the predominantly white female SGA leadership became quite strained. On March 29, when it appeared that Slater was not negotiating in good faith, at least forty-five students went to the chancellor's residence, next-door to Elliott Hall, hoping to get him to put pressure on Slater. Ferguson was not in evidence but he told student leaders next day that he had no power over Slater and was legally obliged to remain neutral.

The crisis came to a head on the night of March 31 when a crowd of 500 (many of them A&T students) attended another rally in Cone Ballroom. The mood was tense. Before long the crowd moved to the Administration (Foust) Building, staged a march around campus, returned to Administration Building, and finally to Cone Ballroom again. Along the way more and more students joined the crowd, which by 9:30 had grown to 1,200. Back at Cone Ballroom, the meeting lasted into the early morning hours as SGA leaders struggled with A&T activists for control. One of the latter, Nelson Johnson, pushed for a march on the chancellor's residence, reportedly threatening to throw bricks at the house or even burn it down if Ferguson did not respond appropriately. SGA President Randi Bryant and other student leaders strongly opposed that proposal. Meanwhile Greensboro police had assembled outside, armed with tear gas, and there were reports that the governor might call out the National Guard. Thinking quickly, Bryant took it upon herself to say that she had just talked with the chancellor and gotten his promise to address the student body the next morning.

The meeting soon broke up and Bryant, along with Katherine Taylor and Presbyterian campus minister Jim Allen, made an urgent post-midnight phone call to Ferguson, asking him to honor her commitment. Already angry at earlier efforts to pressure him and having little additional to say, Ferguson was reluctant. But at length he relented and spent the few remaining hours thinking over what he could say. At the hastily-called convocation in Aycock Auditorium at 9:30 a.m., he repeated that the strike negotiations were in other hands and he had no authority to shape them. William Friday had no direct voice in the matter either, but he drove over from Chapel Hill that morning at Ferguson's request to offer at least moral support. Peaceful campus demonstrations continued.

In fact, Ferguson's obligation of neutrality had not prevented him from working behind the scenes to facilitate negotiations. The initial strike talks had stalled because Slater's local managers had no authority to make concessions and they refused to talk to Henry Frye, a Greensboro lawyer retained by the strikers and students. Frye was respected by moderates of both races locally, but was unknown in Philadelphia where Slater had its headquarters. (He had just entered the state legislature, the first African American elected to that body in the twentieth century; thirty years later he became chief justice of the state supreme court.) On the previous night, even as students demonstrated, Ferguson was on the phone to Philadelphia, telling Slater's top management who Henry Frye was and why it was essential to deal with him. Their response was to send a vice president who not only dealt with Frye but offered more favorable terms than the strikers themselves had originally demanded. The strike ended on April 2.

Ferguson deserved much of the credit he received for dampening down student outrage and ultimately facilitating negotiations. But there is something to be said for the position of the moderate student leaders that he should have intervened sooner than he did to push Slater into good faith negotiations. (As he eventually recognized, they themselves were walking a tightrope between the establishment and militants—many from A&T—who actively courted confrontation.) From their perspective Ferguson was clearly antagonized by the methods they employed, but pressure seemed to bring results. The full extent of their success became clear only later, when they learned of his telephone intervention with Slater. Why then did he make such a point in his Aycock speech the next morning of his powerlessness to intervene?

Students also believed the chancellor was too dependent for information and advice on Business Manager Henry Ferguson. Rightly or wrongly, Henry Ferguson was perceived to be in league with Slater throughout the strike; at one point they even hung him in effigy outside the Administration Building. Students were also quite critical of the general passivity of the faculty during the crisis. Apart from a few generalized expressions of sympathy, very little help was forthcoming from that quarter. Even Chancellor Ferguson's warmest defenders concede broadly that he made some mistakes in this crisis, but that he learned and benefited from them in later emergencies.[27]

There would be other incidents, though nothing quite matching the cafeteria strike. When an A&T student was shot and killed in May 1969, that campus erupted in violence, bringing out National Guardsmen. Coming so soon after the cafeteria strikes on both campuses, there was concern that the contagion might spread to UNCG. It did not, but guardsmen patrolled the UNCG campus for a time, while students (like the city generally) were placed under a nighttime curfew. Black students were even permitted to return to their homes temporarily.[28]

* * *

Peace demonstrations, on and off campus, became almost routine. But when anti-Vietnam activists sought to launch a moratorium in the fall of 1969 with classes suspended for one day, a student poll showed overwhelming opposition not only to the war but to a moratorium. Instead SGA sponsored special seminars and observances on the appointed day, October 15.[29]

Intensity picked up after the U.S. invasion of Cambodia and the ensuing Kent State shootings on May 4, 1970. Students at UNCG as all over the country passed resolutions and staged demonstrations. Music students put on a special performance of Benjamin Britten's War Requiem. When some students called for a boycott of classes to permit discussion of the recent events and their implications, Ferguson appointed a special faculty committee under historian Richard Bardolph to recommend a course of action. Its report, as adopted by the faculty council, permitted penalty-free student class absences and alternative ways to make up work missed in this period; but under orders from UNC headquarters and unlike some other institutions around the country, it provided no suspension of classes or final exams. In fact, class attendance during these days was almost normal.[30]

* * *

Nationally, the Student Power movement aimed to give students a greater voice in university governance. They emerged from this period with a distinctly greater voice but little actual control; administrators and faculty still determined the agenda and made most of the decisions. But they did so with a clearer knowledge of student opinion, based on vivid memories of the students' capacity to make themselves heard. The age of protest led almost everywhere to institutional changes providing student representation on faculty committees, and even on governing boards. (The latter rankled faculty members, who often got no such representation for themselves.) Student representation was spread across a broad spectrum of university affairs, some of it only minimally interesting to the students. Further, what is of interest in periods of white-hot reform activity may not remain so years or decades later. As a result, students did not always rush to enjoy in practice what they had marched or sat-in for in principle.[31]

Much the same was true of student participation in deciding the curriculum. This had traditionally been an area of faculty control. But student demands now brought greater curricular flexibility to many institutions.[32] Students sought first to achieve specific changes—greater choice among courses, more "relevant" offerings such as vocational courses and those dealing with blacks and women, and adoption of the pass/not pass system instead of letter grades. Secondly, some students demanded a major share in the decision process. Faculty members were seldom willing to share much power but many agreed there was a need for substantive changes.

At UNCG, students in 1968 formally requested representation on several faculty committees, ultimately including those on curriculum and academic policies. Ferguson's initial reaction was to allow student members, with voting privileges, on several appointive committees that indicated a readiness to receive them. In addition, the SGA president and vice president were invited to sit in on faculty council meetings. But those concessions did not satisfy. Perhaps the men were more aggressive. Incoming SGA President Lindsay Lamson hit the deck running in 1970, calling for a "thorough review of all university academic policies." The existing regulations, he declared, stifled student initiative and threatened the university with stagnation.[33] In his State of the Campus address in 1971, Lamson specifically embraced Student Power: "Students should be consulted on all decisions at every level of the university." And, he added, it should occur soon enough to let them "examine and criticize any policy *before* it is implemented."[34]

That did not happen. But a wider student membership on committees did come with the adoption of a new instrument of government in 1974. It provided a voting student membership on every faculty committee, including the academic cabinet, the large new faculty advisory body. There was nothing approaching a student majority on most committees, but students won a louder voice—to the degree they chose to use it.[35] When student leaders revisited the question a few years later, militancy had waned and the issue had little further resonance. Indeed, SGA was hard-put to staff the student positions open to them.

Student leaders around the state called for a comparable membership on the UNC board of trustees. It came in 1971, with membership accorded to the student government president from each campus.[36] When reconsolidation came in 1972, with separate boards for each campus, the student government president became a voting member of each.

As early as 1966, students were calling for curricular reform and better teaching. For a few years beginning in 1968, through an organization called SCORE (Student Committee Organized for Research and Evaluation) they sought to identify and reward good teaching. SCORE developed and distributed teaching evaluation questionnaires and offered its own award for distinguished teaching.[37]Even before his landslide victory in 1970, Lindsay Lamson pronounced the curriculum outdated and unfair to students. It should provide more student options along with more interdisciplinary programs.[38] The faculty acquiesced in the pass/not pass option in 1970, permitted students to withdraw from classes more easily in 1971, and went a long way to satisfy the other curricular demands in 1972. Although student input was the major ingredient in most of these changes, the faculty retained relatively firm control of the curriculum.

* * *

Under Lamson, the SGA adopted a new constitution, returning to a bicameral legislature and consolidating the student courts into one. But the issue did not captivate most students, only 2 percent of whom now participated in student government.[39] In 1973, after several years of lagging candidacies for the office of student marshal—long since become ceremonial ushers—the position was made appointive; only the chief marshal remained elective.[40] Even the 2 percent of student government activists were turned off by what they regarded as time wasted in personal posturing and discussion of trivial issues. In 1973 the residents of Hinshaw Dormitory even tried to secede from SGA.[41]

This problem too was nationwide; a number of institutions abolished student government altogether.[42] As Helen Lefkowitz Horowitz points out in her book *Campus Life*, students from less affluent backgrounds were vocationally oriented; they had little interest in student government, or in much of campus life. There were notable exceptions, but much the same was true of older students, those living off campus, and those holding down jobs—all of whom collectively came to comprise the vast majority of UNCG students in these years.[43]

* * *

The last major demonstration on campus, in 1973, was widely attributed to irresponsible behavior by members of the student senate. At UNCG as elsewhere, black students (represented here by the Neo-Black Society) were sometimes guilty of overreaching and gratuitous confrontation.[44] Some white students were resentful and pushed for the removal of NBS's campus funding. They argued that the society refused admittance to whites and was therefore in violation of the civil rights laws and the university's own anti-discrimination regulations. All or nearly all of the 145-odd NBS members at that time were in fact black and they clearly did not relish admitting whites. But there had been a few white members and the society, in order to avoid just such a loss of funding, carefully refrained from closing the door. The NBS found itself caught up in the seemingly insoluble dilemma that blacks have faced from the beginning of the civil rights movement. Seeking equality and acceptance in a majority-white society, they wanted at the same time to preserve their own identity and institutions. When an SGA committee ruled against the white complainants, they appealed to the student senate. That body, in a post-midnight closed session on the night of March 26–27, accepted the charges and voted to withdraw funding from the NBS.[45]

The news got out immediately and some NBS members stormed the meeting room—again Cone Ballroom—and physically assaulted members of the senate, sending one to a hospital emergency room. Less violent NBS adherents made the rounds of the dormitories, recruiting other black students. At about 2:30 a.m., a crowd gathered in front of the chancellor's residence. Once again he, in his bathrobe, invited some of them inside and heard them out. He promised to appoint a faculty review committee the next day. Students then began planning a sit-in at the Administration or Foust Building, to begin in the morning. Not all the protesters were black; some white students also felt the NBS had been treated unfairly. About 300 students gathered in front of Foust Building at 8 a.m. and then occupied the building. The operation was entirely peaceful. They remained until 5 p.m. and returned every morning for a total of four days, until the review committee made its report.

The committee, chaired by psychology professor Kendon Smith, consisted of two black and three white members. It met at once and heard representatives of both sides. On March 30 it reported, upholding the NBS and finding the senate guilty of serious procedural errors. Ferguson accepted that finding, as did the faculty generally. Dean of Students Jim Allen had advised the sit-in demonstrators to keep a narrow path open within the building, enabling employees to reach their offices and avoiding a violation of the 1965 state law against campus disruption.[46]

A number of students, including some SGA officials, were so unhappy with the decision that they appealed it to the board of trustees. Trustees normally confirm their chancellors' actions, but in June, after a hearing in which the student appellants were represented by counsel and the university was not—UNCG had no counsel of its own, and general administration sent none for this occasion—the trustees voted to remand the matter to the student senate for reconsideration. In the fall, after the NBS added some white members and agreed to new non-discrimination rules, its funding was restored.[47]

There remained a feeling among many white students that the NBS was given favored treatment—in its level of funding and its Elliott Hall headquarters. No matter that it was a former storage room, it was thought to exceed what other student organizations received. Tension over NBS funding broke up another senate meeting two years later in 1975, prompting the *Carolinian* to conclude that the problem ran deeper than a simple disagreement over funding; the campus had a real race relations problem.[48] Yet blacks were soon elected to a variety of SGA offices, beginning in 1975 with Donna Benson as attorney general and extending in 1978 to Ralph Wilkerson as SGA president.[49] (Benson would serve years later as a vice president of the UNC system.)

* * *

Although the vast majority of students paid no attention to student government, some of their leaders—echoing militants in other places—continued to push for an equal role with administrators and faculty in running the university. In 1975 SGA President Sean O'Kane himself accused several student senators of political grandstanding—a view shared by Jim Allen. One night in 1976, Ferguson, the vice chancellors, and the deans all met with the senate. In a sometimes rowdy meeting, they stayed up until 11:35 discussing a variety of student requests, including one to gain equal representation with the faculty on all university committees. (Nearly 100 students already served on such committees; it was frequently hard to recruit them and their attendance record was spotty.) Nothing was resolved that night but the students once more were impressed with Ferguson's willingness to hear them out.[50]

* * *

The most permanent changes in these years were also the most traditional. They went back to the Roaring Twenties. Like Julius Foust and each of his successors, James Ferguson faced a student body bent on ever-greater social and personal freedom. Like Foust, he had to retreat from the *mores* that had governed his own generation. And as always, the phenomenon was national if not global. The difference now was that the '60s and early '70s were an age of more general protest, bringing the virtual disappearance of *in loco parentis*. The retreat brought benefits to all. Those claimed for the students were obvious; for faculty members, as David Riesman points out, it meant freedom from unwelcome supervisory and chaperone duties.[51] For administrators—much like restaurant managers with the end of segregation—it brought even greater relief from a burdensome and occasionally dangerous police duty.

But when all was said and done, many students as well as faculty and administrators were repelled by the new anarchy. If the university was no longer a social arbiter, it still had the responsibility to provide personal security and an atmosphere conducive to study. Dormitory counselors were still necessary but under the new dispensation it became harder to find adults willing to take on that duty.[52]

The retreat from *in loco parentis* came as much from the new student diversity as from student rebellion. Male students traditionally received less oversight than female students. Adult students received only the most minimal parietal regulation even if they lived in the dormitories—as most did not. Even teenagers who commuted from home were primarily under the tutelage of their parents. By the process of elimination, revolt was left to the remaining minority of traditional students who lived on campus.[53]

At UNCG, life in the women's residence halls continued for a time virtually unchanged from WC days. Freshmen were still housed in separate dormitories; the other three classes were mixed together. Each hall had a resident woman counselor, of middle age or older, and the larger units had assistant counselors as well. When students began asking in the late '60s for younger and more "aware" counselors, younger women were gradually hired as they became available. Graduate students served frequently as assistant counselors, but they proved unsatisfactory in the top positions; having other responsibilities as students, they were not always available when needed.[54]

During the early '70s dormitory life became unfashionable and the occupancy rate by 1973 slipped down to 80 percent. The decline was attributed largely to flight from dormitory regulations, although these had largely disappeared by 1971; the comparative economy of off-campus housing was a major factor. In any event, the trend reversed; by 1980 the residence halls were again at capacity.[55]

* * *

The regulations in place in 1965 were themselves the survivors of the repeal campaigns of previous generations. In the new environment, even more receptive to change, they fell like tenpins between 1966 and 1972. One of the leaders in this crusade, beginning as a freshman, was the same Randi Bryant who as SGA president faced down the radicals in the cafeteria strike of 1969.[56]

First to go was the dress code. In 1966 Ferguson bowed to student requests to drop the code altogether, trusting them to maintain minimal standards on their own. Skirts, hitherto mandatory on campus, rapidly gave way to bermuda shorts and blue jeans. Not everybody was pleased with the change; reminiscent of their comparative dress codes in an earlier day, even the students at Greensboro College took to criticizing UNCG coeds for their scruffy appearance.[57]

Until 1969 the only alcohol consumed on campus was smuggled in. That year it was permitted in the privacy of students' rooms; by 1973 that restriction was lifted and beer and wine were being served at private functions in the dormitory lounges and Elliott Hall. One of those responsible for the change was Cheryl Callahan, then student president of Elliott Hall. By the time she returned as a student affairs administrator in the late '70s, student government was sponsoring beer blasts in the dormitory quadrangle.[58]

Drugs became a problem in the late '60s. The *Carolinian* reported the presence of marijuana in May 1968, with apparently minuscule student usage and only one case being reported to the administration.[59] A year later city police arrested half a dozen students for use. SGA launched a drug education program and established a special student court to deal with what was clearly a growing problem. The drug court in its first eight months, into 1970, heard eight cases ranging from marijuana possession to the sale of LSD. The health center launched its own counseling program in 1972, using student volunteers. The proportion of students actually doing drugs seems to have been small, with marijuana the drug of choice. Polling showed that UNCG students as a whole were somewhat stricter than the national average in advocating expulsion for students convicted of drug use.[60] Yet "pot parties" were not uncommon in at least the men's dorms. Two alumni recalled the smell of marijuana as so strong that one could almost get stoned walking down the hall.[61] The Residential College drew the greatest attention for drug use, if only because it sought most vigorously to root out the problem. Drug use continued through the '70s, although campus observers thought it had abated by 1976 when beer was permitted as the drug of choice.[62]

By no coincidence, the "hippie" culture invaded Tate Street at the same time. By 1967, street people were taking control of the area nearest to campus, intimidating shoppers and passersby. Students called it "Tate Ashbury." The grassy embankment in front of the music building was so appealing as a gathering place for counter-culture types that it came to be known as Hippie Hill. By 1970, complaints about unpleasant sights, doings, and language there led the university to plant the site with barberry bushes, which caused the offenders to move elsewhere. Then in 1971 motorcycle gangs—considerably more violent—began to congregate in front of next-door Taylor Theater, brandishing knives, throwing bottles, and shouting obscenities at passersby. The music building, with its practice facilities, had to close at night for security reasons. Both the city and the university launched police patrols of the area, leading the gangs also to leave. By 1972 the hippie presence on Tate Street was in decline but it took time for students and other customers to return in force. To project a more hospitable image, local merchants sponsored an arts festival there in 1974.[63]

Dormitory regulations were the issue of greatest concern to students. One of the most aggravating rules was that permitting student dormitory officers to inspect rooms at any time. The main purpose of these searches was to seek evidence of liquor or drug consumption. But inspectors took note of poor housekeeping as well. Students charged that blanket searches, without a specific objective, were a violation of their basic rights of privacy. These searches were abandoned in 1967.[64]

The next major target was the age-old closing hour and weekend restrictions. The great majority of students wanted these regulations reduced or abolished although a few valued them as a security blanket against unwanted male pressures. Most of these restrictions were phased out between 1967 and 1972.[65]

More controversial was the issue of visitation. The regulations governing male visitors in female dormitories had not changed materially from the days of Sue May Kirkland. Randi Bryant (soon to be SGA president) no doubt spoke for a majority in 1966 when she called for an open door to parties and visitors of either sex in student rooms at any time. That was largely realized in 1971 when dormitories were permitted to set their own visitation rules, subject to closing hours ranging from midnight on weeknights to 2 a.m. on Saturdays and Sundays. (UNCG, Ferguson informed interested outsiders, was the last UNC campus to make this concession.) Even that limitation was hardly observed in the men's dormitories. But there were at least a few students who found any regulation of this sort objectionable on principle. Anyone old enough to vote or to fight in the nation's wars, affirmed a *Carolinian* editorial in 1978, was old enough to determine his own sexual activity—subject only to a decent respect for the privacy of others.[66]

The final caveat was well taken. Some students began almost immediately to complain of nocturnal pandemonium in the dorms: parties, shouting in the hallways, and blaring radios, TVs, and stereos. Many girls were so immature, one complained, that they felt compelled to have a boy around in the evenings.[67] The university received an abundance of unwanted publicity in 1972 when a female student went public with complaints against her former roommate. The latter entertained her boyfriend in the room almost every day from noon until closing hours, and several nights a week asked her to leave for an hour so that they could be alone. Although the informant claimed later that the story was exaggerated, the *Charlotte News* stuck by its account. Dr. William McRae, director of the health center, reported at the same time that he was seeing two or three pregnant girls every week; he thought the number would surely be higher if he were not dispensing birth control pills to those most obviously in need. Most of these girls, he added, were fearful of notifying their parents and went out of state to have abortions. Two days after the story broke, passersby found hanging from the McIver statue a sign proclaiming: "Welcome to Sin City. Population: 5,000 pick-ups, 2,000 fags, and 1 virgin."[68]

With more and more students satisfied (if not sated) by the 1971 concessions, they defined campus policy with only slight modification for years to come.[69]

* * *

The honor system remained in place through the '60s, with student government as the enforcement agency. Many students continued to abide by it and resented both fellow students who violated it and faculty members who ignored it by proctoring their exams.[70] But the code had already begun to erode in the '50s where social offenses were concerned; the erosion continued, spreading to the academic side as the student body mushroomed in size and diversity. Reflecting the greater society of their time, students were less and less willing to report each other, especially for the violation of social regulations that they opposed anyway. By 1974 the SGA attorney general confessed that the honor code had broken down. Students did not deserve it any longer, she said, and should consider some alternative. The faculty withdrew its support of the code in 1975, also calling for a new look. A *Carolinian* editorial remarked that, barring a religious conversion, only proctoring would stop student cheaters. Nevertheless, a special faculty-student committee under chemistry professor Walter Puterbaugh labored for two years to produce a new code. In a referendum attracting only 6 percent of the student body it barely mustered the necessary two-thirds favorable vote. Like the old code, it was largely ignored by both students and faculty.[71]

* * *

Campus security was tested in this period as never before, but not primarily for the reasons that come first to mind—the student demonstrations. The occasional protest seems not to have phased the campus police and students did not complain of brutality or heavy-handedness. On the few occasions when a substantial police presence *was* felt to be needed, as with the cafeteria strike and the motorcycle gangs on Tate Street, it was primarily the city police who provided it.

The campus police by 1976 had grown to fifteen officers. As with campus forces around the country there was more and more emphasis on professional training, often in cooperation with the Greensboro police. Since 1963 campus police had had the power to make arrests.[72]

Their greatest challenge came from the university's rising enrollment and its changing academic and social policies. As early as 1966, the increase in evening classes brought demands for better lighting and more frequent campus patrolling at night—near the classroom buildings, the library, the dormitories, and the parking lots. The extension of open hours in the dormitories increased the need still further.[73] More and more girls were afraid to move around campus after dark without substantial escort. There were very few major crimes, but the number of threats, purse snatchings, and minor assaults rose alarmingly. When the student legislature issued a public call for immediate remedial action in December 1969, Ferguson promised more dormitory alarm systems, more campus lighting, and more campus policemen.[74] The rape of a student in 1973 in Peabody Park prompted still further security demands including one—long delayed—for a student escort service to accompany female students on or adjacent to campus at night.[75]

Chapter 28

Student Life: Traditions and the Alumnae/i

If campus life were to continue, new symbols and activities would have to replace those just discarded. Jim Lancaster, '72, who was active in student government and played a part in the demolition derby, soon came to regret much of the destruction. He was not alone; a measure of rehabilitation and substitution came in the 1980s. Meanwhile there was an emptiness, mitigated by a few survivals from the old order.

One was the Alma Mater song, going back to 1910. It survived by a hair; Lancaster recalled that by his own graduation, hardly any student on campus knew that UNCG had an Alma Mater, much less knew its words.[1] Efforts in 1967 and again in the early '80s to replace it with something more "relevant" to a modern coeducational university failed to produce a viable alternative. With only minor verbal changes, therefore, the anthem continued to spread its admonition of service into the new millenium. Printed in the student handbook, it is sung primarily at commencement and Founder's Day, when attendees can consult their printed programs for the words.[2]

The service ideal itself hung on, taking different forms. Golden Chain, the service honorary, survived the revolution and a chapter of Alpha Phi Omega, the national men's service fraternity, was organized in 1969. Its members made themselves useful in a variety of ways, from helping freshmen move into their dormitories on opening day to raising money for cancer research.

APO initiated two particular projects that left their mark on the campus. In 1970 it began the Christmas tradition of lining the campus walks and drives with luminaries, paper bags containing sand and lighted candles.[3] It also helped to save the McIver statue. Beginning in the late 1950s, WC students took to painting, clothing, otherwise decorating, and attaching signs to the statue, which then was located in front of the old McIver Building. Decorating the statue proved to be another institution that spanned the divide. In his new location in front of the library, Charlie (as students called him) became even more the campus bulletin board and graffiti capital. The senior class (while it lasted as an organized entity) annually painted him in its class color, thereby making him an honorary member of the class. Most of the decoration did no physical harm—the paints were usually watercolors—but the statue required periodic cleaning and it was the cleaning solution that took the greatest toll over the years.

Alpha Phi Omega came to the rescue in 1973 with the Rock, a 12.7-ton boulder imported from a quarry in nearby Jamestown. Placed conveniently between the dining halls and the dormitory quadrangle, the Rock served henceforth as Charlie's surrogate, repeatedly painted in every hue and bearing messages of every description. The operative rule was that every message was entitled to at least twenty-four hours before giving way to a successor. Charlie himself continued to receive occasional student decoration, but usually in the form of hats, glasses, or drapery leaving no mark. He received a complete physical rehabilitation in 1991 to mark the centennial.[4]

Students continued to serve the campus and community in a variety of ways. Some chose the Rock to stage charitable fund-raising campaigns. Some helped register voters and distribute campaign literature prior to an important bond referendum. Others participated in voluntary drug intervention programs or manned the campus security escort service.

New traditions did come in time, with the advent of larger size and new student interests. A progressively larger athletic program brought cheerleaders in 1967 and festive fall weekends, dubbed Falderal in 1974. By 1982 it had evolved into a full-blown homecoming.[5]

* * *

One of the great debates on campus from the '60s onward concerned the proper scope of the athletic program. In Woman's College days it was almost entirely intramural. Only in the college's last months, early in 1963, did it break decisively from that tradition, fielding an intercollegiate basketball team. That development came at a time of rising feminism, including much greater emphasis on women's sports. In that environment Woman's College would necessarily have continued to expand its intercollegiate program.[6]

Even with coeducation, the women's sports program expanded dramatically. By 1968 there were five varsity sports: field hockey, fencing, golf, tennis, and basketball. The basketball team won fourth place nationally in 1971 and the golf team captured the national title in 1973. By that time the women's athletic program was regarded as one of the best in the country. Unfortunately, as the competition for scarce funds grew in the '70s, some teams had to be eliminated.[7]

A men's athletic program was seen as one of the surest ways to encourage male enrollment. In 1965, a year after the first male undergraduates appeared on campus, UNCG hired Frank Pleasants to develop both intramural and extramural programs. The intercollegiate program started off with basketball, wrestling, tennis, golf, and cross country. Jim Swiggett, a successful area high school coach, came to coach basketball.[8]

In their first year of competition, 1967–68, the men adopted the name Spartans for their teams. The women soon signed on as well, particularly as the Spartan depicted in the new logo bore a striking resemblance to WC's old helmeted Minerva, retained on the UNCG seal. Whether intended or not, the similarity may have helped to bridge the generational and gender gaps.[9]

Given the much larger female student population from which to draw, it is not surprising that the established women's teams outplayed the early men's teams. (The men's first winning season in basketball came in 1979.) Yet it seems to have taken the advent of males to generate student excitement for the athletic program generally and to move the *Carolinian* beyond its hitherto perfunctory attention to sports. Its coverage now increased exponentially.[10] Intramurals, however, remained under the same blanket of silence that had prevailed since the '50s.

In 1968, the men's and women's intercollegiate programs were consolidated into a division of intercollegiate athletics in the department (soon school) of health, physical education, and recreation (HPER). The intramural program occupied a separate division of HPER.[11] Under this arrangement, athletics remained carefully subordinated to the academic program, in the tradition of Mary Channing Coleman and Ethel Martus. In 1968 the men joined the Dixie Intercollegiate Athletic Conference and with it the National Association of Intercollegiate Athletics (NAIA). In 1974 they moved over to Division III of the National Collegiate Athletic Association (NCAA). The women, meanwhile, affiliated in the early '70s with the new Association of Intercollegiate Athletics for Women (AIAW).[12] The cost of these expanding programs came as always from student fees, which were gradually raised from $4 a year in 1967 to $22 in 1978.

Serious controversy began to develop in the early '70s when student affairs Vice Chancellor Jim Allen and others, including leaders of the Greensboro business community, began pushing for athletic scholarships. They saw these subsidies as the surest way to build up the athletic program, generate a more inviting campus social atmosphere, especially for men, and polish the university's image in the community.[13] Athletic scholarships were multiplying around the country. As they did, UNCG increasingly lost its most promising athletic applicants, male and female; the teams suffered accordingly. The HPER faculty were divided on the issue, but most felt that scholarships would spell the end of HPER control over athletics and, with it, the program's academic orientation. That was also the view of Chancellor Ferguson and majorities of the general faculty and alumnae. They saw athletics as not only tangential to the university's educational purpose, but harmful to the degree that it threatened to divert already scarce funding from the academic program. All but the largest subsidized athletic programs around the country lost money. In 1975, at the recommendation of Ferguson and a special faculty/administrative task force he had appointed, the UNCG trustees voted down athletic scholarships.[14]

The trustees called for revisiting the question in five years; in fact it remained under perpetual discussion. In 1976 a group of Greensboro businessmen led by Mayor Jim Melvin offered the university $60,000 a year for four years to help subsidize the athletic program, particularly basketball. That was too little to underwrite a scholarship program; the remainder would still have to come from student fees. A random survey of 1,200 students in 1977 showed overwhelming favor for a greater athletic presence, including athletic scholarships in the abstract; but fewer than a third favored scholarships if they came out of increased student fees. *Carolinian* editor Peter Rutledge, conceding that his might be a minority view among students, wrote that school pride rested above all on academic standing; he would rather have an MBA from Harvard than from Carolina, he said, even if Carolina could beat Harvard in basketball. Heeding these sentiments, a faculty-student committee reaffirmed the previous recommendation, as did Ferguson. This time a majority of the trustees apparently did not agree, but decided to table the matter until a sunnier day.[15]

Both committees had called for measures to make the athletic program more visible without scholarships. To that end a number of changes were made in the late '70s. The number of teams was reduced, leading to termination of the highly successful women's field hockey and golf teams—sports carrying relatively small scholarship assistance nationwide. With money thereby released, plus higher student fees, the university in 1978 hired its first full-time coaches for men's and women's basketball. Early in 1979 Jim Melvin and others launched a Spartan Club fund-raising drive that netted a modest $2,300 to help keep these measures afloat.[16]

* * *

Seemingly defeated for the time being on athletic scholarships, Jim Allen turned to another possible means of enhancing the undergraduate experience: social fraternities and sororities. They appeared to be on the rise nationally in the '70s[17] and UNCG was one of the few universities in the state without them. This proposal was only a degree less controversial than athletic scholarships. Every campus administration since McIver's had regarded sororities as elitist, divisive, and irrelevant if not subversive of the institution's academic purpose. Many or most faculty and alumnae still held that view. So did the great majority of students who were surveyed on the question in 1965; some even took pride in their freedom from the party school atmosphere they associated with fraternities.[18] The main argument for fraternities now was that, like a strong athletic program, they would foster a campus environment hospitable to traditional college-age students, particularly men. Only with that kind of environment, argued Allen and others, could UNCG hope to compete for students with Chapel Hill, State, Duke, Wake Forest, and other leading campuses. He believed that the university was losing some of its best applicants—measured academically—because of a forbidding social climate. It took him almost as long to win this debate as the athletic one.

A faculty committee recommended against fraternities in 1975, but recurrent student interest prompted a second study in 1977–79. It found that 31 percent of the undergraduates would seriously consider joining a fraternity or sorority if they were available. That was enough to make the committee recommend their establishment for a trial period of five years. With some reluctance, both the faculty and trustees gave their approval to the plan late in 1979, after Ferguson had left office. The initial membership rush took place in 1980.[19]

* * *

The university seems to have stopped taking a religious census of its students after 1971. At that time, Methodists, Baptists, Presbyterians, and Episcopalians continued to lead the other denominations by a wide margin and maintained off-campus ministries. Catholics and Lutherans followed suit by 1975. Other denominational groups including the Jewish Hillel Society held services or conducted programs in Elliott Hall. The Inter-Faith Council continued to hold its annual Moravian candlelight service and love feast at Christmas.[20] Although two successive deans of students were drawn from the Episcopal and Presbyterian ministries in these years, the campus was undeniably more secular. This was especially true in the '60s; like other campuses it saw some revival of religious interest in the '70s.[21] Mandatory chapel was long gone and the ensuing mass meetings disappeared in the mid-1960s.

* * *

The *Carolinian* always suffered in some measure from the absence of a journalism program on campus. Students who were seriously interested in the field transferred away after the sophomore year, leaving the paper in the hands of a fledgling staff. Indeed the paper engendered so much controversy from sarcastic editorials and other improprieties that it narrowly escaped closure in 1964.[22] In 1967 *Cary* doubled its accustomed pace and began publishing twice a week. In 1970 it acquired the means to do its own printing and began carrying UPI coverage of state, national, and international affairs. The editor was elected every year by the student body, with the successful candidate often running unopposed. Successive editors urged that the position become appointive and that overworked staff members receive some financial compensation from advertising revenues—a frequent practice elsewhere.[23]

Undermining that demand was the paper's increasing flirtation with the counter culture. Chancellor Ferguson leaned over backward to avoid censorship. In 1971 he agreed with an off-campus critic that foul language had become all too common in the paper; indeed the editor that year had to face student impeachment charges on that ground. The remedy most often proposed by students, faculty, and administrators was a student media board with the power to appoint editors of the various student publications and to review, advise, and mediate but not censor their staffs. That was finally achieved in 1977.[24]

The paper had already improved markedly. In 1973 it began receiving first class ratings from the National Student Press Association.[25] The issue of salaries would not die, and at one point they were granted. When the student senate withdrew them in 1975, much of the *Cary* staff went out on strike and senators took over as strikebreakers. A student referendum overwhelmingly rejected salaries for all but the top student officials, but that included the *Carolinian* editor. In both 1978 and 1979, *Cary* was one of thirteen first-place winners in a national competition involving more than a hundred major college and university papers.[26]

The literary magazine *Coraddi* was particularly receptive to change. In the '60s it began to include more art work. In the '70s, according to a later admiring retrospective, it experimented with "bold color layouts, freeform verse and material in styles not yet accepted by literary circles" around the land.[27] The staff—all undergraduates—took pride in their product. Many prominent writers appeared in its pages, often when they were yet unknown. In 1967 the magazine took third place (among 131 entries) in the nation's first annual literary magazine contest.[28] Next year, partaking the spirit of the age, the *Coraddi* staff withdrew from the annual spring arts festival, refusing to accept the customary English department voice in the contents of that seasonal issue.[29] The quality of the magazine headed downhill, like the *Carolinian* seemingly finding bottom in 1971. That year the editor prepared a massive single-issue volume, estimated to cost $8,000. That plan, with other irregularities, led the student government finance board to shut down publication for the year.[30] (In a separate incident the editor gained national publicity by participating in a pop-art project—jumping nude into a large bowl of spaghetti.) The student-run arts festival also suspended. But in 1972–73, it and *Coraddi* were revived under less flamboyant management.[31]

* * *

Paradoxically, campus television production preceded a campus radio station by almost a decade. As early as 1925, President Foust applied unsuccessfully for a license to establish a campus education radio station. Later efforts failed for lack of money.[32] Not until 1964 did a campus station become reality. An FM station, it was assigned the call letters WUAG, standing for University At Greensboro. It used old equipment donated by local commercial stations, and with only ten watts of power it barely covered the city of Greensboro.[33]

WUAG's subsequent career was as problematic as its origin. On a number of occasions over the next decade it was forced to cut back its hours of operation or shut down altogether, apparently for budgetary reasons. It was at times an instructional facility, entailing supervision by drama/speech faculty. That caused some students—this was the '60s—to create in 1969 a purely student station, WEHL, located in Elliott Hall. WUAG re-emerged under student control in 1973. By 1977 it had a staff of sixty-five students and played music of every kind, from classical through jazz to bluegrass.[34]

* * *

Inter-society debating had been one of the highlights of student life in the Normal days. Interest died in the 1920s and efforts to revive it on an intercollegiate basis in succeeding decades proved shortlived. Too few students—and faculty—were interested.[35] The picture brightened during the '60s and '70s. A UNCG debate union was founded in 1964, with a modest $1,500 subsidy from the academic affairs budget. By 1969 some twenty students were involved and L. Dean Fadely was hired as a member of the drama/speech department, charged with developing a serious debate program.[36]

Despite a perennially razor-thin budget, the program was successful under Fadely's direction. In 1971 UNCG won first place in a 45-team tournament in Kentucky. It twice won the state championship in 1974 and 1975. Soon afterward, two UNCG debaters garnered a national championship. As successes mounted, both student government and the Alumni Association began subsidizing the team. But these sources were uncertain. When SGA withdrew its funding in 1976 the *Carolinian* protested, noting that the debaters were winning more consistently than any of the athletic teams. From first to last, the forensic effort skirted insolvency. Weary and disgusted, Fadely resigned as coach in 1978. Without him the program itself rapidly died.[37]

* * *

Student social life built on the foundations established in the 1950s when Elliott Hall came into being. It featured informal dances on Saturday nights and free movies on Friday and Sunday nights, with more elaborate dances or parties on special occasions like Christmas and Valentine's Day. For a time beginning in the mid-'60s, Elliott sponsored Saturday afternoon concerts by noted performers like Dione Warwick preceding the evening dance. All these events were heavily attended, as were dramatic productions in Taylor Theater. About a third of the students attended the continuing lecture and concert series, but the proportion was falling. A relic of the distant past survived into the '60s: Sunday and Tuesday afternoon teas for the dwindling numbers of students and faculty who chose to come. In addition to these campus-wide events, individual dormitories and the four classes (while they lasted) sponsored parties or mixers.[38]

Consolidated University Day, which brought busloads of Greensboro students to Chapel Hill or Raleigh at the time of the State/Carolina football game each fall, disappeared after 1965 as the original three campuses began to multiply. But students from the three campuses continued to commingle individually or by groups, as in inter-dormitory mixers. Thus large numbers of male students visited UNCG on weekends, somewhat balancing the girls who left.

As a result, the occasional reference to a suitcase campus whence students fled on weekends, seems overdrawn. Student attitudes were mixed. According to a 1972 survey by SCORE, the student polling organization, slightly over half of UNCG's residential or dormitory students admitted to leaving campus at least two weekends a month. Of those who left, half went home; another quarter went to visit boyfriends or girlfriends. Whatever that may say about campus life, almost 80 percent of those polled said they would recommend UNCG to high school seniors. When SCORE asked another residential sample in 1974 whether they considered UNCG a good school socially, 59 percent responded negatively; 8 percent said yes and 32 percent said sometimes. They approved the institution overwhelmingly on academic grounds and divided equally over whether they were glad to have come to it. A third survey, this time of incoming students in 1978, found that three-quarters of them were satisfied with UNCG's reputation for social activity. As the *Alumni News* pointed out that year, if the campus sometimes seemed deserted on weekends, it was because two-thirds of the students were now commuters.[39]

UNCG was no more exempt from campus fads than it was from campus protest. Most notable was the streaking phenomenon that swept American campuses early in 1974. The *Carolinian* kept its readers apprised of local developments. On one of the first occasions, some 20 streakers ran naked up and down College Avenue. A few nights later, 258 students (75–80 of them women) streaked through the dormitory quadrangle before a crowd of 1,000 to 1,500 cheering spectators. The total number of participants, the paper pointed out, exceeded the 209 who had streaked recently at Chapel Hill; more importantly, the number of women reportedly set a national record. They were urged on by a girl at a microphone on one of the balconies shouting, "We will never put UNC-G on the map unless more girls streak." The quadrangle event—billed as the First National Streaking Competition—was reportedly the best orchestrated of its kind in the state. Campus police intervened at one of the first events, but were overwhelmed by student bystanders determined to support the participants. The fad soon played out, but not before many students had convinced themselves that school spirit was truly alive at UNCG.[40]

Off campus, students continued to patronize the familiar haunts of earlier years. Next-door Tate Street was the chief place of concentration with its movie theater, grocery store, drug store, and several eating places. Many students were surely repelled by the drug scene there in the '70s, but there was no other shopping area within easy walking distance. Students continued to go downtown on occasion, to theaters, stores, and restaurants or cafeterias.[41] The Yum Yum ice cream and hot dog emporium also remained a favorite student hangout. Located at the corner of Spring Garden and Forest Streets since 1921, it moved across Spring Garden in 1974 to make room for the new Mossman administration building.[42]

* * *

The alumni soon came to reflect the new university's growth and diversity. By 1977, after only fourteen years, UNCG produced more graduates than the Normal/NCCW/WC had turned out from 1893 through 1963. The great majority of UNCG graduates, of course, were still female; nevertheless, the Alumnae Association adopted the spelling Alumni in 1964—but delayed applying it to the Alumnae House until 1972.

Relations between the university and the Alumni Association were increasingly clouded by the problems of dual sovereignty. In 1963, as the new university sought to launch its fund-raising activities, the alumni agreed to merge their own annual giving campaign into the larger effort. In return, the association was guaranteed a share of the proceeds for its own activities.[43] That arrangement worked reasonably well during the Singletary and Ferguson years, but there were strains. Although donors to the annual campaign were giving to the university, about 40 percent of the proceeds by 1972 were going to the Alumni Association. That irked the development office, while at the same time the association felt it was still underfunded and understaffed.[44]

Another point of contention was the Alumnae/i House. The Alumnae Association had been largely responsible for building the structure in the 1930s. It operated the building thereafter, sometimes making space available for student organizations and administrative offices. But the house belonged legally to the college/university, on whose land it stood and which regularly paid for its upkeep.[45] In 1965 Chancellor Singletary asked permission to move the chancellor's office temporarily from the old Administration (later Foust) Building to the Pecky Cypress Room in the ground floor of the Alumnae House. The association agreed and the move was made in 1966. But when the chancellor moved out nine years later (into the new Mossman Building) the development office took over the vacated space without any by-your-leave asked or received from the Alumni Association. Like the camel in the tent, it subsequently appropriated the entire ground floor.[46]

Publications were another point of friction. Alumnae Secretary Barbara Parrish had edited the *Alumnae News*, as she found time, until 1963. (In her last year as editor she found time to produce only one issue.) In 1964 the post went to Trudy Atkins, a journalist and MFA graduate of the writing program, who was simultaneously named editor of a new university newsletter. She was paid separately by the association and the university, and predictably it proved impossible to keep the two functions and lines of authority entirely separate.[47] The newsletter went to all alumni while the *Alumni News* went to those who contributed to the university financially. Under Atkins, the *News* returned to quarterly publication and won a national award in 1970 for its public affairs content.[48]

Barbara Parrish continued throughout this period to serve as the association's executive secretary and the university's alumni director. In the latter role she was required after 1962 to report to the director or vice chancellor for development—George Hamer and later Charles Patterson. That arrangement seemed to stamp the alumni as merely a branch of the university's fund raising effort—something even Hamer later regretted. The relationship gradually deteriorated in disputes over money allocation and the proper focus of association activities. In the process Parrish identified herself more and more with the association rather than the university. She tended to ignore Hamer and Patterson except in budgetary matters where their authority was clear. In 1979 the development office, for its part, abruptly moved the alumni records out of the Alumni House without prior notice, generating great anger. As early as 1970 Hamer had urged Ferguson to place the alumni office entirely under university jurisdiction. Ferguson recognized the overall problem but shrank from antagonizing the alumni by shaking up the current relationship. That action awaited his successor.[49]

Part VII
University of North Carolina at Greensboro, 1979–1994

Chapter 29

Administration, the Campus and Student Body

Taking office as chancellor in 1979 was William E. Moran, until now chancellor of the University of Michigan at Flint. The son of Irish immigrants, Moran went to Princeton on an NROTC scholarship, followed by twelve years progressing from the navy to the Harvard Business School, a New York consulting firm, and the Ph.D. program in business administration at the University of Michigan. Finally choosing a career in university administration, he spent five years at the State University of New York campus at Stony Brook working on budget and planning. In 1971, at age 38, he moved on to Flint as its first chancellor. Popular there, he orchestrated the building of a new campus that helped to revitalize the city's core.[1] Moran's fifteen-year span at UNCG was also a period of remarkable growth and achievement. Yet they were years of growing administration-faculty tension faintly reminiscent of the 1950s.

In some ways Moran seemed an ideal fit for UNCG. There was widespread agreement on campus that it too could use some rejuvenation and perhaps a more aggressive leadership style. On the academic side, Moran was a Princeton honors graduate in English with intellectual interests that included a love of poetry. But that was overshadowed in faculty perception by his business background and lack of classroom experience—limited to part-time teaching at Stony Brook and, earlier, at Northeastern University in Boston. After an acquaintance of several years, associates at UNCG characterized the chancellor as scholarly, intelligent, fair, and gentle; yet they judged him also to be distant, formal, reserved, and aloof. He was a detail man, quite ready to delegate tasks but never willing to sign off until he had digested everything personally. Concerned with style as well as substance, he edited every outgoing message that crossed his desk and rewrote more than a few. All this took time. He communicated constantly with the vice chancellors, but for deans, faculty, and students he was noticeably harder to reach than Ferguson, whose door had always been open.[2]

Moran was sensitive to these criticisms and went out of his way to schedule meetings with groups of students, faculty, and staff.[3] But these events tended to be scripted, somewhat formal, and were only partially successful. Moreover, his priorities, particularly in campus expansion, rejuvenation, and athletics seemed to confirm a business orientation that faculty found suspect; indeed he appeared most at ease with business leaders. He joined the boards of several money management companies affiliated with Greensboro's Jefferson-Pilot Life Insurance Company and served as well on the board of an investment firm in Pennsylvania.[4] Where Ferguson had shared faculty concerns and gave them primacy at the cost of physical upkeep, Moran lost popularity as he was forced to address the areas of neglect. As he seemed at times to enjoy the bureaucratic detail from which faculty members typically recoiled, he was unfairly blamed for much of the administrative growth that actually had taken place under Ferguson.

Bureaucratic growth was universal in American higher education—attributable to enrollment growth but also to government regulations and the strings attached to government money. Between 1975 and 1990, as college and university enrollments increased 10 percent, administrative positions rose by 42 percent. In the 1980s administrative budgets grew 26 percent faster than instructional budgets. At UNCG the faculty's percentage of the total workforce fell from 42.3 in 1987 to 37.9 in 1993.[5]

Here as elsewhere, growing layers of bureaucracy muted the faculty voice in university governance. To some degree, faculty members themselves were responsible, but the reasons were complex. Increasingly distracted by the pressure to excel and to publish in their chosen fields, they had less and less time to spend on committee meetings and the like. (In fact, university governance probably suffered more than the students from the imperative to publish or perish; faculty research, it is argued, sharpens teaching performance.) Attendance at faculty council meetings continued to fall. This withdrawal was seldom accompanied by a cheerful agreement to let the administrators fill the void. Like campus leaders everywhere, Moran was too often blamed unfairly for the loss of faculty voice.[6]

The number of vice chancellors was actually cut from six to five under Moran. Only one, Jim Allen in student affairs, remained throughout the period. The first to leave, in 1980, were Henry Ferguson in business affairs and Charles Hounshell, administration and planning. Ferguson's successor, Fred Drake, came from the University of Houston and quickly established a valuable rapport with both Moran and the faculty. One of Moran's early (and popular) moves was to establish an advisory faculty budget committee. Drake worked easily with the committee and won its respect. He remained in office throughout Moran's term. Hounshell's immediate successors, Lawrence Fincher and Richard L. (Skip) Moore, served shorter terms, Moore soon moving over to development. The administration and planning position passed in 1991 to political science head James Clotfelter. One of his assignments was to shore up UNCG's lagging support in the state legislature.[7]

Stanley Jones retired in 1983 as vice chancellor for academic affairs. His successor, Elisabeth Zinser, was recently dean of nursing at the University of North

Dakota. Personally charming but a micromanager whose energy and enthusiasm outpaced her political judgment, Zinser quickly polarized the faculty. She had hardly arrived when she ordered a comprehensive institutional self-study in order to identify the university's strengths, weaknesses, and future course.[8] This is a time-honored technique of new administrators to educate themselves and to raise faculty consciousness about the institution. The problem in this case was that it came hard on the heels of a similar time-consuming exercise required for the SACS re-accreditation of 1982. Zinser's new study generated open hostility among a faculty that already saw itself as overburdened with such chores. The end product, a thick treatise called *Quo Vadimus*, became an object of bitter satire. As opposition far outweighed support for the document, Moran ultimately shelved it.[9] Amid this controversy, Zinser sought career opportunities elsewhere. After a nationally publicized rebuff from the students of Gallaudet University, the institution for hearing-impaired in Washington, D.C., because she was not herself hearing-impaired she departed in 1989 to become president of the University of Idaho. Apart from faculty applause, her departure brought a marked relaxation of turf warfare that Moran had had to mediate between her and other vice chancellors and deans.[10]

Zinser's successor was graduate school Dean Donald V. DeRosa; in 1991 his title of vice chancellor for academic affairs was upgraded to provost. Reporting to him by 1992 were the deans of the college and the six professional schools, the dean of graduate studies, the library director, three associate and assistant provosts, and two program directors. DeRosa's accession was widely welcomed, though he like the chancellor was sometimes faulted for overlong decision-making.

DeRosa had come to campus after the 1984 retirement of John Kennedy, who served for twenty years as dean, then vice chancellor for graduate studies. With DeRosa's promotion, the graduate deanship passed in 1991 to archaeologist Brad Bartel from San Diego State University.

Also leaving in 1984, after a decade as vice chancellor for development, was Charles Patterson. His successor a year later was Bernard Keele of the University of Rochester. Keele quickly made enemies, particularly as he provoked warfare between the Moran administration and the Alumni Association. He left abruptly in 1989, to be replaced by Richard (Skip) Moore, a capable young administrator who had been working his way up through the ranks since arriving in 1984. One of Moore's new assignments—and accomplishments—was to make peace with the alumni.

Registrar Hoyt Price retired in 1987 after twenty-seven years on the job. His unflappable demeanor had won the plaudits of nearly everyone on campus. But the computerization of student records had been neglected. His successor, James Kaiser, an automation expert, set about that task. In 1990 the heretofore-separate administrative and academic computer centers were merged.[11]

Robert Miller stepped down in 1985 as dean of the college of arts and sciences—its only dean since its re-creation in 1969. (A capable and willing administrator, Miller went on to fill a variety of interim positions during the next decade and more.) His successor in the college, Joanne Creighton of Wayne State University, was both capable and innovative. She was also upwardly mobile, departing after five years for Wesleyan University and then the presidency of Mt. Holyoke College. The new dean of arts and sciences in 1990 was English department head Walter Beale.

* * *

Town-gown relations took many forms. The Community Forum of 1976–77 failed from lack of public interest and no doubt also from vocal opposition to campus expansion by the few who did attend. An annual Community Day, launched in 1979, also foundered for lack of public interest.[12] On the other hand, Greensboro residents attended concerts, lectures, and other events despite the parking problems that infuriated students and faculty; these problems were much less severe at night. Pressure by community leaders also helped propel the university toward subsidized athletics in the 1980s.[13] Yet neighbors were alienated by fireworks set off during night-time soccer games as well as disturbances of the peace at off-campus fraternity houses. Opposition to campus expansion gradually died out following major land annexations of the '70s; most of those in the university's path had already been displaced.

One avenue by which Moran reached out to the business community was a series of breakfasts inaugurated in 1984, in which fifty to sixty local businessmen, educators, and government officials listened to faculty members and others speak on topics of mutual interest.[14]

The benefits flowed in both directions. The Greensboro Chamber of Commerce estimated in 1982 that UNCG would spend nearly $9 million that year on goods and services. Its students at the same time would spend about $22 million on clothing, recreation, entertainment, and even automobiles, while off-campus students were expected to spend $16 million more on housing and living expenses. Returning alumni, parents, and other visitors (some 10,000 of them at commencement) would spend millions more at motels, restaurants, service stations, and stores. Moreover, the university helped lure new businesses to the city. All told, the chamber estimated that UNCG would bring some $80 million to the city directly that year. And applying a standard multiplier factor for generated dollars, it was expected to add $147 million altogether to the local economy. These numbers increased with the passing years.[15]

A vital result of Moran's political skills and ties to the business community was greater financial support, from the legislature as well as private donors.

UNCG won a substantial capital improvements appropriation in 1983 despite the Guilford County delegation's continued lack of seniority and political clout in Raleigh. It was owing in large measure to intense lobbying by Moran, former Mayor Jim Melvin, and local businessman Michael Fleming.[16]

Moran actively recruited business leaders for the board of trustees.[17] Under law, four of its members were appointed by the governor and eight by the UNC board of governors; both generally followed recommendations from the chancellor. In 1980 as again in 1990, women were equally represented on the UNCG board, in striking contrast with the other campuses. Blacks held two of the twelve positions in 1980 and one in 1990.[18] Three of the women, Ann Gaither, Katy Bell, and Betty Ervin, all alumnae, served as board chairman in this period—Gaither being the first female chair in the institution's history.

* * *

UNCG continued to struggle with its image. Its growing curricular and extracurricular outreach programs made the old motto, Service, almost as apt as it had been in McIver's day. But like faculty and administrators at metropolitan universities elsewhere, few were familiar with this term or initially attracted to it. Those in the liberal arts particularly clung stubbornly to the ideal of a traditional research university where the arts and sciences held center stage. Only a few, like Stanley Jones and education Professor Roland Nelson (himself a former president of Marshall University in West Virginia) called for this transition with any specificity.[19]

In fact, as Zachary Karabell has noted, it was the new metropolitan universities (along with the community colleges) who manned the front lines of academic change in these years. It was primarily they with their burgeoning enrollments who accommodated the revolution of higher expectations in American education. Jerome Ziegler has called the metropolitan universities the land-grant institutions of the twenty-first century.[20]

Although Moran agreed to have UNCG join the new Coalition of Urban and Metropolitan Universities in 1993,[21] he never identified UNCG specifically in those terms. Along with the faculty planning council he formed in 1980, he and the trustees followed Chancellor Ferguson in pushing for academic excellence within the traditional parameters. Their major concern regarding UNCG's mission was to achieve balance between graduate and undergraduate programs. The planning council in 1983 reaffirmed the centrality of the liberal arts and called for marketing the institution as "a university with a small college atmosphere." When the subject came up a decade later Moran warned against such "pieties" in mission statements, but there was little substantive change. The goal was still to move upward as soon as possible from doctoral to research university *a la*

Chapel Hill and State; general administration denied UNCG's request for that status in 1991.[22] It was not that Moran in any way begrudged community outreach; he advanced it.[23] But neither he nor most of the others in charge saw that activity as changing the university's mission or character.

Interestingly, Moran's departure in 1994 sparked more public debate over the institution's mission than it had seen in a generation. Two articulate department heads, Henry Levinson in religious studies and Shirl Hoffman in exercise and sport science, took this opportunity to advance quite different notions of where the university should head, championing the liberal arts and sciences in the one case and the professional programs in the other as the focal points of future development. Where Levinson urged more limited enrollment with higher admission standards to raise the university's academic standing, Hoffman called for a continued emphasis on professional training that had already, in his words, won national acclaim for UNCG. Neither begrudged the other's existence and both called for an expansion of community service, but the gap was wide. As Hoffman's view more nearly embraced the status quo, it carried an automatic advantage as the university faced the future.[24]

* * *

In the mid-1980s, spurred by signs that both the quantity and quality of student applicants were falling and by the perennial desire to increase male enrollments, the university embarked on a sustained campaign of image enhancement. Over the next several years it overhauled the university publications along with the logo, seal, and colors. In the logo, for convenience sake, the hyphen was dropped from the initials UNC-G. The seal, bearing a profile of the goddess Minerva (or Athena), dated back to Normal days with many variations and had been standardized in 1963; it was now adapted with little change for use by the UNCG Spartans. The colors of the Normal/NCCW/WC from the earliest days had been yellow or gold and white. There was no disposition now to abandon those, but merely to add a darker contrasting color, primarily for athletic uniforms. To that end Moran chose a dark blue that was in fact already in use by Spartan teams.[25] Closely related to this campaign were more substantive changes: the introduction of fraternities, sororities, and athletic scholarships.

* * *

Moran vastly increased the volume of institutional planning. In so doing he reflected current national trends as well as directives from UNC general administration and SACS, the regional accrediting agency.[26] In 1981, after two years' effort, he secured funds to hire a campus physical planner and appointed Robert Trotter to the post.[27] Meanwhile, he launched in 1980 a lengthy all-purpose planning effort that served also as the campus self-study required for the impending SACS reaccreditation. The report, embracing everything from academics to the physical plant, came out early in 1983 and served as a general guide during the remainder of the decade. (This was the predecessor of Elisabeth Zinser's massive additional study, sparking faculty revolt.) It led to a host of specialized studies in the following years—involving administrators primarily—concerning such matters as the physical plant, computing, parking, housing, security, alumni, athletics, student fees, enrollment, curriculum, minority students, and fund raising. Individual academic programs also came under study, a few at a time, involving the faculty.[28] These activities were relatively uncoordinated with each other; surprisingly, Moran resisted until 1992 the idea of an overall planning council to superintend such efforts.[29]

The seemingly perpetual self-study was a major contributor to the faculty apathy and alienation that marked the Moran years. To most of those outside the administrative circle, the process appeared both wasteful and fruitless; there seemed little to show for the substantial commitment of time and energy faculty members had taken from their own professional priorities in the classroom, library, and laboratory.[30] Indeed, Moran's correspondence lends some credence to the widespread perception that administration had become the university's *raison d'etre*, leaving the faculty and students to supporting roles.

* * *

In 1983 Moran hired the John C. Warnecke firm of Washington, D.C. to prepare a comprehensive campus plan, the first in a decade. It called for a mainly pedestrian campus, keeping vehicular traffic and parking at the perimeter. A number of campus streets were to be closed, but that proposal evoked vehement protest and was dropped.[31] In the late '90s a landscaped median was constructed along Spring Garden Street, providing students and other pedestrians better odds to survive the crossing.

The Warnecke plan also called for continued expansion to accommodate anticipated enrollment growth. In general, it accepted the previously drawn "natural boundaries" between Market Street and the Norfolk Southern Railroad on the north and south, and between Tate and Aycock Streets on the east and west. Expansion east of Tate Street—never seriously considered—was precluded by the creation there of a College Hill historic district. That left only the one-block-wide strip between McIver and Tate Streets on the east. Most expansion must still be channeled westward toward Aycock. That busy thoroughfare might eventually constitute as formidable an obstacle as Market Street, but not in the near term.

Despite Moran's repeated efforts to secure funding for purchase of the remaining forty acres within the "natural boundaries," he received money for only fifteen acres by the time he left office in 1994. The acquisition pattern, however slow, was clear enough that most of the remaining residents and businesses had reconciled themselves to the inevitable; nearly all residents were gone by 1994 but several businesses including the Yum Yum were still in place at the dawn of the new millenium.[32]

For the time being, most of the new land went into additional parking lots. In 1982 a student survey showed that parking was, by far, the aspect of UNCG most needing improvement.[33] The problem was largely resolved in the next several years, particularly with the appearance of new lots in the southwest quadrant along Oakland Avenue and Aycock Street. Their construction and maintenance came, as always, from parking fees. Students and faculty willing to pay the mounting fees ($150 per year by 1992) could almost always find a parking place now, followed by up to a five-minute walk.[34]

In the 1990s, these land-consuming lots began giving way to multi-tiered (and more expensive) parking decks. The first was opened in 1994 on Walker Avenue, a block west of the library, the second in 1997 on McIver Street, a block south of Market. Others were in the offing, as surface lots were needed for construction sites. Finally, for those administrators and faculty ready to pay still higher fees, reserved parking spaces appeared next to many campus buildings.[35]

* * *

Unquestionably, the physical plant had deteriorated during Chancellor Ferguson's last years. On Moran's arrival in 1979, he was struck by a pervasive shabbiness, outdoors and indoors.[36] Faculty, staff, and students agreed. The contrast between their own typically drab or crumbling surroundings and outdated equipment on the one hand and the glamorous new Mossman administration building on the other bred no little cynicism. The 1981 self-study found that "years of deferred maintenance and inadequate resources" had resulted in "severe problems."[37] A 1988 state facilities study declared that 34 percent of UNCG's buildings required either "complete replacement, major renovation, or demolition;" an additional 60.5 percent required some degree of renovation, leaving only 5.5 percent in satisfactory condition.[38] Righting these conditions clearly had to be a top priority. They did improve but only gradually, owing to the same budgetary constraints that had hobbled Ferguson.

Paradoxically, the 1988 appraisal came in the midst of a construction boom such as the campus had not seen in years. Apart from the new business and economics building that came into service early in 1980, most of the projects involved non-academic facilities and were financed through student fees, parking fees, and private funding. The construction and repair of academic buildings, by contrast, required legislative appropriations. Although Moran fought hard for these funds they came very slowly.[39] UNCG still ranked low in a legislature populated by Chapel Hill and State graduates who even voted state money for sports arenas at more favored institutions.[40] Ironically, the very progress Moran made on the non-academic front merely confirmed faculty conceptions of him as a corporate executive whose values were not academic. His greatest public relations failure may have lain in not sufficiently communicating the state's arcane budgetary and political constraints to the faculty and students.

The improvements that were realized took many forms. Campus landscaping improved tremendously, with small shrubbery and flower beds appearing all over campus in places that had been wastelands. Peabody Park, whittled away to about twenty acres, remained an eyesore, however, except as student groups sporadically turned their attention to cleaning it up. They sought vociferously to protect the park from further development, threatened in the forms of a new music building and parking lot, both adjacent to Market Street. They defeated the parking lot but not the music building.[41]

The most striking landscape development, in which Moran took great pride, was a terraced plaza with a fountain on the slope behind the dining halls where the Woman's and Kirkland Dormitories once had stood. The project involved closing a block of Gray Drive, thus discouraging some of the cross-campus vehicular traffic. Completed in 1991, the plaza provided an attractive meeting place in the heart of campus. The Rock (the student graffiti center) lay nearby as did a new seventeen-foot clock tower presented by the Class of 1941.[42]

The dining halls themselves underwent a massive renovation, completed in 1988, with modernistic entrance facades on both the College Avenue and plaza sides. From the plaza, one entered through a two-story atrium with large tropical plants into a combination fast-food court and student post office. A stairway led to two cafeterias on the second floor—all replacing the four old dining halls that occupied the same space.[43]

New buildings included a large physical activities complex and a student recreation center, next door to each other on Walker Avenue. The physical activities building, completed in 1989, combined and added to the existing Rosenthal and Coleman Gymnasiums; they had long since failed to serve adequately the growing coeducational student body.[44] The recreation center opened in 1992, embracing among other things an indoor jogging track, gymnasium, and racquetball courts. To make room for it its early predecessor, the 1930s log cabin, was sold and moved off campus.[45]

Another casualty from the '30s was the nine-hole golf course. Virtually abandoned in the '40s to make way for a campus lake, then resurrected in the '50s, it now gave way to still newer priorities. There had long been a shortage of playing fields. The university began using off-campus facilities in 1978 but found them unsuitable. Two of the new priorities were therefore soccer and baseball stadiums.[46] The soccer stadium came in 1991, just as UNCG entered Division I athletics. Although some students objected to this use of student fees, there was an overflow crowd for the first game. The baseball stadium, planned since 1993, followed six years later on recently acquired property across Walker Avenue. As to the golf course, it was reduced by 1998 to a 150-yard fairway, two greens, and a bunker. Unlike the soccer and baseball teams, UNCG golfers played off campus.[47]

Another building need was office space to accommodate the growing bureaucracy. Like some of the athletes, administrators began working in leased quarters off campus. This reached major proportions in 1993 with the lease of a large building on Market and Tate Streets. It soon housed university offices to which students seldom came, such as personnel and development.[48]

The university also negotiated a complex building deal with six of the campus ministries—Baptist, Methodist, Lutheran, Presbyterian, Jewish, and Catholic. They surrendered their present buildings, most of them now engulfed by the spreading campus, in return for a space on which they could jointly construct a new building. The chosen spot was next to the planned parking deck on Walker Avenue; the structure was completed in 1994. Closely related to this question was the perplexing legal issue surrounding the chapel fund that Chancellor Jackson had begun amassing in 1942. By 1991 it had climbed in value to almost $800,000. The university was now debarred by law from using it for a chapel or any other religious purpose; nor could it give the money away, to the campus ministries or anyone else. The ultimate solution, in 1992, was to create a special meeting room (or *kiva* in southwestern Pueblo parlance) in a new University Center that was planned to expand if not replace Elliott Center. The *kiva* would be available for religious as well as secular meetings. Construction was well along by 2003, including the *kiva*.[49]

Besides the physical education complex, three other badly needed academic buildings were either completed or in motion at this time involving business, art, and music. Business will be mentioned shortly. Art and music had outgrown their quarters literally decades earlier. Both had seen their classes and faculty offices shunted into temporary spaces from one end of campus to the other. Now art, or at least the Weatherspoon Gallery, was served first. With the help of Greensboro philanthropists Benjamin and Anne Cone, a new building bearing their name was completed at the corner of Spring Garden and Tate Streets in 1989. Located on the site of Moore's Mineral Springs of yesteryear, construction was difficult and long delayed. Although the building admirably served its purpose, it quickly gained distinction as the homeliest building on campus. Essentially a rectangular brick box, it sported a tower or steeple at one corner that supposedly echoed the College Place Methodist Church across the street. A new music building was still in the planning stage when Moran departed in 1994.

Student housing was also a problem. In 1972 the great majority of resident students were reported as pleased with the upkeep of their dormitories. But when Moran came aboard in 1979, Jim Allen took him on a tour of the dorms that revealed disrepair and shabbiness at every hand.[50] Much of the damage—about $40,000 worth per year—resulted from student vandalism, usually alcohol or drug-related. It was a national phenomenon. Beginning in 1981, students were assessed individually for the damages they caused individually; collective assessments were levied when the culprits could not be identified. During the first year alone this policy brought the vandalism damage down to $5,000. By 1987, over $5 million was committed to dormitory repair and rehabilitation, with very positive results.[51]

Another solution to vandalism—one not wholly anticipated—was the advent of coed dormitories. Not only were women far less prone to vandalism but (it was found) their presence in a building had a civilizing effect on the males in residence. Besieged administrators surely found this a useful argument to advance when irate parents, legislators, and the general public stormed against coed dorms.[52]

Dormitory management was also complicated by the fact that more students (at UNCG and nationally) were choosing to live on campus; their motivation was the higher cost of living off campus, driven by inflation. As a result, the dorms filled and the university began losing qualified applicants who could not afford to live off campus.[53] The university came close to buying a defunct Ramada Inn across from Greensboro College for dormitory use. Instead private individuals bought the high-rise building and operated it as the University Inn for students of several institutions. UNCG welcomed it as an overflow dormitory and began a shuttle bus service to campus. By 1994, as inflation ebbed, nearby landlords were once again urging upon students the economies of off-campus living.[54]

There had been no dormitory construction on campus since the '60s, as commuters accounted for nearly all the subsequent enrollment growth. The next dormitory opened in 1993 at the corner of Spring Garden and Aycock Streets, on the western edge of campus; it was patterned architecturally after the Foust Building. Following the latest trend in residence hall construction, it was an apartment-style complex accommodating about 300 students.[55]

* * *

The late 1970s and early '80s were a period of severe belt tightening in American higher education—for public and private institutions alike. Several factors were responsible: double-digit inflation; the computer revolution with its attendant costs; slackening federal support together with mounting red tape surrounding what remained; and a falling birth rate since 1960 with consequent drops in enrollment.[56] The worst was over by the mid-'80s.[57]

Chancellor Moran arrived in the middle of the trough. North Carolina never slashed its higher education budget as deeply as some states, but retrenchment was the order of the day. In fact Moran was hit with a hiring freeze and a budget reversion on his arrival in 1979; there would be others.[58] By careful management he and Fred Drake saw that the cuts impacted the academic program as little as possible; support services bore most of the burden.[59]

These sporadic cuts only accentuated the longer and deeper funding problem. The revenues of each UNC campus fell into at least four categories, the first three of them depending on legislative appropriations. The first, salary support, varied according to an institution's mission (including the presence of expensive graduate programs), its enrollment, and its student/faculty ratio. In UNCG's case, that ratio (ranging from 14.1 to 15.1) was favorable, making its faculty salary scale reasonably competitive among institutions with relatively few doctoral programs.[60] The second category, the operations budget, covered nearly all other academic costs including physical upkeep; it was perennially the greatest problem area at UNCG. The third category, money for capital improvements such as land acquisition and new construction, also typically lagged. Only the fourth category, for residence halls, athletics, the student union, and other aspects of student life, was financed from student assessments. As already discussed, it was the area most nearly under local control.

Every campus in the system complained of underfunding—probably all of them with reason, given the times and the state's overpopulation of universities. Yet UNCG's claims were among the most pressing. Despite its doctoral mission and large graduate enrollment (second only to Chapel Hill) it ranked fourteenth of fifteen (omitting the School of the Arts) in per-pupil funding in 1977–78; in 1990 it was eleventh. Under the circumstances it was exceedingly difficult to maintain, much less upgrade academic buildings and the facilities within them. The antiquated heating system was kept alive for years on little more than prayer.[61] Moran was apparently the prime mover in getting the state to relax some of its rigid line-item budget restrictions for all UNC campuses, allowing them greater freedom to move appropriated funds from one purpose to another.[62] But his repeated entreaties for better academic and capital improvements funding bore little fruit. The resultant economies took many forms including the substitution of imitation parchment for sheepskin in undergraduate diplomas.[63]

Like his predecessors, Moran argued both in Chapel Hill and Raleigh that the institution had never received the funding appropriate to its status as a doctorate-granting university. As there were no comparable institutions in the UNC system (Chapel Hill and State being research universities, a step higher) he looked farther afield for convincing evidence. An investigation in 1987–90 identified and produced data on six institutions across the country with similar missions, though none really served a metropolitan area or qualified as a metropolitan university: Ball State (Indiana), Northern Illinois, Southern Mississippi, Miami (Ohio), William and Mary (Virginia), and the State University of New York at Binghamton—later replaced by the University of North Texas. Comparing UNCG's support with theirs, its shortfall was about $6.4 million per year. Once again, the deficiency arose from non-salary academic support (where UNCG fell at the bottom) as well as capital improvements money.[64]

Although that $6.4 million represented only a small part of UNCG's total operating revenues of $129 million in 1994, there could be no comprehensive solution without greater state appropriations. Unfortunately, the report appeared during a national economic recession in 1990 and 1991; there was little response to Moran's entreaties until after his departure. In 1995–96 the university even used some of its limited endowment income to pay for urgent repairs that should have come from state money.[65]

Only after a legislative study in 1996 confirmed UNCG's own peer review findings did lawmakers take note, voting an extra $4.5 million to UNCG for general funding and campus renovation, plus $2 million for capital improvements.[66] This was gratefully received but it was a one-shot appropriation. In 1999 another outside study called UNCG the neediest of the UNC campuses. It continued to exist within a skewed budget system—supported fairly adequately on the salary side, its new dormitory and athletic facilities financed by some of the highest student fees in the system, a dilapidated academic infrastructure financed by inadequate state funding, and new construction occurring thanks to successful state bond issues but well behind the university's needs.[67]

* * *

All this added urgency to private fund raising. Around the country as states lowered their levels of support, institutions responded with higher tuition and greater fund raising.[68] In fact, from the 1980s onward the new designation of traditionally public institutions was "public assisted" rather than "public supported."

In 1979–80 UNCG derived 54 percent of its revenues from state appropriations; by 1993–94 it was 45 percent. In both years most of the remainder came from student payments for tuition, fees, room, and board. Private gifts and investment income in 1979–80 amounted to about $1 million, or 2 per cent of total revenues; in 1993–94 it was $4,916,000 or 3.8 percent.[69] The dollar amount was about average for public institutions of its size. About one-third came from alumni, well over the national average, but corporate and foundation support was weak.[70]

Moran sought more. He launched two major fund-raising campaigns, in the early 1980s and again a decade later geared to the university's centennial. The first campaign raised $13.5 million, only $1 million of it from alumni. The great bulk came from the business community as a result of intense wooing by Moran and Vice Chancellor Charles Patterson. (Moran's Jefferson-Pilot board memberships seem to have been aimed directly at improving the university's fund-raising capacity in the corporate community.)[71] The centennial campaign was launched in 1992 with a target of $42 million. When it concluded in 1999 it had raised $55 million.[72]

In 1993–94, Moran's last year, in the midst of the centennial campaign, private gifts plus investment income totaled $5,385,000 or about 4 per cent of total revenues that year—far less than the national average. About 40 per cent of that came from alumni.[73]

Although several individuals in the Greensboro community gave substantial amounts of money in these campaigns and over the years, the prime donor was Joseph M. Bryan of the Jefferson Standard and Pilot Life Insurance companies. A man of great and varied philanthropies throughout the state, Bryan with his wife Kathleen began donating to Woman's College in 1960. Most of their WC/UNCG money went to the business school. In 1968 they endowed a chair in consumer economics that was awarded to Thomas J. Leary, a specialist in the field who was already on the faculty. Leary was a popular teacher whose classes were heavily elected.[74] Unknown to the Bryans he was also an outspoken liberal. In 1972 the *Greensboro Daily News* quoted Leary as calling for restrictions on private property in order to prevent a further maldistribution of wealth. A few days later he wrote a letter to the editor offhandedly referring to "the wealthy (and other tax evaders)." The Bryans were outraged and demanded that Leary be removed from the Bryan chair.[75] Chancellor Ferguson put them off and never mentioned the matter to Leary. But he did virtually everything else in his power to mollify the couple; she received an honorary degree in 1973 and he in 1979. The Bryan professorship remained a sensitive issue, however, apparently clouding all further approaches to them for money.[76]

Chancellor Moran arrived in 1979 and planned to solicit up to $5 million from Bryan in his new fundraising campaign. Informed of the Bryans' feelings about Leary, he removed Leary from the Bryan chair in 1982 with the acquiescence of business school Dean David Shelton and Vice Chancellor Stanley Jones. As before, Leary was neither informed of the reason for his losing the Bryan chair nor advised in any way to curb his public utterances; he suffered no penalty in rank or salary.[77] In 1983 Bryan gave the university $1 million and four years later the business school was named for him.[78] Another $5 million from his estate followed Bryan's death in 1995. His house in the posh Irving Park area of Greensboro soon became the chancellor's residence, replacing the house on campus.[79]

Moran inherited an endowment of about $3.5 million. With careful nurture and a rising market it climbed to over $42 million when he stepped down in 1994. By 2000, it was $112 million.[80] Broadly defined, the endowment consisted of three separate funds, the Endowment Fund, the Excellence Fund, and the Home Economics (later Human Environmental Sciences) Foundation; a Weatherspoon Art Foundation was added later. In 1992 they were reorganized as the University Investment Fund.[81] Meanwhile, in 1981 Moran formed an investment committee of six local businessmen and UNCG administrators to manage all the funds.[82]

Allocation of the income from these investments was governed to some extent by restrictions attached to each fund. Most of the Endowment Fund was earmarked for scholarships. Excellence Fund disbursements went mostly to faculty research grants and salary supplements for the endowed professorships; some were used as seed money to boost additional fund-raising; others helped finance the international studies program, new computer labs, and the move to Division I athletics.[83] The endowed faculty chairs grew both in number and complexity. By 1993 there were a dozen or so, defying any simple categorization or listing.[84]

* * *

Earlier predictions of falling college enrollments in the '80s based on a declining birth rate proved incorrect. Instead they rose owing to greater attendance by both traditional college age people and adults. In fact, the lion's share of growth nationally came from nontraditional students. Half of the increase were over 25 years old; 74 percent were women; 56 percent were part-time. By 1993, 38 percent of all college students were over 25; 56 percent were women; 61 percent had jobs; and 42 percent were attending part-time. Only one-fifth of the total fit the traditional profile: 18 to 22 years old, living on campus, and studying full-time. For many or most of the remainder, as Arthur Levine points out, college was secondary to work and family.[85]

UNCG generally conformed to the new profile. Despite small dips in the early '80s and again in the early '90s, total enrollment grew from 9,925 in 1979 to 12,094 in 1994—a gain of 22 percent. However, that increase was the product of significant qualitative tradeoffs and resultant agonizing along the way. Student demographics were not dramatically different from those established in the '70s. Chancellor Moran made male enrollment an early priority.[86] It did rise during his administration, but only from 30 to 36 percent. Part-time students continued to account for about one-third of the total enrollment—less than the national average. Graduate students comprised about a quarter of the total. UNCG continued to draw more than half of its students from Guilford and adjacent counties in North Carolina, but that dependence was diminishing, from 63 to 57 percent by 1994; just over one-third that year were from Guilford. The same proportion lived on campus.

A UNC system-wide study of 1988 graduates provided an interesting socioeconomic snapshot of the student body at each campus. Forty-seven percent of the UNCG grads were first-generation college graduates; the percentage at Chapel Hill was 24.6. Sixty-five percent of the UNCG grads came from families with incomes over $30,000; at Chapel Hill it was 84.5. Forty-three percent of the UNCG grads received financial aid while in school, compared with 33 percent at Chapel Hill. And 31 percent at UNCG had worked more than 21 hours a week while in school compared with only 11 percent at Chapel Hill.[87]

At UNCG transfer students ranged from a third to half of each fall's entering contingent; a third to half of them, in turn, came from the community colleges. By 1984 the number of transfers was so great that the senior class outnumbered the freshmen.

UNC officials in 1986 set a cap of 18 percent on out-of-state freshmen at each campus.[88] Despite the high out-of-state tuition, UNCG's freshmen class contained about that proportion each year thereafter. About half of these students came from Virginia, Maryland, Pennsylvania, New Jersey, and New York—owing in part to deliberate recruitment by admissions office staff and alumni. There were only 143 foreign students in 1994.[89]

UNCG launched a sustained enrollment management campaign in the '80s. Two of its goals were to expand male and black enrollments, as before. But the greatest and most nagging problems were to maintain total enrollment in a period of declining high school graduation rates in order to maintain state funding, and at the same time maintain or improve academic standards. Ill-prepared freshmen became a national phenomenon in the '70s and '80s; it was reflected in dropping SAT scores almost everywhere. At many institutions the temptation was all but irresistible to keep up enrollments by lowering admission standards. Once admitted, then, poorer students required more of the remedial work that colleges had largely forsworn as early as the 1920s.[90] Instead of openly listing remedial classes as in the 1890s, institutions offered extensive tutorial help, sometimes surreptitiously. They were most apt to provide it for minority and nontraditional students who showed promise but lacked the conventional academic credits. UNCG continued its earlier Special Services program for such students.[91]

Older students were another fairly distinct clientele. The university continued through the '80s to offer evening classes for students with daytime job or family commitments. But these efforts were spotty and the university found itself losing some of its evening "market share" to more aggressive local campuses like Guilford and High Point Colleges.[92] In 1992, the university inaugurated an Adult Continuing and Evening Student (ACES) program to accommodate non-traditional students. One of its purposes, increasingly achieved, was to let students complete all their undergraduate requirements to graduation through evening classes. From the spring of 1993 onward, over 300 such classes were available each semester.[93]

Until 1988, UNCG admitted over 85 percent of its applicants, thereby earning classification as "less competitive" in *Barron's Profiles of American Colleges.*[94] Much of the institution's image problem, in fact, sprang from the impression, shared widely by students, faculty, alumni, and the general public, that virtually everyone could get in.[95] Faculty members noticed a particular drop in the quality of some students by 1993, when admissions standards were lowered and the acceptance rate rose to almost 90 percent.[96]

Until that year, the minimum admission standards included a ranking in the top half of one's high school class, a combined verbal and math SAT score of at least 800, and a predicted grade point average (derived from the other two criteria) of 1.8. That last figure was lowered to 1.5 by 1993 in order to sustain enrollments and already-budgeted state appropriations; after faculty protest it was raised to 2.0 in 1994.[97]

Exceptions had always been made to the 800 minimum SAT score. For black applicants it was 700. Although both Chapel Hill and State had abolished the minimum score altogether, UNCG's faculty held back, seeing that action as a lowering of standards. UNCG finally abandoned its minimum scores in 1994 amid concerns that it could be charged legally with operating a dual racial system.[98] SAT scores remained an ingredient in the mix but high school performance was even more heavily weighted than before in determining the predicted grade point average.[99]

Nevertheless, SAT scores were the most easily measurable and comparable from one place to another. For UNCG (as also Chapel Hill and State) they had peaked in the late '60s, then sank until 1984 as enrollments rapidly mounted. There was now a determined effort to pull the SAT scores back up, even at the expense of curtailing enrollment growth.[100] A Century Scholarship program was devised in 1991 to attract students with scores above 1050; in its second year it attracted ninety students with an average score of 1124.[101]

It was particularly difficult to enhance black enrollment and SAT scores at the same time.[102] Black students on average scored significantly lower on these tests, yet once admitted their retention rates were about the same—sometimes better—than whites. Through intensive recruitment, aided in some measure by the lower SAT minimum for blacks, African-American enrollment grew from 10 percent of the total in 1979 to 12 percent in 1994. This was among the highest at the state's traditionally white campuses. From 1994 onward, UNCG continued actively to recruit black applicants but followed a race-blind selection process among all the applicants. Black enrollment continued to increase nonetheless, reaching 17 percent in 2001. This policy succeeded in part because of the university's relative lack of selectivity overall. At the more competitive institutions like Chapel Hill black/white disparity in qualifications and resultant lower black enrollments continued to be a problem.[103] But UNCG's success could be attributed to other factors as well. Greensboro boasted a growing black middle class that was sending its kids to college. Some of those parents saw UNCG as better academically and safer physically than A&T, the cross-town competition; and enrollment at UNCG by no means precluded social contacts at A&T.

By 1989, the average SAT score at UNCG was back to the 960 level; but in 1994, at 938, it ranked an unenviable seventh in the UNC system. (It remained, nevertheless, higher in most years than the national average.) Twenty-nine percent of the freshmen that year had been in the top fifth of their high school class, compared with 90 percent at Chapel Hill and 59 percent at State. As always at UNCG, the out-of-state students helped bring up the average.[104]

Chapter 30

The Faculty and Curriculum

UNCG could boast a well trained and stable faculty, the SACS accreditation team noted in 1993. Over half were tenured and about 45 percent had been at the university for ten years or longer. Among the full-time faculty, 76 percent held the doctorate or first professional degree.[1] The percentage of women among the full-time faculty rose from 36 to 43 in this period but they were still clustered disproportionately in the lower ranks and among the part-timers.[2]

Efforts to recruit women paled by comparison with the more difficult and less successful campaign to recruit black faculty. One of the greatest handicaps facing the few black faculty and staff members already on hand was the absence of the mutual support network that came with critical mass. Once they were numerous enough to organize in 1985, they set out to provide support for the black students as well. Initially, they almost outdid those students in the stridency of their demands for more aggressive faculty recruitment.[3] From Moran down, the administration and faculty shared these concerns and sought to address them. But earnest effort continued to bring only modest returns; African Americans reached only 3 percent of the full-time faculty during the early '90s. That disappointing outcome evoked anger and charges of bad faith on the part of minority faculty, staff, and students, as well as the Greensboro NAACP.[4] The fact remained that qualified blacks were in short supply everywhere and were gobbled up disproportionately by the institutions paying the highest salaries and those traditionally black.[5] For UNCG the bright spot remained the School of Nursing, where black faculty continued to be successfully recruited.[6]

Adjunct faculty—temporary and part-time teachers—were another story. In 1963 part-timers comprised a third of all faculty members nationally—a proportion that continued to rise. Some were mothers with children at home; some were off-campus professionals or business people; some were partially retired faculty; some were graduate students working toward doctorates; others already had them. For many of these people part-time work was all they desired or could handle, but a great many others—perhaps a majority—would have embraced full-time work joyfully had it been available. Universities had long resorted to part-time teachers when they needed to offer only one or two courses in a given area, or they faced emergencies resulting from sickness or an unexpected enrollment surge. But increasingly the practice became routine.

Part-time and temporary faculty are usually found in the lower ranks. They receive low salaries, few fringe benefits, and have no significant voice in governance or curriculum development. Their exploitation is encouraged by at least two factors: the persistent underfunding of higher education and the flood of new or expectant Ph.D.s into the market. Applicants consistently outnumber the available jobs in most fields; they need work and they are ripe for the picking. In turn, they depress the faculty labor market. As Zachary Karabell points out, part-timers and temporaries have become as vital to the economy of higher education as migrant workers are to agriculture. Everywhere college administrators join to create what is now a permanent underclass, both cheaper and more subject to the whims of management. In the nature of things, they lack even the flagging institutional loyalty of the research-oriented regulars above them. On the other hand, they are frequently superb teachers, especially at the freshman and sophomore level where most are concentrated. By 1993, part-time and temporary faculty including graduate student assistants accounted for 65 percent of the national total. A disproportionate share of those were found at community colleges and other two-year institutions, however.[7]

UNCG followed the trend. At its university debut in 1963 it listed only twenty part-time faculty, or 8 percent of the total; fourteen of them were women.[8] Thirty years later part-timers accounted for 16 percent of the total—a percentage distributed fairly evenly across campus. But they taught 24 percent of all undergraduate credit hours.[9] Another 10 percent or so were full-time, temporary appointees whose status was similar.[10]

* * *

Although faculty salaries at UNCG in the late 1970s were quite competitive nationally, they sank to embarrassing levels during the '80s and '90s. That resulted partly from lagging appropriations and partly from the university's precarious lodgment in the top rank of doctoral universities in the American Association of University Professors' annual salary grading program. If counted as a comprehensive university, the second rank, its salaries would have appeared competitive. In fact, UNCG salaries rose markedly in this period, behind only Chapel Hill and State within the UNC system, but they failed to keep pace with the national increase among doctoral universities.[11]

Several campus studies were made of salary differentials between male and female faculty. In each case they echoed earlier findings that the discrepancies were inconsistent and smaller than those reported for the nation as a whole. Women were still disadvantaged by their disproportionate presence in the lower ranks.[12]

No less interesting, a 1981 campus study found distinct differences in salary levels among the various disciplines. To no one's surprise it found the lowest salaries to be in the languages and humanities. Relative to them, faculty in the natural sciences were higher by about 2 percent, those in the social sciences, fine arts, and nursing by 8 percent, those in music and health/physical education/recreation by 11 percent, those in education and home economics by 13 percent, and those in business and economics by 23 percent.[13]

* * *

The faculty tenure regulations of 1994 were essentially those of the '70s. Good teaching and service were still rewarded more or less, but research and publication remained the pre-eminent criteria for promotion and tenure. Fifty-five percent of the full-time faculty enjoyed tenure in 1994.[14] Retirement regulations followed the changes in federal law. The automatic retirement at age 65 mandated in 1979 was raised to 70 in 1982, then was removed altogether in 1994.[15]

On a number of occasions Chancellor Moran demonstrated clear support of academic freedom and free speech on campus. In 1986 a new state obscenity law reportedly caused two faculty members to alter their course material, involving in one case a course devoted specifically to freedom of speech. The director of Elliott Center removed nude drawings from an art exhibit. Moran overruled that decision and, in the absence of any evidence that the statute was aimed at universities, encouraged faculty members to hold their ground. "Our faculty," he told the trustees, "like faculty in every good University, must decide for themselves what is needed in a particular course.... I do not plan to remove any books from circulation around here or pictures from the galleries in which they have been placed."[16]

Beginning in 1985, the university received a growing volume of complaints from animal rights advocates about experimental research on cats carried out by psychology Professor Walter Salinger. Moran saw these attacks as a threat not only to Salinger but to the university's research programs as a whole. He, Provost DeRosa, and members of the science departments spoke out repeatedly in Salinger's behalf. At the same time, Moran made sure that the university was adhering to all federal and state guidelines governing the use and care of animals. "The position of the University," he announced, "is that our faculty must decide research topics and how research will be conducted."[17] The protests spun on for several years, increasingly accompanied by threats of violence to Salinger and his family as well as the university. Ultimately he felt obliged to give up this aspect of his research.[18]

In 1994, by invitation of a student group, black Muslim leader Khalid Abdul Muhammad was scheduled to speak in Aycock Auditorium. Some weeks earlier

Muhammad had spoken at a campus in New Jersey, making remarks deeply offensive to Jews, Catholics, gays, and others, and intimating that violence might be the only answer to racial discrimination in South Africa. His scheduled appearance at UNCG evoked loud protests. But Moran affirmed his right to come, however hateful his message, given the history of Aycock Auditorium as a place of public assemblage open to any group willing to pay for its use. Even if there were a legal means to prevent Muhammad's appearance, Moran argued, it would not be a good idea. Such restrictions had not worked at other campuses and those choosing to hear him had a right to do so. Muhammad did appear and the event passed without incident save for a venomous post-mortem meeting on campus a few days later.[19]

On other occasions Moran made unheralded defenses of individual faculty members whose research had evoked public criticism.[20] The only significant exception, as mentioned in the preceding chapter, was the taking away of Professor Thomas Leary's Bryan chair in economics in order to secure continued contributions from the Bryan family. Even that action, performed without any substantive penalty, could be defended as only a matter of form.

* * *

When the academic cabinet created in 1974 failed to evoke broader faculty interest or participation in campus governance, Moran encouraged another study of the problem in 1980–81. The faculty government committee under political scientist James Svara followed national trends in proposing to replace the cabinet with a stronger and more representative faculty senate. It also proposed to elevate the elective vice chairman of the faculty council into chairman, replacing the chancellor as presiding officer at faculty meetings. These changes were quite acceptable to Moran but they offended some of those who had fashioned the existing system, and were narrowly defeated.[21]

A decade later, in 1991, as attendance at both council and cabinet meetings dropped to new lows, the faculty adopted a new constitution finally providing for an elected senate of thirty-five members. It became the primary agency of faculty governance, theoretically subject to veto by the general faculty which normally met only twice a year. An elected faculty chair presided over both the senate and general faculty meetings. Based on faculty population, the combined professional schools and library staff held seventeen seats, the college of arts and sciences sixteen. Students lost the symbolic membership they had enjoyed in the academic cabinet.[22] The first senate chair was physics Professor C. Bob Clark.

From the beginning the senate took a much more active part than the cabinet had done. Moran and faculty leaders united in their praise of the new arrangement at the end of the first year.[23] But administrators had second thoughts by 1993 as the senate passed resolutions on a variety of subjects, often requiring extended administrative response. Some now questioned whether the senate had exceeded its powers. Relations continued downhill that year.[24]

* * *

Teaching loads continued to vary across campus, indeed from one department to another in the college of arts and sciences. For full-time, tenure-track faculty the closest to a standard remained three courses per semester, but temporary personnel in the lower ranks often taught four and many senior professors only two. Owing to this divergence, information on the subject was not shared widely, much less publicized on campus.[25]

It was campus service, not classroom performance, that suffered most from the drive for research and publication. Student organizations like the *Carolinian* repeatedly found this to be true as they approached faculty members—often in vain—to serve as their advisors.[26]

The encouragement to research took several forms apart from its priority in promotion and tenure decisions. To the Alumni Teaching Excellence awards, dating from 1963, were added Research Excellence awards in 1989. In each case an award was made to a junior and a senior faculty member each year.[27] Research assignments, the legally mandated equivalent of sabbaticals or research leaves, were still awarded on the basis of full pay for half a year or half pay for a full year. Twenty-three of these were awarded in 1979–80.[28]

Increasingly, government, corporate, and foundation research grants became the keys to professional advancement. They not only enhanced the university's reputation but were somewhat lucrative as well. Under law, UNCG and the state routinely kept 90 percent of the awards beyond the actual cost of the research activity in order to compensate themselves for the overhead costs involved in administering or hosting the projects. In fact, 10 percent of that surplus revenue went to the individual researchers, 15 to 30 percent (the proportions varied over time) to the state, and the remainder to the campus for a variety of academic purposes not necessarily related to research activity. Indeed, these overhead revenues helped significantly to compensate for UNCG's egregious underfunding by the state. The university had ample reason to promote grantsmanship.[29]

In 1979–80 UNCG faculty members won seventy-two grants worth $1,131,000. (This was less than a tenth the amount awarded to each of the two research campuses at Chapel Hill and Raleigh.)[30] Increasingly, the university drew on the proceeds of its fund-raising campaigns to award research grants of its own. Symbolizing this growing emphasis, the research services office in 1986 was enlarged, reorganized, and moved to new quarters in McIver Building.[31]

It took time for the new culture of grantsmanship to take hold, especially in disciplines where outside money had heretofore been scarce to nonexistent. Accordingly, administrators launched a selling campaign including grant-writing workshops.[32] The effort was successful enough that by 1993–94, UNCG faculty won 185 grants worth $16,505,000. The school of education under Dean Edward Uprichard was responsible for almost three-quarters of that total, however; arts and sciences accounted for nearly half of the remainder. As in most of these years, three-quarters of the total amount came from the federal government.[33] Among the UNC campuses, UNCG was sometimes third in the amounts of money awarded, but it was always far behind the two research universities.

* * *

For many or most faculty members, the center of research activity was the library. It was forced to economize even more than usual in these years of inflation (sometimes rampant), budget cutbacks, mounting enrollment, and multiplying graduate programs. Serials subscriptions were cut back at least twice, with faculty cooperation.[34] Nevertheless, the total holdings rose from 556,000 volumes in 1979 to 850,000 in 1994. (Neither figure included documents or microtext; adding these, the total came to 2,274,000 in 1994.)[35] Like other libraries, it looked increasingly at alternatives to the printed page, such as compact disks, for information acquisition and storage. To the dismay of many older faculty, the computer began to replace the card catalog in 1989.[36] Full-time librarians numbered only twenty-two (with forty-eight support staff members) in 1992—about half of the recommended national standard for an institution of its size. Jackson remained an excellent undergraduate library but the collection fell short in many of the fields with new graduate programs.[37] As department heads and administrators had learned, the winning strategy was usually to get the program first then ask for the necessary funds rather than *vice versa*.

University policy still forbade the dispersion of holdings into departmental libraries, owing to a lack of professional facilities or care outside Jackson Library. Contention over this issue centered as before in the school of music, which kept its own collection of scores and other materials in a basement room of the Brown music building that was subject to mold and water damage. The issue was not resolved until the completion of a new music building in 1999 that provided the necessary care and facilities.[38]

Although the university archives dated back to 1942, most administrators ignored the requirement that outdated records be deposited there in timely fashion. Fortunately the presidents' and chancellors' papers—by far the most important—were acquired and preserved virtually intact. From 1974 onward, beginning with the McIver papers, these records were organized and made available under the direction of special collections librarian Emilie Mills.[39] In 1981, without her knowledge, the physical plant sent at least twenty-three file drawers of old records from the Foust Building to the Greensboro landfill. No one could be sure what they contained, but they may well have included the last several years' minutes of Chancellor Jackson's advisory committee.[40]

After eighteen years as library director, James H. Thompson stepped down in 1988 in favor of full-time teaching in the history department, where he remained until retiring in 1994.[41] His successor was associate director Doris Hulbert, who had come from the University of Delaware in 1980.

* * *

As faculty and students came increasingly to rely on films, videotapes, and related technology, a Learning Resources Center was created in 1982 to better serve these needs. Unconnected to the library, it was located in the McNutt Building under the direction of Hugh Hagaman. Of all the underfunded agencies on campus, administrators regarded the LRC as the neediest. Escalating faculty demands for its services, including computer repair, repeatedly went unanswered for lack of personnel or equipment. Vice Chancellor Zinser in 1986 called the situation a "ticking bomb." The bomb never went off, in large measure because departments increasingly resorted to off-campus sources of supply and repair.[42]

Computer facilities suffered similarly. An outside consultant in 1981 pronounced the administrative computer fifteen years out of date.[43] That came a year after the advent of the first academic computer on campus—a VAX machine installed in the new business and economics building. Although many faculty continued to use the computer in the Research Triangle near Raleigh by remote access, the new VAX was quickly flooded with faculty and student users leading to long waits, limited use time, emergency deletion of files, and attendant outrage. Subsequent expansions in capacity never kept up with the rising demand.[44] Additional relief came soon with the advent of micro (later personal) computers. Several schools and departments led the way by 1982, financing small microcomputer laboratories on their own.[45] But these had drawbacks too, apart from installation costs. Not only were the machines incompatible with many others across campus, but departments lacked the money and expertise to service them.[46]

More and more persons called for a campus-wide computer network with centralized control and service, compatible hardware and software, and a cable network linking campus buildings. Progress began in 1985 with the naming of Administration and Planning Vice Chancellor Lawrence Fincher as coordinator and Richard L. (Skip) Moore in academic affairs as chief facilitator.[47] When

Fincher departed next year, Moore took his place. The administrative and academic computer centers were merged and placed under his general direction in 1990.[48] James Clotfelter took over in 1991. Computer capacity grew rapidly in the form of VAX upgrades and new micro labs, with academic and administrative users both benefiting. By 1993 most academic buildings were connected to the network and it was beginning to reach dormitories as well.[49] In the absence of adequate state funding, student computing like athletics came increasingly to be funded through student fees.[50] From this point onward the emphasis was on placing a computer on every faculty desk and within easy access of every student; that was achieved in the mid-'90s.[51]

* * *

Faculty members spent the decade of the 1980s debating the university's undergraduate general education requirements. Following the fashion of its time, the Kupferer plan of 1972 had permitted so many alternative courses to satisfy the general distribution requirements—ultimately there were more than 700 to choose from—that many of its original proponents drew back. In 1978 as in 1945, Harvard provided a new turning point in the evolution of general education, this time toward a more concentrated approach.[52] At UNCG under Dean Robert Miller the college of arts and sciences adopted a more restrictive program for its own majors in 1981. Vice Chancellor Stanley Jones had favored the older latitudinarian approach but with his retirement in 1983 the trend back to stricter requirements gained headway across campus.[53]

Controversy, sometimes intense, developed over the details; more than any issue in memory it tended to pit the arts and sciences faculty against those in the professional schools. From the arts and sciences perspective, the greatest threat came from professional school faculty like the dance professor who reportedly declared that her department was perfectly capable of teaching writing, history, physiology, and aesthetics, and thus should be allowed to offer courses providing distribution credit in those fields.[54] On the other side, many professional school faculty regarded the college (with half of the faculty and students) as trying to aggrandize itself at their expense. They also felt squeezed between the pressures for a continued strong general education requirement (with which many or most of them agreed) and increasingly stringent accreditation requirements from their respective professional associations; as a result their students had less and less opportunity to take free electives. This debate came to a head in April 1988 at a more fully attended faculty council meeting than most of those present had ever seen. Under the leadership of arts and sciences Dean Joanne Creighton, an all but unanimous college faculty pushed through a more structured distribution system involving participation by the schools but leaving the college in firm control.[55]

The new plan was fully implemented in 1991, a decade after the issue arose. Under the acronym AULER (All-University Liberal Arts Requirements) it raised the required minimum of liberal arts hours from thirty-six to forty-five. (That total was reduced if necessary to meet professional accreditation requirements.) These hours were distributed fairly evenly among ten disciplinary areas embracing all or nearly all departments in the college. The central purpose was to allow student choice among a limited number of courses designed in large measure for this purpose, rather than the "cafeteria" menu of 700 departmental courses that had evolved after 1972. In practice, the menu was now shortened to 200.[56] Fairly deep-seated divisions of faculty opinion remained, as displayed in the Levinson-Hoffman debate of 1994 over the university's future, but the AULER regulations were generally accepted and civility returned.[57]

Another national curricular reform of the '80s looked to provide more intensive training in writing. At UNCG the English department set up a writing center in 1985, designed ultimately to provide individualized guidance to students at any level in the college of arts and sciences. It became a mainstay of the writing across the curriculum program adopted by the college in 1989. Instructors in every department were encouraged to designate some of their courses as writing intensive and college majors were required to enroll in at least four of them before graduation.[58]

Still another product of the curricular counter-revolution of the 1980s was the revival of Western Civilization as a core course. Traditionally taught by historians as a history course and ignoring the emerging Third World of Asia, Africa, and Latin America, it encountered increasing opposition and died out in most places during the '70s.[59] It soon came back to life, at UNCG and elsewhere, through the interdisciplinary approach that had remained alive in fond imagination if not in practice. As resuscitated at UNCG in 1981, WCV was a multisectioned, team-taught course required of majors in the college and some of the schools. It retained history as the core ingredient but was coupled in each section with a faculty member from another discipline. The latter usually but not always came from the college.[60] For perhaps a decade the course worked extremely well, owing to dedicated instructors and cooperative department heads. But gradually it fell victim to the traditional problems of interdisciplinary programs. Outside of history, department heads gave it less and less favor either in assigning instructors or allowing them professional credit for their service in the course. As a result, potential instructors themselves were less and less willing to take time from their main teaching and research activities. The interdisciplinary approach to WCV was abandoned in the mid-'90s, leaving it once more essentially a history course with fewer sections, smaller enrollment, and correspondingly less relevance to the general education program.

Students had called for black studies courses since at least the early '70s. Amid evidence of faculty foot-dragging, the calls made little headway until student pressure mounted in 1983.[61] The response at that time, pushed strongly by arts and sciences Dean Robert Miller, was to create a black studies minor drawn primarily from eleven social science and humanities courses. These were added to in the next few years. After 1992 students could use black (by that time African American) studies courses to satisfy some of the distribution requirements for graduation.[62]

* * *

The honors program thrived in these years, with 140 students enrolled in 1993. Most of its alumni went on to graduate or professional schools. For several years beginning in 1992 the program produced its own journal, *Inquiry*, edited and written by student members.[63]

At the opposite end of the spectrum, the need for remedial work increased in company with the percentage of the population who now attended college. For UNCG it was back to Foust's day if not McIver's, except that a large proportion of the recipients were now black. The federally funded student services program continued to help those who showed academic promise but still needed help with college-level reading, writing, math, or study skills. This was a sensitive issue for an aspiring research university. But in addition to individual tutoring and counseling, it offered for those who needed them non-credit courses in algebra and basic writing as well as English as a second language.[64]

* * *

The consortium with A&T, Guilford Tech, and the four private colleges in Greensboro and High Point continued to function through this period. By 1993 Elon College was also a member. UNCG customarily received more students from the other institutions than it sent to them. The main attraction for UNCG students at A&T was still its ROTC program.[65]

The only troubling aspect of this relationship pertained to Guilford Technical Institute. Like every institution of higher education it aspired to higher status—in its case, beginning in 1981, to the level of a community college. One step toward that end was to have its students' transfer credits accepted toward graduation by the neighboring colleges and universities. UNCG had long accepted credits for college-level courses at Guilford Tech that were taught by instructors UNCG furnished or approved; these were regarded as UNCG extension courses. But more than A&T, the private colleges, or even the UNC board of governors, UNCG resisted accepting transfer credits for Guilford Tech's own courses. This led to a succession of uncomfortable consortium meetings until 1983, when Guilford Tech and others became community colleges.[66]

The new community colleges were not automatically equipped to offer college-level programs on their own, and for some time UNCG continued to negotiate the familiar extension agreements. But as Guilford and others in the vicinity developed two-year college-level programs culminating in the associate degree, UNCG increasingly negotiated agreements to facilitate the transfer of their graduates into specific major fields at UNCG. Many were part-time, fully employed students who in the early '90s fit well into the campus's new ACES program for non-traditional students; by 1993 it was enrolling nearly 800 students. UNCG had helped to pioneer these articulation agreements, and in 1997 the board of governors adopted a similar program for the entire UNC system.[67]

Relations with A&T were more tenuous. Many on that campus continued to fear a forced merger with UNCG resulting in the disappearance of their campus and careers. That fear was never fully understood or appreciated at UNCG, where there was little discussion and less sentiment for merger. It seems never to have been seriously contemplated in Chapel Hill, Raleigh, or Washington, and William Moran so reported when confronted with the issue in 1979 before he had even taken office. But such mergers were taking place in other southern states and the cloud continued to hover at A&T.[68]

As a result, intercampus cooperation was often difficult. At UNCG administrators and many campus units ranging from the library to the school of nursing continued to establish or maintain ties with their counterparts at A&T.[69] There were faculty and student exchanges in a number of departments. Pressure for programmatic collaboration continued to come from above. Hardly a new graduate program could be proposed in the '80s without considering a joint undertaking with A&T.[70] The joint master's program in social work was the single example of such collaboration and it took fourteen years to achieve.[71] A joint manuscript and oral history project on Greensboro civil rights history that would also have included the city of Greensboro died from lack of support at A&T despite endorsement by the mayor and the top administrators on both campuses. UNCG eventually conducted the oral history part of the project by itself.[72] In 1984 the board of governors authorized a joint math-science education center, to be established on the A&T campus. It too died from lack of cooperation by A&T.[73]

Despite these setbacks, leaders of the two universities in 1990 planned a more ambitious engineering and science research center. It failed for more complex reasons. The project became enmeshed in rivalries among the educational and business communities in Greensboro, Raleigh, and Winston-Salem as North Carolina State and Wake Forest Universities contemplated similar projects. There was also resentment among UNCG science faculty who felt that Moran and his fellow administrators had pushed the project without adequately consulting those who were expected to operate it. In the end, UNC President C.D. Spangler (William Friday's successor) agreed with the outside consultants who found that the project needed better-funded graduate programs in the sciences and engineering than either UNCG or A&T offered. Nor was there much interest at the state level in granting the two universities' urgent requests to fill those needs.[74]

Chapter 31

The College and Schools

Inadequate financial support, especially for the graduate programs, was obvious to every observer. Moran and other administrators who arrived in these years were immediately struck by it. So were the outside science consultants of 1992 and the visiting SACS accreditation team of 1993. The latter concluded that while the graduate faculty easily passed muster for reaccreditation, "many instructional facilities across campus remain... inadequate for a master's and doctoral level institution." [1]

The graduate program had initially been carried forward by state funds accompanying the rapid enrollment increases of the '60s and early '70s; that increase had slowed down.[2] Masters' programs were expanded and strengthened during the '80s and early '90s, but despite continued interest on campus no doctoral programs were added in the arts and sciences and only a few in the professional schools.[3] The number of doctoral degrees awarded annually in this period fluctuated between 49 and 83, and masters' degrees between 448 and 606. By the mid-'80s the school of education was conferring about half of the doctorates, down from earlier years.[4]

Moran was particularly concerned with the recruitment and funding of graduate students; he claimed to have nearly tripled that funding by 1985.[5] Yet stipends were still too low. Tuition waivers for outstanding out-of-state students remained grossly inadequate by national standards, especially after the legislature increased out-of-state tuition. As a result UNCG was often left with "students of convenience," who for personal reasons had to remain in the Greensboro area. Many of them were good students but as the science consultants remarked, that dependency was "not a good basis for building a graduate program."[6] As a matter of policy most of UNCG's waivers (107 in 1979–80, 139 in 1992–93) went to the schools and departments offering the doctorate.[7]

The graduate program defied easy categorization. In effect, UNCG developed at least two different "graduate schools" in these years. The first embraced many doctoral and some outstanding master's programs like creative writing that attracted students nationwide if not worldwide. The second embraced terminal master's programs like nursing and business administration that served and drew primarily from the surrounding region. The second accorded well with UNCG's metropolitan university status but it was often looked down on by faculty and administrators yearning for research university status. Complicating matters further, there were master's programs in the arts and sciences that, whatever their academic merits, led nowhere in particular, and finally the horde of "special students" referred to in an earlier chapter who for reasons of their own were taking graduate courses without any particular degree program in mind.[8]

* * *

At the undergraduate level, the '80s and early '90s saw a revival of student interest in the arts and sciences, measured both in upperclass enrollments and degrees conferred. Business administration and its near relatives remained strong but they lost the comparative edge they had enjoyed in the '70s. The most popular major in 1994, in terms of degrees awarded, was nursing, followed closely by English and psychology. Education, the old favorite, had fallen to fifth place.[9]

The campus plan of 1983 reaffirmed the primacy of the liberal arts.[10] Their campus home, the college of arts and sciences, claimed 359 faculty members in the fall of 1994, half of the campus total. All the more ironic that it claimed to be the most underfunded unit, with 33 percent less money on a cost-per-credit-hour basis than the campus average. As a result, said Dean Joanne Creighton in 1987, "we do not [presently] function as UNC's preeminent program in liberal studies, but rather, as a regional campus providing, for very many of our students, minimal rather than optimal, programs of liberal study." Creighton found on her arrival in 1985 that the college lacked cohesiveness; faculty now identified primarily with their own departments and disciplines. This was inevitable, and her stalwart efforts to create an *esprit de college* met only modest success. The problem of inadequate financing remained after her departure in 1990 and no doubt contributed to it.[11]

According to Creighton's successor Walter Beale, the sciences and mathematics were the least developed area in the college—perhaps partly a legacy of the Woman's College past. UNCG's transition to a comprehensive doctoral institution, he said, required stronger science and math programs especially as they helped to support existing graduate work in a number of professional fields. Outside consultants agreed, adding in no uncertain terms that existing programs required much better funding before new and more expensive doctorates were contemplated. Given such funding, they favored new programs first in the areas of existing strength—biology, psychology, and related professional programs such as nutrition. Armed with a modest influx of money by 1994, Beale and Provost DeRosa launched a science uplift program. A further recommendation by the consultants—a new science building—became one of the university's leading priorities.[12]

Although the science consultants recommended the institution of a Ph.D. in biology—a perennially deferred hope of many in the department and the administration—the necessary support was still not forthcoming. William Bates replaced the ailing Bruce Eberhart as department head in 1979; he gave way in 1988 to Robert Gatten.[13]

Psychology, with its Ph.D. well established, was clearly the star of the science departments. The Ph.D. clinical program ranked well in a 1983 national survey.[14] The department claimed to bring in a third to half of all the outside grants to UNCG.[15] But all was not rosy. Enrollments stabilized, as everywhere; that plus funding cuts and a change in leadership stalled the dynamism that had animated the department in the '70s. Robert Eason stepped down as head in 1980, to be replaced after two years by Gilbert Gottlieb, a noted developmental psychologist. He commuted from Raleigh several days a week and never fully engaged the department. Moreover, factionalism that had already developed along subdisciplinary lines became worse.[16] Gottlieb gave way in 1986 to Walter Salinger, one of the department's best-known scholars. Salinger received rare praise from a national review panel next year, both for his scholarship and leadership.[17] He gave up the headship in 1993 to another insider, Anthony DeCasper.

The chemistry and physics departments both suffered from inadequate quarters in the 1939 Petty science building. (Even those who knew that the building had been named for faculty pioneer Mary Petty were not above facetious remarks about the "petty sciences" housed within.) The science consultants of 1992 found the chemistry department too small and too lacking in research activity to mount a credible Ph.D. program.[18] The whole campus community was shocked to hear in 1981 of the suicide of chemistry head and faculty leader Walter Puterbaugh—only the most prominent of several chemistry department deaths in these years. Harvey Herman inherited the headship, to be replaced in 1990 by Michael Farona from the University of Akron.[19]

Physics was even smaller, numbering only seven members—of whom four had won campus teaching awards by 1993.[20] Francis McCormack and Gaylord Hageseth, both insiders, served as head during the Moran years. The department added a professional astronomer, Stephen Danford, in 1976, leading eventually to expansion of the departmental name to physics and astronomy. One of Danford's achievements, in company with A&T and Guilford College, was the opening in 1981 of the Three College Observatory, located in adjoining Alamance County. Students from Duke, Chapel Hill, and other regional institutions as well as the three sponsors came to see and use the 32-inch reflective telescope that, under ideal conditions, could detect a 40-watt light bulb in Chicago. In 1994 it was still the largest telescope in the state.[21]

The SACS visiting committee in 1983 characterized both chemistry and physics as "partially-endangered," owing largely to their size, funding, and obsolete facilities.[22] All the more reason for the university to place a new science building near the top of its capital improvements budget.

Mathematics, with over twenty-five members including part-timers, produced about thirty graduates each year and remained an important service department for majors in other fields. Richard Sher and, after 1986, Paul Duvall served as heads. By 1993 the department included three disciplines—mathematics, computer science, and statistics—with undergraduate majors in each and a master's degree in common. Computer science had been added in the '80s after fairly sharp debate as to whether it belonged in mathematics, the business school, or a separate department. A math doctorate remained under study after many years. In a departure from the norm elsewhere in the country the department offered a minor in statistics for doctoral candidates in other fields.[23]

* * *

Communications and theatre, the behemoth of the arts and sciences, consisted of four divisions, each with its own director. They were housed at different times in eight to eleven different buildings. Over this enterprise John Lee Jellicorse presided with great ability for fourteen years, until 1988. His successor, Robert Hansen, had come to campus two years earlier to head the theatre division.[24] With about 800 student majors each year, the department by 1985 offered four bachelor's degrees, each breaking down into two to seven sub-specialties. Its graduate program embraced three master's degrees—of arts, education, and fine arts—similarly bifurcated. The great majority of these degree tracks, with over 90 percent of the majors and graduates, were professional or pre-professional in character.

No surprise that the department unanimously persisted with each change in the college deanship to push for separate school status; it was already administered internally as a school. If that status had been formalized in 1983 its enrollment would have made it the second-largest school on campus, narrowly behind home economics and far outstripping music and nursing.[25] Like Dean Robert Miller before them, neither Joanne Creighton nor Walter Beale would countenance the idea—although Creighton approved the much smaller social work department's request to join home economics. On the other hand, Vice Chancellor Elisabeth Zinser pretty clearly favored the school proposal, regarding the issue as having campus-wide ramifications well beyond the "highly politicized" college under Creighton's leadership. (This came at the height of the campus *Quo Vadimus* debate, pitting the two on opposite sides.) When Creighton responded in kind, Moran ducked, calling for further study.[26] There the matter remained until 1994, by which time the department finally gave up on school status and accepted the alternative of dividing into separate departments. Ultimately there were five, three of them remaining in the college.[27]

Meanwhile, the theatre division, like the campus performing arts generally, experienced simultaneously growing artistic quality and falling box office support—from students, faculty, and the community alike. According to a 1988 study, season memberships had fallen from 1,600 in past years to 300. Although home television surely played a role, the decline also sprang from the explosion of competing community activities such as Greensboro's Community Theatre and Children's Theatre, the Greensboro Symphony, the Eastern Music Festival, and comparable programs in every field; there was even a Greensboro United Arts Council to promote them. As the 1988 study pointed out, UNCG faculty members had taken leading roles in these competing activities; now the university needed somehow to deal with the consequences.[28]

During each academic year the theatre division offered four major plays and a host of other offerings including children's plays and productions directed by MFA students. Music and dance cooperated in a number of these offerings. Each summer brought four repertory productions, offered first on campus and then—through the '80s—at the Parkway Playhouse in the mountains.[29] The playhouse had almost always run a deficit. When massive repairs, including asbestos removal, could no longer be postponed, the university in 1990 regretfully terminated once more its affiliation with the playhouse.[30]

* * *

The social science departments saw their financial and personnel growth level off after 1990, given the university's new priority of lifting up the natural sciences. Political science head David Olson, like John Jellicorse, predated the two-term headship rule and continued to hold the post until 1988.[31] His successor, James Clotfelter, was promoted to vice chancellor, giving way to Lee Bernick in 1991 and Charles Prysby in 1993; all three were insiders, originally recruited by Olson. Department members were actively involved in research—none more so than Olson, who became an authority on European parliamentary systems, particularly those of eastern Europe as the iron curtain collapsed.[32] In 1979 he played the leading role in establishing an interdisciplinary Center for Social Research and Human Services that did consulting work with area governments, schools, and other groups.[33]

Geography was one of the fastest-growing social science departments. By 1992 there were six full-time faculty members and 150 undergraduate majors. This growth occurred under John Hidore, who arrived as head in 1980 and his successor after 1987, John Rees.[34]

The program in social work, originally a part of sociology, achieved department status in 1980. It was a vocational program, and in 1987 received permission to leave the college and join the school of home economics.[35]

* * *

William Lane retired as head of the English department in 1981, to be succeeded in turn by Robert Stephens, Walter Beale (who left in 1990 to become dean of arts and sciences), and James Evans. The department continued to reach most students on campus by virtue of the mandatory freshman composition course, taught primarily by Ph.D. students. The doctoral program itself survived primarily by training people to teach just such courses. Its clientele consisted largely of regional English teachers.[36]

More visible nationally was the MFA in creative writing. Saved from extinction by a last-minute infusion of funds in the early 1980s, the program was rated by one authority in 1994 as fourth in the nation.[37] It was a two-year program with about five faculty members and twenty students involved at a given time. It sponsored a visiting writers program as well as the semi-annual *Greensboro Review*. Robert Watson, who had helped found the program, retired in 1987. Its chief star in the '90s, Fred Chappell, won over the years the Bollingen prize in poetry, UNC's O. Max Gardner award, and an endowed chair; in 1997 he became North Carolina's poet laureate.[38]

* * *

The art department remained largely studio-oriented; the great majority of its members were productive artists who exhibited regularly.[39] Joan Gregory was succeeded as department head by William Collins in 1985 and Kathryn Porter Aichele in 1990.

The department's greatest event by far in these years was completion of the new Weatherspoon Gallery building, named for local benefactors Benjamin and Anne Cone. They were relatives of the Baltimore Cone sisters whose gifts of art had provided the gallery an early boost in 1950. The building's siting and design both generated controversy. The department had always regarded the gallery as an integral part of its teaching program; as such it should be adjacent to the classrooms. Chancellor Moran, however, saw it primarily as a university entity that could serve as a visible gateway to the campus. He prevailed and the building was erected at the corner of Spring Garden and Tate—not far from the art department in McIver Building but on the other side of busy Spring Garden Street.[40]

Once the gallery and department were separated physically the next, even more contentious, step was to separate them administratively. Although the collection arguably had always belonged to the university, it now passed from the department-related Weatherspoon Gallery Association to a new Weatherspoon Arts Foundation answerable directly to the university trustees. By the same token, the gallery director in 1987 began reporting directly to the vice chancellor for academic affairs instead of the department head.[41] Ruth Beesch came as director, replacing Gilbert Carpenter, just as the new building neared completion in 1989. The collection continued to focus on twentieth-century American art.

* * *

In 1979 Dean Robert Miller raised—not for the first time in the institution's history—the possibility of merging the foreign language departments. The issue seemed timely at that point as all three department heads were about to leave office. Miller's reasons centered on the small size of classical civilization and German and Russian, and the operational and cost efficiencies he expected to arise from joining them both to romance languages. The proposal was no more popular this time around; the smaller departments fought it tooth and nail and again prevailed, with general support throughout the college.[42] Until the matter was resolved in 1983, each department remained under an acting head. Romance languages then passed successively into the care of Roch Smith and Mark Smith-Soto. German and Russian went to Robert P. Newton and, in 1991, Joachim Baer.

In the case of classical civilization the interregnum lasted longer as the department, with only three full-time members, had no sufficiently senior person to assume the role on a continuing basis. There was a succession of three acting heads, each the current or past head of another department. In 1986 the department changed its name to classical studies.[43] A year later Douglas Minyard was promoted to head. On his resignation in 1989 for health reasons, the chair rotated between the other two department members, Jeffrey Soles and Susan Shelmerdine. Soles was the department's most visible research scholar, gaining national publicity for his archaeological work unearthing the Minoan civilization in Crete.[44]

The university's international programs barely survived the underfunding and concomitant lack of student interest in the '70s and '80s. But they came back to life in the '90s with the growing general interest in globalization. An office of international programs was established in 1991, headed by Charles H. Lyons from Connecticut State University. Among other things, it soon increased vastly the number of students studying abroad.[45]

* * *

Ann P. Saab inherited the history headship in 1978 from longtime incumbent Richard Bardolph. She in turn gave way in 1984 to Allen Trelease and in 1992 to Steven Lawson from the University of South Florida, a specialist in American civil rights history. History remained a major service department, particularly through its leadership in the Western Civilization course. It was also the largest contributor to the continuing women's studies program although psychology,

English, and other departments also participated. Trelease raised again in 1989 the prospect of a history Ph.D., based on a widely-predicted shortage of college faculty members following the retirement of the large generation that had entered the profession in the '50s and '60s.[46] Although local administrators were again supportive, the proposal failed once more, owing now to the nation's increasing reliance on temporary and part-time faculty to fill vacancies; the expected market explosion never materialized.[47] William Link of the department led in creating the Greensboro civil rights oral history collection in the '80s, originally planned with A&T. As part of the UNCG centennial in 1991–92, he also assembled a university oral history collection of over 160 taped interviews—an invaluable source for this book.[48]

* * *

Women's studies experienced very lean years during the '80s, losing both budget and office space. It survived through the charity of the participating departments and the college of arts and sciences. Conditions improved in the early '90s with the creation and financial support of an outside Friends group. An undergraduate major came in 1991 and a full-time director, Katherine Mille, in 1992.[49]

The Residential College, like women's studies and the interdisciplinary programs in general, "ran on altruism," as a former director put it. It was commonly seen as a stepchild, even by departments that participated in it. Faculty participation was always in jeopardy owing to the well-grounded perception that RC service was a dubious road to professional advancement. Dean Robert Miller, in a real sense its founder, came close to shutting it down in 1981. Yet the RC was a great success in the estimation of its students and those faculty who took the plunge. Its alumni were disproportionately apt to achieve academic honors and to assume student leadership positions during their junior and senior years. They formed their own mini-alumni association and were more likely to stay in contact with each other after graduation. All this in time brought a measure of respect, even money. It became a model for other universities to study.[50]

Cornelia Strong College made its appearance on campus in 1994. Named for the Normal's early mathematics professor, it set up shop in newly renovated Moore/Strong Dormitory. Its avowed models were the undergraduate houses or colleges at Harvard and other campuses. Offering no courses of its own, it had no faculty and escaped RC's perennial headache of faculty recruitment and retention. Its students could remain in the mini-college all four years instead of RC's two. But it sought with some success to recreate the sense of community that had always been one of RC's main drawing cards.[51]

* * *

The school of business and economics continued for years to play catch-up as expanding enrollments outpaced resources. A year after the school moved into its new building in 1980, Dean David Shelton could still report that "only the faculty/student ratio meets even spartan standards for a quality program, and this ratio is growing worse." There was no money to repair, much less replace furniture and equipment when they wore out. If the school were a private business, he added, it would seek protection of the bankruptcy laws.[52] But the school's poverty did not prevent the American Assembly of Collegiate Schools of Business in 1982 from simultaneously accrediting all of its professional programs, graduate and undergraduate—a rare event.[53]

That done, Chancellor Moran stepped in and called for a new dean. In a 1983 press story he credited Shelton with doing "a super job" in his thirteen years at the school's helm; few if any disagreed. But Moran now thought it time for the school to "turn outward" and forge stronger ties with the business community. The need was apparently so urgent that it could not wait a year for the choosing of a permanent successor; business administration professor Robert S. Cline stepped in as acting dean during 1983–84. Shelton returned to teaching economics, remarking that "administration's not much fun these days."[54]

The shakeup may have been part of the university's ongoing courtship of Greensboro philanthropist Joseph M. Bryan. Shelton had often endorsed outside funding and even proposed to name the school for Bryan in return for a suitable donation, but he himself had been an "inside dean," as one admiring faculty member put it later, where the case now called increasingly for an "outside dean."[55] (Direct fund raising was not at issue; the development office was now insisting that it alone be responsible for campus fund raising.)[56] In any event, Bryan money was now forthcoming. Through the earnest efforts of Moran and development Vice Chancellor Charles Patterson, Bryan pledged $1 million in 1983, and the school was named for him in 1987.[57] Another $5 million came from Bryan's estate after his death in 1995.

The B&E faculty were temporarily at sea following Shelton's resignation. They were curious to know if Moran had some major change of direction in mind for the school.[58] In truth, he had none to suggest, lending weight to the suspicion that fund-raising imperatives had motivated the shakeup.

The new dean in 1984 was Philip Friedman from Boston University. In 1985 the school reorganized after a long study that had begun under Shelton. The changes reflected the rapid evolutionary growth of several of the disciplines. There were now five departments—accounting, economics, management and marketing, finance (including insurance), and information systems and operations management.[59] There was also a non-departmental division of business and marketing education, or teacher training, but that field was steadily shrinking (locally as nationally) while other areas such as business computing mushroomed.[60]

Friedman took Moran's cue about turning outward. He established a successful management development program that met on weekends and a dean's advisory committee of Greensboro business leaders. But it was not long before he too was calling attention to the state's low level of operational support. More than Shelton, he ran into internal opposition; some saw him as authoritarian, a perception that he attempted with some success to reverse.[61]

When only conditional reaccreditation came in 1988 it was attributed primarily to a lack of scholarly research in the professional departments. This rekindled longstanding academic differences between those departments and economics, where much if not most of the research activity was centered.[62] The research productivity of the economics faculty was great enough, at least quantitatively, that a 1984 study placed it second among all economics departments in the country not offering the Ph.D. The department had offered to initiate a doctorate in 1983 and again a decade later if additional faculty positions were forthcoming.[63] They were not and the program did not materialize.

Friedman hastened to repair the school's standing, partly by rewarding research activity as never before and partly by reducing so far as possible the school's reliance on adjunct faculty for whom teaching was subsidiary to outside careers. Full accreditation returned in 1989.[64]

Friedman departed in 1990 to become provost of Bentley College in Massachusetts. He was succeeded by Associate Dean James K. Weeks of the management department. The school by this time claimed about eighty faculty, with some 380 graduate and 2,200 undergraduate majors.[65] Although the fact of accreditation placed it among the upper 35 to 40 percent of business schools nationally, it (like UNCG as a whole) served primarily a regional or metropolitan clientele: 70 percent of its students lived in the Triad—the Greensboro, Winston-Salem, High Point area. Eighty percent of the MBA students were part-timers, drawn from the Triad business community. By the mid-'80s they represented more than 150 employers; the larger corporations like R.J. Reynolds, Western Electric, and Burlington Industries paid their employees' expenses.[66] A number of faculty members, particularly in management and accounting, served as consultants to regional businesses.

Dean Weeks, like his predecessors, was urged from above to initiate specialized doctoral programs that would attract national attention. Although he gave research activity a lower priority than did either Friedman or the campus administration, he did push internally for expanded graduate programs. And reflecting a growing concern by 1993 among business schools around the country with globalization, he pushed successfully for a greater international focus in its instruction, research, and outreach programs.[67]

Vital as these matters were for the school's future, they were rivaled if not overshadowed by renewed controversy over the role of economics and over

Weeks himself. The economics faculty in particular saw him as too little concerned with scholarly research and too eager to increase enrollments at the expense of academic standards. Nevertheless, a 1994 study of research productivity among economics departments showed that it continued to rise markedly under Weeks.[68] These disagreements climaxed in the fall of 1994, when the full professors of economics bluntly challenged Weeks's values and priorities as anti-economics and, in effect, anti-intellectual. This in turn reinforced the perception elsewhere in the school that the economists harbored a superiority complex. So Weeks was not alone when at an ensuing faculty meeting he angrily invited the economics department to leave the school, if not the university. That did not happen and the quarrel was papered over, but serious personal, philosophical, and programmatic differences remained.[69] When Chancellor Patricia Sullivan reappointed Weeks to a second term in 1996 over vocal opposition, a number of resignations and retirements followed—involving, as one faculty member put it facetiously, everyone who did not have binding family ties in Greensboro.

* * *

Student enrollment in the school of nursing had stopped growing by 1979 owing to limited opportunities for off-campus clinical training. Admission was necessarily selective, therefore, but not enough to please the state nursing board, who (in the process of reaccreditation) expressed concern in 1982 about faculty overload; the master's degree program was the largest in the state.[70] Faculty overload was not an idle concern. In 1983–84, eighteen of the forty-one faculty members were pursuing doctoral work at universities near and far in response to widespread pressure to achieve that degree as the road to professional advancement. The school's famed *esprit de corps* under Dean Eloise Lewis was reflected in the willingness of senior members to carry extra responsibilities for their juniors pursuing that goal. No doubt at the urging of Chancellor Moran and Vice Chancellor Zinser, the school itself meditated offering a doctoral program.[71]

Eloise Lewis, the school's founding dean, retired in 1985 and the famed faculty morale dropped significantly. Her successor, Patricia Chamings from Emory University, stepped down in 1990, to be followed by Associate Dean Lynne Goodykoontz.[72] By 1993 over half of the faculty held doctorates. The school offered a baccalaureate extension program at Rockingham Community College to the north and both graduate and undergraduate programs in Hickory to the west.[73]

* * *

Lawrence Hart retired in 1981 after fifteen years as dean of the school of music. (Soon afterward he spent a year as acting chancellor of UNC's School of the Arts in Winston-Salem.) His successer at UNCG, Robert Blocker, remained only two years before returning to Texas and the deanship at Baylor University.[74] After a year's hiatus the new dean in 1984 was Arthur Tollefson from the University of Arkansas. Tollefson (like Blocker) was a concert pianist; he had soloed with the San Francisco Symphony at the age of 12. Unlike Blocker, he remained in place for seventeen years.[75]

In 1981–82, Chancellor Moran directed the professional schools that had not already done so to move toward departmentalization comparable to the college of arts and sciences.[76] Music reorganized into five divisions (not departments) in 1982: instrumental; keyboard; vocal studies; music education; and composition, history, and theory.

The school retained its emphasis on performance. It was ranked in the 1980s as one of the top twenty music programs in the country. Its doctoral programs in music education and musical arts or performance (the latter introduced in 1984) were the only ones in the state. An undergraduate concentration in jazz studies was introduced in 1983. There was a great diversity of performance ensembles for both students and faculty; student groups performed in the Kennedy Center, Lincoln Center, and Carnegie Hall.[77] Reminiscent of Wade Brown's old summer music contest for North Carolina high school students was a new summer music camp for fourth graders to high school seniors initiated in 1983 by UNCG band director John R. Locke. By 1990 the camp was the largest in the South, enrolling each year over 1,400 participants from twelve states; by 1995, with over 1,600 students, it was reportedly the largest in the nation. Locke attributed its success to the national reputation of the music faculty, many of whom participated in the program.[78] On the other hand, efforts by Chancellor Moran and Vice Chancellor Zinser in 1987–88 to attract the annual summer Eastern Music Festival away from its longtime home at Guilford College proved unavailing.[79]

One reason for that failure was likely the school's inadequate physical facilities. By 1993 it occupied eight different buildings in whole or in part, four of them former faculty houses dating back to the Foust era. Headquarters remained the 1925 Brown Building, long since outgrown and outmoded. Another perennial concern, the lack of a unified music library under the school's control, also had to await better quarters. Only in 1993 after twenty years' planning did the budgetary stars converge in the form of a successful state bond issue to permit construction of a new building. It was completed in 1999.[80]

* * *

The school of health, physical education, and recreation maintained its national reputation; a 1982 survey placed it sixth among the fifty-eight doctoral-granting schools or departments in the country. In 1987 the physical education department began offering the Ph.D. degree, replacing the older Ed.D.[81] Three members of that department—Diane Gill, Janet Harris, and Daniel Gould—as well as Stephen Anderson of leisure studies served either as presidents of national professional organizations or editors of journals in their fields; Gill and Gould did both.

These achievements came amid a host of handicaps. Like other units, the school had run out of space; by the mid-80's many of its facilities were outmoded and too small to handle the current volume of students. (Although the old physical education requirement had disappeared, about 20 percent of the undergraduates in 1984 still elected PE courses while half participated in campus recreational activities.) PE classes were meeting in Elliott Center and a variety of off-campus sites including a bowling alley and a racquetball club.[82] Faculty offices were similarly scattered. All this ended with the completion of a new state-of-the-art physical activities center in 1989. That facility represented a remodeling of Rosenthal and Coleman, the two existing gymnasiums, plus a new connecting structure forming a single large building. Further, a new recreation building opened next door in 1992, as did soccer and baseball stadiums in 1991 and 1999.

There were also changes in nomenclature. In 1984 the school's instructional divisions became departments and some changed their names in the next several years. Health education became public health education, recreation became leisure studies, and physical education became exercise and sport science. The school itself twice changed names. Having added dance to its already-long title in 1980, forming the acronym HPERD, it became in 1991 simply the school of health and human performance. These changes were more than a little confusing to outsiders, yet all of them reflected significant shifts of emphasis within the respective disciplines, locally and nationally.[83]

The changes complicated life in a number of ways. There were persisting strains between older and younger faculty members who had been hired in different times with different expectations. Senior faculty, going back in some cases to Woman's College days, had won professional recognition through campus service and participation in professional organizations up to the national level. Their juniors, by contrast, came with a stronger expectation of research activity. Fairness to each required in effect twin standards for advancement, providing fertile ground for misunderstanding.

Cutting across that generational divide was a growing separation between the disciplines or departments. The transition from divisions to departments, like the name changes, was more than cosmetic. It brought greater autonomy to units that were maturing in different directions; they had less and less in common. For senior faculty in particular, the result was bittersweet. They welcomed greater freedom to pursue their own agendas, yet lamented the loss of the old common identity within the school.[84]

The most serious disagreement involved the department of public health education. Echoing a rivalry that had festered for decades on this and other campuses, health faculty saw the school as falling increasingly under the domination of the larger physical education department. In 1987 the health department asked unanimously to be moved from HPERD to the school of home economics—now making its own transition in nomenclature to human environmental sciences. The department cited a number of commonalities with that school and its dean was receptive to the transfer. But the dean of HPERD saw it as treason and carried the day with Moran and Vice Chancellor Zinser, who felt that HPERD needed the department more.[85]

Such problems were hardly unique to HPERD—witness the economics controversy. As professional disciplines became more specialized, their faculties had more trouble operating under the same roofs. Vice Chancellor Zinser once cited this process as reason to reorganize the entire campus into more compatible groupings. That never came to pass but if it had, most of the problems would surely have continued.

It was no bed of roses for the deans involved. Margaret Mordy's retirement as dean of HPER in 1979 led a year later to the hiring of Richard Swanson from San Francisco State University. Inevitably, his appointment was controversial. First, Swanson was the first male dean in a school that was still overwhelmingly female. More important, there was little faculty consensus as to what kind of leader the school needed or in what direction he/she should lead it; Swanson represented the highest common denominator.[86] On the job, he proved to be accessible, fair-minded, and well liked inside and outside the school. He played a central role in modernizing the inadequate physical plant. Likely at the instance of Chancellor Moran, he initiated the departmentalization policy that recognized the new realities in the respective fields. Yet some faculty criticized him for permitting if not fostering a decline in the school-wide *esprit de corps* of former years. Probably no one could have satisfied all the divergent expectations. Swanson agreed in 1989 to a reappointment for three years.[87]

His successor in 1992 was Robert Christina of SUNY Buffalo, at the time president of the American Academy of Physical Education.[88] The school in 1993 had forty-five full-time faculty, still divided into four academic departments—dance, exercise and sport science, leisure studies, and public health education—as well as the campus recreation department, supported by student fees.

* * *

Home economics was equally marked by shifting emphases and nomenclature. There was the same generational divide over research expectations and achievements. There were also widening divisions among the constituent disciplines and their faculties—accompanied with fewer fireworks, however. Although home economics programs around the country had begun to adopt new names in the early 1960s, UNCG delayed until 1987 its change to the school of human environmental sciences; the emphasis was increasingly on science. The department of home economics education changed its name twice before disappearing altogether in 1988, its components merging into child development and family relations. That department itself changed names in 1991 to human development and family studies.[89]

Responsible for most of the changes locally was Jacqueline Voss, who in 1982 replaced Dean Naomi Albanese, retiring after twenty-four years. Like Richard Swanson in HPERD, Voss made decentralization one of her first priorities, giving member departments more control over their own budgets and personnel. Hand in hand with that came a higher degree of participatory democracy. Under Albanese the emphasis had been vocational, geared particularly toward training high school teachers in the various department specialties. Under Voss every department rethought its curriculum in light of the vastly greater career opportunities open to women (and not only women) in the field. Every program changed. In clothing and textiles it meant a shift from sewing and styling to textile science. In food and nutrition it brought closure in 1982 of the home ec cafeteria, that time-honored scene of faculty social gatherings, department meetings, and political caucuses. Coming hard on the heels of Voss's arrival, and however justified by shifting curricular needs and economic necessity, the closing made her *persona non grata* for some time among faculty members outside the school.[90]

Across the school, undergraduate majors increased dramatically, as did the employment rate of new graduates. At the graduate level Voss inherited the largest home economics doctoral program in the United States; it was, in fact, larger than the existing faculty could handle. Concerned that the school become known as a degree mill, Voss pushed for higher admission standards that lowered enrollments to more manageable levels. She directed as much money as possible into the promotion of faculty research, particularly among those senior members who had grown up in a different culture. By that means and by tying salary increases to research productivity, the faculty publication rate rose 80 percent by 1985.[91]

Several of the school faculty achieved national recognition. Sheron Sumner in 1987 was elected president of the American Home Economics Association.[92] Betty Feather in 1992 became president of the International Textile and Apparel Association. Gerontologist Vira Kivett won a host of professional honors, including UNC's coveted O. Max Gardner award.

Instructional programs in 1982 were distributed in nine different campus buildings. Headquarters were in the Stone Building, which was not only too small but increasingly obsolete technologically.[93] After a seemingly interminable remodeling that saw much of the school temporarily housed in Curry School's former Park Gymnasium, the Stone Building reopened in 1993.

Dean Voss retired in 1992 after a highly productive ten years in office. Her successor after a two-year hiatus was Helen Shaw, head of the food and nutrition department. The school by then had forty-three full-time faculty in five departments: clothing and textiles; food, nutrition, and food service management; human development and family studies; housing and interior design; and, since 1987, social work. The first three offered the Ph.D. Interior design, failing in its first attempt at accreditation in 1991, achieved that goal two years later. At that time the school as a whole received glowing reviews from another outside accreditation team that praised its research output and services to the region, including the furniture and textile industries. The team pronounced the school one of the best in the nation.[94]

* * *

By the late 1980s, the master's degree had replaced the bachelor's as the most common entry-level credential for public school teachers. Hopeful teachers majored more and more as undergraduates in the subject areas they expected to teach, leaving education courses to the graduate program. Although a few schoolteachers held the doctorate in education, that degree was primarily the preserve of college level teachers and school or community college administrators.[95] In North Carolina by the early 1990s, a significant number of the state's school superintendents and principals held Ed.D. degrees from UNCG.[96]

In the mid-'80s, 12 percent of all UNCG undergraduates and 28 percent of the graduate students were enrolled in teacher education programs. There were 88 such programs scattered around campus, involving 107 faculty members. Only about half of these students were actually enrolled in the school of education. Control of the program similarly remained decentralized, and to no avail did Dean David Reilly repeat the school's longstanding call for centralization in its hands. In response, the multidisciplinary teacher education cabinet that had been in charge since 1974 cited recent approval of the current system by both NCATE (the national accrediting agency) and the state department of public instruction.[97]

Like HPERD and home economics, education received new or refurbished quarters—in its case through a substantial renovation of the Curry Building, completed in 1983. And like other schools it reorganized into departments, also completed in 1983. Most of them offered only graduate instruction; by 1985, the undergraduate programs in education were concentrated in the department of pedagogical studies. That year all the graduate and undergraduate programs were reaccredited with flying colors.[98]

These achievements came despite an atmosphere of almost constant turmoil within the school. In 1985 Dean Reilly tried and failed to abolish the department of curriculum and educational foundations, whose members had opposed his policies.[99] Several faculty members around the school, including Roland Nelson and former Dean Robert O'Kane, resigned or took early retirement. These controversies were at once philosophical and personal. Whatever their merits, Reilly was a divisive figure. This was quite clear by 1981 when he was reappointed for five years; he resigned in 1986.[100]

His successor in 1988 (after a two-year hiatus) was Edward Uprichard of the University of South Florida. Uprichard made it a point to cultivate everyone and was popular with all.[101] He was also a dynamo. In 1989 he established something called the Collegium for the Advancement of Schools, Schooling and Education, a combination think tank, research center, and fund raising agency for educational issues.[102] In 1990 the school, through him, won an $18.5 million grant to operate a southeastern regional education laboratory for the federal government. It was the only such laboratory in the country to be located on a college campus, and the grant was reportedly the largest ever received in the UNC system.[103] In 1991–92 education faculty members received grants totaling $7.3 million, far beyond any previous amount. Two years later the school accounted for 71.6 percent of the entire campus external funding, mostly through the continuing federal grant of 1990.[104]

In a further tribute to Uprichard's credibility, he (and with him the school of education) were given greater authority than before to guide the campus teacher ed program. This was done through a complex new entity called the teacher academy, established in 1993.[105] In 1995, following the resignation of Donald DeRosa, Uprichard became university provost.

In 1993, meanwhile, another round of organizational changes produced five departments: educational research methodology, educational leadership and cultural foundations, counseling and educational development, curriculum and instruction, and library and information studies.[106] In addition to the monetary grants already cited, several of the departments and individual faculty members won national honors in the early '90s. The graduate program in counselor education was judged the best in the nation in 1991 and again in 1994 by its national organization.[107] Jane Myers in that department served in 1990–91 as president of the American Association of Counseling and Development. Jack Bardon in school psychology secured a lifetime achievement award from the National Association of School Psychologists. At home he was possibly the most visible faculty member on campus, at different times chairing one of the major campus-wide planning efforts, heading the faculty council, and serving as acting dean of the school. Marilyn Miller, who came from Chapel Hill to head the library science department in 1987, had already served as president of the American Association of School Librarians; in 1992 she became president of the American Library Association.[108]

At different times the school or its constituent departments offered graduate programs at other campuses—at UNC-Asheville and Charlotte and even in Virginia in the case of library science.[109]

* * *

All told, the university's academic programs—graduate and undergraduate—grew remarkably in size, strength, and diversity during these years. Some of the growth was recognized and rewarded nationally. But much of it reached only a local audience, confirming UNCG's unacknowledged status as a metropolitan university. As always, administrators and faculty wanted still more but found themselves limited by the political and economic imperatives farther upstream.

Chapter 32

Student Affairs

Fewer than a third of the students now lived on campus—it was only a quarter in the fall of 1994.[1] The numbers ebbed and flowed; during inflationary periods students found the dormitories more affordable than off-campus housing and substantially filled them. But the early '90s found larger numbers choosing to rent rooms and apartments in town. One of the reasons they assigned, apart from economics, was lack of privacy in the dorms. In 1990 the dormitories still operated under rules won by the militants back in 1971: every year the residents of each hall voted, within fairly wide parameters, on the permissible visitation hours for guests of either sex. To many in the '90s the outermost limits that had won such wide acceptance in 1971—midnight on weeknights and 2 a.m. on weekends—no longer satisfied. Violations were common and students, in company with their contemporaries across the land, pressed increasingly for unrestricted visitation rights.[2]

In 1993 UNCG, like many other campuses, fell in line—at least on an experimental basis in four dormitories including the new student apartment complex; all guests still had to be signed in and out. In explaining this new concession to trustees and the public, Moran invoked Harriet Elliott's old doctrine of responsible freedom. He pointed to evidence that dormitory residents made better students: they earned better grades, had better access to campus facilities like the library and computer labs, participated more in extracurricular activities, and succeeded better after graduation. The university thus had a responsibility to maximize on-campus residence; he did not mention the financial benefits of full dormitories.[3]

The push for coed dormitories—beyond the existing Residential College—began in 1975. By 1982 there were three, but each represented a special constituency: apart from the RC in Mary Foust Hall they included the international program students in Shaw and graduate students in South Spencer.[4] As soon as it appeared that these halls produced fewer disciplinary problems than the traditional single-sex (particularly male) dorms, administrators proved almost as eager as the students for this experiment to succeed. Their needs were real: in Spring 1983 more than thirty male students were crowded three to a room while more than thirty spaces for women went unfilled. This was no way to recruit male students. Accordingly, the first unspecialized coed dorm made its appearance that fall in Coit Hall. The genders were quartered on alternate floors. Ten years later—by choice of the students and administrators—there were ten coed dorms compared with eight for women and three for men.[5]

Largely for economic reasons, the university cut back on the number of full-time residence hall counselors; there were only two in 1982. The part-time majority were mainly graduate students— particularly those seeking advanced degrees in student development and counseling. Once hired, they underwent an extensive training program.[6]

* * *

The large commuter majority had long been organized. In 1983 they changed their name from the Town Students to the Commuting Students Association—recognizing the many who came regularly from out of town. Their average age in 1988 was 27.[7] More than most student organizations, the CSA suffered from lack of constituent support. The president in 1990 admitted that the organization was run by half a dozen students and was about to collapse from lack of interest. With help from student activity fees, however, it was still alive in 1993, providing its members with monthly deli lunches.[8]

Parking—the perennial commuter concern—no longer approached the crisis proportions of earlier years. As some existing lots gave way to new construction—such as the baseball stadium and the long-awaited music building—new ones appeared, keeping up with rising enrollments. In the fall of 1990, utilization of the 3,000-odd parking spaces exceeded 90 percent only in the "prime time" morning hours of ten and eleven on Wednesdays. The problem for late comers in the morning hours was to find the few empty spaces scattered around campus. The first multi-level deck appeared in 1994. That event opened up parking privileges to freshman and sophomore dormitory students, who had hitherto been forbidden to keep cars on campus. The greatest concern for students and staff now was financial, as the annual fees required to construct and maintain these facilities mounted to $150 by 1992 and kept on rising.[9]

* * *

The office for adult students, established in the early '70s, was superseded in 1992 by a larger Adult, Continuing and Evening Student (ACES) program. It helped non-traditional students of various kinds to earn undergraduate degrees entirely with evening classes. By 1995 some 2,000 students had entered the university through that program.[10]

Women faculty and staff members organized in 1980 and a women's student association followed in 1982. Meanwhile the university established in 1981 a women's resource center with a full-time director to serve all women constituencies on campus. These organizations survived for some years but each suffered in varying degree from lack of interest and hence of financial support.[11]

One of the objections raised back in 1973 to student government funding of the Neo Black Society was that other minorities like gay students would then demand similar recognition and support. A Gay Student Union was in fact organized, winning recognition in 1979. By that time federal court decisions clearly sanctioned such campus organizations, as Vice Chancellor Allen, Moran, and President Friday assured state officials, legislators, alumni, and others who wrote in to query or protest the action. The organization kept a relatively low profile, as did the reportedly large number of gay students on campus as individuals. Its advisor, anthropology professor Tom Fitzgerald, reportedly taught the only course on homosexuality offered in the state.[12] Reorganized in 1981 as the Gay and Lesbian Student Association, it suffered occasional student harassment but such events were rare and the campus gained a reputation as relatively friendly to gays. Student interest in the association waxed and waned, and its continued existence was always problematic.[13]

There was a remaining issue for gay students. Beginning in 1983, they pushed for an official university statement barring discrimination on the ground of sexual orientation. If enacted, it would supplement existing statements regarding race, color, national origin, religion, gender, age, and handicap.[14] Rather surprisingly in the minds of many, the question hung fire for over a decade amid concerns by Moran, campus attorney Lucien Capone, and even the faculty senate that such a declaration might commit the university to official recognition of same-sex relationships and even undesirable organizations like the Ku Klux Klan. These concerns were unpersuasive to the students involved, to UNC system attorney Richard H. Robinson, and to ten other UNC campuses that adopted such declarations. The issue was compromised in 1996 after the faculty senate unanimously approved a resolution condemning discrimination against gays and lesbians.[15]

* * *

Racial tensions continued, fed by the prejudices and stereotypes brought with them by students of both races. Blacks, as the minority, were more conscious of problems. Yet black enrollment rose throughout these years—from 10 percent of the total in 1979 to 12 percent in 1994; the proportion continued to rise thereafter. The level of black discontent varied according to whom one asked. A 1986 campus survey by the institutional research office indicated widespread satisfaction on a variety of fronts, academic and social. In the dining halls, the library, and in social life generally, self-segregation remained the norm, with some notable exceptions.[16] Black girls were elected homecoming queen in 1983 and 1984, but this came from a solid black student vote while whites divided among three other candidates.[17]

The Neo Black Society flourished. According to its faculty advisor RaVonda Webster—herself a member back in the '70s—it verged on having too many leaders. For a time in the '80s there was also a Black Student Alliance composed of the NBS and the black fraternities and sororities. Both undertook to speak for the black students as a whole, although as in every student population comparatively few were active.[18] The leaders pressed for more: more black faculty, more minority scholarship money, a stronger black studies program, and a greater black presence in the curriculum generally. When the university seemed to drag its feet on these issues—all except the scholarship money required faculty action—they announced in 1988 that they would no longer help to recruit prospective black students. The admissions office depended heavily on their assistance.

Moran was as concerned as Ferguson had been to hear and heed black student concerns. He appointed a succession of faculty, staff, alumni, and student committees on the subject, and made good-faith efforts to redress the grievances expressed.[19] In 1979 the university created an office of minority affairs within the student affairs division.[20] In 1982 it began observing Martin Luther King's birthday. Observance of Black History Month followed in 1983. So did a small curricular black studies program. And by 1987 the campus counseling center had a member specializing in minority concerns.[21] Following the 1988 recruitment threat Moran gave blacks even greater visibility in the administration and appointed a faculty committee under psychologist Robert Eason to consider the student demands. Specialized committees followed, charged with addressing the major concerns in detail.[22]

Yet matters continued to deteriorate. The Greensboro branch of the National Association for the Advancement of Colored People charged the university in 1989 with discriminatory hiring and personnel practices. Racial incidents in the dormitories, such as graffiti on walls and some white students masquerading as black cafeteria workers, brought an admonitory letter from the director of residence life. In December Moran addressed the entire campus community, calling attention to these incidents and outlining the steps taken so far to allay black student concerns. After a delay of several months he, Jim Allen, and campus attorney Phyllis Lewis met with NAACP leaders and seem to have allayed their concerns.[23] Yet blacks continued to point out cases of interracial insensitivity. Walter Pritchett, the assistant director of admissions and a member of the Greensboro school board, wrote Moran in 1991 to protest the slighting of blacks in university publications.[24]

Progress, however slow and uncertain, was registered in meeting the student demands of 1988. Additional funds were found for minority scholarships. Vice Chancellor DeRosa and others worked hard to increase the number of black faculty, the hardest nut to crack; in the fall of 1990 they numbered seventeen, or 2.9 percent of the total. Good faith efforts were made to increase the role of multiculturalism in the curriculum. After 1992, African American studies courses could be used to satisfy general education requirements. Minority student applications and enrollments continued to rise almost every year.[25]

* * *

The ARA food service continued to serve the campus. Despite marked improvements in the '70s, students could always find aspects that fell short of perfection. Indeed, a 1981 survey revealed that, on a scale of 1 to 5 where 5 was best and 3 was neutral, students gave only 2.5 or 2.6 ratings to the quality and variety of food and to the variety of places on campus to consume it.[26] Jim Allen's efforts to address these issues had commonly been thwarted by the business office under Henry Ferguson, whose priority was always to keep costs down. With the arrival of Moran and of Fred Drake as vice chancellor for business affairs, more money was allocated to food, to the residence halls, and other aspects of student life. The eating environment improved dramatically with the massive renovation of the dining halls in 1988. A food court with different locations for entrees, vegetables, salads, and beverages cut the time spent in lines. Other fast-food centers were established elsewhere in the building and in Elliott Center. Resident students were still required to purchase a dining plan but their options among alternative plans and the various campus eating venues was almost infinite.[27]

* * *

Academic advising remained in the hands of the faculty, subject to coordination and oversight by a very competent academic advising office. The weakest elements in the system were those faculty and students—not a few in either case—who took the responsibility too lightly. Some faculty members were hard to find or were not knowledgeable and neglected to consult the advising office. Some students, with or without such provocation, bypassed the system, forging advisers' signatures and taking their chances, often with serious consequences. Particularly at risk were freshmen, sophomores, and transfer students who had not settled on a major and thus lacked a secure academic home. For other kinds of advice there were a variety of campus agencies including the counseling and testing center, the office of minority student affairs, and the career planning and placement center.[28]

* * *

The health center by 1981 had grown to five full-time and two part-time physicians, two part-time psychiatrists, fifteen nurses, three technicians, and a part-time pharmacist. These numbers actually declined a little in the next several years as more and more students lived at home and community health services became more readily available to the university.[29] Student patronage declined correspondingly. Faced with that trend along with rising health costs nationwide, the center followed another trend after 1990 by closing on weekends and overnight when student demand had become minimal.[30] William McRae stepped down as director in 1987, after seventeen years. His replacement, Jayne Ackerman, a UNCG graduate and a staff physician since 1978,[31] departed after three years. Her successor, Robert P. Doolittle, was also promoted from within.

* * *

By the early '80s rowdy campus parties awash in beer were asssuming "worrisome dimensions," in Moran's words. The resultant property damage even evoked protest from the insulation company called in to make dormitory repairs. Tighter restrictions, including fewer events at which beer was supplied and in smaller quantities, brought noticeable improvement. As Moran was careful to point out, only a small minority of students was responsible for the damage—which they were required to pay for.[32] Students protested the restrictions but the question largely became moot in 1985, when the state raised the drinking age to 21. Fewer than a third of the resident students met that requirement, and for the rest the campus became legally dry. Though some found means to evade the rules, campus drinking dropped significantly; so, in the view of many students, did the quality of campus social life. Yet by 1995, at least nationally, drinking gradually lost favor among collegians on and off campus.[33]

Drug use fluctuated. A citywide drug raid in 1981 brought the arrest of eleven UNCG students including the outgoing editor of the *Carolinian*—in his case for the possession, sale, and delivery of marijuana. Some of the others faced charges relating to LSD, cocaine, or hashish. In 1988 the UNC system adopted a new drug policy.[34] During the next academic year fourteen students were suspended, expelled, or placed on probation—rather higher than the average for the sixteen campuses. Infractions gradually diminished for a few years, only to double in 1993–94.[35] In 1997 UNCG was billed in the *Chronicle of Higher Education* as tenth in the nation for drug arrests. With fewer than 13,000 students but 109 arrests in the survey year of 1995, it was the smallest school to make the list. (Actually, it was in fairly distinguished company, including the flagship campuses of the Universities of California, Michigan, Wisconsin, Maryland, Arizona, and New Jersey [Rutgers].) The best interpretation that red-faced campus officials could put on the report was that it was a tribute to UNCG's law enforcement efficiency and comprehensive reporting. Students said it confirmed their regular observations. Hard drug use was rare, they said, but marijuana was "widely used and easily available." A dormitory adviser reported that on any given night he could find twenty or thirty rooms with towels stuffed under the doors, a common indicator of pot-smoking within.[36]

Vying for attention with alcohol and drugs was the demand, first raised in 1988, for condom machines in every residence hall. This came amid reports that 48 percent of all college students visiting campus health centers around the country were infected with a sexually transmitted disease. At UNCG the health center already sold condoms—about 400–500 packs of three in 1988–89. A student survey showed overwhelming support for the request for machines. Also supportive were a faculty committee and health center director Jayne Ackerman, a recognized authority on the subject. Moran approved the request in 1990.[37]

* * *

The campus mail service had occupied many places since 1892. In 1986 it moved to a recently vacated U.S. branch post office on Tate Street; student mail was delivered to the dormitories as before.[38] But three years later dormitory delivery was discontinued and the operation moved to the newly-renovated dining hall complex, next to the fast food emporia. For resident students eating in the dining halls this location was almost as convenient as dormitory deliveries. But the 7,800 commuters, who had previously received campus mail at home, now had to traipse across campus on foot, often in the dark, since there was next to no parking space in the vicinity. Although the arrangement saved the university thousands of dollars a year in postage and overhead costs, it infuriated two-thirds of the student body.[39]

The campus bookstore had always been a college or university operation, with most of the profits going to scholarships. Students through the years had grumbled at the real or perceived results of a monopoly: high prices and indifferent service. In 1985 competition appeared in the form of Addams Bookstore, taking over the former movie theater on Tate Street. Two years later the university leased its campus store to Barnes & Noble. Students appreciated the competition, often finding lower prices and better service at Addams but greater selection on campus.[40]

* * *

Tuition, fees, and financial aid reached a higher level of controversy in these years than at any time in the institution's history. Nationally, college tuition charges rose by 92 per cent between 1980 and 1995, *after* adjustment for inflation. The UNC system had long prided itself on providing North Carolinians an inexpensive, quality education. Its average tuition charges were among the lowest in the nation and rose less than the national average in these years. (This applied to in-state students; out-of-state tuition was among the highest in the nation since legislators paid no political price for increasing it.) However, holding the line led to underfunding and came at very real cost to the quality and reputation of programs at virtually every campus.[41] Until the late '90s, tuition was essentially uniform across the system. Variation arose rather from the student fees levied by each campus.

At UNCG escalating fees evoked more complaint than the tuition increases. In 1979–80 in-state tuition and fees together totaled $603. By 1993–94 that figure had nearly tripled to $1,727, over half of it in fees; at $881, they were the highest in the UNC system. Responsible in no small measure was the university's new commitment to subsidized athletics. State law required these costs to be paid either by student fees or private donations. As a new competitor at this level, UNCG could boast only small donations. And as a former woman's college, the handicap was doubly large: most WC alumnae were downright hostile to the new departure. Hence the athletic fee of $34.50 in 1979–80 reached $235 in 1993–94, over a quarter of the fee total.[42]

Another reason for higher fees lay in the growing number of students requiring financial aid and counseling. This too was a national phenomenon, as more and more of the population attended college. The problem was exacerbated by federal government cutbacks in student loan funds, which colleges and universities tried to replace on their own.[43] And even as federal aid funds shrank, the complexity and cost of handling them continued to grow.

At UNCG half of all students by 1981 received financial aid in the form of grants, scholarships, work-study jobs, or loans. Three-quarters of the aid came from the federal government, 20 per cent from the state, and the remaining 5 percent from private sources.[44] During the 1980s, as the university sought to attract better students, more and more scholarship money was awarded on the basis of merit as opposed to financial need.[45] At the same time—following national trends—students worked longer hours at jobs, resulting in lighter course loads and longer times to graduation.[46]

* * *

Every generation complained of student apathy; this one was no exception. Colleges and student bodies around the country differed markedly. In general, the larger the proportion of students who held jobs, the less apt they were to become involved in campus life. Students were largely career-oriented. Older and commuter students in particular saw campus life and student government as extraneous to their own lives.[47]

At UNCG all of these factors operated to discourage widespread interest or participation. As an adult student wrote the *Carolinian*, it's not that we don't care about student government or athletics, but they're not high priorities with us.[48] In 1981 a student competition offering a $200 prize for the best new university song failed to attract a single entry. Laura Weill Cone's entry of 1910 continued to reign. Student turnout at athletic events was abysmal, even when the Spartan women were second in the nation in Division III basketball.[49]

Apathy was also conspicuous in matters of governance. For years student representatives had been appointed to serve on standing committees of the faculty, including the academic cabinet. Their service was spotty at best.[50] The same was true of student government itself. Despite the *Carolinian's* vigorous and perennial promotion of student voter turnout, it occasionally sank to 3 or 4 percent. A straw poll for the U.S. presidency in 1980 brought out only 619 voters in a student body of 10,000; Jimmy Carter won narrowly over Ronald Reagan. The choice of a student government president in 1981 required seven ballots over a period of eight months. Although 1,600 students took part in the first balloting, only 681 votes were cast in the seventh; of these, only 646 were legitimate as tellers discarded write-in votes for Richard Nixon, Mickey Mouse, and other ineligibles. The delay was occasioned by a number of irregularities, including vote-stealing and unrelated criminal charges against one of the winning candidates; it was not a shining hour for the university. A few students called for the abolition of student government altogether as the University of Texas had just done. The *Alumni News* contacted the living ex-presidents for their reactions. The most common and entirely reasonable response was that the campus had changed so much and the student body had become so diverse by age, residence, and life experience that traditional student government was no longer relevant to most of them.[51]

Although repeated condemnation by the *Carolinian* and student leaders of apathy, indifference, and scandal continued to go unheeded, student government survived.[52] As in every generation, there was repeated tinkering or even replacement of the constitution in the never-ending quest for a perfect system.[53] In 1983 for the first time in eleven years a woman, Kim Theriault, was elected SG president.[54] Men continued to predominate, though not invariably, in the years ahead. Black candidates also frequently won the presidency and other offices; in 1994 both the president and vice president were black females.

The student marshals continued to serve as ushers at formal campus events. In the early '80s they began electing their own chief marshal rather than subjecting that official to popular election by a student body largely ignorant of the office. In an effort both to reward scholarship and upgrade the marshals' status, they were now chosen on the basis of academic excellence. To qualify, a student had to have completed at least thirty semester hours with a grade point average of at least 3.65 out of a perfect 4.0. The honor was real, as fewer than 3 percent of the student body met the standard.[55]

* * *

There were signs of a renewed interest in old student traditions. In 1982, after a lapse of many years, the *Carolinian* began running articles on them.[56] (Such articles used to be annual events, to acquaint incoming freshmen with the campus culture.) In 1985, after a lapse of fifteen years, student leaders revived the old class organization, freshman through senior. Each class elected officers. In cooperation with a delighted Alumni Association they set out to revive some of the old traditions as well, beginning with sister classes. Among the new undertakings: freshmen promised to help recruit new students; sophomores, to sponsor a commencement activity for their sister seniors; juniors, help the incoming freshmen to organize; and seniors, to organize and lead the new effort as a whole. Class rings would return; sweaters would replace the old jackets.[57] As it turned out, these initiatives met only indifferent support and most of them were short-lived.[58]

Nevertheless there remained a core of activists to keep at least some of the old flags aloft. The *Carolinian* threatened to suspend publication in 1980 if more students did not join the staff, but it carried on, even garnering second-place honors in the annual Columbia University student newspaper competition. (First place was reserved for the top 10 percent of contestants.) In succeeding years *Cary* frequently alternated between first and second rank. Even so, it was not always easy to recruit a good editor; the same talents commanded more money with less responsibility on one of the Greensboro papers.[59] The quality of the paper varied from year to year, from editor to editor. Rare was the case where a red-faced editor had to apologize for such gaffes as, in 1991, accusing Chancellor Moran of nepotism in hiring his wife as an assistant; in fact Donna Moran, the assistant, was no relation.[60]

Coraddi, the student literary magazine, continued to appear, its frequency depending on the annual appropriation from student fees.[61] The yearbook *Pine Needles* was also financed by student fees until 1981. Its student volunteers then dwindled in number and quality deteriorated correspondingly. When students were given the option to buy it with their own funds, they opted out overwhelmingly. The publication hung on by its fingernails during the '80s, finally expiring in 1993 when only 170 of 12,000 students bought copies.[62]

WUAG, the campus radio station, also survived lean years. In 1982 it became a joint arm of the student media board and the communication and theatre department. Students remained in charge of day-to-day operations, some earning academic credit in the process. By 1993 the staff numbered over seventy-five. In addition to news and sports, it offered "album-oriented rock and jazz in a progressive, non-commercial format." Its reach was still limited to the city of Greensboro.[63]

Public television in North Carolina gradually moved away from the original concept in the 1950s of regional production centers at such places as UNCG in favor of centralization at the main studios in Chapel Hill. Indeed programming was increasingly national. In 1981 the UNCG television center lost its affiliation with the UNC-TV station. It became primarily an instructional arm of the communication and theatre department, many of whose majors were headed toward careers in television.[64]

* * *

Through the service fraternities and otherwise, students continued to volunteer time and energy to a variety of helpful, even necessary activities. Some manned telephones in a university fund-raising campaign.[65] Others launched the campus recycling effort. Randy McCracken, a junior, began that operation in September 1989; by the following April he had a staff of fifty students who were gathering 1,600 pounds a week from ninety campus collection boxes. A business management class conducted an audit of campus paper usage and recommended that the university itself adopt a systematic recycling program. Its response was characteristically cautious; Chancellor Moran and Vice Chancellor Drake looked at the issue primarily in terms of cost effectiveness. But the state government was itself moving toward mandatory recycling and the university followed suit perforce. In 1993 recent alumnus John Bonitz was appointed campus recycling coordinator, charged with setting up the program, or rather, inheriting it from the students.[66]

* * *

As to student social life, the term "suitcase college" was still prevalent. Not all students shared this view but it was common enough to concern university planners in the early '80s. One alumna remembered that so many girls left campus on weekends as to equalize the gender balance at those times.[67] A survey of 1988 graduates registered widespread satisfaction with the university, both academically and socially. Over a third of the respondents had not used campus-sponsored recreational opportunities but of those who did, three-quarters indicated satisfaction. The same proportion said they would come back to UNCG if they were starting over. This was a UNC system survey, however, and the system-wide responses to those two questions were somewhat more enthusiastic than UNCG's. As late as 1996 the university was battling a perception that—except for those who lived in smaller units like the Residential or Cornelia Strong Colleges—it was not a student-friendly campus.[68]

There were popular events, however. Falderal, evolving into Homecoming by 1982, grew in tandem with the sports program. In fact, much of the planning was done by staff members in development and student affairs.[69] Students elected a homecoming queen each year, despite a 1982 student senate resolution condemning it as sexist and potentially racist.[70] The former concern was resolved in time by choosing a king as well; racism was not a problem as a number of African Americans were chosen. Men's soccer games provided the main athletic interest. The springtime equivalent to Homecoming was Spring Fling, in 1993 featuring a campus carnival with hot air balloon rides.[71]

Off campus, there was still Tate Street. Although the university continued into the '80s to warn incoming freshmen not to go there, the drugs and crime of earlier days were largely gone, giving way at worst to panhandlers. The restaurants offered a real ethnic mix. Individual businesses opened and closed over the years but in general they formed a community with common interests; they were at least as stable as the student population on whom they depended. In 1992 and 1993 the merchants promoted what they hoped would be an annual Tate Street festival, reminiscent of but bigger than similar events there twenty years earlier.[72]

* * *

Over the years the campus continued to support a University Concert and Lecture Series, supported by student fees and box office receipts. The events were open to students free (they paid their fees at registration) and to faculty, staff, and the general public for a charge. Many were held in Aycock Auditorium. The programs included such artists and groups as Wynton Marsalis, Isaac Stern, the San Francisco Opera, the Hague Philharmonic, the North Carolina Symphony (long an annual event), the Alvin Ailey American Dance Theatre, and also relatively little known musical or dance troupes, hopefully on their way up. According to a five-year report in 1985, students averaged from nearly a third to nearly half of the concert/lecture series audiences. In addition, the music, theater, and dance divisions regularly produced plays and concerts, open to students and the public on the same terms. They were held in different venues, such as Aycock, Taylor Theater, the music building recital hall, and a dance theater in the new physical education complex. Still further, student fees continued over many years to support a dual film series including both art or classic films and popular movies; the latter generally showed on weekends.[73]

* * *

Vice Chancellor Jim Allen's hard-fought campaign for fraternities and sororities came to fruition just as Moran stepped aboard in 1979. As approved by the faculty and trustees, hazing was to be banned along with racial and religious discrimination. By Fall 1981, seven fraternities and seven sororities were officially recognized and struggling to achieve critical mass. The initial five-year probation period expired and the system achieved full recognition in 1984.[74]

The university at first provided no separate on-campus housing for fraternities and sororities.[75] Meeting initially in small rooms in Elliott Center, some gradually acquired housing of their own off campus. Sigma Phi Epsilon acquired the Market Street home of Wade R. Brown, long-ago head of the music department. The rule against on-campus housing was gone by 1987 when four sororities were assigned floors in a high-rise dormitory. By 1993 the university was moving toward the allocation of campus property near Aycock and Spring Garden Streets for the construction of separate houses by those organizations that could afford them.[76]

Student reception of the Greek way of life was by no means overwhelming; in 1987 there were six sororities with about 250 members and six fraternities with 150 men.[77] Although there was the predictable friction with neighbors over nocturnal noise and other events, the fraternal organizations in general were good citizens. They were active in university fund-raising and other good works.[78] They were by no means the elitist cabal that McIver and his contemporaries had feared.

* * *

Seven religious denominations had campus ministries by 1987: Methodist, Lutheran, Baptist, Presbyterian, Catholic, Episcopal, and Jewish. Most surrendered their buildings to occupy a new joint structure, completed in 1994. Chancellor Moran credited the clergy assigned to all of these ministries with providing a vital counseling function supplementary to that of the university itself. He also acknowledged their help as mediators in occasional inter-group or interracial difficulties.[79]

* * *

Nationwide, campus crime rose in the '80s and '90s, particularly on urban campuses subject to spill-over from surrounding neighborhoods. Colleges and universities beefed up campus security. It was partly a matter of self-defense for administrators; by the late '80s students were going to court and winning settlements against campuses where they had suffered injury. Campus police more and more resembled city police in their training, technology, mobility, and professionalism. The greatest difference probably lay in their broader understanding and tolerance of adolescent excess so long as it stopped reasonably short of criminality. Many campus forces shared jurisdiction over neighboring off-campus areas where students frequently needed the most protection.[80]

All these things obtained at UNCG, where campus police were fully-sworn law officers and did a lot of off-campus patrolling. The force totaled sixteen in 1979 when Security Director Jerry Williamson described campus crime as decreasing in violence but increasing in everything else. By 1992 the force numbered over thirty full-time officers and support personnel.[81] The most prevalent offenses included petty theft, marijuana possession, and vandalism. The last was still a problem in the dormitories; in 1979 the dean of students had to forbid the ever-popular panty raids and the women's retaliatory sorties because students of both sexes were beginning to trash each other's quarters in the process. Williamson attributed 90 per cent of the violence, especially vandalism, to drinking. As already pointed out, tighter campus regulations and statewide raising of the drinking age to 21 in 1985 brought a marked decline in these offenses.[82]

Increasingly after 1975, the campus police relied on student auxiliaries for routine duties. These ranged from handing out parking tickets to manning the campus escort service.[83] In 1982 that service provided a walking escort—for female students only—until midnight when the police took over. By 1985, with only four student escorts on duty each night, demand often exceeded capacity.[84] In 1988 the campus police provided them with vans. Thus equipped, they operated all over campus as well as to student parking lots off campus.[85]

Despite these increased services, plus better lighting and emergency telephones dotted around campus, violent crime was always a danger. There were no murders, and rapes were comparatively rare but in 1984 a student was raped at knife point in a third-floor practice room in the music building, a place where music students could hardly avoid going at night. Lax security in that building was strengthened immediately.[86]

* * *

Diversity was increasingly the essence of student life in these years. It could hardly be otherwise among a student body comprising almost every age group, marital and familial status, economic standing, and place of domicile. Despite valiant efforts to balance the gender ratio it seemed permanently fixed at two-thirds female. An even larger proportion lived off campus, either at home with families or in rental housing. No surprise, therefore, that the few restrictions on student freedom surviving the '60s and '70s continued to recede. Even a student body still predominantly female found trouble identifying with the older mores and traditions of a residential woman's college. Some institutions, like student government, the *Carolinian*, and *Coraddi* did survive along with the old buildings, but in large measure it was a different place.

Chapter 33

Dispute and Departure

Chancellor Moran faced an undeniably tough assignment. He found a university expanding rapidly in size and complexity with no clear consensus as to its future direction or even its current identity. Different constituencies, on and off campus, pushed in different directions. None could expect adequate funding. No great surprise therefore that Moran found himself embroiled in controversy almost from the beginning. He was never popular with the faculty. The blame lay with both sides. However sincere his words and actions in behalf of academic freedom, however much he spared the faculty from mandated budget cuts, however successful his fund-raising and impressive the physical improvements it brought, his managerial orientation and somewhat formal demeanor put off a faculty that was itself increasingly self-absorbed, with little understanding either of his priorities or of the world in which he had to operate. Despite an air of outward civility, neither seemed able to communicate effectively with the other.

Nor did Moran voice a compelling new vision for the university. A leader who charts a new direction engenders controversy. Moran engendered controversy while pursuing the same research-university agenda that had animated the Ferguson administration and that appealed so naturally to faculty members. He was blamed, sometimes fairly and sometimes not, for bureaucratic growth, perpetual self-study, slow decision-making, tolerating for too long truly unpopular administrators like Vice Chancellors Zinser and Keele, subordinating all priorities to the financial bottom line, and for not listening to opinions at variance with his own. His closest relations were apparently with the off-campus business community—an important constituency but not the only one to cultivate. Otherwise, he sometimes displayed a political tin ear that by 1994 had antagonized elements of every major campus constituency.

No controversy equaled that over intercollegiate athletics—specifically athletic scholarships and the move to NCAA Division I. Chancellor Ferguson had opposed this idea and a divided board of trustees shelved it until after his retirement. It was clearly on the front burner in 1979 when members of the chancellor search committee, especially trustee Chairman Louis Stephens (president of the Pilot Life Insurance Company) and Greensboro Mayor Jim Melvin, made plain to the finalists that this item ranked high on their agenda.[1] Like Vice Chancellors Jim Allen and Charles Patterson, its prime sponsors on campus, their aim was to create a campus environment more attractive to traditional undergraduates—especially males—and engender greater community support for the university. The admissions staff too argued in 1981 that a more visible athletic program was one of the best ways to enhance the university's public image.[2] For over a century American colleges had leveraged athletic prowess into higher status, more dollars, and even by some alchemy greater academic recognition in the community.

At UNCG, many faculty members supported the initiative for these reasons, but most were opposed—often vehemently. Many regarded UNCG as uniquely blessed in its freedom from a large and distracting athletic program. Conspicuous in that camp were most of the physical education faculty, for whom the specter of athletic domination of the academic program was most immediate.[3] Although the alumni were never polled on the question, it is safe to say that the majority—certainly of the WC alumnae—were opposed. Current students favored the idea in the abstract but divided when they learned that most of the financial support would have to come from student fees. Student turnout at athletic events under the present dispensation was in the neighborhood of 100 to 200, the *Carolinian* reported in 1979—this in a student body of 10,000. Nor did attendance rise dramatically in the next few years when more competitive teams were fielded at the same NCAA Division III level.[4]

Moran was fully alert to these cross currents. Never one to rush headlong, he took seven years to weigh the pros and cons. By that time UNCG was the only UNC campus, apart from the School of the Arts, that did not offer athletic scholarships. In studying the experience of regional institutions that did have subsidized programs, attention focused on basketball as the most affordable high-visibility sport; football was ruled out as too expensive. Other sports would be subordinate to basketball.[5]

Although the final decision was long deferred, the drift was clearly toward subsidies and eventual membership in NCAA's Division I. Moran indicated repeatedly that his main if not sole reservation was financial; even a minimal Division I program would cost about half a million dollars a year more than the university was presently allocating to athletics. Preliminary steps went forward nonetheless. Following a national trend, the university in 1981 withdrew its women's programs from the AIAW and entered them alongside the men in the NCAA's Dixie Conference.[6]

At the same time, the athletic program was reshuffled on campus, moving out of the school of health, physical education and recreation. Although Dean Richard Swanson remained personally in charge of the program, he now reported directly to the chancellor.[7] Student fees were raised and several sports were eliminated, freeing money to beef up the eight teams—four women's and four men's—that remained. Of these, five teams (both men and women) won conference championships in 1981–82. In 1982 the women's basketball team under Coach Lynne Agee was second in the nation in Division III and one of its members, Carol Peschel, became the institution's first All-American. Similar victories accumulated in the next several years. Between 1982 and 1988, the men's soccer team under Coaches Mike Berticelli and Michael Parker won that division's national championship four times.[8]

One could argue—as Moran's overall planning committee in effect did—that with this level of success the university should declare victory and remain in Division III. It could not afford and should not aspire to big-time athletics, the committee recommended in March 1983; there were higher priorities elsewhere.[9]

The university continued its move toward the big time. In September 1983 Nelson Bobb, the assistant athletic director at Cornell University, was hired as UNCG's first full-time athletic director, replacing Tony Ladd. For the moment Bobb too opposed a move to Division I but he looked forward confidently to further expansion of the Division III program. Reporting to him by 1984 were four full-time coaches—two women and two men—each coaching two sports. In 1985 Moran appointed David Knight of the chemistry department as UNCG's first representative to the NCAA.[10]

Moran and fellow administrators saw changing demographics as posing a critical challenge to UNCG. The pool of 18-year-olds was predicted to drop through the 1980s and '90s. UNCG was already seeing in the early '80s a declining number of applicants from the high schools, and among these a decreasing trend in SAT scores; transfer applications were down as well. Something was needed to raise both the numbers of applicants (particularly males) and their academic standing. The clearest antidote appeared to be a more attractive extracurricular life, and the best way to that end was the higher sports visibility that athletic scholarships could provide.[11] They were buoyed by further polls of the student body that revealed continuing interest in higher levels of competition, i.e., athletic scholarships, even at the cost of higher student fees. In November 1986 the student legislature formally endorsed the move.[12] The only obstacle was funding, and this was diligently pursued. The goal was pledges amounting to at least $500,000 a year for five years.[13]

Faculty members expected or at least hoped to have some voice in the decision.[14] But administrators knew the drift of faculty opinion and studiously avoided any formal expression of it; the final decision, after all, lay with the trustees. As it turned out, the only collective voice the faculty got was an unscheduled and reluctantly-conceded straw poll at a faculty council meeting in November 1986. The vote was fifty-six opposed to the change and thirty favoring it. This poll had no effect on the outcome; the decision had long since been made, subject to funding.[15]

The funding campaign was well along but by no means complete when the trustees finally voted in February 1987 to enter Division I; it was unanimous, with two abstentions.[16] The expansion of the existing program over the last several years had pointed the way. A massive new physical activities complex was under construction, with a soccer stadium and other facilities in contemplation. Long before the decision was made, supporters and fund-raisers had gone public with the cry: "Division I in '91."[17]

As actually accomplished by 1991, the transition was a major achievement. Heretofore no university had made the jump from Division III to Division I in so little time; only three years (1988–91) were spent in Division II. Once the move was completed, UNCG in 1992 affiliated with the Big South conference, consisting of smaller Division I schools—the best affiliation currently available to it. The university fielded fourteen intercollegiate teams—the NCAA minimum. (Although the number of teams was evenly divided between men and women, the budget ratio favored men by about 55 percent to 45 percent.) The women's softball and men's soccer teams won conference championships in 1994.[18]

Even critics had to agree that Moran, Bobb, the coaches, and everyone else involved had provided a textbook example of how such an operation should be run. Owing to careful advance planning and continuing oversight there was no whiff of scandal. Coaches were paid from athletic funds, not from state-funded faculty lines. Out-of-state tuition waivers were not used to subsidize athletes. A new Spartan Fund (later Club) was established to conduct athletic fund raising, but it remained under control of the university development office. The athletic department consistently emphasized and rewarded academic achievement on the part of its athletes. They were admitted on the same basis as other students and subject to the same regulations. With some special tutoring and other oversight their academic averages were just under those of the student body at large, and their graduation rate was higher. Even the majority of faculty who opposed the new departure could cite no pressure for grades or other favors from the athletic department. From 1987 to 1992 the effort had cost almost $10 million, apart from building construction. Student athletic fees rose from $100 to $190 a year in that time and paid 80 percent of the program costs; the remaining 20 percent (including the scholarships themselves) came from gifts and gate receipts.[19]

Athletic boosters at UNCG swam against several strong currents. One was of course its history as a woman's college, coupled with the trend toward female majorities at campuses across the country. A second obstacle was the high cost of Division I programs, particularly new ones where there was little immediate prospect of the gate receipts and outside funds that come with a history of success. A third was Greensboro's location in a region long under the spell of nearby

Atlantic Coast Conference football and basketball teams: Chapel Hill, State, Wake Forest, and Duke. Fourth was a seemingly contradictory national trend in the '90s of antagonism toward big-time college athletics.[20] Most important perhaps was the continuing predominance at UNCG of commuter students, many of them with adult responsibilities and preoccupations at home. Women and commuters each comprised at least two-thirds of the student body through the turn of the century, despite Division I athletics.[21]

Even into Division I, the turnout at athletic events remained poor—worse than poor at women's games although UNCG fielded one of the best women's basketball teams in the country. Over 21,000 fans attended the men's soccer games in the new stadium in 1991, but next year attendance fell off by a third.[22] Similarly, attendance was outstanding at a new basketball series with A&T in the Greensboro Coliseum in 1993, featuring both men's and women's games, but the seats were embarrassingly empty at regular season games—male and female. (Student admission for these events was free.) The trend continued for years despite many successful seasons, depressing the coaching staff and making their job of recruitment harder.[23]

At the same time costs continued to rise, leading to growing resentment at the program. Its visible monuments rankled most. Following completion of the new physical education complex in 1989 there followed in fairly rapid succession a soccer stadium, a recreation building, and a baseball stadium. At a time when academic programs all over campus were starved for funds, immense anger was generated among both faculty and students over the administration's seemingly skewed priorities. In fact, only the PE complex was paid for with state funds, but the niceties of UNC budgeting were never widely understood. Students generally recognized that the bulk of the athletic program—including the monuments—came from student fees. By 1992 they were the highest in the UNC system and would remain at or near the top through the decade.[24] Nevertheless the student legislature that year, backed by the *Carolinian*, supported higher fees, citing athletics as one of the programs meriting greater support. But when fees mounted by 1995 to $920 with $265 going to intercollegiate athletics, and more was requested for the following year, many students protested vehemently.[25] In vain.

Moran continued to justify the athletic program as enhancing student life, even at its current state of development. On the verge of leaving office in 1994 he called for "one more leap forward," from the current support level of $3 million per year to $4.5 million. That increase, he felt, was probably needed to bring the program to the "Colonial Conference level of competition"—the level needed to "engage fully both the student body here and the Triad." Since he continued to oppose the use of state money for athletics—something other campuses earned criticism for doing routinely—that leap would inevitably require still higher fees and more private dollars. His immediate successors upheld the commitment to Division I.[26]

Amidst continuing successes on field and court, UNCG in 1997 moved up a step to the Southern Conference—VMI, Davidson, the Citadel, etc. And amidst the still-higher fees required to fund the program, many students and faculty continued to protest that it was not worth the price. Athletics, they said, were forcing student morale downward, not upward.[27]

The student recreation program had no part in this controversy; it had been a campus fixture for generations and remained so. In fact it received a major boost with completion of the new recreation building at the corner of Walker and Aycock in 1992. Many faculty members used the facility too. A healthy recreation program contributed to the same positive campus atmosphere that animated proponents of the athletics program, but it was far less expensive and controversial. Under the continuing direction of Ellen Greaves, the recreation program embraced intramurals, club sports, and individual fitness activities. The intramural and club sports involved competition between men's, women's, and coed teams. Both included a wide variety of sports or activities, from rugby and fencing to billiards and basketball. Unlike the intramurals, the club sports were intercollegiate. The Piney Lake field campus, south of Greensboro, provided a venue for some of these activities.[28]

* * *

Simultaneous with the athletics controversy was another, bordering on open warfare, with the Alumni Association. UNCG's alumni came rather quickly to reflect the diversity of the student body. As Arnold Grobman said of urban university alumni everywhere, they were a mixed bag: twenty-somethings who had spent four years in the dormitories, middle-aged men and women who had attended college part-time, often at night, and transfer students who had done much of their work elsewhere. All these might share a common gratitude for the educational and career opportunities the university provided, and that might well translate into financial contributions down the road. But such disparate populations were little apt to share campus memories or joyful reunions together.[29] The diversity led to specialized alumni organizations. Black alumni at UNCG formed their own council, subordinate to the main Alumni Association, in 1981. Alumni of certain graduate degree programs followed suit.[30]

By 1987 the Alumni Association numbered about 10,000 members: former students who within the year had donated money to the university. They represented about 20 percent of all living alumni. Most of the active, interested members were still Woman's College graduates, who accordingly dominated the alumni board. Their financial support fell off after 1988 as long-standing tension between the university and the Alumni Association erupted into open conflict; unrestricted gifts were particularly hard-hit.[31]

Disagreement had existed for decades over the allocation of alumni gifts. It reached crisis proportions in the 1980s as the university grew steadily more dependent on outside funding, which always started with the alumni. That concern was seldom mentioned in the ensuing debates, but it represented the greatest tangible change from years past when differences were papered over in the interest of comity.[32]

Chancellor Ferguson like his own predecessors had shrunk from antagonizing the alumni by pushing for a clearer resolution of the legal and financial problems between them. Moran also recognized the importance of alumni support.[33] But the stakes were climbing and he raised the subject soon after his arrival in 1979. He questioned whether he was free legally to accept money given to the university, a branch of the state, and then turn over part of it to support the Alumni Association, a private entity. In the same vein, he asked whether it was either legal or practical to have in one person a university alumni director reporting to the chancellor and an alumni secretary reporting to the alumni board of trustees; Barbara Parrish had performed this balancing act since 1955. A third question involved control of the Alumni House, largely built and managed by the alumni but belonging legally to the university which maintained and increasingly occupied it. Other issues involved control over alumni programming and the *Alumni News*.[34]

Moran's preferences over the next several years varied from an independent Alumni Association to a purely advisory one within the university. He said the latter was the most common model within the UNC system but he remained flexible. Discussions dragged on inconclusively for several years amidst rising tension, particularly on the alumni side.[35]

In 1985 Bernard Keele arrived as vice chancellor for development. He had several alumni concerns and lost little time in provoking conflict over them. The first was that, out of unrestricted alumni gifts to the university in 1984–85 totaling only $235,000, a full 85 percent was earmarked for support of alumni operations. Seeing alumni activity as little more than a branch of university fund-raising, Keele begrudged its taking so much of this income. Second, he was troubled by the relative absence of blacks, males, and younger alumni in the association leadership. And third, the association had too few active chapters around the country.[36]

These concerns were legitimate and merited attention but Keele's hamhanded approach to them, apparently sanctioned by Moran, needlessly embittered relations. Without prior notification the university in 1985 reduced the Alumni Association staff (all of them paid by the university) from seven and a half positions to four; the subtracted positions were moved to the development office. Next year, at Moran's direction, the university ceased paying the association its accustomed share of alumni gifts, explaining that as gifts to the university they could not legally be transferred to a private entity. (Moran later argued that despite this bookkeeping shift the university's total outlay for alumni support actually rose in the following years.) In 1987 the development office, again without prior notice, took possession of the alumni records; these were the vital database for alumni fund raising and Keele regarded them as state records. (Moran later retreated from this position.) In 1989 Moran ruled that the remaining Alumni Association personnel would be regarded as university rather than association employees. And the *Alumni News*, always funded by the university but like the alumni director and staff jointly affiliated, was now to be a university publication with alumni input.[37]

The association vigorously protested these actions as they occurred. It showed no sign of backing down, and Moran proposed in 1986 that both sides appoint committees to examine and state their positions. They did so, issuing lengthy reports in 1988. The alumni cited a history of amicable relations over many years and attributed the present conflict primarily to Keele. Their president, Catherine Vaughn, initially praised Moran for his fairness and conciliatory style. Although the principals on both sides remained civil, such concessions quickly evaporated. The administration report cited the legal and political ambiguities of dual sovereignty over the years but failed to make clear what tangible damage had resulted. It offered the association two choices: accept a supportive role within the university or become an independent, self-supporting entity. At issue were not only the reporting relationship and the allocation of unrestricted alumni gifts but control of the Alumni House and the *Alumni News*. The alumni leaders continued to seek a middle ground.[38]

For many alumni it seemed as if the university was beating up on its mother. Betty Ervin—daughter-in-law of the late Senator Sam Ervin—who inherited the alumni presidency from Catherine Vaughn in June 1988 and became its chief negotiator, wrote Moran that fall: "It is truly beyond comprehension that a respected university would alienate and attempt to eviscerate its alumni association as this one is doing."[39] Even George Hamer, the development director who had urged Chancellor Ferguson in 1970 to take full control of the alumni office, thought the university was acting too harshly now. He urged that the association be made self-supporting with power to raise money on its own, as before 1963.[40] Moran by now had come to favor his other main alternative, a purely advisory Alumni Association within the university, but he was prepared to accept independence if that was what the alumni wanted.[41]

The university held the upper hand financially and even legally—it received the backing of the state attorney general's office in 1990. But it was losing the all-important battle for public opinion, particularly alumni opinion, at a time when it needed outside funding as never before.[42] Moran's case was legalistic and his successive explications of it could hardly be otherwise. Although Bernard

Keele abruptly departed the scene in 1989 amid rumors that he had been fired, relations continued to spiral downward. Late that year, as a desperation measure, both parties agreed to mediation by Greensboro's Center for Creative Leadership. The process took nearly a year.[43]

The upshot was a compromise agreement in November 1990, engineered on the university's part by Keele's successor Richard L. (Skip) Moore. Not surprisingly, the alumni refused to accept an advisory status within the university. Instead they chose a partial independence, returning to the dues system abandoned in 1963. They were given three years to reach financial self-sufficiency. On its part the university agreed to a continuation of the dual position and dual allegiance of alumni director and secretary. The *Alumni News* was recognized as an alumni rather than a university publication, in return for which the association agreed to pay its costs. The university also retreated from its earlier claims to full control of the Alumni House, leaving the existing management/upkeep arrangements in place. Both parties were guaranteed access to the alumni records. The university received full access to unrestricted alumni donations and the association got most of the other things it had claimed, with the responsibility to pay for them. Alumni leaders confessed trepidation about that aspect. They quickly set out to solicit donations and recruit dues-paying members.[44]

As soon became clear, financial independence was not in the cards. Only the largest university alumni associations have enough critical mass to support themselves wholly. UNCG had about 61,000 identified living alumni in 1994–95.[45] Some 3,000 were dues-paying members of the association; several hundred others (including some non-alumni supporters like William E. Moran) were life members. Together they generated only a third of the income the association needed. Accordingly, the university agreed to continue paying an annual subsidy; it was lowered from $50,000 to $35,000 in the year 2001. The alumni director/executive secretary and virtually all the staff were still paid by the university. In 1998 the association agreed to merge the *Alumni News* into a new *UNCG Magazine*, supported by the university but including alumni class notes. Overall, the arrangement bore a striking resemblance to the *status quo ante* in 1985, or even 1963.[46]

Meanwhile, as the war had raged, Barbara Parrish was clearly a partisan of the Alumni Association. She had intended for some time to retire, delaying only until a settlement made it easier to recruit a successor. In the event, she chose to step down in December 1989 after Moran denied her any further reporting relationship to the association. Relations were then at their lowest ebb. Parrish was in poor health and died in May 1991.[47] Her successor, Associate Director Brenda Cooper, '65, was soon charged with implementing the new agreement along with Skip Moore and the new alumni President Ann McCracken. Cooper herself retired in 1995. In keeping with national trends toward the professionalization of such positions, her own successor Joan Glynn was not a WC/UNCG alumna.[48] Betty Ervin, alumni president during the darkest days and arguably the most militant of them, was elected to the UNCG board of trustees in 1993; in 1999 she became its chairman. The war was over.

* * *

The alumni war had hardly settled before the new senate provided a forum for faculty discontent. It was hardly unique to UNCG; according to surveys in the 1980s, two-thirds of American faculty members rated their administrators as only poor to fair and leaning toward autocracy. As institutions grew in size and complexity, their leaders inevitably were seen more as managers than fellow-scholars. And as work-place conditions deteriorated from flagging financial support, faculty members saw themselves losing status.

If sagging morale produced adversarial feelings, it seldom bred militancy. In the conservative '80s AAUP chapters waned or disappeared and fewer than a third of all four-year institutions adopted collective bargaining.[49] The explanation lay largely in the growing pressure to publish, leading faculty to identify more with their disciplines than their institutions.

UNCG was no exception. Typically blamed for sagging morale here were inadequate funding, the athletics issue, lower admission standards, perpetual self-study, and an entrepreneurial atmosphere fostered by the growing bureaucracy. To the degree that blame was personalized, it centered on Moran and Elisabeth Zinser. But compared with the fear and enmity engendered by Edward Kidder Graham in the '50s, resentment was muted. The campus AAUP chapter withered away by the mid-'90s, a victim of the growing apathy already observable under Ferguson. As attendance fell off at faculty meetings and other events, absences were rationalized by the self-fulfilling excuse that all the important decisions were made by the bureaucrats, and by the more credible explanation that there were always more urgent professional claims on one's time. Moran won good marks initially by instituting a faculty advisory budget committee; but before long administrators were studiously ignoring it until after the decisions were made. Other committees registered the same complaint. Perhaps the greatest anger was among those faculty leaders who did devote long hours to their tasks but still felt left out of the loop. That anger crystallized in the new faculty senate in 1992.[50]

Moran like Ferguson was troubled by the general trend. To the extent he understood its causes he sometimes lacked means—financial or otherwise—to reverse them. More importantly, both sides were responsible for a communication gap that lessened mutual understanding.[51] Moran's efforts to communicate with the faculty through meetings with individual departments and otherwise were undercut by the absence of a common culture; he really was a manager and they really were not. His strenuous efforts to improve funding and to shield faculty from recurrent budget cuts were mostly unknown to a faculty who made little effort to understand the budget process, or faculty government generally. His relations with the student body suffered similarly. The *Carolinian* in 1990 said he had a visibility problem and should "come out of the shadows."[52]

In March 1988 former sociology head Daniel Price wrote Moran warning him of "seriously low" faculty morale, centered just then on Elisabeth Zinser's new planning document, *Quo Vadimus*. College faculty in particular saw this prolix volume as an attack on the liberal arts and feared an administration effort to force it on the university from above.[53] Moran's shelving of *Quo Vadimus* and Zinser's departure were widely hailed, therefore, but there were other sore points.

The joint engineering and science research center projected with A&T in 1991–92 originated with the two university administrations. At UNCG anyway, the science departments had almost no input in its planning. Faculty senate chair Bob Clark (of the physics department) blamed this on Moran's "'top-down' administrative style."[54] Then, despite a senate resolution asking for faculty consultation before any further big programmatic changes, administrators announced a new plan to offer more degree programs in the evening. Faculty members learned of this too on television.[55] In neither case did they register much opposition to the projects involved; resentment sprang rather from the lack of prior consultation in matters requiring faculty action to implement. Such consultation had been regarded as a given for decades past. Accordingly, the university's accreditation self-study report of 1992 acknowledged "top-down" administrative problems as well as communication barriers ascribable to both sides.[56]

Campus morale remained a leading issue for the next two years. Outside consultants on the projected engineering-science center noted the problem, saying it was worse than at other institutions they had seen.[57] The senate assumed a degree of activism not seen in faculty government for years. It held roundtable discussions on administration-faculty relations and in the fall of 1992 established a committee to study the "status, rights and privileges of faculty members." It also called for faculty participation in the periodic review of higher administrators. (Moran, in fact, was reviewed by a committee of the trustees in the summer of 1993; its report was not released.)[58]

The faculty status committee issued its final report in January 1994. This nine-page document, approved unanimously by the senate, was popularly named for committee chairman Charles Tisdale—the same who had introduced the 1971 amendment to the tenure regulations assigning primacy to teaching over research and publication. The 1994 report praised Moran and his colleagues for improving the campus physically and visually, for a variety of "exciting program developments" in the academic area, for making the best of tight budgets, and for raising outside funds on an unprecedented scale. Turning to faculty morale, it admitted that the problem was as much national as it was local. Yet the local issue needed addressing. Like comedian Rodney Dangerfield (who was not mentioned) the UNCG faculty felt they lacked respect; they had too little voice in shaping policy, even in academic matters where they were directly involved. The report cited a variety of examples: the evening class program, the disregard of the budget committee until after issues were decided, the lowering of admission standards, a recent shakeup of the admissions and financial aid offices without any faculty input, and the introduction of subsidized athletics despite widespread opposition. Reflecting Tisdale's and others' long-time concerns, it questioned once again the primacy of research grants and publication over classroom teaching and professional service. Moran took the criticisms in good part and promised to respond constructively.[59]

* * *

Bureaucratic administration also antagonized students. One galling example for the commuter student majority was placing their mailboxes near the dining hall where there was no parking space.[60] Far more serious was the financial aid crisis of 1993. The process of awarding aid had already slowed down in recent years with the growing number of student applicants and ever-more-complex reporting requirements by the federal government. Those delays had caused discomfort and no little anger before the process came to a virtual standstill in 1993.[61] Financial aid director Marleen Ingle and her staff hunkered down to process the paperwork, refusing for long periods even to answer the telephone. Actual and prospective students, unable to learn when or whether they would receive financial aid, faced alternative necessities of dropping out of school, taking additional jobs, or being evicted from their rooms or apartments for nonpayment of rent. The result for UNCG was a public relations nightmare.[62]

Ingle's superiors, particularly Associate Provost Anne Steele, attributed much of the problem to slowness in computerizing student records. When they called in Registrar James Kaiser, a computer expert, to remedy the deficiency it actually worsened the problem temporarily; so did the ensuing resignation of Ingle and 80 percent of her staff.[63] The case was by no means clear-cut. Ingle had held the post since 1980 and otherwise compiled an enviable record. She had won a number of regional and national honors and served in 1992 as president of the Southern Association of Student Financial Aid Administrators.[64]

Lagging automation extended also to the admissions office, according to an outside consultant hired by Anne Steele in 1992. In this case too there was much to praise in the record of its director since 1985, Charles Rickard.[65] He had served previously as admissions director at the University of Michigan's Flint campus under Moran, who was instrumental in hiring or promoting him at both institutions.[66] Soon after arriving at UNCG Rickard took the lead in organizing the admissions directors of the UNC system, serving successive terms as their chairman and as a unifying force among a highly competitive group. Keeping track of each other's activities, they admired Rickard's work at UNCG. With this statewide visibility he was frequently called upon by general administration to chair committees and help formulate policy.[67] On campus, he was repeatedly praised by Moran, Zinser, and others for his success in recruiting students.

The reaction of Steele and Provost DeRosa to the consultant's report was to reorganize the admissions office as well, in effect forcing Rickard out; he left in 1993 for Kent State University.[68] Their next move was to consolidate admissions, financial aid, and the registrar's office under a single head—temporarily DeRosa himself.[69] To cope with the shambles in financial aid they hired in 1994 a private agency temporarily to process applications. Conditions improved but the operation was still in trouble as Moran left office that summer.[70]

All this came at a time when national demographics threatened to curtail enrollments and thus the university's per-student state funding. To prevent that it lowered admission standards to what seemed unprecedented levels, with predictable results in the freshman class. Moran, Steele, and DeRosa were blamed for the morass. Steele departed abruptly in November 1994, soon after Moran, and DeRosa followed in 1995 to become president of the University of the Pacific in California.

* * *

Moran received a final setback early in 1994, this time from the board of trustees. It involved the siting of the long-awaited and much-needed new music building. Moran, music Dean Arthur Tollefson, and campus planners all favored a location at the southeast corner of campus, on Tate Street behind the new Weatherspoon Gallery building. That location was reasonably adjacent to other campus buildings frequented by music students. Its importance to Moran was reflected in his lengthy and able supporting statement. It was bitterly opposed, however, by the director and friends of the Weatherspoon, who feared that it would cut off future expansion of the gallery.[71] The leading alternative was at Market and McIver Streets, the northeast corner of campus. As Market was one of the city's main arteries, trustees felt that a new "signature" building there might better showcase the campus to outsiders. From the students' perspective, that site was closer to the dormitories (for the minority who lived in dormitories) but farther from other classroom buildings. It would also bring further incursion into Peabody Park. Both locations were convenient to commuters and the general public, and either one would be served by a new parking deck.

The trustees had the final voice. Their decision, overriding Moran, the dean, and the planners, was first signaled in a unanimous committee vote on February

8, 1994, then ratified by the full board on February 10.[72] Nationally, university trustees feel most at home dealing with questions of bricks and mortar where they are most apt to have personal experience.[73] In this case they apparently did not see their action as a slap at Moran, for whom they had genuine regard. Nonetheless, it represented one of the few such reversals in the institution's history.

* * *

On February 9, the morning after the trustee committee vote, Moran awoke (as he later reported) fully and finally determined to resign as chancellor. He so reported to the full board next day, making August 15 the effective date. He and his wife had discussed the matter for two years, he explained, but problems kept arising to delay it; now, after fifteen years—far longer than average for campus leaders—most of the things he could do were done. He drove to Chapel Hill and informed President C.D. Spangler, saying that UNCG needed "new leadership, fresh ideas, and a new face." He would not say what role was played by the senate's critical vote and he mentioned the music building only in neutral terms as a problem now settled. Whatever the mixture of reasons, he had given no advance notice and everyone was surprised, including trustees who had voted against him on the building site and now tried vainly to dissuade him.[74]

As is customary, speeches were made and articles written citing Moran's accomplishments, and they were considerable. Despite the recurrent faculty discontent, or perhaps because of it, he himself claimed that his greatest satisfaction arose from the university's academic progress since 1979. This included many more graduate programs, much greater scholarly activity and creative work by the faculty, and many more research grants. The endowment had risen more than eleven-fold, to $42.4 million, one of the best performances in the nation. Easiest to perceive visually were eight new buildings, not yet including the music building.

Supporters praised Moran's determined support of athletics. Faced with clear pressure from the business community to introduce athletic subsidies, clear opposition from most faculty and alumni, and ambivalent student attitudes, he went ultimately with the business community. Faculty opponents, on the other hand, attributed his tendency to delay important decisions like this as betraying an unreadiness either to make big decisions or to provide the university with clear direction. No one ever questioned Moran's intelligence, his dedication to the university, or his even temper—some said his grace—both in governing and in leaving.[75]

Moran taught a semester in the business administration department, then took a two-year leave of absence to re-enter the investment business with which he had maintained a board-member relationship since 1969. He came back in January 1997 to teach another semester, then retired at age 65.[76]

Epilogue

1994–2003

History did not end in 1994 when the preceding chapters broke off. By 2002, enrollment climbed to 14,000 but the mix had hardly changed: two-thirds of the students were still female and close to three-quarters now lived off campus. Graduate students accounted for 23 percent of the total. African American enrollment reached 18 percent—a remarkable achievement viewed from the perspective of, say, 1980. At the same time admissions standards and SAT scores rose from the basement of the early '90s; the freshman average in 2002 was 1034.[1]

It had not escaped the notice of female graduates—always the vast majority—that in all its years as a woman's college and then a predominantly female university, the institution had never had a female president or chancellor. That changed in 1994. When it proved impossible to identify a successor to Chancellor Moran before his departure in August, UNC President C.D. Spangler named as acting chancellor N.C. State University graduate school Dean Debra W. Stewart. He had already made it known that the time was likely ripe for UNCG to have a woman chancellor on a continuing basis.[2] Stewart was immensely popular during her semester at the helm but she rejected pleas to become a candidate for the job permanently. Her successor in January 1995 was Patricia A. Sullivan, vice president for academic affairs and recently interim president of the Texas Woman's University. Provost Donald DeRosa resigned the following summer to become president of the University of the Pacific, and Sullivan promoted education Dean Edward Uprichard to succeed him.

Sullivan herself had been a controversial choice with many of the faculty but she set out at once to cultivate all campus constituencies, with success. The Sullivan-Uprichard team won widespread support. There was no decapitation of lesser administrators. A gradual rotation of vice chancellors saw longtime student affairs head Jim Allen retire and development chief Skip Moore leave to head a local charitable foundation.

One hallmark of the Sullivan administration has been to emphasize more than ever before the university's ties to the surrounding region. The term metropolitan university has not been used, but it becomes more and more a reality. By 2003, UNCG estimated that it contributed 6,439 jobs and $541 million to the economy of Guilford County—even more to the Greensboro, Winston-Salem, High Point Triad.[3] Sullivan herself invoked informally the name University of the Triad. Under her aegis new campus agencies have been established to serve specific population groups in the region such as recent Hispanic, Asian, and other immigrants. In 1997 the university announced a Fast Forward program permitting area high school students to take college level courses in their schools for UNCG credit.[4] Community service and teaching were assigned greater weight—or so it was hoped—in faculty tenure decisions.[5] By all of these means it was hoped to spur even greater community support, economic and otherwise, for the university.

UNCG has continued to rely on temporary and part-time faculty, as have the UNC system and the nation. New academic programs are continually added to the curriculum, as are accelerated master's degrees and overtures toward online education.

Despite the physical improvements achieved by Chancellor Moran, a UNC systemwide study tagged UNCG in 1999 as the neediest of all the campuses in terms of physical maintenance.[6] Paradoxically, as administrators wrestled with that perennial headache, new construction proceeded apace, paid for from other budget sources. The baseball stadium and the new music building came into service in 1999. Elliott University Center underwent by 2003 a massive renovation and expansion, closing much of Forest Street. A third parking deck is underway at the south end of Forest, near the railroad, and a new arts and sciences classroom building is planned for 2005 on the site of Park Gymnasium nearby. On the east side of campus a new science building has arisen on McIver Street, much of it also permanently closed to vehicular traffic. College Avenue is finally becoming a pedestrian mall, closed to all but emergency vehicles. To the north, the remains of Peabody Park face a major refurbishment, with paved trails, stream restoration, and a 270-foot bridge leading to the new music building.[7]

The athletics controversy has simmered down. Most opponents of the subsidized program have accepted their defeat but students still protest the ever-increasing fees for that purpose. The teams often do well but turnouts continue to disappoint. Persons on and off campus nevertheless credit the program with raising the university's visibility and, they continue to hope, its fund-raising prospects.[8]

The larger identity problem has also abated in an atmosphere of rising morale among faculty, students, and alumni.[9] The overall comfort level appears higher than it has been in many years.

Notes

Preface Note

1. Karabell, *What's College For?*, p. xiv; Johnson and Bell, *Metropolitan Universities*, esp. pp. xiii–xv, 3, 7–15, 23–26, 41, 219–25, 230, 243, 343–45. See also the 1994 debate over UNCG's mission by faculty members Henry S. Levinson and Shirl J. Hoffman, Greensboro *News & Record*, 27 Sept., 6 Oct. 1994.

Chapter 1 Notes

1. Ayers, *Promise of the New South*, pp. 417–18.
2. U.S. Commissioner of Education., *Report*, 1890–91, *House Executive Documents*, 52 Cong./1 sess., #1, Part 5, vol. 5, part 1 (Serial 2938), pp. 7–31; Bowles, *Good Beginning*, pp. 4–5.
3. Leloudis, *Schooling the New South*, pp. 11–12, including quotation.
4. Leloudis, *Schooling the New South*, pp. 20–33.
5. See this view attributed to McIver, in Coon, "Charles Duncan McIver and His Educational Services," p. 332.
6. Leloudis, *Schooling the New South*, p. 70. For the UNC summer school, see Coyner, "The South's First University Summer Normal School," pp. 173–82. My discussion of McIver, his colleagues, and their campaign is heavily dependent on a number of studies, the best being the two listed first here: Leloudis, *Schooling the New South*, pp. 37–38, 60–72; Dean, "Covert Curriculum," pp. 25–48; Daniels, *Tarheel Editor*, pp. 370–72, 457–61; Dabney, *Universal Education*, I, pp. 193–209; Holder, *McIver of North Carolina*; Eaton, "Edwin A. Alderman," pp. 207–08; Malone, *Edwin A. Alderman*, pp. 36–47, 257; Elmer Johnson, "James Yadkin Joyner," pp. 360–64. See also Alderman's appreciative "Charles D. McIver of North Carolina."
7. Leloudis, *Schooling the New South*, pp. 73–90 (quotation on p. 89); Alderman, "Charles D. McIver," pp. 103–04; Daniels, *Tarheel Editor*, pp. 370–72, 457–61; E.J. Forney, in *Alumnae News*, 34 (Nov. 1945), pp. 4–5.
8. Friedlander, "A More Perfect Christian Womanhood," pp. 75–76.
9. *Raleigh News & Observer*, 25 May 1893, in College Scrapbooks, I.
10. Charles D. McIver, undated autobiographical sketch, McIver Papers; William C. Smith, "Charles Duncan McIver," p. 280; Dean, "Covert Curriculum," pp. 47–48.
11. See, e.g., *Raleigh Morning Post*, 19 May 1900.
12. Leloudis, *Schooling the New South*, pp. 98–99; Dean, "Covert Curriculum," p. 52.
13. Daniels, *Tarheel Editor*, p. 457.
14. *Greensboro Workman*, 13 June 1891, in College Scrapbook, I; McIver, 8 Aug. 1899, to Josephus Daniels, McIver Papers.
15. William C. Smith, "North Carolina State Normal and Industrial College," pp. 154, 157–58; Dean, "Covert Curriculum," pp. 68–69.
16. E.J. Forney, in *Alumnae News*, 34 (Nov. 1945), pp. 4–5. W.C. Smith attributes the dropping of coeducation to its unpopularity in the legislature. "North Carolina State Normal and Industrial College," p. 157.
17. *North Carolina Laws*, 1891, chapter 139.
18. *North Carolina Laws*, 1891, chapter 139.
19. McIver, 8 Aug. 1899, to Josephus Daniels, McIver Papers. For accounts of the subsequent auction, see in particular Richard Bardolph, "Why Greensboro?," *Alumni News*, 74 (Fall 1985), pp. 26–29 and (Winter 1986), pp. 26–29. See also Directors' Minutes, 9 June 1891 (embracing events of June 9–12); Directors' report to the governor, with the minutes of 20 Dec.

1892; reminiscence of one of the directors, in *Raleigh News & Observer*, 15 Feb. 1893, College Scrapbook, I; *Greensboro Record*, 18 June 1891, in College Scrapbook, I, containing a list of the Greensboro subscribers; Julius I. Foust, 27 Nov. 1940, to Rachel [Clifford], Foust Private Papers; Foust, College History draft, pp. 33–37; *Alumni News*, 56 (Fall 1967), pp. 20–21.

20. The credibility is supported by news that an equivalent referendum in Graham brought only two negative votes. "Director," *Raleigh News & Observer*, 15 Feb. 1893, in College Scrapbook, I.

21. Directors' report to the governor, with the Minutes of 20 Dec. 1892; Bardolph, "Why Greensboro?," *Alumni News*, 74 (Fall 1985), p. 28. For the Agricultural and Technical college, see Gibbs, *History of the North Carolina Agricultural and Technical College*, p. 7; Harris, "Publicly Supported Negro Institutions in North Carolina," p. 287; Logan, "The Movement in North Carolina to Establish a State Supported College for Negroes," p. 179.

22. James A. Leach, quoted in Julius Foust to Rachel [Clifford], 27 Nov. 1940, Foust Private Papers.

23. S.M. Finger, 26 March, 10 June 1891, to McIver; Edwin Alderman, 11 June (postcard), 13 June 1891, to McIver, McIver Papers; McIver, 6 June 1891, to Finger, Supt. Of Public Instruction Papers, N.C. Archives; Directors' Minutes, 12 June 1891; Leloudis, *Schooling the New South*, pp. 90–91.

24. Notes of Richard Bardolph interview with Mrs. Mabel Merritt, ca. 1981, UNCG Archives.

25. For Pullen, see sketch by Jerry L. Cross in William S. Powell, ed. *Dictionary of North Carolina Biography*, 6 vols. Chapel Hill: University of North Carolina Press, 1979–96, 5: 155–56.

26. Report of site committee, in Directors' Minutes, 20 May 1892; Directors' report to the governor, with their Minutes of 20 Dec. 1892; Foust, College History draft, pp. 38–40, 130.

27. Richard Bardolph, "A Historic Site," *Alumni News*, 67 (Spring 1979), inside front cover; Foust, College History draft, p. 41; E.M. Goodwin, 25 Sept. 1891, and S.M. Finger, 11 Dec. 1891, to McIver, McIver Papers; report of the Building Committee, and directors' report to the governor, with the Directors' Minutes of 20 May 1892, 23 May 1895, and 20 May 1896; National Register of Historic Places, inventory nomination form, n.d., Moran Papers, A-General, 1980; *Greensboro Daily News*, 30 Oct. 1980, sec. B-1, p. 7.

28. Directors' Report, 20 Dec. 1892.

29. Directors Report, 20 Dec. 1892; S.M. Finger, 28 July 1892, to McIver, with undated newspaper clipping, McIver Papers; *Raleigh News & Observer*, 15 July 1892, in College Scrapbook, I; Foust, College History draft, pp. 40–41.

30. S.M. Finger, 30 Aug. 1892, to McIver, McIver Papers; Virginia Lathrop, "McIver House," *Alumnae News*, 41 (Fall 1952) pp. 1–2; *Carolinian*, 24 Oct. 1952, p. 4; Satterfield, *Charles Duncan McIver*, p. 48.

31. Directors' report to the governor, with Minutes of 20 Dec. 1892; *Decennial* (1902), p. 13.

32. Report by S.M. Finger, with Directors' Minutes, 20 May 1892; McIver to wife, 28 Feb. 1894, McIver Papers.

33. Directors' Minutes, 23 May, 27 June 1895; McIver, biennial report, with Directors' Minutes of 17 Dec. 1896; Foust, College History draft, 75–76; *Greensboro Patriot*, 3 July, 25 Sept. 1895, in College Scrapbook, IV.

34. McIver biennial report, with Directors' Minutes, 17 Dec. 1896; *Greensboro Patriot*, 3 July, 25 Sept. 1895, in College Scrapbook, IV.

35. McIver biennial report, with Directors' Minutes, 17 Dec. 1896; Directors' Minutes, 18 May 1897; *State Normal Magazine*, I (June 1897), 122; V (Dec. 1900), 85; *Greensboro Record*, 10 March 1898, in College Scrapbook, VII; *State Normal Magazine*, 2 (April 1898), 256. For

an account of the unusual granite blocks found on campus and used in the wall, see *Greensboro Record*, 31 Jan. 1898, in College Scrapbook, VII. For the fountain, see *State Normal Magazine*, 5 (Dec. 1900), 85.

36. *Charlotte Observer*, 21 Nov. 1897, and *Greensboro Record*, 10 March 1898, in College Scrapbook, VII; *Greensboro Record*, 26 Sept. 1898, in ibid, VIII; Report of J.L. Ludlow, 17 Nov. 1899, following Directors Minutes, 12 Jan. 1900.

37. Directors Minutes, 20 June, 20 Dec. 1900; report of J.Y. Joyner and E.J. Forney, 20 Dec. 1900, Normal School reports, McIver Papers.

38. *Greensboro Record*, 10 March 1898, in College Scrapbook, VII.

39. McIver, biennial report, 18 Dec. 1902, with Directors' Report, 1902, pp. 21–22. For the naming, see Lula Martin McIver, 8 May 1942, to Frances G. Satterfield, Satterfield Papers, UNCG.

40. McIver, [23 July 1901], to wife, McIver Personal Papers; McIver, 5 Sept. 1901, to George Foster Peabody, McIver Letterbooks; McIver, biennial report, 15 Sept. 1904, with Directors' Report, 1904, p. 19.

41. *State Normal Magazine*, 6 (Oct. 1902), pp. 68–69.

42. McIver biennial report, 15 Sept. 1904, with Directors' Report, p. 19.

43. *Greensboro Record*, 12 April 1902, in College Scrapbook, X; McIver, 3 Nov. 1902, to George Foster Peabody, 11 April 1905, to W.H. Osborne, and 16 May 1906, to J.L. King, McIver Letterbooks; Foust, biennial report, 15 Sept. 1918, with Directors' Report, 1918, p. 11.

44. For retrospective accounts of the building and its uses at the time of its demolition in 1949, see *Alumnae News*, 38 (Aug. 1949), pp. 1–2; *Greensboro Daily News*, 20 Nov. 1949, in Vertical File: Students' Bldg.

45. McIver, 13 Jan. 1902, to Curry, McIver Letterbooks.

46. J.L.M. Curry, 6 July 1891, to McIver, McIver Papers.

47. Winston, 22 June 1891, to McIver, McIver Papers.

48. *Catalog*, 1892–93, p. 42.

49. M.C.S. Noble, 23 May 1892, to McIver, McIver Papers.

50. Schmidt, *Liberal Arts College*, pp. 103–07 (quotation on p. 103); Veysey, *Emergence of the American University*, pp. 268, 302–05; Donovan, "Changing Conceptions of the College Presidency," pp. 42–48; Rourke & Brooks, *Managerial Revolution in Higher Education*, pp. 4–5.

51. McIver, 6 Nov. 1903, to D.B. Johnson, McIver Letterbooks.

52. Board resolution, 20 June 1900, McIver Papers.

53. Cornelia Strong et al., Coit obituary statement [1944], Jackson Papers.

54. Virginia Brown Douglas, in *Alumnae News*, 55 (Jan. 1967), p. 5.

55. Oeland Barnett Wray, 3 March 1935, to Julius Foust, Alumnae Letters, Foust Papers.

56. Directors' Minutes, 17–18 Dec. 1896; Letters to Julius Foust from Nettie Allen Deans, 18 Oct. 1934; Oeland Barnett Wray, 3 March 1935; and Vaughn Holloman, 11 March 1935, Alumnae Letters, Foust Papers; Forney, *Leaves from the Stenographers' Note Books*, p. 9; DeVane, "County Fair," pp. 15–19 (inc. Yadkin quote); *Alumni News*, 61 (Fall 1977), 2.

57. Foust, College History, Notes: Appropriations; and draft, pp. 64–76.

58. Daniels, *Editor in Politics*, pp. 319–24; Harlan, *Separate and Unequal*, pp. 60–62.

59. Rudolph, *American College and University*, pp. 430–32. See also Fosdick, *Adventure in Giving*, pp. 1–22; Curti, *Social Ideas of American Educators*, pp. 283–85; Hofstadter and Metzger, *Development of Academic Freedom*, pp. 457–58.

60. For an annual breakdown of Peabody donations, see W.M. Murray, 14 Oct. 1960, to Otelia Connor, Vertical File: Peabody Education Trust Fund. For J.L.M. Curry's relations

with the Normal, see Curry, 6 July, 6 Aug. 1891, to McIver; S.M. Finger, 13 June 1893, to McIver; D.L. Russell, 3 Sept. 1897, to McIver, McIver Papers; Foust, College History draft, pp. 41–42.

61. Letters of McIver, 2 June 1894, to Josephus Daniels, S.M. Finger, and W.J. Bryan; to D.E. McIver, 4 June 1894, McIver Papers.

62. Curti, *Social Ideas of American Educators*, pp. 281–82; Leloudis, *Schooling the New South*, pp. 130–32; Cooper, *Walter Hines Page*, pp. 141–44; Sellers, "Walter Hines Page," pp. 485–94. The speech appears in Page, *Rebuilding of Old Commonwealths.*

63. Oeland Barnett Wray, 3 March 1935, to Julius Foust, Alumnae Letters, Foust Papers.

64. Betty Anne Ragland Stanback, interview with Emma Speight Morris, in *Alumni News*, 55 (Fall 1966), pp. 5–6.

65. Forney, *Leaves from the Stenographers' Note Books*, p. 4.

66. For examples of devotion, see letters to McIver from Cornelian Society members, 12 May 1894, Gertrude Mendenhall, 25 May 1894, and the Class of 1894, 16 June 1894, in McIver Papers; Holder, *McIver of North Carolina*, pp. 132, 223–24, 254. For more mixed alumna views, see Vaughn Holoman, 11 March 1935, to Julius Foust, Alumnae Letters, Foust Papers; Mozelle Olive Smith, in Richard Bardolph, "The Centenary Project," *Alumni News*, 73 (Winter 1985), pp. 12–13.

67. Phoebe Pegram Baughan, in *Alumnae News*, 25 (April 1937), p. 5; Lula McIver, [9 March 1895], to McIver; Annie McIver, 10 March 1895, to McIver, McIver Personal Papers; College News, *State Normal Magazine*, I (March 1897), pp. 26–27; *Greensboro Record*, 26 Feb., 1 March 1897, in College Scrapbook, V.

68. Oeland Barnett Wray, 3 March 1935, to Julius Foust, Alumnae Letters, Foust Papers.

69. McIver, 3 Nov. 1904, to Mrs. J.H. Moseley, McIver Letterbooks.

70. Annie H. Saunders, 25 March 1935; Eunice K. Rankin, 27 May 1935, to Julius Foust, Alumnae Letters, Foust Papers; Forney, *Leaves from the Stenographers' Note Books*, p. 22; Dean, "Covert Curriculum," p. 137.

71. Julia Pasmore, 21 May 1935, to Julius Foust, Alumnae Letters, Foust Papers.

72. *North Carolina Statutes*, 1891, chapter 139, section 6.

73. Satterfield, *Charles Duncan McIver*, p. 46.

74. Dean, "Learning to be New Women," pp. 292–94. Quotation from McIver, "Two Open Fields," *State Normal Magazine*, I (Mar. 1898), p. 18. For an account of how the supposed public school reforms worked out in practice in North Carolina during the Progressive era, see Kousser, "Progressivism."

75. Dean, "Covert Curriculum," p. 22; "Learning to be New Women," pp. 295–97.

76. For former students' testimony on McIver's evangelical message, see letters to Julius Foust from Ida Wharton Grimes, 10 April 1935 and Eunice Rankin, 27 May 1935, Alumnae Letters, Foust Papers.

77. Faculty Council Minutes, 24 March, 16 Sept. 1902; McIver, "Current Problems in North Carolina," pp. 297–98; Leloudis, "School Reform in the New South," pp. 886–891, 898–900; Leloudis, *Schooling the New South*, pp. 154–55; Link, *Paradox of Southern Progressivism*, pp. 134–38; Dean, "Learning to be New Women," pp. 294–95.

78. *Greensboro Daily News*, 11 Oct. 1925, in Faculty File.

79. For accounts of the educational crusade in the South, with McIver's role in it, see Ayers, *Promise of the New South*, pp. 418–19; Link, *Paradox of Southern Progressivism*, pp. 124–38; Woodward, *Origins of the New South*, pp. 400–06; Mitchell, "From Black to White," pp. 343–46.

80. Curry, 6 July, 6 Aug. 1891, to McIver, McIver Papers.

81. S.M. Finger, 10 Jan. 1891, 26 March 1894, to McIver, McIver Papers; McIver, 18 Feb. 1897, to wife, McIver Personal Papers; Foust, College History draft, p. 80; Prather, *Resurgent*

Politics, p. 51. For the national debate, see Harper, *Century of Public Teacher Education*, pp. 108–11; Borrowman, *Liberal and Technical in Teacher Education*, pp. 89, 119–21.

82. Dixie Lee Bryant, "Reminiscences Concerning the Early Curriculum," typewritten ms., n.d., Faculty File: Bryant.

83. George T. Winston, 19 March 1897, to McIver, McIver Papers.

84. *Catalog*, 1892–93, p. 18.

85. "The Basic Aims of Woman's College," 23 Oct. 1957, in Study & Planning Committee, Blackwell Papers.

86. Leloudis, *Schooling the New South*, pp. 111–12; Dean, "Covert Curriculum," pp. 277–78; Holder, *McIver of North Carolina*, pp. 136–41.

87. McIver, 5 Feb. 1901, to wife, McIver Personal Papers; Foust, College History draft, p. 64.

88. Leloudis, *Schooling the New South*, pp. 109–19; Dean, "Covert Curriculum," pp. 274–79; Gobbel, *Church–State Relationships*, pp. 133–50, 168–71; Foust, College History draft, pp. 57–63; Link, *Paradox of Southern Progressivism*.

89. McIver, 11 April 1902, to Mrs. J.H. Bunting; 9 Jan. 1905, to Mrs. W.G. Randall; 17 Jan. 1905, to Charles B. Aycock, in McIver Letterbooks; Julius Foust, 15 Nov. 1928, to Fred W. Morrison, Foust Papers; Bratton, "Cradled in Conflict," pp. 77–99.

90. Notes and minutes of student meetings, February and April 1893, in McIver Papers.

91. Leloudis, *Schooling the New South*, pp. 119–20; Dean, "Covert Curriculum," pp. 279–80. For McIver's hand in mobilizing student support for the school, see McIver, 24 Feb. 1897, to wife, McIver Personal Papers.

92. McIver to wife, 7 July 1905, McIver Personal Papers; Holder, *McIver of North Carolina*, pp. 244–46.

93. Re the governorship, see McIver, 23 April 1896, to the *Greensboro Patriot*, McIver Papers. Re the UNC presidency, see R.H. Battle, 8 July 1896, to McIver, McIver Papers; McIver to wife, 12 July 1896, McIver Personal Papers; McIver, 16 July 1896, to [Maude] Bunn, La–Ly, Blackwell Papers, 1960; Raleigh *News & Observer*, 18 July 1896, in College Scrapbook, VIII, pp. 181–82. Re both opportunities, see Holder, *McIver of North Carolina*, pp. 166–69.

94. Raleigh *Morning Post*, 19 May 1900, in College Scrapbook, IX, p. 92; McIver to wife, 29 June 1904, McIver Personal Papers.

95. McIver, 24 Jan. 1904, to George Foster Peabody, McIver letterbooks; McIver, 25 Jan. 1904, to Hoke Smith and Thomas W. Dockery, 4 Feb. 1904, to McIver, McIver Papers.

96. Daniels, *Tarheel Editor*, pp. 461–63; Daniels, in W.C. Smith, ed., *Charles Duncan McIver*, pp. 231–34; McIver, 29 March 1906, to W.T. Carrington, McIver Letterbooks; Holder, *McIver of North Carolina*, pp. 253–54.

Chapter 2 Notes

1. Directors' Minutes, 20 May 1892; printed faculty list (with salaries written in), McIver Papers, 1894. My discussion of the charter faculty, their recruitment, origins, and credentials owes a great deal the to perceptive discussions in Leloudis, *Schooling the New South*, pp. 91–93; Dean, "Learning to be New Women," p. 289; and particularly in Dean, "Covert Curriculum," pp. 79, 82–92. See also McCandless, "Progressivism and the Higher Education of Southern Women," p. 312; faculty biographical sketches in Bowles, *Good Beginning*, pp. 31–67, and Camp, *Some Pioneeer Women Teachers*.

2. Holder, *McIver of North Carolina*, p. 133.

3. "History of Shorthand Writing in North Carolina," *State Normal Magazine*, 5 (Oct. 1900), pp. 5–8; *Carolinian*, 12 Dec. 1929, pp. 1, 2; 5 March 1948, p. 6; *Alumnae News*, 34 (Nov.

1945), pp. 4–5; 36 (May 1948), pp. 7–8; 45 (July 1957), pp. 7–8; Julius Foust, 6 Oct. 1941, to Edna Forney, Foust Private Papers; Faculty Council Minutes, 17 May 1948.

4. McIver, 10 Jan. 1906, to H.S. Kellogg, McIver Letterbooks; Obituary in *State Normal Magazine*, 10 (Dec. 1905), pp. 95–96.

5. McIver, 13 April 1904, to J.S. Jarman, McIver Papers; Camp, *Some Pioneer Women Teachers*, pp. 90–93 (quotation, p. 90); *Greensboro Record*, 16 Dec. 1939, in Faculty File: Gove; *Alumnae News*, 36 (May 1948), pp. 9–10; Bowles, *Good Beginning*, pp. 39–40.

6. Foust, College History draft, pp. 70–71; Camp, *Some Pioneer Women Teachers*, pp. 41–41; Bowles, *Good Beginning*, p. 34; Bryant, "Reminiscences Concerning the Early Curriculum," and Notations, typewritten ms., ca. 1940, in Faculty File: Bryant; Bryant, 7 June 1905, to McIver, McIver Papers; Bryant, [2 Dec. 1940], to Anna Gove, Gove Papers.

7. Camp, *Some Pioneer Women Teachers*, pp. 36–37; *Alumnae/i News*, 24 (Nov. 1935), pp. 12–13; 28 (April 1940), p. 10; 61 (Winter 1973), p. 8; Vaughn Holoman, 11 March 1935, to Julius Foust, Alumnae Letters, Foust Papers; Holder, *McIver of North Carolina*, p. 133.

8. Mendenhall, 3 March 1891, to Lula McIver, McIver Personal Papers; Camp, *Some Pioneer Women Teachers*, pp. 127–29; Gilbert, *Guilford: A Quaker College*, pp. 170, 181–82.

9. Dean, "Learning to be New Women," p. 289.

10. Dean, "Covert Curriculum," pp. 85–92.

11. Johnson, "James Yadkin Joyner," pp. 360–64; Bowles, *Good Beginning*, p. 40; Leloudis, *Schooling the New South*, p. 152.

12. Lewis, *Philander Priestley Claxton*, pp. 31–36, 42–47, 65, 70–81, 87; *State Normal Magazine*, 6 (Feb. 1902), pp. 244–45; 6 (April 1902), p. 364; *Alumni News*, 55 (Jan. 1967), p. 4; Bowles, *Good Beginning*, p. 38.

13. Camp, *Some Pioneer Women Teachers*, p. 162; Bowles, *Good Beginning*, pp. 42–43; Turrentine, *Romance of Education*, pp. 120–26.

14. Camp, *Some Pioneer Women Teachers*, pp. 152–53; Virginia T. Lathrop, in *Alumnae News*, 40 (Feb. 1952), pp. 10–12; Bowles, *Good Beginning*, pp. 41–42.

15. Petty, 18 May 1911, to Julius Foust; Minnie L. Blanton, 5 April 1918, to Foust, Foust Papers; Camp, *Some Pioneer Women Teachers*, pp. 154–55; *Alumnae News*, 12 (Oct. 1923), pp. 13–14; 40 (Feb. 1952), pp. 10–12; Bowles, *Good Beginning*, p. 43. For librarianship as the worst-paid profession, see Hamlin, *University Library*, p. 131.

16. Sharpe, 8 May 1905, to McIver, Mc, McIver Papers; *Alumnae News*, 33 (July 1944), p. 24; 54 (Summer 1966), p. 6; Bowles, *Good Beginning*, p. 45.

17. Letters from Georgia State College faculty members in behalf of Mrs. Phillips, 9–11 Aug. 1903, McIver Papers; McIver to wife, [15 Aug. 1903], McIver Personal Papers; McIver, 5 Aug., 5 Sept. 1903, to Mrs. Phillips, 23 Nov. 1903 to H.S. Kellogg, 26 July 1904 to Mrs. Phillips, 29 July 1904 to Lula M. Cassidy, McIver Letterbooks; Mrs. Phillips, annual report, 1904, McIver folder, McIver Papers; Mrs. A.R. Phillips, "Suggestions for a Vacation," *State Normal Magazine*, 8 (June 1904), pp. 179–86; account of commencement in ibid., p. 243; Minnie Jamison, Domestic Science in the Early Days, Faculty File: Jamison; Dillon, *Ulrich Bonnell Phillips*, pp. 5–6, 155; Roper, *U.B. Phillips*, pp. 6–7.

18. Obituary, with Faculty Council Minutes, 17 April 1944; Julius Foust to Cora Strong, 10 April 1944, Foust Private Papers (also in Faculty File: Coit); *Alumnae News*, 33 (Nov. 1944), pp. 4–5; Camp, *Some Pioneer Women Teachers*, pp. 51–53; Bowles, *Good Beginning*, pp. 43–44.

19. Camp, *Some Pioneer Women Teachers*, pp. 104–06; *Alumnae News*, 36 (May 1948), pp. 4–5; Obituary, with Faculty Council Minutes, 20 Sept. 1948; *Carolinian*, 20 Feb. 1948, in Faculty File, Jamison; Bowles, *Good Beginning*, pp. 44–45.

20. *State Normal Magazine*, 5 (Oct. 1900), pp. 32–33; 7 (Feb. 1903), pp. 159–60; *Alumnae News*, 32 (April 1944), p. 7; 33 (Nov. 1944), pp. 2–3; obituaries in Faculty File.

21. *Charlotte Observer*, [Jan. 1902], in College Scrapbook, X; Vaughn Holoman, 11 March 1935, to Julius Foust, Alumnae Letters, Foust Papers.

22. McIver, 18 Dec. 1902, to D.C. Gilman, McIver Letterbooks; Pearson, *Adventures in Bird Protection*, pp. 64–67, 70–71, 79–87; Orr, *Saving American Birds*, pp. 1–5, 8, 32, 76–78, 86–143, 156–57; Gilbert, *Guilford: A Quaker College*, pp. 205–08; Virginia Brown Douglas, in *Alumni News*, 70 (Fall 1981), pp. 17–19. Re the museum, see Orr, *Saving American Birds*, p. 89; *Carolinian*, 26 Feb. 1943.

23. *State Normal Magazine*, 10 (Nov. 1905), pp. 18–19; *Alumnae News*, 31 (Nov. 1942), p. 17; 44 (April 1956), p. 8; *Greensboro Daily News*, 25 Sept. 1939, 30 June 1940, 20 Feb. 1956, in Faculty File.

24. Rudolph, *American College and University*, p. 398; Veysey, *Emergence of the American University*, pp. 320–22.

25. See faculty salary list in Directors' Minutes, 19 May 1897.

26. See printed list of the faculty in *Catalog*, 1892–93, pp. 4–7.

27. Winston, 22 June 1891, to McIver, McIver Papers.

28. Printed faculty list, 1892–93, with handwritten salaries, McIver Papers, 1894; faculty list with salaries, in Directors' Minutes, 19 May 1897; Dean, "Covert Curriculum," pp. 78, 80; Veysey, *Emergence of the American University*, p. 390; Leslie, *Gentlemen and Scholars*, pp. 167–68; Rossiter, *Women Scientists... to 1940*, pp. 17, 197–98. For McIver's views on salaries, see McIver to T.D. Bratton, 21 Feb. 1903, and to M.O. Winfrey, 2 April 1906, McIver Letterbooks. For a series of faculty requests for salary increases in 1905, likely inspired by McIver himself prior to a board meeting, see his papers for early June 1905.

29. McIver, 21 Feb. 1903, to T.D. Bratton, and 27 May 1905, to Cora Strong, McIver Letterbooks.

30. Veysey, *Emergence of the American University*, p. 358; Geiger, *To Advance Knowledge*, p. 69; Harper, *Century of Public Teacher Education*, pp. 116–17.

31. *Catalog*, 1892–93, p. 42; McIver, 2 Jan. 1894, to A.M. Kellogg, McIver Papers; McIver, biennial report, in Directors' Minutes, 17 Dec. 1896; McIver, in *State Normal Magazine*, 6 (June 1902), pp. 443–44. See list of faculty activities during the summer of 1906, in ibid., 10 (Aug.) 1906, pp. 222–27.

32. McIver, 2 Aug. 1904, to Josephus Daniels; 18 Dec. 1902 to D.C. Gilman; 21 July 1906 to E.W. Gudger, McIver letterbooks.

33. The following discussion of the Normal curriculum draws heavily on Dean, "Covert Curriculum," pp. 97–148.

34. Rudolph, *Curriculum*, p. 170.

35. McIver to Howard Russell Butler, 16 Nov. 1901, McIver Papers.

36. Wechsler, *Qualified Student*, pp. viii–ix, 4; Rudolph, *Curriculum*, pp. 159–61; Rudolph, *American College and University*, pp. 281–83; Jencks and Riesman, *Academic Revolution*, pp. 279–80; Leslie, *Gentlemen and Scholars*, pp. 222–24; Gordon, *Gender and Higher Education*, pp. 168–72.

37. *Catalog*, 1892–93, pp. 46–47; McIver, biennial report, in Directors' Report, 1892–94, p. 9; Foust, College History draft, pp. 49–54.

38. McIver, report, with Directors' Report, 22 Dec. 1892.

39. Laura Coit, 11 Nov. 1901, to McIver, McIver Papers; Dean, "Covert Curriculum," p. 148n.

40. *North Carolina Public Laws*, 1897, chapter 230.

41. Bowles, *Good Beginning*, pp. 12–13.

42. Ethel Wicker, 4 July 1892, and Ethel Finlator, 28 June, 11 July 1892, to McIver, McIver Papers. For other examples, see McIver Papers, May to Sept. 1892, repeated in later years.

43. *Catalog*, 1892–93, pp. 36–37; McIver, 1 Aug. 1906, to Josephus Daniels, McIver Letterbooks.

44. McIver, 4 June 1894, to L.B. Edwards, McIver Papers.

45. President's report, 1902, in *State Normal Magazine*, 7 (Feb. 1903), pp. 163–64; Faculty Council Minutes, esp. 9, 27 May, 16 Sept. 1905; McIver, 25 July 1905, to J.T. Alderman; 23 Aug. 1905, to N.A. McLeod, McIver Letterbooks; *State Normal Magazine*, 10 (Nov. 1905), p. 20; 10 (Aug. 1906), pp. 255–56, 295–96; Foust, College History draft, pp. 97–107.

46. *Catalog*, 1892–93, p. 22; Bowles, *Good Beginning*, p. 94.

47. Eells, *Degrees in Higher Education*, pp. 90–91.

48. Butts, *College Charts Its Course*, pp. 240–42; Rudolph, *American College and University*, p. 303.

49. Foust, College History draft, p. 50.

50. Foust, College History Draft, p. 85; Dean, "Covert Curriculum," p. 99.

51. Normal School, biennial report, 1892–94, pp. 7–9.

52. Bryant, "Reminiscences Concerning the Early Curriculum," typewritten ms., Faculty File: Bryant.

53. Hofstadter and Metzger, *Development of Academic Freedom*, pp. 359–60.

54. Dean, "Covert Curriculum," pp. 150–52.

55. Claxton, pedagogy department annual report, 18 April 1898, and anonymous report, [1898], on practice school, in Miscellaneous Papers, Box 138, McIver Papers; Claxton, 20 May 1899, to McIver, McIver Papers; Nettie M. Allen, "Our Training School," *Alumnae News*, 4 (April 1916), p. 5; Bowles, "Curry School: A Proving Ground," *Alumni News*, 55 (Fall 1966), pp. 14–15.

56. Claxton, pedagogy department annual report, 18 April 1898, Miscellaneous Papers, Box 138, McIver Papers.

57. McIver, circular letter, 22 Aug. 1898, to citizens and property holders of Blowing Rock; McIver, 2 Sept. 1899, to Dear Sir, McIver folder, McIver Papers.

58. McIver, circular letter, 24 Nov. 1902, to county school superintendents, McIver folder, McIver Papers; McIver, 22 Dec. 1904, to C.G. Wright, McIver Letterbooks.

59. McIver, 12 March 1906, to county school superintendents; similar letter, 17 March 1906, to prospective students, McIver Papers.

60. Foust, College History draft, pp. 85–86; Dean, "Covert Curriculum," p. 99.

61. *State Normal Magazine*, 5 (Dec. 1900), p. 82; 5 (Feb. 1901), pp. 141, 153; McIver, 25 Aug. 1905, to Mrs. J.H. Withers, McIver Letterbooks.

62. *Catalog*, 1892–93, p. 18.

63. Rury, *Education and Women's Work*, p. 148.

64. *Catalog*, 1892–93, p. 18; McIver, printed prospectus, June 5, 1893, McIver Papers; Jamison, "Domestic Science in the Early Days," Faculty File: Jamison; Dean, "Covert Curriculum," pp. 100–01.

65. Richard Bardolph, "Physical Culture," *Alumni News*, 81 (Spring 1992), p. 17.

66. *Catalog*, 1892–93, p. 30; McIver, biennial report, with Directors' Minutes, 17 Dec. 1896; *State Normal Magazine*, I (Feb. 1898), p. 203; Mary Settle Sharpe, annual report, 19 April 1898, Miscellaneous Papers, Box 138, McIver Papers; Sharpe, 8 May 1905, to McIver, Mc folder, McIver Papers; Richard Bardolph, "Physical Culture," *Alumni News*, 81 (Spring 1992), pp. 17–18; Dean, "Covert Curriculum," pp. 206–08, 214; O'Neill, "History of the Physical Education Department," pp. 16–19; Means, *History of Health Education*, pp. 65–66; Newcomer, *Century of Higher Education*, pp. 101–02; Rice et al., *Brief History of Physical Education*, pp. 213–16; Hackensmith, *History of Physical Education*, pp. 400–01; Earnest, *Academic Procession*, pp. 177–78.

67. McIver report, 1893–94, with Directors' Minutes, 21 June 1894.

68. Lula M. McIver, 21 May 1942, to Guy Lyle, Correspondence, Office of Librarian Records; Annie Petty, in *Carolinian*, 1913, pp. 74–75; Maude B. Goodwin, in *Alumnae News*,

2 (Jan. 1913), p. 3; "The New Library," ibid., 12 (Oct. 1923), 12–14; Holder, "History of the Library of the Woman's College," pp. 7–18; UNCG Library, *Library Columns*, 29 (Oct. 1991), pp. 3–5.

69. *State Normal Magazine*, 1 (Dec. 1897), pp. 157–58; 4 (March 1900), pp. 64–65.

70. Walter Hines Page, 21 Oct. 1901, to McIver; McIver, 15 Nov. 1901, to Andrew Carnegie; McIver & Osborn, 3 Dec. 1901, to Carnegie, McIver Papers; Holder, "History of the Library of the Woman's College," pp. 22–25, 29–30. Re Carnegie, see Lagemann, *Politics of Knowledge*, pp. 16–20.

71. List of servants, 1894–95, McIver Papers, 1894.

72. For the African-American neighborhood, originally called Rhode Island and later the Warren Street community, see *Greensboro News & Record*, 15 Feb. 1986, in College History File.

73. *Carolinian*, 1913, pp. 79–80. Re William Peoples in particular, see J.A. Leach, 28 Dec. 1928, to Julius Foust, Foust Papers; *Carolinian*, 23, 30 May 1929; *Alumnae News*, 22 (July 1933), p. 20; W.C. Jackson, 8 Sept. 1948, to H.L. Trigg, Jackson Papers; Hicks, *My Life With History*, p. 119.

74. Edmund Faribault, 4 Jan. 1900 and undated [1903], to McIver; Laura Coit, 31 Oct. 1903, to McIver, McIver Papers; *State Normal Magazine*, 8 (Oct. 1903), p. 28.

75. *Decennial*, 1902, p. 149; *Carolinian*, 4 Oct. 1935, 21 Oct. 1938; *Greensboro Daily News*, 2 Oct. 1938. Robinson apparently planned to retire in 1944, then remained until it became mandatory two years later. *Greensboro Daily News*, 11 June 1944; Jackson, 2 July 1945, to Ezekiel Robinson, Jackson Papers; *Greensboro Record*, 2 Dec. 1960; Funeral obituary program, 3 Dec. 1960, all in Faculty File; *Alumnae News*, 33 (July 1944), p. 8; Dean, "Covert Curriculum," pp. 132, 290–92n.

Chapter 3 Notes

1. McIver report, 1892, with Directors' Minutes, 20 Dec. 1892, pp. 69–70; Foust, College History draft, p. 42.

2. Emily Asbury Yoder, in *Alumni News*, 63 (Summer 1975), p. 20. For the quotation, see Lilee to Gibby (Frances Gibson Satterfield), 27 Oct. 1937, Satterfield Papers, and Holder, *McIver of North Carolina*, p. 128.

3. McIver, 18 Feb. 1893, to Walter Hines Page, McIver Papers.

4. Reports of McIver and Directors, with Directors' Minutes, 20 Dec. 1892, pp. 63, 76; McIver, report, 1893–94, with Directors' Minutes, 21 June 1894; annual report, 18 Dec. 1902, in *State Normal Magazine*, 7 (Feb. 1903), pp. 160–61; McIver, 27 Sept. 1901, to Minnie Pepper; 18 Nov. 1902 to L.E. Snead; 26 Nov. 1902 to B.R. Lacy; 3 June 1903 to Mrs. W.D. Huff, McIver Letterbooks.

5. Laura Coit, 11 Jan. 1904, to McIver, McIver Papers.

6. *Catalog*, 1896–97, pp. 50–51. These annual data are conveniently brought together in subsequent published Directors' Reports, most comprehensively in 1916, p. 10.

7. McIver, 9 Sept. 1901, to J.F. Cook, McIver Letterbooks; Laura Coit, in *Carolinian*, 12 Dec. 1929.

8. Holder, *McIver of North Carolina*, p. 121.

9. Foust, College History notes: Expenditures, Foust Papers; Richard Bardolph, in *Alumni News*, 70 (Spring 1982), p. 15.

10. *Catalog*, 1892–93, pp. 43–44; McIver biennial report, with Directors' Minutes, 1–2 Dec. 1898.

11. *State Normal Magazine*, 5 (Dec. 1900), pp. 74–75; McIver, 12 June 1906, to B.R. Lacy, McIver Letterbooks; Richard Bardolph, in *Alumni News*, 70 (Spring 1982), p. 15.

12. *Catalog*, 1892–93, pp. 39–41; Fodie Buie Kenyon, in *Alumnae News*, 16 (Nov. 1926), pp. 16–17; Dean, "Covert Curriculum," pp. 115, 117–18.

13. Dean, "Covert Curriculum," pp. v–viii, xiv–xv, 119–20.

14. Maude B. Goodwin, in *Alumnae News*, 2 (Jan. 1913), p. 3; Fodie Buie Kenyon, in ibid., 16 (Nov. 1926), p. 17; [Minnie Jamison], "In The Early Days," typed ms., Faculty File: Jamison; Lillian G. Crisp, in *Carolinian*, 1913, p. 81.

15. Maude B. Goodwin, in *Alumnae News*, 2 (Jan. 1913), p. 2; Phoebe Pegram Baughan, in ibid., 25 (April 1937), p. 4; Fodie Buie Kenyon, in ibid., 30 (Nov. 1941), p. 13; (Feb. 1942), p. 4; [Minnie Jamison], "In The Early Days," Faculty File; Emily Asbury Yoder, "Recollections" (1956), and Sudie Israel Wolfe, "Memories," both handwritten mss., Alumni Association records, 1899–1988; Kathrine [sic] M. Robinson, in *Carolinian*, 1913, pp. 61–64; Dean, "Covert Curriculum," pp. 136–42; Holder, *McIver of North Carolina*, p. 129; Foust, College History draft, pp. 40–41, 48.

16. McIver, 7 Feb. 1894, to Maxcy L. John, McIver Papers.

17. Legislative committee report, in *Greensboro Patriot*, 10 March 1897, in College Scrapbook, V.

18. Directors' report, with Minutes of 20 Dec. 1892; Report of J.L. Ludlow, 27 Nov. 1899, following Directors' Minutes of 12 Jan. 1900; N.C. Board of Health, Report on the Sanitary Inspection of the State Institutions.... 1895, Vertical File: Typhoid Epidemic.

19. McIver correspondence, July–August 1895, McIver Papers; *Greensboro Record* and *Greensboro Patriot*, both 25 Sept. 1895, in College Scrapbook, IV; Report of building committee, 19 March 1896, with Directors' Minutes, 20 May 1896; McIver biennial report plus addenda, with Directors' Minutes, 17 Dec. 1896.

20. [Minnie Jamison], "In the Early Days," Faculty File; Holder, *McIver of North Carolina*, pp. 141, 270; E.J. Forney, obituary statement re Lula M. McIver, 30 April 1945, Jackson Papers.

21. "Miss Boddie," *Alumnae News*, 24 (Nov. 1935), 12.

22. Foust, College History draft, p. 46.

23. A.C. McAlister to S.M. Finger, 15 June 1892, McIver Papers.

24. Phoebe Pegram Baughan, in *Alumnae News*, 25 (April 1937), p. 5.

25. [Ruth Fitzgerald], "Sue May Kirkland," in Camp, *Some Pioneer Women Teachers*, pp. 114–16 including quotations (also in Faculty File: Kirkland); Raleigh *News & Observer*, 15 July 1892, in College Scrapbook, I (re music teaching); Virginia Brown Douglas, in *Alumni News*, 55 (Jan. 1967), pp. 3, 5; Vaughn Holoman, 11 March 1935, to Julius Foust, Alumnae Letters, Foust Papers; Obituary remarks, *Alumnae News*, 19 (Oct. 1914), pp. 4–5, 8–9, 11; Dean, "Covert Curriculum," pp. 92–95.

26. Martha E. Winfield, in *Alumnae News*, 10 (March 1921), p. 3.

27. Dean, "Covert Curriculum," pp. 158–61.

28. *Greensboro Record*, 16 Dec. 1939, in Faculty File: Gove.

29. *Carolinian*, 1913, p. 72; Anna Gove, 3 July 1947, to Clara Byrd, Vertical File: Infirmary; Nancy Beam Funderburk, Gove obituary remarks, *Carolinian*, 6 Feb. 1948.

30. McIver biennial report, with Directors' Minutes, 17 Dec. 1896.

31. *Greensboro Record*, 16 Dec. 1939, in Faculty File: Gove.

32. LeDuc, *Piety and Intellect at Amherst*, pp. 119–22; Solomon, *In the Company of Educated Women*, p. 105.

33. *Charlotte Democrat*, 3 April 1891, in College Scrapbook, I.

34. Adelphian Society Minutes, Spring 1893 to 11 Nov. 1893; Cornelian Society Minutes, October–November 1893; Minnie Jamison, handwritten ms. on the founding of the two societies, in Vertical File: Adelphian Society; [Jamison], "In the Early Days," Faculty File: Jami-

son; Fodie Buie Kenyon, in *Alumnae News*, 30 (Feb. 1942), p. 5; Nettie Allen Deans, 18 Oct. 1934, to Julius Foust, Alumnae Letters, Foust Papers; Dean, "Covert Curriculum," pp. 173–75, 181. E.J. Forney's account, *Leaves from the Stenographers' Note Books*, p. 18, written years after the events, conflicts in some essential details with the original records in the two sets of society minutes.

35. Dean, "Covert Curriculum," pp. 175–76; letters to Julius Foust from Nettie Allen Deans, 18 Oct. 1934, and Oeland Barnett Wray, 3 March 1935, Alumnae Letters, Foust Papers; Emily Herring Wilson, interview with Jane Summerell, in *Alumni News*, 61 (Winter 1973), pp. 7–8.

36. McIver biennial report, *State Normal Magazine*, 6 (June 1902), p. 446.

37. Agreement by the fourteen students to disband, 12 March 1896, McIver Papers; Directors' Minutes, 20 May 1896, limiting secret organizations to the literary societies; "Adelphian Literary Society," *Carolinian*, 1913, pp. 264–65. Dean, "Covert Curriculum," pp. 166–73.

38. Dean, "Covert Curriculum," pp. 176–78; letters to Julius Foust from Nettie Allen Deans, 18 Oct. 1934, Oeland Barnett Wray, 3 March 1935, Eunice K. Rankin, 27 May 1935, and Marion Stevens Hood, 15 March 1935, Alumnae Letters, Foust Papers; "Adelphian Society," *Carolinian*, 1913, p. 266.

39. Dean, "Covert Curriculum," pp. 161–62.

40. Raleigh *News & Observer*, 2 Dec. 1894, in College Scrapbook, IV, 67.

41. *State Normal Magazine*, 4 (May 1900), p. 116.

42. Dean, "Covert Curriculum," pp. 182–84.

43. Newcomer, *Century of Higher Education*, pp. 117–18; Schmidt, *Liberal Arts College*, pp. 142–43.

44. Dean, "Covert Curriculum," pp. 254–57, 260; "College News," *State Normal Magazine*, 1 (March 1897), pp. 28–29; 5 (Feb. 1901), pp. 142–43; Foust, College History draft, p. 51; Virginia Terrell Lathrop, "Development of the Societies," *Alumnae News*, 42 (Spring–Summer 1953), p. 12.

45. Trudy Atkins, 25 Oct. 1979, to W.E. Moran, VC for Development, Moran Papers; Statement of Jim Rogerson et al., December 1983, and copy of seal with legend "Adopted August 14, 1963," in Vertical File: Seal.

46. *Carolinian*, 1913, p. 107.

47. Maude B. Goodwin, "A Message from the Class of 1893," *Alumnae News*, 2 (Jan. 1913), 2; Minnie Jamison, handwritten ms., page on college colors, copy in Vertical File: Colors. Cf., "A Question of Color," *Alumnae News*, 75 (Winter 1987), 22.

48. "The Red and White Reunions," *Alumnae News*, 12 (July 1923), p. 12; Dean, "Covert Curriculum," pp. 198–200.

49. Commencement coverage in June issues of *State Normal Magazine*; Dean, "Covert Curriculum," pp. 200–02; Virginia Brown Douglas, in *Alumni News*, 55 (Jan. 1967), p. 3; *Carolinian*, 23 Sept. 1955, p. 8; 22 April 1982, p. 3. For the daisy chain's adoption, with variations, see *State Normal Magazine*, 3 (June 1899), p. 534; 4 (June 1900), p. 156; 5 (June 1901), p. 271; 6 (June 1902), p. 468; 7 (June 1903), p. 318. For its use elsewhere, see Schmidt, *Liberal Arts College*, p. 142; Earnest, *Academic Procession*, p. 194.

50. Marsden, *Soul of the American University*, p. 333; Crawford, *College Girl*, pp. v–vi.

51. See McIver, 6 July 1906, to Myron T. Scudder, McIver Letterbooks.

52. Julius Foust, 27 Oct. 1909, to M. Luther Canup, Foust Letterbooks.

53. Richard Bardolph, in *Alumni News*, 69 (Summer 1981), pp. 9–10; H. Hoyt Price, 21 Feb. 1972, to John L. Sanders, Q–R, Ferguson Papers. For evening vesper services, see [Minnie Jamison], "In the Early Days," Faculty File: Jamison.

54. The last quotation is from Holder, *McIver of North Carolina*, p. 135. The others are from Dean, "Covert Curriculum," pp. 154–57.

55. Dean, "Covert Curriculum," pp. 154–58, 186–93; Bertha M. Lee, "The Young Women's Christian Association," *Decennial*, 1902, pp. 106–07; Holder, *McIver of North Carolina*, pp. 134–35. For Etta Spier, see her obituary in S, Jackson Papers, 1939.

56. Dean, "Covert Curriculum," pp. 232–34; letters to Julius Foust from Nettie Allen Deans, 18 Oct. 1934, Oeland Barnett Wray, 3 March 1935, Eunice K. Rankin, 27 May 1935, and Eugenia Harris Holt, [1935], Alumnae Letters, Foust Papers.

57. Dean, "Learning to be New Women," pp. 289–91.

58. Dean, "Covert Curriculum," pp. 222–24, 226, 229. Quotations are on pp. 222, 226; Dean, "Learning to be New Women," pp. 291–92.

59. McCandless, "Progressivism and the Higher Education of Southern Women," p. 311; Requardt, "Alternative Professions," pp. 275–80.

60. Newspaper clippings in College Scrapbook, VI, and VII, pp. 44, 61–62.

61. *State Normal Magazine*, passim. For Daphne Carraway, see 5 (April 1901), pp. 202–03, 218.

62. McIver biennial report, 1892, with Directors' Minutes, 20 Dec. 1892, pp. 75–76; *Catalog*, 1901–02, pp. 49–50; Julia Dameron, 20 Oct. 1895, to mother, Williams/Dameron Papers; McIver, 18, 22 Nov. 1902, to H.M. Joyce and A.C. Trotter, McIver Letterbooks; Maude B. Goodwin, in *Alumnae News*, 2 (Jan. 1913), p. 3; Fodie Buie Kenyon, in ibid., 16 (Nov. 1926), pp. 17–18, and 30 (Feb. 1942), p. 5; Virginia Brown Douglas, in ibid., 55 (Jan. 1967), p. 5; Letters to Julius Foust from Oeland Barnett Wray, 3 March 1935, Nettie Allen Deans, 18 Oct. 1934, and Marion Stevens Hood, 15 March 1935, Alumnae Letters, Foust Papers; Dean, "Covert Curriculum," pp. 251–53; Richard Bardolph, "Centenary Project," *Alumni News*, 72 (Fall 1983), pp. 10–12.

63. *State Normal Magazine*, 7 (Oct. 1902), p. 75; Eleanor D.T. Kennedy, in *Alumni News*, 62 (Summer 1974), p. 2.

64. Confessions and correspondence, 1897, in McIver Papers; Leloudis, *Schooling the New South*, p. 262, n65; Dean, "Covert Curriculum," pp. 256–57.

65. McIver, 24 March 1903, to G.W. Graham, Jr., McIver Letterbooks.

66. McIver to wife, 9, 10, 11 Oct. 1904, McIver Papers.

67. McIver, 9 Oct. 1903, to M.C. Teague, McIver Letterbooks.

68. *Catalog*, 1892–93, p. 44.

69. Dean, "Covert Curriculum," pp. 258–60.

70. Mary Wiley diary, 30 Oct. 1892, 14 March 1893, 17 Jan. 1894, Calvin Wiley Papers.

71. *State Normal Magazine*, 1 (Feb. 1898), p. 203; 7 (Oct. 1902), pp. 68–69; Dean, "Covert Curriculum," p. 206; O'Neill, "History of the Physical Education Department," p. 18; Lojko, "Effects of Societal and Cultural Changes," pp. 30–31; Earnest, *Academic Procession*, p. 177.

72. *State Normal Magazine*, 4 (March 1900), pp. 64–65; (May 1900), p. 115, photo opp. p. 152; (June 1900), p. 173; Dean "Covert Curriculum," pp. 203, 213–15; Lojko, "Effects of Societal and Cultural Changes," pp. 1, 35–40.

73. *State Normal Magazine*, 5 (April 1901), p. 219; Lojko, "Effects of Societal and Cultural Changes," p. 40.

74. Bowles, *Good Beginning*, pp. 117–18; Dean, "Covert Curriculum," pp. 229–32.

75. Editorial, *State Normal Magazine*, 1 (Dec. 1897), pp. 154–55.

76. Julius Foust, 9 Nov. 1907, to W.R. Coppedge, Foust Letterbooks; W.C. Smith, "North Carolina State Normal," pp. 164–65.

77. Leloudis, *Schooling the New South*, p. 105.

78. Dean, "Covert Curriculum," pp. 248–50; Anne Wall, in *Alumnae News*, 36 (May 1948), p. 13.

79. McIver, 20 Feb. 1905, to William W. Boddie, McIver Letterbooks.

80. Byrd, "History of the Alumnae Association," pp. 1–6; Richard Bardolph, in *Alumni News*, 75 (Winter 1987), p. 16.

81. Directors' Minutes, 27 June 1895, 17 Dec. 1896, addenda; McIver correspondence, July–August 1895, McIver Papers; *Greensboro Record*, 28 Jan. 1893, 24 June, 28 June, 13 July 1895; *Greensboro Patriot*, 25 Sept. 1895, in College Scrapbook, I.

82. Directors' Minutes, 12 Jan. 1900, with attached reports; "The Cause of the Epidemic at the State Normal College," copied from *The Biblical Recorder*, 20 Dec. 1899, Vertical File: Typhoid Epidemic.

83. McIver correspondence, November 1899–January 1900, McIver Letterbooks and Papers; Newspaper clippings for same period, College Scrapbook, VIII, IX, including W.P. Beall, in North Carolina Board of Public Health *Bulletin*, Feb. 1900, pp. 77–80; *State Normal Magazine*, 4 (March 1900), p. 57; Foust, College History draft, pp. 86–87; Dean, "Covert Curriculum," p. 297.

84. Millie Archer, in *State Normal Magazine*, 8 (Feb. 1904), p. 115.

85. Official statement of Board of Directors, 30 Jan. 1900, Vertical File: Typhoid Epidemic; C.H. Mebane et al., draft report, 21 Dec. 1900, McIver Papers; Foust, College History draft, pp. 88–89.

86. McIver, 24 Jan. 1904, to George Foster Peabody and, same date, to Robert C. Ogden, McIver Letterbooks; Laura Coit, 13 Feb. 1904, to John J. Fowler; McIver, 20 Feb. 1904, to R.F. Beasley; Coit, 26 Feb. 1904, to Renny Lee Davis, McIver Papers; Millie Archer, in *State Normal Magazine*, 8 (Feb. 1904), pp. 114–16; [Minnie Jamison], "In the Early Days," Faculty File: Jamison; Eugenia Harris Holt, n.d. (1935), and Lizzie Stokes, 18 March 1935, to Julius Foust, Alumnae Letters, Foust Papers; Interview with Rena Bridgman Lupton, *Alumni News*, 65 (Winter 1977), p. 11; Mildred Rankin, "Reminiscences of the Fire," *Carolinian*, 1913, pp. 65–67; Notes of telephone conversation (1968) with Josephine Scott Hudson, Vertical File: Bell; Holder, *McIver of North Carolina*, pp. 232–36. Scott, who became ill from exposure, never returned to the college. But sixty-five years later, by then the sister of one North Carolina governor and aunt of another, she was belatedly honored at the UNCG Founders Day ceremony. Bessie Heath Daniel, 27 May 1968, to Clora McNeill (Foust); Daniel, 28 April 1969, to J.S. Ferguson; Certificate honoring Josephine Scott Hudson, 6 Oct. 1969, Ferguson Papers.

87. McIver, 27 Jan. 1904, to Wallace Buttrick, McIver Letterbooks.

88. Emily Semple Austin, in Forney, *Leaves from the Stenographers' Note Books*, p. 22; Vaughn Holoman, 11 March 1935, to Julius Foust, Alumnae Letters, Foust Papers; Foust, College History draft, pp. 135–37.

89. McIver, 24 Jan. 1904, to George Foster Peabody, McIver Letterbooks; McIver, 25 Jan. 1904, to Hoke Smith; Thomas W. Dockery, 4 Feb. 1904, to McIver, McIver Papers.

90. Emma Speight Morris, in *Alumnae News*, 24 (Nov. 1935), p. 5; 55 (Fall 1966), p. 21; McIver, 2 Feb. 1904, to Warren H. Manning; 5 Feb. 1904, to P.P. Claxton, McIver Letterbooks.

91. McIver, 24 Jan. 1904, to Robert C. Ogden, McIver letterbooks; Faculty Council Minutes, 25 Jan. 1904.

92. McIver, 15 June 1904, to Board of Directors, McIver Papers; *State Normal Magazine*, 9 (Oct. 1904), pp. 32–33; Richard Bardolph, in *Alumni News*, 75 (Spring 1987), pp. 16–20; *Carolinian*, 14 May 1954.

93. McIver, 13 Feb. 1905, to R.T. Gray; 15 March 1905, to Andrew J. Conner, McIver Letterbooks.

94. W.C. Smith, in *State Normal Magazine*, 10 (Aug. 1906), p. 222, and 11 (Nov. 1906), pp. 78–80; Vaughn Holoman, 11 March 1935, to Julius Foust, Alumnae Letters, Foust Papers.

95. Satterfield, *Charles Duncan McIver*, p. 58; Holder, *McIver of North Carolina*, pp. 256–58; Daniels, *Tarheel Editor*, pp. 459–60; W.C. Smith, "Charles Duncan McIver," pp. 7–47; *State Normal Magazine*, 11 (Nov. 1906), pp. 1–108.

Chapter 4 Notes

1. Directors' minutes, 19 Sept., 19 Nov. 1906; Foust, College History draft, p. 114; Orr, *Charles Brantley Aycock*, p. 357.

2. E.C. Brooks, 22 Nov. 1906, to Julius Foust, J.Y. Joyner, 29 July, 7 Oct. 1909, to Foust, Foust Papers; Foust, 30 May 1907, to G.C. Royall, and 3 June 1907, to Gov. R.B. Glenn, Foust Letterbooks; Correspondence, 9 May to 11 June 1907, Foust Private Papers; Joyner, 13 April 1907, to B.F. Aycock, and 13, 16 May 1907, to Foust; Foust, 13, 14 May 1907, to Joyner; B.F. Aycock, 15 May 1907, to Joyner, Joyner Papers, N.C. Archives; Bratton, *East Carolina University*, pp. 71–72; Bratton, "Cradled in Conflict," p. 96; Directors' Minutes, 28 May 1907.

For evidence of a lifelong Joyner-Foust friendship, see Foust, 6 March 1940, to Joyner, College History correspondence, Foust Papers. Many years later, P.P. Claxton's biographer claimed that Claxton had been offered the presidency at this time, but turned it down. There is no evidence for this in the records and Joyner (who as board president would have known) denied that Claxton had ever been offered the job. Lewis, *Philander Priestley Claxton*, p. 143; W.C. Jackson, 18 Oct. 1948, to Joyner, and Joyner, 26 Oct. 1948, to Jackson, Jackson Papers.

Although Foust and the Normal students opposed the East Carolina charter, Foust set out to mend fences once the decision was made. See letters to Foust from J.A. Gordon, 16 Jan. 1907 and Thomas J. Jarvis, 2 Feb. 1907, Foust Papers; Foust, 7 Dec. 1907, to Laura Coit, Foust Letterbooks; Vaughn Holoman, 11 March 1935, and Marion Stevens Hood, 15 March 1935, to Foust, Alumnae Letters, Foust Papers.

3. McIver, 18 June 1906, to J.B. Aswell, McIver Letterbooks.

4. See Julius Foust, 6 Dec. 1913, to R.L. Doughton, Foust Letterbooks; Ava Jordan Tate, 31 March 1935, to Foust, Alumnae Letters, Foust Papers; *Alumni News*, 60 (Fall 1971), pp. 9–11.

5. Walter Clark, 2 Aug. 1899, to McIver, McIver Papers; Foust, 28 Jan., 4 Feb., 2 April 1913, to Daisy B. Waitt, Foust Letterbooks.

6. *Alumnae News*, 5 (June 1916), pp. 4–5.

7. Foust, 22 March 1917, to Minnie M. Brown, Foust Papers; *Alumnae News*, 31 (Feb. 1943), pp. 6–7.

8. Foust, College History draft, pp. 114–15. UNCG *Fact Book*, 1995–96, p. I-5. The Normal's appropriation actually exceeded the university's in some years at the turn of the century. See State Treasurer, Biennial reports.

9. See *State Normal Magazine*, 13 (March 1909), p. 142; 17 (March, April 1913), pp. 335–36, 407; Foust, 9 Feb. 1919, to Adelaide Van Noppen, Foust Papers.

10. Foust, College History draft, p. 161.

11. See Foust, 4 Oct. 1919, to E.W. Gudger, and Gudger, 18 Oct. 1919, to Foust, Foust Papers.

12. Faculty Council Minutes, 28 Jan. 1907; Directors' Minutes, 18 Jan. 1908, 12 Jan. 1909, 22 May 1911, 1 Jan. 1915; W.C. Smith, 13 Nov. 1908, to Foust; Foust, 13 Sept. 1919, to Jackson, Foust Papers; Foust, 17 March 1910, 13 May 1914, to D.B. Johnson, Foust Letterbooks.

13. Jackson, 31 Oct. 1949, to E.W. Gudger, Jackson Papers; Obituaries in Jackson Papers, 1948; Faculty Council Minutes, 15 Nov. 1948; Faculty File.

14. Warren H. Manning, 16 March, 18 June 1908, 22 Dec. 1917, to Foust; Manning, "View of Campus," Jan. 1909; Foust, 12 June 1908, to Manning; Pencilled notes from [Charles C. Hook], 9 Feb. 1909, to Foust, Foust Papers; Directors' Executive Committee Minutes, 7 July, 28 Dec. 1917.

15. McIver, 19 Jan. 1906, to Wallace Buttrick, and 20 Jan. 1906, to W.P. Bynum, McIver Papers.

16. Deeds, 19 Dec. 1908; Foust, 12 Jan. 1914, to James R. Young and, 6, 8 May 1918, to Mrs. J.A. Brown, Foust Papers; Foust biennial reports, 1908, p. 7, 1918, pp. 11–12, with Directors' Reports; Directors' Executive Committe Minutes, 22 Feb. 1910, 9 Sept. 1913, 3 Aug. 1916, 7 July 1917; Directors' Minutes, 27 April 1918, 21 May 1919; Foust, College History draft, pp. 130–35.

17. Directors' Minutes, 19 Sept. 1906, 27 May 1907; Foust, College History draft, pp. 130–32.

18. Foust, 22 Nov. 1917, to James R. Young, Foust Papers.

19. Foust, 11 Feb. 1913, to R.A. Doughton, and Directors' report, 1917, Foust Papers; *State Normal Magazine*, 12 (June 1908), p. 192; *Carolinian*, 1913, pp. 72–73; Foust, College History draft, pp. 140–41.

20. Fund-raising letter from Gertrude W. Mendenhall et al., 8 Oct. 1906, Vertical File: McIver Statue; Directors' Report, 15 Sept. 1912, pp. 25, 27; J.Y. Joyner, 23 Dec. 1909, to Lula M. McIver, Foust Papers.

21. F.W. Ruckstuhl, 4 Jan. 1915, to Foust; Foust, 15 Jan. 1915, to Ruckstuhl, Foust Papers; Charles M. Adams, 1 May 1962, to James W. Patton, K–M, Singletary Papers.

22. For the first three years, see Foust, 2 Oct. 1909, to J.Y. Joyner, Foust Letterbooks; *State Normal Magazine*, 14 (Nov. 1909), pp. 26–28; 15 (Nov. 1910) p. 127; 16 (Nov. 1911) p. 110. See also W.C. Jackson, 31 Oct. 1947, to Mrs. M.B. Satterfield, Alumnae, Jackson Papers. For 1913 and later, see Foust, 16 Aug. 1913, to J.H. Small, Foust Letterbooks; Foust, 27 July 1921, to Charles E. Maddry, Foust Papers.

23. *State Normal Magazine*, 15 (May 1911), p. 409; 18 (May 1914), p. 533; Marion Stevens Hood, 15 March 1935, and Celeste Jonas Gibson, 25 March 1935, to Foust, Alumnae Letters, Foust Papers; Katherine G. Rogers, 12 Jan. 1982, to Richard Bardolph, Alumni Association Records, 1899–1988.

24. *State Normal Magazine*, 17 (Nov. 1912), p. 97; 18 (Oct. 1913), p. 58; Directors' Minutes, 26 May 1913; Directors' Report, 1914, p. 10; Foust, 12 Jan. 1914, to J.R. Young, Foust Papers; Richard Bardolph, notes of interview with Mrs. Robert Merritt and Robert Merritt, Jr., ca. 1981, UNCG Archives.

25. Permit, 12 July 1910, from Greensboro Dept. of Health, D, Foust Papers.

26. Foust, 26 March 1917, to J.L. King; 28 Sept. 1917 to J.D. Grimes; 7 Nov. 1917, to J.G. Hanner; 1 Jan. 1918, to David White, Foust Papers, 1917; Report of G.W. Hinshaw, with Directors' Executive Committee Minutes, 28 Dec. 1917; Foust correspondence with C.D. Benbow, 21 July 1917, 29 March 1923 ff, in B, Foust Papers, 1923; Foust, College History draft, p. 141.

27. G.W. Hinshaw report, Directors' Executive Committee Minutes, 28 Dec. 1917; *Alumnae News*, 42 (Spring–Summer 1953), p. 8; *Greensboro Daily News*, 1 July 1953, in Faculty File.

28. Directors' Report, 1916, p. 10.

29. Foust, College History draft, p. 79.

30. For the Serbian girls, see W.C. Jackson, 1 May 1919, to Foust; Foust, 1 May 1919, to Jackson and 8 Dec. 1919 to Ida Gordner [sic], Foust Papers.

31. Directors' Minutes, 21 May 1919.

32. Annie Goodloe Randall, 23 July 1909, to Foust, Foust Papers; Foust, 26 July 1909, to Belle Andrews, 26 or 27 July 1909 to Annie G. Randall, and 8 Oct. 1913 to Blanche Hamilton, Foust Letterbooks; *State Normal Magazine*, 15 (Oct. 1910), pp. 46–47.

33. Foust, 17 Nov. 1914, to Annie J. Gash, Foust Letterbooks.

34. *State Normal Magazine*, 13 (June 1909), pp. 172–75.

35. Foust, 7 Oct. 1908, to Peabody Board, Foust Letterbooks; Directors' Report, 1910, p. 16.

36. Interview in *Alumni News*, 61 (Winter 1973), p. 6.

37. Foust, 8 Aug. 1910, to Kirkland, Foust letterbooks. See also W.C. Smith, 12 June 1909, to Foust, Foust Papers.

38. Richard Bardolph, in *Alumni News*, 72 (Fall 1983), p. 11. See also E.W. Gudger, 21 June 1914, to Foust, Foust Papers; Directors' Executive Committee Minutes, 12 Oct. 1914; Directors' Minutes, 1 Jan. 1915. For King, see *Carolinian*, 18 Nov. 1938, p. 1.

39. For national developments, see Newcomer, *Century of Higher Education*, pp. 118–19; Rudolph, *American College and University*, p. 369.

40. Jane Summerell, in *Alumni News*, 61 (Winter 1973), p. 7.

41. *State Normal Magazine*, 14 (May 1910), pp. 180–84, 221–24 (quotation on pp. 222–23); 15 (Oct. 1910), p. 45; Foust, 5 May 1911, to Mary Frances Wickliffe, Foust Letterbooks; *Carolinian*, 1913, p. 279.

42. *State Normal Magazine*, 16 (April 1912), pp. 389–90.

43. Gladys Avery Tillett, in *Alumni News*, 55 (July 1967), pp. 12–13, and 65 (Spring 1977), p. 19; May Worth Rock, 28 March 1935, and Caroline Goforth Hogue, 10 March 1935, to Foust, Alumnae Letters, Foust Papers.

44. Foust, 24 July 1913, to Willie May Stratford; 26 Oct. 1914, to W.A. Wilkinson, and Laura Coit, 11 Dec. 1914, to Willie May Stratford, Foust Letterbooks; Directors' Minutes, 1 Jan. 1915.

45. Constitution, in *Student Handbook*, 1915–1916, pp. 37–48.

46. Foust, 30 Sept. 1915, to Rosa Blakeney; Foust, 30 April 1915, to presidents of Wellesley, Randolph-Macon, Bryn Mawr, Smith, Mt. Holyoke, and Sweet Briar Colleges, Foust Letterbooks; Gladys Avery Tillett in *Alumni News*, 55 (July 1967), p. 13.

47. See Ruth Kernodle, 21 Jan. 1918, to Laura Coit; Adelaide Van Noppen, 13 Dec. 1918, 25 April 1919, to Foust, Foust Papers.

48. Richard Bardolph, in *Alumni News*, 72 (Winter 1984), pp. 12–13; Bowles, *Good Beginning*, pp. 145–46.

49. *State Normal Magazine*, 21 (May 1917), p. 257; Foust, 26 April 1918, to Helen H. Law, Foust Papers.

50. W.C. Jackson, 7 May 1919, to T.R. Hodges, Foust Papers.

51. Directors' Minutes, 27 April 1918.

52. See *State Normal Magazine*, 14 (Jan., March 1910), pp. 87–89, 156–57, 162; 15 (Jan. 1911), pp. 221–22; 16 (Dec. 1911), 149–50; 22 (May, June 1918), pp. 263, 298; *Carolinian*, 13 Dec. 1928, p. 3.

53. See description of the marshals' role in *Student Handbook*, 1917–18, pp. 30–31.

54. Bowles, *Good Beginning*, p. 135.

55. *State Normal Magazine*, 17 (April 1913), pp. 402–03.

56. *State Normal Magazine*, 13 (Jan. 1909), p. 78.

57. Faculty Council Minutes, 26 Feb. 1912, 28 April 1913; Eleanor Morgan Phipps, in *Alumni News*, 56 (Spring 1968), p. 3.

58. Glassberg, *American Historical Pageantry*, pp. 35–37, 96–101, 137, 191; Rice, *Brief History of Physical Education*, p. 245.

59. Trelease, *Changing Assignments*, pp. III-170–77; *Greensboro Daily News*, 19 May 1912, 20 May 1916; *State Normal Magazine*, 20 (April–May 1916), pp. 302–03; *Alumnae/i News*, 36 (May 1948), p. 15; 54 (Summer 1966), pp. 2–7; Katherine G. Rogers, 12 Jan. 1982, to Richard Bardolph, Alumni Association Records, 1899–1988. For some of the sacrifices entailed, see *State Normal Magazine*, 16 (Nov. 1911, April 1912), pp. 104, 394–95; letters to Foust from Ava Jordan Tate and May Worth Rock, 31 March 1935, and Arnette Hathaway Avery, 30 April 1935, Alumnae Letters, Foust Papers.

60. See Foust, 30 Sept. 1908, to Henry Weil, Foust Letterbooks. For an account of a supposedly typical chapel service in 1914, see *Carolinian*, 1914, pp. 198–99.

61. *State Normal Magazine*, 11 (March 1907), pp. 232–33; Marion Stevens Hood, 15 March 1935, to Foust, Alumnae Letters, Foust Papers. For a printed list of the course offerings in Fall 1917, see Vertical File: Religious Activities. For the national background, see Marsden, *Soul of the American University*, pp. 334–35; Altbach, *Student Politics in America*, pp. 29–30, 51.

62. See *Carolinian*, 1913, pp. 242–44; *Catalog*, 1916–17, pp. 135–36; Richard Bardolph, in *Alumni News*, 72 (Winter 1984), p. 12.

63. *State Normal Magazine*, 23 (Oct. 1918), p. 2; Foust, 14 Sept. 1918, to Gertrude Weil; 7 March 1919, to Lucy Crisp; Crisp, 29 March 1919, to Foust; Foust, 23 Oct. 1919, to Florence Stephenson, Foust Papers; *N.C. Community Progress*, 3 (Nov. 5, 1921), pp. 1–2, in Vertical File: YWCA Hut; Foust, College History draft, p. 152; *Carolinian*, 23 Oct. 1942, p. 6; Trelease, *Changing Assignments*, pp. III-116–19.

64. For Laura Cone, see Faculty Council Minutes, 26 Oct. 1909; *Alumni News*, 58 (Spring 1970), pp. 42–43; 69 (Winter 1981), p. 14; Dean, "Covert Curriculum," p. 190; *Carolinian*, 31 Oct. 1952, p. 3.

65. *State Normal Magazine*, 13 (Nov. 1908), p. 26.

66. *Student Handbook*, 1910–11, p. 19; Foust, 26 Nov. 1941, to Clara Byrd, Foust Private Papers; *Carolinian*, 31 Oct. 1952, p. 3; *Alumni News*, 64 (Winter, Spring 1976), pp. 34, 41.

67. For a statement of the obligation, see Foust's remarks to the 1909 graduating class, in *State Normal Magazine*, 13 (June 1909), pp. 194–95.

68. Rudolph, *American College and University*, pp. 356–59.

69. Marion Stevens Hood, 15 March 1935, to Foust, Alumnae Letters, Foust Papers; Foust, 26 Nov. 1941, to Clara Byrd, Foust Private Papers. For an alternative suggestion that the motto originated with the first graduating class of 1893, see Maude Broadaway Goodwyn, in *Alumnae News*, June 1912, p. 2.

70. Folder of student statements concerning their personal donations to the war effort, Foust Papers, 1917; Foust, 21 Nov. 1917, to S.L. Alderman; 1 Aug. 1918 to D.H. Hill, Foust Papers; Foust, College History draft, pp. 147–62; "Farming for Uncle Sam, 1918," in Marjorie Craig Diary, UNCG Archives; Trelease, *Changing Assignments*, pp. III-106–10. For Vassar College—where over 200 students volunteered—see Horowitz, *Alma Mater*, p. 297.

71. *State Normal Magazine*, 14 (Jan. 1910), p. 104. For the national background, see Lee, *Campus Scene*, pp. 13–14; Solomon, *In the Company of Educated Women*, pp. 111–13; Flexner, *Century of Struggle*, pp. 248–93, 306, 319.

72. *State Normal Magazine*, 16 (April 1912), pp. 341–48; 17 (March 1913), pp. 328–29; 18 (April 1914), pp. 440, 447–48; 19 (March 1915), pp. 219–20.

73. For Foust's support, see Foust, 28 May 1918, to Sen. Lee S. Overman; 3 June 1918, to Julia Dameron, Foust Papers.

74. Harriet Elliott, 12 May 1946, to Robert B. House, in Dean of Women, VC for Student Affairs records; *Alumni News*, 55 (July 1967), p. 12; 73 (Fall 1984), pp. 8–9; Dean, "Learning to be New Women," pp. 298–302.

75. *Carolinian*, 29 March 1935, pp. 1, 3; *Alumni News*, 63 (Spring 1975), p. 20.

76. *State Normal Magazine*, 21 (May 1917), pp. 252; 22 (March–June 1918), pp. 211, 253, 331–32; 33 (May–June 1919), pp. 242–44; *Alumnae/i News*, 7 (June 1918), p. 5; 8 (Aug. 1919), passim; 73 (Fall 1984), pp. 10–11; [Virginia Terrell Lathrop], "The Spirit of Anna Howard Shaw," Vertical File: Anna Howard Shaw; *Carolinian*, 6 Feb. 1948.

77. Anne Wall, in *Alumnae News*, 36 (May 1948), p. 13.

78. Foust, 3 March 1917, to R.G. Kittrell, Foust Papers.

79. Foust, 24 June 1915, to Rachel S. Lynch, Foust Letterbooks; Foust, 11 Dec. 1919, to W. Vaughan Howard, Foust Papers.

80. McIver, 2 April 1906, to J. Alex Moore, McIver Letterbooks.

81. *State Normal Magazine*, 10 (Aug. 1906), pp. 254, 300–02; 12 (Nov. 1907), p. 41; Byrd, "History of the Alumnae Association," p. 6.

82. Foust, 7 June 1907, to Lewis Dull, Foust Letterbooks; Byrd, "History of the Alumnae Association," pp. 6–13; Richard Bardolph, in *Alumni News*, 75 (Winter 1987), pp. 16–19, and 76 (Spring 1988), pp. 16–17.

Chapter 5 Notes

1. Kimmel, "Catalogue Study of the Faculty," Table I.

2. Foust, 8 June 1908, to I.C. Pratt; 10 Sept. 1910, to Mrs. H.R. Bryan, Foust Letterbooks.

3. Harriet Elliott, 8 April 1913, to Foust, Foust Papers.

4. Foust, 9 July 1917, to Sallie Guerrant, Foust Papers; Foust, 29 March 1913, to Isabel E. Lord; Foust, 31 Jan. 1914, to officials at Johns Hopkins, Chicago, and Columbia Universities, Foust Letterbooks. See also, re married women, Mrs. W.K. Hartsell, 22 June 1909, to Foust, Foust Papers.

5. See, for example, *State Normal Magazine*, 13 (Nov. 1908), pp. 35–38.

6. See Foust, 7 July, 10 Aug. 1908, to Julia Dameron, Foust Letterbooks.

7. Foust, 24 June 1907, to Viola Boddie, and 3 July 1907 to Melville Fort, Foust Letterbooks.

8. *State Normal Magazine*, 14 (May 1910), pp. 231–32.

9. Foust, 19 Feb. 1915, to R.A. Merritt, Foust Letterbooks; Joyner, 12 June 1916, to Foust; Foust, 21 July, 5 Aug. 1916, to Merritt, Foust Papers.

10. W.C. Smith, 29 April 1919, to Foust, Foust Papers.

11. Earnest, *Academic Procession*, pp. 277, 295; Foust, 21 Feb. 1911, to L.V. Bassett, Foust Letterbooks.

12. Foust, 17 Feb. 1919, to A.M. Scales, Foust Papers.

13. Foust, 4 Feb. 1918, to Francis W. Shephardson, and 3 June 1918 to Julia Dameron, Foust Papers.

14. Foust, circular letter, 25 June 1917, to certain faculty; Elva Barrow, 28 June 1917, to Foust; Foust, 24 July 1917, to Barrow, Foust Papers.

15. Directors' Minutes, 21 May 1919. For the national background, see Metzger, "Academic Tenure in America," pp. 123–35.

16. Directors' Executive Committee Minutes, 28 Dec. 1915; Foust, 10 May 1915, to W.C.A. Hammel, Foust Papers.

17. See McIver, in *State Normal Magazine*, 10 (March 1906), 212, 296.

18. Foust, 4 March 1916, to Miss I.L. Pratt; E.W. Gudger, 7 June [1915], to Foust; W.C.A. Hammel, 19 June 1917, to Foust; Foust, 16 Oct. 1917, to Mrs. W.N. Hutt; Foust, 24 March, 7 July 1919, to Julia Raines; Raines, 4 April 1919, to Foust; Raines, 14 July 1919, to J.Y. Joyner; Melville W. Fort, 8 Feb. 1920, to Foust, and Foust, 11 Feb. 1920, to Fort, Foust Papers; W.C. Jackson, 2 Nov. 1944, to E.W. Gudger; Gudger, 13 Nov. 1944, to Jackson, Jackson Papers.

19. Foust, 10 June 1907, to E.E. Balcomb, and 19 June 1909, to Charles R. Van Hise, Foust Letterbooks.

20. Foust, 4 Aug., 1 Sept. 1911, to E.E. Balcomb; Foust, 7 Sept. 1911, to Josephus Daniels; Balcomb, 2 June 1912, 30 Jan., 3, 10 April, 15 May 1913, to Foust; Foust article for Raleigh *News & Observer* [1913], Foust Papers; Foust, 17 Oct. 1913, to Clarence Poe, and 3 Nov. 1913 to P.P. Claxton, Foust Letterbooks. For comparable developments at George

Peabody College for Teachers in Nashville, see Hoffschwelle, "Science of Domesticity," pp. 659–68.

21. *Catalogs*, 1913–20; Foust-Balcomb correspondence, 18 March to 18 July 1919; Mrs. E.E. Balcomb, 29 Aug. 1919, to Laura Coit, Foust Papers.

22. *State Normal Magazine*, 18 (Oct. 1913), p. 57.

23. *Greensboro Daily News*, 8 Feb., 22, 23 March 1918; Correspondence of Foust with Reincken and Schoch, 13, 18 Feb., 1 July [June], 5, 22 June, 4, 25, 26 July, 5 Aug. 1918, 7 April 1919, Foust Papers; Directors' Minutes, 27 April, 18 June 1918.

24. Faculty Council Minutes, 10 May, 13 Sept. 1909; Foust, 26 April 1909, to F.P. Venable, Foust Letterbooks; Hermann H. Hoexter, 15 Oct. 1909, to Foust, Foust Papers; Veysey, *Emergence of the American University*, pp. 304–05.

25. Foust, 25 April 1911, to C.L. Coon, Foust Letterbooks.

26. Mary T. Moore report, Faculty Council Minutes, 23 Oct. 1911.

27. Foust, 20 Nov. 1913, 16 Jan. 1914, to C.G. Vardell, Foust Letterbooks.

28. *Catalog*, 1911–12, pp. 20, 27.

29. E.W. Gudger, 22 Oct. 1917, to Foust, Foust Papers.

30. See Foust, annual report, in Directors' report, 1918, pp. 12–13.

31. Foust, 22 Jan. 1911, to R.T. Vann; Foust, 20 May 1915, to W.D. Magginnis, Foust Letterbooks; W.C. Smith, n.d. [1917], to Directors, Foust Papers.

32. In Memoriam, Julius I. Foust, in Faculty Council Minutes, 21 Oct. 1946; Foust, 6 Sept. 1941, to W.C. Smith, College History correspondence, Foust Papers; Foust, College History draft, pp. 116–18. For Foust's aspirations for the college over the years, see his letters, 18 May 1911, to Eleanor J. Gladstone, 2 April 1913, to Daisy B. Waitt; 28 Jan. 1914, to J.L. Jarman, Foust Letterbooks; 3 Aug. 1916, to T.W. Bickett, Foust Papers; and, 17 June 1942, to Mrs. T.B. Edmunds, Foust Private Papers.

33. For alumnae views, see Frances Womble et al., 22 Dec. 1916, to Board of Directors, Foust Papers; Foust, 26 July 1913, to Isabelle L. Pratt, Foust Letterbooks. For student opinion, see *State Normal Magazine*, 21 (Feb. 1917), p. 139.

34. Alumnae committee, 16 Nov. 1918, to the Board; Adelaide Van Noppen, 4 Dec. 1918, to Foust; Foust, 3, 13 Feb. 1919, to Laura Coit; Foust, 17 Feb. 1919, to Julia Dameron, Foust Papers; Directors Minutes, 25 Feb. 1919; *North Carolina Public Laws*, 1919, chap. 199.

35. Faculty Council Minutes, 24 March 1919; Laura Coit, 24 March 1919, to Foust; Foust, 21 April 1919, to the Faculty, Foust Papers.

36. For background concerning the regional accrediting agencies, see Selden, *Accreditation*, pp. 31–32, 38–40; Rudolph, *Curriculum*, pp. 221–26; McCandless, "Progressivism and the Higher Education of Southern Women," p. 318.

37. For Jackson's views as given in campus talks, see *Carolinian*, 30 April, 7 May 1921, 15 July 1922, 3 March 1923, 16 Feb. 1928, 2 May 1929; *Alumnae News*, 18 (Nov. 1929), pp. 7–8.

38. W.C. Jackson, 4 Oct. 1940, to Ernest J. Arnold, and 9 March 1950 to W.D. Carmichael, Jackson Papers. See testimony of former students Virginia Terrell Lathrop and Gladys Avery Tillett, respectively, in *Alumni News*, 62 (Spring 1974), pp. 12–15, and 65 (Spring 1977), p. 19.

39. *Carolinian*, 28 Oct. 1922, p. 1.

40. Caroline Goforth Hogue, 10 March 1935, to Foust, Alumnae Letters, Foust Papers; *Alumnae News*, 36 (Nov. 1947), pp. 3–4; 55 (July 1967), pp. 6, 12–13; 65 (Spring 1977), pp. 17–18; Virginia Terrell Lathrop, *Asheville Citizen-Times*, 26 Aug. 1973, in Vertical File: Women's Suffrage; Annie Lee, "Pen Feathers," *Winston-Salem Journal & Sentinel*, 17 Aug. 1947, and Frank P. Hobgood ms., both in Harriet Elliott folder, Jackson Papers, 1947.

41. For Elliott's marketability, see Jackson, 17 May 1917, to Foust, and Elliott, 15 May 1919, to Foust, Foust Papers.

42. *Catalogs*, 1907–20; H.H. Beneke, 26 June 1919, to Foust, Foust Papers; Harriet Elliott, 22 Feb. 1943, to E.E. Pfaff, Dean of Women Papers, VC Student Affairs records; Glenn R. Johnson, in *Alumnae News*, 34 (April 1946), p. 2. For Jackson and Elliott's efforts to upgrade the history offerings, see Jackson, 27 March 1919, to Foust, Foust Papers.

43. See letters to Foust from Caroline Goforth Hogue, 10 March 1935, and May Worth Rock, 28 March 1935, Alumnae Letters, Foust Papers.

44. See E.W. Gudger to Foust, 23 May 1908, 18 May, 22 Oct. 1917, Foust Papers.

45. Correspondence between Gudger and Foust, 5, 10 Feb., 25 March, 3 April 1919, 23 March, 21 April, 10 May, 1 July 1920, Foust Papers.

46. Mary Wyche, 15 Nov. 1907, to Foust, with printed open letter, Foust Papers; Foust, 27 Sept., 1912, to Wyche, Foust Letterbooks.

47. See unidentified newspaper clipping on Matheson's arrival, in Faculty File. Foust's letterbooks and papers are full of correspondence concerning these cases, from March 1914 through February 1915.

48. Faculty Council Minutes, 11 June, 3 Aug. 1912; Foust, 12 July 1912, to Julia Dameron, and 11 Feb. 1913 to R.A. Doughton, Foust Letterbooks; W.C. Smith, in *Alumnae News*, 1 (Nov. 1912), p. 4; Foust article for Raleigh *News & Observer* [1913]; John H. Cook, summer school report, 16 Dec. 1925, Foust Papers; Jim Clark, in *Alumni News*, 68 (Summer 1980), p. 6.

49. Summer Session report, 1922, Directors' Reports, 1922, p. 35.

50. *Catalog*, 1914–15, pp. 146–50; Charles M. Adams, 20 Nov. 1962, to L.R. Wilson, Vertical File: Male Students.

51. Foust, 19 Sept. 1911, to J.L. Mann, Foust Letterbooks; J.L. Mann, 1 Aug. 1913, to Foust, with accompanying agreement between city and college; Greensboro Board of Commissioners, minute [1915]; Foust, 7 Jan. 1916, to J.G. Foushee; 6 March 1916, to T.J. Murphy; 19 Dec. 1916, to J.H. Ackerman, Foust Papers; Elisabeth Bowles, in *Alumni News*, 55 (Fall 1966), pp. 15, 23.

52. Foust, 15 March 1918, to five Curry teachers; 15 April 1918, to Frederick Archer; 12 Aug. 1918, to H.B. Smith; 23 Sept. 1918, to Henry Louis Smith, Foust Papers.

53. [Jamison], "Domestic Science in the Early Days," Faculty File: Jamison; Matthews, "*Just a Housewife*," pp. 157–66.

54. Foust, 25 Aug. 1914, to Kate R. Styron, Foust Letterbooks; E.W. Gudger, 13 Nov. 1944, to W.C. Jackson, Jackson Papers.

55. Faculty Council Minutes, 8 Nov. 1915, 27 Nov. 1916; Foust, 28 Nov. 1916, to Mary Petty, and 5 June 1917, to J.Y.Joyner, Foust Papers.

56. Blanche Shaffer, 7 May 1918, to Foust; Foust, 10 May, 27 July, 13 Aug. 1918, 24 March 1919, to Shaffer, Foust Papers.

57. See Foust, 18 Jan. 1913, to Senators F.M. Simmons and Lee S. Overman, and 12 June 1914 to Gov. Locke Craig, Foust Letterbooks; and Foust's protracted correspondence with President D.H. Hill and Mrs. Jane McKimmon of the A&M College, July 1914 to Nov. 1915, in the Foust Letterbooks and Papers. For discussions of the Smith-Lever and Smith-Hughes Acts of 1914 and 1917, see Brubacher and Rudy, *Higher Education in Transition*, p. 233; Matthews, "*Just a Housewife*," pp. 157–58; McCandless, "Progressivism and the Higher Education of Southern Women," p. 310. For the Normal's early activities, see Frances Jordan, in *Alumni News*, 53 (Winter 1965), p. 12.

58. Hamlin, *University Library*, p. 71.

59. Foust, 2, 10 Dec. 1909, to J.Y. Joyner, and 12 Jan., 1 Feb. 1910, to Wickliffe Rose, Foust Letterbooks; [Jamison], "Domestic Science in the Early Days," Faculty File: Jamison.

60. Foust, 24 June 1915, to Rachel S. Lynch, Foust Letterbooks.

61. See Foust, 18 Jan. 1913, to Senator F.M. Simmons, and 3 Nov. 1913 to P.P. Claxton, Foust Letterbooks; Foust article for the Raleigh *News & Observer*, [1913], and Minnie L. Jamison, 12 Jan. 1914, to Bessie C. Leftwich, Foust Papers.

62. Minnie L. Jamison, 12 Jan. 1914, to Bessie C. Leftwich, and Foust, 28 Feb. 1914, to Clarence Poe, Foust Letterbooks; Directors' Exec. Com. minutes, 9 Sept. 1913, 26 Jan. 1914; *Alumnae News*, 2 (Feb. 1914), p. 3; *State Normal Magazine*, 18 (March 1914), pp. 376–77; *Carolinian*, 1915, p. 167; [Jamison], "Domestic Science in the Early Days," Faculty File: Jamison.

63. Foust, 27 Oct. 1916, to Jane S. McKimmon, Foust Papers.

64. See *State Normal Magazine*, 11 (Jan. 1907), pp. 161–63.

65. Foust, in *State Normal Magazine*, 11 (June 1907), pp. 272–73; H.H. Hoexter, 21 May, 28 July, 15 Oct. 1909, to Foust; A.S. Hill, 31 May 1912, to Foust; C.J. Brockmann, 16 May 1912, to Foust; Foust, 1 June 1921, to A.T. Allen, Foust Papers; Foust, 21 July, 21 Aug. 1909, to Hoexter; 15 Aug. 1910, to Charles J. Brockmann; 15 Aug. 1910, 24 May 1912, to A.S. Hill; 8 June 1911, to R.P. Womble, Foust Letterbooks; E.W. Gudger, 13 Nov. 1944, to W.C. Jackson, Jackson Papers.

66. Hermione Warlick Eichhorn in *Alumnae/i News*, 39 (Feb. 1951), p. 9, and 63 (Fall 1974), pp. 12–15. See also May Worth Rock, 28 March 1935, to Foust, Alumnae Letters, Foust Papers; Virginia Lathrop, *Greensboro Daily News*, 30 Oct. 1938, in Faculty File: Wade Brown.

67. *Alumni News*, 57 (Spring 1969), p. 40.

68. Wade Brown, *North Carolina State High School Music Contest-Festival*, pp. 9–10.

69. See Cahn, *Coming on Strong*, p. 26.

70. See *New York Times Magazine*, 15 Jan. 1995; Umstead, in *Alumni News*, 83 (Summer 1995), pp. 2, 4–5.

71. *Carolinian*, 1913, pp. 311–12; Physical Education department, report, 1917–18, HPERD records; O'Neill, "History of the Physical Education Department at the Woman's College," pp. 19–24; Richard Bardolph, "Physical Culture," in *Alumni News*, 81 (Spring 1992), p. 18. For the national background to these developments, see Rice, *Brief History of Physical Education*, pp. 249, 293, 299–302; Hackensmith, *History of Physical Education*, pp. 400–01.

72. Hygiene reports, 31 Jan., 7 June 1921, Foust Papers.

73. *State Normal Magazine*, 13 (June 1909), pp. 236–37 (for the first Field Day); 16 (Oct. 1911), p. 41 (for camping trip); O'Neill, "History of the Physical Education Department," pp. 20, 106–10, 117; Lojko, "Effects of Societal and Cultural Changes," pp. 43–44.

74. *State Normal Magazine*, 17 (Dec. 1912, April 1913), pp. 137, 406; 20 (Nov. 1915), p. 63.

75. Fay Davenport, 15 March 1919, to Foust; Foust, 19 March 1919, to Davenport, Foust Papers. For continuing student support for intercollegiate sports, see *State Normal Magazine*, 23 (March–April 1919), pp. 146–47.

76. Cahn, *Coming on Strong*, pp. 23–27.

77. Amy Homans, 17, 19, 24 March, 23 April, 4, 7 May 1909, 6 Dec. 1912, to Foust, Foust Papers. For Homans herself, see Rice, *Brief History of Physical Education*, pp. 235–36.

78. See the lengthy correspondence between Foust and physical education director Fay Davenport between January 25 and June 24, 1919, Foust Papers.

Chapter 6 Notes

1. Foust, 9 July 1920, to James R. Young, Foust Papers.

2. See these writings by Horowitz: *Alma Mater*, pp. 314–16; "Designing for the Genders," pp. 451–60; "Smith College," pp. 99–100.

3. See *Alumnae News*, 19 (Nov. 1930), pp. 12–13.

4. Foust, 12 March 1926, to J.L. Nelson, Board folder, Foust Papers; *Carolinian*, 11, 18 March 1926.

5. Foust, 10 March 1926, to W.R. Taylor, and 22 March 1926 to C.H. Mebane with accompanying newspaper clipping, Board folder, Foust Papers; *Alumni News*, 61 (Fall 1972), p. 4; 64 (Summer 1976), p. 20; 65 (Fall 1976), pp. 7–8; *Greensboro Daily News*, 5 Sept. 1976; *Greensboro News & Record*, 23 Sept. 1990; OH: Roger F. Davis, 19 March 1990.

6. *Alumni News*, 65 (Fall 1976), p. 8.

7. Report of Clyde R. Place, 23 April 1923, Building folder, and W.C. Smith, 14 Dec. 1923, to Foust, Foust Papers.

8. Trudy W. Atkins, in *Alumni News*, 63 (Spring 1975), pp. 7–8; Creese, "Architecture and Learning," pp. 244, 270, 282; Turner, *Campus*, pp. 215–20, 245.

9. Foust report, 30 Nov. 1922, Building folder; Draft budget request, 1 Dec. 1924, Budget folder; Foust, 25 Sept. 1928, to the Alumnae, and 21 Feb. 1929 to Mary Lou Fuller, Foust Papers; *Carolinian*, 27 Sept. 1929, esp. p. 6.

10. *Catalog*, 1921–22, p. 30; OH: Mary Elizabeth Keister, 24 Sept. 1990, and Mary Hooke Moore, 23 Oct. 1990; Directors' Minutes, 3 June 1921, 31 July 1923, 14 May 1924; Corresp. between Foust and J.D. Franks, 13 May to 1 Sept. 1924; Foust, 24 May 1924, to City Manager P.C. Painter, and 22 July 1924 to Mayor Claude Kiser; C.C. Hudson, 19 July 1924, to Foust, and Foust to Hudson, 1 Aug. 1924; Draft budget request, 1 Dec. 1924, Budget folder; Foust, 13 Aug. 1928, to Henry Burke, Budget Bureau folder, Foust Papers.

11. Foust correspondence with C.D. Benbow, 29 March to 20 July 1923; State Health Inspection report, 19 April 1923; R.S. Curtis, 19 Nov. 1923, to Foust, all in B folder, Foust Papers; Foust report, with Directors' reports, 1926, p. 15. For an account of college farm operations in 1922–23, see *Carolinian*, 11 Nov. 1922, 8 Dec. 1923.

12. *Carolinian*, 18 March 1922, 19 May 1923; 6 June 1931; *Student Handbook*, 1927–28, p. 117; *Catalog*, 1931–32, p. 27; Foust, 1 April 1932, to Bess Goodykoontz, Foust Papers; *Alumnae/i News*, 17 (July 1928), p. 12; 71 (Winter 1983), 9.

13. *Carolinian*, 17 Sept. 1921, p. 2; Foust, 26 April 1922, to Carroll G. Pearse; 23 Dec. 1922 to J.D. Murphy; 15 March 1923 to Mrs. Kemp Funderburk, Foust Papers.

14. Foust, College History draft, p. 128.

15. Faculty Council Minutes, 9 Sept., 12 Dec. 1921, 7 Sept. 1922; Foust, 17 Dec. 1921, to W.C. Smith; Foust, report to Directors, [Feb. 1922], Faculty, General folder, and 29 May 1922, Board folder; Foust, 9 Feb. 1922, to the faculty, and 14 March 1922, to Dept. Heads in the Liberal Arts, Foust Papers; Foust, biennial report, 1 Dec. 1922, with Directors' Reports, pp. 4–9; *Catalog*, 1921–22, pp. 11–12; Foust, College History draft, pp. 125–29.

16. Foust, 17 Dec. 1921, to W.C. Smith; 9 Feb. 1922, to Faculty; 16 Feb. 1922, to Mrs. J.A. Brown; Brown, 20 Feb. 1922, to Foust, Foust Papers.

17. See the correspondence between Foust and Mendenhall, 1 March to 22 June 1922; Foust report to the Directors, 29 May 1922, Board folder; Foust report to the faculty, 22 June 1922, Faculty, General folder; Foust, 29 Aug. 1924, to Sue Stone Durand, Foust Papers.

18. Foust, [Feb. 1922], to the Directors, Faculty, General folder; Foust, 21 April 1922, to J.D. Murphy, Foust Papers; Faculty Council Minutes, 5, 12 Dec. 1921. These Faculty Council Minutes record only the approval or rejection of motions, not divisions in the voting.

19. Harriet Elliott, 22 Feb. 1943, to E.E. Pfaff, and [1946], to Gladys [Avery Tillett], Dean of Women Papers, VC Student Affairs Records; Elliott, 21 Aug. 1944, to John Lockhart, E, Jackson Papers.

20. Foust, 10, 20 Feb. 1926, to J.D. Murphy, Board folder, and 21 June 1928, to Harriet Elliott, Foust Papers.

21. Foust, 13 Jan. 1926, to Gertrude Weil; 21 Jan., 10, 20 Feb. 1926, to J.D. Murphy; 18 Feb. 1926, to Mrs. W.T. Bost; 16 Jan. 1932, to J.L. Nelson; Foust, report, 26 May 1932 (last in Board folder), Foust Papers.

22. *North Carolina Public Laws*, 1929, ch. 223, sec. 2; Foust, 15 Feb. 1929, to A.D. MacLean; 15 Feb. 1929, to George R. Ward; O. Max Gardner, 11 May 1929, to Foust, Board folder, Foust Papers.

23. Veysey, *Emergence of the American University*, p. 308.

24. See W.C. Jackson, 1 June 1922, and W.C. Smith, 16 Feb. 1924, to Foust, Foust Papers.

25. Foust, 22 Feb. 1922, to J. Foster Searles; 3 March 1925, to Joe Rosenthal; Clora McNeill, 12 Nov. 1927, to Rosenthal; Rosenthal, 14 Nov. 1927, to Foust; Clora McNeill, 25 Nov. 1927, to A.T. Allen; Henry Foust, 3 Jan. 1928, to Foust; Foust, 7 March 1928, to Beverley R. Tucker; R.D. Douglas, 22 Sept. 1930, to Foust; Foust, 6 Jan. 1931, to J.D. Murphy, and 22 Feb. 1933, to F.L. Robbins, Foust Private Papers; Foust, 10 Aug. 1927, to J.A. Gray, and accompanying correspondence re Hege, G–I folder; Foust, 30 April 1928, to H.G. Chatham; 4 Sept. 1928, 9 Feb. 1929, to Mina (Mrs. Henry) Weil, Foust Papers.

26. Foust, 7 Oct. 1931, to Easdale Shaw; 10 Oct., 8 Dec. 1931, to Fred Morrison; 29 Aug. 1932, to Henry Burke; F.P. Graham, 9 Dec. 1933, to Foust, last in Graham folder, Foust Papers.

27. *Carolinian*, 29 Jan., 19 Feb. 1921, 3 March 1923; Clara Byrd, in *Alumnae News*, 10 (March 1921), p. 4; Foust, College History draft, pp. 182, 185–89.

28. Wilson, *University of North Carolina Under Consolidation*, pp. 117–18.

29. See Foust, 13 April 1916, to Ceasar Cone; 26 Feb., 30 April 1926, to John D. Rockefeller, Jr.; 27 Feb. 1926, to Benjamin N. Duke; 9 June 1926, to J.L. Nelson, Board folder; W.W. Brierley, 1 July 1926, to Foust, Education folder, Foust Papers.

30. Foust, 6 Sept. 1923, to Faculty; 12 Sept. 1923, to W.C. Jackson; Jackson, 14 Sept. 1923, to Foust; Lenoir Chambers, 5 Dec. 1923, to Jackson; Foust, 12 Dec. 1923, to Chambers; J. Arthur Dunn, 9 May 1928, to Foust; Foust, 16 May 1928, 5 July 1929, to Dunn, Foust Papers; *Carolinian*, 27 March 1930.

31. Foust, report on reorganization [1922]; Foust, 12 April 1924, to F.M. Bralley; 19 June 1924, to Eva M. Locke; 21 Jan. 1927, to Helen Barton, Foust Papers; Metzger, "Academic Tenure in America," pp. 123–28, 134–35.

32. For an endorsement of Foust's respect for academic freedom, see Magnhilde Gullander, 3 July 1934, to Foust, Foust Private Papers, and OH: Key L. Barkley, 7 June 1991. For further evidence of underground opposition, see E.C. Lindeman, 29 May 1922, to Foust, Lindeman folder, Foust Papers.

33. Minnie L. Jamison, 17 March 1923, 30 May 1924, to Foust; Foust, 8 Nov. 1923, 4 June 1924, to Jamison, all I–J folders, Foust Papers.

34. Foust correspondence with R. March Merrill, 2 March to June 1922; Foust, 2 May 1922, to D.B. Johnson, Foust Papers.

35. Foust, 19 Aug. 1922, to Majel W. Wood, Foust Papers.

36. J.P. Givler, 23 June 1924, to Foust; Foust, 25 June 1925, to Givler, Foust Papers. For age discrimination, see Foust, 28 Feb. 1924, to Amy J. Stevens, Foust Papers.

37. Foust, 2 June 1926, to Mrs. Henry Weil, Foust Papers.

38. *Carolinian*, 10 April 1920, p. 5; Foust, 2 Nov. 1931, to John H. Cook, Foust Papers.

39. A.W. McAllister, 24 March 1921, to Foust; Foust, 29 March, 11 April 1921, to McAllister, Foust Papers. For Lindeman's professional activity, see *Carolinian*, esp. 27 March, 3 April 1920; *Alumnae News*, 9 (April 1920), p. 5.

40. Anonymous letter, 16 May 1921, to Foust, Foust Papers.

41. Foust, 13 April 1922, to E.C. Brooks; 14 Feb. 1923, to Herbert W. Mumford; 13 Feb. 1925, to Minnie McIver Brown, Foust Papers.

42. Gate City Klan #19, 16 Feb. 1922, to Foust, Lindeman Folder, Foust Papers.

43. Lindeman, 22 Feb. 1922, to Foust, with accompanying statement of same date, Lindeman folder, Foust Papers.

44. Directors' Minutes, 31 May 1922; Foust, 1 March, 21 April, 10 May 1922, to J.D. Murphy; Lindeman, 4 April, 29 May 1922, to Foust; C.H. Mebane, 9 May 1922, to Foust; Foust, 10 May, 13 June 1922, to Mebane; 11 May 1922, to J.L. Nelson; R.D.W. Connor, 12 May 1922, to Foust; Foust, 15 May 1922, to Connor; *Survey* article, 20 May 1922, pp. 267–68; Lindeman, 24 May 1922, to Paul L. Benjamin (the *Survey* editor); Foust, 26 May 1922, to Lindeman; draft statements for Board, [May 1922], all in Lindeman folder, Foust Papers; Foust, 13 Feb. 1925, to Minnie McIver Brown, Board folder, Foust Papers; Foust, 7 Feb. 1941, to W.C. Jackson, Foust Private Papers; *Greensboro Daily News*, 9, 10 May 1922.

45. *Carolinian*, 23 May 1929; *Who Was Who in America*, 3 (1951–60), p. 520.

46. Foust, 13 Feb. 1925, to Minnie McIver Brown; 1 April 1925, to J.D. Murphy; J.L. Nelson, 14 May 1925, to Foust; Foust, draft report [May 1925], Board folder, Foust Papers; A.S. Kiester, 10 March 1925, to Foust, Foust Papers; Keister, 28 April 1974, to Willard B. Gatewood, Jr. (my thanks to Professor Gatewood for a copy); Gatewood, *Preachers, Pedagogues and Politicians*, pp. 120–22; *Greensboro Daily News*, 2 July 1956. See also the Keister Incident folder, Foust Papers. For contemporary clippings on the Keister controversy, see Faculty File: Keister.

47. Foust, 13 Feb. 1925, to Minnie McI. Brown; 1 April 1925, to J.D. Murphy (including quotation); Foust, draft report, [May 1925], Board folder, Foust Papers.

48. Foust, 13 Feb. 1925, to Minnie McI. Brown, Board folder; 21 April 1925, to E.W. Gudger, Keister Incident folder; 8 March 1925, to H.W. Chase, Foust Papers; Gatewood, *Preachers, Pedagogues and Politicians*, pp. 125–30, 146, 183, 198, 223; Marsden, *Soul of the American University*, pp. 321–24.

Chapter 7 Notes

1. Faculty listings in *Catalogs*, 1919–20 and 1929–30; *Carolinian*, 29 Sept. 1923; J.P. Givler, 4 Nov. 1924, to Foust, Foust Papers. See also OH: Key L. Barkley, 7 June 1991.

2. Foust, 29 April 1922, to H.W. Odum, Foust Papers.

3. Foust, 20 Aug. 1924, to Laura Coit; 25 Nov. 1924, to E.E. Balcomb, Foust Papers.

4. Cott, *Grounding of Modern Feminism*, pp. 218–19; Carter, "Academic Women Revisited," p. 675.

5. Faculty listings in *Catalogs*, 1919–20 and 1929–30; Chafe, *Paradox of Change*, p. 101; Cott, *Grounding of Modern Feminism*, pp. 221–22, 227–28.

6. OH: Louise Ward, 14 May 1991; Mary Elizabeth Keister, 24 Sept. 1990.

7. Earnest, *Academic Procession*, pp. 277, 295; Bowen, "Faculty Salaries," p. 10; Foust, 4 March 1920, to J.D. Murphy, Foust Papers.

8. Rossiter, *Women Scientists... to 1940*, pp. 197–98; W.C. Smith, 20 July 1919, to Foust; Martha Winfield, 7 Aug. 1920, to Laura Coit, Foust Papers.

9. Foust, 7 Sept. 1921, to D.B. Johnson, Foust Papers. The overall salary averages in those two years were $2,044 and $2,678. Faculty salary lists, 1920–21, 1929–30, Foust Papers. See also Graham, "Expansion and Exclusion," pp. 765–66.

10. W.C. Smith, 26 July 1922, to Foust; Foust, 28 Nov. 1924, to Virginia Ragsdale, Foust Papers.

11. Foust, 29 Aug. 1919, to D.B. Johnson, Foust Papers.

12. Correspondence between Foust and Aladdin Co., July to Sept. 1920, Foust Papers; *Carolinian*, 25 Sept. 1920; Foust report, with Directors' Report, 1920, p. 12.; Foust, College History draft, p. 145.

13. Foust, 3 Jan. 1923, to Baxter Durham; W.C. Jackson, 14 July 1923, to Ethelyn A. Dewey; Foust, 15 Dec. 1923, to W.N. Everett, Foust Papers.

14. W.C. Smith, 12 March 1924, 28 April 1925, to Foust; Foust, 2 May 1925, to Smith, Foust Papers.

15. Foust, 17 March 1925, to Faculty Cabinet, Faculty folder; Foust, 8 May 1928, to Mary M. Petty, Foust Papers; Faculty Cabinet Minutes, 18 March 1927; Mary Taylor Moore, 16 Feb. 1948, to W.C. Jackson, Jackson Papers.

16. Foust, 30 March 1920, to E.W. Gudger, Foust Papers. For the similar picture in women's colleges generally, see Rossiter, *Women Scientists... to 1940*, pp. 22–23.

17. Foust-Lindeman correspondence, 1 Sept. to 6 Dec. 1921; Foust, 17 Dec. 1921, to C.A. Williams; 27 Oct. 1922, to John H. Cook, Foust Papers.

18. Faculty Cabinet Minutes, 8, 20 Dec. 1922.

19. *Catalog*, 1921–22, p. 43.

20. Faculty Council Minutes, 9 Sept. 1918; *Catalog*, 1918–19, pp. 44–51; 1929–30, pp. 36–39; Foust, College History draft, pp. 118–19, 125. For broader accounts of general education and the distribution system in this period, see Butts, *College Charts Its Course*, pp. 243–46; Rudolph, *Curriculum*, pp. 256–57; Thomas, *Search for a Common Learning*, pp. 57–64, 69, 85–87.

21. Faculty Council Minutes, 3 Feb. 1930; *Carolinian*, 25 Sept. 1930.

22. Foust, 26 April 1922, to Carroll G. Pearse, Foust Papers.

23. Registrar's report, 18 Dec. 1924, M, Foust Papers.

24. W.C. Jackson, 11 March 1920, to Foust; Foust, 7 April 1922, to Jackson, Foust Papers.

25. OH: Mary Bailey Williams Davis, 23 Feb. 1990; Mary Elizabeth Keister, 24 Sept. 1990; Elizabeth Yates King, 9 April 1991.

26. For Hicks's memories of NCCW, see his autobiography, *My Life With History*.

27. Kendrick obituaries, 28–29 Oct. 1946, in Faculty File.

28. Foust, 22 July 1921, to W.C. Smith, Foust Papers.

29. W.R. Taylor, 30 March 1922, 8 Jan. 1924, 22 Sept. 1925, 31 Oct. 1928, to Foust, Foust Papers; Taylor, 31 Aug. 1936, to W.C. Jackson, Jackson Papers; *Alumni News*, 61 (Fall 1972), pp. 2–3; J.S. Ferguson remarks at dedication of Taylor Theater, 1967, Speeches, Ferguson Papers.

30. *Carolinian*, 5 Oct. 1934; Trelease, *Changing Assignments*, p. II-57; Herman Middleton, in *Alumni News*, 64 (Summer 1976), p. 20. For Taylor's off-campus business, see *Greensboro News & Record*, 23 Sept. 1990.

31. Foust, 16 Oct. 1917, to Mrs. W.N. Hutt, Foust Papers.

32. W.C. Smith, 20 July 1919, to Foust, Foust Papers; Camp, *Some Pioneer Women Teachers*, pp. 193–95; Weatherspoon obituary, 26 May 1939, in Faculty File. For a divergent student view, see Katherine G. Rogers, 12 Jan. 1982, to Richard Bardolph, Alumni Association Records, 1899–1988.

33. E.M. Weatherspoon, 1 March 1922, to Laura Coit, with Faculty Cabinet Minutes, 1922–30. For the first art graduate, see "Department of Art and Weatherspoon Art Gallery," Art Center, Moran Papers, 1982.

34. See Rudolph, *Curriculum*, pp. 265–67.

35. Mary T. Moore, 18 April 1919, to Victoria C. Bagier, Foust Papers.

36. W.S. Barney, 11 June, 1 Aug. 1919 to Foust, Foust Papers.

37. *Alumnae/i News*, 42 (Spring–Summer 1953), p. 7; 57 (Spring 1969), p. 40.

38. W.C. Smith, 28 March 1923, to Foust, Foust Papers; "Memorial to Miss Caroline Schoch," 1961, Faculty File.

39. Registrar, 8 Jan. 1914, to Nettie Wysor, Foust Letterbooks; Mary Taylor Moore, 2 April 1919, to Foust, Foust Papers.

40. Foust, 20 July 1918, to Viola Boddie; Boddie, 8 April 1919, to Foust; W.C. Smith, 28 March 1923, to Foust, Foust Papers. For student recollections of Miss Boddie, see Kathrine Robinson Everett, in *Alumni News*, 70 (Fall 1981), p. 22; Katherine G. Rogers, 12 Jan. 1982, to Richard Bardolph, Alumni Association Records, 1899–1988.

41. W.C. Smith and W.S. Barney, 20 Sept. 1924, with draft of college budget request for 1925–27, Budget folder, Foust Papers.

42. John H. Cook, 13 March 1928, to W.C. Jackson; Foust, 5 Jan. 1929, to Viola Boddie; Cook, 7 Jan. 1929, to Foust; Foust 14 Jan. 1929, to Cook, Foust Papers.

43. Foust, 22 Oct. 1924, 17 June 1925, to Gertrude Mendenhall; Mendenhall, 23 Oct. 1924, to Foust; Foust remarks about Mendenhall at 1926 commencement, Foust Papers.

44. *Alumnae News*, 37 (Aug. 1948), p. 16.

45. J.P. Givler, 20 Jan. 1922, to Foust, Foust Papers.

46. J.P. Givler, 20 Jan., 28 May 1922, 13 Oct. 1928, 15 June 1931, to Foust; Smith, 28 April 1925, to Foust, Foust Papers.

47. W.T. Wright, 24 Feb. 1928, to W.C. Smith, Budget folder; Foust, 20 March 1928, to Smith; Foust correspondence with Wright, 7 March to 20 June 1928, Foust Papers.

48. Anna J. Reardon, in *Alumnae News*, 33 (Feb. 1945), p. 5.

49. Richard Bardolph notes on interview with Mabel (Mrs. Robert) Merritt, ca. 1981, UNCG Archives; J.A. Highsmith, in *Alumnae News*, 33 (April 1945), p. 2.

50. J.A. Highsmith report, 23 May 1924, Dept. Reports; Foust, 19 Nov. 1924, to John H. Cook; Cook, 24 Nov. 1924, to Foust, Foust Papers; Faculty Cabinet Minutes, 17 Nov. 1924 (with letter from Highsmith, 17 Nov. 1924, to W.C. Smith), 24 Feb., 18 March 1925.

51. J.A. Highsmith, 24 Sept. 1928, to Foust, Budget folder, Foust Papers; OH: Key L. Barkley, 7 June 1991.

52. Foust, 26 April, 25 May 1932, to J.A. Highsmith, Foust Papers.

53. Geiger, *To Advance Knowledge*, p. 110; Herbst, *And Sadly Teach*, pp. 169–89; Borrowman, *Liberal and Technical in Teacher Education*, pp. 129–30; Tyack, *Turning Points*, pp. 417–19.

54. John H. Cook, in *Alumnae News*, 13 (Jan. 1925), p. 13.

55. Gobbel, *Church-State Relationships*, pp. 213–14.

56. John H. Cook, in *Alumnae News*, 13 (Jan. 1925), pp. 12–13.

57. Faculty File: John H. Cook.

58. J.H. Cook, 6 May 1919, to Foust, Foust Papers. See on this question, Borrowman, *Liberal and Technical in Teacher Education*, pp. 140–47.

59. Foust, 19 Nov. 1924, 20 March 1928, to J.H. Cook; Cook, 3, 4 April 1928, to Foust, Foust Papers.

60. Foust, 31 Jan. 1941, to W.C. Jackson, Foust Private Papers; *Carolinian*, 13 Feb., 24 April 1930.

61. Elisabeth Bowles, "Curry School," in *Alumni News*, 55 (Fall 1966), p. 23.

62. J.H. Cook, 19 May 1921, 28 March 1923 (with accompanying statement re Curry building), 30 Sept. 1925, to Foust; Foust, 6 Dec. 1924, to Edward Conradi; 6 Dec. 1921, to E.C. Brooks; 3 Jan. 1923, to Baxter Durham, Foust Papers.

63. J.H. Cook report, 1 Dec. 1928, Dept. Reports, Foust Papers.

64. Foust, 11 Dec. 1920, to E.C. Brooks; 15 Jan. 1924, to J.H. Cook, Foust Papers.

65. J.H. Cook, summer session reports, [1924], 16 Dec. 1925, 1 Dec. 1928, Dept. Reports; Cook, 23 Jan. 1929, to Foust; Foust, 5 Feb., 27 April 1929, to Cook, Foust Papers; *Alumnae/i News*, 13 (April 1925), p. 11; 68 (Summer 1980), p. 6. Re the percentage of elementary school teachers with bachelor's degrees, see Borrowman, *Liberal and Technical in Teacher Education*, p. 189.

66. OH: George Dickieson, 20 March 1990; Wade Brown, 13 June 1921, to Foust, Foust Papers.

67. See *Carolinian*, 11 March 1926, 12 Feb., 24 Sept. 1931.

68. *Alumni News*, 63 (Fall 1974), p. 14.

69. Wade Brown, *North Carolina State High School Music Contest-Festival*, pp. 10–20, 40; *Alumnae News*, 39 (Feb. 1951), p. 9; Sunderman, *Historical Foundations of Music Education*, pp. 255–57.

70. Foust, 17 July 1922, to Lelia A. Styron; report, 26 May 1932, Board folder, Foust Papers; W.C. Jackson, in *Alumnae News*, 28 (Nov. 1939), p. 8.

71. Rossiter, *Women Scientists... to 1940*, pp. 199–202; Hoffschwelle, "Science of Domesticity," pp. 669–74.

72. Foust, 1 April 1932, to Edwin H. Scott, Foust Papers; Helen Canaday et al., *History of the School of Human Environmental Sciences* (hereafter cited as *History of HES*), p. 9.

73. Faculty Cabinet Minutes, 18 March 1927; Canaday, *History of HES*, pp. 8, 93–94, 141; OH: Emeve Singletary, 24 Oct. 1990; Trelease, *Changing Assignments*, pp. II-63–65.

74. *Carolinian*, 14 Feb., 14 March 1929; *Alumnae News*, 17 (April 1929), p. 11; School of Home Economics, Position Statement, Jan. 1978, Home Ec, Ferguson Papers; Canaday, *History of HES*, p. 18.

75. Foust, 27 Nov. 1909, to Wallace Buttrick; 17 Feb. 1910, to Andrew Carnegie, Foust Letterbooks.

76. C.B. Shaw, "The Library," unidentified clipping in Vertical File: Library History.

77. *Carolinian*, 23 Sept. 1925, 22 Nov. 1930.

78. Hamlin, *University Library*, p. 131.

79. Foust, 17 March 1920, to C.B. Shaw; Shaw, 20 March, 30 April 1920, to Foust; Annie F. Petty, 5 April 1920, to Foust; Foust, 12 June 1920, to Petty, Foust Papers; *Carolinian*, 20 Sept. 1919, 25 Sept. 1920; Holder, "History of the Library of the Woman's College," pp. 38–39, 55.

80. Foust, 20 March 1928, to C.H. Stone, and [Anna Reger}, "Training for Librarianship at Woman's College," with Reger, 4 Nov. 1957, to Gordon Blackwell, in Correspondence, Office of Librarian Records; *Alumnae News*, 17 (July 1928), pp. 25–26; Holder, "History of the Library of the Woman's College," pp. 57–61.

81. Foust, 23 April 1919, to John H. Cook; Foust-Chase correspondence, 30 March to 12 April 1923; W.C. Jackson, 5 Nov. 1924, to Foust, Foust Papers.

82. Faculty Council Minutes, 19 Feb. 1920; *Catalog*, 1919–20, pp. 55–56.

83. Alumni Association, "The Class of 1917," [1967], p. 19, UNCG Archives.

84. See W.C. Smith, 3 April 1923, to Faculty Cabinet, Foust Papers; Faculty Council Minutes, 21 May 1924; Wilson, *University of North Carolina Under Consolidation*, p. 349.

85. *Alumnae News*, 36 (July 1947), p. 40.

86. Faculty Council Minutes, 10 Oct. 1921; Policy statement on extension work, n.d. [after April 28, 1921]; Charles B. Shaw, 19 Oct. 1921, to Foust (and Faculty); [Shaw], report on extension work, [Jan. 1923]; Foust, 30 Aug., 16 Sept. 1923, to W.C. Jackson; 6 Sept. 1923, to Faculty; Jackson, 20 Sept. 1923, to Foust, Foust Papers; Charles B. Shaw, in *Alumnae News*, 11 (Jan. 1923), p. 13; *Catalog*, 1926–27, pp. 244–47.

87. W.H. Livers, extension division report, 1 Dec. 1928, Dept. Reports, Foust Papers. See list of courses offered in 1927–28, in K–L folder, 1928, Foust Papers.

88. Foust-Gove correspondence, 11 May to 24 July 1920; Gove, 31 Jan. 1921, to T.A. Storey, and Gove report, 31 Jan. 1921, in Hygiene folders; J.P. Givler, 20 Jan. 1922, to Foust, Foust Papers.

89. Foust, 23 Oct. 1924, to Mary C. Coleman, Foust Papers.

90. Gove, 2 Aug. 1920, to Foust; Mary C. Coleman, 3 Aug. 1920, to Foust; Foust, 3 Aug. 1920, to Fay Davenport, Foust Papers; Faculty Council Minutes, 20 Sept. 1920.

91. Coleman biographical listing in School of HPERD records; Umstead, "Mary Channing Coleman," esp. pp. 8–10, 16–19, 32–39, 47, 50, 129–32, 152–56; *Alumnae News*, 36 (Nov. 1947), p. 6; Gerber, *Innovators and Institutions*, pp. 311–12; OH: Sallie Robinson, 11 Oct. 1990.

92. Foust report, with Directors' Reports, 1926, p. 15; Umstead, in *Alumni News*, 62 (Winter 1974), pp. 7–8; O'Neill, "History of the Physical Education Department," pp. 27–28, 96, 98; Rice, *Brief History of Physical Education*, p. 300.

93. Faculty Council Minutes, 23 Jan. 1923.

94. Department of Health, proposal for a physical education major, 18 March 1922, with Faculty Cabinet Minutes; Umstead, "Mary Channing Coleman," pp. 56, 60–64, 70–71; O'Neill, "History of the Physical Education Department," pp. 25–31.

95. Physical Education department annual reports, 1 June 1923, and [1928], Foust Papers; Anna Gove, 5 July, 8 Sept. 1923, to Foust; Foust, 10, 15 July, 16 Sept. 1923, to W.C. Jackson; 6 May 1925, to Mary C. Coleman, Foust Papers; Physical Education department annual report, [1928–29], General Correspondence, HPERD Records; *Alumnae News*, 18 (July 1929), p. 19; Umstead, "Mary Channing Coleman," pp. 55, 61, 73; *Carolinian*, 15 Oct. 1943.

96. *Carolinian*, 2 Oct. 1920, pp. 5–6; [Mary C. Coleman], untitled description of Athletic Association programs, [ca. 1922], Athletic Association, HPERD Records; Physical Education department report, 1 June 1923, Foust Papers; Physical Education department report, 30 May 1924, General Correspondence, HPERD Records.

97. Physical Education department annual report, [1928], Foust Papers; *Carolinian*, 19 Oct., 2 Nov. 1928, 24 Oct. 1929; Umstead, "Mary Channing Coleman," pp. 71–74, 151–52. For national background, see Cahn, *Coming on Strong*, pp. 55–66, 97–100; Guttmann, *Women's Sports*, pp. 135–37, 140–41; Gerber, *American Woman in Sport*, pp. 65–74; Rice., *Brief History of Physical Education*, pp. 277–78.

Chapter 8 Notes

1. Horowitz, *Alma Mater*, pp. 277, 282–84; Earnest, *Academic Procession*, pp. 264–70; Dean, "Learning to be New Women," pp. 305–06.

2. Foust report, 10 May 1924, with Directors' Executive Committee Minutes, 13 May 1924. See also Foust, 20 Nov. 1923, to Nell Farrar; 11 July 1929, to Lillian Killingsworth; 11 July 1929, to Martha Winfield, Foust Papers.

3. Foust, 12 July, 29 Aug. 1924, to Sue Stone Durand, Foust Papers.

4. Foust, 1 April 1925, to J.D. Murphy; Foust, draft report, [1925], Board folder; Foust, 6 July 1933, to Alice Armfield, Foust Papers.

5. *Carolinian*, 12 Dec. 1929. See also the memories of historian John D. Hicks on the faculty during the single year 1922–23, in his *My Life With History*, p. 118.

6. Foust report, 10 May 1924, Directors' Executive Committee Minutes, 13 May 1924; Foust, 12 July 1924, to Sue Stone Durand, Foust Papers; Harriet Elliott, 21 Aug. 1944, to John Lockhart, E, Jackson Papers.

7. *Carolinian*, 1, 15, 29 March 1924, 28 March, 2 May 1929.

8. See Mattie Erma E. Parker, 22 Feb. 1971, to J.S. Ferguson, O'Shea folder, Ferguson Papers.

9. Levine, *American College*, pp. 126–31.

10. Foust, 31 Oct. 1921, to J. Henry Highsmith; Completed SACS form, n.d., S folder, 1923; Mary Taylor Moore, 24 May 1928, to Foust, Foust Papers; *Catalog*, 1926–27, p. 52.

11. *Alumnae News*, 18 (July 1929), p. 7; 28 (Nov. 1939), p. 8; OH: Mary Jane Wharton Sockwell, 8 March 1990.

12. Faculty Admissions Committee report, 1 Oct. 1928, F, Foust Papers.

13. Faculty Council Minutes, 17 May 1926; *Alumnae News*, 14 (April 1926), p. 7.

14. Registrar report, 1 Dec. 1928, Dept. Reports, Foust Papers.

15. Foust, 12 July 1923, to W.C. Jackson; 15 Dec. 1923, to W.N. Everett, Foust Papers.

16. Foust, 5 Jan. 1925, to H.G. Connor, Budget Commission folder; 23 Nov. 1925, to Edward Conradi, F, Foust Papers.

17. *Carolinian*, 10 Feb. 1928.

18. *Carolinian*, 9, 16 May, 27 Sept., 17 Oct. 1929, 13 April 1934.

19. *Carolinian*, 10 Oct., 14 Nov. 1929.

20. *Carolinian*, 24 Sept. 1921, 21 Jan. 1922, 7 Feb. 1929, 5 May 1932; Dining room regulations, 30 Jan. 1923, in Faculty-Student Joint Advisory Committee Records; Hope Coolidge, 30 April 1928, to Foust; Foust, 17 June 1932, to Henry Burke, Foust Papers; *Alumnae News*, 21 (Nov. 1932), p. 21.

21. See Foust-Beall correspondence, 4–8 Sept. 1919, Foust Papers.

22. Boynton, "Development of Student Health Services," p. 6; Ruth Collings report, 1945–46, H, Jackson Papers.

23. Foust, 30 March 1932, to James P. Kinard, Foust Papers.

24. "Expenses," typed ms. in College History notes, Foust Papers; Summary table of education costs per capita, 1920–31, Budget folder, 1929, Foust Papers.

25. *Greensboro News & Record*, 25 Oct. 1987; Faculty File: Hawkins; Richard Bardolph, in *Alumni News*, 70 (Spring 1982), p. 15.

26. *Alumni News*, 63 (Summer 1975), pp. 3–4.

27. Hope Coolidge, 13 April 1923, to Foust; correspondence between Foust, Laura Coit, and Mary M. Sloop, July–Nov. 1923, 17 April 1924; Foust, 18 July 1932, to C.A. Shore; 22 July 1932, to student applicants, Foust Papers.

28. *Carolinian*, 11 Feb. 1926; Foust, 13 Nov. 1925, to Mrs. T.S. Sharp, Foust Papers.

29. *Carolinian*, 27 Sept. 1919, 8 April 1922.

30. OH: Louise Falk, 20 March 1990; Adelaide Holderness, 26 April 1990; W.W. Martin, 8 Sept. 1928, to Profs. Bates et al., Foust Papers.

31. *Carolinian*, 15 March 1928, 28 Feb. 1929, 20 Feb., 6, 13, 27 March 1930.

32. Foust to Emma King, 14 July 1921, 6 April 1922, 21 March, 11 April, 16, 30 June, 5 July 1924; Faculty Council Minutes, 7 Sept. 1922; Nell Farrar report, 14 March 1923; Foust report, with Executive Commitee Minutes, 13 May 1924; Foust to Farrar, 25 Feb., 25 March, 1924; Foust to Sue Stone Durand, 24 June, 5, 10, 12 July 1924, Foust Papers; Emma King to Anna Gove, 23 June 1924, and Gertrude Mendenhall to Gove, 1 July 1924, Gove Papers.

33. Foust to J.D. Murphy, 5 April, 10, 17 May 1928; J.L. Nelson, 19 May 1928, to Foust; Foust to Mrs. J.A. Brown, 14 Aug. 1928, all in Board folder; Foust to Annie (Mrs. Kemp) Funderburk, 22, 31 March 1928; Foust-Durand correspondence, 10–16 May 1928; Foust to Edith A. Sprague, 10 July 1928; Foust to Iva L. Peters, 3 Sept. 1928; Foust to N.A. Pattillo, 22 June 1932, Foust Papers; Foust to Annie [Funderburk], 10 March 1928; Foust to J.D. Murphy, 16 May 1928; Foust to Durand, 17 May 1928, Foust Private Papers.

34. See *Carolinian*, 19, 26 April, 1928; 7 Feb., 30 May, 24 Oct. 1929.

35. OH: Mary Jane Wharton Sockwell, 8 March 1990; Faculty Council Minutes, 24 Sept. 1928; Foust to Mrs. R.O. Everett, 28 Nov. 1928, Foust Papers; Foust letters to Lillian Killingsworth, Nov. 1934, Foust Private Papers.

36. Brubacher and Rudy, *Higher Education in Transition*, pp. 342–44; Rudolph, *American College and University*, p. 460; Faculty Cabinet Minutes, 10 Feb. 1926, Jan. 1929. For Freshman Week, see *Carolinian*, 28 Sept. 1928; *Alumnae News*, 17 (Nov. 1928), pp. 8–9.

37. Foust report, Directors' Reports, 1928, pp. 14–16; Foust to H.W. Chase, 11 May 1928; Foust to C.G. Woodhouse, 12 Dec. 1928 and Woodhouse report, 13 Feb. 1929, Institute folder;

Foust, 10 April 1929, to Henry Burke, Budget Bureau folder; Foust-Woodhouse correspondence, June–July 1928, Dec. 1928–Jan. 1929, Foust Papers; Rossiter, *Women Scientists...to 1940*, pp. 264, 387n33 (Rossiter errs in calling Woodhouse a Republican); Office of Historian, U.S. House of Representatives, Women in Congress, 265–66.

38. Frank P. Graham, 7 May 1934, to Foust; Foust, 14 May 1934, to Jane Summerell, Foust Papers; W.C. Jackson, 21 July 1934, to C.G. Woodhouse, Jackson Papers; Foust, 6 March 1935, to Woodhouse; Woodhouse, 14 March 1935, 21 Nov. 1944, to Foust, Foust Private Papers; Harriet Elliott, [Nov. 1946], to Gladys Tillett, Tillett Papers.

39. Altbach, *Student Politics*, p. 20; Fass, *Damned and Beautiful*, pp. 194–97, 434 n67; Earnest, *Academic Procession*, pp. 264–70; McCandless, "Preserving the Pedestal," pp. 46–53.

40. *Carolinian*, 15 Nov. 1940, 20 Feb. 1948; Horowitz, *Alma Mater*, p. 288.

41. *Student Handbook*, 1922–23, p. 37; 1931–32, p. 36; *Carolinian*, 12 Nov. 1921, 17 April, 25 Sept., 9 Oct. 1930; 15 Nov. 1940; Sybil Mann, State of the Senate address, 28 Sept. 1982, SGA Minutes. For national background, see Brubacher and Rudy, *Higher Education in Transition*, pp. 344–46.

42. *Carolinian*, 29 Sept. 1927, 15 Nov. 1928, 28 Feb. 1929.

43. *Carolinian*, 27 Sept., 3 Oct. 1929.

44. *Carolinian*, 28 March, 25 April, 8 June 1929, 1 May 1930.

45. OH: Key L. Barkley, 7 June 1991; *Carolinian*, 11 Feb. 1932; Foust, 12 May 1932, to M. Jamison and L. Killingsworth, Foust Papers. See also Fass, *Damned and Beautiful*, pp. 205–07, 310–19.

46. Faculty Council Minutes, 6 May 1932.

47. OH: Mary Jane Wharton Sockwell, 8 March 1990.

48. Foust, 29 Sept. 1923, to W.C. Jackson; Foust, 21 May 1924, to D.B. Johnson; Jackson, 14 Feb. 1928, to E.H. Miller; Foust, 3 May 1933, to A.D. Davis, Foust Papers; Student-Faculty Advisory Committee Minutes, 2 Oct. 1923.

49. Fass, *Damned and Beautiful*, pp. 195, 294–97; Lee, *Campus Scene*, p. 29; Durden, *Launching of Duke University*, pp. 261–62.

50. Foust, 24 March 1931, to Parents of Students; SGA, [1931], to Board; letters from board members to Foust, Nov. 1931, Board folder; Lillian Killingsworth, 12 Dec. 1931, to Foust, K folder; Foust, 5 Jan. 1932, to SGA Legislative Board, and other contents of 1931 Smoking folder, Foust Papers; *Alumnae News*, 20 (Feb. 1932), pp. 20–21.

51. OH: Louise Ward, 14 May 1991; McCandless, "Preserving the Pedestal," pp. 53–54, 61–62.

52. *Alumnae News*, 36 (May 1948), p. 15.

53. Summary of May Day ceremonies, 1926–1935, Alumni Association Records, 1899–1988; Vertical File: May Day.

54. *Carolinian*, 22 May 1920, 28 May, 4 June 1921; *Pine Needles*, 1925, p. 230; OH: Eleanor Vanneman Bennett, 20 Sept. 1990; Vertical File: Park Night; *Alumnae News*, 17 (July 1928) p. 12; Cheryl Junk, "Our Motto, 'Service' Will Remain," Feb. 1995, ms. in possession of the author.

55. See *Carolinian*, 25 Oct. 1919, 6 Oct. 1923; *Alumnae News*, 14 (Jan. 1926), pp. 17–18; Almeida, "Lifting the Veil," pp. 12–13.

56. Foust, 20 March 1924, to M.C. Coleman, Foust Papers.

57. See *Carolinian*, 11 Jan. 1929.

58. *Carolinian*, 25 Feb. 1922.

59. W.R. Taylor, 30 March 1922, to Foust, Foust Papers; Faculty Cabinet Minutes, 21 Feb., 16 May 1929; *Carolinian*, 12 Jan. 1928, 28 March, 2 May 1929, 11 Dec. 1930.

60. *Carolinian*, 19 May 1923, 14 Feb., 23 March 1925, 30 Sept. 1926, 7 June 1930; OH: Mary Jane Wharton Sockwell, 8 March 1990. For variant student opinions of the societies as

they evolved in the `20s, see *Carolinian*, 2, 9 Feb., 1 March 1924, 19 Oct., 13 Dec. 1928, 7, 28 March, 20 Nov. 1929, 6 June 1931.

61. Foust, 11 March 1924, to the Students; 12 Feb. 1925, to Rosalynd Nix, Foust Papers; *Carolinian*, 14, 21 Feb., 19 Nov. 1925, 7, 14 March 1929; Almeida, "Lifting the Veil," pp. 23–25.

62. Minnie Jamison, 1 Dec. 1931, to Foust, Foust Papers.

63. G.K. Ferguson, 30 Aug. 1918, to Adelaide Van Noppen, Vertical File: *Carolinian*; *Carolinian*, 19 May 1919; Arnette Hathaway Avery, 30 April 1935, to Foust, Alumnae Letters, Foust Papers; Alonzo Hall, in *Alumni News*, 61 (Summer 1973), p. 18; Richard Bardolph, ibid., 75 (Fall 1986), p. 25.

64. *Carolinian*, 20 Sept. 1919; Bowles, *Good Beginning*, p. 142.

65. *Carolinian*, 18 March, 29 April 1926; 12 Dec. 1929, p. 1; OH: Eleanor Vanneman Bennett (*Carolinian* editor in 1925–26), 20 Sept. 1990.

66. *Alumnae News*, 41 (Summer 1952), pp. 8; 56 (Spring 1968), p. 5; "Coraddi, A Retrospective," *Coraddi*, Spring 1989, p. 46.

67. *Pine Needles*, 1920—; R.H. Nason, 8 Oct. 1924, to Foust, Foust Papers; *Carolinian*, 17 Jan. 1925; *Alumnae News*, 41 (Summer 1952), p. 8.

68. Fass, *Damned and Beautiful*, pp. 136–39; Marsden, *Soul of the American University*, pp. 344–45, 359.

69. *Carolinian*, 30 April 1921, 9, 15, 23 Feb., 1, 15 Nov. 1924, 19 May 1925, 16 Dec. 1926, 30 Oct. 1930, 20 March, 14 May, 24 Sept. 1931; Foust, 22 Sept. 1921, to Faculty; W.C. Jackson, 1 April 1924, to Foust; Foust, 6 Nov. 1924, to the Class Presidents; G.W. Thompson, 10 March 1925, to Wade Brown; A.P. Kephart, 12 March, 2 Nov. 1925, to Foust; Foust, 4 Nov. 1925, to Kephart, C folder; Foust, 5 May 1926, to Katherine Sherill, Foust Papers.

70. Faculty Council Minutes, 7, 18 Sept. 1922, 15 April 1924; 17 Oct. 1927; *Carolinian*, 14 Oct. 1922, 17 Feb. 1923, 19 May 1925, 27 Feb. 1942; Foust, 23 Oct. 1928, to the Students; 27 Oct. 1928, to A.P. Kephart, Foust Papers.

71. H. Hoyt Price, 21 Feb. 1972, to John L. Sanders, Q–R, Ferguson Papers.

72. Junk, "Waiting Task," pp. 2–3.

73. Taylor, "On the Edge of Tomorrow," pp. 7–8, 14–18, 27–39, 43, 96–99, 124, 147, 150.

74. *Carolinian*, 6 Oct. 1923, 1, 15, 29 March 1924, 7 Oct., 25 Nov. 1926; Almeida, "Lifting the Veil," pp. 55–69; Junk, "Waiting Task," pp. 2–3.

75. Foust, 21 Oct. 1925, to Elizabeth Webb; 17 May 1928, to V.L. Roy; 10 Dec. 1928, to Miss A.G. Taylor, Foust Papers.

76. W.C. Jackson, 12 Feb. 1929, to Foust; Foust, 15 Feb. 1929, to Jackson, Foust Papers.

77. Wade R. Brown, 20 Sept. 1935, to W.C. Jackson, Jackson Papers.

78. *Carolinian*, 17 Jan. 1929.

79. *Alumnae News*, 49 (Jan. 1961), p. 8.

80. Chafe, *Paradox of Change*, pp. 111–12; Cookingham, "Bluestockings, Spinsters and Pedagogues," p. 351; Palmieri, *In Adamless Eden*, Table 10.

81. Anne Wall, in *Alumnae News*, 36 (May 1948), p. 13.

82. Foust, 17 March 1920, to Trevor Arnett, Foust Papers.

83. Foust, 21 Jan. 1926, to Frank P. Bachman, Foust Papers; *Carolinian*, 27 Nov. 1929.

84. List of graduates who obtained doctorates, [1957], G, Blackwell Papers.

85. Scott, *Southern Lady*, pp. 117–18.

86. Rudolph, *American College and University*, pp. 428–29.

87. OH: Brenda Cooper, 25 April 1991.

88. Clara Byrd correspondence, 27 Jan. to 15 Feb. 1923; Byrd annual report, 1937, Byrd Papers; *Alumnae News*, 28 (Nov. 1939), p. 12.

89. George A. Holderness, 21 Jan. 1921, to Foust; Laura Coit, 14 Dec. 1923, to Mrs. Ben S. Guion; Foust, 27 March 1933, to Laura Weill Cone, Foust Papers; Clara Byrd, 10 Oct. 1935, to W.C. Jackson; Jackson, 26 May 1939, to Executive Committee, UNC Trustees, Jackson Papers; Byrd, 7 March 1940, to Foust; Foust, 21 March 1940, to Byrd, Foust Private Papers; Alumnae Association Trustees minutes, 5 June 1922, 6 Jan. 1940, Alumni Association Records; Barbara Parrish, 20 Oct. 1987, to Betty Bullington, Alumni Association Records, 1899–1988.

Chapter 9 Notes

1. *Alumnae News*, 23 (Feb. 1935), p. 10.
2. Faculty Council Minutes, 15 Jan. 1931, 6 Feb., 27 April, 11, 23 May 1933; *Alumnae News*, 19 (Feb. 1931), pp. 18–19.
3. Earnest, *Academic Procession*, pp. 295–96; Geiger, *To Advance Knowledge*, pp. 249–50; *Alumnae News*, 23 (Feb. 1935), p. 9; B.B. Kendrick, 14 Nov. 1942, to F.P. Graham, Jackson Papers.
4. Foust, 10 July 1933, to C.E. Teague, Budget folder, Foust Papers.
5. C.G. Woodhouse, 11 March 1932, to Foust, Foust Papers.
6. Foust reports, in Directors' Reports, 1930, pp. 3–4; 1932, pp. 1–4; OH: Janice Hooke Moore, 23 Oct. 1990.
7. *Carolinian*, 25 Sept. 1930.
8. *Alumnae News*, 23 (Feb. 1935), p. 10; Earnest, *Academic Procession*, p. 296; Levine, *American College*, pp. 185–93.
9. Mildred Pearson, 1 Sept. 1931, to Laura Coit, Foust Papers, 1931.
10. Foust, 30 July 1932, to Walter Murphy, Foust Papers.
11. Foust correspondence with George M. Swift, 16, 20, Sept. 1931, and W.A. Brock, Jan. 1932, Foust Papers.
12. Foust, College History draft, pp. 77–78.
13. Harriet Elliott, 21 Aug. 1944, to John Lockhart, Jackson Papers; OH: Ruth Whalin Cooke, 4 Sept. 1990; Mary Elizabeth Keister, 24 Sept. 1990.
14. Brubacher and Rudy, *Higher Education in Transition*, pp. 380–81.
15. *North Carolina Public Laws*, 1931, chapter 202; Lockmiller, *Consolidation*, pp. 4–5, 8–16, 31, 33–34; Gatewood, *Eugene Clyde Brooks*, pp. 254–56.
16. Wilson, *University of North Carolina, 1900–1930*, pp. 22–23, 223–27, 379–81, 536–37; Dean, *Women on the Hill*, pp. 7–10.
17. Wilson, *University of North Carolina, 1900–30*, pp. 575–77; Wilson, *University of North Carolina Under Consolidation*, pp. 4–5, 16. See Faculty Cabinet Minutes, 14 April, 3 Nov. 1924, and Foust report, with minutes of 17 Nov. 1924; Foust, 5 Jan., 4 Nov. 1924, to H.W. Chase; W.C. Smith, 5 Nov. 1924, to Foust, Foust Papers.
18. Gatewood, *Eugene Clyde Brooks*, p. 255; Foust, 15 Nov. 1928, to Fred W. Morrison, Foust Papers.
19. Foust, 18 Feb. 1931, to Alumnae, and responses, Consolidation folder, Foust Papers; Foust, College History notes, Foust Papers; Faculty Council Minutes, 15 Jan., 2 March 1931; Gatewood, *Eugene Clyde Brooks*, pp. 256–59; Lockmiller, *Consolidation*, pp. 28–29; Ashby, *Frank Porter Graham*, pp. 108–10; Morrison, *Governor O. Max Gardner*, pp. 95, 161–63; *Alumnae News*, 19 (April 1931), pp. 5–7; 20 (July 1931), p. 11; 21 (Feb. 1933) p. 23.
20. See Foust, 7 Nov. 1931, to M.C. Huntley, A, Foust Papers; Faculty Council Minutes, 6 May 1932.
21. Lockmiller, *Consolidation*, pp. 103–04.

22. Minutes of board's first meeting, 11 July 1932, Consolidation folder, Foust Papers; Laura Cone, in *Alumnae News*, 23 (Nov. 1934, p. 8.

23. Lockmiller, *Consolidation*, pp. 51–56.

24. Faculty Council Minutes, 1 May 1933; Foust, 3 May 1933, to Graham, G folder, Foust Papers. For the trustees' executive committee, see Julius D. Grimes, 12 Dec. 1955, to L.P. McLendon, McLendon Papers, SHC.

25. See Ashby, *Frank Porter Graham*, esp. pp. 114, 118–19, and Link, *William Friday*, pp. 68–69, 74.

26. Lockmiller, *Consolidation*, p. 108n.

27. See Jackson, 1 April 1935, to Josephus Daniels and, July 1935, to F.P. Graham, Jackson Papers.

28. Statement by Dean Harriet Elliott and faculty committee, UNC Trustees Minutes, 30 May 1936; W.W. Pierson, 21 Nov. 1939, to F.P. Graham, Jackson Papers.

29. Special Information Under Budget Memorandum #209, 27 Jan. 1933, Budget folder, Foust Papers; Vance Littlejohn, "Graduate Education at the Woman's College," [March 1962], Gr, Singletary Papers; Lockmiller, *Consolidation*, pp. 61–62, 71, 73–76, 80.

30. See Foust, 8 Dec. 1940, to May Tomlinson, Foust Private Papers; Clora M. Foust, 18 Jan. 1949, to Gov. W. Kerr Scott, Clora Foust Correspondence, Foust Papers.

31. Foust, 13 June 1932, to N.C. Commission on University Consolidation, Consolidation folder, Foust Papers; Foust, 2 March 1945, to Frank Hutton, Foust Private Papers.

32. C.W. Phillips, 23 July 1932, to Foust; Foust, 29 July 1932, to Phillips, Foust Papers; Faculty Council Minutes, 12 Sept. 1932.

33. Registrar's report, 14 Dec. 1932; *Greensboro Record*, 5 Dec. 1963, in Vertical File: Coeducation; *Alumnae/i News*, 21 (Nov. 1932), pp. 14–15; 21 (April 1933), p. 8; 53 (Fall 1964), pp. 16–17, 22, 26.

34. OH: Key L. Barkley, 7 June 1991; Physical Education department annual report, 1932–33, Foust Papers; OH: Elizabeth Yates King, 9 April 1991.

35. *Carolinian*, 1, 15 Dec. 1932.

36. Clora Foust, 14 June 1933, to Angus McLean; Julius Foust, 11 Oct. 1934, to George F. Zook; 8 Dec. 1940, to May Tomlinson, Foust Private Papers; Wyatt Taylor, 31 July 1936, to W.C. Jackson, Jackson Papers; *Carolinian*, 1 Dec. 1932, p. 3; *Pine Needles*, 1933, p. 164; Foust, College History notes, Foust Papers; OH: Key L. Barkley, 7 June 1991.

37. Telegram, Henry M. London, 13 June 1933, to Foust; Foust, 14 July [June] to London, Board folder, Foust Papers.

38. Foust, 13, 14 June, 1 Sept. 1933, to Graham, G, Foust Papers; Greensboro newspaper clippings, 7–8 Sept. 1933, in Vertical File: Coeducation.

39. UNC Trustees minutes, 8 July 1932, Foust Papers; W.C. Jackson, 12 June 1945, to H. Hugh Altvater; 20 July 1948, to J.A. Highsmith et al., Jackson Papers. For home economics, see Katherine Taylor, 13 Jan., 13 May 1949, to Jackson; Jackson, 23 May 1949, to Taylor, Jackson Papers.

40. Foust, 14 June 1933, 21 June 1934 (not sent), to F.P. Graham; 14 May 1934, to Jane Summerell, Foust Papers; Clora Foust, 13 June 1933, to Dear Henry, Clora Foust correspondence, Foust Papers. See also Clora Foust, 14 June 1933, to Angus McLean, Foust Private Papers.

41. Foust, 7 April 1936, to B.B. Kendrick; 25 July 1936, to F.P. Graham, Foust Private Papers. For Harriet Elliott's hostility to Foust, see Elliott, 13 Aug. 1933, to Gertrude Weil, G. Weil Papers, and [1946] to Gladys [Tillett], Dean of Women Papers, VC Student Affairs Records.

42. B.B. Kendrick, 16 May 1934, to F.P. Graham, Subgroup 2, series 3, subseries 1, Graham Papers, UNC Archives.

43. Foust-Graham correspondence, 23 May to 21 June 1934, Foust Papers; Ashby, *Frank Porter Graham*, pp. 114–19.

44. See Foust, 4, 18 July 1934, 16 Jan. 1936 (never sent), to F.P. Graham; 6 Nov. 1934 to Lillian Killingsworth; 9 Nov. 1934, to R.D.W. Connor, Foust Private Papers; Clora Foust, draft letter, 8 May (1938?), to Graham; Clora Foust, "Two Men," 1968, Clora Foust correspondence, Foust Private Papers.

45. Foust, 11 Oct. 1934, to George F. Zook, Foust Private Papers; Foust, College History draft and notes.

46. Ashby, *Frank Porter Graham*, p. 118; Virginia T. Lathrop, in *Alumnae News*, 39 (Aug. 1950), p. 8.

47. For the politics involved in the 1945 name change, see Morrison, *Governor O. Max Gardner*, pp. 213–15.

48. Lockmiller, *Consolidation*, esp. pp. ix–xi, 97–112; Wilson, *University of North Carolina Under Consolidation*, esp. p. vii.

49. Jackson-Howard Odum correspondence, 30 Jan. to 1 March 1937, Jackson Papers.

50. Lockmiller, *Consolidation*, pp. 138–39.

51. Jackson, 27 Jan. 1941, to T.T. Murphy; 4 April 1945, to Doak S. Campbell, Jackson Papers.

Chapter 10 Notes

1. See [Harriet Elliott], Analysis of the Organization of the Woman's College U.N.C., [1945], Dean of Women Papers, VC Student Affairs Records.

2. See Advisory Committee Minutes, 6 March 1944.

3. Alumnae House Committee minutes, 5 Jan. 1937, Alumni Association Records. For the national trend, see Finkelstein, *American Academic Profession*, pp. 28–29.

4. Jackson, 12 June 1945, to H.H. Altvater, Jackson Papers.

5. Faculty Council Minutes, 10 Sept., 10 Dec. 1934.

6. *Alumnae News*, 32 (Nov. 1943), p. 5.

7. Jackson, 1 Jan. 1935, to F.P. Graham, Jackson Papers; *Alumnae News*, 36 (May 1948), pp. 7–8.

8. Vita, Laura Hill Coit, 28 Feb. 1944, Jackson Papers. See the extensive correspondence concerning Coit in the 1937 Foust Private Papers.

9. Jackson, Memorandum of Administrative Changes, 1 April 1939; Jackson, 15 Feb. 1949, to G.P. Wilson, Jackson Papers; Jackson, 9 May 1949, to Mildred Newton, Vertical file: Admissions.

10. Advisory Committee Minutes, 12, 14 June 1935; Josephine Hege, [1935], to Jackson, Jackson Papers; Harriet Elliott, 5 Nov. 1940, to Mrs. C.H. Elliott, Harriet Elliott Collection.

11. Elliott, Suggestions for a Building Program…21 Aug. 1944, Dean of Women, Building Program; Elliott, pencilled draft speech, n.d., Dean of Women, Speeches, both in VC Student Affairs Records.

12. See Dodds, *Academic President*, pp. 14–16; Finkelstein, *American Academic Profession*, pp. 27–29.

13. Advisory Committee Minutes, 1935–47, with prefatory remarks; Jackson, speech to faculty, 14 Sept. 1936; Jackson, biennial report, 1934–36 (I–K folder); Jackson report for 1934–44 [1944]; Jackson, 29 July 1948, to E.R. Isbell (Q–R); 11 May 1949, to W.D. Carmichael, Jackson Papers; [Harriet Elliott], Analysis of the Organization of the Woman's College U.N.C., [1945], Dean of Women Papers, VC Student Affairs Records; Faculty Council Minutes, 15 Nov., 18 Dec. 1944, 16 May 1949; OH: Key L. Barkley, 7 June 1991. The information on rival slates was supplied to the author by Richard Bardolph, 30 Oct. 2000.

14. Alumnae House Committee minutes, 5 Jan. 1937, Alumni Association Records.

15. Faculty Council Minutes, 1 Oct., 19 Nov. 1945; Brief Summary of Faculty Regulations...Concerning Curriculum, Dec. 1953, including Faculty Council Minutes, 8 May 1935, and Jackson, 2 Oct. 1945, to Department Heads, in Committee folder, E.K. Graham Papers, 1953.

16. See Henry W. Lewis, 10 Sept. 1968, to Administrative Council, A, Ferguson Papers.

17. *Alumnae News*, 39 (Aug. 1950), pp. 5–7; Magnhilde Gullander, 2 March 1954, to Gordon Gray, subgroup 2, series 3, subseries 1, controversy over faculty relations, Gray Papers, UNC Archives; OH: Laura Anderton, 19 Jan. 1990; Harriet Kupferer, 27 Oct. 1989; May Lattimore Adams, 5 April 1991; Ruth Whalin Cooke, 4 Sept. 1990; Mereb Mossman, 4 Oct. 1989; Esther B. Matthews, 7 Feb. 1991; Anna J. Reardon, 20 Sept. 1990; Ann B. Currin, 7 March 1990; Marjorie Burns, 8 Jan. 1991; For Jackson as a benign figure dominated by Harriet Elliott, see OH: Key L. Barkley, 7 June 1991.

18. Degree citation, 30 May 1949, B folder, Jackson Papers. See Chapter 14, below, for more on Jackson, the college, and segregation.

19. Jackson, 3 June 1947, 1 June 1948, to F.P. Graham; Graham, 23 June, 3 Oct. 1947, to Jackson; Jackson, speech to alumnae, April 1949, Jackson Papers; Faculty Council Minutes, 18 April 1949; Virginia T. Lathrop, in *Alumnae News*, 39 (Aug. 1950), p. 9.

20. Visiting Committee report following visit of 29–30 April 1948, Jackson Papers.

21. Jackson, 3 June 1947, to F.P. Graham; speech to alumnae, April 1949; 3 March 1950, to Susie Sharpe, Honorary degrees folder, Jackson Papers.

22. The best accounts of Elliott's bureaucratic career are Link, *Harriet Elliott*, pp. 45–68, and Jeffreys-Jones, *Changing Differences*, pp. 84–93. See also Elliott, 1 Jan., 11 Dec. 1941, to Julius Foust, Foust Private Papers; letter of Henry Morgenthau in *Alumnae News*, 36 (Nov. 1947), p. 5; Ware, *Partner and I*, pp. 202–03; Swain, *Ellen S. Woodward*, pp. 71–72, 163, 167–69; Vera Largent, "Harriet Wiseman Elliott," *Notable American Women*, I, pp. 572–74; Virginia T. Lathrop, "Harriet Elliott," *Alumni News*, 55 (July 1967), pp. 6–11.

23. Elliott, 1 Jan., 11 Dec. 1941, to Julius Foust, Foust Private Papers; 30 April 1943, to Katherine Rogers, Dean of Women, Correspondence with former students, VC Student Affairs Records.

24. Advisory Committee Minutes, 6 July 1935; interview with Charles Phillips, in *Alumni News*, 67 (Fall 1978), p. 17.

25. F.P. Graham, 21 June 1935, to Jackson, Jackson Papers; Faculty Council Minutes, 9 Sept. 1935.

26. See *Alumni News*, 67 (Fall 1978), pp. 18–19; James Ferguson, speech for Charlie Phillips Appreciation Dinner, 24 Jan. 1972, Ferguson Papers; *Greensboro Daily News*, 23 Jan. 1972; Greensboro *News & Record*, 4 Jan. 1989.

27. V.T. Lathrop report, 12 March 1940, Jackson Papers; Lathrop report, 9 April 1941, Foust Private Papers; *Greensboro Daily News*, 3 Dec. 1974.

28. *Carolinian*, 9 May 1947, 17 Nov. 1955; Doris W. Betts, in *Alumni News*, 55 (July 1967), p. 29.

29. Faculty Council Minutes, 20 March, 17 April 1944.

30. Alumnae Trustees report, 5 Oct. 1946, Alumni Association Records; *Greensboro Daily News*, 28, 30 Nov. 1946; *Greensboro Record*, 28, 29 Nov. 1946.

31. Harriet Elliott, [1946], to Gladys [Tillett], Tillett Papers; see also Elliott, 10 April 1946, to Tillett, ibid.; Jackson, 11 Feb. 1947, to Calvin Warfield, Jackson Papers.

32. Jackson, 4 April 1945, to Doak S. Campbell; Jackson correspondence, 1946, Building folder, Jackson Papers; Jackson statement, with letter of Greensboro citizens, 19 Nov. 1946, to UNC Trustees et al., and local newspaper clippings, Nov. 1946–Feb. 1947, in Vertical File: College History: Consolidation; Harriett Elliott, [1946], to Gladys [Tillett], Tillett Papers.

33. Julius Foust, 8 Dec. 1940, to May Tomlinson, Foust Private Papers; Dean, *Women on the Hill*, pp. 9–16.

34. Julius Foust, 2 March 1945, to Frank Hutton; Hutton, 6 March 1945, to Foust, Foust Private papers; *Greensboro Daily News*, 28, 30 Nov. 1946; *Greensboro Record*, 28, 29 Nov. 1946. For Clara Byrd, see OH: Evon Dean, 28 March 1990.

35. Alumnae Association Minutes, 1 June 1946, 25 Jan. 1947, Alumni Association Records; Laura W. Cone, in *Alumnae News*, 35 (Feb. 1947), p. 10; Jackson, 7 Feb. 1945, to George Penny, Jackson Papers; *Greensboro Record*, 4 Feb. 1947; Gallien, "Coeducational Transition," pp. 5–6. See faculty and student discussion of the issue, in Faculty Council Minutes, 22 April, 18 Nov. 1946, and *Carolinian*, 25 Oct., 13 Dec. 1946.

36. Faculty Council Minutes, 18 Nov. 1935.

37. Committee on Five Year Plan, minutes, 18 June 1938, Alumni Association Records; Clara Byrd, 16 Feb. 1939, to Mrs. Henry D. Holoman, Byrd Papers; "A Birthday Gift to the Woman's College for its Fiftieth Anniversary," 22 March 1941, Alumni Association Records.

38. College-Alumnae Committee minutes, 20 April 1946, Minutes & Reports, Clara Byrd Papers; [Clara Byrd], 12 June 1946, to Jackson; Alumnae Association Trustees' minutes, 14 Feb. 1948; Jackson, 5 March 1948, to Mrs. Carlton Jester, Alumni Association Records; C.W. Phillips, in *Alumnae News*, 37 (Aug. 1948), p. 18; Dale F. Keller, 8 Jan. 1962, to Louis R. Wilson, U–W, Singletary Papers.

39. Jackson, 3 Feb. 1943, to Mrs. Henry Pfeiffer; 3 June 1948, to Katherine G. Rogers; 12 Dec. 1949, to Mrs. M.B. Satterfield, Jackson Papers; *Carolinian*, 9 Oct., 13 Nov. 1942.

40. Phyllis Lewis, 5 May 1986, to W.E. Moran, Ca–Ch, Moran Papers; Lucien Capone, 28 Oct. 1991, to Moran, with Trustees' Minutes, 7 Nov. 1991; Remarks of Chancellor William Moran, Faculty Senate Minutes, 1 April 1992.

41. *Catalog*, 1946–47, pp. 42–43; University Support Organizations, Major Gifts folder, Moran Papers, 1982; Otis Singletary, 3 Sept. 1963, to Frank H. Kenan, Ho–S, Singletary Papers.

42. See Jackson, 4 Nov. 1946, to Mrs. P.P. McCain, Alumnae, Jackson Papers.

43. James Ferguson, Speech for Charlie Phillips Appreciation Dinner, 24 Jan. 1972, Ferguson Papers.

44. [N.C. Budget Bureau], *The Budget*, 1929–31, p. 147; 1935–37, p. 302; 1945–47, p. 529; 1947–49, p. 497.

45. Jane Summerell et al., [1916], to Foust, Vertical File: Alumni Association, Historical Material; Foust, 9 Oct. 1919, to Adelaide Van Noppen, Foust Papers; Clara Byrd, 8 March 1943, to Foust, College History letters, Foust Papers.

46. *Alumnae News*, 11 (Jan. 1923), pp. 10–12; *Carolinian*, 8 Nov. 1924, p. 4.

47. Clara Byrd, 9 Nov. 1925, to Beardsley Ruml, Byrd Papers; Richard Bardolph, in *Alumni News*, 76 (Spring 1988), pp. 16–20; 77 (Summer 1989), pp. 16–19.

48. Clara Byrd, in *Alumni News*, 55 (Jan. 1967), pp. 20–23; Richard Bardolph, ibid., 79 (Spring 1991), pp. 12–17.

49. Dale F. Keller, 28 Dec. 1961, to L.R. Wilson, W, Singletary Papers; Wilson, *University of North Carolina Under Consolidation*, p. 97.

50. *Carolinian*, 22 April 1938, 10 March 1939.

51. Excerpt from UNC Trustees' minutes, 2 Oct. 1944, in Jackson Papers; Alumni Association Trustees' minutes, 5 Oct. 1944, Alumni Association Records; Jackson, 19 Nov. 1945, to Julius Foust, Foust Private Papers.

52. To the City Council of Greensboro, [5 March 1946], and newspaper clippings in Vertical file: Walker Ave. Closing; [Jackson], "Reasons for Closing Walker Ave.," (likely notes for a speech he gave in a public meeting in Aycock Auditorium, 17 Dec. 1946), G, Jackson Papers. The Walker Avenue closure constitutes a significant item in Jackson's papers, 1945–48.

53. Jackson report, 31 May 1947, and F.P. Graham remarks, 28 May 1949, in Alumnae Association annual meeting minutes, Alumni Association Records.

54. [W.D. Carmichael], 1 March 1941, to Guy R. Lyle, Library folder, Jackson Papers; Jackson, Statement of Building Program for 1945–47, [1945], Building folder, Jackson Papers; Trustees' Visiting Committee Reports, April 1948.

55. Trustees' Visiting Committee Reports, April 1948.

56. Jackson, 13 Aug. 1949, to W.D. Carmichael, Jackson Papers; Minutes of Trustee Building Committee and its executive committee, 6 May, 23 July, 6 and 23 Sept. 1949, in K–L, E.K. Graham Papers, 1950.

57. Newspaper clippings and other documents in Vertical file: Library Fire; Sampson, "After the Fire," pp. 434–35; Holder, "History of the Library of the Woman's College," pp. 63–65; Guy Lyle, 24 Oct. 1939, to W.C. Jackson, in Correspondence, Office of Librarian Records.

58. See Charles Adams, 6 Oct. 1948, to Karl Brown; 20 Oct. 1951, to Anne Coogan; Librarian report, 30 June 1950, in Correspondence, Office of Librarian Records; Minnie M. Hussey and Marjorie Hood, in *Alumnae News*, 37 (Feb. 1949), p. 4; Adams, "Library First on Building Program," pp. 1772–77.

59. *Alumnae News*, 37 (Nov. 1948), p. 8; Adams, "Woman's College Library," pp. 135–36. See also *Carolinian*, 18 April 1952.

60. Harriet Elliott, Suggestions for a Building Program, 21 Aug. 1944, Building Program, Dean of Women Papers, VC Student Affairs Records; City fire inspection reports, 10 Feb., 24 Sept. 1947, F, Jackson Papers.

61. Trustees' Building Committee Minutes, 23 July 1949; Jackson, 13 Aug. 1949, to W.D. Carmichael, and 8 Sept. 1949, to Tartt Bell, Building folder, Jackson Papers.

62. Virginia T. Lathrop, in *Alumnae News*, 41 (Fall 1952), pp. 1–2.

63. *Carolinian*, 27 March, 24 April 1930; 6 June, 24 Sept., 1, 22 Oct. 1931; 14 Dec. 1933; Statement of J.P. Givler and Biology department, 1 March 1946, with additional pages, Building folder, Jackson Papers; Jackson, 27 March 1947, to Mrs. F.S. Miles, Jackson Papers; OH: Mary Lou Merrill, 16 Feb. 1990.

64. Thomas W. Sears, 2 Dec. 1922, to Julius Foust; Foust, 22 May 1924, to College Park, Inc., Foust Papers.

65. Julius Foust, 2 May 1931, to Hugh M. Gordon, Foust Papers; Jackson, 9 March 1935, to the faculty; 9 June 1948, to Ethel Martus, Jackson Papers; O'Neill, "History of the Physical Education Department," p. 100; *Carolinian*, 14 Dec. 1933, 30 March 1934, 22 March 1935, 5 Nov. 1954.

66. *Greensboro Record*, 18 Feb. 1941; *Carolinian*, 7, 16, 21 Feb. 1941. For details of lake construction, see Jackson correspondence with John D. Spinks, 31 July 1939 to 2 Dec. 1940, Jackson Papers.

67. See Trelease, *Changing Assignments*, pp. I-125–29.

68. *Carolinian*, 17 Nov. 1954.

69. George R. Ross, 25 Aug. 1931, to Julius Foust; Foust, 27 Aug. 1931, to Ross, Foust Papers.

70. Sale notices, 6 Nov. 1945, Jackson Papers; Foust-Jackson correspondence, 29 Oct. to 19 Nov. 1945, Foust Private Papers; *Carolinian*, 9 Nov. 1945, 3 Oct. 1947.

Chapter 11 Notes

1. Mary T. Moore, 16 Feb. 1948, to Jackson, Jackson Papers; List of faculty, 1929–30 to 1951–52, dated 18 June 1953, K–L, E.K. Graham Papers.

2. Faculty listings in *Catalogs* for 1934–35 and 1949–50.

3. Harriet Elliott, 26 March 1945, to Jackson, Dean of Women Papers, VC Student Affairs Records. For Jackson's agreement with this position, see Jackson, 29 July 1941, to McKee Fisk, and 11 Jan. 1944, to Haywood Parker, Jackson Papers.

4. See OH: Harriet Kupferer, 27 Oct. 1989.

5. Jackson, 4 Feb. 1935, to Alice C. Strong, Jackson Papers.

6. Jackson correspondence with F. McNutt and Eunice Lloyd, 24 June to 17 Oct. 1941, Jackson Papers.

7. See Winfield H. Rogers, 13 Dec. 1941, to Jackson, Jackson Papers.

8. Jackson, 8 May 1941, to Guy H. Wells; Trustees' Visiting Committee report, 26 May 1944, B folder, Jackson Papers. See also Table V in the study of male and female faculty salaries, 1935–65, by an AAUP committee in 1965, headed by Margaret Hunt, in VC Academic Affairs Records, 1941–84: AAUP Statistics.

9. Advisory Committee Minutes, 26 May [1937]; Harriet Elliott, 18 June 1943, to Jackson; Jackson, 22 June 1943, to Elliott; Gregory Ivy, 4 Sept. 1945, to Jackson; J.A. Highsmith, 25 Nov. 1947, to Jackson, Jackson Papers.

10. Leonard B. Hurley, search committee report, 27 May 1936; Jackson, 20 July 1949, to Gregory Ivy; Ivy, 24 July 1949, to Jackson, Jackson Papers.

11. Jackson, 27 June 1949, to the faculty, Jackson Papers.

12. Julius Foust, 18 Feb. 1926, to A.T. Allen, Foust Papers; Jackson, 5 Nov. 1934, to M.C. Huntley; Dean of Administration report, 15 Jan. 1936; Jackson, 24 Jan. 1936, to Nora Thompson Gerberich, Jackson Papers; Advisory Committee Minutes, 21 May, 22, 28 June 1935, 23 March 1937.

13. Jackson, 8 May 1941, to Guy H. Wells; 11 Jan. 1944, to Haywood Parker; 24 Aug. 1945, to Calvin N. Warfield; contents of Faculty folder, 1945; Trustees' Visiting Committee report, 26 May 1944, B folder, Jackson Papers; Advisory Committee Minutes, 29 Aug.1944, 18 March, 17 April 1945.

14. H. Hugh Altvater, 20 April 1942, to Jackson; Ruth Collings, 9 March 1942, to Jackson; B.B. Kendrick, 14 Nov. 1942, to F.P. Graham; W.S. Barney, 11 Sept. 1946, to Jackson, Jackson Papers.

15. Jackson, salary recommendations, 19 April 1945, G folder; Jackson, 21 July 1947, to Faculty; 30 June 1948, to F.P. Graham, Jackson Papers; Faculty Council Minutes, 19 March, 30 April, 1 Oct. 1945, 21 April 1947; Trustees' Visiting Committee report, April 1948; John C. Lockhart, 8 May 1948, to Arch T. Allen, Visiting Committee, Jackson Papers.

16. UNC Administrative Council Minutes, 15 May 1949, and Jackson, 1 Aug. 1949, to Susan Barksdale, Jackson Papers.

17. Julius Foust, 1 Jan. 1920, to J.D. Murphy, Foust Papers. For TIAA, see Brubacher and Rudy, *Higher Education in Transition*, pp. 384–86.

18. Julius Foust, 28 April 1928, to H.W. Chase, Foust Papers; Trustees' resolutions, 5 June 1934, L–M folder; Jackson, 12 May 1939, to W.C. Smith; 5 Nov. 1940, to J.M. Lear, Jackson Papers.

19. For Weatherspoon's desperate plight, see Minnie McIver Brown, 22 Aug. 1932, to Julius Foust, and Trustees' Executive Committee Minutes, 28 Sept. 1932, Consolidation folder; John H. Cook, 21 Aug. 1933, to Foust, Foust Papers; Jackson, 12, 27 Sept. 1934, to Weatherspoon, Jackson Papers.

20. L.R. Wilson, *University of North Carolina Under Consolidation*, pp. 124–35; UNC Administrative Council Minutes, 16 April 1948, Jackson Papers; Jackson, 3 June 1947, to Caroline Schoch; 14 Dec. 1948, to Cornelia Strong; 9 March 1950, to W.D. Carmichael, Jackson Papers; enclosure with John C. Lockhart, 5 Jan. 1951, to E.K. Graham, R, Graham Papers; Virginia T. Lathrop, 8 Feb. 1959, to Gordon Blackwell, Blackwell Papers.

21. Jackson, 13 May 1941, to W.S. Barney, Jackson Papers.

22. J.P. Givler, 16 March 1945, to Jackson; list of secretaries (Department Recommendations folder); W.S. Barney, 11 Sept. 1946, to Jackson (Faculty Budget folder); Gregory Ivy, 10 March 1947, to Jackson, Jackson Papers.

23. OH: Key L. Barkley, 7 June 1991.

24. Advisory Committee Minutes, 23 March 1938; Kearney, "All Out For Victory," pp. 32–33.

25. Jackson, 29 Jan. 1937, to W.S. Barney, Jackson Papers; Barney, 24 May 1951, to E.K. Graham, Graham Papers.

26. Jackson, 13 July 1936, to Frank P. Graham; memo of conversation with Graham, 20 July 1936; 20 July 1936, to Gregory Ivy; 7 Sept. 1936, to Charlotte Kohler, Jackson Papers; Faculty Council Minutes, 20 Nov. 1939.

27. See Advisory Committee Minutes, 16 May 1937; OH: Hollis Rogers, 10 April 1990.

28. *Carolinian*, 13 Jan. 1939; Faculty Council Minutes, 20 Nov. 1939.

29. Advisory Committee Minutes, 3 June 1941; Committee on Rank and Promotion report, 11 March 1942, C folder; Jackson, 1 March 1946, to Austin L. Venable; 23 Oct. 1946, to F.P. Graham, Jackson Papers; AAUP, *Policy Documents and Reports*, 1995 ed. (AAUP, Washington, D.C.), p. 4. For his successor's impatience with Jackson's laxity in this respect, see E.K. Graham, 8 Nov. 1954, to Elizabeth Adams, B of T, Graham Papers.

30. A.B. Andrews, 6 Feb., 26 June 1936, to Jackson, with accompanying report, 25 June 1936, F, Jackson Papers.

31. Registrar report, 18 March 1949, Q–R, Jackson Papers.

32. Jackson, 30 June 1948, to F.P. Graham, Jackson Papers; OH: Mereb Mossman, 4 Oct. 1989, Vance Littlejohn, 23 Oct. 1989; Kearney, "All Out For Victory," p. 36.

33. Jackson, draft speech to faculty, 14 Sept. 1936, Jackson Papers.

34. Jackson report, 1934–44, Jackson Papers.

35. OH: Hollis Rogers, 10 April 1990. See also J.P. Givler, 6 Feb. 1940, to Jackson, Jackson Papers; E.K. Graham, 28 Nov. 1951, to Howard B. Adelmann, Faculty folder, Graham Papers.

36. Jackson, 24 Aug. 1945, to C. Warfield, and 20 Oct. 1945, to F.P. Graham; Graham, 2 Dec. 1945, to Jackson, W, Jackson Papers.

37. *Charlotte Observer*, 15 Dec. 1940, and *Greensboro Daily News*, 20 Dec. 1970, in Vertical File: Psychology; *Carolinian*, 13 March 1942, 3 Oct. 1947.

38. UNC Administrative Council Committee report, [1946], Jackson Papers; Trustees' Visiting Committee Report, 1953, pp. 12–13.

39. Faculty Council Minutes, 21 April 1947; Jackson, 4 Feb. 1949, to Lois Bowden, Jackson Papers.

40. Advisory Committee Minutes, 17 March, 24, 26 May [1937]; Subcommittee on Faculty Needs report, 6 Dec. 1937, with Advisory Committee Minutes, 15 Dec. 1937.

41. Jackson, 18 April 1939, to Allen Tate; 2 July 1942, to Alexander Guerry, Jackson Papers.

42. OH: Phillip Morgan, 3 April 1990.

43. Faculty Council Minutes, 1 Oct. 1945.

44. For divergent views on this point, see John L. Caldwell, 28 Aug. 1939, to E.J. Forney, Jackson Papers; OH: Elizabeth Vezell Griffin, 7 May 1991.

45. Comparative List of Courses Given at Five Representative Colleges of About the Same Enrollment, Consolidation folder, Foust Papers, 1931.

46. OH: Harriet Kupferer, 27 Oct. 1989; Anne Young Oakley, 16 April 1991; Laura Anderton, 19 Jan. 1990; Richard Bardolph, 14 May 1991.

47. Faculty-Student Joint Advisory Committee Minutes, 26 Oct. 1921; Faculty Council Minutes, 7 Nov. 1921; Julius Foust, 26 Feb. 1929, to Florence Eckert, Foust Papers.

48. Press release re Phi Beta Kappa, 11 Dec. 1934, Jackson Papers; Faculty Council Minutes, 2 March 1931, 10 Dec. 1934; *Alumnae News*, 19 (July 1930), pp. 29–30; 44 (Oct. 1955), p. 13; (April 1956), p. 20; OH: Key L. Barkley, 7 June 1991. It may well have been Foust who brought Phi Beta Kappa to the campus. For differing views on this, see Magnhilde Gullander, 3 July 1934, to Foust, with Mrs. Foust's marginal notation, Foust Private Papers, and OH: Key L. Barkley, 7 June 1991. For the national background within Phi Beta Kappa, see Current, *Phi Beta Kappa*, pp. 143–44.

49. Plan for Awarding Honors, adopted by Faculty Council, 22 April 1946, Jackson Papers; Faculty Council Minutes, 20 Jan. 1947.

50. Faculty Council Minutes, 17 March, 21 April 1947; Plan for Honors Work, [ca. 1947], Vertical File: Honors Program; Helen Barton, in *Alumnae News*, 36 (Feb. 1948), p. 9.

51. Eells, "Norms for Honorary Degrees," pp. 378–79.

52. Advisory Committee Minutes, 1 Feb., 15 Nov. 1938, 12 Nov. 1943; Faculty Council Minutes, 18 Oct., 15 Nov. 1943; Jackson-F. P. Graham correspondence, 1–16 Nov. 1938, Jackson Papers.

53. [W. D. Carmichael], 8 Feb. 1950, to F. P. Graham; Jackson, 16 Feb. 1950, to Graham, Jackson Papers.

54. See Jackson's letter of condolence, 26 June 1950, Jackson Papers.

55. Faculty Cabinet Minutes, 13 Jan. 1928; *Carolinian*, 23 Jan. 1930; Faculty Council Minutes, 8 Jan. 1935, 21 April, 20 Oct. 1941, 20 March, 17 April, 15 May 1944; Trustees' Visiting Committee Report, April 1948. See also the Quarter System and S folders, Jackson Papers, 1944.

56. Ashby, *Graham*, 118–19.

57. Julius Foust, [1929], to Director of the Budget and the Advisory Budget Commission, Budget folder, Foust Papers; Jackson report, 1934–44, Jackson Papers, 1944.

58. Kearney, "All Out For Victory," pp. 45–49.

59. Harriet Elliott, 23 Nov. 1942, to Jackson, Jackson Papers; Elliott, 22 Feb. 1943, to E.E. Pfaff, Dean of Women Papers, VC Student Affairs Records.

60. [Vance Littlejohn,] Graduate Education at the Woman's College, [March 1962], Gr–Gu, Singletary Papers; Margaret Edwards, Home Economics Department report, 22 March 1938; Jackson, 27 Aug. 1938, to N.C. Newbold; 1 Nov. 1944, to Archibald Henderson, Jackson Papers.

61. Jackson report, 15 Jan. 1936, Dean of Administration Reports; Advisory Committee Minutes, 7, 9 April 1936.

62. See Jackson, 17 Aug. 1939, to H.R. Douglass and, 13 Aug. 1941, to W.C. Ryan, Jackson Papers.

63. Faculty Council Minutes, 20 Oct. 1941, 19 Jan. 1942, 18 April 1949; F.H. McNutt, 9 Sept. 1957, to W.M. Whyburn, Graduate Council Papers, 1950–59, in VCAA Records, 1941–84. Re McNutt, see Eugenia Hunter and Charles E. Prall, 30 Nov. 1953, to Edna Arundel, G folder, E.K. Graham Papers. Re the MFA degree, see Vertical File: Creative Arts Program; *Alumnae News*, 37 (May 1949), p. 9; 38 (May 1950), p. 7.

64. F.H. McNutt, Graduate School report, 22 July 1949, G folder, Jackson Papers; [Vance Littlejohn], Graduate Education at Woman's College, [March 1962], Gr–Gu, Singletary Papers.

Chapter 12 Notes

1. Faculty File: Charles H. Stone; Holder, "History of the Library of the Woman's College," pp. 56–62.

2. Kaser, "Century of Academic Librarianship," pp. 223, 226–27; Faculty File: Guy R. Lyle.

3. Faculty File: Charles M. Adams; J.S. Ferguson, Speech at Friends of Library meeting, 16 April 1969, Speeches, Ferguson Papers. For the national library construction boom, see Hamlin, *University Library*, pp. 68, 73–74.

4. Helen Ingraham, 17 April 1945, to Charles Adams, Jackson Papers.

5. Guy Lyle, 21 Oct. 1936, to Jackson; Jackson, 28 Nov. 1936, to Lyle, Jackson Papers.

6. Lyle, 17 Nov. 1941, to A.S. Keister; 27 Nov. 1941, to M.K. Hooke, Correspondence, Office of Librarian Records.

7. Committee to Study Staff Status, records and reports, [early 1942], and Charles Adams correspondence on this issue, Dec. 1948, [Jan. 1949], Dec. 1951–April 1952, Nov. 1954–April 1955, in Correspondence, Office of Librarian Records; Faculty Library Committee, 16 April 1955, to F.H. McNutt, Committees F–T, Graham Papers; Faculty Council Minutes, 16 May 1955.

8. Jackson, 6 July 1935, to Charles Stone; Elizabeth Sampson, 1 Oct. 1935, to the faculty, Jackson Papers; *Catalog*, 1935–36, p. 34; Wilson, *University of North Carolina Under Consolidation*, p. 181.

9. Guy Lyle, "The Library of the Woman's College of the University of North Carolina: The Present and the Future," [1939], with Correspondence, Office of Librarian Records; Mereb Mossman, 22 June 1956, to W.W. Pierson, Pierson Papers. For book ordering, see Julius Foust, 15 Oct. 1931, to James P. Kinard, Foust Papers.

10. [Treva W. Mathis], College Collection report, [13 July 1944], Vertical File: College Collection; C.M. Adams report, 1947–48, in Correspondence, Office of Librarian Records; Holder, "History of the Library of the Woman's College," pp. 94–96.

11. See Smith obituaries in S folder, Jackson Papers, 1944.

12. See Harriet Elliott, 18 Dec. 1939, to Mrs. Lionel Weil, Dean of Women Papers, VC Student Affairs Records; Jackson, 6 Feb. 1941, to Julius Foust, Foust Private Papers; Jackson, 24 March 1941, to Gertrude Rainey; F.P. Graham and Jackson, 26 March 1941, to English department, Jackson Papers.

13. For Friedlaender, see OH: Eleanor Dare Taylor Kennedy, 5 Feb. 1991.

14. Clara Byrd, 26 May 1930, to Rosa Blakeney Parker, Alumni Association Records; Advisory Committee Minutes, 15 Dec. [1937].

15. Waldron, *Close Connections*, pp. 175–76, 184–85; Caroline Gordon, 16 June 1975, to James H. Thompson, Faculty File: Caroline Gordon. See also Jackson, 2 July 1942, to Alexander Guerry, Jackson Papers; Faculty File: Allen Tate.

16. Jarrell, ed., *Randall Jarrell's Letters*, p. 425; Current, *Phi Beta Kappa*, pp. 188–89.

17. "Peter Taylor's Homecoming," *UNCG Bulletin*, Spring 1992, pp. 4–5; Greensboro *News & Record*, 12 Nov. 1991.

18. Watson, Forward to *Greensboro Reader*, [Chapel Hill, UNC Press, 1968], in Vertical File: English Department, Creative Writing; Peter Taylor and Robert Watson, in Lowell et al., *Randall Jarrell*, pp. 248–49, 258.

19. Greensboro *News & Record*, 16 Sept. 1990, 12 Nov. 1991; Robert Watson, in *Alumae/i News*, 52 (Jan. 1964), p. 8; 57 (Spring 1969), p. 2; Reminiscences of Jarrell's students, in ibid., 54 (Spring 1966), pp. 19 ff; OH: Robert Watson, 21 March 1990; Jarrell, *Randall Jarrell's Letters*, pp. 175, 182, 185, 201–02; Pritchard, *Randall Jarrell*, pp. 154–58, 193–94, 276–78.

20. Marc Friedlaender, 17 April 1947, to L.H. Hubbard and, 26 May 1947, to Jackson, Jackson Papers; Robert Watson, Forward to *Greensboro Reader*(Chapel Hill, UNC Press, 1968), in Vertical File: English Department, Creative Writing; *Alumnae/i News*, 35 (July 1946), p. 10; 38 (May 1950), pp. 7–8; 42 (Spring–Summer 1953), p. 10; 57 (Spring 1969), pp. 3–4, 6–7.

21. *Greensboro Daily News*, 27 Nov. 1947; *Alumnae News*, 36 (Feb. 1948), p. 7; Jackson, 1 March 1948, to F.P. Graham; Jackson, opening remarks to second session of the forum, 11 Nov. 1948, Jackson Papers.

22. W.R. Taylor, 26 March 1935, to Curriculum Committee (including quotation); 2, 26 Aug. 1935, 31 Aug. 1936, to Jackson, Jackson Papers; Faculty Council Minutes, 18 Oct. 1937.

23. W.R. Taylor report, 15 June 1939, Jackson Papers.

24. W.R. Taylor correspondence, 1946, Jackson Papers; OH: Herman Middleton, 19 Feb. 1990.

25. Reports on Burnsville School of Fine Arts, Jackson Papers, 1947–1949; C.W. Phillips, 11 Oct. 1949, to W.D. Carmichael, B folder, Jackson Papers; W.R. Taylor statement, 8 March 1956, W.D. Carmichael Papers; Gordon W. Pearlman, in *Alumni News*, 57 (Winter 1969), pp. 39–41; W.C. Burton, in Greensboro *News & Record*, 1 Aug. 1993; Vertical File: Burnsville School of Fine Arts.

26. W.C. Burton, in Greensboro *News & Record*, 1 Aug. 1993; OH: Herman Middleton, 19 Feb. 1990.

27. W.R. Taylor, 3 Oct., 22 Nov. 1947, to Jackson; Jackson, 15 June 1949, to Taylor and England; Dramatic Activities Board minutes, 27 Sept., 10 Nov. 1949; Ione H. Grogan, 4 Nov. 1949, to Jackson; Vance T. Littlejohn, 22 Nov. 1949, to Jackson; Taylor, 9 Jan. 1950, to L.B. Hurley; Hurley, 6 March 1950, to Jackson, Jackson Papers; Advisory Committee minutes, 21 Nov. 1949, in Dramatic Arts Department folder, Gordon Gray Papers, subgroup 2, series 3.

28. Levine, *American College*, p. 97.

29. Advisory Committee Minutes, 21, 23 July 1935; *Greensboro Daily News*, 13 Jan. 1985; *Alumnae/i News*, 34 (Nov. 1945, pp. 2–4; 75 (Fall 1986), p. 4.

30. *Catalog*, 1935–36, pp. 73–76; Bonnie Angelo, in *Alumnae News*, 38 (May 1950), p. 7.

31. See Lamar Dodd, 30 March 1942, to Jackson, and Jackson correspondence with E.W. Gudger, 24 Oct.–2 Nov. 1944, Jackson Papers.

32. *Alumnae/i News*, 34 (Nov. 1945), p. 3; 38 (Feb. 1950), p. 2; 75 (Fall 1986), p. 4; Vertical File: Art Department, Weatherspoon Art Gallery.

33. Gregory Ivy, 7 July 1938, to Jackson, Jackson Papers; *Alumnae News*, 34 (Nov. 1945), p. 4.

34. Faculty File: Burton B. Kendrick.

35. Advisory Committee Minutes, 28 May, 5 June 1946, 13 March, 16 June 1947; Magnhilde Gullander, 5 May 1946, to Jackson; Louise Alexander et al., [1946], to Jackson; A.C. Hall et al., 22 May 1946, to Jackson; C.D. Johns, 31 May 1946, 29 May , 10 June 1947, to Jackson; Marc Friedlaender, [late 1946], 15, 21 May 1947, to Jackson; C.D. Johns memorandum, 13 July 1947, Jackson Papers.

36. C.D. Johns, 17 March 1946, to Jackson, Jackson Papers.

37. OH: Richard Bardolph, 14 May 1991.

38. Louise Alexander, 5 Aug. 1912, to Julius Foust; Foust, 6 Aug. 1912, to Alexander, Foust Papers; *Carolinian*, 5 March 1936; Harriet Elliott, [Nov. 1946?], to Gladys Tillett, Tillett Papers (re dinner on election night); Taylor, "Woman Suffrage Movement," p. 181; Richard Bardolph, in *Alumni News*, 73 (Fall 1984), p. 11; 73 (Spring 1985), p. 12; Faculty File: Louise Brevard Alexander.

39. C.D. Johns, 17 March 1946, to Jackson, Jackson Papers; OH: Janice Hooke Moore, 23 Oct. 1990; Marjorie Burns, 8 Jan. 1991; Eleanor Dare Taylor Kennedy, 5 Feb. 1991; Susannah Thomas Watson, 7 Feb. 1991; Lula Hoskins, 8 April 1991; Eleanor Lloyd, 9 April 1991; Laura Brown Quinn, 6 May 1991.

40. *Alumnae News*, 37 (May 1949), pp. 4–5; Faculty File: Louise Brevard Alexander.

41. Jackson report, Dec. 1936, Dean of Administration Reports; Advisory Committee Minutes, 22 March 1937, 29 May 1939, 25 Feb., 29 April 1942; Jackson correspondence with John A. Clark, 1939–46, especially Aug. 1941, Feb.–May 1942, Feb.–June 1945, and Feb. 1946; Jackson, 9 Aug. 1945, to Otho B. Ross; Jackson, 28 Dec. 1945, to F. P. Graham, Jackson Papers.

42. Jackson, 11 May 1949, to Warren Ashby; L.O. Kattsoff, 12 Nov. 1949, to Jackson, Jackson Papers; *Carolinian*, 3 Oct. 1985; Greensboro *News & Record*, 3 Oct. 1985.

43. Jackson report, Dec. 1936, Dean of Administration Reports; Advisory Committee Minutes, 21 May, 28 June, 3, 6, 19, 23 July 1935; Jackson, 26 June, 21, 29 July 1935, to Viola Boddie; 6 Aug. 1935, to F.P. Graham, Jackson Papers.

44. Advisory Committee Minutes, 22 March 1937; C.C. Jernigan, 13 April 1938, 28 May 1942, to Jackson; Clyde Pharr, 10 July 1949, to Jackson; Jackson, 13 Aug. 1949, to W.D. Carmichael, Jackson Papers; Jernigan, in *Alumnae News*, 35 (April 1947), pp. 2–3.

45. John H. Cook, 20 March 1924, to Julius Foust, Department Reports folder; Foust, 20 March 1928, to Cook; J.P. Givler, 15 June 1931, to Foust (Budget folder); Givler, 18 July 1931, to Charles Crittenden, and Foust, 6 Aug. 1931, to Crittenden, Faculty folder, Foust Papers; Advisory Committee Minutes, 9 April 1937; Jackson, 20 Aug. 1937, to E. Edna Arundel, Jackson Papers.

46. Jackson, 20 Aug. 1937, to Edna Arundel, Jackson Papers; Advisory Committee Minutes, 10 Jan. 1938.

47. Advisory Committee Minutes, 3 May 1938; 29 March, 15 April 1940; 29 April 1942; Jackson, 4 May 1942, to Edna Arundel, Jackson Papers.

48. Glenn Johnson, in *Alumnae News*, 34 (April 1946), pp. 2–3; *Charlotte Observer*, 9 Nov. 1941, in Vertical File: Sociology.

49. Mereb Mossman, 27 July 1937, to Glenn R. Johnson; Jackson, 26 May 1948, to W.D. Carmichael, Jackson Papers; OH: Mereb Mossman, 4 Oct. 1989.

50. J.P. Givler, 13 Oct. 1928, to Julius Foust, Budget folder, Foust Papers.

51. Newspaper clipping, 17 Nov. 1935, in College Scrapbook, 1935–36; Julius Foust report, 1930, with Directors' Reports; Archie Shaftesbury, 15 June 1931, to Mary Taylor Moore, and other items in Vertical File: Summer Session, Beaufort and Beaufort Summer School; Shaftesbury, 4 Aug. 1938, to Jackson, Jackson Papers; *Alumnae/i News*, 26 (Feb. 1938), p. 7; 35 (July 1946), p. 1; 55 (July 1967), p. 31; *Carolinian*, 12 March 1948; *Greensboro Daily News*, 25 April 1954. For the marine lab closing, see Victor Cutter, 13 July 1953, to E.K. Graham; John C. Lockhart, 29 July, 9 Dec. 1953, to Graham, E.K. Graham Papers.

52. OH: Mary Jane Wharton Sockwell, 8 March 1990; J.P. Givler, 10 Jan. 1941, to Jackson, Jackson Papers; E.K. Graham, 28 Nov. 1951, to Howard B. Adelmann, Graham Papers.

53. Jackson, 3 Sept. 1934, to Mary Petty, Jackson Papers; *Alumni News*, 60 (Summer 1972), p. 19.

54. *Alumnae News*, 33 (Feb. 1945), p. 5; 35 (Feb. 1947), p. 11; OH: Anna Joyce Reardon, 20 Sept. 1990; Reardon, 15 May 1941, to Calvin Warfield; Jackson, 18 Feb. 1947, to J.W. Harrelson; A.D. Shaftesbury et al., 25 April 1947, to Jackson; Jackson, 19 Aug. 1947, to F.P. Graham; 4 Oct. 1947, to Muriel Kestner, Jackson Papers.

55. Calvin Warfield, 21 March 1938, to Jackson; Florence Schaeffer, 22 Jan. 1946, to Jackson, Jackson Papers.

56. *Charlotte Observer*, 15 Dec. 1940, in Vertical File: Psychology; *Alumnae News*, 33 (April 1945), p. 2; 42 (Spring–Summer 1953), p. 6; OH: Key L. Barkley, 7 June 1991; Laura Brown Quinn, 6 May 1991.

Chapter 13 Notes

1. F.H. McNutt, 24 June 1941, to Jackson; Jackson, 7 July 1941, to McNutt; 15 Dec. 1941, to Eunice Ann Lloyd; McNutt, 27 Jan. 1942, to Lloyd; Ruth Fitzgerald, 2 April 1942, to Jackson; McNutt, 9 March 1942, to Jackson, Faculty folder, Jackson Papers.

2. Ralph Brimley, 23 Feb. 1947, to Jackson; Jackson, 21 March 1947, to Brimley, Jackson Papers.

3. Jackson, 10 May 1947, 5 March 1949 to Dennis H. Cooke; Cooke, 13 May 1947, to Jackson; Jackson, 5 May 1949, to Charles E. Prall; 17 May 1949, to W.D. Carmichael, Jackson Papers.

4. Jackson, 12 Jan. 1942, to Julius Foust, Foust Private Papers; W.R. Johnson, "Teachers and Teacher Training," p. 243; Armstrong, *The College and Teacher Education*, pp. 242–45, 249–50.

5. "Woman's College Will Have Kindergarten," 8 Aug. 1935, Curry School Records, 1902–69, School of Education Records; OH: Ruth Elliott, 29 Oct. 1990; Nancy White, 4 Dec. 1989.

6. Albert Keister, 31 May 1940, to Jackson, Jackson Papers.

7. John C. Lockhart, 29 Nov. 1943, to B.L. Smith; F.H. McNutt, Education Department budget request, 13 July 1944; Jackson, 9 Aug. 1944, to Alvin T. Haley, Jackson Papers.

8. OH: May Lattimore Adams, 23 Feb. 1990; Betty Brown Jester, 22 March 1990.

9. George M. Joyce, 15 Feb. 1936, to Jackson; Jackson, 30 May 1940, to J.F. Miller, Jackson Papers; Jackson report, Dec. 1936, Dean of Administration Reports; Jackson, in *Alumnae News*, 28 (Nov. 1939), p. 8.

10. Jackson, 30 May 1940, to J.F. Miller; Vance Littlejohn, 11 July 1944, to Jackson, Jackson Papers; Faculty Council Minutes, 20 March 1944; OH: Paula Andris, 23 April 1991.

11. McKee Fisk, in *Alumnae News*, 32 (Feb. 1944), pp. 4–5; Vance Littlejohn, 11 July 1944, 15 March 1945, 19 Sept. 1946, to Jackson, Jackson Papers; OH: Vance Littlejohn, 23 Oct. 1989.

12. *Alumnae News*, 22 (July 1933), p. 20.

13. Jackson, 10 Dec. 1945, to F.P. Graham; 4 Feb. 1949, to Margaret Edwards; 23 May 1949, to Katherine Taylor, Jackson Papers.

14. Faculty File, Margaret Edwards; *Alumnae News*, 35 (April 1947), p. 6; 49 (Oct. 1960), p. 10; Canaday, *History of the School of Human Environmental Science*, p. 24.

15. Canaday, *History of the School of Human Environmental Science*, pp. 9, 22, 25.

16. Margaret Edwards, 8 July 1944, to Jackson, Faculty folder, Jackson Papers; *Greensboro Daily News*, 2 Nov. 1941, in Vertical File: Home Economics.

17. Advisory Committee Minutes, 27 May 1936; Faculty File: H.H. Altvater.

18. H.H. Altvater, 1 Feb., 25 March 1937, to Jackson; 26 Nov. 1937, to J.C. Pfohl, in Correspondence, Music School Records.

19. *Carolinian*, 10 Oct. 1941; Altvater report, 1936–37; Altvater, 8, 24 May 1944, to Jackson, Faculty folder, Jackson Papers; Telephone interview, 16 Sept. 1998, with Herbert Hazelman.

20. *Carolinian*, 28 Nov. 1941; Faculty File: H.H. Altvater; Vertical File: Greensboro Orchestra; H.H. Altvater, 3 Nov. 1948, to Jackson; "The Greensboro Orchestra: Its History and Development," [March 1946], A folder, Jackson Papers; OH: George Dickieson, 20 March 1990; Telephone interview with Herbert Hazelman, 16 Sept. 1998.

21. *Alumnae News*, 23 (Feb. 1935), p. 7; Brown, *North Carolina State High School Music Contest-Festival*, pp. 20–45. For debate over Brown's conduct as director and the college's connection with it, see Jackson, 11 Oct. 1934, to James C. Harper et al., and Harper's response, 12 Oct. 1934, Jackson Papers.

22. C.E. Teague, 14, 21 April 1941, to W.D. Carmichael, Vertical File: Business Office; H.H. Altvater, 20 April 1942, to Jackson; Jackson, 30 June 1948, to F.P. Graham; 8 May 1947, to Altvater, Jackson Papers.

23. OH: Phillip Morgan, 3 April 1990; Frances Ashcraft McBane, 19 Feb. 1991; Esther Bagwell Mathews, 7 Feb. 1991; Graduates, School of Music, 1910–1960, VC Academic Affairs Records, 1941–84: Music.

24. Mary C. Coleman, 9 March 1935, to Jackson; Jackson, 1 June 1935, to Anna Gove, Jackson Papers; Advisory Committee Minutes, 29 May 1935.

25. Watson, "Ethel...Lawther," pp. 1, 48–50, 57, 65–66, 69. For Coleman's death see Umstead, "Mary Channing Coleman," p. 160.

26. Physical Education Department budget requests, [1944]; Ethel Martus, 15 March 1948, to Jackson, F.P. Graham folder, Jackson Papers; O'Neill, "History of the Physical Education Department," pp. 32–38, 41.

27. *Alumni News*, 71 (Winter 1983), pp. 8–9; Umstead, "Mary Channing Coleman," pp. 95–96; Watson, "Ethel...Lawther," pp. 119–22.

28. Jackson, 17 Dec. 1935, to W.C. Smith; John H. Cook, 31 July 1939, to Jackson; Jackson, 19 Dec. 1941, to W.W. Pierson, Jackson Papers; Jackson report, 15 Jan. 1936, Dean of Administration Reports; Jackson report, 1934–44, Jackson Papers, 1944; Advisory Committee Minutes, 9 Nov., 15 Dec. 1937, 15 Nov. 1938; Faculty Council Minutes, 21 Nov. 1938, 20 March 1944.

29. Jackson, 25 July 1945, 24 July 1946, to C.W. Phillips; 30 June 1948, to F.P. Graham, Jackson Papers; Eugenia Hunter and Charles E. Prall, 30 Nov. 1953, to Edna Arundel, G, E.K. Graham Papers.

30. Jackson, 13 Aug. 1941, to W. Carson Ryan, Jackson Papers; Jackson report, 1934–44, Jackson Papers, 1944.

31. C.W. Phillips, 26 Sept. 1950, to E.K. Graham, E folder; F.H. McNutt, 13 July 1953, to Mereb Mossman, Appendix C, Departments folder, E.K. Graham Papers; Gordon Blackwell, 1 July 1960, to Wm. Friday, E, Blackwell Papers.

32. F.H. McNutt, evening college proposal, [6 Nov. 1945], E folder; Jackson, 19 Nov. 1945, to McNutt; 5 Dec. 1946, to Eric W. Rodgers, Jackson Papers; Grady Lane, 16 Sept. 1950, to E.K. Graham, F–G; C.W. Phillips, 26 Sept. 1950, to Graham, E, Graham Papers.

33. Jackson, 19 Nov. 1945, to F.H. McNutt; 22 Aug. 1946, to F.P. Graham; 11 Sept. 1946, to W.T. Bost; 5 Dec. 1946, to Eric W. Rodgers, Jackson Papers.

34. E.K. Graham, 22 Nov. 1952, to Gordon Gray, G, Graham Papers.

Chapter 14 Notes

1. OH: May Lattimore Adams, 23 Feb. 1990; Jackson, 8 April 1935, to Margaret Bunn, Jackson Papers.

2. *Alumni News*, 67 (Fall 1978), p. 18; Report of conference, 7 Aug. 1935, with Jackson, 8 July 1936, to Kent Blair, N–P folder, Jackson Papers; Advisory Committee Minutes, 28 May 1936.

3. Advisory Committee Minutes, 23 March, 14 May 1937.

4. *Carolinian*, 6 Nov. 1942; *Alumnae News*, 31 (Feb. 1943), p. 1; 34 (Feb. 1946), p. 2; Jackson report, 1934–44, [1944], Jackson Papers; Faculty Council Minutes, 17 April 1944; E.K. Graham, 7 Dec. 1954, to Bill Sharpe, Graham Papers.

5. Special Information...for Fiscal Year 1932–33, 27 Jan. 1933, Budget folder, Foust Papers; "Enrollment," in Jackson report, 1948–49, C, Jackson Papers.

6. List of town students, 30 Dec. 1949, E, Jackson Papers.

7. *Carolinian*, 6 Nov. 1942; Harriet Elliott, "Suggestions for a Building Program," 21 Aug. 1944, E, Jackson Papers; OH: Ruth Elliott, 29 Oct. 1990; Eleanor Dare Taylor Kennedy, 5 Feb. 1991; Margaret Daniel Thurston, 10 Sept. 1990.

8. Memorandum, 23 Jan. 1939, to Jackson, S, Jackson Papers; Julius Foust, 10 April 1944, to Cornelia Strong, Foust Private Papers.

9. Julius Foust, 9 Oct. 1931, to Josephus Daniels, Foust Papers.

10. See OH: Harriet Kupferer, 27 Oct. 1989; Mazie Bullard, 26 Jan. 1990.

11. [Mildred Newton,] List of Students by Counties and States, 8 Dec. 1942, Jackson Papers.

12. Advisory Committee Minutes, 23 March, 14 May 1937; Jackson, in *Alumnae News*, 28 (Nov. 1939), p. 8; Jackson report, 1934–44, [1944]; {Mildred Newton], List of Students by Counties and States, 22 Nov. 1948, Jackson Papers. For the United States, see Jencks and Riesman, *Academic Revolution*, p. 169.

13. OH: Mereb Mossman, 4 Oct. 1989.

14. Wilson, *University of North Carolina Under Consolidation*, p. 114; *Carolinian*, 16 Jan., 9 April 1948.

15. Faculty Council Minutes, 18 Nov. 1946; OH: Ruth Elliott, 29 Oct. 1990; Margaret Daniel Thurston, 10 Sept. 1990.

16. Harriet Elliott, 28 June 1944, to Jackson, Jackson Papers; OH: Harriet Kupferer, 27 Oct. 1989; Beverly Bell Armfield, 6 Sept. 1990; Frances Ashcraft McBane, 19 Feb. 1991; Betsy Umstead, 7 Dec. 1989; Anne Young Oakley, 16 April 1991; "Dining Hall Etiquette," [1950], Vertical File: Dining Halls.

17. Expenses, 1892–1940, in Foust, College History notes.

18. Jackson, 18 Jan. 1939, to W.R. Clegg; 22 June 1945, to Mrs. J.T. Kenyon, Jackson Papers.

19. Levine, *American College*, pp. 196–201; Ware, *Holding Their Own*, p. 57; Earnest, *Academic Procession*, pp. 301–02.

20. *Carolinian*, 15 Nov. 1935, 10 Dec. 1937; 4 Oct. 1940.

21. Edna Forney, 12 Feb. 1943, to Clora & Julius Foust, Foust Private Papers; OH: Margaret Daniel Thurston, 10 Sept. 1990; Nancy White, 4 Dec. 1989.

22. Cornelia Strong, 2 May 1946, to Jackson; C.W. Phillips, 4 March 1947, to John Lockhart, Jackson Papers; *Carolinian*, 7 Oct. 1949.

23. "History of the Class Chairman," Am–Ay, Singletary Papers, 1963.

24. For the issue of counselor-academic rivalry at Smith, see Harriet Elliott, 30 Nov. 1942, to Ione Grogan; and at WC, Elliott, 28 June 1944, to Jackson, both in Jackson Papers.

25. Dean of Administration Reports, Dec. 1936; Harriet Elliott, in *Alumnae News*, 24 (April 1936), pp. 6–9; Elliott, 30 March, 10 June 1942, 23 March 1943, to Jackson, Jackson Papers; Elliott, 28 June 1944, to Jackson, Dean of Women Papers, VC Student Affairs Records; Jackson report, 1934–44, [1944], Jackson Papers.

26. Dean of Women report, 1937–38, and Harriet Elliott, excerpts from "The Counselor's Guide Book," 1945, in "Summary of Miss Elliott's Philosophy," Dean of Women Papers, VC Student Affairs Records; *Alumni News*, 53 (Winter 1965), p. 22; Interview with four former counselors, in ibid., 66 (Spring 1978), pp. 8–10; OH: Elizabeth Booker, 17 May 1991.

27. Dean of Women report, 1937–38, Dean of Women Papers, VC Student Affairs Records; Harriet Elliott, 21 Aug. 1944, to John Lockhart, E, Jackson Papers; *Alumni News*, 55 (July 1967), pp. 6, 8.

28. Katherine Taylor, Residence Department report, in Jackson report, 1948–49, C, Jackson Papers; OH: Laura Anderton, 19 Jan. 1990; *Alumnae News*, 38 (May 1950), p. 5; Link, *Harriet Elliott*, pp. 30–31.

29. Advisory Committee Minutes, 5 March 1943, 13 March 1944, 16 July, 21 Sept. 1946; Harriet Elliott, 23 March 1943, to Jackson, Jackson Papers; Elliott, 15 July, 9 Sept. 1946, to Jackson, Dean of Women Papers, VC Student Affairs Records; Katherine Taylor, 9 May 1949, to Jackson, Jackson Papers.

30. See Harriet Elliott, 21 Aug. 1944, to John Lockhart, E, Jackson Papers.

31. Jackson, 10 Jan. 1948, to Richard Bardolph, Jackson Papers.

32. [Harriet Elliott], "Analysis of the Organization of the Woman's College U.N.C.," [1945], Dean of Women Papers, VC Student Affairs Records; Dean of Academic Advising, Self Study and Plan, May 1985, Self Study and Plans, Assistant VC Academic Affairs Records.

33. Harriet Elliott, in *Alumnae News*, 24 (April 1936), p. 8; Dean of Women report, 1937–38, and Elliott, 28 June 1944, to Jackson, Dean of Women Papers, VC Student Affairs Records; Elliott, 21 Aug. 1944, to John Lockhart, E, Jackson Papers; Link, *Harriet Elliott*, pp. 31–34.

34. *Carolinian*, 15 Feb., 27 Sept. 1935; 7 May 1937; 9 Feb. 1945, 14 Jan. 1949; Mary Jo Rendleman, 1 Aug. 1942, to Jackson, Jackson Papers; Elliott, 28 June 1944, to Jackson, Dean of Women Papers, VC Student Affairs Records; Link, *Harriet Elliott*, pp. 32–42.

35. For alumnae memories, see OH: Elizabeth Yates King, 9 April 1991; Susannah Thomas Watson, 7 Feb. 1991; Harriet Kupferer, 27 Oct. 1989; Jane L. Joyner, 19 Feb. 1990; Beverly Bell Armfield, 6 Sept. 1990; Evon Dean, 28 March 1990; Nancy White, 4 Dec. 1989; Betsy Umstead, 7 Dec. 1989. For faculty and staff recollections, see OH: Vance Littlejohn, 23 Oct. 1989; Richard Bardolph, 14 May 1991; Mazie Bullard, 26 Jan. 1990; Key L. Barkley, 7 June 1991. Re male faculty dance escorts, see *Carolinian*, 11 May 1945; Key L. Barkley, 6 May 1994, to Jamie Sykes, Alumni Association Records.

36. OH: Key L. Barkley, 7 June 1991; Susannah Thomas Watson, 7 Feb. 1991. See also Kearney, "All Out For War," pp. 18–22.

37. *Carolinian*, 15 Nov. 1940; Jackson report, 1934–44, [1944], Jackson Papers.

38. Dean of Women report, 1937–38, Dean of Women Papers, VC Student Affairs Records.

39. Faculty Council Minutes, 15 Jan. 1934, 16 March 1942, 27 Sept., 18 Oct. 1943; *Carolinian*, 27 Feb., 20, 27 March, 2, 23 Oct. 1942, 15 Dec. 1944, 4 May 1945, 8 Feb. 1946; Vertical File: Honor Policy; Kearney, "All Out for Victory," 13–14; OH: Betsy Umstead, 7 Dec. 1989; Phillip Morgan, 3 April 1990.

40. OH: Harriet Kupferer, 27 Oct. 1989.

41. *Carolinian*, 1 April 1938; 7, 14, 28 Feb., 6 March 1941; 20 Feb., 13 March 1942; 26 Feb. 1943; 14 Feb. 1947; 5 Nov., 10 Dec. 1948. See also Jackson, 15 Jan. 1948, to W.D. Carmichael, Jackson Papers. For an ardently contested debate over alleged student apathy in 1942, see the "Needles Knitting Controversy," SGA Records.

42. See Katherine Taylor, Residence Department report, in Jackson report, 1948–49, Jackson Papers; OH: June Rainey Honeycutt, 10 May 1997.

43. *Carolinian*, 24 Sept. 1937; OH: Harriet Kupferer, 27 Oct. 1989; Esther Bagwell Matthews, 7 Feb. 1991; Lucy Horne Heath, 28 Feb. 1991.

44. *Carolinian*, 15 Nov. 1935.

45. *Carolinian*, 7 Oct. 1938.

46. *Carolinian*, 12 Oct. 1934, 13, 27 Oct. 1939; OH: Betsy Umstead, 7 Dec. 1989; Mary Miller, 17 Sept. 1990; Nancy White, 4 Dec. 1989; Mary Eppes Turner, 26 Feb. 1991; Beverly Bell Armfield, 6 Sept. 1990; Anne Young Oakley, 16 April 1991; Frances F. Brinkley, 19 Feb. 1990; Eleanor Dare Taylor Kennedy, 5 Feb. 1991; Lucy Horne Leath, 28 Feb. 1991; Esther Bagwell Matthews, 7 Feb. 1991; Kearney, "All Out For Victory," pp. 11–13, 17, 23–25.

47. Link, *Harriet Elliott*, p. 35.

48. Harriet Elliott, draft speech to alumnae, [ca. 1935], Speeches, Dean of Women Papers, VC Student Affairs Records; OH: Anna Joyce Reardon, 20 Sept. 1990.

49. *Carolinian*, 22 March 1935; OH: Mary Eppes Turner, 26 Feb. 1991; Eleanor Dare Taylor Kennedy, 5 Feb. 1991; Betsy Umstead, 7 Dec. 1989; Harriet Kupferer, 27 Oct. 1989; Katherine Taylor, Residence Department report, in Jackson report, 1948–49, Jackson Papers; Kearney, "All Out For Victory," pp. 13, 17–18, 29.

50. *Carolinian*, 15 Nov. 1935; 10 March, 27 Nov. 1936; 21 Oct. 1938; 19 Jan. 1940; *Alumnae News*, 32 (Nov. 1943), p. 4; *Student Handbook*, 1935–36, p. 64.

51. Richard MacKenzie, Emily Harris, and Harriet Elliott correspondence, 23 July to 5 Oct. 1938; James E. Davis and Jackson correspondence, 31 Oct., 3 Nov. 1939; Katherine Tay-

lor, 10 Nov. 1947, to Jackson; Taylor, Residence Department report, in Jackson report, 1948–49, Jackson Papers; OH: May Lattimore Adams, 23 Feb. 1990.

52. OH: Edna Richardson Watson, 10 May 1991; Harriet Kupferer, 27 Oct. 1989; Margaret Daniel Thurston, 10 Sept. 1990; Betsy Umstead, 7 Dec. 1989; *Alumni News*, 62 (Summer 1974), pp. 4–5.

53. *Alumni News*, 62 (Summer 1974), pp. 8–9.

54. OH: Ruth Whalin Cooke, 4 Sept. 1990; Esther Bagwell Matthews, 7 Feb. 1991.

55. Harriet Elliott and Mary Eppes, 27 Sept. 1941, to the faculty, Vert. File: World War II (Misc.); C.E. Teague, weekly reports, 29 Sept., 6 Oct., 24 Nov. 1941, Vertical File: Business Office; Jackson, 22 Oct. 1941, to Leon R. Meadows; 11 Sept. 1945, to Col. Paul R. Yountz, Jackson Papers; Faculty Council Minutes, 20 Oct. 1941; *Alumnae News*, 32 (Nov. 1943), pp. 3–4; OH: Margaret Daniel Thurston, 10 Sept. 1990; Harriet Kupferer, 27 Oct. 1989; Eleanor Dare Taylor Kennedy, 5 Feb. 1991; Marjorie Burns, 8 Jan. 1991; Key L. Barkley, 7 June 1991; Jim Schlosser, in Greensboro *News & Record*, 1 March 1993; Kearney, "All Out For Victory," pp. 25–28.

56. Religious Affiliations of Students, 1939–40, R, Jackson Papers. In January 1939 Jackson reported 43 Catholics and 69 Jews. Jackson, 18 Jan. 1939, to Arthur H. Compton, Jackson Papers.

57. Julius Foust, 30 April 1932, to James P. Kinard, Foust Papers; Altbach, *Student Politics*, pp. 98–99.

58. Ernestine Halyburton, 1 April 1932, to Julius Foust, Foust Papers; Dean of Administration Reports, Dec. 1936; Jackson report, 1934–44, [1944], Jackson Papers.

59. Dean of Administration Reports, Dec. 1936; *Carolinian*, 6 Nov. 1936; *Greensboro Daily News*, 8 Oct. 1942; Jackson report, 1934–44, [1944], Jackson Papers.

60. Advisory Committee Minutes, 20 Sept. 1936; *Carolinian*, 27 Feb. 1942.

61. *Carolinian*, 3 Nov. 1939, 28 Nov. 1941; *Alumni News*, 82 (Fall 1992), p. 2.

62. Jackson, 17 July 1940, to Guy R. Lyle, Jackson Papers; OH: Jane L. Joyner, 19 Feb. 1990; Nancy White, 4 Dec. 1989; Frances F. Brinkley, 19 Feb. 1990; Betsy Umstead, 7 Dec. 1989.

63. OH: Eleanor Dare Taylor Kennedy, 5 Feb. 1991; Dacia L. King, 25 Oct. 1990.

64. Faculty Council Minutes, 21 April 1948, 21 Feb. 1949; *Carolinian*, 14 May 1948; *Alumnae News*, 37 (Aug. 1948), p. 12.

65. Altbach and Peterson, "Before Berkeley," pp. 6–7, 13.

66. *Carolinian*, 17, 24 April 1936; "Kearney, All Out For Victory," p. 38; OH: Key L. Barkley, 7 June 1991.

67. *Greensboro Daily News*, 30 May 1937; Almeida, "Lifting the Veil," pp. 79–82; OH: Susannah Thomas Watson, 7 Feb. 1991.

68. "Statement by Dr. W.C. Jackson regarding interracial activity at St. Mary's House, April 19, 1946," dated 27 Feb. 1952, Q–R, E.K. Graham Papers, 1952.

69. Jackson, 21 Jan. 1935, to Wade Brown; 27 Sept. 1935, to Lee M. Brooks, Jackson Papers; OH: Susannah Thomas Watson, 7 Feb. 1991.

70. Wade R. Brown, 11 May 1935, to Jackson; Jackson, 20, 27 May, 17 June 1935, to Charlotte Hawkins Brown; Brown, 14 June 1935, 1 March 1937, to Jackson, Jackson Papers; Advisory Committee Minutes, 15 May 1935, 5 March 1937.

71. Archie D. Shaftesbury, 3 Dec. 1941, to W.R. Taylor, Jackson Papers.

72. Jackson correspondence with W.D. Carmichael and others, 21 Nov. to 3 Dec. 1947, C folder; Jackson, 5 Dec. 1947, to Maxine Garner; 19 July 1949, to Governor W. Kerr Scott, Jackson Papers.

73. Jackson, 27 Jan. 1948, to Lyda Gordon Shivers, Jackson Papers.

74. Goolsby, *Letters Lost and Found*, Introduction and pp. 68–76.

75. Kearney, "All Out For Victory," pp. 39–44, 51–52; OH: Nancy White, 4 Dec. 1989.

76. *Carolinian*, 10, 20 March, 6 Nov. 1936; 21 May, 5 Nov. 1937; 26 Feb. 1942; 22 Oct. 1943; 25 Feb. 1944; 27 Feb. 1948; Rat Day Banquet speech, [1942], Vertical File: Adelphian Society; Virginia T. Lathrop, in *Alumnae News*, 42 (Spring–Summer 1953), p. 13; OH: Jane L. Joyner, 19 Feb. 1990; Hilman Thomas Watkins, 6 March 1990; Betsy Umstead, 7 Dec. 1989.

77. *Carolinian*, 13 Nov. 1936, pp. 2, 3; 5 Nov. 1937; Ruth Collings, 11 Nov. 1939, to Jackson; Jackson, 26 Oct. 1945, to Sarah Moss, Jackson Papers.

78. *Carolinian*, 15 Oct. 1943, 27 Oct. 1944; *Alumnae News*, 36 (Nov. 1947), pp. 25, 27; Trelease, *Changing Assignments*, pp. III-208–13; OH: Beverly Bell Armfield, 6 Sept. 1990.

79. *Carolinian*, 3 March 1939.

80. OH: Mary Vance McAdams Whitcomb; Jane L. Joyner, 19 Feb. 1990; Kearney, "All Out For Victory," pp. 14–16.

81. OH: Harriet Kupferer, 27 Oct. 1989.

82. OH: Ruth Whalin Cooke, 4 Sept. 1990; Jane L. Joyner, 19 Feb. 1990; Frances F. Brinkley, 19 Feb. 1990; Betsy Umstead, 7 Dec. 1989.

83. Jackson, 30 Jan. 1945, to Gov. R. Gregg Cherry, Jackson Papers.

84. *Carolinian*, 6 Nov. 1920; 23 Sept., 12 Nov. 1925; 1Oct. 1931; 3 Nov. 1944; 3 Oct. 1947, pp. 2, 6; Jackson, 15 May 1945, to John C. Lockhart, Jackson Papers; OH: Margaret Daniel Thurston, 10 Sept. 1990; *Alumnae News*, 33 (April 1945), p. 5.

85. *Greensboro Daily News*, 29 April 1938; OH: Margaret Coit Elwell, 10 May 1991; *Alumnae/i News*, 41 (Summer 1952), p. 8; 56 (Spring 1968), p. 5; 57 (Spring 1969), pp. 3–4; *Coraddi*, Spring 1989, p. 46.

86. M.C. Coleman, 21 May 1943, to Jackson, with enclosure, "History of Sports Day," Jackson Papers.

87. *Carolinian*, 2 May 1941, 26 Feb. 1942; M.C. Coleman, 30 Sept. 1941, 21 May 1943, to Jackson, the last with enclosure, "History of Sports Day," Jackson Papers; OH: Key L. Barkley, 7 June 1991; O'Neill, "History of the Physical Education Department at the Woman's College," p. 54.

88. *Carolinian*, 26 Feb. 1942; OH: Marjorie Burns, 8 Jan. 1991.

89. Pamela Grundy, paper delivered to the Historical Society of North Carolina, 4 April 1997.

90. *Carolinian*, 17 March 1944, 12 Nov. 1948, 11 Feb. 1949; UNCG Trustees' Minutes, 19 Feb. 1987, Item II: Upgrading Intercollegiate Athletics; Ware, *Holding Their Own*, pp. 61–62; Cahn, *Coming on Strong*, pp. 66–68, 89, 101–04, 108; Jones, "History of Women's Intercollegiate Athletics," pp. 44–45, 82, 84–85; O'Neill, "History of the Physical Education Department at the Woman's College," pp. 54, 57–58, 117.

91. F.H. McNutt et al., 18 Dec. 1941, to W.W. Pierson, Jackson Papers.

92. [Jackson?], undated statement supporting proposed Woman's College building program for 1945–47, Building folder, Jackson Papers, 1946; "Percentage of Students... Qualifying for Certification," Institutional Studies, 1952–53, VC Academic Affairs Records, 1941–84.

93. Chafe, *Paradox of Change*, pp. 116–18, 121.

94. Clara Byrd, Notes (Memorandum) of 21 July 1931, Byrd Papers; Alumnae House Committee report, 6 Oct. 1939, in Alumnae House Committee, Minutes & Reports, Byrd Papers; Alumnae Assn. Annual Meeting minutes, 8 June 1940, Alumni Association Records.

95. Julius Foust, 27 March 1933, to Mrs. Julius (Laura) Cone, Foust Papers; Charles W. Tillett-W.C. Jackson correspondence, 23–29 Oct. 1935; Jackson, 28 April 1939, to Rosa B. Parker; 9 June 1939, to Clara Byrd; Sadie [McCain], 28 May 1942, to Jackson, Jackson Papers; Sadie [McCain], [ca. 1940], 21 March [1940], 28 Jan. 1942, to Harriet Elliott; Elliott, memorandum for her files, 20 March 1940; Elliott, 30 Jan. 1942, to McCain, Dean of Women Papers, VC Student Affairs Records; Sadie [McCain], 25 April (1940), to Clora Foust; 13 Jan. 1942, to Julius Foust; May Tomlinson, 5 Dec. 1940, 22 March 1941, 9, 12 Jan. 1942, to J. Foust; Clara Byrd, 25 Jan. 1941 (two letters, in Alumnae House folder), 17 March, 26 May 1941, to

J. Foust; Lula Martin Dickinson, 28 Oct. 1942, to J. Foust; J. Foust, 17 Nov. 1942, to Dickinson, Foust Private Papers.

96. Clara Byrd, 10 Oct. 1935, to Jackson, Jackson Papers; Byrd, 3 June 1940, to Sadie [McCain], Byrd Papers; *Alumnae News*, 30 (July 1941), pp. 5–6.

97. Jackson, 22 Feb. 1936, to Mrs. R.H. Leslie, Jackson Papers; Advisory Committee Minutes, 7 April 1936.

98. Jackson, 28 April 1939, to Rosa B. Parker; 9 June 1939, to Clara Byrd; College financial statement, June 1947, Alumnae folder, Jackson Papers; Harriet Elliott, 12 June 1939, to Sadie [McCain], Dean of Women Papers, VC Student Affairs Records; Alumnae Trustees' minutes, 6 Jan. 1940, Alumni Association Records.

99. [May Tomlinson], pencilled note to Jackson, [1944], Jackson Papers.

100. Jackson, memorandum, 10 June 1947; Jackson, 27 Sept. 1947, to Mrs. Richard P. McCormick, Alumnae folder, Jackson Papers; Alumnae Trustees' minutes, 25 June, 19 Sept. 1947, Alumni Association Records; OH: Betty Brown Jester, 22 March 1990.

101. Jackson, 20 Oct., 31 Dec. 1947, to Mrs. M.B. Satterfield, Alumnae folder, Jackson Papers; *Alumnae News*, 38 (Aug. 1949), p. 14; Jane W. Sockwell, 20 July 1950, to E.K. Graham, Graham Papers; Alumnae Trustees' minutes, 11 Nov. 1950, Alumni Association Records.

Chapter 15 Notes

1. Harriet Elliott, 5 Sept. 1941, to F.P. Graham, Jackson Papers.

2. Alumnae Trustees' minutes, 5 Oct. 1948, Alumni Association Records; Rachel M. Clifford, 6 Oct. 1948, to F.P. Graham; Martha Fowler, 10 Dec. 1948, to Graham, subgroup 2, series 3, subseries 1, F.P. Graham Papers; Helen C. White, 16 Dec. 1948, to Graham, and Frances Gibson Satterfield, 11 March 1950, to Gladys Tillett, Gladys Tillett Papers; Student Suggestions About the New Chancellor [1948], Student Government Association Records. (Clifford's letter is also in Alumni Association Records, 1894–1987; Fowler's is also in Legislative Lobbying, Student Government Association Records, 1949).

3. Newspaper clipping, May 1950, Box 20, E.K. Graham Papers.

4. Dodds, *Academic President*, pp. 29, 43–52.

5. See Graham, 13 June 1952, to Gordon Gray; 18 March 1955, to F.H. McNutt, Committees F–T; Graham-Jackson correspondence, March 1955, H; Graham, 4 Oct. 1955, to Jackson, I–L, Graham Papers.

6. See Graham, 20 Feb. 1953, to Albert Keister, Committees, Graham Papers; Trustees' Visiting Committee, notes of meeting with Graham and Dean Taylor, 25 Feb. 1954, Graham Papers; Josephine Kremer, 6 March 1954, to Gordon Gray, Subgroup 2, series 3, subseries 2, Gray Papers. See also the impressions of the later Chancellor Gordon Blackwell in 1959, after talking with Graham and faculty members: Blackwell, 10 Feb. 1959, to Doris Betts, Blackwell Papers.

7. On the point of management style, see Magnilde Gullander, 2 March 1954, to Gordon Gray, Subgroup 2, series 3, subseries 1, Gray Papers.

8. Faculty Council Minutes, 23 Oct. 1950; Graham, 10 Aug. 1954, to Gordon Gray and J. Harris Purks, G; 16 Dec. 1955, to Trustees' Visiting Committee, Board folder, Graham Papers.

9. Graham, Memo to faculty, 16 Nov. 1950; Graham, 9 Dec. 1950, to Gordon Gray; "Alleged Complaints... With Regard to the Chancellor...," *Greensboro Record*, 16 February [1954], Faculty folder, Graham Papers; Faculty Council Minutes, 27 Nov. 1950.

10. Faculty Council Minutes, 15 May 1951, with Graham's statement; Advisory Committee report, 26 April 1951, Committees; Graham, 12 May 1951, to Gordon Gray; Graham, un-

dated notice to the faculty [May 1951]; Marc Friedlaender, 12 May 1951, and Vera Largent, 15 May 1951, to Graham, D; Graham, 29 Oct. 1951, to Laura Weill Cone, Alumnae Assn.; Graham, 13 June 1952, to Ruth E. Eckert, G; Administrative Council Minutes, 19 Nov. 1954, A; Graham, 18 March 1955, to Franklin H. McNutt, Committees F–T, Graham Papers; Ruth A. Shaver, 11 March 1954, to Gordon Gray, in Controversy over Faculty Relations, Subgroup 2, series 3, subseries 1, Gray Papers; OH: Vance Litttlejohn, 23 Oct. 1989; Richard Bardolph, 14 May 1991; Gail Hennis, 18 Jan. 1990.

11. Administrative Council Minutes, 19 Jan., 18 Feb., 8 March 1955, A; Graham, 7 March 1955, to Harris Purks, Committees A–E; Graham, 18 March 1955, to F.H. McNutt, Committees F–T, Graham Papers. The 1947–55 records of the advisory committee are among the few important college records to have disappeared.

12. LeBlanc, "Concept of General Education," pp. 88–90, 124, 579–80, 583. See also Rudolph, *Curriculum*, pp. 256–64; Thomas, *Search for a Common Learning*.

13. W.S. Barney, 22 March 1950, to Mereb Mossman, General Education Steering Committee Records. The Faculty Council minutes for Fall 1949 are lost; those for Spring 1950 don't mention this committee.

14. Graham, Outline of remarks at faculty meeting, 16 Oct. 1950, Faculty, Graham Papers; Faculty Council Minutes, 23 Oct. 1950, 27 Nov. 1950, 27 Nov., 12 Dec. 1951, 19 May 1953; General Education Steering Committee Records, esp. minutes of 11 Dec. 1950, report of [Jan. 1952], and grant application of 25 Oct. 1952; Graham interview in *Carolinian*, 20 Nov. 1953.

15. Graham, 10 March 1951, to Ralph McDonald, General Education, Graham Papers.

16. Graham, report to the faculty on General Education, 15 Dec. 1953; Trustees' Visiting Committee, notes of meeting with Graham and Dean Taylor, 25 Feb. 1954, Graham Papers; Curriculum Committee minutes, 14 Jan. 1954; Curriculum Committee to the faculty, 15 Jan. 1954, Curriculum Committee Records; Faculty Council Minutes, 15 Dec. 1953, 19 Jan. 1954; *Carolinian*, 20 Nov., 18 Dec. 1953; Magnhilde Gullander, 2 March 1954, to Gordon Gray, Controversy over Faculty Relations, Subgroup 2, series 3, subseries 1, Gray Papers; Gullander, statement of 9 March 1956 to W.D. Carmichael, Carmichael Papers.

17. Faculty Council Minutes, 29 Jan. 1954. See also the Gullander references in the preceding note.

18. Graham, 26 May 1954, to Advisory Committee on General Education, Educational Steering Committee Records.

19. OH: Kendon Smith, 18 Oct. 1989.

20. See Graham, 7 April 1951, to Clarence H. Faust; 27 April 1951, to Thomas S. Hall, General Education; 26 Sept. 1952, to F.H. McNutt, A–G; 19 Dec. 1953, to Leonard S. Cottrell, Jr.; Trustees' Visiting Committee, notes of meeting with Graham and Dean Taylor, 25 Feb. 1954, Graham Papers.

21. See clippings, 1954–56, in Graham Papers, Box 20; Alumni Association Records, 1899–1988; Magnhilde Gullander, three undated memos [1954–55] to W.D. Carmichael, Carmichael Papers.

22. Alphabetical list of faculty members, [1954], with indications of support or opposition to Graham, in Subgroup 2, series 3, subseries 1, Gordon Gray Papers (A minus sign in this list indicates opposition; an exclamation point, support for Graham.); OH: Janice Hooke Moore, 23 Oct. 1990; Eugene Pfaff, 24 Jan.1990; Jarrell, *Randall Jarrell's Letters*, p. 406.

23. Louise Alexander and Magnhilde Gullander, statements to the Carmichael committee, March 1956, Carmichael Papers; Jarrell, *Randall Jarrell's Letters*, pp. 402–05; letters to Gordon Gray from Coy T. Phillips, Magnhilde Gullander, 2 March 1954; Meta Helena Miller, 5 March 1954; Ruth A. Shaver, 11 March 1954; [Harris Purks], undated notes on Graham controversy; Notes of conferences with faculty members, 4–5 March 1954, all in

Subgroup 2, series 3, subseries 1, Gray Papers; OH: Betsy Umstead, 7 Dec. 1989; Richard Bardolph, 14 May 1991; Kendon Smith, 18 Oct. 1989; May Lattimore Adams, 5 April 1991; Phillip Morgan, 3 April 1990; Vance Littlejohn, 23 Oct. 1989; Gail Hennis, 18 Jan.1990; Lenoir C. Wright, 9 Feb. 1990; Hollis Rogers, 10 April 1990; Betty Brown Jester, 22 March 1990; Brenda Cooper, 25 April 1991; Jean Buchert, 19 Jan. 1990; Robert Darnell, 19 March 1990; Louise Falk, 20 March 1990; George Dickieson, 20 March 1990; Betty Brown Jester, 22 March 1990; Elizabeth Holder, 27 April 1990; Franklin Parker, 21 Feb. 1990; Robert Watson, 21 March 1990; June Rainey Honeycutt, 10 May 1997. For a refutation of the charge against Katherine Taylor by one who claimed to know, see statement, 26 March 1956, in Ellen Griffin Papers.

24. See Link, *William Friday*, pp. 73–81.

25. See notes of these conferences and related correspondence in Subgroup 2, series 3, subseries 1, Gordon Gray Papers.

26. V.T. Lathrop, 30 June 1954, to L.P. McLendon, McLendon Papers; Richard H. Robinson, in *Alumni News*, 82 (Summer 1994), p. 41. See Graham's notes of his conversations with Lathrop on 24–25 Sept. 1954, K–L, Graham Papers.

27. Faculty Council Minutes, 18 Oct. 1955.

28. Katherine Roberts, 20 Feb. 1956, to Graham, Departments, Graham Papers.

29. Statements of Thomas Turner, 8 March 1956, and Magnhilde Gullander, 9 March 1956, to W.D. Carmichael, Carmichael Papers.

30. Newspaper clippings, 1–2 June 1955, in Alumni Association Records, 1899–1988.

31. Carmichael committee report, 12 May 1956, in UNC Trustees' Minutes, 28 May 1956; also in *Greensboro Daily News*, 29 May 1956. Re Katherine Taylor, see ibid., 26 March 1956; *Catalogs*, 1952–60.

32. Graham, 13 March 1955, to Mereb Mossman, and 13 Aug. 1955, to Harris Purks, in Subgroup 2, series 3, subseries 1, Gordon Gray Papers; Graham, 16 June, 7 Sept., n.d. Oct. 1955, to Harris Purks, P, Graham Papers; Mossman-Graham correspondence, May–December 1955, Graham Papers; OH: May Lattimore Adams, 5 April 1991.

33. Student Legislature minutes, 17 Oct. 1951, Student Government Association Records; *Carolinian*, 24 May 1952.

34. Kay Neelands, 18 Feb. 1954, to Graham, Faculty, Graham Papers.

35. *Carolinian*, 19 Feb. 1954, 10 Nov. 1955, 9 March 1956.

36. Student Legislature minutes, 23 May 1956, Student Government Association Records; *Greensboro Record*, 24 May 1956.

37. *Coraddi*, Fall 1954, p. 15; Student Legislature minutes, 15 Dec. 1954; Debbie Marcus, [16 Dec. 1954], to [Diana Chatham]; "Results of student poll, 17 Dec. 1954, in *Coraddi* Censure," Student Government Association Records; *Carolinian*, special issue, 16 Dec. 1954, and separate editorial of same date; Off-campus newspaper clippings, Vertical File: Coraddi Controversy; Graham, 16 Dec. 1954, to *Coraddi* staff, and on same date to student body; Trustees' Visiting Committee Minutes, 28 Dec. 1954; Graham correspondence with faculty and others, Dec. 1954 and Jan. 1955, C, Graham Papers; English Department minutes, 10 Jan. 1955, English Department Records. For the Rogers resignation, see also Leonard B. Hurley, 7 Jan. 1955, to Graham, VC Academic Affairs Records, 1941–84: English; [Katherine Taylor], Comments on the Lane Kerr Story in the *Greensboro Daily News*, [ca. 18 April 1956], I–L, Graham Papers.

38. Magnhilde Gullander, statement to Carmichael committee, 9 March 1956, Carmichael Papers.

39. Graham, 14 Jan. 1955, to L.C. MacKinney, C, Graham Papers. See also Graham statement to UNC *Daily Tar Heel*, 17 Feb. 1955, D, Graham Papers.

40. *Alumni News*, 72 (Fall 1983), p. 7; OH: Brenda Cooper, 25 April 1991.

41. Newspaper clippings, 14–18 Oct. 1955, Alumni Association Records, 1899–1988; Magnhilde Gullander, 16 Oct. 1955, to Graham, Q–R, Graham Papers; William N. Felt, 6 March 1956, to Wm. Friday, Carmichael Papers; OH: George Dickieson, 20 March 1990; Betty Brown Jester, 22 March 1990. For the role of Virginia Terrell Lathrop and Alumnae Secretary Betty Brown Jester, see Richard H. Robinson, in *Alumni News*, 82 (Summer 1994), p. 41.

42. *Greensboro Daily News* and *Greensboro Record*, 27 Feb. 1956, in newspaper clippings, Alumni Association Records, 1899–1988.

43. Link, *William Friday*, pp. 86–88.

44. Wm. Friday, 1 March 1956, to WC faculty and administrators, with Trustees' Visiting Committee report, 1956.

45. Newspaper clippings, in Box 20, Graham Papers, and in E.K. Graham Controversy, Alumni Association Records, 1899–1988. See also a fragmentary surviving interview with Louise Alexander, in Carmichael Papers. Most of the surviving statements were given originally to the Hanes committee and then transferred at their authors' request to the Carmichael committee. See Carmichael Papers, March 1956.

46. UNC Trustees Minutes, 28 May 1956; (the committee report also is in *Greensboro Daily News*, 29 May 1956, in Box 20, Graham Papers); Link, *William Friday*, p. 88.

47. Obituaries in *Greensboro Daily News*, 16 March 1976; *Alumni News*, 64 (Summer 1976), p. 20.

48. Elizabeth Hathaway, 29 May 1957, to W.W. Pierson, Pierson Papers; *Alumnae News*, 45 (July 1957), p. 11; OH: Donald Russell, 14 Feb. 1990; George Dickieson, 20 March 1990; May Lattimore Adams, 5 April 1991.

49. Trustees' Visiting Committee minutes, 24 Oct. 1956, and Pierson, 14 Dec.1956, to Rosa B. Parker, B. of T., Pierson Papers.

50. Ethel Martus, 13 Aug. 1960, to Gordon Blackwell, Departments M–S, Blackwell Papers; OH: Harriet Kupferer, 27 Oct. 1989; M. Elaine Burgess, 8 Nov. 1990.

51. See Pierson, 13 July 1956, to Mereb Mossman, Pierson Papers.

52. *Greensboro Daily News*, 23 March 1956.

53. OH: Gordon Blackwell, 12 Nov. 1990; Otis Singletary, 9 Nov. 1989; Paula Andris, 23 April 1991; Kendon Smith, 18 Oct. 1989; Richard Bardolph, 14 May 1991; Tommie Lou Smith, 18 Sept. 1990; George Dickieson, 20 March 1990; Robert Watson, 21 March 1990; May Lattimore Adams, 5 April 1991.

54. Amy M. Charles, 27 Jan. 1977, to James S. Ferguson, in Correspondence, Faculty Welfare Committee Records; OH: Jean Buchert, 19 Jan., 22 Feb. 1990; Phillip Morgan, 3 April 1990; Jane Mitchell, 29 Nov. 1990; Paula Andris, 23 April 1991; Richard Bardolph, 14 May 1991; Elisabeth Bowles, 4 Dec. 1990.

55. OH: Mereb Mossman, 11 Oct. 1989; Mossman, speech to American Business Women's Assn., 17 June 1971, Mereb Mossman Papers, VC Academic Affairs Records.

56. See Committees folders, 1956–57, Pierson Papers.

57. Jackson, 17 Sept. 1947, to Lois V. McClure, Committees folder, Jackson Papers.

58. George L. Simpson, Jr., "Gordon Williams Blackwell," *Popular Government*, 25 (Oct. 1957), pp. 30–33, in Vertical File: Chancellor, Blackwell; *Alumnae News*, 46 (Oct. 1957), pp. 2–3; OH: Gordon Blackwell, 12 Nov. 1990.

59. Self-study folders, 1957–58, Blackwell Papers; OH: Gordon Blackwell, 12 Nov. 1990; Richard Bardolph, 14 May 1991; Donald Russell, 14 Feb. 1990; Kendon Smith, 18 Oct. 1989.

60. Blackwell, 29 July 1960, to Wm. Friday, Home Economics folder, Blackwell Papers; OH: Gordon Blackwell, 12 Nov. 1990; King, *Multicampus University*, p. 38.

61. Academic Policies Committee report, 29 Oct. 1960, B. of T., Pierson Papers; OH: Donald Russell, 14 Feb. 1990.

62. Pierson, 17 April 1961, to faculty, Pierson Papers; OH: Otis Singletary, 9 Nov. 1989.

63. OH: Robert Calhoon, 1 Feb. 1990 (quotation); Blackwell Robinson, 14 Nov. 1990.

64. OH: Otis Singletary, 9 Nov. 1989.

65. OH: Donald Russell, 14 Feb. 1990; Richard Bardolph, 14 May 1991; George Dickieson, 20 March 1990; Tommie Lou Smith, 18 Sept. 1990; Nancy Fogarty, 27 March 1990; Brenda Cooper, 12 Nov. 1990; M. Elaine Burgess, 8 Nov. 1990; Gail Hennis, 18 Jan. 1990; Gayle Fripp, 29 Nov. 1990.

66. Elaine Penninger and John E. Bridgers, 16 March 1963, to Singletary; Singletary, 21 March 1963, to Penninger & Bridgers, Pa–Pr, Singletary Papers; *Carolinian*, 5 April 1963; OH: Gayle Fripp, 29 Nov. 1990.

67. Mereb Mossman, 22 May, 4 June 1956, to Graham, G–H, Graham Papers; Pierson, 9 July 1956, to Wm. Friday, F; Blackwell, 14 June 1957, to Pierson, Pre-July 1 folder, Pierson Papers.

68. Graham, 8 Feb. 1953, to Mereb Mossman, M, Graham Papers; R.E. Godfrey, 15 May 1959, to Gordon Blackwell, Q–R, Blackwell Papers.

69. OH: Gordon Blackwell, 12 Nov. 1990.

70. Charles Phillips, 14 Jan. 1952, to Graham, P; Graham, 13 May 1955, to Gordon Gray; Graham, 22 Nov. 1955, to Phillips, D, Graham Papers; Faculty file: Phillips.

71. A.A. Wilkinson, 9 July 1956, to Pierson; Mrs. Ed M. Anderson, 30 July 1956, to Wm. Friday; Friday, 6 Aug. 1956, to Mrs. Anderson, N; Pierson, 9 July 1956, to Friday, F; Trustees' Visiting Committee minutes, 24 Oct. 1956, B. of T., Pierson Papers; Visiting Committee Reports, 1956–58.

72. See Lee Rigsby, 2 Nov. 1962, to Mereb Mossman, VC Academic Affairs Records, 1941–84: Music.

73. [Graham], Remarks to the Advisory Budget Committee, 14 Sept. 1954, Budget, Graham Papers.

74. Graham, 20 Jan. 1955, To be Read at House Meetings, Budget, Graham Papers.

75. [N.C. Budget Bureau], *The Budget*, 1957–59, pp. 293–432.

76. Blackwell, 2 Jan. 1959, to R.E. Lee, La–Lu; Correspondence in Legislative Program folder, Jan.–Feb. 1959, Blackwell Papers; Bratton, *East Carolina University*, pp. 295–96.

77. Gordon Gray, 5 Oct. 1951, to Dear Colleague, Correspondence, Office of Librarian Records; "Report on Alumnae Fund... December 8, 1951," Alumni Association Records; Louise Dannenbaum Falk, 15 Dec. 1951, to the faculty, Vertical File: Alumnae Annual Giving; Gordon Gray, 10 Nov. 1954, to Graham, G; Graham, 23 Sept. 1955, to J. Harris Purks; Paul H. Davis, 11 Nov. 1955, to Graham; Graham, 22 Nov. 1955, to Charles W. Phillips, D, Graham Papers; Dale F. Keller, 8 Jan. 1962, to Louis R. Wilson, U–W, Singletary Papers.

78. Blackwell, 21 March 1958, to R.J. Spac, Sp–St, Blackwell Papers; OH: Gordon Blackwell, 12 Nov. 1990; Dale F. Keller, 8 Jan. 1962, to Louis R. Wilson, U–W, Singletary Papers.

79. Blackwell, 11 Jan. 1958, to W.D. Carmichael; 25 Nov. 1958, to Mrs. Aaron Turner, Sp–St; 13 June 1960, to Mrs. Ed Anderson, A, Blackwell Papers; Dale F. Keller, 8 Jan. 1962, to Louis R. Wilson, and Singletary, 19 Jan. 1962, to Wilson, U–W, Singletary Papers.

80. Home Economics Foundation folder, 1959, Blackwell Papers; Dale F. Keller, 8 Jan. 1962, to Louis R. Wilson, U–W, Singletary Papers.

81. [Blackwell], Memorandum to the Files, 19 Jan. 1960, F, Blackwell Papers; North Carolina Colleges report, 25 July 1963, Q–R, Singletary Papers.

82. King, *Multicampus University*, p. 21; W.M. Murray, 6 July 1961, to [Trustees'] Committee on Use, Acquisition, and Disposition of Real Estate, M–N, Singletary Papers.

83. Blackwell, 14 Oct. 1957, as quoted in Henry L. Ferguson, 14 Oct. 1968, to Bruce Eberhart, Buildings and Grounds Committee folder, Office of Librarian Records. See also that committee's report, [May 1958], in Correspondence, ibid.

84. W.M. Murray, 25 Aug. 1958, to Blackwell, Sp–St; Explanation of Requests, [1958], Capital Improvements, Blackwell Papers.

85. Florence Schaeffer, 21 Oct. 1950, to Graham; Building Committee minutes, 27 Oct. 1950, and Graham, 28 Feb. 1951, to R.E. Little, Building; Trustees' Visiting Committee minutes, 19 April 1952, and Graham, 15 July 1952, to Gordon Gray, Board; College requests to Advisory Budget Commission, 13 Aug. 1952, Budget 1; Needs for Physical Plant... 1955–57, [1954], Budget; Graham, 15 June 1955, to Gray, Board; Estimates... for Permanent Improvements... 1957–59, 10 July 1956, Budget 1, Graham Papers; Trustees' Visiting Committee report, 1956, B. of T., Pierson Papers; Trustees' Building Committee minutes, 5 Aug. 1957, B. of T.; Explanation of Requests, [1958], Capital Improvements; Blackwell, 15 July 1958, to Calvin Leonard, E, Blackwell Papers; Trustees' Visiting Committee report, 1957. For opposition by Chancellor Jackson and students to such an extension of College Avenue, see Jackson, 27 March 1947, to Mrs. F.S. Miles, Jackson Papers; Student Legislature minutes, 19 May 1952, Student Government Association Records. For the proposed arts building, see *Carolinian*, 15 Jan. 1954.

86. See W.C. Jackson, 27 March 1947, to Mrs. F.S. Miles, Jackson Papers; Trustees' Visiting Committee minutes, 19 April 1952, and subsequent committee report, Board, Graham Papers; Student Legislature minutes, 19 May 1952, Student Government Association Records; Committee on Markers..., 28 Oct. 1959, to Blackwell, M, Blackwell Papers.

87. Jackson, 19 Jan. 1948, to W.D. Carmichael; Carmichael, 12 Feb. 1948, to Herman G. Baity, Jackson Papers; D.F. Ashton, 11 April 1952, to Graham; Graham, 14 April, 17 Dec. 1952, to Ashton, A; Trustees' Visiting Committee minutes, 19 April 1952, and subsequent committee report, Board; College budget requests, 13 Aug. 1952, Budget 1; State Board of Health report, 7 May 1953, A, Graham Papers; *Carolinian*, 5 Nov. 1954, 2 Oct. 1957; *Alumnae News*, 45 (Jan. 1957), p. 7.

88. See Vertical File: Infirmary, 1951–53.

89. Correspondence between E.K. Graham, Gordon Gray, Charles Phillips, and Wade Davis, 29 March–23 Nov. 1954, D, Graham Papers; Draft letter, [Ernest V. Holmes], 27 Oct. 1955, to Arthur S. Flemming, D, Graham Papers; Trustees' Executive Committee Minutes, 13 Feb. 1956; W.M. Murray, 9 Dec. 1958, to Wm. Friday, F; Blackwell, 28 April 1960, to Murray, M, Blackwell Papers; Henry Ferguson, 18 Oct. 1963, to Friday, F, Singletary Papers.

90. See Turner, *Campus*, pp. 260, 264.

91. Trudy W. Atkins, in *Alumni News*, 63 (Spring 1975), pp. 8–9; Watson, "Ethel Loroline Martus Lawther," pp. 80, 82.

92. Blackwell, 18 Dec. 1958, to Bruce Benward, Departments H–M, Blackwell Papers.

93. See Harriet Elliott, 28 Sept. 1938, to Mollie, Dorothy, and Mae, in Building Program, Dean of Women Papers, VC Student Affairs Records; [Elliott?], "Why We Need a Student Union Building ...," [1942], Jackson Papers; Katherine Taylor, in *Alumni News*, 55 (July 1967), pp. 14–15.

94. Dale F. Keller, 31 Oct. 1961, to A.H. Shepard, Sa–So, Singletary Papers.

95. Trustees' Visiting Committee Minutes, 19 April 1952, Board, Graham Papers.

96. Explanation of [Capital Improvement] Requests, [1958], Capital Improvements; W.M. Murray, 25 Aug. 1958, to Blackwell, Sp–St; Request for Capital Improvements, [1959], Legislative Program; Capital Improvements Request, 1960, Budget, Blackwell Papers; Murray, 29 March 1961, to Frank B. Turner, A, Pierson Papers; Trustees' Visiting Committee report, 1961, p. 23.

97. J.P. Givler, 13 Oct. 1928, to Julius Foust, Budget, Foust Papers; 12 Feb. 1937, to Jackson, Science Building, 1940, Jackson Papers; "The Building for the Social Studies and the Humanities," [1952], R, Graham Papers; Statement on McIver Building, 6 Nov. 1956, M, Pierson Papers.

98. Trustees' Visiting Committee Minutes, 19 April 1952; John C. Lockhart, 24 April 1952, to Trustees' Visiting Committee; Visiting Committee report, [June 1952], B; Waldo C. Cheek, 31 July 1952, to Graham, C; "The Building for the Social Studies and the Humanities," [1952], R; D.S. Coltrane, 9 March 1956, to Mrs. William A. Miller, M, Graham Papers; Pierson, "McIver Building," 12 July 1956, Speeches; Statement on McIver Building, 6 Nov. 1956, M, Pierson Papers; Newspaper clippings in Vertical File: McIver Building; *Alumnae News*, 44 (April 1956), p. 9.

99. Directors' Minutes, 26 May 1913; Correspondence in M, Graham Papers, 1956; *Alumnae News*, 44 (April 1956), p. 9; 45 (Jan. 1957), p. 3; Pierson, "McIver Building," 12 July 1956, Speeches, Pierson Papers; *Alumnae News*, 49 (Jan. 1961), p. 3.

100. See *Carolinian*, 30 Sept., 21 Oct. 1960; Buildings and Grounds Committee minutes, 10, 17, 24 Oct. 1960, Correspondence, Buildings and Grounds, Office of Librarian Records; OH: Donald Russell, 14 Feb. 1990. For Randall Jarrell's characterization, see *Alumni News*, 63 (Spring 1975), p. 9. For photos of the two buildings, see Trelease, *Changing Assignments*, pp. I-52–62.

101. Academic Policies Committee report, Oct. 1962, Ba–Bo, Singletary Papers.

102. Trustees' Building Committee minutes, 5 Aug. 1957; Faculty Buildings and Grounds Committee minutes, 29 Sept., 15 Dec. 1959, Correspondence, Office of Librarian Records; Chancellor's Cabinet minutes, 23 Feb. 1960, Chancellor's Cabinet Records; *Carolinian*, 18 March 1960.

103. Blackwell, 3 Nov. 1958, to Wm. Friday, Capital Improvements, Blackwell Papers; Henry L. Ferguson, 26 April 1971, to Trustees' Building Committee, B. of T. (1), Ferguson Papers.

104. Blackwell, 17 March 1958, to Wm. Friday; Charles M. Adams, 28 May 1958, to ?, Mc–Mu; Blackwell, Capital Improvements Request..., 4 Jan. 1960, Ca–Ch, Blackwell Papers; Adams, "Woman's College Library," p. 136; Trustees' Visiting Committee Report, 1961, p. 23; Wm. Friday, 29 June 1963, to the UNC faculties, F, Singletary Papers.

105. Chancellor's Cabinet Minutes, 3 Feb. 1960; Correspondence in A–Alum, 1960, Blackwell Papers. For the chancellor's residence, see Wendell M. Murray, 24 June 1961, to Wm. Friday, M, Pierson Papers.

Chapter 16 Notes

1. E.K. Graham, 16 April 1952, to Paul W. Gates, Faculty folder; Robie [Macauley], 23 May 1953, to Marc [Friedlaender], General Education, Graham Papers; William R. Mueller, 9 Dec. 1957, to Blackwell, Study and Planning Committee, Blackwell Papers; OH: Harriet Kupferer, 27 Oct. 1989.

2. "A Statistical Composite of the Faculties of the Consolidated University of North Carolina," n.d., in Faculty, 1951–1972, VC Academic Affairs Records, 1941–84; Institutional Self-Study report, 1962, Tables VIII-7–8; *Catalogs*, 1951–52, 1962–63.

3. Bernard, *Academic Women*, pp. 38–61, 190–91. See also Carter, "Academic Women Revisited," pp. 675–78; Cott, *Grounding of Modern Feminism*, pp. 218–28.

4. Rossiter, *Women Scientists... 1940–1972*, pp. xv–xvii, 227–30; Graham, "Expansion and Exclusion," pp. 764–72. For a later protest over the preference for male faculty at WC, see OH: Susannah Thomas Watson, 7 Feb. 1991.

5. Graham, 1 July 1952, to Deans and Department Heads, Departments A–G, Graham Papers; Blackwell, 18 May 1959, to Eleanor F. Dolan, American folder, Blackwell Papers. For the national impact of nepotism rules, see Dolan and Davis, "Antinepotism Rules," pp. 285–92.

6. See Richard Bardolph, in *Alumni News*, 63 (Spring 1975), p. 25; John Beeler, 4 Nov. 1978, to Frank Melton, H, Ferguson Papers; OH: Robert Watson, 21 March 1990.

7. OH: Otis Singletary, 9 Nov. 1989.

8. Unsigned ms., 19 Oct. 1953, in Faculty, 1951–1972, VC Academic Affairs Records, 1941–84; Graham, 9 Oct. 1954, to Gordon Gray, B. of T., Graham Papers; Institutional Self-Study Report, 1962, Tables VIII-2, 4, 6, 8; ibid., Fifth Year report, 1967, IV, Table I.

9. "A Statistical Composite of the Faculties of the Consolidated University of North Carolina," n.d., in Faculty, 1951–1972, VC Academic Affairs Records, 1941–84.

10. Graham, 28 June 1952, to C. Vann Woodward, Faculty, Graham Papers.

11. Institutional Self-Study report, 1962, Tables VIII-1–9; ibid, Fifth Year report, 1967, IV, Table II. For national figures on the possession of the doctorate, see Seymour Harris, *Statistical Portrait*, p. 497.

12. See Geiger, *Research and Relevant Knowledge*, pp. 92–94, 157–58, 163–66.

13. OH: Rosemary McGee, 21 May 1990; Gail Hennis, 18 Jan. 1990; Lenoir C. Wright, 9 Feb. 1990; Jean Buchert, 19 Jan. 1990; Jane Mitchell, 29 Nov. 1990.

14. OH: Laura Anderton, 19 Jan. 1990; Kendon Smith, 18 Oct. 1989; Harriet Kupferer, 27 Oct. 1989; M. Elaine Burgess, 8 Nov. 1990. For the faculty Research Society and Warren Ashby's agency in establishing it, see Nomination of Warren Ashby . . . , [1982], B, Moran Papers; OH: Laura Anderton, 19 Jan. 1990.

15. Graham, 13 March 1951, to John Gardner, General Education; 15 April 1952, to Robert F. Thorne, B, Graham Papers.

16. Graham, 9 Oct. 1954, to Gordon Gray, B. of T., Graham Papers.

17. Charles Adams [?], 20 March 1953, to Gordon Gray, in Mission of the Library, Office of Librarian Records; Victor Cutter report, 12 June 1953, Department Annual Reports, Graham Papers.

18. Deans' Council Minutes, 18 Feb. 1957; Temporary Research Council, minutes of first meeting, 24 June 1957, and F.H. McNutt, 28 June 1957, to Faculty, Q–R, Pierson Papers; Woman's College Research Council, Announcement of Spring Term Grants-In-Aid, [1957–58], and Research Council . . . report, 1966–67, Vertical File: Research Council; Blackwell, 27 Sept. 1958, to Trustees Visiting Committee, B. of T., Blackwell Papers.

19. C.M. Adams and Mereb Mossman, 21 May 1957, to the faculty, F, Pierson Papers.

20. *Carolinian*, 19 Feb. 1958. See also *Alumnae News*, 46 (April 1958), p. 11.

21. Deans' Council Minutes, 30 Oct. 1958, 28 April 1960, 16 Feb. 1961, 19 Jan. 1962; Institutional Self-Study Report, 1962, p. VIII-64.

22. Blackwell, 5 Dec. 1957, to Amy Charles, Study and Planning Committee, December folder; 27 Sept. 1958, to Trustees Visiting Committee, B. of T., Blackwell Papers.

23. Graham, 2 Dec. 1953, to John C. Cairns, C, Graham Papers.

24. F.H. McNutt, 6 March 1958, to Blackwell, Faculty folder, Blackwell Papers; Academic Policies Committee Minutes, 12 March 1958; Blackwell remarks, in Faculty Council Minutes, 20 May 1958; Blackwell, "A Proposal for a System of Faculty Leaves," [May 1958], Admissions, Blackwell Papers.

25. Mereb Mossman, 9 Dec. 1959, to Dexter Perkins, Departments E–H; 10 Feb. 1960, to Blackwell, Da–Du, Blackwell Papers; Institutional Self-Study report, 1962, p. VIII-66.

26. Marcia Jones and Bonnie Frazer, in *Carolinian*, 26 March 1963.

27. For the still-strong faculty-student rapport in the 1950s, see Graham, 9 Oct. 1954, to Gordon Gray, B. of T., Graham Papers; OH: Gail Hennis, 18 Jan. 1990; Jean Buchert, 19 Jan. 1990; Emilie Mills, 30 Jan. 1990. For a suggestion that it was fading by 1962, see the college's Self-Study Report that year, pp. X-17–18.

28. See Mereb Mossman, 10 Feb. 1960, to Blackwell, Da–Du, Blackwell Papers.

29. Blackwell, 27 Sept. 1958, to Trustees Visiting Committee, B. of T., Blackwell Papers; Institutional Self-Study report, 1962, p. VIII-64.

30. Faculty Council Minutes, 23 Oct. 1950; Graham, 28 Sept. 1950, to J.S. Doolittle, D; 25 Jan. 1952, to R.D. Wellons and, 11 Feb. 1952, to Logan Wilson, W–Z; 8 Nov. 1954, to Elizabeth Adams, B. of T.; 22 Nov. 1955, to J.D. Messick, M; 16 Dec. 1955, to Trustees' Visiting Committee, Board folder, Graham Papers.

31. Academic Policies Committee Minutes, 10 June 1959; Blackwell, 12 June 1959, to Wm. Friday, Faculty carbons folder, Blackwell Papers; Deans' Council Minutes, 24 Sept. 1959; Institutional Self-Study Report, 1962, pp. VIII-67–69; King, *Multicampus University*, p. 27.

32. OH: Jean Buchert, 22 Feb. 1990.

33. Graham, 9 Feb. 1952, to faculty and administrative staff, P; 17 March 1952, 3 Aug. 1953, to Gordon Gray, G. Gray folders; 16 April 1952, to Paul W. Gates, Faculty folder; Trustees' Visiting Committee minutes, 19 April 1952, Board folder, Graham Papers; "Criteria for Faculty Promotions and Appointments," 28 April 1952, in Faculty Council Minutes, 27 May 1952, 21 April 1953; Graham, 18 Nov. 1955, to L.P. McLendon, McLendon Papers; Mereb Mossman, 23 Aug. 1963, to Edmund Berkeley, Departments A–H, Singletary Papers.

34. Keller, *Academic Strategy*, p. 10; Bowen, "Faculty Salaries," pp. 9–18; Faculty salaries and promotions, 1955–56 to 1961–62, Fa, Singletary Papers, 1961.

35. Pierson, 4 Oct. 1956, to W.H. Plemmons, O–P; 7 Dec. 1956, to Wm. Friday, Q–R, Pierson Papers; Blackwell statement on resignations from the faculty, 30 April 1959, Re–Ru, Blackwell Papers.

36. *AAUP Bulletin*, June 1963, p. 174; Trustees' Visiting Committee Report, 1963, p. 17.

37. Graham, 11 Sept. 1953, to W.D. Carmichael, C; 9 Oct. 1954, to Gordon Gray, B. of T., Graham Papers. See also Ethel Martus, 28 March 1956, to Graham, Budget (2), Graham Papers. For a faculty vote favoring across-the-board increases, see Academic Policies Committee report, 13 Nov. 1959, UNC Visiting Committee, VC Academic Affairs Records, 1941–84.

38. For UNC policy at this time, see Graham, 12 Dec. 1952, to the faculty, Faculty folder, Graham Papers; Academic Policies Committee Minutes, 12 Dec. 1962. See also Graham, 12 May 1952, to Virginia T. Lathrop, Board folder; Administrative Council Minutes, 24 Nov. (2d meeting), 8 Dec. 1954, 2 Feb. 1955, A folders, Graham Papers; Pierson, 5 Nov. 1956, to Wm. Friday, Q–R, Pierson Papers; Deans Council Minutes, 15 Nov. 1956.

39. Graham, 4, 28 May 1955, to J. Harris Purks, P; 6 Feb. 1956, to Wm. Friday, E–F, Graham Papers; Academic Policies Committee Minutes, 26 Nov. 1957.

40. Academic Policies Committee Minutes, 14 Nov.1956.

41. See Graham, Mossman, and Schaeffer correspondence, 1955, in Departments A–D (original and carbon); Graham, 12 July 1955, to J. Harris Purks, P, Graham Papers.

42. Pierson, 7 Nov. 1956, to Wm. Friday, Q–R, Pierson Papers; Mereb Mossman, 29 July 1960, to Registrar, and Mossman, 24 Oct. 1960, to Deans and Department Heads, in Saturday Classes, VC Academic Affairs Records, 1941–84; Deans' Council Minutes, 29 Nov. 1962, 28 Feb. 1963.

43. OH: Otis Singletary, 9 Nov. 1989.

44. Graham, 22 Oct. 1955, to Shahane Taylor (p. 2), T; Memorandum for the Visiting Committee, 16 Dec. 1955, Board folder, Graham Papers; Committee on Faculty Governance, notes, 18 Dec. 1970, Assistant VC Academic Affairs Records.

45. AAUP membership list, 1 March 1962, Al–As, Singletary Papers.

46. Blackwell, 5 May 1959, to faculty; 28 Oct. 1959, to Richard Bardolph et al.; Bardolph, 9 Oct. 1960, to W.W. Pierson, Faculty Welfare Committee Records, 1959–77.

47. Institutional Self-Study Report, 1962, pp. VIII-70, 85.

48. OH: Kendon Smith, 18 Oct. 1989.

49. OH: Phillip Morgan, 3 April 1990; Craig Dozier, 20 Oct. 1990; Paula Andris, 23 April 1991.

50. See Singletary, 6 Sept. 1962, to Kenneth Batchelor, Ba–Bo, Singletary Papers.

51. Graham, 7 April 1951, to Clarence H. Faust, General Education, Graham Papers.

52. Institutional Self-Study Report, 1962, pp. VII, 1–2, 8–10; Committee minutes and correspondence in Admissions folder, 1958, Blackwell Papers; Summary Report on Admissions, 1961–62, UNC Visiting Committee, VC Academic Affairs Records, 1941–84.

53. Faculty Council Minutes, 18 Jan. 1960.

54. "Admissions Research at the Woman's College," 1959, Admissions Research, VCAA Papers, 1941–84.

55. *Alumnae News*, 44 (April 1956), pp. 13–14.

56. R.E. Godfrey, 26 Sept. 1956, to Mereb Mossman; Academic and Personnel Committee et al., 21 May 1957, to Faculty Council, Academic and Personnel Committee Records, VC Academic Affairs Records, 1941–84; Faculty Council Minutes, 15 Oct. 1957.

57. English Department staff minutes, 13 Dec. 1954; Deans Council Minutes, 8 Nov. 1954, 17 March 1955; *Carolinian*, 16 March 1955, pp. 1, 2, 4.

58. Committee on Grading report, [Nov. 1958], Academic Policies Committee Records; Blackwell correspondence, 29 Jan.–27 Feb. 1959, Gra, Blackwell Papers. See also Grade Summary, Fall Term, 1949–50—1950–55, U–Z, Graham Papers, 1955.

59. Faculty Council Minutes, 20 March 1951, 17 March 1953; Student-Faculty Committee on Evaluation of Teaching report, 7 March 1952; Graham, 21 March 1952, to John W. Riley, Committees folder; Lyda Gordon Shivers, 17 May 1954, to Evaluation Committee, Committees folder, Graham Papers; *Carolinian*, Feb. 1953 (special issue); 20 March, 17 April 1953; Student Legislature minutes, 18 March 1953, Student Government Association Records.

60. Paul Diederich observations, 10 March 1953, in Faculty-Evaluation, 1952–53, VC Academic Affairs Records, 1941–84.

61. Survey of Student Opinion on General Education, May 1953, General Education, Graham Papers.

62. *Catalog*, 1946–47, p. 71; 1962–63, p. 56.

63. Visiting Committee report, in Institutional Self-Study, 1962; Jordan Kurland, "Curriculum Changes," *Alumnae News*, 52 (April 1964), pp. 6–7.

64. Office of Registrar, "Distribution of Bachelors Degrees . . . ," 1951–56 and 1958–62, in HEW, Annual Reports, 1956–66, and UNC-Visiting Committee, 1962, respectively, VC Academic Affairs Records, 1941–84.

65. See Riesman, *On Higher Education*, pp. 212–13.

66. [Vance Littlejohn], "Graduate Education at the Woman's College," [March 1962], Gr–Gu, Singletary Papers.

67. Academic Policies Committee report, 6 Nov. 1958, in UNC Visiting Committee, VC Academic Affairs Records, 1941–84; Trustees' Visiting Committee reports . . . 1958; Graduate School, Report to the Visiting Committee, [1960], Vertical File: Graduate Administrative Board.

68. Donald B. Anderson, 31 Aug. 1961, to Wm. Friday, Subgroup 3, Series 3, Subseries 1, Friday Papers, UNC Archives; Anderson, 26 Oct. 1961, to Alexander Heard et al., G, Singletary Papers; "The Graduate Program," in Information Supplied to State Board of Higher Education, 20 Feb. 1970, BHE, Ferguson Papers; King, *Multicampus University*, p. 53.

69. See OH: Nancy White, 4 Dec. 1989.

70. Comparative library figures for 1951–52, in Library, General, VC Academic Affairs Records, 1941–84.

71. Wilson, *University of North Carolina Under Consolidation*, pp. 181, 361, 381; Visiting Committee report, in Institutional Self-Study, 1962, pp. 18–19; Library Statistics, in Library, Fifth Year Report to SACS, May 1967, Mission of the Library, Office of Librarian Records. For Smith College, see Boroff, *Campus USA*, p. 138.

72. Charles M. Adams, [7 March 1956], to Department Heads and Faculty, Vertical File: Library (General).

73. Whiton Powell, "Library Service for the Proposed Graduate Program in Home Economics," March 1958, Vertical File: Library (General).

74. Ethel Martus, 2 May 1958, to Blackwell, Departments N–S, Blackwell Papers; C.M. Adams, 12 Nov. 1959, to Glenda Graybeal, Correspondence, Office of Librarian Records; Winston-Salem *Journal & Sentinel*, 8 March 1959, in Vertical File, Library (Special Collections); Watson, "Ethel Loroline Martus Lawther," pp. 90–97.

75. Helen Thrush and Charles Adams, 12 April 1954 (two letters) to Graham, Correspondence, Office of Librarian Records.

76. For the primacy of the WC records schedule, see Christopher Crittenden, 30 July 1963, to Members of the Advisory Committee on College and University Records, and the committee minutes, 13 Aug. 1963, in Correspondence, Office of Librarian Records. For the interminable process of getting the schedule drawn up and approved, see Correspondence, 17 Dec. 1957 to 29 Nov. 1962, Office of the Librarian Records.

77. James Thompson, 4 June 1975, to J.S. Ferguson, J–M, Ferguson Papers.

78. Brubacher and Rudy, *Higher Education In Transition*, pp. 287–88; Hamlin, *University Library*, p. 137.

79. Institutional Self-Study, 1962, p. IX-24; *Alumnae News*, 44 (April 1956), p. 10.

80. Library Staff, with UNCG Library, Fifth Year Report to SACS, May 1967, Mission of the Library, Office of Librarian Records.

81. Visiting Committee report, Institutional Self-Study, 1962, p. 23.

82. Hamlin, *University Library*, pp. 65, 128.

83. C.M. Adams, 29 March 1955, to Guy R. Lyle; 31 March 1955, to David H. Clift, and correspondence, 21 Dec. 1957 to 27 Jan. 1958, Correspondence, Office of Library Records; draft letter from Martha Hodges, 20 March 1959, La–Lu, Blackwell Papers.

Chapter 17 Notes

1. Arthur Dixon, 17 April 1958, to Blackwell, Departments A–E; Blackwell, 5 May 1959, to E.K. Graham, Gra, Blackwell Papers; [W.W. Pierson], "Some Comments to the Visiting Committee ...," [Fall 1960], B. of T., Pierson Papers. For Friedlaender's departure see Richard Bardolph, in *Alumni News*, 82 (Spring 1993), p. 10.

2. See Mereb Mossman, "Statement on the Basis for a Drama Program at Woman's College," 21 Nov. 1952, Committee on Dramatics, 1952–53, VC Academic Affairs Records, 1941–84; Graham, 5 June 1953, to L.B. Hurley; 11 June 1953, to Katherine Taylor, M; Mossman, 7 Dec. 1953, to Graham, Departments, Graham Papers. For Taylor's view of these events, see Taylor, 8 March 1956, to W.D. Carmichael, Carmichael Papers.

3. OH: Herman Middleton, 19 Feb. 1990.

4. Herman Middleton, 28 May 1960, to Mereb Mossman, Drama Department, VC Academic Affairs Records, 1941–84; *Alumnae/i News*, 52 (Jan. 1964), pp. 4–5; 61 (Spring 1973), pp. 21–24; Greensboro *News & Record*, 23 Sept. 1990; OH: Herman Middleton, 19 Feb. 1990.

5. Blackwell, 30 Jan. 1960, to Wm. Friday, Departments A–H, Blackwell Papers; OH: Herman Middleton, 19 Feb. 1990; *Alumnae News*, 52 (Jan. 1964), pp. 4–5; Self-Study, 1985: Communication & Theatre, Provost Records.

6. Wilson, *University of North Carolina under Consolidation*, pp. 390–92; King, *Multicampus University*, pp. 16–17. For WUNC-TV's primacy among university-sponsored TV stations, see David Davis, in Annual Meeting minutes, 4 June 1955, Alumni Assn. Records. For

a list of the TV credit courses offered at WC, 1955–59, see T folder, Blackwell Papers. For an attack on the intellectual content of WC's TV offerings by a loyal alumna, see Doris Betts, 1 Oct. 1958, to Administrator, WUNC, Woman's College, T, Blackwell Papers.

7. Correspondence in B folders, 1951–54, Graham Papers (esp. Graham, 25 June 1954, to Gordon Gray); "The Burnsville School of Fine Arts, 1950–1954," C, Graham Papers, 1955; W.R. Taylor, 8 March 1956, to W.D. Carmichael, Carmichael Papers; *Alumnae News*, 40 (Feb. 1952), p. 6; [Katherine Taylor], Comments on Lane Kerr Story in *Greensboro Daily News*, [April 1956], I–L, Graham Papers. For W.C. Burton's lamentation over the move from Burnsville, see his *Greensboro Daily News* column, in Vertical File: Parkway Playhouse Clippings.

8. Trustees' Visiting Committee Minutes, 19 April 1952, B, and 24 Oct. 1956, B. of T., Graham Papers; Gregory Ivy, n.d. (recd. 14 June 1952), to Graham, Departments A–G, Graham Papers; Requested Adjustments to the Recommended Budget, 1959/61: Capital Improvements, [1959], Budget, Blackwell Papers.

9. Barbara Parrish, 2 May 1961, to David C. Huntley, Alumni Association Records, 1899–1988; *Carolinian*, 12 May 1961; Department of Art, 1 Nov. 1961, to Singletary, Departments, Singletary Papers.

10. *Alumni News*, 75 (Fall 1986), p. 4.

11. See Gregory Ivy's remarks in Trustees' Visiting Committee Minutes, 20 Dec. 1954, B. of T., Graham Papers; John D. Kehoe and John P. Sedgwick, 23 April 1963, to Donald B. Anderson, B, Singletary Papers.

12. Trustees' Visiting Committee Report, 1959, p. 17; *Carolinian*, 12 May 1961; *Campus Calendar*, 2 Dec. 1985 to 12 Jan. 1986, p. 2.

13. See Lee Rigsby, 12 Feb. 1963, to Gov. Terry Sanford, Departments Ho–S, Singletary Papers.

14. Lee Rigsby, in *Alumnae News*, 52 (Jan. 1964), p. 7.

15. See H.H. Altvater, 25 Sept. 1950, to Graham, Departments, Graham Papers; OH: George Dickieson, 20 March 1990; Phillip Morgan, 3 April 1990.

16. *Greensboro Record*, 1 June 1955, and *Greensboro Daily News*, 2 June 1955, in Box 20, Graham Papers; OH: George Dickieson, 20 March 1990; Robert Darnell, 19 March 1990. For glimpses of Dean Marquis' leadership style, see his Annual Music Faculty Evaluation… 1954–55, in Music, VC Academic Affairs Records, 1941–84; and Marquis, 14 May 1956, to Wm. Friday, Departments, Graham Papers.

17. For evidence of the demoralization, see the transcript of a telephone conversation, 10 April 1959, between Dean Mossman and Bruce Benward of the University of Arkansas, who had just refused appointment as music dean following a visit to campus; and Blackwell, draft notes for a talk to the music faculty, 21 April 1959, in Departments-Music, Blackwell Papers. See also Lee Rigsby, 14 Sept. 1961, to Mossman, in Correspondence, School of Music Records.

18. Miles Wolff et al., solicitation for the Symphony Society, January 1960; [George Dickieson], "History of the Greensboro Orchestra," [1961], in Greensboro Orchestra, School of Music Records; Dickieson, 13 Feb. 1969, to James S. Ferguson, Depts. M–S, Ferguson Papers; OH: George Dickieson, 20 March 1990.

19. Minutes of History Department meeting with the chancellor, 6 Sept. 1950; Graham, 13 Dec. 1950, to Paul W. Gates; 31 May 1951, to Fletcher M. Green, Departments folders; 22 Sept. 1951, to Mereb Mossman, Faculty, Graham Papers.

20. Graham, 16 April 1952, to Paul W. Gates; Graham correspondence with J.H. Hexter, May-June 1952, Faculty; Goldwin Smith, 3 Sept. 1952, to Graham; Graham, 28 Nov. 1952, to Frederick Marcham, S–So; 27 March 1953, to Robert R. Palmer; Magnhilde Gullander, 30 Nov. 1953, to Graham; Vera Largent to Graham, recd. 23 Nov. 1953, H; Graham, 14 May 1953, to C. Vann Woodward, T–Z, Graham Papers.

21. Graham, 10 July 1954, to History Department, Departments, Graham Papers.

22. *Carolinian*, 23 Nov., 16 Dec. 1960.

23. *Catalogs*, 1956–1962.

24. Graham, 25 March 1955, to Mereb Mossman, Department carbons, Graham Papers; Mereb Mossman, Memo Re Spanish Teaching, 29 April 1955, Romance Languages, General, VC Academic Affairs Records, 1941–84.

25. Meta Miller, 30 Oct. 1961, to Singletary, Departments; Sanford Newell, 14 Feb. 1962, to Singletary, Departments E–S, Singletary Papers.

26. William R. Barrett, German Department report, 2 June 1953, Department Annual Reports, Graham Papers.

27. Academic Policies Committee Minutes, 8 Dec. 1959; Mereb Mossman, 5 March 1957, to W.W. Pierson, Q–R, Pierson Papers.

28. Mereb Mossman, 5 Nov. 1959, to Meta Miller; 20 Nov. 1959, to Blackwell, Departments Me–R, Blackwell Papers; Anne F. Baecker, 1 Dec. 1961, to Mossman; 10 Feb. 1962, to Academic Policies Committee; Academic Policies Committee minutes, 14 Feb. 1962, in Academic Policies Committee Records; Baecker, 5 July 1966, to Mossman, Teaching, Singletary Papers.

29. Self Study, 1985, International Studies and Latin American Studies, Provost Records; *Catalog*, 1962–63, pp. 74–75.

30. Mereb Mossman, 15 May 1959, to Virginia Farinholt, J–K, Blackwell Papers; "Junior Year Abroad Program at Woman's College," March 1961, Vertical File: Junior Year Abroad.

31. Chafe, *Civilities and Civil Rights*, p. 115; Greensboro *News & Record*, 3 Oct. 1985; Henry Frye, in *Carolinian*, 31 Oct. 1985.

32. Warren Ashby, 29 Jan. 1953, to Graham, Departments, Graham Papers; OH: M. Elaine Burgess, 8 Nov. 1990.

33. Acadamic Policies Committee Minutes, 12 Oct. 1960, 10 May 1961, 17 Jan., 14 Feb. 1962; Faculty Council Minutes, 20 March 1962; *Carolinian*, 3 Oct. 1985.

34. *Carolinian*, 13 Feb. 1953; Warren Ashby, 10 May 1956, to Mereb Mossman, Departments, Graham Papers; Ashby, 20 Sept. 1956, to Mossman, Committees, Pierson Papers; Marsden, *Soul of the American University*, pp. 337–41, 359, 394–95.

35. Graham, 28 Nov. 1951, to Howard B. Adelmann, Faculty; 15 April 1952, to Robert F. Thorne, B; 5 Aug. 1952, to Gordon Gray, C, Graham Papers.

36. OH: Hollis Rogers, 10 April 1990.

37. Elizabeth Duffy, 2 June 1953, to Graham; Katherine Roberts, 8 July 1953, to Graham; Correspondence from outside referees, 1953, Committees, Graham Papers; OH: Kendon Smith, 18 Oct. 1989. For Duffy's professional standing, see her obituary (as Elizabeth Duffy Bridgers) in *Greensboro Daily News*, 20 Dec. 1970, in Vertical File: Elizabeth Duffy.

38. OH: Kendon Smith, 18 Oct. 1989. See also Personality Report, in Graham, 18 March 1955, to Gordon Gray, Gordon Gray folder, Graham Papers.

39. See correspondence of Smith, Graham, and Mossman, 11 May to 6 Oct. 1954, Departments; Kendon Smith, 25 Feb. 1955, to Graham, Departments M–S, Graham Papers; Katherine Taylor, 3 July 1957, to Blackwell, H, Blackwell Papers; Trustees' Visiting Committee minutes, 24 Oct. 1956, B. of T., Pierson Papers; Smith to Mossman, 6 Nov. 1958, in Psychology, VC Academic Affairs Records, 1941–84; Minutes of Singletary meeting with Trustees' Visiting Committee, Nov. 1961, B. of T., Singletary Papers; Ruth Collings, in *Alumnae News*, 52 (Oct. 1963), p. 8.

40. "Sociology," [1957], in Sociology, General, VC Academic Affairs Records, 1941–84.

41. Donald B. Anderson, Diary Note on Conversation with Chancellor Singletary, 28 Dec. 1961, Subgroup 3, Series 3, Subseries 1, Wm. Friday Papers; OH: Harriet Kupferer, 27 Oct. 1989.

42. See Graham, 5 Sept. 1950, to Margaret Edwards, Departments; Memorandum of phone conversation between Graham and W.D. Carmichael, 8 Sept. 1950, C; Graham, 24 April 1951, to Gordon Gray, Gordon Gray folder; 14 July 1951, to Betty B. Jester, Alumnae Assn. folder; 5 Sept. 1951, to Ruby Morgan, M; 20 Sept. 1951, to Ralph W. Cummings, H; Frances N. Miller, 24 Sept. 1951, to John C. Lockhart, Departments; Graham, 23 June 1953, to Nancy Hall Copeland, B, Graham Papers.

43. Josephine Kremer, 6 March 1954 (two letters), to Gordon Gray, Subgroup 2, Series 3, Subseries 2, Gray Papers; Graham, 22 April 1954, to Mrs. Ed M. Anderson, A, Graham Papers. For biographical information on Dean Roberts, see *Alumnae News*, 40 (Feb. 1952), p. 1; newspaper clippings, Faculty File.

44. *Alumnae News*, 40 (Feb. 1952), p. 8; Katherine Roberts, 21 April 1955, to Graham, Departments E–H, Graham Papers; Roberts, 31 July 1956, to W.W. Pierson; Carey H. Bostian, 2 Aug. 1956, to Pierson, Home Economics, Pierson Papers; Dean Roberts's remarks to the faculty committee appointed to recommend her successor, 19 July 1956, in Committee to Recommend a Dean, 1956–58, Home Economics, VC Academic Affairs Records, 1941–84.

45. Josephine Kremer, 6 March 1954 (two letters), to Gordon Gray, Subgroup 2, Series 3, Subseries 2, Gray Papers; Graham, 22 April 1954, to Mrs. Ed M. Anderson, A, Graham Papers; Kremer, 4 Nov. 1955, to Robert M. Hanes et al., Carmichael Papers; Dean Roberts's remarks, 19 July 1956, in Committee to Recommend a Dean, 1956–58, Home Economics, VC Academic Affairs Records, 1941–84.

46. OH: Gordon Blackwell, 12 Nov. 1990.

47. Wilson, *University of North Carolina Under Consolidation*, pp. 353–54; OH: Vira Kivett, 21 Feb. 1990.

48. OH: Vira Kivett, 21 Feb. 1990; Clara Ridder, 19 Nov. 1990; May Lattimore Adams, 5 April 1991.

49. J.A. Davis, 29 July 1960, to Blackwell; Blackwell, 29 July 1960, to Wm. Friday; Davis, 8 Aug. 1960, to Blackwell (including the quotations), Home Economics, Blackwell Papers.

50. Donald B. Anderson, 15 Aug. 1961, to Wm. Friday; Anderson, Diary Note on conversation with Otis Singletary, 28 Dec. 1961, Subgroup 3, Series 3, Subseries 1: General, Friday Papers; OH: Vance Littlejohn, 23 Oct. 1989.

51. Visiting Committee report, Institutional Self-Study, 1962, pp. 43–44.

52. *Carolinian*, 8 Dec. 1954; Naomi Albanese, 3 March 1959, to Blackwell, Departments-Home Economics, Blackwell Papers; James S. Ferguson et al., 8 July 1968, to Board of Directors, Sigmond Sternberger Foundation, M–N, Ferguson Papers; Canaday et al., *History of the School of Human Environmental Sciences*, pp. 96–97.

53. *Greensboro Daily News*, 23 Jan. 1966.

54. East, *Home Economics*, pp. 49–50.

55. "Role of the School of Home Economics in the Consolidated University," 23 Oct. 1959, Departments-Home Economics, Blackwell Papers; Wilson, *University of North Carolina Under Consolidation*, p. 354.

56. Faculty Council Minutes, 18 May 1942; Harriet Elliott, 23 Nov. 1942, to Jackson, Jackson Papers; [E.K. Graham], "Chronological Outline of Developments Bearing on ... Nursing at Woman's College," 1 Nov. 1951, N, Graham Papers.

57. Graham, 7 Jan. 1951, to Robert House, H, and the correspondence among Graham and others in N, 1951, Graham Papers.

58. Academic Policies Committee Minutes, 14 Dec. 1960; Faculty Council Minutes, 21 Feb. 1961.

59. Graham, 30 March 1954, to Gordon Gray, N, Graham Papers; Curriculum Committee Minutes, 14 April 1955; Correspondence in N, 1956, Pierson Papers; *Alumnae News*, 45

(Oct. 1956), pp. 5, 14; (July 1957), p. 13; Singletary, 1 Dec. 1961, to Louis R. Wilson, U–Z; Alice C. Boehret, 11 Sept. 1964, to Mereb Mossman and Singletary, Departments Ho–S, Singletary Papers; Eloise R. Lewis, 26 July 1967, to Mary McRee, Nursing School, VC Academic Affairs Records, 1941–84: Nursing School; OH: Eloise Lewis, 24 Jan. 1990.

60. [E.K. Graham], "Notes on conference with Dr. Vance T. Littlejohn, 28 Sept. 1954," 2 Oct. 1954, Graham Papers; Administrative Council minutes, 21 Feb. 1956, A, Graham Papers; Graham, 4 June 1956, to W.W. Pierson, G, Pierson Papers.

61. Mereb Mossman, 24 March 1953, to Graham, N–P, Graham Papers; Blackwell, 19 April 1960, to Vance Littlejohn, Departments A–H, Blackwell Papers.

62. Special Committee report, [1957], Vertical File: Commercial Department.

63. See Mereb Mossman, 13 April 1953, to Graham, Departments, Graham Papers.

64. *Carolinian*, 21 Oct. 1966; Correspondence in Departments A–E, 1966; Statement Concerning Termination of the One-Year Commercial Course . . . , [1967], Departments A–D; Ferguson, Speech at Commercial Class commencement, 1967, Speeches, Ferguson Papers; *Alumni News*, 55 (July 1967), p. 17.

65. Ruth Collings, 23 May 1951, to Graham (with Collings, 30 Jan. 1954, to Gordon Gray); Collings, 30 Jan. 1954, to Graham, Ma; Correspondence, Jan.–Feb. 1955, Departments M–S; Administrative Council minutes, 6 Dec. 1955, A, Graham Papers; W.W. Pierson, 17 June 1957, to Blackwell, Pre-July 1 folder, Blackwell Papers; Alice Schriver, 6 March 1963, to Singletary, Departments A–Hi, Singletary Papers; Watson, "Ethel Loroline Martus Lawther," pp. 110–11.

66. Ethel Martus, 15 Feb. 1954, to Graham, in Visiting Committee, B. of T.; Graham, 22 April 1954, to Mrs. Ed M. Anderson, A, Graham Papers; OH: Gail Hennis, 18 Jan. 1990; Rosemary McGee, 21 May 1990; Sallie Robinson, 11 Oct. 1990; Donald Russell, 14 Feb. 1990; Watson, "Ethel Loroline Martus Lawther," pp. 108–37, 227.

67. W.M. Murray, 4 July 1960, to W.D. Carmichael, P, Blackwell Papers; Singletary, Memorandum re Piney Lake, 28 Feb. 1962, P, Singletary Papers; Watson, "Ethel Loroline Martus Lawther," pp. 97–103; *Alumnae News*, 45 (Oct. 1956), p. 6; *Carolinian*, 1 Oct. 1956; Vertical File: Piney Lake.

68. Tyack, *Turning Points*, pp. 419–20. See also Selden, *Accreditation*, pp. 63–65; Earnest, *Academic Procession*, pp. 284–86; W.R. Johnson, "Teachers and Teacher Training," pp. 243–45.

69. See student requirements, in *Catalogs*, 1929–30, 1939–40, 1949–50, 1962–63; Education faculty, 19 April 1972, to James Ferguson, Schools E–H, Ferguson Papers.

70. *Carolinian*, 20 Feb. 1953. See also letters to the editor, 8 Dec. 1954, and 13 Oct. 1961; and editorials, 20 April 1956 and 26 March 1958.

71. *Alumnae News*, 40 (May 1952), pp. 10–11.

72. OH: Kendon Smith, 18 Oct. 1989; Education faculty, 19 April 1972, to James Ferguson, Schools E–H, Ferguson Papers.

73. Academic Policies Committee Minutes, 9 Jan. 1963.

74. Kenneth E. Howe, Faculty Announcement, 17 May 1966, Departments A–E, Singletary Papers.

75. Academic Policies Committee Minutes, 11 April, 8 Oct., 14 Nov. 1962; 3, 9, 11 Jan., 13 March, 2 April 1963; W. Earl Armstrong, 5 Sept. 1962, to Singletary; Donald B. Anderson, 11 Sept. 1962, to Singletary; Singletary, 30 Oct. 1962, to Armstrong, NCATE, Singletary Papers; Institutional Self-Study, 1962: supplementary report for 1963–64.

76. Dean's Council Minutes, 28 March 1962; OH: Donald Russell, 14 Feb. 1990; Lois Edinger, 11 Sept. 1990; Elisabeth Bowles, "Curry School," *Alumni News*, 55 (Fall 1966), p. 23.

77. "Renovation and Enlargement of Curry Building," [1958], Curr, Blackwell Papers.

78. Correspondence and Teacher Education Council minutes in Curry School, 1959, Blackwell Papers; Curry Study Committee, majority and minority reports, 25 May 1962, Cu; Kenneth E. Howe, 24 Aug. 1962, to Singletary, Departments E–S, Singletary Papers.

79. Summer Session report: Total Enrollment and Courses Offered, 1956–61, with Summer Session Council minutes, July 1961, Sp–Su, Singletary Papers.

80. [J.A. Davis], Report on the Graduate School, [Fall, 1960], B. of T., Pierson Papers; Institutional Self-Study, 1962: supplementary report for 1962–63.

81. Extension Advisory Board Minutes, 1 Feb. 1960, Extension Division, VC Academic Affairs Records, 1941–84.

82. Trustees' Visiting Committee report, 1959, pp. 15–16.

Chapter 18 Notes

1. "Students by Counties ..., First Semester 1950–51," 1950, E, Graham Papers; "Number of Students Enrolled... 1953–59," Student Statistics, VC Academic Affairs Records, 1941–84; Registrar's Office, "Students Enrolled by North Carolina Counties... 1956–1962," 1963, B. of T., Singletary Papers. For the UNC limit on out-of-state students see King, *Multi-campus University*, pp. 21–22.

2. Admissions Office, Number of students registered ..., 25 Sept. 1950, E, Graham Papers; W.M. Murray, 20 Feb. 1961, to Wm. Friday, M; H. Hoyt Price, 12 Dec. 1960, to Mereb Mossman, E, Pierson Papers; *Student Handbook*, 1957–58, p. 113.

3. Blackwell, 16 Oct. 1959, to Kenneth Holland; 19 Oct. 1959, to Organization of American States; 29 Oct. 1959, to American Friends of the Middle East, Fa–Fr, Blackwell Papers.

4. Registrar's report, with Directors' Report, 1932.

5. Registrar's Office, "Number and Percent of Students Transferring ..., 1944–53," 26 July 1954, G; Graham, 11 Feb. 1954, to faculty, S, Graham Papers; Registrar's Office, report on transfer students, 30 July 1954 (in Transfer Credit folder), "Number and Classification of Transfer Students ..., 1953–57," (in Student Statistics), and Admissions Office, Table IV: "Number and Classification of Transfer Students ..., 1957–65" (in UNC-Visiting Committee), VC Academic Affairs Records, 1941–84.

6. *Carolinian*, 4 March 1957; Statement of Jane Summerell, 3 May 1945, Alumni Association Records, 1899–1988; Statement of Chancellor Blackwell, Deans' Council Minutes, 18 Jan. 1958; OH: Hilman Thomas Watkins, 6 March 1990; "Reasons Students Transfer from UNCG," 20 Nov. 1963, T, Singletary Papers.

7. Statement of Registrar Rollin Godfrey in unidentified newspaper clipping [ca. 1954], Alumni Association Records, 1899–1988.

8. Mereb Mossman, 10 Nov. 1959, to Trustees' Visiting Committee, B. of T.; Blackwell, 23 Feb. 1960, to Wm. Friday, Da–Du, Blackwell Papers; "The Withdrawal from College Prior to Graduation of Freshmen Entering in September 1953–1957," Withdrawals, VC Academic Affairs Records, 1941–84; "Reasons Students Transfer from UNCG," 20 Nov. 1963, T, Singletary Papers.

9. Graham, 11 Feb. 1954, to faculty, S, Graham Papers; "Parental Occupation, Education, Size of Home Community of Freshmen ...," Institutional Studies, 1952–53, VC Academic Affairs Records, 1941–84.

10. See OH: Laura Anderton, 19 Jan. 1990; Sallie Robinson, 13 March 1990.

11. *Greensboro Record*, 3 Feb. 1956; K. Taylor, 8 Feb. 1958, to Blackwell, T, Blackwell Papers; F.H. McNutt, 1 Feb. 1957, to Editor, *Greensboro Daily News*, B, Pierson Papers.

12. *Carolinian*, 3 Nov. 1955, 19 Jan., 15 Oct. 1956, 9 Oct. 1959, 13 Jan. 1961; Dale F. Keller, reports on food service, Sept.–Oct. 1961, D; Keller, 21 Dec. 1961, to Singletary, Fe–Fr, Single-

tary Papers; Institutional Self-Study, 1962, Visiting Committee report, p. 31; *Alumni News*, 66 (Spring 1978), p. 9; OH: Sallie Robinson, 11 Oct. 1990; Emilie Mills, 30 Jan. 1990; Betty Hobgood Eidenier, 29 March 1991. For the business end of the food service, see Wendell M. Murray, 28 July 1959, to Wm. Friday, M, Blackwell Papers; Henry L. Ferguson, 29 March 1963, to Sadye Dunn, F, Singletary Papers.

13. Ruth Collings, in *Alumnae News*, 52 (Oct. 1963), p. 8; *Greensboro Daily News*, 9 June 1963, in Faculty File: Collings. For Collings' statement of the health service's functions in 1955, see [UNC] Council on Student Affairs, minutes, Chapel Hill, 24 Feb. 1955, Appendix 2, U–Z, Graham Papers.

14. Ruth E. Boynton report, 27–28 Feb. 1958, Departments H–M, Blackwell Papers.

15. *Catalog*, 1961–62, p. 26.

16. [Katherine Taylor], "An Evaluation of Student Welfare Services . . . ," [1958], Sp–St; Blackwell, 2 Sept. 1960, to Wm. Friday, St–Su, Blackwell Papers; Institutional Self-Study report, 1962, pp. X 45–46. For a listing of all the loan funds and their amounts, see *Catalog*, 1956–57, pp. 57–58.

17. Admissions Office report, Oct. 1961, A; Singletary report, 30 June 1962, C–Cl, Singletary Papers; Blackwell, 28 July 1958, to Ellen Winston; 31 Oct. 1958, to Pierce T. Angell, S–Sc, Blackwell Papers.

18. Singletary report, 30 June 1962, C–Cl folder, Singletary Papers; Press release, Dec. 1961, and related correspondence, Sa–So, Singletary Papers.

19. See correspondence in Sa–Sc folder, Singletary Papers, 1962.

20. Katherine Taylor, Student Activities report, 16 June 1953 (received), Department Annual Reports, Graham Papers; Taylor, 14 Feb. 1963, to Singletary, St–Su, Singletary Papers; Institutional Self-Study report, 1962, pp. X 44–45.

21. Taylor, Student Activities report, 16 June 1953 (received), Department Annual Reports; Trustees' Visiting Ccommittee minutes, 19 April 1952, Board folder, Graham Papers; *Alumnae News*, 44 (Jan. 1956), p. 17; Kathleen P. Hawkins, 13 Feb. 1957, to Pierson, F, Pierson Papers.

22. Katherine Taylor to Graham (received 17 Jan. 1951); Graham, 12 May 1951, to Gordon Gray; Graham, [1951], notice to the faculty concerning the Mossman and Taylor appointments, D, Graham Papers.

23. Graham, 3 Aug. 1953, to Gordon Gray, N–P, Graham Papers.

24. J.S. Ferguson, in *Alumni News*, 60 (Summer 1972), p. 18; Emily Herring Wilson, in Greensboro *News & Record*, 3 April 1994; OH: Gordon Blackwell, 12 Nov. 1990; Rosemary McGee, 21 May 1990; Sallie Robinson, 13 March 1990; May Lattimore Adams, 5 April 1991; Nancy Fogarty, 27 March 1990.

25. Katherine Taylor, Student Activities report, 16 June 1953 (received), Department Annual Reports, Graham Papers; *Alumnae News*, 40 (May 1952), p. 7. For the change in mail service, see *Carolinian*, 18 Sept. 1959.

26. Institutional Self-Study Report, 1962, pp. X 2, 4–8; [Katherine Taylor], "An Evaluation of Student Welfare Services . . . ," [1958], Sp–St; Blackwell, 18 May 1960, to the faculty, A–Alum, Blackwell Papers; Mereb Mossman, 28 Oct. 1960, to Trustees' Visiting Committee, B. of T., Pierson Papers; Dale F. Keller, 18 Dec. 1961, to A.H. Sheperd, Jr., K–M, Singletary Papers; Tommie Lou Smith, in *Alumni News*, 53 (Winter 1965), pp. 22–23; OH: Laura Anderton, 19 Jan. 1990; Tommie Lou Smith, 18 Sept. 1990; Elizabeth Booker, 17 May 1991; Brenda M. Cooper, 12 Nov. 1990. The lack of coordination between academic and social counseling by 1962 is criticized in the SACS accreditation team's report that year. Institutional Self-Study, 1962, Visiting Committee Report, pp. 25–28.

27. Religious Activities Center, "Denominations Listed and Preferences by Students, 1954/55–1958/59"; "Denominations Having Student Organizations, Fall 1958," Q–R, Blackwell Papers.

28. Blackwell, 7 May 1958, to Harry G. Long, Jr., Q–R; [Katherine Taylor], "An Evaluation of Student Welfare Services," [1958], Sp–St, Blackwell Papers.

29. K. Taylor, 17 Sept. 1957, to W.H. Plemmons, Q–R, Blackwell Papers; OH: Carol Bryden Passmore, 2 Feb. 1991.

30. *Catalog*, 1951–52, p. 39; K. Taylor, "An Evaluation of Student Welfare Services," [1958], Sp–St, Blackwell Papers; Altbach, *Student Politics*, pp. 169–70; *Carolinian*, 9 April 1954; Inter-Faith Council report, 1954–55, Vertical File, I–F Council; Blackwell, "Discussion at Luncheon with Ministers," 15 Jan. 1959, Re–Ru, Blackwell Papers.

31. Inter-Faith Council Chapel Committee, 19 Oct. 1955, to Presidents and Advisors... and... the faculty, Vertical File: I–F Council.

32. Singletary, 28 Nov. 1961, to the students, Sp–Su, Singletary Papers; *Carolinian*, 8 Dec. 1961; OH: Betty Hobgood Eidenier, 29 March 1991.

33. Graham, 23 June 1952, to Vermont Royster, Sp–Sz, Graham Papers; Institutional Self-Study, 1962, Visiting Committee report, p. 32.

34. Pre-School Conference, September 7–9, 1953, in Pre-School Conference, VC Academic Affairs Records, 1941–84.

35. *Carolinian*, 3 Oct. 1952.

36. *Carolinian*, 21 March 1958; Institutional Self-Study Report, 1962, pp. X 27–31; ibid., Visiting Committee report, p. 32.

37. OH: June Rainey Honeycutt, 10 May 1997; *Carolinian*, 19 Sept. 1957.

38. *Alumnae News*, 40 (Aug. 1951), p. 12; *Carolinian*, 9 March, 26 Oct. 1951; 22 Feb. 1952; 1, 8 March 1963.

39. Strobel, "Ideology and Women's Higher Education," pp. 172–75; *Carolinian*, 11 Jan. 1952.

40. Advisory Committee report, 26 April 1951, with clipping from *Carolinian*, 9 Feb. 1951, Committees folder; Graham, 10 Jan. 1953, to Victor Bryant, B. of T., Graham Papers; Administrative Council minutes, 19 Nov. 1958, in Chancellor's Cabinet Records; Trustees' Visiting Committee Reports, 1958, p. 17 (including quotation); *Carolinian*, 11 Feb. 1959; Deans' Council Minutes, 22 Nov. 1960.

41. *Carolinian*, 23 Feb. 1962; 15 March, 18 Oct. 1963; Katherine Warren, 17 April 1962, to Singletary, Se–So; Katherine Taylor, "A Slice of Campus Life," 30 June 1962, T; Barbara Vern Davis, 17 Oct. 1962, to Singletary, Sp–St, Singletary Papers.

42. Blackwell, 4 Dec. 1958, to Roger C. Kiser, J–K; Blackwell, Talk to Student Assembly, 9 Feb. 1960, Da–Du, Blackwell Papers; "Outline of Events Pertaining to Sit-Down Strike ....," in Sit-Down Demonstrations, Virginia Lathrop Papers, UNCG; *Carolinian*, 12 Feb., 1 April 1960; Clarence L. Harris (Woolworth store manager), account of the sit-ins, [1981], in Vertical File: Sit-Ins; OH: Gordon Blackwell, 12 Nov. 1990; Mereb Mossman, 11 Oct. 1989; Richard Bardolph, 14 May 1991; Brenda Cooper, 25 April 1991; Claudette Graves Burroughs-White, 25 Feb. 1991; Edith Mayfield Wiggins, 8 May 1991; Emilie Mills, 30 Jan. 1990; Franklin Parker, 21 Feb. 1990; Ann Dearsley-Vernon (one of the three WC students) in *Alumni News*, 68 (Spring 1980), pp. 7–8, 29; *UNCG Magazine*, 2 (Summer 2000), pp. 12–19; Chafe, *Civilities and Civil Rights*, pp. 83–98; Wolff, *Lunch at the 5 & 10*, pp. 43–55, 79, 115–16, 127. For Curry School segregation, see correspondence in Curry School folders, 1957–58, Blackwell Papers. For national background to these events, see Altbach and Peterson, "Before Berkeley," pp. 11–13; Altbach, *Student Politics*, p. 199.

43. Chafe, *Civilities and Civil Rights*, pp. 110–13, 119–48.

44. OH: M. Elaine Burgess, 8 Nov. 1990; Carol Bryden Passmore, 2 Feb. 1991.

45. Myrna Lee et al., 22 March 1962, to Carol Furey; Sina I. McGimpsey et al., 27 Feb. 1963, to Singletary; Katherine Taylor, notes of conference with Mr. Apple of the Do-Nut Dinette, 13 March 1963; Taylor, conference with Mr. Eugene Street, 14 March 1963; Richard

G. Apple, 28 March 1963, to Singletary; Taylor, 15 May 1963, to Singletary; "HELP *ALL* W.C. STUDENTS," [16 May 1963]; "Students Who Signed Call to Boycott," 16 May 1963, all in Ne–O, 1963; Singletary, 2 April 1963, to Sherry Mullins, St–Su; Singletary, 18 March 1966, to Ann Flack Boseman, Ac–Al, Singletary Papers; Student Legislature Resolution, 13 March 1963, and Anne Prince, SGA President, 23 May 1963, to J.S. Longdon, Student Government Association Records; Acad. Policies Committee Minutes, 13 March, 2 April 1963; *Carolinian*, 26 April 1963; OH: Brenda Cooper, 12 Nov. 1990; M. Elaine Burgess, 8 Nov. 1990; *Alumni News*, 63 (Spring 1975), pp. 13–14; 70 (Winter 1982), p. 18.

46. Anne Prince, 31 Oct. 1963, to Michael H. Lawler, Correspondence, Student Government Association Records.

47. See statement by Chancellor Pierson in *Alumnae News*, 49 (Jan. 1961), pp. 2, 12.

48. *Student Handbook*, 1957–58, pp. 79–93; OH: Vira Kivett, 21 Feb. 1990; Carol Bryden Passmore, 2 Feb. 1991; Robert Watson, 21 March 1990.

49. See Kendon Smith, 28 Jan. 1960, to Edna Arundel, Committee on Academic Counseling, VC Academic Affairs Records, 1941–84.

50. Blackwell, 23 March 1959, to senior class, Students folder, Blackwell Papers; *Alumnae News*, 48 (Jan. 1960), p. 12; George W. Hamer, 28 March 1963, to Wm. Friday, F, Singletary Papers.

51. Trustees' Visiting Committee minutes, 19 April 1952, Board folder, Graham Papers; Administrative Council minutes, 5 Nov. 1958, 4 March 1959, 26 April 1960, Chancellors' Cabinet Records; Buildings and Grounds Committee minutes, 3 April [1959], Correspondence, Office of Librarian Records; *Carolinian*, 27 Oct., 20 Nov., 4 Dec. 1959.

52. Faculty Council Minutes, 21 Feb., 20 March 1962, 21 May 1963; OH: Henry Ferguson, 12 April 1990.

53. Graham, 9 Oct. 1954, to Gordon Gray, B. of T., Graham Papers; Katherine Taylor, 22 Jan. 1959, to Blackwell, Re–Ru, Blackwell Papers; Taylor, Student Affairs report, 1963, B. of T., Singletary Papers; OH: Henrietta Huffines, 20 May 1991; Brenda Cooper, 12 Nov. 1990; Gayle Fripp, 29 Nov. 1990.

54. Newspaper clippings in Vertical File: Consolidated University Day; *Alumnae News*, 42 (Fall 1953), p. 7; 47 (Oct. 1958), p. 10.

55. *Carolinian*, 16 Feb., 20 April 1951; Societies report, [1953], Vertical File: Societies; *Alumnae News*, 41 (Winter 1953), p. 9.

56. Alumnae from the early '60s recalled that the marshals were chosen on the basis of academic achievement. OH: Janet Harper Gordon, 28 March 1991; Betty Hobgood Eidenier, 29 March 1991.

57. *Student Handbook*, 1952–53, p. 115; 1962–63, p. 129.

58. See Nell Siceloff, [Sept. 1950], to Margaret [Miller], Vertical File: Adelphian Society; *Carolinian*, 11 Nov. 1960.

59. *Carolinian*, 12 Nov. 1958; 13 Nov. 1959, 11 Nov. 1960; *Alumnae News*, 49 (Oct. 1960), p. 11. For the '60s, see OH: Brenda Cooper, 12 Nov. 1990; Betty Hobgood Eidenier, 29 March 1991.

60. OH: Vira Kivett, 21 Feb. 1990; Claudette Graves Burroughs-White, 25 Feb. 1991; Gayle Fripp, 29 Nov. 1990; Brenda Cooper, 12 Nov. 1990.

61. OH: Brenda Cooper, 12 Nov. 1990; Betty Hobgood Eidenier, 29 March 1991.

62. Dramatic Activities Board minutes, 4 Oct., 8 Dec. 1949, Jackson Papers; *Carolinian*, 15 Oct. 1954; *Greensboro Daily News*, 23 Oct. 1954, in Vertical File: May Day.

63. Pamela Grundy, paper given to Historical Society of North Carolina, 4 April 1997.

64. Watson, "Ethel Loroline Martus Lawther," pp. 164–65; Jones, "History of Women's Intercollegiate Athletics," pp. 50–52, 88; OH: Sallie Robinson, 11 Oct. 1990.

65. Jones, "History of Women's Intercollegiate Athletics," p. 102.

66. "Estimates of the Amounts Required for Permanent Improvements... 1957–59," 10 July 1956, Budget (1) folder, Graham Papers; OH: Henrietta Huffines, 20 May 1991.

67. Pierson, 15 Aug. 1956, to Sheriff John P. Walters, U–Z, Pierson Papers; Henry Ferguson, 25 June 1963, to Sheriff Clayton H. Jones, F, Singletary Papers; OH: Henry Ferguson, 12 April 1990.

68. Trudy Atkins in *Alumni News*, 65 (Fall 1976), p. 11.

69. Strobel, "Ideology and Women's Higher Education," pp. 181–85; "First Occupation Entered by Woman's College Graduates... Classes of 1952–1959," 1 Nov. 1959, PTA-Poc, Blackwell Papers.

70. Julia Mauldin, 25 Nov. 1957, to Blackwell, Acad.–Alum., Blackwell Papers; Institutional Self-Study Report, 1962, pp. XIII 4–6.

71. Betty B. Jester, 24 April 1951, to Virginia T. Lathrop, in Correspondence, 1950–79, Alumni Association Records, 1899–1988; Alumnae Fund Committee minutes, 17 Nov. 1953, Alumni Association Records; OH: Mary Jane Wharton Sockwell, 8 March 1990.

72. Henry R. Sims, "College and Alumni Relationships," [1954], Alumni Association Records.

73. Mrs. L.H. Swain, Feb. 1952, to the Active Members of the Alumnae Association, Alumni Association Records, 1899–1988.

74. Graham, 29 Oct. 1951, to Mrs. Julius (Laura) Cone, Alumnae Assn. folder; Graham, 4 Aug. 1953, to Gordon Gray, Gray folder; Graham, 25 June 1954, to Gray, A, Graham Papers; correspondence of Curtis P. Fields and Gordon Gray, July 1952 to July 1953, Subgroup 1, series 4, Consultants, Gordon Gray Papers; OH: Betty Brown Jester, 22 March 1990.

75. OH: Betty Brown Jester, 22 March 1990; May Lattimore Adams, 5 April 1991; *Alumnae News*, 43 (Fall–Winter 1954, p. 2.

76. Richard H. Robinson, in *Alumni News*, 82 (Summer 1994), p. 41.

77. Chancellor's Office, "Supplement to Personnel Report... Re Barbara Parrish," 5 May 1955, Gordon Gray folder; Graham, 15 June 1955, to Gray (including quotation), Board folder, Graham Papers; Graham, 5 May 1955, to Annie Lee Singletary; [Marion Sifford, Alumnae Committee], 12 May 1955, to Annie Lee Singletary (in Committee to Recommend a Secretary papers); and Alumnae Board minutes, 3 June 1955, Alumni Association Records, 1899–1988; Institutional Self-Study Report, 1962, p. XIII 2.

78. Barbara Parrish, statement to William Friday et al., 8 March 1956, in E.K. Graham Controversy, Alumni Association Records, 1899–1988; Alumni Association Board minutes, 1 June 1956, in Alumni Association Minutes, 1955–60.

79. Institutional Self-Study Report, 1962, p. XIII 1.

Chapter 19 Notes

1. Correspondence between John W. Clark, Graham, and Gordon Gray, 6–17 Feb. 1951, Gordon Gray folder, Graham Papers.

2. Graham, in *Alumnae News*, 40 (Aug. 1951), p. 19. See also Graham, 25 Jan. 1952, to Alfred G. Ivey, H–J, Graham Papers; Civil Rights History Interviews: Franklin & Jennie Parker, 26 March 1987.

3. Graham, 11, 13 April 1951, to Gordon Gray, K–L, Graham Papers; Graham, 10 April 1951, to Charles Adams; Adams, 12 April 1951, to Graham (with accompanying memorandum); Adams, 14 June 1951, to Graham; correspondence on this question between Graham, Adams, and others, 24 March to 3 June 1952, K–L, Graham Papers (also in Correspondence,

Office of Librarian Records.); Adams, 11 Oct. 1954, to Graham, Correspondence, Office of Librarian Records; "Use of Woman's College Library by A. & T. [and other college] Students, 1953–58," [1958], La–Li, Blackwell Papers; *Carolinian*, 7 March 1952; OH: Charles Adams, 6 April 1990.

4. Graham, 29 Oct. 1951 to F.D. Bluford, S; 25 June 1951, to Albin Pakutis, N; 7 March 1952, to W.C. Archie, A; 9 April 1952, to Elizabeth Duffy, R, Graham Papers. See also Graham, 2 Feb. 1953, to Ernest Ball, B; 7 Oct. 1953, to Warren Ashby, A; 31 Oct. 1953, to A.C. Hall, K–L; 10 Sept. 1955, to Katherine Roberts, Departments carbon copies, Graham Papers.

5. Lou Ann Lewis Locke, in *Alumni News*, 70 (Spring 1982), p. 2; *Carolinian*, 11 Jan. 1952; Extract from Student Legislature minutes, 7 Jan. 1953, with Graham, 16 Feb. 1953, to Gordon Gray, Gray folder, Graham Papers.

6. OH: Eugene Pfaff, 24 Jan. 1990; Franklin Parker, 21 Feb. 1990; Civil Rights Oral History Interviews: Helen Ashby, 25 March 1987; Franklin & Jennie Parker, 26 March 1987.

7. Obituary in Greensboro *News & Record*, 3 Oct. 1985; Nomination of Warren Ashby for the Gladys Strawn Bullard Award, [1982], B, Moran Papers; Chafe, *Civilities and Civil Rights*, pp. 115–16.

8. Warren Ashby, 14 Oct. 1955, to Graham, F, Graham Papers; Faculty Council Minutes, 18 Oct., 15 Nov., 13 Dec. 1955; Vertical File: Black Students at UNCG, including clippings from *Greensboro Record*, 8 Dec. 1955 and *Greensboro Daily News*, 15 Dec. 1955; Draft resolutions and press release, Oct., Dec. 1955; Student Legislature minutes, 7 Dec. 1955; News release, 8 Dec. 1955, and accompanying public reactions, Se–So, Graham Papers.

9. Wilson, *University of North Carolina Under Consolidation*, pp. 387–88; Link, *William Friday*, pp. 83–84, 249–50.

10. Graham, 26 April 1951, to Franklin H. McNutt and Mildred Newton, A; Administrative Council minutes, 13 March 1956, A; Graham, 7 April 1951, to Gordon Gray, N; 26 March 1953, to Katherine Roberts, Departments folder, Graham Papers.

11. Graham, 20 March 1951, to Gordon Gray, B; Gray, 23 March 1951, to Graham, Gordon Gray folder, Graham Papers.

12. *Carolinian*, 14 March 1952, 15 Oct. 1954, 9 March 1956.

13. Trustees' Visiting Committee minutes, 19 April 1952, Board folder, Graham Papers; *Carolinian*, 1 Oct. 1954; Strobel, "Ideology and Women's Higher Education," pp. 168–69.

14. Meeting on Selective Admissions, 9 Nov. 1955, minutes and rough notes; Ibid., 22 Nov. 1955, rough notes, in Admissions, General Policies, VC Academic Affairs Records, 1941–84; Institutional Self-Study Report, 1962, pp. VII 1–2, 8–10.

15. See the explanation, probably by William Whatley Pierson, who chaired the UNC committee that devised the three-campus policy and, ironically, presided as chancellor over the admission of WC's first two black students. Memorandum re University Testing System, [1956], A, Pierson Papers.

16. Pierson, 17 Aug. 1956, to Sam O. Worthington, S–Se, Pierson Papers; Blackwell, 2 Feb. 1959, to Mrs. John F. McNair, J–K, Blackwell Papers.

17. Pierson, 24 Sept. 1956, to Clifton F. West, S–Se (including quotation); Newspaper clipping of Pierson speech to Greensboro Kiwanis Club, [1956], Biography folder, Pierson Papers; *Greensboro Daily News*, 11 Sept. 1956; OH: Mereb Mossman, 11 Oct. 1989; Kendon Smith, 18 Oct. 1989; Betsy Umstead, 7 Dec. 1989; Franklin Parker, 21 Feb. 1990; Robert Watson, 21 March 1990; Charles Adams, 6 April 1990; Richard Bardolph, 14 May 1991.

18. Sam O. Worthington, 14 Aug. 1956, to Pierson; Pierson, 17 Aug. 1956, to Worthington, S–Se, Pierson Papers. For background information on Smart and Tillman and college reactions to their admission, see *Greensboro Daily News*, 14 Aug., 11, 12 Sept. 1956; *Greensboro Record*, 14, 16 Aug. 1956, in Vertical File: Black Students at UNCG.

19. JoAnne Smart Drane, in *Alumni News*, 68 (Spring 1980), pp. 9–11, 30; OH: Gordon Blackwell, 12 Nov. 1990; Mereb Mossman, 11 Oct. 1989; Franklin Parker, 21 Feb. 1990; Claudette Graves Burroughs-White, 25 Feb. 1991; Edith Mayfield Wiggins, 8 May 1991; Janet Harper Gordon, 28 March 1991; Emilie Mills, 30 Jan. 1990; "Enrollment Figures on Negro Students, 1959–1960," 14 Oct. 1959, E, Blackwell Papers; Ad Hoc Committee on University Racial Policies report, Table I: Enrollment of Negro Students . . . , [1969], Ad Hoc Committee folder, Ferguson Papers.

20. Ad Hoc Committee on University Racial Policies report, [1969], p. 10, Ad Hoc Committee folder, Ferguson Papers; OH: Edith M. Wiggins, 8 May 1991; Janet Harper Gordon, 28 March 1991; Emilie Mills, 30 Jan. 1990; Diane Oliver, in *Alumni News*, 63 (Spring 1975), pp. 13–15.

21. See L. Robert Grogan, 10 May 1958, to Mereb Mossman, Na–Nu, Blackwell Papers; John Harris and John Reitzel, "Prediction of Negro Freshman Performance in a Predominantly Non-Negro University" [WC/UNCG, 1961–64], I–L, Singletary Papers, 1966; Tommie Lou Smith report, 18 March 1970, Appendix III: Students Graduating Four Years After Admission as Freshmen, B. of T. Visiting Committee folder, Ferguson Papers; OH: Kendon Smith, 18 Oct. 1989.

22. *Alumni News*, 63 (Spring 1975), pp. 13–15.

23. Newcomer, *Century of Higher Education*, pp. 38–41; Lee, *Campus Scene*, pp. 164–65.

24. Gallien, "Coeducational Transition," pp. 89–90.

25. C.W. Phillips, 19 May 1956, to William D. Carmichael; Graham, 29 May 1956, to Wm. Friday, A, Graham Papers; Graduate School report, Nov. 1963, B. of T., Singletary Papers.

26. King, *Multicampus University*, pp. 44–51; Link, *William Friday*, pp. 160–69; Gallien, "Coeducational Transition," pp. 92–95, 104–05. For Friday's role, see also Thomas J. Pearsall, 31 Jan. 1963, to Singletary, Pa–Pr, Singletary Papers.

27. Institutional Self-Study Report, 1962, p. VI 8; Link, *William Friday*, p. 167.

28. Alumnae Association Trustees resolution, 1 Dec. 1962, Pearsall Committee folder, Singletary Papers. For alumnae leaders' agonizing over the question, see Coeducation Polling folder, 23 Feb. to 19 March 1963, Alumni Association Records, 1899–1988.

29. OH: Brenda Cooper, 12 Nov. 1990; Betty Hobgood Eidenier, 29 March 1991; Carol Bryden Passmore, 2 Feb. 1991; *Carolinian*, 13 April, 11 May 1962 (for student opinion), and 11 Jan., 15 Feb. 1963 (for editorial support).

30. OH: Harriet Kupferer, 27 Oct. 1989; Nancy White, 4 Dec. 1989.

31. Donald B. Anderson, Diary note on conversation with Otis Singletary, 28 Dec. 1961, Subgroup 3, series 3, subseries 1, Friday Papers, UNC Archives; [Singletary], "Miscellaneous Thoughts re Coeducation at Woman's College," [1962], and "Thoughts on the Pearsall Committee," 9 Aug. 1962, Pearsall Committee folder, Singletary Papers; OH: Gordon Blackwell, 12 Nov. 1990; Singletary, 9 Nov. 1989.

32. The fullest discussion of the local coeducation debate is Gallien, "Coeducational Transition." See esp. pp. 94–99, 106–14. For Dean Taylor's statement, see OH: Robert Darnell, 19 March 1990. For other opinions on both sides, see the correspondence in the Pearsall Commmittee folder, 1962, Singletary Papers; Amy M. Charles, 12 May 1963, to Wm. Friday, Co–Cu, Singletary Papers; OH: Susannah Thomas Watson, 7 Feb. 1991.

33. OH: Gordon Blackwell, 12 Nov. 1990; Mereb Mossman, 11 Oct. 1989; Otis Singletary, 9 Nov. 1989; Gail Hennis, 18 Jan. 1990; Paula Andris, 23 April 1991; Herman Middleton, 19 Feb. 1990; Kendon Smith, 18 Oct. 1989; Gallien, "Coeducational Transition," pp. 101–02, 108. For the recurrent view that WC had been neglected, see Victor S. Bryant, 31 July 1957, to Blackwell, B. of T.; Blackwell, 24 Feb. 1959, to George Tindall and, 24 Feb. 1959, to William Sanders, Legislative Program folder; Blackwell, 9 Sept. 1960, to Terry Sanford, Sa–Se, Blackwell Papers; *Greensboro Daily News* editorial, 20 Nov. 1962; *Carolinian*, 15 Feb. 1963; Gallien, "Coeduca-

tional Transition," pp. 101–02, citing an interview with Mereb Mossman, 24 Oct. 1985; OH: Gordon Blackwell, 12 Nov. 1990; Gail Hennis, 18 Jan. 1990; Paula Andris, 23 April 1991.

Chapter 20 Notes

1. *Alumni News*, 53 (Winter 1965, p. 27; (Summer 1965), pp. 2–3; OH: Otis Singletary, 9 Nov. 1989.

2. Academic Policies Committee, report to Trustees Visiting Committee, Nov. 1963, B. of T., Singletary Papers. See also report of Mereb Mossman, 14 Nov. 1963, to Trustees Visiting Committee, in same folder; Bell I. Wiley, 28 Feb. 1964, to Singletary, A–Al, Singletary Papers.

3. *Carolinian*, 16 Oct. 1964, 26 March 1965; Monette Weaver, in *Carolinian*, 4 Nov. 1966.

4. OH: Otis Singletary, 9 Nov. 1989; Gail Hennis, 18 Jan. 1990.

5. OH: Gail Hennis, 18 Jan. 1990; Rosemary McGee, 21 May 1990; Robert Eason, 14 Feb. 1996; Robert Calhoon, 1 Feb. 1990; Nancy White, 4 Dec. 1989.

6. For Singletary's preference of Ferguson as successor, see Singletary, 20 Dec. 1966, to Ferguson, Personal folder, Ferguson Papers; OH: Henry Ferguson, 12 April 1990; Richard Bardolph, 14 May 1991.

7. Wm. Friday's remarks, Board of Trustees minutes, 15 Sept. 1978, B. of T., Ferguson Papers; *Carolinian*, 30 Sept. 1966; 13 Jan. 1967; 19 Sept. 1978 (for Friday's statement); *Alumni News*, 55 (Jan. 1967), inside of front cover; OH: Robert Calhoon, 1 Feb. 1990; Blackwell Robinson, 14 Nov. 1990. See the outpouring of congratulations in Ferguson's Papers, 1967.

8. Helen Yoder (Ferguson's secretary), in *Greensboro Daily News*, 16 Sept. 1978; OH: James Lancaster, 24 Jan. 1991; Henry Ferguson, 12 April 1990; Stanley Jones, 27 Dec. 1990; James Allen, 11 Sept. 1990; Kendon Smith, 18 Oct. 1989; Harriet Kupferer, 27 Oct. 1989; Jean Buchert, 22 Feb. 1990; Robert Eason, 14 Feb., 13 March 1996.

9. Ferguson, 12 June 1967, to Curt [Lamar]; 4 Oct. 1967, to Wendell H. Stephenson, Personal folder, Ferguson Papers.

10. Ferguson, undated speech to Executive Institute, "Problems of Achieving Effectiveness in the Chancellor's Office," Speeches, Ferguson Papers. For student social demands on Ferguson, see OH: James Lancaster, 24 Jan. 1991.

11. Robert M. Calhoon, "Samuel E. McCorkle and James S. Ferguson," address, UNCG, 17 Oct. 1995, in Faculty File: Calhoon; Calhoon, in *Alumni News*, 79 (Winter 1991), p. 2.

12. Ada M. Fisher, 2 Nov. 1984, to Chairman, Board of Governors, N, Moran Papers.

13. For Frances Ferguson's illness and his own decision to step down, see Ferguson, 9 Jan. 1979, to William T. Haywood, Personal folder, Ferguson Papers.

14. Cremin, *American Education*, p. 561. See also Harold T. Shapiro, "University Presidents—Then and Now," in Bowen and Shapiro, *Universities and Their Leadership*, pp. 73–74; McLaughlin and Riesman, "The President," pp. 182–83.

15. E.K. Graham, 4 June 1956, to W.W. Pierson, G, Pierson Papers; Dean of the Faculty, B Budget Request, 10 June 1964, B, Singletary Papers.

16. OH: Robert Miller, 23 Jan. 1990; Lawrence Hart, 25 Sept. 1990; Robert Eason, 13 March 1996.

17. See articles marking the event in *Greensboro Daily News*, 7 Feb. 1971.

18. See OH: Stanley Jones, 27 Dec. 1990; Robert Miller, 23 Jan. 1990; Lawrence Hart, 25 Sept. 1990; Robert Eason, 13 March 1996.

19. See OH: Jean Buchert, 22 Feb. 1990.

20. OH: Stanley Jones, 27 Dec. 1990.

21. OH: Robert Miller, 23 Jan. 1990; Robert Eason, 13 March 1996.

22. See organizational chart, March 1974, H, Ferguson Papers.

23. Ferguson, 19 July 1978, to Theodore Mahaffey, A, Ferguson Papers.

24. OH: James H. Allen, 11 Sept. 1990; Stanley Jones, 27 Dec. 1990; Robert Eason, 13 March 1996.

25. Singletary, 26 Oct. 1964, to J.S. Ferguson, D, Singletary Papers; OH: May Lattimore Adams, 5 April 1991.

26. *Greensboro Record*, 12 Jan. 1964.

27. Ferguson, Statement to Trustees' Visiting Committee, 27 April 1968, B. of T. Visiting Committee folder; Ferguson, draft of annual report, 1968, Ca–Cl, Ferguson Papers. For Smyth, see *Greensboro Daily News*, 19 May 1968; Faculty File: Smyth; Deans' Council minutes, 5 May 1971, in Dean of Students, VCAA Records; *Carolinian*, 23 March 1971.

28. Changes Affecting Student Life, in 1972 Institutional Self-Study, Fifth Year Report, 1977; James H. Allen, 20 Jan. 1975, to Faculty and Staff, Stu–Stu Govt., Ferguson Papers; OH: James Allen, 11 Sept. 1990.

29. Institutional Self-Study Report, 1972, pp. 94–96.

30. Organization chart, April 1979, O folder, Moran Papers.

31. OH: Paula Andris, 23 April 1991.

32. Wilson Davis, 13 March 1975, to Charles Patterson, N, Ferguson Papers. See also News Bureau section of C&D Budget Request for 1975–77 (booklet), in Ferguson Papers, 1974.

33. Brubacher and Rudy, *Higher Education in Transition*, pp. 379–80.

34. Institutional Self-Study, 1962: Report of Visiting Committee, pp. 5–6, and ibid., supplementary report for 1962–63, pp. 6–7; Donald J. Reichard, 15 Sept. 1981, to A. Lawrence Fincher, I folder, Moran Papers.

35. John Harris, 25 Oct. 1966, to Singletary et al., I–L, Singletary Papers; Ferguson, speech, Problems of Achieving Effectiveness in the Chancellor's Office, p. 8, Speeches, Ferguson Papers.

36. A. Lawrence Fincher, 9 Sept. 1982, to UNCG Board of Trustees, B. of T., Moran Papers.

37. Donald J. Reichard, 15 Sept. 1981, to A. Lawrence Fincher, I folder, Moran Papers.

38. Turner, *Campus*, pp. 249–50; King, *Multicampus University*, p. 21. For UNCG, see Six Associates, "Residential Planning for Peabody Park," May 1965, rev. Jan. 1967, in Vertical File: Peabody Park.

39. Institutional Self-Study Report, 1972, pp. 524–26. The SACS visiting team agreed. Ibid., Visiting Committee report.

40. Charles Hounshell, 13 Nov. 1972, to Jerry W. Johnson, Q–R, Ferguson Papers.

41. Dober and Associates, 14 Aug. 1974, to C.D. Hounshell, with Deans Council Minutes, 3 Oct. 1974; Ferguson, 25 Jan. 1977, to Neill McLeod, Executive Committee Meetings, Alumni Association Records, 1899–1988; Campus Planning Committee, [1978], Operating Procedures, Ci–Co, Ferguson Papers; Remarks by W.E. Moran, in Notes on Meeting of the Arts & Sciences Administrative Council, 16 Nov. 1979, in Arts & Sciences College, VCAA Records; W.E. Moran, 11 Nov. 1980, to Robert B. Muir, in Lands, Buildings, and Equipment, UNCG Planning Process, 1980–83; OH: Henry Ferguson, 12 April 1990; Robert Eason, 13 March 1996; Institutional Self-Study Report, 1992, pp. 97–98. For the campus planning committee, see Jack Jezorek, 8 Nov. 1976, to The University Community, Vertical File: Campus Planning Committee.

42. Ferguson, statement on campus expansion, 3 April 1965, M–N, Ferguson Papers; *Greensboro Daily News*, 4 Sept. 1965; *Alumni News*, 53 (Spring 1965), pp. 19–21; OH: Henry Ferguson, 12 April 1990.

43. OH: Henry Ferguson, 12 April 1990.

44. McNeill Smith, 21 Jan. 1963, to Singletary, Sh–Sp, Singletary Papers; H.L. Ferguson, 24 Sept. 1965, to Robert Barkley, I–L; and H.L. Ferguson, Statement to Trustees' Visiting Committee, 9 Dec. 1965, B. of T., Ferguson Papers; Proposed Resolution Designating the College

West Redevelopment Area ..., 20 April 1966, with April 15 supporting document, P–R, Singletary Papers; Correspondence in I–L, Singletary Papers, 1966; *Greensboro Daily News*, 26 April, 2, 3, 7, 9, 15, 18 May, 20, 22 June 1966; *Carolinian*, 4 Nov. 1966.

45. Charles W. Phillips, in *Alumni News*, 67 (Fall 1978), p. 19; *Carolinian*, 21 Nov. 1967.

46. Wm. Friday, 14 Aug. 1963, to Hugh Cannon, L–M; Singletary, Transmittal of capital improvement estimates, [1966], Ca–Ch, Singletary Papers; Correspondence in B. of T, folder, 1968, and Henry L. Ferguson, 9 Aug. 1968, to Felix Joyner, Ca–Cl; Resolution Authorizing the Purchase of Property... for Campus Parking, [1974], B. of T., Ferguson Papers; Deans' Council Minutes, 23 Jan. 1969; OH: Henry Ferguson, 12 April 1990. For the acquisition process, by 1972, see UNCG Trustees' minutes, 14 Sept. 1972, B. of T., Ferguson Papers.

47. Henry L. Ferguson, 10 Feb. 1964, to A.H. Shepard, I–M; Trustees' Building Committee minutes, 12 July 1966, B. of T., Singletary Papers; Anthony Lord, Residential Planning for Peabody Park, Feb. 1965, O–Pen, Ferguson Papers; Trustees' Visiting Committee, annual report, 1966, p. 42.

48. H.L. Ferguson, 2 Jan. 1970, to N.H. Gurley, O–P, Ferguson Papers; *Carolinian*, 14 Sept. 1973.

49. Trustee Visiting Committee, annual report, 1966, p. 42; Singletary, 18 Oct. 1966, to Ellen Griffin et al., Depts. G–M, Singletary Papers; *Alumni News*, 60 (Fall 1971), p. 41; Proposed Capital Improvement Project: Convert Golf Course to Outdoor Physical Education Facilities, 28 Jan. 1972, Schools E–H, Ferguson Papers; *Greensboro Daily News*, 3, 9 May 1966; Greensboro *News & Record*, 30 June 1998.

50. H.L. Ferguson, 27 Sept. 1963, to T.M. McKnight, T, Singletary Papers; Anne Prince, Report to Visiting Committee, 15 Nov. 1963, in Minutes, SGA Records; OH: Henry Ferguson, 12 April 1990.

51. *Carolinian*, 9 Dec. 1966, 24 Feb. 1967, 25 March 1976; Royce G. McCombs, 18 July 1968, to Ferguson, T; Trustee minutes, 6 July 1972, B. of T.; Charles W. Patterson, 13 Feb. 1976, to Ferguson, Com, Ferguson Papers; OH: Mary Lou Merrill, 16 Feb. 1990.

52. *Greensboro Daily News*, 4 Sept. 1965; Singletary, notes of talk to trustees, [1966], B. of T.; UNCG Capital Improvement Estimates, [1966], Ca–Ch, Singletary Papers.

53. H.L. Ferguson, 9 Sept. 1975, to Mrs. Lora M. Silver, T; H.L. Ferguson, 9 Sept. 1976, to Board of Trustees, B. of T., Ferguson Papers; *Carolinian*, 6 April 1976.

54. E.S. Wilkinson, 10 Sept. 1971, and H.L. Ferguson, 22 Sept. 1971, to Faculty, Deans, Department Heads, and Staff, Ta–Tr, Ferguson Papers; *Carolinian*, 30 Sept. 1971.

55. Ferguson remarks, Trustees' Minutes, 6 July 1972; Clarence Shipton, 1 Sept. 1972, to Ferguson, B. of T.; Ferguson, 13 March 1974, to Mrs. Jesse Lee Heptinstall, Traffic, Ferguson Papers; Amy Charles, in *Carolinian*, 30 March 1976; Remarks by Charles Church, Deans' Council Minutes, 31 March 1976.

56. *Carolinian*, 29 Aug., 5 Sept., 24 Oct. 1974; Office of Institutional Research, Commuters and Parking at UNCG, October 1975, Com–Cons, Ferguson Papers; Remarks of Charles Church, Deans' Council Minutes, 31 March 1976; Joseph W. Guyton, 8 Nov. 1977, to James T. Laumann, Ti–Tri, Ferguson Papers.

57. Report to Board of Trustees on Campus Parking, 13 April 1978, B. of T.; Ferguson, 18 July 1978, to Wm. Friday; Mayor Jim Melvin, 11 Sept. 1978, to Charles W. Allen, Tr–Tu, Ferguson Papers; *Greensboro Daily News*, 7 May 1978.

58. *Greensboro Record*, 18 July 1978; H.L. Ferguson, 30 Aug. 1978, to Board of Trustees; Report on Parking, 15 Sept. 1978, in Parking, VCAA Records; Trustees' minutes, 15 Sept. 1978, B. of T., Ferguson Papers; *Carolinian*, 31 Aug., 26 Sept., 24 Oct. 1978; 27 Feb. 1979.

59. *Alumni News*, 54 (Summer 1966), pp. 16–17; "The University of North Carolina at and IN Greensboro," *Greensboro Business*, Sept. 1966, pp. 2, 11, in D, Singletary Papers.

60. Ferguson, 27 Jan. 1966, to McNeill Smith; Smith, 26 Aug. 1966, to Singletary; Ferguson, 20 Sept. 1966, to Smith, F–G, Ferguson Papers.

61. Turner, *Campus*, pp. 267, 271, 294–97.

62. Trudy Atkins, in *Alumni News*, 63 (Spring 1975), pp. 9–11.

63. OH: Paula Andris, 23 April 1991.

64. Henry Ferguson, 27 Nov. 1967, to Frank S. Turner, Ca–Co, Ferguson Papers.

65. Ferguson, 4 March 1968, to Mrs. Robert D. Douglas, D; The Preservation of Foust Administration Building, 8 Oct. 1973, Al–App; Virginia Brown Douglas and Clora McNeill Foust, 18 Jan. 1974, to Ferguson, and Ferguson replies to them, 24 Jan. 1974, Ac–Ad, Ferguson Papers.

66. Institutional Self-Study Report, 1972, pp. 509–10.

67. Ferguson remarks, in Deans' Council Minutes, 27 Jan. 1970; OH: May Lattimore Adams, 5 April 1991; Jean Buchert, 22 Feb. 1990; Robert Eason, 13 March 1996; M. Elaine Burgess, 8 Nov. 1990; William Moran, 28 Jan. 1991.

68. Lawrence Hart, 24 April 1974, and William K. McRae, 2 May 1974, to Henry Ferguson, Schools: M–N, Ferguson Papers.

69. Herman Middleton, 18 Nov. 1963, to H.L. Ferguson, Depts. A–Hi, Singletary Papers; Lawrence Hart, 10 April 1970, to Ferguson, Music/Nursing, Ferguson Papers; Capital improvement requests, 28 Jan. 1972, with Deans' Council Minutes, 9 Feb. 1972, and in B & C Budget Requests for 1975–77 (booklet), Ferguson Papers, 1974; H.L. Ferguson, 10 Sept. 1975, to L. Felix Joyner, Am–Arc, Ferguson Papers; *Greensboro Daily News*, 5 Sept. 1976.

70. Randolph Bulgin et al., 28 Sept. 1965, to Ferguson, M–N, Ferguson Papers; Capital improvement requests for 1965–67, Ca–Ch, Singletary Papers, 1966. Regarding the infirmary, see William G. Morgan, 15 Jan. 1969, to Katherine Taylor, I–J, Ferguson Papers.

71. See Ferguson correspondence on handicapped access, Nov. 1973, Arts/Sciences, Ferguson Papers.

72. Trustee Visiting Committee Reports, 1963, pp. 15–17; 1964, pp. 36–41 (quotation on p. 36).

Chapter 21 Notes

1. Geiger, *Research and Relevant Knowledge*, p. 264; Freeland, *Academia's Golden Age*, p. 382; Keller, Academic Strategy, pp. 24–25.

2. Freeland, *Academia's Golden Age*, pp. 414–17.

3. Link, *William Friday*, pp. 171–85; King, *Multicampus University*, pp. 92–135, 163–64. See Chancellor Ferguson's endorsement of the law in a memorandum to the faculty, 10 Nov. 1971, Higher Ed, Ferguson Papers.

4. See trustee lists in the annual catalogs, 1972–73ff.

5. Gallien, "Coeducational Transition," pp. 6–7, 14.

6. See John W. Kennedy, 6 Oct. 1970, to Ferguson, G, Ferguson Papers; OH: Robert Eason, 14 Feb. 1996.

7. *Carolinian*, 30 Sept. 1966.

8. Institutional Self-Study Report, 1992, pp. 38–39. See Ferguson's remarks to the faculty, Faculty Council Minutes, 17 Sept. 1974.

9. Geiger, *Reseach and Relevant Knowledge*, pp. 266–68.

10. Ferguson, 3 May 1976, to Gordon W. Sweet, Se–Su, Ferguson Papers; UNCG *Fact Book*, 1979–80, p. 74.

11. OH: Henry Ferguson, 12 April 1990.

12. Ferguson, 7 April 1975, to McNeill Smith; Ferguson, 18 April 1975, to Wm. Friday, B, Ferguson Papers; Deans' Council Minutes, 7, 9, 23 April 1975.

13. Ferguson, 27 Dec. 1977, to Wm. Friday, B, Ferguson Papers, 1978; *Alumni News*, 66 (Winter 1978), p. 12; 66 (Spring 1978), p. 11. For the classification of institutions, see Table 2–1, p. 14, in Board of Governors, Comparative Study of Baccalaureate and Master's Program Offerings, 8 Dec. 1978, HEW folder, Ferguson Papers.

14. OH: Otis Singletary, 9 Nov. 1989; statements by Vice Chancellors John W. Kennedy, James H. Allen, and Charles W. Patterson, 5–17 Sept. 1979, Chancellors' Cabinet Records. For ties to the 1972 reconsolidation in particular, see OH: Robert Eason, 14 Feb. 1996; James H. Allen, 11 Sept. 1990.

15. Institutional Self-Study Report, 1972, pp. 102–03, 249, 656–59; *Carolinian*, 12 Dec. 1969.

16. For an appeal not to repudiate the WC heritage, see Jean Eason, 6 July 1979, to Task Force on Extended University, in Extended University, Assistant VCAA Records. For a good discussion of the Golden Age view and some of the problems of the 1970s, see Herbert Wells, in *Alumni News*, 65 (Summer 1977), pp. 1–4.

17. Statements of Vice Chancellors James H. Allen and Charles W. Patterson, 10, 17 Sept. 1979, Chancellor's Cabinet Records; OH: James H. Allen (including the Arnold King reference); Richard Bardolph, 14 May 1991; William Lane, 15 Nov. 1990; James Lancaster, 24 Jan. 1991; Fred Chappell, 7 March 1991; Ruth Whalin Cooke, 4 Sept. 1990; Peggy Whalen-Levitt, 21 May 1991; Emily Herring Wilson, in Alumni News, 70 (Winter 1982), pp. 18–19.

18. For discussion about the urban university idea, see Deans' Council Minutes, 14 July 1971, 17 April 1974, 7 May 1975; Trustees' Visiting Committee Minutes, 25 April 1972, p. 6, in B. of T., Ferguson Papers; Institutional Self-Study Report, 1972, pp. 102, 249; ibid., First Follow-Up Report, 1973, p. 5; OH: Stanley Jones, 27 Dec. 1990.

19. Freeland, *Academia's Golden Age*, pp. 118, 356–70, 375; Berube, *Urban University*, pp. 14–15. For an interesting look at Northern Illinois University, a campus similarly situated, see Hodgkinson, *Institutions in Transition*, esp. pp. 194–95.

20. Geiger, "Research Universities," p. 73.

21. See George Hamer, 8 March 1972, to Leo J. Heer, Deg–Du, Ferguson Papers.

22. OH: George Hamer, 12 Dec. 1990; Alumni Annual Giving Council Minutes, 25 Feb. 1975, and related documents in Af–Al, Ferguson Papers, 1975.

23. George Hamer, Report to the Visiting Committee, 15 Nov. 1963, B. of T., Singletary Papers; Tables: UNC-G Private Support and Alumni/University Annual Giving, 1963–83, Chancellor's Cabinet Records, 12 Sept. 1983.

24. *Carolinian*, 15 Jan. 1980; UNCG *Fact Book*, 1979–80, p. 74.

25. William E. Moran, 27 March 1980, to L. Felix Joyner, VC Development, Moran Papers.

26. George Hamer, Report to Trustees' Visiting Committee, 22 April 1968, B. of T. Visiting Committee folder; Statement to Board of Directors of the Excellence Fund, 8 Jan. 1974, E folder; J.S. Ferguson, The Excellence Fund—Private Support for Public Higher Education, 20 Feb. 1979, L–No, Ferguson Papers.

27. Ferguson, 1 Aug. 1968, to Wm. Friday, D, Ferguson Papers.

28. Margery Davis Irby, in *Alumni News*, 55 (Jan. 1967), pp. 24–25; Herbert Wells, Undergraduate Admissions, Dec. 1975, in Admissions Office, 1973–78, VCAA Records, 1935–87.

29. Deans' Council Minutes, 22 Sept. 1971; Stanley Jones, 27 June 1977, to Ferguson; Robert W. Hites, 14, 27 June, 29 Nov. 1977, to Ferguson, in Al (1); Jones, 24 Aug. 1977, to Academic Deans, Ad–Af, Ferguson Papers; Academic Support Unit/Program Self-Study and Plan for the Admissions Office, [1985], pp. 2–3, in Self Study & Plans, Assistant VCAA Records.

30. Eleanor S. Morris, Request for Funding Scholarship Finalists' Visit to Campus, [1975], Af–Al, Ferguson Papers.

31. Lucas, *Crisis in the Academy*, pp. 15–17; Enrollment, in Information Supplied to State Board of Higher Education, 20 Feb. 1970, BHE, Ferguson Papers.

32. *Alumni News*, 54 (Summer 1966), p. 9; Chart: Male Enrollment, B. of T./B. of G., Moran Papers, 1979.

33. See Report, Committee to Bring Suggestions...on Improving Male...Enrollment, M–N, Ferguson Papers, 1967; OH: Stanley Jones, 27 Dec. 1990; Robert Miller, 23 Jan. 1990; Gallien, "Coeducational Transition," pp. 115–16.

34. Table: Enrollment Figures...1962–1968, E folder; Donald J. Reichard, 5 Oct. 1977, to Ferguson, I folder; Stanley Jones to Academic Deans, 24 Aug. 1977, Ad–Af, Ferguson Papers; Table: Trends in UNC-G Enrollment In Relation to Tuition Changes, 1971–83, in Enrollment (General), Assistant VCAA Records.

35. Institutional Self-Study Report, 1972, p. 142; Table 8: Residence Status of Entering Students...1978–79, A folder, Ferguson Papers.

36. Average SAT Total Scores of...Entering Freshmen, 1970–86, Enrollment, [1986], Moran Papers; SGA Meeting with the Visiting Committee, [May 1972], SGA folder, Ferguson Papers; OH: Peggy Whalen-Levitt, 21 May 1991.

37. Ferguson, 8 Aug. 1977, to Wm. Friday, Sa–Sc, Ferguson Papers.

38. UNCG *Fact Book*, 1979–80, pp. 18, 20.

39. *Alumni News*, 69 (Fall 1980), p. 20; Office of Institutional Research, Demographic Characteristics of Commuting Students, 17 Dec. 1975, Com–Cons, Ferguson Papers.

40. Freeland, *Academia's Golden Age*, pp. 379–80.

41. Office for Adult Students, To the Faculty: 19 March 1975, Fall 1976, Fall 1977, in Vertical File: Adult Students; *Carolinian*, 26 Feb. 1973, 6 Dec. 1979.

42. UNCG *Fact Book*, 1995–96, p. I-5; Illustrative Materials for the University of North Carolina at Greensboro, 14 Nov. 1975, B. of G., Ferguson Papers; Materials for Visit of Advisory Budget Commission, 28 Sept. 1978, Bo–Bu, Ferguson Papers.

43. Donald J. Reichard, Some Quantitative Changes, 1967–1977, 5 Oct. 1977, I folder, Ferguson Papers.

44. UNCG *Fact Book*, 1979–80, p. 26.

45. Herbert Wells, Undergraduate Admissions, Dec. 1975, pp. 17, 23–26, in Admissions Office, 1973–78, VCAA Records, 1935–87; Table IV: Number and Classification of Transfer Students...1969–1978/79, A folder, Ferguson Papers, 1979.

46. Herbert Wells, Undergraduate Admissions, Dec. 1975, pp. 11–14, in Admissions Office, 1973–78, VCAA Recs., 1935–87.

47. OH: James H. Allen, 11 Sept. 1990; Anna Joyce Reardon, 20 Sept. 1990; Tom Kirby-Smith, 10 Sept. 1990; Laura Anderton, 19 Jan. 1990.

48. *Alumni News*, 62 (Spring 1974), p. 40.

49. Figures 7, 9, in A. Lawrence Fincher, Strategic Planning Model of Enrollment, 6/18/84, E, Moran Papers; UNCG *Fact Book*, 1979–80, p. 29.

50. Factors in the Choice of UNC-G, 14 June 1979, A, Ferguson Papers; Ravitch, *Schools We Deserve*, p. 29; Boyer, *College*, pp. 25–27.

51. See Johnson and Bell, eds., *Metropolitan Universities*.

52. General Comments, on survey of student applicants who chose to go elsewhere, [1971], Admis folder; Factors in the Choice of UNC-G, 14 June 1979, A, Ferguson Papers.

53. Robert W. Hites, July 1976, to Herbert Wells, in Admissions-Special Recruiting, Assistant VCAA Records.

54. Donald J. Reichard, 14 June 1978, to Robert Hites and Herbert Wells, Admissions Office folder, Assistant VCAA Records; Results of Survey Administered to Entering Students, esp. Table 3, in Report...from the Committee on Fraternities and Sororities, with Academic Cab-

inet Minutes, 21 Feb. 1979; Office of Institutional Research, Modifying the HEW-OCR Survey of Students Not Returning . . . , [1976], Table 1, in Retention Study, Assistant VCAA Records.

55. Office of Institutional Research, Highlights from the Spring 1979 Survey of Student Perceptions . . . , Oct. 1979, in Race Relations, Assistant VCAA Records.

56. Warren Ashby, 21 July 1971, to Stanley Jones, in Deans' Council, VCAA Records, 1941–84; Ashby, 5 April 1978, to Ferguson, HEW, Ferguson Papers.

57. For detailed accounts of the drawn-out HEW-UNC controversy basically favorable to the UNC position, see Link, *William Friday*, pp. 249–366, and King, *Multicampus University*, pp. 204–41. For a shorter and less sympathetic view, see Halpern, *On the Limits*, pp. 169–74, 210–31. For Chancellor Ferguson's view of the controversy, echoing that of UNC administrators, see Deans' Council Minutes, 10 Feb. 1970, 21 March 1973; Ferguson, 10 Jan. 1974, to the Faculty, EEO folder; Ferguson, 8 Feb. 1978, to the Faculty, and Ferguson, 2 May 1978, to Thomas Scullion and Dianne Harrison, HEW; Ferguson, 28 March 1978, to V. Lane Wharton, F, Ferguson Papers. A large part of the correspondence relating to the controversy as it affected UNCG can be found in the HEW folders of Ferguson's papers from 1970 onward. Other materials can be found in the Deans' Council Minutes.

58. Research Triangle Institute, draft report, 30 May 1977, in Remedial Education, Assistant VCAA Records; Marie E. Darr, Admissions Officer's Observations and Recommendations, May 1971, in Admissions Office, VCAA Records.

59. Ferguson, 1 March 1967, to Warren Ashby, Depts. N–P; Ferguson, 13 April 1970, to Elsa McKeithan, B, Ferguson Papers. For black faculty, see Ferguson, 1 March 1967, to Edna Douglas, M–N, Ferguson Papers.

60. Keller, *Academic Strategy*, pp. 17–18; Bowen and Bok, *Shape of the River*, pp. 4–8.

61. Marie E. Darr, Admissions Officer's Observations and Recommendations, May 1971, in Admissions Office, VCAA Records; Chancellor Ferguson, in transcript of trustees' meeting, 11 April 1974, B. of T.; Ferguson, 11 July 1977, to Wm. Friday, HEW; Robert W. Hites, 11 July 1978, to Stanley Jones, with accompanying reports, HEW; Minority Presence Student Recruitment Questionnaire, 1978–79, [1979], HEW, Ferguson Papers.

62. Table I, in Report of Ad Hoc Committee on University Racial Policies, Ad Hoc Comm. folder, [1969], Ferguson Papers; Chart: Fall Term Enrollment by Race, 1970–79, [1979], B. of T./B. of G., Moran Papers.

63. UNCG *Fact Book*, 1979–80, p. 22; *Alumni News*, 64 (Winter 1976), p. 15.

64. *Alumni News*, 58 (Summer 1970), p. 9; 64 (Winter 1976), p. 15; Institutional Self-Study Report, 1972, p. 127; Ferguson, 30 June 1977, to Cleon F. Thompson, with enclosure, Sp, Ferguson Papers; Research Triangle Institute, draft report, 30 May 1977, in Remedial Education, Assistant VCAA Records.

65. *Carolinian*, 21 May 1965.

66. Ad Hoc Committee on University Racial Policies report, [Aug. 1969], Ad Hoc Comm. folder, Ferguson Papers.

67. Marilyn M. Barker, Admissions Policies Committee minutes, 20 Feb. 1984, in Admissions Policies Committee, VCAA Records.

68. Office of Institutional Research, Highlights from the Spring 1979 Survey of Student Perceptions . . . , Oct. 1979, in Race Relations, Assistant VCAA Records.

69. Keller, *Academic Strategy*, p. 18.

70. Geiger, *Research and Relevant Knowledge*, pp. 262–63.

71. Faculty Council Minutes, 19 May 1964.

72. See Odessa Patrick and Ernestine Small, in *Alumni News*, 68 (Spring 1980), pp. 12–14; OH: Catherine Turner, 1 Oct. 1990.

73. Table: UNCG Full-Time Work Force Complement, 1975–86, Chancellor's Cabinet Records, 11 Dec. 1986.

74. OH: Jeannette Dean, 16 March 1990; H.L. Ferguson, 16 July 1963, to Singletary, F, Singletary Papers; Table: Ethnic Census Survey Summary, [1972], O–Po, Ferguson Papers.

75. Ad Hoc Committee on University Race Policies report, [Aug. 1969], pp. 32–37, Ad Hoc Comm. folder, Ferguson Papers.

76. Correspondence in N–Non, 1969, Ferguson Papers.

77. H.L. Ferguson, 11 May 1971, to Ferguson, N, Ferguson Papers; Ad Hoc Committee on Faculty Governance, minutes, 11 Nov. 1971, in Faculty Governance Committee Minutes, Assistant VCAA Records.

78. Notes on Open Forum Held Regarding Report on Faculty Governance . . . , 20 March 1972, in Faculty Governance Committee Minutes, Assistant VCAA Records; Elizabeth Booker and Paula Osborne, 28 April 1972, "Greetings!!", in AASA, Assistant VCAA Records; Elizabeth Booker, 3 Aug. 1972, to Ferguson; Ferguson, 8 Aug. 1972, to Booker; Stanley Jones, 27 Sept. 1972, to Elizabeth Sellers, Ca–Com; AASA Executive Committee, 13 March 1975, to Deans, Department Heads and Directors, A–Ad, Ferguson Papers.

79. *Carolinian*, 11 April 1978; Ferguson, 15 Sept. 1967, to John W. Kennedy and Mereb Mossman, U–Y, Ferguson Papers; Deans' Council Minutes, 10 Feb. 1970.

80. Deans' Council Minutes, 10 Feb., 14 April 1970; 14 July 1971; 13 Sept. 1972; Institutional Self-Study, 1972, Fifth Year Report, 1977, pp. 13–14; Ann P. Saab, 4 Feb. 1982, to Wm. E. Moran, Consent Decree folder, Moran Papers; OH: Stanley Jones, 27 Dec. 1990; Paula Andris, 23 April 1991. Many records of these joint dealings are in A&T State U., Comm. in Cooperation With, VCAA Records.

81. Richard Bardolph, 8 May, 17 Sept. 1970, to Robert L. Miller, in N.C. A&T, 1970–73, VCAA Records.

82. Deans' Council Minutes, 25 April 1972; Sarah V. Kirk and Virginia J. Stephens, 24 June 1986, to Nathan F. Simms and Elisabeth A. Zinser, Arts & Sciences: Social Work, Moran Papers.

83. Eloise R. Lewis, 18 March 1974, to Stanley Jones, in Cooperation with A&T, VCAA Records.

84. See, besides the report from Eloise Lewis just cited, the other correspondence in Cooperation with A&T, VCAA Records, and Deans' Council Minutes, 1 May 1974, 1 Sept. 1975; Summary of Program Development, Library Science/Educational Technology Division, 9 June 1978, in School: Education, Ferguson Papers; Nursing School, annual reports, 1977–78, pp. 89–90, 96–97; 1978–79, p. 102.

85. Stanley Jones, 22 June 1977, to Glenn F. Rankin, Schools: B/E–Ed, Ferguson Papers. For President Friday's concern in 1977 about possible duplications at UNCG and A&T, see the notes of a conference between UNC and UNCG administrators, 20 Oct. 1977, in Graduate School, Moran Papers, 1980, and Friday, 1 Nov. 1977, to Lewis C. Dowdy and James S. Ferguson, Deans' Council Minutes, Nov. 1977.

86. Ferguson, 21 Nov. 1969, to William E. Highsmith, Al–Ay, Ferguson Papers.

87. See the extensive correspondence filed under "Consortium" in the Ferguson Papers of 1970 and 1971.

88. Deans' Council Minutes, 28 Feb. 1973, 9 April 1975, Feb. 1978, March 1979; Table: Greater Greensboro Consortium, Report on Interchange of Students, Fall . . . 1982, in Greensboro Consortium, Assistant VCAA Records; Ann P. Saab, 4 Feb. 1982, to Wm. E. Moran, Consent Decree, Moran Papers.

89. Academic Policies Committee Minutes, 13 Sept. 1973; *Carolinian*, 27 Sept. 1977; Ferguson and Lewis C. Dowdy, 24 Aug. 1978, to Wm. Friday, Budget, Moran Papers, 1980.

90. Academic Policies Committee Minutes, 8 Oct. 1970, 17 May, 29 July 1971, 12 May, 14 Sept., 9 Nov. 1972, 8 March 1973; Deans' Council Minutes, 25 April, 18 Oct. 1972; Robert L. Miller, 23 Feb. 1973, to Stanley L. Jones, all in Academic Policies Committee Records.

91. Institutional Self-Study, 1972, Fifth Year Report, 1977, p. 22.

92. See correspondence in Academic Policies Committee folder, 1972, Ferguson Papers.

93. Background of Guilford Technical Institute's College Transfer Program, with Raymond J. Needham, 13 April 1982, to Wm. E. Moran, and Admissions Policies Committee Minutes, 26 Oct. 1982, in Guilford Technical Community College, VCAA Records.

Chapter 22 Notes

1. These are the author's counts from the annual catalogs, omitting *emeriti*. Faculty totals vary from one source to another, only sometimes arising from the enumeration of just full-time faculty. All faculty (and student) totals are approximate.

2. Stanley Jones, 21 March 1976, to Ferguson, Ac, Ferguson Papers.

3. Geiger, *Research and Relevant Knowledge*, pp. 218–19; Bowen and Rudenstine, *In Pursuit of the PhD*, pp. 9–10; Freeland, *Academia's Golden Age*, p. 381.

4. Harris, *Statistical Portrait*, p. 497.

5. The 70 percent figure for 1979 is a compromise between 69 and 71 percent given in two divergent sources. For 1963, see Institutional Self-Study, 1962: Fifth Year Report, 1967, p. IV-2. For 1979, see Institutional Self-Study Report, 1992, p. II-35, and UNCG *Fact Book*, 1979–80, p. 63.

6. West, "Women Faculty," p. 26; Finkelstein, *American Academic Profession*, pp. 39–40, 181; Graham, "Expansion & Exclusion," pp. 768–73; Bowen and Schuster, *American Professors*, pp. 55–57; Astin and Bayer, "Sex Discrimination in Academe," pp. 335–45; Chamberlain, *Women in Academe*, pp. 124, 258, 260.

7. Table I: Number of Full-Time Faculty by Sex with Highest Degree, First Semester 1963–64, [1963], Faculty folder, Singletary Papers.

8. Institutional Self-Study, 1972, Visiting Committee Report, p. 77.

9. John L. Saunders, Academic and Non-Academic Employment by Sex and Race at UNC-G, 21 July 1971, Equal folder, Ferguson Papers; Mereb Mossman, in *Alumni News*, 59 (Fall 1970), pp. 19–20; Gallien, "Coeducational Transition," p. 101. For the desire to attract male students, see OH: Jane Mitchell, 29 Nov. 1990.

10. UNCG *Fact Book*, 1979–80, pp. 59, 61.

11. Institutional Self-Study, 1972, Fifth Year Report, 1977, pp. 27–29; Table 3: Teaching Faculty Data 1973–74, 1978–82, in Affirmative Action, p. 12, UNCG Planning Process, 1980–83.

12. Ferguson, 3 Feb. 1978, to Linda W. Little, Alumni Assn. folder, Ferguson Papers.

13. Ferguson, 24 May 1977, to the Faculty, A–Ac, Ferguson Papers.

14. Keller, *Academic Strategy*, p. 10; Lewis, *Marginal Worth*, p. 23; Bowen and Schuster, *American Professors*, pp. 80–81, 84, 88–89, 95, 101–02.

15. Annual compensation tables in *AAUP Bulletin/Academe*, spring or summer issues, 1964, 1969, 1973, 1979; David Shelton, 3 May 1966, to UNCG Chapter of AAUP, Sa–Sc, Singletary Papers; John Harris, 8 Sept. 1966, to Singletary, Am–As, Singletary Papers; Table: Consolidated University, Average Salaries and Faculty Structure, 17 April 1968, I folder, Ferguson Papers.

16. Institutional Self-Study Report, 1972, pp. 330–31.

17. Mereb Mossman, 14 Nov. 1963, to Visiting Committee, B. of T., Singletary Papers; Singletary, annual report, 30 June 1966, Ca–Ch, Singletary Papers.

18. See Ferguson, 11 May 1967, to Wm. C. Friday, F, Ferguson Papers.

19. Finkelstein, *American Academic Profession*, p. 194.

20. See Astin and Bayer, "Sex Discrimination in Academe," pp. 342, 345; Cox and Astin, "Sex Differentials in Faculty Salaries," pp. 290–98; Johnson and Stafford, "Earnings and Promotion of Women Faculty," pp. 901–02; Bellas, "Faculty Salaries," p. 73; Chamberlain, *Women in Academe*, p. 262.

21. Margaret Hunt, Report of the AAUP Committee on the Salaries of Men and Women Full-Time Faculty Members, 23 Feb. 1966, in AAUP Statistics, VCAA Records. (See also her tables of 1 April 1965 in ibid.); Institutional Self-Study Report, 1972, pp. 336–37, and ibid., Visiting Committee report, p. 77; Affirmative Action, p. 34, in UNCG Planning Process, 1980–83; Academic Salary Averages... 1972–73, with Deans' Council Minutes, 10 Jan. 1973.

22. Institutional Self-Study, 1972, Visiting Committee report, p. 42; Stanley L. Jones, 17 April 1973, to Robert L. Miller, Arts/Sciences, Ferguson Papers.

23. Academic Policies Committee Minutes, 9 Jan. 1964; Deans' Council Minutes, 27 Jan. 1970; Institutional Self-Study Report, 1972, pp. 338–40.

24. Jencks and Riesman, *Academic Revolution*, pp. 14–19; Boyer, *College*, p. 5; Lewis, *Marginal Worth*, pp. 50–51; Freeland, *Academia's Golden Age*, pp. 96–97.

25. Faculty Council Voting Privilege, with Faculty Council Minutes, 21 May 1963.

26. J.A. Bryant, 14 Dec. 1966, to Ferguson; Ferguson, 20 Dec. 1966, to Bryant, F–G, Ferguson Papers; *Campus Calendar*, 10–23 Feb. 1986; OH: Betsy Umstead, 7 Dec. 1989; Paula Andris, 23 April 1991; Nancy White, 4 Dec. 1989.

27. Faculty Governance Committee minutes, 18 Dec. 1970, 10 May 1971, 16 Nov. 1972, Assistant VCAA Records; Faculty Council Minutes, 21 April 1971, 19 March 1974; Margaret Hunt, Statement, 21 Nov. 1972, Faculty folder, Ferguson Papers; Instrument of Government... July 1, 1974, in Faculty Governance, 1970–76, Ad Hoc Committee Records.

28. Academic Policies Committee minutes, 17 Jan. 1962, Academic Policies Committee Records.

29. Dean of the Faculty, Notes on Academic Matters for the Visiting Committee ..., 7 Dec. 1965, B. of T., Ferguson Papers; OH: Robert L. Miller, 23 Jan. 1990; Kendon Smith, 18 Oct. 1989.

30. Robert L. Miller, 27 Jan. 1969, to Mereb Mossman, D; Stanley L. Jones, 13 July 1973, to Ferguson, A–Ac, Ferguson Papers; Administrative Council minutes, 9 Nov. 1973, in Arts & Sciences College, VCAA Records; Robert L. Miller, 9 Sept. 1974, to Stanley Jones, with list of department heads and dates of appointment, in Arts & Sciences, Headship Review Process, VCAA Records; OH: Robert L. Miller, 23 Jan. 1990; William Lane, 15 Nov. 1990.

31. Faculty Council Minutes, 21 May 1963; Ferguson, 31 Aug. 1971, to Wm. Friday, U–Y, Ferguson Papers; Deans' Council Minutes, 10 Sept. 1971; OH: Helen A. Thrush, 20 Sept. 1990; Elisabeth Bowles, 4 Dec. 1990.

32. Institutional Self-Study Report, 1962, p. X-17.

33. Faculty Governance Committee minutes, 4 Nov. 1971, Assistant VCAA Records.

34. James H. Allen, 28 Oct. 1977, to Ferguson; Ferguson, 31 Oct. 1977, to Randy Sides, SGA-Summer, Ferguson Papers; Trustee Minutes, 17 Feb. 1978.

35. Faculty Governance Committee minutes, 4 Nov. 1971, Assistant VCAA Records; OH: Cheryl Callahan, 19 Jan. 1990.

36. See OH: Rosemary McGee, 21 May 1990; Kendon Smith, 18 Oct. 1989.

37. Faculty Council Minutes, 15 April 1969.

38. Ernest A. Lynton, in Johnson and Bell, *Metropolitan Universities*, p. xix.

39. Lewis, *Marginal Worth*, pp. 28–30.

40. See Alexander E. Sidorowicz, "The Outreach Role of the Fine and Performing Arts," in Johnson and Bell, *Metropolitan Universities*, p. 299.

41. Lewis, *Marginal Worth*, pp. 1–7, 28–36, 46, 53–57, 66–67.

42. For discussion of this issue, in addition to those already cited, see Hexter, "Publish or Perish," pp. 60–77; Lucas, *Crisis in the Academy*, pp. 190–94; Clark, "Small Worlds, Different Worlds," p. 25; Boyer, *College*, pp. 4, 121–25; Cross, "Improving the Quality of Instruction," pp. 289–90.

43. See discussion in Deans' Council Minutes, 11 Dec. 1969; OH: Robert Miller, 23 Jan. 1990.

44. See *Carolinian*, 19 Feb. 1965, 17 Feb. 1967; Report of Self-Study Committee on Planning for the Future, p. III-99, preceding Deans' Council Minutes, 14 July 1971; OH: Rosemary McGee, 21 May 1990; Marian Solleder, 11 Dec. 1990.

45. SGA Minutes, 11 Oct. 1971; AAUP Chapter, 14 Oct. 1971, to the Faculty, in AAUP Correspondence, VCAA Records; Faculty Council Minutes, 19 Oct. 1971 (the vote was postponed apparently to November, but it was not found in the November or December minutes); Institutional Self-Study Report, 1972, pp. 632–36; *Alumni News*, 60 (Winter 1972), p. 13; OH: C. Bob Clark, 8 Nov. 1990.

46. Stanley L. Jones, 7 Oct. 1977, to Academic Deans, in Arts & Sciences College, with Administrative Council minutes, VCAA Records; *Carolinian*, 8 May 1972.

47. See the explanation of how the system worked, in Singletary, 22 July 1966, to Carl Frischknecht, T–W, Singletary Papers; Ferguson, 23 April 1969, to Committee for the Evaluation of the Alumni Teaching Excellence Awards, T, Ferguson Papers.

48. Richard Cox, 19 May 1978, to Mrs. Bern F. Bullard, Te–Ti; Eloise R. Lewis, 23 March 1979, to Ferguson, T, Ferguson Papers.

49. *Carolinian*, 12 March 1968, 29 April 1969; Madeleine Bombeld, 9 Dec. 1970, to Dear Professor, Sco–So, Ferguson Papers; Deans' Council Minutes, 24 Oct. 1968, 8 Dec. 1970, 12 Jan. 1971; Vertical File: SCORE; Institutional Self-Study Report, 1972, pp. 200–02.

50. Report of the Ad Hoc Committee ... to Evaluate Teaching Effectiveness, 1 Aug. 1974, with Deans' Council Minutes, 30 Oct. 1974; ibid., 3 Oct. 1977.

51. Deans' Council Minutes, 25 Feb. 1965; 6 Sept., 1 Dec. 1966; 6 April 1967; Kenneth Howe, 4 Oct. 1965, to Mereb Mossman, Teaching loads, Ferguson Papers; John Beeler et al., 5 May 1966, to Richard Bardolph, Teaching, Singletary Papers; Institutional Self-Study Report, 1972, pp. 341–44.

52. Ferguson, 12 Jan. 1966, to Wm. Friday, Q–R; John W. Kennedy, 20 Dec. 1967, to Rudolph Pate, Q–R; Mereb Mossman, [May 1970], to Deans and Department Heads, and 29 Sept. 1970, to Ferguson; Ferguson, 14 Oct. 1970, to Mossman, Q–R, Ferguson Papers; Sponsored Research and Special Projects, 1966–68, in UNC-Visiting Committee, 1968, VCAA Records; Jean Eason, A Proposal, Sept. 1979, Sponsored Programs, Moran Papers.

53. Mereb Mossman, 14 Nov. 1963, to Visiting Committee, B. of T., Singletary Papers; Deans' Council Minutes, 18 Nov. 1965; Institutional Self-Study Report, 1972, pp. 323–24.

54. Research Assignments/Leaves of Absence, 1977–82, R, Moran Papers, 1984. For national background, see Geiger, *To Advance Knowledge*, 75; Brubacher and Rudy, *Higher Education in Transition*, p. 386; Eells and Hollis, *Sabbatical Leave*, pp. 1–15; Blackwell, *College and University Administration*, p. 36.

55. Institutional Self-Study Report, 1972, pp. 322–23.

56. Deans' Council Minutes, 26 Oct. 1967; Ferguson, 6 March 1973, to Raymond H. Dawson, B. of G.; Ferguson, 2 Sept. 1976, to the Faculty, Ac, Ferguson Papers.

57. Full-Time Faculty and Administrators with Tenure, 1973–74 and 1982–83, in Academic Affairs: General Information, VCAA Records; *Alumni News*, 63 (Winter 1975), p. 33. For national figures, see Bowen and Schuster, *American Professors*, pp. 44–45.

58. Report to the Visiting Committee by Representatives of the [AAUP] Chapter, Nov. 1965, B. of T.; Ferguson, 6 April 1972, to James Cooley, Am, Ferguson Papers. For national background concerning the AAUP, see Ladd, *Professors, Unions*, pp. 41–43.

59. King, *Multicampus University*, pp. 57–67; Link, *William Friday*, pp. 109–41. For UNCG's reaction, see the Speaker Ban folder, 1963, and B. of T. folder, 1966, in the Singletary Papers, and the 1965 Speaker Ban folders in the Ferguson Papers.

60. See Ferguson, 16 Feb. 1970, to Opal L. Raymer, and 29 April 1970, to Mrs. I. Frank Peake, Cl–Co, Ferguson Papers.

Chapter 23 Notes

1. Report of All-University Calendar Committee, [1966], Ca–Ch, Singletary Papers.

2. Nancye Baker, Presentation to Visiting Committee, 9 Dec. 1965, B. of T.; Student Resolution Concerning Academic Calendar Change, [1968], A; Ferguson, 12 May 1971, to Marsha Dishman, Ca–Co, Ferguson Papers; Report of All-University Calendar Committee, [1966], Ca–Ch, Singletary Papers; Faculty Council Minutes, 18 Nov. 1969, 20 Jan., 15 Dec. 1970, 16 Nov. 1971.

3. Faculty Council Minutes, 18 Nov. 1969, 20 Jan. 1970.

4. Deans' Council Minutes, 7 April 1960, 23 Jan. 1964, 6 Sept. 1966, 23 Feb. 1967, 6 Oct. 1970, 12 Jan., 3 March 1971, 6 Sept. 1972; Academic Policies Committee Minutes, 7 Jan., 11 Feb. 1971; Faculty Council Minutes, 12 April 1971; David Shelton, 21 July 1970, to Mereb Mossman, Bus/Econ School, and Stanley L. Jones, 12 Nov. 1973, to Lawrence E. Hart, Music School, both in VCAA Records; Clarence Shipton, 12 Oct. 1970, to Ferguson, D, Ferguson Papers.

5. Stanley L. Jones, 25 Oct. 1973, to Academic Deans, in Evening Classes, VCAA Records; Herbert Wells, 25 July 1974, to Ferguson, with Deans' Council Minutes, 14 Aug. 1974; H. Hoyt Price, 6 Feb. 1975, to Deans and Department Heads, with Deans' Council Minutes, 12 Feb. 1975; Summary of Evening Offerings and Enrollments, 1976–78, in Evening Classes, VCAA Records; *Greensboro Daily News*, 19 Nov. 1978, in Vertical File: Acad. Affairs; *Alumni News*, 68 (Fall 1979), pp. 8–9.

6. Tommie Lou Smith, 11 Feb. 1964, to Singletary, Am–As, Singletary Papers; Associate Dean, annual report, 23 June 1967, in Associate Dean's Office, VCAA Records; Office of the Dean of Academic Advising, Self-Study and Plan, May 1985, in Self-Study and Plans, Assistant VCAA Records; *Alumni News*, 53 (Winter 1965), pp. 22–23; OH: Tommie Lou Smith, 18 Sept. 1990; Elizabeth Booker, 17 May 1991.

7. Levine and Weingart, *Reform of Undergraduate Education*, pp. 112–13, 120–25; Lamont, *Campus Shock*, 57–64; Herbert Wells, in *Alumni News*, 63 (Summer 1975), p. 17.

8. Herbert Wells, 30 Oct. 1975, to Stanley L. Jones, A–Ad, Ferguson Papers; H. Hoyt Price, 24 Jan. 1975, to Stanley Jones, in Grades 1969–82; Donald J. Reichard, 23 April 1980, to Academic Deans et al., in Grade Distribution Data; and Herbert Wells, 17 Sept. 1980, to Walter Puterbaugh, in Grade Point Averages, all in Assistant VCAA Records; *Alumni News*, 62 (Spring 1974), p. 40; 63 (Summer 1975), p. 17; 64 (Spring 1976), p. 19; 64 (Summer 1976), pp. 1–3; *Carolinian*, 29 Sept. 1977. For later years, see Bob Newton, 4 Dec. 1989, to Donald V. DeRosa, I (letter), Moran Papers, 1990; UNCG *Fact Book*, 1995–96, pp. IV-12, 16–19.

9. Minutes of Singletary meeting with Visiting Committee, Nov. 1961, B. of T.; Mereb Mossman, Report to Visiting Committee, 26 Oct. 1962, Ba–Bo; Summary of Program Developments in the Three-Year Master's Program . . . , 1961–1962, [1962], H, all in Singletary Papers; *Alumni News*, 53 (Fall 1964), pp. 6–7; *Catalog*, 1966–67, pp. 80–83; Self Study, 1985: Honors Program, Provost Records.

10. Enrollment in the Honors Program, 1962–68, with Faculty Council Minutes, 15 April 1969; Program for Especially-Gifted Students, in Honors Council, VCAA Records; Self Study, 1985: Honors Program, Provost Records; OH: Peggy Whalen-Levitt, 21 May 1991.

11. J. Formby, [15 Dec. 1969], and Elaine Burgess, 5 March 1971, to Honors Council, in Honors Council, VCAA Papers; Herbert Wells, 22 March 1974, to Mrs. Arnetha T. Robinson, in Honors Program, Assistant VCAA Records.

12. Tables: Bachelor's Degrees, and Master's and Doctor's Degrees Conferred at North Carolina Colleges and Universities, 1974–75, [1975], J–M; Degrees Conferred, 1976–77, B. of G., [1977], Ferguson Papers.

13. Table: Degrees Granted by the University . . . , 1970–75, [1976], Q–R, Ferguson Papers.

14. Rudolph, *Curriculum*, pp. 245–55; Lamont, *Campus Shock*, pp. 46–53; Freeland, *Academia's Golden Age*, pp. 109–11, 407–09. See also Millett, *Academic Community*, pp. 126–28; Boyer, *College*, 3–4; Keller, *Academic Strategy*, pp. 15–16; Levine and Weingart, *Reform of Undergraduate Education*, pp. 8, 20–24, 51.

15. Final Report of the Committee to Review General Degree Requirements (Kupferer Committee), March 1972, with Faculty Council Minutes, 18 April 1972; Institutional Self-Study report, 1972, pp. 105–15, 183–84; Ibid., Visiting Comm. report, pp. 17–18; *Alumnae/i News*, 52 (April 1964), pp. 6–7; 61 (Spring 1973), p. 14; OH: Robert Miller, 23 Jan. 1990; Robert Calhoon, 1 Feb. 1990. For the general education requirements in 1966 and 1976, see *Catalog*, 1966–67, pp. 59–63; 1976–77, pp. 75–81.

16. Ferguson, Report to Board of Directors of the Excellence Fund, 4 Dec. 1972, Ex, Ferguson Papers.

17. Faculty Council Minutes, 21 March 1978; Stanley L. Jones, 31 July 1980, to John Merriman, with Physical Education Proposal of 16 Nov. 1977, in Curriculum Committee, VCAA Records.

18. Academic Policies Committee Minutes, 10 Oct. 1963; *Alumni News*, 61 (Spring 1973), p. 14.

19. Clarence O. Shipton, 1 March, 27 Oct. 1967, to Ferguson; Shipton, 19 April 1967, to Mereb Mossman, D, Ferguson Papers; Shipton, 24 Jan. 1969, to William V. Graves, Dean of Students for Student Services Records, 1967–83.

20. See the correspondence and other documents in ROTC, VCAA Records, and ROTC, Assistant VCAA Records.

21. Gallien, "Coeducational Transition," pp. 107–08; Freeland, *Academia's Golden Age*, p. 107.

22. James Ferguson, in *Alumni News*, 53 (Fall 1964), pp. 4–5.

23. Donald J. Reichard, 3 July 1992, to Wm. E. Moran, copy in possession of author; OH: Robert Miller, 23 Jan. 1990; C. Bob Clark, 8 Nov. 1990; Kendon Smith, 18 Oct. 1989; Richard Bardolph, 14 May 1991; Robert Eason, 14 Feb. 1996; Stanley Jones, 27 Dec. 1990; Hollis Rogers, 10 April 1990; Mereb Mossman, 11 Oct. 1989.

24. Registrar, Earned Degrees Conferred . . . 1975–1979, in Enrollments, Assistant VCAA Records.

25. John W. Kennedy, 21 Oct. 1971, to Ferguson; Kennedy, 10 Dec. 1971, to Edwin L. Lively, Grad School folder, Ferguson Papers; Deans' Council Minutes, 13 Sept. 1972, 29 July 1977 with John W. Kennedy, 3 Aug. 1977, to Deans, Department Heads et al.; Institutional Self-Study Report, 1972, pp. 590–91.

26. News Release, [May or June] 1967, M–N, Ferguson Papers; Deans' Council Minutes, 19 May 1971.

27. History of Position No. 867, with Stanley L. Jones, 19 July 1973, to John W. Kennedy, Gr; Assistantships 1968–69—1977–78, Grad Sc–St, 1978; John W. Kennedy, 8 March 1979, to Ferguson, G, all in Ferguson Papers.

28. Appendix B: Analysis of Tuition Waivers... 1977–1978, in Graduate School, General, VCAA Records; Strengthen Graduate Assistants, in Change Budget Requests, 1981–83, Budget folder, Moran Papers, 1980. For the damage done to graduate work, see the budget request rationale just cited plus H.T. Kirby-Smith, 10 Oct. 1972, to William Lane, Te–Tu, Ferguson Papers.

29. See Powell, "Collection Development," pp. 60–61.

30. Rothstein, "Service to Academia," pp. 101–02.

31. Institutional Self-Study, 1962, Fifth Year report, 1967, p. V-11; UNCG *Fact Book*, 1979–80, p. 71; [James H. Thompson], statement on the library, ca. 1979, in Library, General, VCAA Records; Hamlin, *University Library*, pp. 125, 129–31.

32. Library, Fifth Year report, May 1967, in Mission of the Library, Office of Librarian Records.

33. *Carolinian*, 22 Sept. 1970; J.H. Thompson, 24 April 1972, to N.H. Gurley, O–Po, Ferguson Papers.

34. James H. Thompson, in *Alumni News*, 62 (Spring 1974), pp. 3–6; Jackson Library... Mission and Goals Statement, 5 Jan. 1984, Vertical File: Library (General).

35. James H. Thompson, 18 Jan. 1973, to Stanley L. Jones, S–Sch; Ferguson, 29 June 1977, to Wm. Friday, Sa–Sc, Ferguson Papers; [James H. Thompson], statement on the library, ca. 1979, in Library, General, VCAA Records; OH: Nancy Fogarty, 27 March 1990; James Thompson, 4 April 1990; Emilie Mills, 30 Jan. 1990. For the faculty status of librarians, see Academic Policies Committee Minutes, 2 April 1963; Singletary, 19 April 1963, to John Beeler, Am–Ay; Singletary, 11 Nov. 1963, to Wm. Friday, L–M, Singletary Papers; Institutional Self-Study Report, 1972, pp. 376–77; Thompson, 13 Oct. 1972, to Ferguson, University Code, Ferguson Papers; Report of Library Committee on Status and Library Governance, 29 Nov. 1972, in Vertical File: Library Committee on Status ....; Ferguson, 2 Sept. 1976, to the Faculty, in Academic Freedom and Tenure Committee Records; OH: Nancy Fogarty, 27 March 1990; Hamlin, *University Library*, p. 76; Downs, "Role of the Academic Librarian," pp. 498–99; Rothstein, "Service to Academia," p. 102.

36. Edmund Berkeley, [Jan. 1967], to Charles Adams, L; James H. Thompson, 28 March 1975, to Ferguson, D, Ferguson Papers; Thompson, 4 June 1975, to Ferguson; Thompson, 29 March 1976, to Emilie Mills; Mills, 29 March 1976, to Vice Chancellors and Deans, with responses; Mills, 7 July 1977, to Hugh Hagaman; Thompson, annual report, 1976–77, in Archives, VCAA Records; OH: Emilie Mills, 30 Jan. 1990.

37. Cora Paul Bomar, 22 Oct. 1957, to Gordon Blackwell; [Anna Reger], Training for Librarianship at Woman's College, with Reger, 4 Nov. 1957, to Blackwell, in Correspondence, Office of Librarian Records.

38. Correspondence, 22 Oct. 1957 to 11 Sept. 1961, in Office of Librarian Records; Elinor Yungmeyer, 28 July 1978, to Mary Frances Johnson, in Schools: Education, Ferguson Papers; Self Study, 1985: Education, Library Science & Educational Technology, Provost Records; Visiting Team Report on the Department of Library and Information Studies, [1988], Education: LIS Accreditation, Moran Papers.

39. Correspondence in Cl–Cu, Blackwell Papers, 1959.

40. Information Supplied to State Board of Higher Education, 20 Feb. 1970, pp. 15–16, BHE, Ferguson Papers; OH: Paula Andris, 23 April 1991.

41. Roscoe J. Allen, 13 March 1974, to Ferguson; Ferguson, 2 April 1974, to Allen; Joseph R. Denk, 14 Nov. 1974, to Ferguson, C; B & C Budget Request for 1975–77 (1974), pp. 6, 14, 32; T.W. Hildebrandt, 28 June 1978, to Ferguson, Comm–Comp, Ferguson Papers; *Student Handbook*, 1977–78, pp. 24–25; James W. Crews, 15 Nov. 1978, to Stanley L. Jones, in Computer Education/Science, VCAA Records; Report of the University Committee on Comput-

ing and Related Technology, April 1984, pp. 6–8, in Computing & Related Technology, VCAA Records; Terry G. Seaks et al., Report of Committee on Computing Needs, 5 Dec. 1980, in Computing Needs, Business/Economics School Records.

Chapter 24 Notes

1. Developments in the Undergraduate Program in the College of Arts and Sciences, [March 1970], Arts & Sciences, Ferguson Papers. For early thoughts about a computer science program, see the reports and correspondence, 1978–80, in Computer Education-Computer Science, VCAA Records.

2. E.E. Posey, 6 Aug. 1979, to R.L. Miller, Arts & Sciences, Moran Papers; OH: Mereb Mossman, 11 Oct. 1989; Robert Miller, 23 Jan. 1990.

3. Bruce Eberhart, Plans for Development of New Programs in Biology, [May 1966], Teaching, Singletary Papers; College Science Improvement Program, grant application, 31 Jan. 1967, p. 15, N–P; Biology Department-UNC-G, [ca. April 1968], B. of T. Visiting Committee; William Wells, 17 Dec. 1968, to John W. Kennedy, Departments A–E; Allen Tucker, 20 April 1970, outside comment on the Ph.D. in biology, Arts/Sciences; Ferguson, 30 July 1970, to William Wells, BHE; Bruce M. Eberhart, 11 Aug. 1970, to [John W.] Kennedy, Arts/Sciences; William Wells, 25 Aug. 1970, to Kennedy, Arts/Sciences; Robert M. Johnson, 16 Feb. 1971, to Kennedy, Arts/Sciences; Ferguson, 30 July 1971, to Wm. Friday, BHE; Stanley L. Jones, 3 May 1974, to Robert W. Williams, Degree Programs, Ferguson Papers; OH: Mereb Mossman, 11 Oct. 1989; Robert Miller, 23 Jan. 1990; Hollis Rogers, 10 April 1990; Robert Eason, 14 Feb. 1996.

4. Self Study, 1985: Biology, Provost Records.

5. E.K. Graham, 6 Jan. 1956, to Mereb Mossman, Departments, Graham Papers; Donald B. Anderson, Report to the Chancellor and Dean of the Faculty, [rec'd. 10 March 1964], Sa–So, Singletary Papers; OH: Sherri Forrester, 14 Dec. 1989; Mary Katsikas, 6 Feb. 1990; Walter Puterbaugh, in *Alumni News*, 60 (Summer 1972), p. 19.

6. Walter Puterbaugh, Ten Year Projection, 15 July 1966, Teaching, Singletary Papers; College Science Improvement Program, grant application, 31 Jan. 1967, pp. 22–26, Departments N–P, Ferguson Papers; OH: Sherri Forrester, 14 Dec. 1989; Mary Katsikas, 6 Feb. 1990 (incl. quotation).

7. Donald B. Anderson, Report to the Chancellor and Dean of the Faculty, [rec'd. 10 March 1964], Sa–So, Singletary Papers.

8. Clifton Bob Clark, 22 April 1968, to Trustees' Visiting Committee, B. of T. Visiting Committee, Ferguson Papers; OH: C. Bob Clark, 8 Nov. 1990.

9. Institutional Self-Study, 1972, Visiting Committee report, p. 41. See also OH: Robert Eason, 14 Feb. 1996.

10. Kendon Smith, 30 June 1966, to Mereb Mossman, Teaching, Singletary Papers; College Science Improvement Program, grant application, 31 Jan. 1967, pp. 40–43, Departments N–P, Ferguson Papers; OH: Kendon Smith, 18 Oct. 1989.

11. Frank W. Finger, 18 Aug. 1969, and Donald B. Lindsley, 19 Aug. 1969, to Ferguson, Departments M–S, Ferguson Papers; OH: Robert Eason, 14 Feb. 1996.

12. Robert Eason, 31 Oct. 1967, to Mereb Mossman, Departments N–P, Ferguson Papers; Report on the Clinical Psychology Program . . . , [July 1981], Arts/Sciences: Psychology, Moran Papers; OH: Kendon Smith, 18 Oct. 1989; Robert Eason, 14 Feb. 1996; Gail Hennis, 18 Jan. 1990.

13. See [W.W. Pierson], Some Comments to the Visiting Committee . . . , [Fall 1960], B. of T., Pierson Papers.

14. [J.A. Bryant], English Department Staff, 1964–1965, [1964], Departments A–Hi, Singletary Papers.

15. John W. Kennedy, 14 May 1965, to Ferguson, G; J.A. Bryant, 2 July 1965, to Ferguson, with departmental Ph.D. proposal of 30 June 1965, Departments A–E, Ferguson Papers; OH: Robert Watson, 21 March 1990.

16. See J.A. Bryant, 21 Jan. 1966, to Mereb Mossman, Departments A–E, Singletary Papers; Alumni Assn. Board of Trustees minutes, 29 May 1969, Al–Ay, Ferguson Papers; OH: Fred Chappell, 7 March 1991.

17. Self Study, 1985: English, Provost Records; OH: William Lane, 15 Nov. 1990.

18. Leonard B. Beach, 18 Nov. 1966, to Ferguson; J.W. Ashton, 29 Nov. 1966, to Ferguson, Departments A–E, Ferguson Papers.

19. See Robert O. Stephens et al., 20 Nov. 1968, to Ferguson, Departments E–G, Ferguson Papers; OH: William Lane, 15 Nov. 1990; Tom Kirby-Smith, 10 Sept. 1990; Robert Watson, 21 March 1990; Gail Hennis, 18 Jan. 1990.

20. For earlier efforts to upgrade the writing program, see Robie Macauley and Lettie Rogers, 28 May 1952, to E.K. Graham et al., Departments A–G, Graham Papers; J.A. Bryant, 1 Oct. 1963, to J.S. Ferguson and Mereb Mossman, in English Department, VCAA Records.

21. Rosemary Yardley, in Greensboro *News & Record*, 9 Nov. 1994; Robert Watson, in *Alumni News*, 57 (Spring 1969), pp. 2–5; T. Kirby-Smith, 9 Feb. 1972, to Robert Watson et al., Gr; Kirby-Smith, 10 Oct. 1972, to Wm. Lane, Te–Tu; Kirby-Smith, 1 Oct. 1973, to John W. Kennedy, and 12 Nov. 1973, to Wm. C. Friday, Arts & Sciences, Ferguson Papers; OH: Robert Watson, 21 March 1990; Fred Chappell, 7 March 1991; Tom Kirby-Smith, 10 Sept. 1990; Fred Chappell interview in *Carolinian*, 30 March 1989; Finley, "A Noble Tradition," pp. 53–56. For Jarrell's death, see Meyers, "Death of Randall Jarrell," pp. 450–67.

22. Fred Chappell et al., Report on the Writing Program ..., Feb. 1979, Arts/Sciences, Ferguson Papers.

23. Fred Chappell, 1 Oct. 1968, to Dear Mac [Randolph Bulgin], Co, Ferguson Papers; *Carolinian*, 22 April 1966; OH: Fred Chappell, 7 March 1991; Tom Kirby-Smith, 10 Sept. 1990; *UNCG Bulletin*, (Spring 1992), p. 3; UNCG, *Campus* newsletter, v. 28, no. 10 (Nov.–Dec. 1978, p. 1.

24. Herman Middleton, 2 Jan. 1973, to Pearl G. Bradley, Arts/Sciences, Ferguson Papers.

25. [Herman Middleton], Department of Drama and Speech, the Next Ten Years, 1967–1977, [1966], Teaching, Singletary Papers.

26. See Robert L. Miller, 8 Nov. 1972, to Stanley L. Jones, Arts/Sciences Departments, Ferguson Papers.

27. Robert L. Miller, 8 Nov. 1972, to Stanley L. Jones, Arts/Sciences Departments, Ferguson Papers; Self Study, 1985: Communication & Theatre, Provost Records.

28. John Lee Jellicorse, 21 Feb. 1978, to Robert L. Miller, Arts/Sciences, Departments A–C, Ferguson Papers; Communication and Theatre department, Proposal for a School of Communication and Theatre, [1985]; Jellicorse, 11 Feb. 1979, to Stanley L. Jones, in Parkway Playhouse, VCAA Records; OH: Herman Middleton, 19 Feb. 1990.

29. W.C. Burton, in *Alumni News*, 61 (Spring 1973), pp. 22–25; OH: Herman Middleton, 19 Feb. 1990; John Jellicorse, 30 May 1979, to Robert L. Miller, Communication & Theatre, General, VCAA Records.

30. *Carolinian*, 11 Feb. 1966; *Greensboro Daily News*, 27 Feb. 1966, 28 Feb. 1967; *Alumni News*, 57 (Winter 1969), pp. 40–41; *Catalog*, 1971–72, p. 72; John Lee Jellicorse, Statement... Relevant to... Parkway Playhouse, 22 March 1975, Arts/Sciences, Ferguson Papers; *Coraddi*, May 1979, pp. 10–11; OH: Herman Middleton, 19 Feb. 1990.

31. "Gilbert F. Carpenter ...," nomination statement for the O. Max Gardner Award, with Eloise Lewis, 10 Jan. 1972, to Helen Yoder, Ga–Go; Table: SACS, UNCG Survey by Depart-

ment, [1977], So, Ferguson Papers; Department of Art and Weatherspoon Art Gallery, [1982], Art Center, Moran Papers; Greensboro *News & Record*, 2 Oct. 1986; OH: Gilbert Carpenter, 27 April 1990.

32. Morrison, *Rise of the Arts*, p. 31.

33. *Alumnae/i News*, 52 (Jan. 1964), p. 14; 59 (Summer 1971), pp. 12–13; "Weatherspoon Art Gallery," [1978], Academic Affairs, Ferguson Papers; James E. Tucker, 22 Sept. 1980, to E. Michael Lowder, W, Moran Papers; Fred L. Drake, 22 March 1984, to Hubert B. Humphrey, Weatherspoon, Moran Papers; *Carolinian*, 20 Jan. 1976; OH: Gilbert Carpenter, 27 April 1990.

34. *Greensboro Daily News*, 6 May 1979.

35. Lee Rigsby, 12 Feb. 1963, to Gov. Terry Sanford, Departments Ho–S, Singletary Papers; Alumnae Association Board of Trustees minutes, 31 May 1963, Alumni Association Records, 1899–1988; Covington and Ellis, *Terry Sanford*, pp. 308–09.

36. *Carolinian*, 9 April 1954; Arts Festival Committee, annual report, 11 May 1960, Arts Festival, VCAA Records; OH: Robert Watson, 21 March 1990; Jean Buchert, 19 Jan. 1990.

37. See OH: Gilbert Carpenter, 27 April 1990; Tom Kirby-Smith, 10 Sept. 1990.

38. See the correspondence in Unicorn Press, 1971–73, VCAA Records, and Un, Ferguson Papers, 1972; Wm. Friday, 24 Jan. 1973, to Ferguson, U, Ferguson Papers; correspondence between Joan Gregory et al. and Wm. Moran, 18 Oct., 26 Nov. 1979, U–W, Moran Papers; OH: Tom Kirby-Smith, 10 Sept. 1990.

39. Warren Ashby, 1 Dec. 1966, to John W. Kennedy, Departments N–S; George Schrader, 15 Jan. 1969, to Ferguson; Arthur C. Danto, 20 Jan. 1969, to Ferguson; Robert Rosthal, 22 May 1969, to Philosophy Search Committee, Departments M–S, Ferguson Papers.

40. Annual UNC–G Symposium in Philosophy, Narrative Statement, [1982], Arts/Sciences, Moran Papers.

41. Developments in the Undergraduate Program in the College of Arts and Sciences, [17 March 1970], Arts/Sciences; Alan B. Anderson, What is Religious Studies?, 7 Oct. 1978, Arts/Sciences, Departments E–R, Ferguson Papers.

42. J.A. Highsmith, 1 Dec. 1938, to W.C. Jackson; Jackson, 15 Dec. 1938, to Highsmith, H, Jackson Papers.

43. Advisory Committee Minutes, 3 June 1942; W.C. Jackson, 5 March 1947, to L.B. Hurley; Jackson, 17 Sept. 1947, to Lois V. McClure; Jackson, 9 Oct. 1947, to Clarence P. Shedd, Committees, Jackson Papers; Administrative Council minutes, 6 April 1955, A, Graham Papers; Thomas J.C. Smyth, 7 Sept. 1966, to Singletary, Departments N–S, Singletary Papers; William H. Poteat, Summary of Comments on a Department of Religion at UNC-G, [Sept. 1967]; R.L. Miller, 19 Nov. 1969, to Mereb Mossman, in Religious Studies, VCAA Records; Committee on a Program in Religion, 13 Dec. 1967, to Ferguson, Departments R–S; [Mereb Mossman], "B" Budget Requests for 1969–71 Biennium, 8 July 1968, Budget folder; Ferguson, 11 Feb. 1970, to Wm. Friday; Developments in the Undergraduate Program in the College of Arts and Sciences, [17 March 1970]; Mossman, 29 Sept. 1970, to Ferguson, Arts/Sciences, Ferguson Papers.

44. *Catalog*, 1971–72, pp. 276–77; 1981–82, pp. 223–25. For a history of religious studies as an academic field, see Hart, *The University Gets Religion*.

45. Paul B. Courtright, 21 Feb. 1984, to William E. Moran, Arts/Sciences, Religious Studies, Moran Papers.

46. SACS Commission on Colleges, UNCG, Survey by Department, [1977], So, Ferguson Papers.

47. See the Current-Mossman correspondence, 4 April–28 May 1963, in Departments A–Hi; Richard Bardolph, 25 July 1966, to Mereb Mossman, Teaching, Singletary Papers; Ferguson, 11 May 1967, to Wm. Friday, F, Ferguson Papers; *Alumni News*, 53 (Winter 1965), p. 27.

48. Allen W. Trelease, Interim report, departmental committee on the Ph.D., 1969, Departments E–Hi; [John W. Kennedy, Statement to the Visiting Committee, 23 March 1970], B. of T. Visiting Committee folder; Proposal for Doctor of Philosophy Degree in History, [April 1970], Budget folder; Ferguson, 30 July 1970, to William Wells, Bureau of Higher Education folder, Ferguson Papers; Richard Bardolph, 1 Sept. 1974, to Robert L. Miller, in History, VCAA Records; OH: Mereb Mossman, 11 Oct. 1989; Richard Bardolph, 14 May 1991; Robert Miller, 23 Jan. 1990.

49. Margaret Hunt, 18 Jan. 1966, to Richard Bardolph, Departments G–M; Bardolph, 25 July 1966, to Mereb Mossman, Teaching, Singletary Papers; Hunt, 21 Feb. 1967, to Bardolph, and, same date, to Ferguson, Departments G–H; Robert L. Miller, 3 Dec. 1968, to Mossman, Departments H–M, Ferguson Papers; Bardolph, 6 Nov. 1969, to Miller; Miller, 6 Nov. 1969, to Mossman, in Political Science, VCAA Records.

50. See the correspondence in Arts/Sciences, Ferguson Papers, 1971.

51. Academic Policies Committee Minutes, 13 May, 8 Dec. 1959, 14 Nov. 1963; Self Study, 1985: Geography, Provost Records; OH: Craig Dozier, 20 Oct. 1990.

52. Institutional Self-Study, 1972, Visiting Committee report, p. 22.

53. Alvin H. Scaff and Harriet J. Kupferer, 1 Dec. 1972, to Robert Miller; Miller, 23 Jan. 1973, to Scaff; Miller, 16 Aug. 1973, to Scaff and Kupferer, Sociology & Anthropology, General, VCAA Records; Kupferer and Scaff, 12 Feb. 1973, to Miller; Miller, 13 March 1973, to Stanley L. Jones; Jones, 30 March 1973, to Ferguson, Arts/Sciences, Ferguson Papers.

54. Institutional Self-Study, 1972, Visiting Committee report, p. 22; Alvin H. Scaff, 14 Dec. 1976, to Robert L. Miller; Scaff, [recd. 20 Dec. 1976], to Social Work Faculty, Arts/Sciences; Ferguson, 12 April 1977, to Miller, Arts/Sciences; correspondence, 1978, in Arts/Sciences: Social Work, Ferguson Papers; Deans' Council Minutes, 12 Jan. 1977, p. 5; Self Study, 1985: Social Work, Provost Records; OH: Harriet Kupferer, 27 Oct. 1989.

55. Deans' Council Minutes, 19 April 1972; *Alumni News*, Summer 1973, p. 26; Greensboro *News & Record*, 15 April 1990.

56. Burton R. Clark, 5 Jan. 1970, to Ferguson, Arts/Sciences; [John W. Kennedy, Statement to Trustees' Visiting Committee], 23 March 1970, B. of T. Visiting Committee folder, Ferguson Papers; Institutional Self-Study, 1972, Visiting Committee report, pp. 22–23.

57. Table: SACS, UNCG Survey by Department, [1977], So, Ferguson Papers; Institutional Self-Study, 1972, Visiting Committee report, p. 20; Robert L. Miller, 23 Feb. 1978, to Departments of History and Classical Civilization, Arts/Sciences, Departments A–C, Ferguson Papers.

58. Table: SACS, UNCG Survey by Department, [1977], So, Ferguson Papers.

59. [Charles Blend], 31 Jan. 1964, to Mereb Mossman; Stanley L. Jones, 5 March 1973, to George E. McSpadden, in Romance Languages, General, VCAA Records; George E. McSpadden, 6 Oct. 1972, to James S. Ferguson et al., Ex, Ferguson Papers; *Greensboro Daily News*, 20 July 1975; OH: George McSpadden, 1 Dec. 1990.

60. Table: SACS, UNCG Survey by Department, [1977], So, Ferguson Papers; Anne F. Baecker, 5 July 1966, to Mereb Mossman, Teaching, Singletary Papers; Baecker, 27 Nov. 1974, to Stanley L. Jones, in German/Russian Department, VCAA Records; Self Study, 1985: German & Russian, Provost Records.

61. Ferguson, 1 March 1973, to William E. Highsmith, As-Ay; Bert A. Goldman, 28 March 1974, to Stanley L. Jones, Acad A, Ferguson Papers; James C. Cooley et al., 17 Sept. 1982, to Wm. E. Moran, Deans' Council Records; Self Study, 1985: World Literature, Provost Records.

62. L.C. Wright, 17 May 1968, to Mereb Mossman, B, Ferguson Papers.

63. R.L. Miller, 21 Jan. 1969, to Ada M. Fisher, with notes of Afro-American Studies Committee meeting, 7 Feb. 1969, in Afro-American Studies, VCAA Records; Afro-American Studies Committee minutes, 27 Feb., 20 March 1969, and proposal for a new history course, 10 March 1969, in Ad–Af, Ferguson Papers; *Carolinian*, 28 Feb. 1969; OH: Robert Miller, 23 Jan. 1990.

64. Riesman, *On Higher Education*, pp. 141–48. See also Berube, *Urban University*, pp. 80–96; Record, "Black Studies Movement," pp. 192–202.

65. Chamberlain, *Women in Academe*, pp. 134–47; Deans' Council Minutes, 6 March 1973; Committee on Women's Studies to the Faculty Council, with Faculty Council Minutes, 19 March 1974; *Catalog*, 1978–79, p. 266; Self Study, 1985: Women's Studies, Provost Records; Caryn McTighe Musil, 31 May 1988, to W.E. Moran, Women's Programs, Moran Papers; OH: Robert Miller, 23 Jan. 1990; *Carolinian*, 24 Feb. 1977; 25 Feb. 1988.

66. Jencks and Riesman, *Academic Revolution*, p. 500.

67. See the correspondence in L–M, Ferguson Papers, 1969; Arts & Sciences Administrative Council minutes, 1 May 1970, in Arts/Sciences, Ferguson Papers; Warren Ashby, annual report, 26 July 1971, Q–R, Ferguson Papers; Institutional Self-Study Report, 1972, pp. 208–09; OH: Robert Miller, 23 Jan. 1990; Robert Calhoon, 1 Feb. 1990. For a statement of faculty skepticism, see Amy M. Charles, 8 Nov. 1972, to Ferguson and Stanley Jones, Ca–Com, Ferguson Papers.

68. OH: Robert Miller, 23 Jan. 1990; Miriam C. Barkley, 9 May 1991; Margaret Griffin, 7 May 1991; David Boutwell, 16 May 1991; *Carolinian*, 26 Sept. 1978, 17 Jan. 1985 (interview with Murray Arndt). For drug use, see Murray Arndt, 7 Jan. 1971, to Clarence Shipton, and Warren Ashby, annual report, 26 July 1971, Q–R, Ferguson Papers.

Chapter 25 Notes

1. David Shelton, 28 March 1969, to Ferguson et al.; Summary, by Employer, of Applicants Admitted as...Graduate Students...1967–69, Departments E–Hi, Ferguson Papers.

2. J.W. Kennedy, 15 Aug. 1966, to Mereb Mossman, Teaching, Singletary Papers; Self Study, 1985: Economics, Provost Records.

3. David Shelton, 17 Oct. 1969, to Kenneth Black, S–Sch, Ferguson Papers.

4. Herbert Wells, 30 Sept. 1983, to Elisabeth Zinser, Enrollment, Moran Papers.

5. See [John W. Kennedy], Statement of the Department of Economics...[re] Business Administration, [1963], B; Kennedy, 15 Aug. 1966, to Mereb Mossman, Teaching, Singletary Papers; Kennedy, 13 Oct. 1966, to Singletary, Departments A–E, Ferguson Papers; David Shelton, 27 April 1967, to Ferguson, Departments E; Kennedy, 20 Nov. 1968, to Ferguson, Budget; Shelton, 29 March 1969, to Ferguson et al., Departments E–Hi; Ferguson, 7 Oct. 1969, to W. Marlin Pickett, S–Sch, Ferguson Papers.

6. David Shelton, 20 Nov. 1968, to Robert L. Miller, Departments A–E; Shelton, 29 March 1969, to Ferguson et al.; Richard W. Fortner, 16 July 1969, to Ferguson, and Max D. Richards, Report on Proposals ..., [3 Oct. 1969], Departments E–Hi; Ferguson, 7 Oct. 1969, to W. Marlin Pickett; Shelton, 17 Oct. 1969, to Kenneth Black, and Black, 10 Nov. 1969, to Ferguson, S–Sch; Shelton, 16 Feb. 1970, to Ferguson and Mereb Mossman; Shelton, 30 Oct. 1970, to W.S. Markham, Departments B–H; Ferguson, 5 Sept. 1973, to Wm. C. Friday, S–Sch, Ferguson Papers; Shelton, 24 Oct. 1973, to Stanley L. Jones, Bus/Econ School, VCAA Records. For early outside evaluations of the school and its programs, see the reports by Richard Fortner, Max Richards, and Kenneth Black, above, and the SACS accreditation team, in Institutional Self-Study, 1972, Visiting Committee report.

7. David Shelton, 24 Jan., 11 May 1972, to Ferguson and Stanley Jones, School of B&E, Ferguson Papers; Shelton, 5 Dec. 1979, to Charles W. Patterson, in Development Office, B&E School Records; Shelton, 27 July 1981, to William E. Moran and Stanley L. Jones, B&E, Moran Papers; Stanley Jones, 14 Nov. 1975, to Sean O'Kane, in Enrollment Controls, Assistant VCAA Records; Shelton, 13 Aug. 1975, to Ferguson, Schools: B&E–Ed, Ferguson Papers.

8. Table: SACS: UNCG, Survey by Department, [1977], So, Ferguson Papers; David Shelton, 28 Sept. 1977, to Stanley Jones, in Academic Affairs, Correspondence, B&E School Records.

9. David Shelton, 20 April 1968, to Trustees Visiting Committee, B. of T., Visiting Committee; Shelton, 28, 29 March 1969, to Ferguson et al., Departments E–Hi, Ferguson Papers.

10. David Shelton, Report to Trustees' Visiting Committee, 21 April 1972, B. of T., Ferguson Papers; Shelton, 28 Sept. 1977, to Stanley Jones, in Academic Affairs, Correspondence, B&E School Records; Dwight L. Gentry, 11 Feb. 1980, to John W. Kennedy, Bus/Ec School, Moran Papers.

11. David Shelton, 1 Sept. 1972, to Ferguson and Stanley Jones, School of B&E, Ferguson Papers; Shelton, 28 Sept. 1977, to Stanley Jones, in Academic Affairs, Correspondence, B&E School Records; James W. Crews, The Department of Business and Distributive Education, 31 Oct. 1977, Vertical File: Business & Distributive Education; Self Study, 1985: Business Information and Support Systems, Provost Records.

12. David Shelton, 1 Sept. 1972, to Ferguson and Stanley Jones, B&E School, Ferguson Papers; Shelton, 28 Sept. 1977, to Stanley Jones, in Academic Affairs, Correspondence, B&E School Records; James W. Crews et al., 23 March 1983, to David Shelton, B&E, Moran Papers.

13. Wilson Davis, Press release, 13 Aug. 1974, in Vertical File: Center for Applied Research; Editorial Policy of *North Carolina Review of Business and Economics*, [1984], in N.C. Review, B&E School Records.

14. Amy M. Charles, 4 April 1963, to Singletary; Mereb Mossman, 14 Nov. 1963, to Sam Ragan, Deptartments Ho–S; Hilda Starbuck, 12 May 1963, to Gov. Terry Sanford, Co–Cu, Singletary Papers; OH: Walter Wehner, 12 Nov. 1990.

15. For outside consultants' evaluation of the school in connection with the Ed.D., see William N. Reeves, 20 Sept. 1967, and Clifton Burmeister, 2 Oct. 1967, to Ferguson, Departments M, Ferguson Papers.

16. Lawrence Hart, School of Music, in Informational Summary on Faculty, Students, and Programs, [1978], in Chancellor Selection, 1978–79, VCAA Records; Table: SACS, UNCG Survey by Department, [1977], So, Ferguson Papers.

17. OH: Lawrence Hart, 25 Sept. 1990.

18. OH: Lawrence Hart, 25 Sept. 1990; Frances Ashcraft McBane, 19 Feb. 1991. For the strings division, see George Dickieson, 13 Feb. 1969, to Ferguson, Depts. M–S, Ferguson Papers, and OH: Robert Darnell, 19 March 1990.

19. OH: Lawrence Hart, 25 Sept. 1990; Richard Cox, 4 June 1974, to Ferguson, Schools M–N, Ferguson Papers.

20. Lee Rigsby, 27 Nov. 1963, to Mereb Mossman, in Music, VCAA Papers; George Dickieson, 13 Feb. 1969, to Ferguson, Departments M–S, Ferguson Papers; OH: George Dickieson, 20 March 1990; Lawrence Hart, 25 Sept. 1990.

21. Lawrence Hart, School of Music, in Informational Summary on Faculty, Students, and Programs, [1978], in Chancellor Selection, 1978–79, VCAA Records.

22. Faculty File: Naomi Albanese; Canaday et al., *History of...HES*, p. 47.

23. Naomi Albanese to Ferguson, 20 Aug. 1968, Departments H–M; Albanese, 5 Sept. 1969, to Ferguson, S–Sch, Ferguson Papers; Draft Report, *Home Economics Review*, Dec. 1979, Table 2, in Home Ec, Moran Papers, 1980; School of Home Economics, Faculty Degree Status, 1969–70, in Home Ec, General, VCAA Records.

24. AHEA, Team Visitors' Report, 11 May 1972, in School: Home Ec, Ferguson Papers; Jacqueline H. Voss, 17 Feb. 1986, to William Moran and Elisabeth Zinser, pp. 6, 13, Home Ec, Moran Papers; Canaday et al., *History of...HES*, pp. 42–43, 52.

25. Home Economics, Review of Department Chairmen and Department Organization, VCAA Records; Draft Report of Home Economics Review, Dec. 1979, Tables 2–6, in Home

Ec, Moran Papers, 1980; Jacqueline H. Voss, 17 Feb. 1986, to William Moran and Elisabeth Zinser, Home Ec, Moran Papers; Canaday et al., *History of...HES*.

26. Naomi Albanese, 20 May 1974, to Ferguson, Schools: Home Ec; Ferguson, 13 March 1975, to Albanese, Schools: Home Ec, Ferguson Papers; Home Economics Foundation, Board minutes, 25 Jan. 1983, Home Ec, Moran Papers; Canaday et al., *History of...HES*, p. 9.

27. Donald B. Anderson, 10 Dec. 1962, to Naomi Albanese, Home Ec, Singletary Papers; OH: Mereb Mossman, 11 Oct. 1989.

28. Graduate Administrative Board minutes, 15 March 1965, in Correspondence, Office of Librarian Records; Vance T. Littlejohn, 17 Dec. 1965, to A.K. King, Departments G–H, Ferguson Papers; Canaday et al., *History of...HES*, pp. 36–37; John W. Kennedy, 29 Jan. 1970, to Naomi Albanese, G, Ferguson Papers; Draft Report of Home Economics Review, Dec. 1979, p. 13–15, Home Ec, Moran Papers, 1980.

29. Canaday et al., *History of...HES*, pp. 141–42; Vertical File: Home Management Houses.

30. Ferguson et al., 8 July 1968, to Board of Directors, Sigmond Sternberger Foundation, M–N, Ferguson Papers; Press release, 26 March 1973, Vertical File: Child Care Facilities; Correspondence in Ga folder, Ferguson Papers, 1974; Faculty File: M.E. Keister; *Alumni News*, 62 (Fall 1973), pp. 16–18; Canaday et al., *History of...HES*, pp. 96–97.

31. Faculty Council Minutes, 4 May 1936.

32. See correspondence in the Home Ec (1970) and Schools-Home Ec (1971) folders, Ferguson Papers; OH: Gilbert Carpenter, 27 April 1990.

33. Correspondence in Schools: Home Ec, 1971; Schools: H–M, 1972; School: HPERD, 1973; and Schools: Home Ec, 1974, Ferguson Papers; Stanley Jones, memorandum of meeting with Henry Foscue, 8 Sept. 1971, in Home Ec, Interior Design, VCAA Records; Faculty Council Minutes, 21 Jan. 1975; Self Study, 1985: Housing and Interior Design, Provost Records; OH: Clara Ridder, 19 Nov. 1990; Mary Miller, 17 Sept. 1990; Gilbert Carpenter, 27 April 1990.

34. Alice C. Boehret, 31 Jan., 22 Oct. 1963, to Singletary, Departments Ho–S; clippings in Departments Ho–S, 1964, Singletary Papers; Benjamin Cone, 12 April 1965, to Thomas White, Departments M–S, Ferguson Papers.

35. Singletary, 18 Jan. 1966, to Wm. Friday; Mildred L. Montag, Report of consultation visit, 20 Jan. 1966, Departments N–S, Singletary Papers; Lyda Gordon Shivers et al., 14 Jan. 1966, to Mereb Mossman, Departments N–S; Ferguson, 21 Feb. 1967, to Claiborne T. Smith, Departments N–P, Ferguson Papers; Self Study, 1985: Nursing Graduate Program, Provost Records; OH: Eloise Lewis, 24 Jan. 1990; Faculty File: Eloise Lewis; Eloise Lewis, in *Alumni News*, 60 (Summer 1972), p. 4; 81 (Spring 1992), pp. 6–7.

36. SACS, UNCG Survey by Department, [1977], So, Ferguson Papers.

37. Nursing School annual report, 1972–73, pp. 33–34, Nursing School Records; OH: Eloise Lewis, 24 Jan. 1990; Margaret Landon, 17 Sept. 1990; Margaret Klemer, 25 Oct. 1990; Catherine Turner, 1 Oct. 1990. For Lewis's record in recruiting black faculty, see Summary Report on Affirmative Action...1973–1978, pp. 5–6, in UNCG Affirmative Action Plan (Revision II), 17 July 1978, in Affirmative Action, Ferguson Papers.

38. Eloise R. Lewis, 29 March 1973, to Stanley L. Jones, in Nursing, VCAA Records; "Special Problems," in Nursing School annual report, 1978–79, Nursing School Records; Eloise R. Lewis, 27 Sept. 1983, to Elisabeth A. Zinser, in Enrollment Management, Assistant VCAA Records.

39. Graduate Administrative Board minutes, 15 March 1965, in Correspondence, Office of Librarian Records; Deans' Council Minutes, 17 Feb. 1971; OH: Gail Hennis, 18 Jan. 1990. For an appraisal of the department in 1966 and its readiness to offer the doctorate, see J.W. Kistler, Evaluation of a Proposal...for...the Doctor of Education...in Physical Education, [23 May 1966], Departments G–M, Singletary Papers.

40. Watson, "Ethel Loroline Martus Lawther," pp. 113–19; SACS, Commission on Colleges, Survey of UNCG, [1977], So, Ferguson Papers.

41. [Ethel Martus], Projections for the Next Ten Years... July 1966, Teaching, Singletary Papers; Watson, "Ethel Loroline Martus Lawther," 227–28; OH: Rosemary McGee, 21 May 1990; Betsy Umstead, 7 Dec. 1989.

42. *Alumni News*, 61 (Fall 1972), p. 29.

43. Faculty File: Marie Riley; *Carolinian*, 29 March 1975, 22 April 1976, 5 April 1979.

44. Piney Lake Field Campus, [1979], T, Ferguson Papers.

45. Kenneth E. Howe, 12 Feb. 1962, to Singletary and Mereb Mossman, Departments E–S, Singletary Papers; OH: Lois Edinger, 11 Sept. 1990; Jane Mitchell, 29 Nov. 1990; Jordan, *Women of Guilford*, p. 156. For background information on Edinger, see Raleigh *News & Observer*, 6 Oct. 1963, in Faculty File: Edinger.

46. OH: Lois Edinger, 11 Sept. 1990.

47. Kenneth Howe, 14 May 1966, to Mereb Mossman, Teaching, Singletary Papers; UNC-G Graduate Degrees Conferred, School of Education Percentage, 1977–1979, in Budget Review, School of Education, 11 Feb. 1980, Education, Moran Papers.

48. Ravitch, *Schools We Deserve*, p. 96.

49. Ravitch, *Schools We Deserve*, p. 95.

50. Report to the State Evaluation Committee on Teacher Education ..., 1–2 Nov. 1971, N; A.K. King, 14 April 1972, to Ferguson, Schools E–H; Rolf W. Larson, 26 May, 26 June 1972, to Ferguson, N, Ferguson Papers; Institutional Self-Study, 1972, Visiting Committee report, pp. 47–48; Deans' Council Minutes, 31 May 1972.

51. Education Faculty, 19 April 1972, to Ferguson, Schools E–H, Ferguson Papers; Deans' Council Minutes, 31 May 1972; Academic Policies Committee Minutes, 13 June 1972.

52. George McSpadden, 8 June 1972, and Walter Puterbaugh, 9 June 1972, to Robert L. Miller, N, Ferguson Papers.

53. Stanley L. Jones, draft memo, 1 June 1972, to Ferguson, with Deans' Council Minutes, 31 May 1972; Ferguson, 14 Jan. 1974, to the Faculty, Te; Jones, draft memo, 28 Sept. 1976, to Deans Council, Tea; Report of the Committee to Evaluate... Teacher Education, [9 May 1978}, Academic Cabinet, Ferguson Papers.

54. David H. Reilly, Self-Evaluation, Fall 1985, Education, Moran Papers; B.J. Chandler and William C. Self, Report on the School of Education, ca. March 1975, Schools B&E–Ed; Rolf W. Larson, 10 Oct. 1975, to Ferguson, NCATE; Ferguson, 10 Feb. 1976, to the Faculty, M–Na, Ferguson Papers; Self Study, 1985: Education, Dean's report, pp. 12–14, Provost Records.

55. Stanley L. Jones, 14 April 1975, to David H. Reilly; Ferguson, 6 May 1975, to Jones and to Reilly, NCATE, Ferguson Papers; William C. Self and B.J. Chandler, Report to Dean David H. Reilly, ca. April 1978, in Education School, VCAA Records; OH: Stanley Jones, 27 Dec. 1990.

56. Lawrence O. Haaby, Report of Revisitation ..., [Jan. 1964?], N–O; Kenneth E. Howe, Faculty Announcement, 17 May 1966, Departments A–E, Singletary Papers; Donald Russell et al., Report of the Ad Hoc Committee ..., [5 Dec. 1966], Departments A–E; Report and Recommendations on Curry High School, [1967]; Robert M. O'Kane, 21 Dec. 1967, to Ferguson, Departments E, Ferguson Papers; OH: Lois Edinger, 11 Sept. 1990.

57. Robert M. O'Kane, 16, 24 Jan., 13 Feb. 1968, to Ferguson; Ferguson, 19 Feb. 1968, to Wm. Friday; Press release, ca. 26 Feb. 1968; Ferguson and O'Kane, 26 Feb. 1968, to Parents of Curry Students, Cr–Cu; Ferguson, 3 March 1970, to Lawrence Hart, A–Ad; Kenneth E. Howe, 26 March 1970, to Ferguson, Fe–Fo, Ferguson Papers; Correspondence in Curry School folder, 1970, Ferguson Papers; Faculty Council Minutes, 26 Feb. 1968; Bryce Perkins, 14 Jan., 28 May, 22 Oct. 1969, to Robert M. O'Kane; Perkins, 8 Jan. 1970, to Curry Parents, Education School

Records, 1957–72; *Alumni News*, Fall 1969, p. 17; Academic Policies Committee Minutes, 12 Feb. 1970, as revised 5 March 1970; OH: Jeannette Dean, 16 March 1990; Elisabeth Bowles, 4 Dec. 1990; Jane Mitchell, 29 Nov. 1990.

58. Institutional Self-Study, 1962: Supplementary report, 1963–64, p. 24.

59. Chart: Summer Session Enrollments, [1964], D–E, Singletary Papers; Summer Session Council, annual report, 1974–75, in Continuing Education, 1974–79, VCAA Records; Summer Session report, [May 1982], Table I, Deans' Council Records. An apparent decline in summer school enrollments after 1976 followed a change in reporting practice, now omitting students who were enrolled in summer programs apart from the regular summer session. Beth Baldwin, 11 July 2000, to John Young, in author's possession.

60. Deans' Council Minutes, 27 Feb. 1974.

61. Notes from Summer Session Council, 15 July 1971, Deans' Council Minutes; Herbert Wells, 17 Oct. 1972, to Deans and Department Heads, Su–Sw, Ferguson Papers; Beth Baldwin, 11 July 2000, to John Young, in author's possession.

62. See Ernest A. Lynton and Daniel W. Shannon, in Johnson and Bell, *Metropolitan Universities*, pp. xvi, 251–54.

63. Ferguson, 3 May 1974, to Faculty and Staff, Continuing Ed, Ferguson Papers.

64. Deans' Council Minutes, 5 May 1970.

65. Institutional Self-Study, 1972, Fifth Year report, 1977, pp. 19–25.

Chapter 26 Notes

1. OH: Betty Hobgood Eidenier, 29 March 1991; Pat Cross, 15 May 1991; Lori Bushell, 18 April 1991; *Carolinian*, 1, 8 Oct. 1965; 18 Oct. 1968; 17, 22 Feb. 1972; *Alumni News*, 54 (Winter 1966), p. 22; 61 (Spring 1973), pp. 12–14.

2. OH: Lenoir C. Wright, 9 Feb. 1990; Laura Anderton, 19 Jan. 1990; Jane Mitchell, 29 Nov. 1990; Rosemary McGee, 21 May 1990; Franklin Parker, 21 Feb. 1990; Harriet Kupferer, 27 Oct. 1989.

3. *Carolinian*, 4, 18 Oct. 1968.

4. H.L. Ferguson, 17 April 1969, to Frank B. Turner, Ca–Ch, Ferguson Papers; *Alumni News*, 53 (Fall 1964), p. 20; *Carolinian*, 24 Sept. 1965. For the Wesley Long Hospital dormitory, see Wm. Friday, 16 Sept. 1965, to B. Everett Jordan, D, Ferguson Papers.

5. *Greensboro Record*, 11 Sept. 1964; *Carolinian*, 23 Oct. 1964; OH: Jeannette Dean, 16 March 1990.

6. *Carolinian*, 9 April 1965, 18 Sept. 1968; *Alumni News*, 55 (Jan. 1967), p. 25; 61 (Spring 1973), pp. 12–14; Excellence Fund Directors minutes, 4 Dec. 1972, Ex; Long Range Plan 1978–1983, [1978]: Office of Residence Life, Long Range Planning, Ferguson Papers. For Spencer Hall, see Shirley K. Flynn, 28 April 1975, to Academic Deans, in Residence Life, VCAA Records; James H. Allen, 10 July 1975, to Ferguson, Af–Al, Ferguson Papers.

7. See Johnson and Bell, *Metropolitan Universities*, pp. 51–60, 80.

8. Office of Institutional Research, Demographic Characteristics of Commuting students, 17 Dec. 1975, Com–Cons, and Survey of Commuter Students, 1976, Institutional Research, Ferguson Papers.

9. Carol D. Eustis, State of Campus address, 8 Feb. 1967, Minutes, SGA Records; OH: Martha Carson Isgett, 24 Sept. 1991; James Lancaster, 24 Jan. 1991. For some of the advantages and disadvantages of commuter life, see Jencks and Riesman, *Academic Revolution*, pp. 52–53, 182–84.

10. *Alumni News*, 66 (Spring 1978), p. 41.

11. See Ravitch, *Troubled Crusade*, pp. 210–11; Lee, *Campus Scene*, pp. 144–50; Lamont, *Campus Shock*, pp. 23–32; Lyons, "Adjustment of Black Students," esp. pp. 463–65. For a particular look at the problem on the Chapel Hill campus, which did not differ greatly from UNCG in this respect, see Kleinbaum, "Minority Experience . . . ."

12. For the graduate students' discrimination charge, see Helen [Yoder], 26 June 1968, to Ferguson; John W. Kennedy, 3 July 1968, to Ferguson, with enclosures; The Negro Graduate Students, 3 July 1968, to Mereb Mossman, all in Gra–Gre, Ferguson Papers. For the 1975 questionnaire, see Results of Minority Student Questionnaire... [June 1975], Admin Cou, Ferguson Papers; *Alumni News*, 65 (Spring 1977), pp. 4–5.

13. For the views of black students generally, see *Carolinian*, 27 Feb. 1968; *Alumni News*, 58 (Summer 1970), pp. 10–15 (including those of Ada Fisher); 61 (Winter 1973), pp. 4–5; 63 (Spring 1975), pp. 12–13; OH: Eula Vereen, 28 March 1991; Charles W. Cole, 5 Feb. 1991. For divergent recollections among white alumnae and faculty, see OH: Betty Hobgood Eidenier, 29 March 1991; Peggy Whalen-Levitt, 21 May 1991; Martha Carson Isgett, 24 Sept. 1991; Miriam C. Barkley, 9 May 1991; and Robert Calhoon, 1 Feb. 1990. For faculty tributes to Fisher, see OH: Hollis Rogers, 10 April 1990; Brenda Cooper, 12 Nov. 1990.

14. Programs and Activities Serving Minority Students . . . . [1971] So–Sp, Ferguson Papers.

15. OH: Charles W. Cole, 5 Feb. 1991.

16. Yvonne Cheek et al., 15 Nov. 1966, to Ferguson, D, Ferguson Papers.

17. *Carolinian*, 15 Nov. 1971.

18. Results of Minority Student Questionnaire... [June 1975], pp. 10–12, Admin–Cou, Ferguson Papers. See the announcement of the 1973 arts festival program in Stanley L. Jones, 5 Feb. 1973, to the Faculty, in Neo-Black Society, VCAA Records.

19. *Carolinian*, 26 April, 25 Oct. 1963; 26 April 1968; 11 Nov. 1971; 13, 16, 30 Nov. 1972.

20. Loeb, *Generation at the Crossroads*, pp. 44–46.

21. UNCG *Fact Book*, 1979–80, p. 24. For out-of-state tuition, see table accompanying Donald J. Reichard, 4 Sept. 1980, to Moran, Moran Papers.

22. OH: Roger F. Davis, 19 March 1990.

23. Kathleen P. Hawkins, Report to the Visiting Committee, 9 Dec. 1965, B. of T., Ferguson Papers; Eleanor Morris, Student Financial Aid, 23 March 1970, B. of T. Visiting Committee, Ferguson Papers; UNCG *Fact Book*, 1979–80, p. 23.

24. Margery D. Irby, 26 Oct. 1965, to Ferguson, Student folder, Ferguson Papers; Institutional Self-Study report, 1972, pp. 469–75.

25. *Carolinian*, 8, 15 Nov., 6 Dec. 1963.

26. *Carolinian*, 17 April, 2 Oct. 1964; *Alumni News*, 53 (Fall 1964), p. 21; OH: Henry Ferguson, 12 April 1990; Betty Hobgood Eidenier, 29 March 1991.

27. *Carolinian*, 20 Nov., 18 Dec. 1964, 12 Feb., 19 Nov. 1965, 25 Feb., 30 Sept., 7 Oct. 1966, 31 Oct. 1967, 12 Nov. 1968, 23 Sept. 1969; Singletary, draft annual report, 30 June 1966, Ca–Ch, Singletary Papers; K. Gilliam, Report, [SGA] Food Services Committee, 19 Oct. 1966, SGA Records; Student Legislature resolution, [30 April 1969], and Ferguson, 20 June 1969, to Thomas J.C. Smyth, Fo; Harry Manley, 10 Feb. 1971, to Susan Ruzicka, and Ferguson, 11 Feb. 1971, to All Persons Using the UNC-G Dining Hall, Fe–Fo, Ferguson Papers; Institutional Self-Study, 1972: Student report, p. 11, and University report, pp. 433–36.

28. *Carolinian*, 16 Jan., 12 Sept. 1975, 22 March 1977; *Alumni News*, 65 (Winter 1977), pp. 4–5; 65 (Spring 1977), pp. 12–13; *Student Handbook*, 1977–78, pp. 27–28.

29. Staff Nurses, 23 Nov. 1964, and "Just for the University from Faculty Members," 23 Nov. 1964, to Ferguson; Olivia Abernethy, 3, 8 Dec. 1964, and Owen W. Doyle, 8 Dec. 1964, to Ferguson, G–M; "University of North Carolina-Greensboro," [Jan. 1965]; [Katherine Taylor], Report on of Charges Made Against the Infirmary, [Jan. 1965]; Ferguson, 9 June 1965,

to George Hamer, H–I; Owen W. Doyle, 13 July 1973, to Ferguson, Stu–Sum, all in Ferguson Papers; *Carolinian*, 20 Nov., 4 Dec. 1964, 24 Sept. 1965.

30. Osa S. McAdoo, 15 March 1968 to Wm. Friday; McAdoo et al., 18 March 1968, to Ferguson; William G. Morgan, 24 April 1968, to Ferguson, I folder; Dare H. Filipski, 18 March 1977, to James H. Allen, Tuition, all in Ferguson Papers.

31. Owen W. Doyle, 31 March, 27 April 1970, to Ferguson; Katherine Taylor, 18 May 1970, to Ferguson; John R. Curtis, 19 May 1970, to Ferguson; Harry Manley, 10 Sept. 1970, to Wilson Davis; Manley, 10 Sept. 1970, to Ferguson, all in H, Ferguson Papers.

32. Ferguson, 5 June 1970, to John R. Curtis, H, Ferguson Papers.

33. For the "pill bill," see Student Legislature minutes, 19 April 1967, SGA Records, 18, 21 April, 5 May 1967; Correspondence, 1967, in P, Ferguson Papers.

34. OH: William McRae, 17 Dec. 1990; Institutional Self-Study report, 1972, pp. 436–39; [McRae], Student Health Service, with Ferguson, 21 Feb. 1972, to Richard H. Robinson, Stu; Owen W. Doyle, 13 July 1973, to Ferguson, Stu–Sum, Ferguson Papers.

35. Mereb Mossman, 17 Aug. 1964, to Singletary, Ci–Cu, Singletary Papers; William H. Friedman, 3 Nov. 1964, to Mossman, C; Friedman, 9 Sept. 1965, to Mossman; Friedman, 8 Dec. 1965, to Trustees' Visiting Committee, Con–Cur; Harry Manley, 14 Jan. 1971, to Ferguson, Student; Ferguson, 8 Aug. 1977, to Wm. Friday, Sa–Se, Ferguson Papers; *Student Handbook*, 1977–78, pp. 25–27.

36. *Carolinian*, 21, 23 Jan., 7 March, 4, 18 Sept., 2 Oct. 1975; *Alumni News*, 64 (Fall 1975), pp. 21–22.

37. H.L. Ferguson, 18 June 1975, to Deans, Directors and Department Heads, J–M, Ferguson Papers.

38. *Alumni News*, 63 (Fall 1974), back cover.

39. *Carolinian*, 20 Oct. 1970, 18 May 1971.

40. James H. Allen, 12, 30 July 1973, to Steve Levkoff; Helen [Yoder], 26 July 1973, to [Ferguson], Stu Con–Sum; Wm. Friday, 18 Feb. 1974, to the Chancellors; Ferguson, 25 Feb. 1974, to Richard H. Robinson, Boo–Bu, Ferguson Papers; OH: Henry Ferguson, 12 April 1990.

Chapter 27 Notes

1. See Altbach, "Students," pp. 213–15; Ravitch, *Troubled Crusade*, pp. 222–24; Horowitz, *Campus Life*, pp. 221–41; Lee, *Campus Scene*, pp. 136–43; Loeb, *Generation at the Crossroads*, p. 263; Heineman, *Campus Wars*, passim.

2. *Carolinian*, 25 Feb. 1966 (marriage mill quote), 13 May 1966. For other charges of student apathy at UNCG, see *Carolinian*, 26 Feb., 8, 15 Oct. 1965, 9, 21 Feb., 1 March, 10 May 1968, 17, 24 Feb., 10 March 1970, 16 Feb. 1971, 15 Feb. 1977; OH: Peggy Whalen-Levitt, 21 May 1991.

3. Charlotte Dawley, Report on Transfers ..., [1966], U–W, Singletary Papers. Randolph Bulgin, in *Carolinian*, 15 Oct. 1965. See also issues of 26 Feb., 8 Oct. 1965, 11 Nov. 1966.

4. Interview with James Allen, *Greensboro Record*, 22 March 1971; Deans' Council Minutes, 5 May 1971; *Carolinian*, 16 Sept. 1971; *Alumni News*, 65 (Fall 1976), pp. 2–4; 65 (Summer 1977), pp. 3–4.

5. *Carolinian*, 7 Feb. 1978, 23, 27, 29 March, 30 Aug. 1979.

6. *Carolinian*, 5, 19 (including quotation), 22 March, 2 April 1965.

7. *Carolinian*, 18 April, 1978; Newspaper clipping, 16 April 1978, in Ralph Wilkerson papers, SGA Records.

8. *Carolinian*, 7 May 1965.

9. *Alumni News*, 58 (Summer 1970), p. 5; 68 (Summer 1980), pp. 2–5; *Carolinian*, 30 Jan., 30 Oct. 1975; OH: Gail Hennis, 18 Jan. 1990; Nancy Fogarty, 27 March 1990; James Lancaster, 24 Jan. 1991; Cheryl Callahan, 19 Jan. 1990.

10. Singletary, 18 March 1966, to Ann Flack Boseman, Ac–Al, Singletary Papers; *Carolinian*, 12 March 1965; King, *Multicampus University*, pp. 70–73. The fullest study of the speaker ban controversy is Billingsley, *Communists on Campus.*

11. OH: M. Elaine Burgess, 8 Nov. 1990; Kendon Smith, 18 Oct. 1989; Robert Watson, 21 March 1990; James H. Allen, 11 Sept. 1990.

12. Jane Ann Ward, [Fall 1967], to Faculty Members, B–Boa, Ferguson Papers.

13. Katherine Taylor, Report on Conference, [2 Nov. 1967], B–Boa, Ferguson Papers.

14. Faculty Council Minutes, 21 Nov. 1967; Janyce Brewer and Thomasine Oliver, 27 Nov. 1967, to Ferguson, B–Boa, Ferguson Papers; Clippings in Vertical File: Black Power Forum; Ada M. Fisher, 21 June 1973, to Ferguson, Neo-Black Soc, Ferguson Papers; Jane Ann Ward, in *Alumni News*, 56 (Winter 1968), pp. 20–21.

15. Ferguson, draft annual report for 1967–68, [1968], Ca–Cl, Ferguson Papers.

16. See Jim Allen's tribute to Ferguson in this respect, in OH: James Allen, 11 Sept. 1990. For a similar tribute to Allen, see Greensboro *News & Record*, 28 June 1996.

17. Ada M. Fisher, 24 Feb. 1985, to Chairman, Board of Directors, Buildings, Moran Papers.

18. *Carolinian*, 30 April 1968.

19. See, e.g., Ferguson, 30 Oct. 1968, to Mrs. William D. Leetch, M–N, Ferguson Papers.

20. Student Legislature minutes, 24 April 1968, SGA Records; Ferguson, 7 May 1968, to Anne Hurst; Speech of Jane Ann Ward, 7 May [1968], St–Su, Ferguson Papers.

21. Daisy Chain Chairman report, 1968, in Class Records, Class of 1971, VC Student Affairs Records; *Carolinian*, 4 Oct. 1968, 2 Oct. 1970, 30, 30 April, 30 Sept. 1971; OH: Brenda Cooper, 12 Nov. 1990; Betty Hobgood Eidenier, 29 March 1991; Lori Bushell, 18 April 1991; James Lancaster, 24 Jan. 1991; Miriam C. Barkley, 9 May 1991.

22. Penny Kay Cooper, "Rat Day 1965–66," and "Attention Freshmen and Sophomores," in Class Records, Class of 1968, VC Student Affairs Records; Sharon Mills, "Air Your Griefs," ibid., Class of 1971; *Carolinian*, 11 Oct. 1968, 28 Oct. 1969.

23. Institutional Self-Study, 1962: Visiting Committee report, p. 39; Barbara Parrish, annual report, 1969–70, 1970–71, 1971–72, and Alumni Association Trustees minutes, 13–14 Feb. 1970, Alumni. Assn. Records, 1899–1988.

24. Student Legislature minutes, 8, 29 April, 18 Nov. 1970; Correspondence, in SGA folder, 1970; Ferguson, 22 Feb. 1971, to Caroline Russell, Ferguson Papers; *Carolinian*, 20 Nov. 1970; OH: James Lancaster, 24 Jan. 1991.

25. *Carolinian*, 10 May 1968.

26. Link, *William Friday*, pp. 145–56; King, *Multicampus University*, pp. 74–77, 81, 84–85.

27. The best day-by-day account of the strike is a Cafeteria Strike Chronology, in the Appendix to the Report of the Ad Hoc Committee on University Racial Policies, Ad Hoc Committee folder, [1969], Ferguson Papers. That appendix includes other important documents, including the best statement of the student view, by Sherri Wood and Karen Bickett. See also correspondence, March–April 1969, in Fo, Ferguson Papers; Vertical File: Service Employees, March 1969; Deans' Council Minutes, 27 March 1969; Faculty Council Minutes, 28 March, 1, 15 April 1969. The *Carolinian* suspended publication during the strike, resuming three weeks later. See its issues of 28, 29 March, 18 April, 9 May 1969. For accounts of the strike by participants and close bystanders, see James S. Ferguson and Randi Bryant Strutton, in *Alumni News*, 68 (Fall 1979), pp. 2–6; Robert M. Calhoon, in ibid., 79 (Winter 1991), pp. 2–4; OH: James Allen, 11 Sept. 1990; Henry Ferguson, 12 April 1990; M. Elaine Burgess, 8 Nov. 1990; Robert Calhoon, 1 Feb. 1990; Cheryl Callahan, 19 Jan. 1990; Brenda Cooper, 25 April 1991;

James Lancaster, 24 Jan. 1991. For another brief overview of the event, see Link, *William Friday*, pp. 154–55.

28. Thomas J.C. Smyth, Notice, 22 May 1969, in Disorders on Campus, VCAA Records; OH: Cheryl Callahan, 19 Jan. 1990. For the black student holiday, see OH: Charles W. Cole, 5 Feb. 1991.

29. Katy Gilmore et al., Official Statement in re Vietnam Moratorium, 24 Sept. 1969, and Student Legislature resolution, 9 Oct. 1969, V–Z, Ferguson Papers; *Alumni News*, 58 (Fall 1969), p. 7.

30. "STRIKE STRIKE STRIKE . . . , [5 May 1970]; SGA et al., Petition, 11 May 1970; Richard Bardolph, 11 May 1970, to Ferguson; Ferguson, 11 May 1970, to Faculty and Students, in Faculty folder; Documents in Student Unrest folder, 1970; Ferguson, "The May Crisis," Chancellor's newsletter column, 31 Aug. 1970, N, Ferguson Papers; Faculty Council Minutes, 11 May 1970; SGA Resolutions and other materials in Disorders on Campus, VCAA Records; Alumni Assocation Board of Trustees minutes, 28 May 1970, Alumni Assn. Records, 1899–1988. For the War Requiem, see Jack M. Jarrett, 7 July 1970, to Benjamin Britten, Music/Nursing, Ferguson Papers; OH: Walter Wehner, 12 Nov. 1990.

31. Riley, "Student Participation in Governance," pp. 240–46.

32. See Rudolph, *Curriculum*, pp. 270–73.

33. Lindsay Lamson, in *Alumni News*, 58 (Summer 1970), pp. 5–6; *Carolinian*, 17 March 1970.

34. Academic Policies Committee Minutes, 10 Oct. 1968, 16 Jan., 8 May, 13 Nov. 1969, 15 Jan. 1970; Faculty Council Minutes, 21 Oct. 1969; Student Legislature minutes, 19 March 1969, with statement on Student Participation in Academic Policy Formation; and Lindsay Lamson, State of the Campus address, 15 Feb. 1971, in Minutes, SGA Records.

35. Instrument of Government, 1 July 1974, in Faculty Governance Committee, Assistant VCAA Records.

36. Correspondence in B. of T., 1971, Ferguson Papers; Steve Underwood, 1 Nov. 1972, to Margaret Hunt, in Faculty Governance Committee, Assistant VCAA Records.

37. Randi Bryant, in *Carolinian*, 9 Dec. 1966; Vertical File: SCORE.

38. Student Legislature minutes, 19 March 1969, with statement on Student Participation in Academic Policy Formation, and Lindsay Lamson, State of the Campus address, 15 Feb. 1971, in Minutes, SGA Records; Deans' Council Minutes, 5 May 1970; *Carolinian*, 17, 24 March 1970, 16 Sept. 1971; Lindsay Lamson, in *Alumni News*, 58 (Summer 1970), pp. 5–6.

39. Institutional Self-Study Report, 1972, pp. 454–62.

40. *Carolinian*, 1 March, 1 Nov. 1968; James H. Allen, 22 Aug. 1973, to Ferguson; Ferguson, 31 Aug. 1973, to Cheryl Sosnik, Stu Con–Sum, Ferguson Papers.

41. *Carolinian*, 16 Sept. 1971; Residents of Hinshaw Hall statement, [1 Oct. 1973]; Ferguson, 8 Oct. 1973, to the Residents of Hinshaw Hall, H, Ferguson Papers; OH: Timothy Bottoms, 3 Oct. 1990; David Boutwell, 16 May 1991; Michael Dana, 9 May 1991.

42. *Alumni News*, 70 (Winter 1982), pp. 1–2, 18–19.

43. Horowitz, *Campus Life*, pp. 250–52. See also Altbach, "Students," pp. 212–13.

44. See Horowitz, *Campus Life*, pp. 241–42.

45. *Carolinian*, 12, 15, 18, 22 Feb., 1, 5, 22, 28 March 1973; Neo Black Society papers, 1973, in SGA Records. For an insider's account of the NBS by one of its founders, see Ada M. Fisher, 21 June 1973, to Ferguson, Neo-Black Soc., Ferguson Papers.

46. Deans' Council Minutes, 28 March 1973; Ferguson, 31 March 1973, to Jacqueline Coleman, NBS; Transcripts of trustees' meeting, 12 April 1973, B. of T., Ferguson Papers; Academic Policies Committee Minutes, 5 April 1973; *Carolinian*, 28 March, 3, 9, 12 April 1973; OH: Kendon Smith, 18 Oct. 1989; Robert Miller, 23 Jan. 1990; Evon Dean, 28 March 1990; Robert Calhoon, 1 Feb. 1990.

47. Deans' Council Minutes, 9 May 1973; Correspondence, 31 March to 13 June 1973, B. of T.; James H. Allen, 15 Oct. 1973, to Richard H. Robinson, Neo Black Soc., Ferguson Papers.

48. *Carolinian*, 23, 30 Jan. 1975, 27 Oct. 1977; Results of Minority Student Questionnaire... [June 1975], pp. 10–12, Admin–Cou, Ferguson Papers; *Alumni News*, 65 (Spring 1977), pp. 4–5; OH: Carol Bottoms, 18 May 1991; Timothy Bottoms, 3 Oct. 1990; Michael Dana, 9 May 1991.

49. *Alumni News*, 68 (Spring 1980), p. 15.

50. Sean O'Kane, statement, [Oct. 1975], Acad. Cabinet (2), Ferguson Papers. Deans' Council Minutes, 24 Nov. 1976 (pp. 3–7), 8 Dec. 1976; *Alumni News*, 65 (Winter 1977), p. 1. For statements of the student position on university governance, see *Student Handbook*, 1977–78, pp. 173–74, and Randolph W. Sides, State of the Campus address, 17 Jan. 1978, St–Su, Ferguson Papers.

51. Riesman, *On Higher Education*, p. 82.

52. Lamont, *Campus Shock*, pp. 9–10.

53. See Ravitch, *Troubled Crusade*, p. 225.

54. Dean of Women, Summary Report to... the Trustees, Dec. 1965, B. of T.; Shirley K. Flynn, 30 July 1970, to Ferguson, Co–Cr, Ferguson Papers; Rosemary McGee, 7 Dec. 1966, to Eloise Lewis, in Application to Establish the School, Nursing School Records; OH: Martha Carson Isgett, 24 Sept. 1991; Peggy Whalen-Levitt, 21 May 1991.

55. *Alumni News*, 69 (Fall 1980), p. 21.

56. Student Legislature minutes, 16 March 1966, SGA Records; *Carolinian*, 17 Nov., 9 Dec. 1966.

57. Student Legislature minutes, 12, 19 Oct. 1966, SGA Records; Rosemary McGee, 26 Oct. 1966, to Ferguson; Ferguson, 16 Nov. 1966, to Nancy Dunn, St–Su; Eula Mae Jarrett, 24 April 1967, to [Rosemary] McGee; McGee, 27 April 1967, to Eula Mae Jarrett, Co–Cu; Ferguson, 1 May 1968, to Robert S. Fullerton, U–W, Ferguson Papers; *Carolinian*, 4 March, 7 Oct. 1966, 20 Oct., 2 Dec. 1967; *Alumni News*, 55 (Jan. 1967), pp. 8–9; OH: Peggy Whalen-Levitt, 21 May 1991.

58. *Carolinian*, 7, 18 March 1969, 25 March, 23 Sept. 1976, 14, 26 Sept., 24 Oct. 1978; James H. Allen, 28 Sept. 1973, to Ferguson; Ferguson, 5 Oct. 1973, to Allen, Al–App; Ferguson, 31 Dec. 1974, to Wm. Friday, Stu Aff; Ferguson, 5 March 1976, to Sean O'Kane, Al, Ferguson Papers; OH: Cheryl Callahan, 19 Jan. 1990; Miriam C. Barkley, 9 May 1991; Carol Bottoms, 18 May 1991.

59. *Carolinian*, 3 May 1968.

60. *Alumni News*, 58 (Spring 1970), pp. 38–39; Wm. K. McRae, 14 April 1972, to [Ferguson]; McRae, 14 Sept. 1972, To Whom It May Concern, Stu, Ferguson Papers. See also correspondence in Deg–Du, 1970, Ferguson Papers; OH: Miriam C. Barkley, 9 May 1991.

61. James H. Allen, 20 Sept. 1973, to Richard H. Robinson, Stu Act–Aid, Ferguson Papers; OH: Timothy Bottoms, 3 Oct. 1990; Carol Bottoms, 18 May 1991.

62. Murray Arndt, 7 Jan. 1971, to Clarence Shipton; Warren Ashby, Residential College annual report, 26 July 1971, Q–R, Ferguson Papers; *Alumni News*, 65 (Fall 1976), pp. 2–4; *Carolinian*, 21 Feb. 1978.

63. Clarence O. Shipton, 18 Dec. 1967, to H.L. Ferguson, S; "A graduate of the university," 17 April 1969, to Ferguson, U; Mrs. Ben Stockard, 24 May 1969, to Ferguson, H; Ferguson, 7 March 1970, to Wm. Friday, T; Correspondence, June 1971, in Ta–Tr, all in Ferguson Papers; *Greensboro Daily News*, 15 June 1970; *Carolinian*, 17 Feb. 1972; *Alumni News*, 62 (Summer 1974), pp. 6–7; Greensboro *News & Record*, 19 May 1985; OH: Miriam C. Barkley, 9 May 1991; Jeanette Dean, 16 March 1990.

64. *Carolinian*, 4 March, 17 Nov., 13, 16 Dec. 1966; Jeanne Young, 30 April 1967, to Carol Eustis, Student folder, Ferguson Papers.

65. *Carolinian*, 17 Nov. 1966, 27 Oct. 1967, 6, 13, 21 Feb., 5 April, 19 Nov., 13 Dec. 1968, 2, 16, 23, Oct., 4 Dec. 1970; Ferguson, 17 May 1967, to Anne Hurst, Student folder; SGA Meeting with Visiting Committee, [May 1972], SGA folder, Ferguson Papers; OH: Peggy Whalen-Levitt, 21 May 1991; Cheryl Callahan, 19 Jan. 1990.

66. Student Legislature minutes, 12 Oct. 1966, 6, 21 March 1968, 15 Feb. 1971, SGA Records; *Student Handbook*, 1977–78, pp. 244–47; Ferguson, 11 March 1971, to Mrs. L.J. Manley; Richard H. Robinson, Development of the Current Visitation Policy . . . , with Robinson, 17 June 1971, to the Chancellors, Deg–Dr, Ferguson Papers; *Carolinian*, 17 Nov. 1966, 5, 23, 26, 30, April, 10 May 1968, 16 Feb. 1971, 8 Dec. 1977, 14 Feb. 1978; *Alumni News*, 66 (Spring 1978), pp. 2–3; OH: Cheryl Callahan, 19 Jan. 1990; Miriam C. Barkley, 9 May 1991; Carol Bottoms, 18 May 1991; Timothy Bottoms, 3 Oct. 1990.

67. Carol Barnhill, [ca. 9 March 1971], to Dean Shirley Flynn, Deg–Dr, Ferguson Papers.

68. For correspondence, press coverage, and other attention to the incident, see U–W folder, 1972, Ferguson Papers (containing a copy of the sign); Vertical File: Visitation Policy in Dormitories; *Carolinian*, 17, 22 Feb. 1972; Student Senate minutes, 16 Feb. 1972, SGA Records; Alumni Association Trustees minutes, 23 March 1972, Alumni Association Records, 1899–1988.

69. Report of the Ad Hoc Committee to Review Visitation Policy, [1976], U–V, Ferguson Papers; James H. Allen, Review of Policies Related to Student Housing, 12 Sept. 1985, with Trustee Minutes, 12 Sept. 1985; *Alumni News*, 65 (Winter 1977), p. 4.

70. *Carolinian*, 19 Feb., 17 Dec. 1965.

71. *Carolinian*, 4 Feb., 21 March 1974, 25 Sept., 2, 9, 23 Oct. 1975, 26 April, 8 Dec. 1977, 5 Dec. 1978; Faculty Council Minutes, 18 March 1975, 18 Jan., 3 May 1977; *Alumni News*, 64 (Spring 1976), pp. 10–11; OH: James Lancaster, 24 Jan. 1991. For a statement of student court procedures in 1972, see Institutional Self-Study report, 1972, pp. 462–65. For the honor code adopted in 1977, see *Student Handbook*, 1977–78, pp. 224–44.

72. *Carolinian*, 27 April 1976; OH: Henry Ferguson, 12 April 1990; Clarence O. Shipton, 18 Dec. 1967, to H.L. Ferguson, S, Ferguson Papers. For more on Alexander, see *Greensboro Daily News*, 8 June 1969. For the national background, see Fisher and Sloan, *Campus Crime*, pp. 12–14.

73. *Carolinian*, 14 Oct., 11 Nov. 1966, 3 March, 7, 10 Nov. 1967, 14 Feb. 1969.

74. Correspondence, 1969, in Sco–Sto; Katy Gilmore, 4 Jan. 1970, to Ferguson, Stu–Su; H.L. Ferguson, 29 Sept. 1970, to Ferguson, Sc–So; Lindsay Lamson, 4 May 1971, to Harry S. Manley, Sco–Sm, Ferguson Papers; Lindsay Lamson, State of the Campus address, 15 Feb. 1971, in Minutes, SGA Records.

75. Resolutions, 1973, in Minutes, SGA Records; *Carolinian*, 27 Sept. 1973.

Chapter 28 Notes

1. OH: James Lancaster, 24 Jan. 1991.

2. Commencement Committee minutes, 10 Feb. 1967, Co–Cu; Ferguson, 26 Sept. 1967, to Jane Ann Ward, U–Y, Ferguson Papers; *Alumni News*, 64 (Winter 1976), p. 34; 64 (Spring 1976), p. 41; *Carolinian*, 22 Jan. 1981; Correspondence in Alma Mater, 1979–82, Music School Records.

3. *Carolinian*, 7 Oct. 1969, 23 Sept. 1971; Steve Gilliam, Press release, 16 Dec. 1977, in Vertical File: Luminaries; OH: Cheryl Callahan, 19 Jan. 1990.

4. *Carolinian*, 20 Oct. 1959, 26 Feb., 4 March 1960, 21 April, 2 May 1967, 30 Sept. 1971, 17 Aug. 1973, 16 April 1987, 27 Oct. 1988, 3 Oct. 1991; Greensboro *News & Record*, 1 Dec.

1990, 10 May 1991; Barbara Parrish, 30 March 1967, to N.H. Gurley, Al–Ay; Rosemary McGee, 21 April 1967, to Gurley, D; J.S. Ferguson, 3 Feb. 1969, to H.L. Ferguson, U; Ferguson, 23 March 1977, to Mrs. E.A. Habel, Alumni Assn. folder, Ferguson Papers; *Today on Campus* newsletter, 12 April 1985; OH: Cheryl Callahan, 19 Jan. 1990.

5. For cheerleaders, see correspondence from Kathy Pritchard and June Galloway, Oct.–Nov. 1967, Departments G–H, Ferguson Papers; *Carolinian*, 29 Oct. 1968. For Falderal and Homecoming, see Barbara Parrish, annual report, 1974–75, in Miscellaneous, Alumni Association Records, 1899–1988; Tentative programs in F, Ferguson Papers, 1974; *Carolinian*, 8 Oct. 1974.

6. See Guttmann, *Women's Sports*, pp. 142, 209, 212–14; Cahn, *Coming on Strong*, pp. 246–49, 259.

7. [Ethel Martus], Projections for the Next Ten Years, July 1966, Teaching, Singletary Papers; Jones, "History of Women's Intercollegiate Athletics at UNCG," pp. 32, 53–56; Cahn, *Coming on Strong*, p. 250; Guttmann, *Women's Sports*, pp. 220–21; Watson, "Ethel Loroline Martus Lawther," pp. 165–66; *Alumni News*, 73 (Winter 1985), pp. 15, 30; OH: Martha Carson Isgett, 24 Sept. 1991.

8. Clarence O. Shipton, 5 Dec. 1966, to Ferguson, D; Report, Committee on Improving... Male... Enrollment, [1967], M–N, Ferguson Papers; *Carolinian*, 29 Sept. 1967; *Alumni News*, 61 (Spring 1973), pp. 12–13; Jones, "History of Women's Intercollegiate Athletics at UNCG," pp. 53, 99; OH: Charles W. Cole, 5 Feb. 1991.

9. *Today on Campus* newsletter, 23 Sept. 1983, in Vertical File: Spartans.

10. See esp. *Carolinian*, 2 Dec. 1967, 19 Nov. 1992.

11. *Alumni News*, 74 (Fall 1985), p. 30.

12. School of HPER, White Paper for Steve Underwood ..., Jan. 1973, Stu Con–Sum, Ferguson Papers; Jones, "History of Women's Intercollegiate Athletics at UNCG," pp. 29–30, 53–55, 99; Cahn, *Coming on Strong*, pp. 248–49; Guttmann, *Women's Sports*, pp. 212–13.

13. Hargrove (Skipper) Bowles, 23 June 1970, to Ferguson, Al–Ay; Ferguson, 7 Sept. 1971, to Walter Puterbaugh, As–Ay, Ferguson Papers.

14. Report of the Task Force on Intercollegiate Athletics, Jan. 1975; Ferguson, 21 March 1977, to Board of Trustees, B. of T., Ferguson Papers; Trustees' Minutes, 10 April 1975; *Greensboro Daily News*, 30 July 1979.

15. Intercollegiate Athletics at UNCG, A Special Report ..., 1 Feb. 1977; Report... Regarding the Future of Intercollegiate Athletics at UNC-G, March 1977, and other contents in Intercoll. Athletics folder; Statement of James S. Ferguson, 14 April 1977, Speeches, Ferguson Papers; Committee on Intercollegiate Athletics Records, 1976–77; Trustees' Minutes, 14 April 1977; *Carolinian*, 12, 26 Sept. 1974, 29 March 1975, 3 Dec. 1976 (including quotation), 22, 24 March, 29 Nov. 1977; *Alumni News*, 65 (Winter 1977), p. 6; 65 (Spring 1977), p. 42; *Greensboro Daily News*, 11 Feb. 1977; Jones, "History of Women's Intercollegiate Athletics at UNCG," pp. 55–64, 118–26; OH: James H. Allen, 11 Sept. 1990; Louise Falk, 20 March 1990.

16. Shirley McDevitt, 20 Feb. 1979, to [Charles W.] Patterson, I folder, Ferguson Papers; Jones, "History of Women's Intercollegiate Athletics at UNCG," pp. 63–64, 124–26.

17. Horowitz, *Campus Life*, pp. 21, 260–61.

18. *Carolinian*, 30 April 1965; OH: Carol Bottoms, 18 May 1991.

19. Student Senate minutes, 19 Sept. 1978, SGA Records; Academic Cabinet Minutes, 21 Feb. 1979 (incl. Report... from the Committee on Fraternities and Sororities), 14 March 1979; Faculty Council Minutes, 20 March 1979; UNG Trustees' Minutes, 13 Nov. 1979 (incl. Report... from [a third] Committee on Fraternities and Sororities); *Carolinian*, 20, 26 Sept. 1978; *Alumni News*, 65 (Winter 1977), p. 5; 67 (Spring 1979), pp. 6, 23; OH: James H. Allen, 11 Sept. 1990.

20. Information Sheet on Denominations ..., [1971], I folder; Katherine Taylor, Report to the Visiting Committee, [1965], B. of T.; Ferguson, 15 Jan. 1970, to Nancy Beamer Hiatt,

Q–R; Katherine Taylor, annual report, 24 April 1972, B. of T., Ferguson Papers; Trustees' Visiting Committee, annual report, 1964, p. 39.

21. *Alumni News*, 65 (Fall 1976), p. 4.

22. *Carolinian*, 2 Nov. 1962, and Spring 1964, esp. 24 April.

23. *Carolinian*, 10 March, 14 April 1970, 23 March, 28 Oct. 1971.

24. J.A. Bryant, 5 March 1968, to Ferguson, Departments E–G; Ferguson, 17 Nov. 1969, to Thomas J.C. Smyth, O–P; Ferguson, 12 Nov. 1971, to Mrs. John A. Boren, Ca–Co, Ferguson Papers; *Carolinian*, 28 Oct. 1971; *Student Handbook*, 1977–78, pp. 153–57.

25. *Carolinian*, 4 April 1974.

26. *Carolinian*, 7, 29 March, 16 April, 6 Oct. 1975; 13 April 1978, 24 April 1979; Press release, 13 April 1978, Vertical File: *Carolinian*.

27. *Alumni News*, 56 (Spring 1968), p. 5; *Coraddi*, Spring 1989, p. 48 (including quotation).

28. J.A. Bryant, 19 April 1967, to Ferguson, Departments E, Ferguson Papers; *Carolinian*, 20 Nov. 1964, 27 Oct. 1967.

29. *Carolinian*, 12, 15 March 1968; Randolph Bulgin, 1 Oct. 1968, to Mereb Mossman, Co, Ferguson Papers.

30. Fred Chappell, 21 Jan. 1971, to Shirley K. Flynn; Ruth Buker et al., 19 Feb. 1971, to Pat O'Shea, Con–Cu, Ferguson Papers; *Alumni News*, 59 (Spring 1971), pp. 26–27; *Carolinian*, 12 Jan., 16, 26 Feb. 1971.

31. Tom Kirby-Smith, 9 April 1973, to English Staff, Arts/Sciences, Ferguson Papers; *Coraddi*, 1967–79. For the spaghetti incident, see *Alumni News*, 59 (Spring 1971), pp. 27–28; *Greensboro Daily News*, 19 Feb. 1971.

32. Julius Foust, 18 Dec. 1925, to Sen. Lee S. Overman, Foust Papers; L.B. Hurley, 22 March 1946, to W.C. Jackson, Faculty folder; Hurley, 15 May 1950, to Jackson, Budget, Jackson Papers; Emil W. Young, Preliminary Report . . . , 11 July 1960, and Dale F. Keller, 25 Sept. 1961, to Otis Singletary, T, 1961, Singletary Papers.

33. Otis Singletary, 16 Oct. 1963, to Wm. C. Friday, Q–R; Bill Young, 8 July 1964, to Singletary, Q–R, Singletary Papers; *Alumni News*, 53 (Fall 1964), p. 23.

34. Clarence O. Shipton, 11 Feb. 1966, to Mereb Mossman, P–R, Singletary Papers; Amy M. Charles, 5 April 1967, to Emil Young, Correspondence, Faculty Welfare Committee Records; *Carolinian*, 16 Feb., 15 March, 10 May 1968, 2 May 1969, 4 Dec. 1972, 17 Aug. 1973; *Alumni News*, 63 (Summer 1975), p. 17; 65 (Spring 1977), p. 15.

35. *Carolinian*, 18 May 1934, 24 May 1935, 11 Dec. 1936, 28 Nov. 1941, 20 Feb., 25 Sept. 1953; Advisory Committee Minutes, 27 Nov., 7 Dec. 1936; Mereb Mossman, 16 Oct. 1962, to Donald K. Springen, in Drama/Speech Department, VCAA Records.

36. Correspondence, 1964–69, in Debating, VCAA Records; *Carolinian*, 9 Oct. 1964, 10 Nov. 1967, 27 Feb. 1968, 17 Oct. 1969, 13 Feb. 1970.

37. Herman Middleton, 28 May 1971, to Ferguson, Arts & Sciences folder; Ferguson, 14 Sept. 1972, to Alumni Annual Giving Council, Alumni folder; L. Dean Fadely, 13 May 1975, to Ferguson; Stanley L. Jones, 9 July 1975, to Ferguson; Ferguson, 15 July 1975, to Alumni Annual Giving Council, Af–Al, Ferguson Papers; Fadely, 10 Dec. 1975, to John Lee Jellicorse, in Communication & Theatre, Debating, VCAA Records; Jellicorse, 4 April 1980, to Robert L. Miller, in Communication & Theatre, General, VCAA Records; *Carolinian*, 9 Dec. 1971, 4 April, 7 Nov. 1974, 22 Sept., 4 Dec. 1975, 20 Jan., 12 Feb. 1976, 29 April, 5 May 1977, 31 Jan., 11 April 1978.

38. Student Orientation Committee, 7 Sept. 1967, to Ferguson, F; Katherine Taylor, annual report, 24 April 1972, B. of T., Ferguson Papers; *Alumni News*, 55 (Jan. 1967), p. 9; SCORE surveys of Nov. and Dec. 1972, in SCORE, Assistant VCAA Records; *Carolinian*, 1 March 1979; OH: James H. Allen, 11 Sept. 1990; Lori Bushell, 18 April 1991.

39. SCORE surveys of Nov. and Dec. 1972, in SCORE, Assistant VCAA Records; Poll of 15 April 1974, Sa–Sm, Ferguson Papers; Results of Survey Administered to Entering Students, esp. Table 3, in Report... from the Committee on Fraternities and Sororities, with Academic Cabinet Minutes, 21 Feb. 1979; *Alumni News*, 66 (Spring 1978), p. 41; OH: David Boutwell, 16 May 1991.

40. *Carolinian*, 4, 21 March, 19 Sept. 1974. For administrative reaction, see Ferguson statement and James H. Allen to All Members of the University Community, both of 6 March 1974, Sp–Su, Ferguson Papers.

41. For a survey of where students went off campus and spent money in 1965, see Norman W. Schul and Charles R. Hayes, Preliminary Report, UNCG Economic Impact, May 1965, Tables VIII–X, S folder, Ferguson Papers.

42. *Alumni News*, 62 (Summer 1974), pp. 8–9.

43. Report of Alumni Association restructuring committee, 1988, pp. 82–83, Alum. Assn. folder, Moran Papers.

44. Alumnae Annual Giving Council minutes, 15 July 1963, A–Al, Singletary Papers; George W. Hamer, 9 June, 3 July, 21 Aug., 12 Oct. 1972, to Ferguson, Alumni folder; Charles W. Patterson, 5 May, 14 July 1976, to Barbara Parrish, Al, Ferguson Papers; Hamer, 29 June 1988, to William Moran, Alumni, Moran Papers; Gist of Discussion with Dr. Ferguson, [ca. Nov. 1972], Executive Committee, and Barbara Parrish, 6 Aug. 1988, to William Moran, Alumni Association Records, 1899–1988; OH: Brenda Cooper, 25 April 1991; Adelaide Holderness, 26 April 1990.

45. See Gordon Blackwell, 8 July 1960, to Barbara Parrish, A&T–Alum folder, Blackwell Papers.

46. Barbara Parrish, 6 Aug. 1988, to William Moran, Alumni Association Records, 1899–1988; George Hamer, 29 June 1988, to W.E. Moran, Alumni, Moran Papers; OH: Paula Andris, 23 April 1991; Susannah Thomas Watson, 7 Feb. 1991.

47. *Alumnae News*, 51 (1962–63, esp. inside front cover); 52–53 (1963–65); Alumni Association Board of Trustees minutes, 31 May, 1 June 1963, Alumni Association Records, 1899–1988; Barbara Parrish, 23 Nov. 1970, to Mrs. John H. Geis; Mrs. H.H. Walston, 18 Dec. 1970, to Ferguson, in Executive Committee, ibid.; Trudy Atkins, 15 Oct. 1970, to George W. Hamer, Al–Ay, Ferguson Papers.

48. Institutional Self-Study Report, 1972, p. 481; *Greensboro Daily News*, 28 Aug. 1970.

49. Singletary, 24 Oct. 1966, to C.P. Deyton, A; Ferguson, 10 March 1967, to Charles S. Davis, Al–Ay; Charles W. Patterson, 5 May, 14 July 1976, to Barbara Parrish, Al, Ferguson Papers; Parrish, 24 June 1976, to Carol Christopher Maus, Alumni Association Records, 1899–1988; George W. Hamer, 15 June 1970, to James S. Ferguson, with Hamer, 12 May 1988, to William Moran; Charles W. Patterson, 19 July 1988, to Moran, Alumni, Moran Papers; Gladys Strawn Bullard et al., 27 June 1979, to the Alumni Board, Executive Committee, Alumni Association Records, 1899–1988; OH: Brenda Cooper, 25 April 1991; Susannah Thomas Watson, 7 Feb. 1991.

Chapter 29 Notes

1. OH: William E. Moran, 20 Feb. 1990; *Greensboro Record*, 20 April 1979.

2. For faculty views, mostly critical, see OH: C. Bob Clark, 8 Nov. 1990; Kendon Smith, 18 Oct. 1989; Richard Bardolph, 14 May 1991; Jean Buchert, 22 Feb. 1990; M. Elaine Burgess, 8 Nov. 1990; Harriet Kupferer, 27 Oct. 1989; Gilbert Carpenter, 27 April 1990. For similar views by a trustee and administrator, respectively, see OH: Louise Falk, 20 March 1990, and Joanne Creighton, 9 April 1990.

3. See Robert M. O'Kane, 24 Oct. 1979, to Moran, and Moran, 12 Nov. 1979, to O'Kane, Education, Moran Papers.

4. OH: William E. Moran, 20 Feb. 1990; Moran, Notice of Intent to Engage in External Professional Activity for Pay, 3 Nov. 1983 and 26 Sept. 1986, E folders; Moran interview with Angela Brown, 30 Nov. 1990, enclosed with Mary Jellicorse, 31 Jan. 1991, to Wilson Davis, Personal, Moran Papers; *Greensboro Record*, 20 April 1979; Greensboro *News & Record*, 28 April 1985.

5. Lewis, *Marginal Worth*, pp. 139–41; Jim Clotfelter, 19 Jan. 1994, to Moran, Adm. & Planning, Moran Papers.

6. See Keller, *Academic Strategy*, pp. 34–37; OH: Betsy Umstead, 7 Dec. 1989.

7. See Clotfelter's preparations for this activity in Legislative Matters, 1991, Moran Papers.

8. See the charge to her planning task force, in Deans' Council Records, 24 April 1985.

9. For the *Quo Vadimus* controversy in 1988, see the extensive correspondence in Arts & Sciences, Depts.: Communication and Theatre; in VCAA-Quo Vadimus; Notes of College of Arts & Sciences council meetings, 24 March, 7 April, 3 Oct. 1988, Arts & Sciences, General, all in Moran Papers; Academic Cabinet Minutes, 6 April, 7 Sept., 5 Oct., 2 Nov. 1988; *Carolinian*, 17 March, 14 April 1988. For later comments about Zinser from a subordinate dean and the faculty chairman, respectively, see OH: Joanne Creighton, 9 April 1990; Jean Buchert, 22 Feb. 1990.

10. For an admiring and largely autobiographical post-Gallaudet interview with Zinser, see *Winston-Salem Journal*, 10 April 1988. For examples of turf struggles, see Zinser, 25 July 1988, to Moran, HES; Zinser, 20 Feb. 1989, to James H. Allen, F; and correspondence among Zinser, Moran, Fred Drake, and others, 3 Oct. to 10 Nov. 1988, in VCAA, Moran Papers.

11. Richard L. Moore, Reorganization of Campus Computing, 26 July 1990, w/Trustee Executive Committee Minutes, 26 July 1990.

12. Faculty Government Committee, [Feb. 1980], to Faculty Council, Faculty Government Committee, VCAA Records; *Carolinian*, 29 March 1977.

13. See UNCG Planning Process, 1980–83: External Relations, pp. 30–33.

14. See the University Breakfasts folders, Moran Papers.

15. *Alumni News*, 70 (Winter 1982), pp. 4–5; (Spring 1982), p. 11. For the impact in 1987–88, see Greensboro *News & Record*, 21 Aug. 1989.

16. See the correspondence in HPERD, 1982–83, and Michael Fleming, 25 April 1986, to Moran, B. of T., Moran Papers.

17. See Moran, Memo to the File, 3 June 1986, B. of T., Moran Papers.

18. Table 2: Race and Sex Profiles for Individual Boards, 2/6/80, B. of G./B. of T.; Members of the Board of Trustees, 1 Aug. 1990, B. of T., Moran Papers.

19. See Stanley Jones, 17 Aug. 1979, to Moran, in Deans' Council Records; letters to Moran from John W. Kennedy, 5 Sept. 1979; James H. Allen, 10 Sept. 1979; Charles W. Patterson, 17 Sept. 1979, and Chancellor's Cabinet Minutes, 24 Sept., 1 Oct. 1979, in Chancellor's Cabinet Records; Roland H. Nelson, 5 Nov. 1979, to Moran, Education, Moran Papers; and OH: Robert Eason, 13 March 1996; Greensboro *News & Record*, 27 March 1983, pp. B1, 8. For discussions of the transition problem nationally, see Ernest A. Lynton and Jerome M. Zeigler, in Johnson & Bell, *Metropolitan Universities*, pp. xiii–xiv, 224–25; and Elliott, *Urban Campus*, p. 34.

20. Karabell, *What's College For*, p. xiv; Ziegler, in Johnson & Bell, *Metropolitan Universities*, pp. 219–20.

21. Correspondence, Oct.–Nov. 1993, in Co, Moran Papers.

22. Summary of Chancellor Moran's remarks to the Planning Council, September 23, 1981, Campus Planning; Moran, 9 Dec. 1981, to Jack Bardon and Gail Hennis, Campus Design; Moran, 5 Dec. 1983, to Faculty and Staff, Campus Plan; Robert Miller, 14 Aug. 1990, to Donald DeRosa, Inst. Mission Review; C.D. Spangler, 3 Dec. 1991, to Committee on Educational Planning, Policies and Programs, in Engineering & Science Center; Moran, UNCG Mis-

sion/Program Planning, remarks to faculty senate, 4 Dec. 1991, Engineering & Science Center; Moran, 13 March 1992, to Roch Smith et al., Inst. Mission Review; [Moran], 28 Aug. 1992, to Don/Jim [DeRosa/Clotfelter]; Moran, 3 Sept. 1992, to Roy Carroll, J–L; Moran, 11 Feb. 1993, to Denise Baker et al., Mission, Moran Papers; Greensboro *News & Record*, 27 March 1983, pp. B1, 8; UNCG Program Authority/Mission, 1991–2001, [Jan. 1991], pp. 1–4, in UNCG Program & Mission, 1991–2001; OH: William Moran, 20 Feb. 1990, 28 Jan. 1991.

23. See, e.g., the correspondence in International Programs, 1993; Moran, 8 Oct. 1993, to Donald DeRosa, Bond Issue, Moran Papers.

24. Greensboro *News & Record*, 27 Sept., 6 Oct. 1994.

25. Larry Hargett, 1 Oct. 1981, to Moran, ICA; Bernard B. Keele, 28 April 1986, to Ty Buckner et al.; Miriam Holland, 11 Aug. 1986, to Moran, Development; Excerpt from Comments of William E. Moran, Faculty Council, 18 Nov. 1986, ICA; Richard L. Moore, 24 May 1993, to Faculty & Staff, VC Development, Moran Papers; Acad. Cabinet Minutes, 5 Feb. 1986; Deans' Council Records, June 1986, 29 April 1992, 31 March 1993; Chancellor's Cabinet Minutes, 1 March 1993. For the hyphen, see Greensboro *News & Record*, 22 Jan. 1986; Bernard B. Keele, 31 Jan. 1986, to Vice Chancellors, Deans, & Directors, Development, Moran Papers. For the logo, see Moran, 29 April 1980, to Faculty and Staff, w/Chancellor's Cabinet Minutes, 28 April 1980; Richard L. Moore, 13 May 1992, to Moran, VC Development, Moran Papers; Vertical File: Logo, and Development & University Relations. For the seal, see Trudy Atkins, 25 Oct. 1979, to Moran, VC Development; Jack Bardon and Gail Hennis, 31 Jan. 1984, to Moran, U, Moran Papers; Academic Cabinet Minutes, 3 April 1985; Vertical File: Seal. For the colors, see Tony Ladd, 21 March 1977, to James H. Allen, School (HPERD-Home Ec), Ferguson Papers; Nelson E. Bobb, 17 Nov. 1983, to Moran, and Moran, 21 Nov. 1983, to Bobb, ICA, Moran Papers; Vertical File: Colors.

26. For academic planning nationally, see Keller, *Academic Strategy*. For UNC directives, see Wm. Friday, administrative memorandum on long-range planning, 22 May 1984, in Deans' Council Records.

27. Moran, 28 Sept. 1979, to Louis C. Stephens, L; Fred L. Drake, 4 Dec. 1981, to the Faculty, Campus Construction/Design, Moran Papers.

28. *Greensboro Daily News*, 7 Sept. 1980; [Elisabeth Zinser], Academic Plan for the Development of the University, w/Zinser, 28 Sept. 1983, to Moran, Campus Planning, Moran Papers; [Zinser], Charge to Deans Council for Academic Planning, 7 Dec. 1983, Deans' Council Records; [Zinser], *Quo Vadimus*, 1987. For a summary of planning efforts from 1980 to 1991, see Institutional Self-Study Report, 1992, pp. 60–70, 84–91. For Moran's view of the Quo Vadimus study, see Moran, 7 Oct. 1993, to Donald DeRosa, Unit Planning, Moran Papers. For others' views, see the correspondence in VCAA-Quo Vadimus, 1988, Moran Papers.

29. For the advisory planning council, see Richard L. Moore, 20 May 1988, to Moran, VC Adm. & Planning; Moran, 6 Dec. 1991, to Provost, Vice Chancellors et al., O–P; Jim Clotfelter, 4 Jan. 1994, to Moran, Adm. & Planning, Moran Papers; Institutional Self-Study Report, 1992, pp. 97–98.

30. See Institutional Self-Study Report, 1992, pp. 88–89.

31. Physical Master Plan, w/Orientation for New Members, 8 March 1984, B. of G., Moran Papers; Greensboro *News & Record*, 22 Oct., 16 Nov. 1984.

32. Moran, 20 Nov. 1986, to C.D. Spangler, B of T; Moran, 27 Aug. 1987, to Charles Hayes, B. of T.; J. Douglas Galyon, 4 April 1989, to Moran, B. of T.; Fred Drake, 19 Feb., 20 Nov. 1992, to L. Felix Joyner; Philip H. Richman, 1 Aug. 1994, to Joyner; Richman, 1 Aug. 1994, to Moran, VC Bus. Aff., Moran Papers; Trustee Minutes, 29 Sept. 1994, w/Land Acquisition background information; Greensboro *News & Record*, 29 April 1990, 13 Oct. 1996.

33. Planning Process, 1980–83: Student Life, Table 1, p. 27; ibid.: Land, Buildings, & Equipment, pp. 71–72.

34. See Dorothy F. Sutton, 6 Nov. 1979, to Moran, Traffic/Parking; H.L. Ferguson, [Parking] Action Item, 18 Dec. 1979, B. of T./B. of G., Moran Papers; *Carolinian*, 27 Aug. 1981, 26 Aug. 1982, 24 Aug. 1989, 16 April 1992, 30 Sept. 1993.

35. General Faculty Minutes, 17 Nov. 1992; UNCG *Bulletin*, Fall 1993, pp. 15–17; Physical Plan for Development of the Campus, in Faculty Senate Minutes, 1 March 1995; Greensboro *News & Record*, 20 Aug. 1997.

36. H.S. Odom, 5 March 1980 (two memos), to Lawrence Hart, Music, Moran Papers; OH: William Moran, 20 Feb. 1990, 28 Jan. 1991; Robert Eason, 13 March 1996.

37. Planning Process, 1980–83: Land, Buildings & Equipment, p. 10, 12 (incl. quotation); Stanley Jones, 16 Oct. 1981, to Lawrence Fincher, Budget, Moran Papers.

38. Greensboro *News & Record*, 10 Feb. 1986; UNCG Program and Mission, 1991–2001, p. 29.

39. OH: Fred Drake, 15 Feb. 1990.

40. See Greensboro *News & Record* editorial, 8 Feb. 1996.

41. *Carolinian*, 14 Nov. 1991, pp. 8, 15; Greensboro *News & Record*, 30 Oct. 1994, 10 Feb., 16 March 1995; Board of Trustees Minutes, 17 Nov. 1994, 9 Feb. 1995; Board of Trustees, Statement Regarding the Location and Planning for the School of Music Building, 5 Dec. 1994, Vertical File: Music Bldg. (New); Campus Planning Committee report, 29 March 1995, w/Faculty Senate Minutes, 26 April 1995.

42. *Carolinian*, 31 Jan. 1991; Press release: New Clocktower, 1993, OIS News Releases.

43. *Campus* newsletter, 8–22 Aug. 1988, and Press release: "One of the Finest in the Country," 7 Nov. 1988, both in Vertical File: Dining Halls; Greensboro *News & Record*, 15 Nov. 1988.

44. Tony Ladd, Project Planning Guide, Physical Activity Complex, 30 June 1980, PE Bldg., Moran Papers.

45. *Carolinian*, 27 Aug. 1992; *Alumni News*, 82 (Winter 1993), p. 7; Greensboro *News & Record*, 11 July 1990.

46. Ellen Greaves, 13 June 1979, to David Payne; Payne et al., 6 Sept. 1979, to Board of Trustees, B. of T./B. of G.; David B. Knight, 2 Aug. 1988, to Moran, Intercoll. Athletics, Moran Papers.

47. Greensboro *News & Record*, 8 Sept. 1991, 30 June 1998; *Carolinian*, 12 Sept. 1991; Fred L. Drake, 4 May 1993, to James Allen; David B. Knight, 14, 15 Sept. 1993, to Moran, ICA: Baseball, Moran Papers.

48. Fred L. Drake, 4 Dec. 1992, to Executive Committee, Excellence Foundation, VC Bus. Aff., Moran Papers; Annual Report of Property Purchased or Leased, 23 Sept. 1993, w/Trustee Minutes, 23 Sept. 1993.

49. Ron Moss et al., 1 July 1984, to Moran, R; Correspondence, 1986, in Ca–Ch, 1987–88 in Chapel Fund, 1989 in Ch–Co, 1990 in Chan–Chap, and 1992 in Ch; Board of Trustees Agenda, 8 Nov. 1990, Ca–Ce; Demolition of University-Owned Structures, 15 June 1994, B. of T., 15 June 1994, Moran Papers; Trustees Minutes, 12 Sept., 7 Nov. 1991, 9 April 1992; Faculty Senate Minutes, 1 April 1992; Correspondence in Vertical File: Associated Campus Ministries and Chapel Fund; Greensboro *News & Record*, 27 Nov., 7, 26 Dec. 1988, 19 Feb., 16 Dec. 1989, 9 Nov. 1990, 10 April 1992, 15 Oct. 1994; *Carolinian*, 16 April 1992.

50. Institutional Self-Study, 1972, Student Report, p. 14; OH: James Allen, 11 Sept. 1990; Moran, 9 Jan. 1980, to Henry L. Ferguson, VC Bus. Aff., Moran Papers. See also *Carolinian*, 27 Aug. 1981, 18 Nov. 1982.

51. Cherry Callahan, 8 Oct. 1980, to James H. Allen, w/enclosure from Helen P. Yoder, D; Robert T. Tomlinson, 2 Aug. 1982, to John E. Helmintoller, and Tomlinson, 26 Aug. 1982, to Mr. & Mrs. Calvin M. Price, R; Fred L. Drake, 5 June 1987, to Don Huffman, VC Bus. Aff., Moran Papers; Student Senate minutes, 20 Jan. 1981, SGA Records.

52. Asst. VC Terry Ford, in *Carolinian*, 27 Aug. 1981; Robert T. Tomlinson, 21 Oct. 1982, to Janet Yates, R; Tomlinson, 27 Feb. 1985, to James H. Allen, R, Moran Papers; *Carolinian*, 7 Feb. 1984.

53. *Carolinian*, 30 Aug., 6 Sept. 1979, 11 Sept. 1980; Planning Process, 1980–83: Student Life, p. 54.

54. Robert T. Tomlinson, 20 Nov. 1987, to Amy Weaver, Student Affairs, Moran Papers; *Carolinian*, 3 Sept. 1987, 8 Sept. 1988, 7 Sept. 1989, 8, 15 April, 2 Sept. 1993, 31 March 1994.

55. Greensboro *News & Record*, 25 Aug. 1993; *Carolinian*, 2 Sept. 1993.

56. Keller, *Academic Strategy*, pp. 3–12. See also Geiger, "Research Universities," pp. 68–70; Geiger, *Research and Relevant Knowledge*, pp. 311–12; Loeb, *Generation at the Crossroads*, pp. 46–47; Nichols, "Federal Science Policy & Universities," pp. 199–204.

57. Callan, "Government & Higher Education," pp. 11–12.

58. Chancellor's Cabinet Minutes, 1, 8 Oct. 1979; Notes for the Record, 5 Feb. 1982; Moran, 8 Feb. 1982, to the Vice Chancellors; Fred L. Drake, 8 Oct. 1982, to Moran; Moran, 12 Oct. 1982, to Faculty Council, Budget; Drake, 8 May 1984, to David J. Pratto, Budget; Donald V. DeRosa, 15 May 1990, to Moran, Budget, Moran Papers; Institutional Self-Study Report, 1992, p. 233; OH: Fred Drake, 15 Feb. 1990.

59. See Moran, 19 Aug. 1991, to Betty Ann Marcus, Tuition & Fees, Moran Papers.

60. For the student/faculty ratio, see Institutional Self-Study Report, 1992, p. 152; Reaffirmation Committee report, p. 34; Donald J. Reichard, 17 June 1994, to David R. Soderquist, Enrollment Management Committee Records.

61. Fred L. Drake, 4 April 1990, to Moran, Chancellor's Cabinet Records. For the student/faculty ratio in 1982, see Donald J. Reichard, 12 May 1982, to A. Lawrence Fincher, Budget, Moran Papers. For an enlightening description of the budget-making process at UNC campuses in the '80s, see UNCG Planning Process, 1980–83: Budgetary Resources, pp. 53–63. For a 1992 update, see Institutional Self-Study Report, 1992, pp. 228–35.

62. W.R. Davis, 4 Oct. 1991, to Moran; Moran, 17 Oct. 1991, to Davis, B. of G., Moran Papers; Moran, address to faculty, 20 Aug. 1993, Vertical File: Office of Chancellor; Greensboro *News & Record*, 12 Oct. 1991.

63. Stanley L. Jones, 8 Dec. 1981, to Hoyt Price, Deans' Council Records.

64. Deans' Council Notes, 7, 28 Oct. 1987; Moran, 15 June 1990, to C.D. Spangler, and other correspondence in National Reference Study, 1990, Moran Papers; UNCG Program & Mission, 1991–2001, [Jan. 1991], pp. 22–25, and Appendix II; Institutional Self-Study Report, 1992, pp. 159–60 and passim; Moran, 2 Dec. 1992, to Priscilla Taylor, B. of G., Moran Papers; OH: Moran, 28 Jan. 1991; James Allen, 11 Sept. 1990; Fred Drake, 15 Feb. 1990.

65. See Moran, 7 June 1994, to C.D. Spanger; Moran, 20 July 1994, to William F. Little, Budget, Moran Papers; Faculty Senate Minutes, 6 Sept. 1995, 13 March 1996; General Faculty Minutes, 13 March 1996; Greensboro *News & Record*, 15, 18 (editorial) March 1996. For UNCG's operating revenues and expenditures, 1990–94, see UNCG *Fact Book*, 1994–95, p. V-1.

66. *Campus* newsletter, 2 Sept. 1996.

67. *UNCG Magazine*, 2 (Summer 2000), p. 2.

68. Geiger, "Research Universities," pp. 68–70; Geiger, *Research and Relevant Knowledge*, pp. 311–14.

69. Planning Process, 1980–83: Budgetary Resources, p. 78; UNCG *Fact Book*, 1997–98, p. V-1.

70. Gifts, Grants & Bequests, 1979–80, [1980], VC Development, Moran Papers; Planning Process, 1980–83, External Resources, pp. 23–25, 55–61.

71. Moran, 13 Jan. 1981, to Louis C. Stephens, Development;Summary of Alumni Private Gift Support Through Prospectus III, w/Richard L. Moore, 9 Oct. 1987, to Cathy Stewart

Vaughn, Administration, Moran Papers; Vertical File: Prospectus III Campaign; Faculty Senate Minutes, 22 April 1992.

72. Greensboro *News & Record*, 15 April 2000.

73. UNCG *Fact Book*, 1997–98, pp. V-1; Sources of Support, 1993–94, (1994), Excellence Foundation, Moran Papers; Geiger, *Research and Relevant Knowledge*, p. 312.

74. *Carolinian*, 30 Oct. 1975.

75. *Greensboro Daily News*, 13 (p. B-14), 17 June 1972; J.M. Bryan, 16, 19 June 1972, to James S. Ferguson; Ferguson, 3 July 1972, to Bryan, Bryan Papers, UNCG.

76. Charles Patterson, 23 Aug. 1976, to David Shelton, Development Office, Business/Economics School Records, 1973–84.

77. David H. Shelton, 5 Dec. 1979, to Charles W. Patterson, Development Office, Business/Economics School Records, 1973–84; Copies of Leary's *Greensboro Daily News* letter and Bryan's response are in B, Moran Papers, 1980; Moran, 2 July, 7 Oct. 1981, to Stanley L. Jones; Jones, 16 Nov. 1981, to Moran, B&E; Moran, 2 July 1984, to E.S. (Jim) Melvin, and other 1984 correspondence in B, Moran Papers.

78. Joseph M. Bryan, 3 Aug. 1983, to Moran, Development: Prospectus III, Moran Papers; Greensboro *News & Record*, 31 July, 1 Nov. 1987; *Campus*, 10–23 Aug. 1987, pp. 1, 8.

79. UNCG *Bulletin*, Fall 1995, p. 8; Cline, *Adding Value*, pp. 259–60, 334, 343.

80. Greensboro *News & Record*, 7 March 1994; Chancellor's Report, 1999–2000, p. 23.

81. Moran, 2 Dec. 1992, to Elisabeth A. Zinser, University Investment Committee; Moran, Remarks, 10 Aug. 1994, Development-Benefactors, Moran Papers.

82. Moran, 17 Feb. 1983, to Michael Weaver, U; Responsibilities of the University Investment Committee, 11 Nov. 1980 (rev. 7 Aug. 1990), Univ. Invest. Comm., Moran Papers.

83. Moran, 11 Sept. 1981, to Richmond G. Bernhardt, Excellence Fund; Tables: Endowment Income by Purpose, Year Ended 30 June 1991, Univ. Invest. Comm., 1992; [Wilson Davis], Story Suggestions and Background Material, [Jan. 1994], I (letter), Moran Papers.

84. See the correspondence in VCAA Records: Professors, Named, Policies; and "Named and Endowed Professorships," May 1986, N–O; Moran, 4 Jan. 1985, to Joanne Bluethenthal, Arts/Sciences: Religious Studies; Donald V. DeRosa, 10 Dec. 1992, to Moran, Excellence Fdn.; DeRosa, 25 Oct. 1993, to William F. Little, Acad. Aff., Moran Papers.

85. Astin, "Educating Women," p. 480; Levine, "How the Academic Profession is Changing," pp. 6–7.

86. Moran, 5 Aug. 1980, to Stanley Jones, VCAA, Moran Papers.

87. Table 6: Variables Related to Persistence by UNC Institution, UNC Board of Governors, draft report: Analysis of Retention and Graduation .... Jan. 1991, w/Raymond Dawson, 21 Nov. 1990, to The Chancellors, Acad. Aff., Moran Papers.

88. King, *Multicampus University*, p. 22.

89. Robert W. Hites, 5 Dec. 1983, to Elisabeth Zinser, Admissions, Moran Papers. Unless otherwise cited, the foregoing data were drawn primarily from different editions of the UNCG *Fact Book*.

90. Levine, "How the Academic Profession is Changing," pp. 7–9; Boyer, *College*, pp. 30–32, 77–79, 140–42; Keller, *Academic Strategy*, pp. 16–17; Lucas, *Crisis in the Academy*, pp. 97–99, 107, 110–11. For SAT scores, see Ravitch, *Schools We Deserve*, pp. 48–49; William Beaver, "Is It Time to Replace the SAT?" *Academe*, 82 (May/June 1996), pp. 38–39.

91. Schrag, "End of the Second Chance?", pp. 72–74; Alvin J. Schexnider, 21 Jan. 1986, to Ansley A. Abraham, Q; Jerry Harrelson, 25 May 1994, to Donald V. DeRosa, Admissions, Moran Papers.

92. Herbert Wells, 23 Sept. 1983, to Elisabeth Zinser, Enrollment Management, Assistant VCAA Records.

93. UNCG Establishing New ACES Program . . . , OIS News Release, 7 February 1992; UNCG Offering 318 Evening Courses . . . , ibid., 16 Nov. 1992.

94. Richard L. Moore, 9 Feb. 1988, to Moran, VC Adm & Planning, Moran Papers.

95. See, e.g., Questions to Moran from Walter Beale and another member of the English department, [1982], Arts/Sciences, Moran Papers; Gaylord Hageseth, 23 Feb. 1994, to Enrollment Management Committee, Enrollment Management Committee Records; *Carolinian*, 16 Sept. 1993; OH: Betsy Umstead, 7 Dec. 1989; Tom Kirby-Smith, 10 Sept. 1990; Lori Bushell, 18 April 1991; Pat Cross, 15 May 1991; Robert Eason, 14 Feb. 1996.

96. Steve Danford, 30 April 1993, to Moran, Enrollment Management Committee Records; *Triad Style*, 15 June 1995; Greensboro *News & Record*, 1 Oct. 1995.

97. Faculty Senate Minutes, 6 Oct. 1993; Deans' Council Notes, 19 Jan. 1994; Enrollment Management Committee, 3 May 1994, to the Faculty, Enrollment Management Committee Records. For an exceptional faculty statement of concern for the university's enrollment and related problems, and for an administration critique of the report, see the Enrollment Management Committee's sixteen-page letter to the Faculty, 3 May 1994, and Donald J. Reichard, 13 May 1994, to Richard L. Moore, both in Enrollment Management Committee Records; Donald V. DeRosa, 6 June 1994, to Moran, Admissions, Moran Papers.

98. Greensboro *News & Record*, 26, 29 May 1994.

99. Robert W. Hites and Paul Lindsay, 14 March 1984, to Admissions Policy Committee; Admissions Policy Committee minutes, 19 Sept. 1983, 19 March, 16 April 1984; Admissions Policy Committee, 2 April 1984, to Academic Cabinet, VCAA Records: Admissions Policy Comm.; Donald V. DeRosa, 6 June 1994, to Moran, Admissions, Moran Papers; Stephen Danford, 6 Aug. 1994, to Donald DeRosa; DeRosa, 26 Aug. 1994, to Steve C. Danford, Enrollment Management Comm. Records; General Faculty Minutes, 1 March 1995; Faculty Senate Minutes, 5 April, 6 Sept., 4 Oct. 1995. For black student exceptions to the 800 SAT minimum before 1994, see Charles E. Rickard, 5 Oct. 1989, to Admissions Policies Committee, Intercoll. Athletics, Moran Papers; Greensboro *News & Record*, 29 May 1994.

100. SAT Score Trends, 1962–1988, [1989], Admissions, Moran Papers; Elisabeth A. Zinser, 2 April, 23 Sept. 1986, to Alvin J. Schexnider; Schexnider, 12 April, 2 Oct. 1986, to Zinser; Zinser, 13 Oct. 1986, to Moran; Moran, 28 March 1988, to Chuck Rickard, Admissions; Zinser, 18 April 1986, to Schexnider; Skip Moore, 8 Sept. 1986, to File; Enrollment Discussion, 22 March 1988; Moran, 20 Oct. 1988, to Don V. DeRosa et al.; Fred L. Drake, 28 Oct. 1988, to Moran; Richard L. Moore, 5 Nov. 1990, to Moran, Enrollment; Moran, 28 Nov. 1989, to DeRosa and Rickard, E, Moran Papers; Charles E. Rickard, 8 Sept. 1986, to Schexnider, Enrollment Projections, Assistant VCAA Records; Deans' Council notes, 11 Feb. 1987; Greensboro *News & Record*, 19 Sept. 1989: People and Places.

101. Donald V. DeRosa, 28 May 1992, to Moran, Discretionary Allocation Requests, Moran Papers.

102. Alvin J. Schexnider, 2 Oct. 1986, to Elisabeth A. Zinser, Admissions; Donald V. DeRosa, 6 June 1994, to Moran, Admissions, Moran Papers.

103. Greensboro *News & Record*, 13 Dec. 1997, 30 June 1998.

104. *Statistical Abstract of Higher Education in North Carolina*, 1994–95, pp. 131, 133, 138.

Chapter 30 Notes

1. Institutional Self-Study, 1991–92, Reaffirmation (Visiting) Committee report, 1993, p. 18; UNCG *Fact Book*, 1979–80, p. 63; *Statistical Abstract of Higher Education in North Carolina*, 1994–95, p. 101.

2. UNCG *Fact Book*, 1979–80, pp. 59, 61; 1994–95, p. I-21; Richard L. Moore, 14 Feb. 1990, to Beverly S. Pugh, Adm. & Planning, Moran Papers.

3. Executive Committee of the Black Faculty and Staff Association, 25 Sept. 1986, to Moran, B, Moran Papers.

4. UNCG *Fact Book*, 1997–98, p. I-14; *Carolinian*, 18 Feb. 1988; Alma S. Adams, Greensboro Branch, NAACP, 31 Aug. 1989, to Moran, Minority Affairs, Moran Papers.

5. For the university's considerable affirmative action efforts, see the Affirmative Action folders in each year's Moran Papers; the Meetings folder in his papers for 1988; and Greensboro *News & Record*, 25 Jan. 1998. For the national picture in the '80s, see Keller, *Academic Strategy*, pp. 17–18; Bowen and Schuster, *American Professors*, pp. 152–55.

6. Stanley L. Jones, 5 Aug. 1980, to Moran, Deans' Council Records.

7. Jencks and Riesman, *Academic Revolution*, p. 188; Bowen and Schuster, *American Professors*, pp. 60–65; Leslie et al., *Part-Time Faculty*, pp. 3–7, 18–29; Levine, "How the Academic Profession is Changing," p. 14; *Academe*, 84 (Jan.–Feb. 1998), pp. 54–57; Karabell, *What's College For?*, pp. 192–95, 204–06; Gappa and Leslie, *Invisible Faculty*, xii–xiii, 1–6, 12, 24–31, 34–36, 84, 91–95.

8. Table II: Number of Part-Time Faculty by Sex with Highest Degree, First Semester 1963–64, [1963], Faculty folder, Singletary Papers.

9. Full-Time and Part-Time Instructional Faculty... 1989–1993, Enrollment Management Committee Records; SACS Commission on Colleges, Institutional Profile form, Fall 1993, p. 3, in Self-Study, Moran Papers.

10. Bob Clark, 8 Jan. 1992, to Moran et al., Fa, Moran Papers.

11. These figures are obtained by averaging the grades received for each of the four academic ranks (professor down to instructor) in each year. See *Academe*, appendixes to the spring or summer issues each year. See also Donald J. Reichard, 30 June 1993, to Moran, I (letter), Moran Papers. For UNCG's placement as a doctoral vs. a comprehensive university in this context, see Institutional Self-Study, 1991–92, Reaffirmation (Visiting) Committee report, 1993, pp. 30–31.

12. College Salary Study Committee, 12 Nov. 1980, to Administrative Council, and the committee's report, 12 Dec. 1980, in VCAA Records: Arts & Sciences College; Barry T. Hirsch and Karen Leppel, "Sex Discrimination in Faculty Salaries: Evidence from an Historically Women's University," July 1981, Salary Study, Moran Papers; Faculty Salary Study Committee report, 15 May 1981, w/Trustees' Minutes, 17 Sept. 1981; Faculty Salary Committee, annual report, 1993–94, w/Faculty Senate Minutes, 27 April 1994. For the national picture, see Glazer-Raymo, *Shattering the Myths*, pp. 81–89.

13. Barry T. Hirsch and Karen Leppel, "Sex Discrimination in Faculty Salaries: Evidence from an Historically Women's University," July 1981, Salary Study, Moran Papers.

14. See report of Jean Buchert, Academic Cabinet Minutes, 2 Oct. 1985; Jack I. Bardon and Eleanor F. McCrickard, 20 June 1989, to Academic Cabinet, w/Academic Cabinet Minutes, 6 Sept. 1989; Joseph E. Johnson, 11 May 1993, to the Faculty, Faculty Senate, Moran Papers; UNCG *Fact Book*, 1994–95, pp. I-22–23. See also Greensboro *News & Record*, 24 May 1994.

15. Moran, 12 Sept. 1979, to the Faculty; Moran, 1 Nov. 1982, to Stanley L. Jones et al., Academic Affairs, Moran Papers; Wm. Friday, Administrative Memorandum #207, 17 Sept. 1984, VCAA Records: Retirement Policies.

16. Greensboro *News & Record*, 18, 19 Aug. 1986; Academic Cabinet Minutes, 10 Sept. 1986; Trustees Minutes, 11 Sept. 1986.

17. Academic Cabinet Minutes, 7 Feb. 1990.

18. For the large volume of correspondence and other materials on this subject, see R (1985), Research (1987), and Animal Research (1988–91), Moran Papers; Academic Cabinet

Minutes, 2 Nov. 1988; Trustees' Minutes, 8 Feb., 8 Nov. 1990; *Carolinian*, 20 April 1989, 1, 15 Nov. 1990; Vertical File: Animal Rights. For national background on the animal research controversy, see Nichols, "Federal Science Policy and Universities," p. 210.

19. Moran, 15 Feb. 1994, to Faculty and Staff, Vertical File: Office of Chancellor; *Carolinian*, 24 Feb. 1994; Greensboro *News & Record*, 2 March 1994.

20. See Moran, 16 June 1989, to Annie Lee Singletary, and Rebecca G. Adams, 23 June 1989, to Moran, Arts & Sciences: Depts.; Moran, 24 May 1994, to Tom Monk, Arts & Sciences College, Moran Papers.

21. James Svara, 25 April 1980, to Moran and Walter Puterbaugh, w/Academic Cabinet Minutes, 30 April 1980; Remarks of Amy Charles, Academic Cabinet Minutes, 5 May 1982; Amy Charles, 27 April 1983, to Moran, Arts & Sciences, Moran Papers.

22. Academic Cabinet Minutes, 5 Sept. 1990, 6 Feb. 1991; Constitution of the Faculty, w/Moran, 14 Feb. 1991, to the Faculty, Faculty Council, Moran Papers; Ad Hoc Committee on Elections and Transition, 20 Feb. 1991, to the Deans Council, Deans' Council Records, 20 Feb. 1991; *Carolinian*, 24 Jan. 1991.

23. See remarks by Moran and Bob Clark, Faculty Senate Minutes, 22 April 1992; Institutional Self-Study, 1992: Supplement, 1993, pp. 45–46.

24. Donald V. DeRosa, 19 Aug. 1993, to Moran, and Moran, 1 Sept. 1993, to Robert Cannon et al., Faculty Senate, Moran Papers; Institutional Self-Study, 1992: Reaffirmation (Visiting) Committee report, 1993, p. 73.

25. See graph and table showing faculty course loads and teaching loads, Fall 1990, in Enrollment Management Committee Records.

26. *Carolinian*, 12 April, 27 Sept. 1990. See also Randolph Bulgin, in Academic Cabinet Minutes, 5 Sept. 1984; Faculty Senate Minutes, 4 Oct. 1995.

27. See Description of Awards Made at Honors Convocation, May 4 1993, T, Moran Papers.

28. Data on research assignments, 1977–82, [1984], R; Table: Research Assignments 1993–1994, [1992], Research, Moran Papers.

29. See Use of Indirect Cost Recovered: Guidelines . . . , 4 April 1985, Research, Moran Papers, 1992; Correspondence in I (letter) folder, Moran Papers, 1994; Provost DeRosa remarks, Faculty Senate Minutes, 13 Jan. 1993; L. DiAnne Borders, Overhead Receipts and the Budget Process, w/Faculty Senate Minutes, 17 April 1996. For overhead revenue as compensation for state underfunding, see Moran, remarks to the faculty senate, 2 March 1994, p. 4, B. of T., Moran Papers.

30. UNCG, Sponsored Programs Activities, Se–St, [1984], Moran Papers; UNCG Planning Process, 1980–83: External Resources, p. 87.

31. *Campus* newsletter, 30 March–12 April 1987; Greensboro *News & Record*, 6 Sept. 1989.

32. Donald V. DeRosa, 7 Aug. 1987, to Moran and Elisabeth Zinser; Moran, 28 Oct. 1987, to C.D. Spangler, Jr.; DeRosa, 14 Dec. 1987, to Patricia Chamings et al., Research, Moran Papers.

33. UNCG *Fact Book*, 1994–95, pp. VIII-1, 4–6.

34. James H. Thompson, 27 Nov. 1979, to Charles W. Patterson, Chancellor's Cabinet Records, 11 Feb. 1980; Thompson, 6 Dec. 1979, to Moran, VCAA Records: Library, General; Thompson, 14 Oct. 1981, to Vice Chancellor Jones, L; Doris Hulbert and Marla Edelman, 15 Oct. 1990, to the Faculty; Hulbert, 21 Nov. 1990, to Paul Duvall et al., Library, Moran Papers.

35. UNCG *Fact Book*, 1994–95, p. VIII-8.

36. Greensboro *News & Record*, 17 Oct. 1990; *Carolinian*, 20 Sept. 1990.

37. Institutional Self-Study Report, 1992, pp. 167–70; Ibid., Reaffirmation (Visiting) Committee Report, 1993, pp. 62–64; OH: Nancy Fogarty, 27 March 1990.

38. Aubrey S. Garlington, 29 Nov. 1979, to Moran; Elisabeth Zinser, 20 Sept. 1988, to James Thompson and Arthur Tollefson, Music, Moran Papers; Thompson, 8 Jan. 1987, to Zinser et al., Library Director Records: Academic Affairs.

39. Moran, 5 April 1983, to Vice Chancellors et al., VCAA Records: Archives; James H. Thompson, 3 Dec. 1984, to Moran, L; Betty Carter, 17 July 1986, to Emilie Mills; Mills and Thompson, 29 July 1986, to Moran, Library, Moran Papers; OH: Emilie Mills, 30 Jan. 1990.

40. *Greensboro Daily News*, 14 Jan. 1982; James Thompson, 14 Jan. 1982, to Vice Chancellor Jones, L, Moran Papers.

41. Wilson Davis, Press Release, 6 Dec. 1988, in Faculty File: Thompson.

42. Stanley L. Jones, 28 April 1982, to Faculty and Staff, Vertical File: LRC; Current Condition of the Learning Resources Center, June 4, 1984, VCAA Records: LRC; Richard L. Moore, 7 March 1986, to Elisabeth Zinser, and Zinser, ca. 13 March 1986, to Moran, L, Moran Papers; Institutional Self-Study Report, 1992, pp. 171–74.

43. R.C.F. Bartels, Comments Relating to Campus Computing, [Oct. 1981], Computing, Moran Papers.

44. University Committee for Computing and Related Technology, final report, April 1984, Deans' Council Records; *Carolinian*, 17 Nov. 1981; Charles A. Church et al., 20 Jan. 1983, to Stephen Danford; Albert Link, 7 Oct. 1983, to Elisabeth Zinser, Computing, Moran Papers.

45. T.W. Hildebrandt, 5 April 1982, to Stanley L. Jones; Jones, 14 May 1982, to Moran; Jere Hershey, 29 Sept. 1982, to Moran, Computing, Moran Papers.

46. Stephen C. Danford, 17 May 1984, to Elisabeth Zinser, VCAA Records: Computer Education/Computer Science.

47. Moran, 15 Feb. 1985, to Elisabeth Zinser, and other correspondence that year in Computing, Moran Papers.

48. Richard L. Moore, 5 July 1990, to Vice Chancellors and Deans, Admin. & Planning, Moran Papers; Division of Administration and Planning, annual report, 1990–91, VC for Adm./Planning, Annual Reports.

49. Stephen Danford, 25 May 1987, to Elisabeth Zinser, Computing, Moran Papers; Institutional Self-Study Annual Report, 1992, pp. 175–77; James Clotfelter, 14 Dec. 1992, to Provost and Deans, Deans' Council Records, 16 Dec. 1992.

50. *Carolinian*, 27 Feb. 1992; Greensboro *News & Record*, 12 Feb. 1999.

51. Faculty Senate Minutes, 28 April 1993; Brian Long, UNCG Creating High-Tech Computing Environment . . . , OIS News Releases, 13 Jan. 1994.

52. LeBlanc, "Concept of General Education, pp. 519—31; Lucas, *Crisis in the Academy*, pp. 144–45; Boyer, *College*, pp. 83–87.

53. More Structured Approach, News Bureau Press Release, 11 Aug. 1981, VCAA Records: Arts & Sciences, Curriculum Revisions; *Carolinian*, 3 Sept. 1981; OH: Robert Miller, 23 Jan. 1990.

54. Terrance McConnell, 23 Oct. 1986, to Roch Smith, w/Academic Cabinet Minutes, 5 Nov. 1986.

55. Faculty Council Minutes, 20 April 1988; Joanne V. Creighton, 7 Sept. 1988, to Jack Bardon; Bardon, 12 Sept. 1988, to Creighton, Faculty Council, Moran Papers.

56. Jim Barborak, 12 Oct. 1988, to Faculty Council, with summary of new AULER regulations, in Vertical File: Curriculum Committee; UNCG to Implement New Liberal Education Requirements . . . , OIS News Release, 23 Aug. 1991.

57. Institutional Self-Study, 1992, Reaffirmation (Visiting) Committee report, 1993, pp. 15–16.

58. Writing Skills Getting Special Emphasis . . . , OIS News Release, 27 April 1990; *Carolinian*, 22 April 1993.

59. Allardyce, "Rise and Fall of the Western Civilization Course," pp. 718, 726–29.

60. Arts and Sciences grant proposal, [1988], Appendix F, in Arts & Sciences, Grant, Moran Papers.

61. *Carolinian*, 11 Nov. 1971; *Greensboro Daily News*, 25, 27 March 1983; James H. Allen, 30 March 1983, to Moran, VCAA Records: Black Studies; Black Studies Committee report, 20 April 1983; Student Senate resolution, ca. 29 April 1983; and Deans' Council Minutes, 4 May 1983.

62. *Greensboro Daily News*, 29 June 1983; *Catalog*, 1986–87, pp. 315–16; 1993–94, pp. 45, 340–41; *Carolinian*, 24 March 1988, 27 April 1989.

63. UNCG Honors Program Provides Environment for Gifted Students . . . , OIS News Release, 22 April 1992; *Alumni News*, 82 (Winter 1993), p. 5.

64. Elisabeth A. Zinser, 13 Dec. 1984, to Moran, C; Alvin J. Shexnider, 21 Jan. 1986, to Ansley A. Abraham, Q; Moran, 18 Sept. 1989, to Raymond H. Dawson; Roch C. Smith, 21 Sept. 1989, to Donald V. DeRosa, VCAA; Table, Fall Remedial Enrollments: Traditional Freshmen, 8 Feb. 1993; Donald V. DeRosa, 11 April 1994, to William F. Little, Academic Affairs, Moran Papers. See also Bob Newton, 12 May 1988, to Moran, Arts & Sciences, Depts., German, Moran Papers.

65. Ann P. Saab, 4 Feb. 1982, to Moran, Consent Decree; Elisabeth A. Zinser, 23 July 1986, to Moran and Frederick L. Drake, Co, Moran Papers; *Catalog*, 1993–94, p. 23.

66. Correspondence and committee minutes, 1982–83, in VCAA Records: Guilford Technical Community College; Moran, 28 April 1982, to Ray Needham, T, Moran Papers; Deans' Council Minutes, 26 May 1982.

67. Correspondence in Technical and Community Colleges, 1988, and T, 1989, 1991, 1993; Donald V. DeRosa, 11 March 1993, to Moran, Excellence Foundation; Moran, 10 Nov. 1993, to Vice President Little, Enrollment, Moran Papers; Deans' Council Minutes, 30 March 1994; *Catalog*, 1993–94, p. 18; Greensboro *News & Record*, 5 Aug. 1997.

68. *Greensboro Daily News*, 27 April 1979; *Carolinian*, 27 Feb., 30 Aug. 1979; Edward B. Fort, 17 Jan. 1991, to A&T Student Body, Engineering & Science Center; Moran, 23 May 1994, to Deloris Boone and Velma Speight, Intercollegiate Athletics, Moran Papers; Greensboro *News & Record*, 18 Aug. 1997.

69. For the library, see James H. Thompson, 12 Feb. 1980, to David Payne, L, Moran Papers.

70. See the remarks of William Friday concerning UNCG's long-range plan, 26 Aug. 1980, Long Range Plan, Moran Papers.

71. Moran, 9 Sept. 1980, to William C. Friday, Long Range Plan; 1988 correspondence in HES; Mary E. Wakeford, 23 April 1991, to Donald DeRosa, School: HES; William F. Little, 23 Dec. 1993, to Moran, HES, Moran Papers; Greensboro *News & Record*, 30 Aug. 1993, 18 Aug. 1997.

72. See the correspondence in Civil Rights History, 1983; C, 1984; and Ch–Ci, 1985, Moran Papers; Deans' Council Records, 30 Sept. 1986.

73. William Friday, 30 July 1984, to Moran; Elisabeth A. Zinser, 6 Aug. 1984, to Moran, VCAA; Gaylord Hageseth, 24 March 1988, to Elisabeth Zinser, VCAA-Quo Vadimus; Elisabeth A. Zinser, 15 Feb. 1988, to Moran, VCAA, Moran Papers.

74. Moran, 19 April 1990, to Walter Massey, Acad. Affairs; Correspondence in Engineering & Science Research Center folders, 1990–92, Moran Papers; Academic Cabinet Minutes, 16 Jan. 1991; Greensboro *News & Record*, 16 Jan., 9 March, 25 April 1991, 18 Aug., 13 Dec. 1997, 19 May 1999.

Chapter 31 Notes

1. OH: William Moran, 20 Feb. 1990, 28 Jan. 1991; Report of the Consultants to the Science Planning Committee, [1992], Engineering-Science Research Center, Moran Papers; In-

stitutional Self-Study, 1991–92, Reaffirmation (Visiting) Committee report, 1993, pp. 18, 19 (incl. quotation), 22, 24.

2. Statement accompanying John W. Kennedy, 10 Aug. 1982, to Moran, Deans' Council Records.

3. John W. Kennedy remarks, Chancellor's Cabinet Minutes, 26 July 1982; Stanley L. Jones remarks, Deans' Council Minutes, 13 July 1983; Memorandum to File, 20 July 1988, Grad School, Moran Papers; Moran remarks, 2 March 1994, p. 6, w/Faculty Senate Minutes, 6 April 1994.

4. Tables 6–7 in Education: Dean's Report, 1985 Self-Study, Provost's Records; *Statistical Abstract of Higher Education in North Carolina*, 1994–95, p. 91; UNCG *Fact Book*, 1994–95, pp. II-1, 22–24.

5. Moran, 4 March 1985, to Elisabeth Zinser, G, Moran Papers. But cf. Table accompanying Donald V. DeRosa, 14 July 1986, to Moran, Grad School, Moran Papers.

6. John W. Kennedy, Nonresident Tuition proposal, with Kennedy, 27 May 1980, to Moran, VCAA Records: Out-of-State Tuition Waivers; Moran, Guest Column, Greensboro *News & Record*, 6 March 1983; Arthur R. Tollefson, 3 Sept. 1985, to Marleen Ingle, Music; Report of the Consultants to the Science Planning Committee, [1992] (including quotation), Engineering-Science Research Center, Moran Papers.

7. Analysis of Tuition Waivers Granted, Fiscal 1979–1980, and Table I, with Donald V. DeRosa, 15 June 1993, to Jasper D. Memory, Grad School, Moran Papers.

8. I am indebted to Ann P. Saab for this characterization of the complex graduate program.

9. Strategic Analyses of Comparative Undergraduate UNCG and UNC Enrollments by Discipline, Fall 1982–Fall 1992, w/James Clotfelter, 28 Jan. 1994, Enrollment, Moran Papers. For degrees awarded, see UNCG *Fact Book*, 1994–95, pp. II-19–21.

10. Greensboro *News & Record*, 27, 30 March 1983.

11. Joanne V. Creighton, Reflections on the College of Arts and Sciences, Sept. 1987, pp. 3, 13 (quotation), Arts & Sciences: General, Moran Papers; OH: Joanne Creighton, 9 April 1990. For faculty statistics, see UNCG *Fact Book*, 1994–95, pp. I-15, 17.

12. Walter H. Beale, 11 March 1992, to Donald V. DeRosa; DeRosa, 6 April 1994, to Moran, Acad. Affairs, Moran Papers; Beale remarks, in Faculty Senate Minutes, 7 Oct. 1992, 3 March 1993; Beale, remarks to College Assembly, 7 Dec. 1993, Arts/Sciences; Report of the Consultants to the Science Planning Committee, [1992], Engineering-Science Research Center; Beale, 21 July 1993, to DeRosa, with Science Planning Report, and DeRosa, 31 Aug. 1993, to Beale, Academic Affairs, Moran Papers.

13. For Dean Robert Miller's appraisal of the department in 1983 under Bates' leadership, see Miller, 14 March 1983, to Stanley L. Jones, Arts & Sciences, Moran Papers. See also Donald V. DeRosa, Observations on the Graduate Program Review of the Ph.D. Program in Psychology, Sept. 1987, Graduate School; and Report of the Consultants to the Science Planning Committee, [1992], Engineering-Science Research Center, Moran Papers.

14. Robert Eason, 31 Jan. 1983, to Moran et al., Arts & Sciences, Moran Papers; *Campus Calendar*, 7–20 Feb. 1983, in Vertical File: Psychology; 1985 Self-Study: Psychology, Provost Records; Report of Site Visit for APA Accreditation, 2–3 Feb. 1987; ibid., 7–8 Oct. 1991, Arts & Sciences: Psychology, Moran Papers.

15. Gilbert Gottlieb, 12 Oct. 1984, to Moran, Arts & Sciences: Psychology, Moran Papers. See also Donald V. DeRosa, 20 Sept. 1985, to Moran, G, Moran Papers.

16. OH: Robert Eason, 14 Feb., 13 March 1996.

17. James J. Jenkins et al., Review of Graduate Program in Psychology [at UNCG, ca. June 1987]; Walter Salinger, 26 June 1987, to Donald V. DeRosa; Joanne V. Creighton, 29 July 1987, to DeRosa; DeRosa, Observations on the Graduate Program Review of the Ph.D. Program in Psychology, Sept. 1987, Graduate School, Moran Papers.

18. Program Review of the Chemistry Department, 5 Feb. 1988, VCAA, Moran Papers; *Carolinian*, 11 Sept. 1981; Report of the Consultants to the Science Planning Committee, [1992], Engineering-Science Research Center, Moran Papers.

19. Stanley L. Jones, 21 May, 6 July 1982, to Moran, Arts & Sciences, Moran Papers.

20. Institutional Self-Study, 1991–92: Reaffirmation (Visiting) Committee report, 1993.

21. Physics Department Self-Study and Planning Report, 1985 Self-Study: Physics, Provost Records; *UNC-G Bulletin*, Dec. 1981, p. 10; *Alumni News*, 70 (Spring 1982), p. 11; 79 (Summer 1991), pp. 10–11; Viewing Dates are Scheduled for Three College Observatory, OIS News Release, 14 Feb. 1994.

22. Institutional Self-Study, 1983: Visiting Committee report, pp. 12–13; Equipment Summary Statement, [1988], VCAA, Moran Papers.

23. 1985 Self-Study: Math, Provost Records; Institutional Self-Study, 1991–92, Reaffirmation Committee report, 1993; Report of the Consultants to the Science Planning Committee, [1992], Engineering-Science Research Center; Walter H. Beale, 21 July 1993, to Donald V. DeRosa, with Science Planning Report, and DeRosa, 31 Aug. 1993, to Beale, Academic Affairs, Moran Papers. For the development of computer science at UNCG, see correspondence, 1978–80, in VCAA Records: Computer Education/Computer Science; Terry G. Seaks, 7 Aug. 1978, to Stanley L. Jones; Seaks, 25 Sept. 1981, to Moran; R.C.F. Bartels, Comments Relating to Campus Computing, [1981], Computing, Moran Papers; Jere [Hershey], [n.d.], to Philip [Friedman], B&E School Records, 1984–85: Computing in SBE Programs.

24. For the difficult decision to replace Jellicorse, see Jellicorse, 15 June 1983, to Moran, and Moran, 23 Aug. 1983, to Jellicorse, Arts & Sciences; Joanne V. Creighton, 11 Sept. 1987, to Elisabeth Zinser, and Creighton, 27 Oct. 1987, to Members of the Communication and Theatre Department, Arts & Sciences: General; Moran, 3 March 1988, to Zinser, Arts & Sciences: Communication & Theatre, Moran Papers. For Hansen's original recruitment in 1986, see Jellicorse, 29 June 1986, to Moran, Arts & Sciences: Communication & Theatre, Moran Papers.

25. 1985 Self-Study Report: Communication & Theatre, pp. 6–7, 10, 24, 27–35, 42–58, 83, 85, Provost Records.

26. John Lee Jellicorse, 9 February 1984, to Elisabeth Zinser, VCAA Records: Communication & Theatre, General; Joanne V. Creighton, 4 Feb., 11 Sept. 1987, to Zinser; Creighton, 27, 29 Oct. 1987, to Members of the Communication & Theatre Department, Arts & Sciences: General; Zinser, 23 March 1988, to Moran (including quotation); Moran, 7 Nov. 1988, to Robert C. Hansen, and other 1988 correspondence in Arts & Sciences: Communication & Theatre; Hansen, 11 April 1990, to Moran, ibid., Moran Papers; OH: Herman Middleton, 19 Feb. 1990.

27. National Association of Schools of Theatre, Visitors' Report, [Feb. 1994], esp. pp. 5–6; Optional Response to the Visitors' Report, [March 1994]; John Lee Jellicorse, 7 May 1994, to Moran, Arts & Sciences; Walter H. Beale, 21 Sept. 1993, to Donald V. DeRosa, Grad School, Moran Papers; Deans' Council notes, 14 Sept. 1994.

28. Committee on University Performing Arts Program, Report, 15 April 1988, pp. 4–13, w/Deans' Council Records, 25 Jan. 1989.

29. *Catalog*, 1986–87, pp. 364–65.

30. VCAA Records: Parkway Playhouse, 1976–84; Sam Zachary, 5 April 1990, to Robert C. Hansen; Hansen, 5 April 1990, to Moran; Moran, 9 April 1990, to Raymond H. Dawson, Arts & Sciences: Communication & Theatre, Moran Papers; OH: Herman Middleton, 19 Feb. 1990.

31. See Dean Robert L. Miller's assessment in Miller, 28 May 1982, to Stanley L. Jones, Arts & Sciences, Moran Papers.

32. See Olson correspondence in VCAA Records: Political Science, General, 1980–82; and Olson, 30 April, 4 Nov. 1993, to Moran, Arts & Sciences, Moran Papers.

33. 1985 Self-Study: Center for Social Research, Provost Records; Robert L. Miller, 28 May 1982, to Stanley L. Jones, Arts & Sciences, Moran Papers.

34. 1985 Self-Study: Geography, Provost Records; John Rees, 27 Aug. 1992, to Moran, G, Moran Papers.

35. Correspondence, 1980, in Arts & Sciences: Social Work, Moran Papers.

36. 1985 Self-Study: English, Provost Records; Denise N. Baker, 30 April 1990, to Robert Miller, Arts & Sciences: English, Moran Papers; OH: Tom Kirby-Smith, 10 Sept. 1990.

37. Lee Zacharias, [June 1980], to Moran et al., Arts & Sciences: English; Moran, 23 Aug. 1983, to Amy Charles, Arts & Sciences, Moran Papers; Finley, "A Noble Tradition," p. 56.

38. Master of Fine Arts in Creative Writing, 1985 Self-Study: English, Provost Records; Walter H. Beale, 15 July 1988, to Donald DeRosa, Graduate School; Beale, 14 Oct. 1992, to Richard L. Moore, Centennial Campaign; C. Barry Chabot, Consultant's Report on the English Department, Spring 1994, w/Donald V. DeRosa, 13 July 1994, to Moran, Arts & Sciences College, Moran Papers; Kurt C. Ward, "Fred Chappell," *The UNCG Graduate*, Spring 1998, pp. 2–5; Vertical File: Creative Writing Program; Faculty File: Fred Chappell, Robert Watson; OH: Robert Watson, 21 March 1990; Fred Chappell, 7 March 1991; Tom Kirby-Smith, 10 Sept. 1990.

39. 1985 Self-Study: Art, p. 4, Provost Records.

40. Moran, 13 Jan. 1981, to the File, W; Brooks Graham, 9 Feb. 1981, to the File, W; and other 1981 correspondence in W and Arts Center; and 1983, Art Center, Moran Papers; OH: Gilbert Carpenter, 27 April 1990; *Greensboro Daily News*, 27 Oct. 1981, 16 Sept. 1983; *Campus Calendar*, 26 Sept.–9 Oct. 1983; Greensboro *News & Record*, 24 Oct., 12 Nov. 1989.

41. Correspondence in Weatherspoon, 1984–89, and Art Center, 1988, Moran Papers; Academic Cabinet Minutes, 7 Sept. 1988; Trustees' Minutes, 15 Sept. 1988.

42. Robert L. Miller, 30 Oct. 1979, to James Svara; Philip A. Stadter, 5 Dec. 1979, to Miller; Stanley L. Jones, 21 May 1982, to Moran, Arts & Sciences; Jones, 25 Oct. 1982, to Robert P. Newton, Academic Affairs; Jones, 20 April 1983, to Miller, VCAA, Moran Papers; Correspondence in VCAA Records: German & Russian Dept., 1980; Foreign Languages Merger, 1980–81, and Languages Department Proposal, 1982–83.

43. 1985 Self-Study: Classical Civilization, Provost Records; William G. Lane, 11 Feb. 1986, to Joanne V. Creighton; Moran, 17 March 1986, to Lane, Arts & Sciences: Classical Civilization, Moran Papers.

44. *New York Times*, 28 Nov. 1989; Greensboro *News & Record*, 13 Dec. 1989.

45. Report of the Ad Hoc Committee on International Programs, 18 April 1990, School: Music; Correspondence in International, 1991; International Programs at UNCG—a Status Report, w/Moran, 12 July 1994, to H. Michael Weaver, Development-Benefactors, Moran Papers.

46. William G. Bowen and Julie Ann Sosa, *Prospects for Faculty in the Arts and Sciences* (Princeton, 1989).

47. James H. Thompson, 6 Feb. 1990, to Allen W. Trelease, Arts & Sciences: History; Donald V. DeRosa, 29 Jan. 1992, to Walter H. Beale, Arts & Sciences, Moran Papers; Deans' Council Minutes, 8 May 1991.

48. Greensboro *News & Record*, 1 Oct. 1992.

49. 1985 Self-Study: Women's Studies, Provost Records; Elisabeth J. Natalle, The Status of Women's Programs [at UNCG], 31 July 1987, Women's Programs; correspondence and reports in Women's Studies, 1989, 1991–92, and W, 1992, Moran Papers; Sally S. Cone, 18 April 1993, to Moran, and Moran, 30 April 1993, to Cone, B. of T., Moran Papers; *Carolinian*, 25 Feb. 1988, 22 Feb. 1990, 22 Aug. 1991.

50. Robert L. Miller, 2 June 1980, to Stanley L. Jones, with accompanying report, VCAA Records: Residential College; 1985 Self-Study: Residential College, including report by Richard T. Whitlock, Provost Records; Greensboro *News & Record*, 1 Nov. 1995.

51. Correspondence, 1994, in Ca–Co, Moran Papers; Robert J. O'Hara, 19 May 1994, to Enrollment Management Committee, Enrollment Management Committee Records; Greensboro *News & Record*, 26 Oct. 1994.

52. David Shelton, 27 July 1981, to Moran and Stanley L. Jones, B&E, Moran Papers.

53. David H. Shelton, 8 Feb. 1982 to Moran et al., with report of the AACSB visiting team; Shelton, [25 April 1982], to Wilson Davis; Lawrence E. McKibbin, 21 May 1982, to Moran, B&E, Moran Papers.

54. *Greensboro Daily News*, 18 Feb. 1983; Minutes of special meeting, 23 Feb. 1983, Faculty Meeting Minutes, B&E School Records, 1973–84.

55. David H. Shelton, 5 Dec. 1979, to Charles W. Patterson, w/minutes of 11 Feb. 1980, Chancellor's Cabinet Records; [Shelton], "The Joseph McKinley and Kathleen Price Bryan College of Administrative and Economic Sciences," [1980], B&E, Moran Papers.

56. David H. Shelton, written communication with the author, Aug. 2001.

57. Joseph M. Bryan, 3 Aug. 1983, to Moran, Development: Prospectus III, Moran Papers.

58. Minutes of special meeting, 23 Feb. 1983, B&E Faculty Meeting Minutes; Robert S. Cline, 26 April 1983, to B&E Faculty, Missions & Goals, B&E School Records, 1973–84; Gerald L. Hershey et al, 28 Feb. 1983, to Moran, B&E, Moran Papers.

59. Philip Friedman, 19 Nov. 1984, to SB&E Faculty; Friedman, 10 Dec. 1984, to Elisabeth A. Zinser; Proposal for Reorganization, 15 Feb. 1985; Zinser, 3 April 1985, to Raymond Dawson, Reorganization, B&E School Records, 1984–85.

60. Jere Hershey, 4 Oct. 1982, to David Shelton, w/Faculty Meeting Minutes, B&E School Records, 1973–84; 1985 Self-Study: Business Information & Support Systems, Provost Records.

61. Friedman, 3 Dec. 1987, to Elisabeth A. Zinser, esp. pp. 10–11, B&E, Moran Papers; Terry Seaks, 23 Aug. 2001, to the author.

62. M. Gene Newport, 11 April 1988, to Philip Friedman; Albert N. Link, 18 April 1988, to Moran; Terry G. Seaks, 29 April 1988, to Moran; Elisabeth A. Zinser, 12 July 1988, to Friedman, B&E, Moran Papers.

63. Albert Link, 4 Oct. 1983, to Robert S. Cline, Faculty Staffing & Recruiting, B&E School Records, 1973–84; Link, 21 Nov. 1983, to Moran; Stuart Allen, 15 Nov. 1993, to Moran, B&E, Moran Papers.

64. Friedman, 30 Jan. 1989, to American Assembly of Collegiate Schools of Business; Friedman, 18 April 1989, to Bryan School Faculty et al., School: B&E, Moran Papers.

65. Friedman, 1 June 1990, to Bryan School Faculty and Staff, School: B&E, Moran Papers; OIS News Release, 10 May 1991.

66. 1985 Self-Study: Business Administration, p. 105, Provost Records.

67. James K. Weeks, 24 Aug. 1991, to Donald V. DeRosa; DeRosa, 3 Sept. 1991, to Weeks, B; Weeks, 10 Aug. 1992, to Bryan School Faculty, School: B&E; Weeks, 25 Oct. 1993, to B&E Faculty, B&E, Moran Papers.

68. Stuart Allen, 4 Aug. 1994, to Jim Weeks, copy in author's possession.

69. Stuart Allen et al., 27 Sept. 1994, to Jim Weeks; Weeks, 18 Oct. 1994, to Bryan School Faculty; Joseph E. Johnson, 20 Oct. 1994, to Weeks; Terry Seaks, 18 Feb. 1998, 23 Aug. 2001, to the author, all in the possession of the author; Terry G. Seaks, 17 Nov. 1994, to Donald DeRosa, B&E School, Debra Stewart Papers.

70. Eloise R. Lewis, 27 Sept. 1983, to Elisabeth A. Zinser, Enrollment Management, Assistant VCAA Records; N.C. Board of Nursing, General Summary and Recommendations of Survey Visit, Feb. 1982, and School of Nursing Response; Anna Kuba, 4 May 1982, to Lewis, Nursing, Moran Papers.

71. Eloise R. Lewis, 2 Nov. 1984, to Elisabeth A. Zinser, Nursing School, General, VCAA Records; Nursing School, annual report, 1984–85, p. 149; Draft Notes, Joint Retreat of Task

Force on Academic Planning, 17 July 1985, Deans' Council Records; [Patricia Chamings], Doctoral Education in Nursing at UNC-G, w/Zinser, [October 1985], to Moran; Zinser, 28 Oct. 1985, 1, [ca. 30] April 1986, to Moran, Nursing, Moran Papers.

72. Patricia A. Chamings, 24 May 1990, to Donald V. DeRosa; DeRosa, 24 May 1990, to Nursing Faculty; DeRosa, 11 June 1991, to Moran; DeRosa, 1 July 1991, to Daphine D. Doster, Nursing, Moran Papers; OH: Catherine Turner, 1 Oct. 1990.

73. Moran, 17 Nov. 1992, to C.D. Spangler; William F. Little, 1 Dec. 1992, to Moran, Nursing, Moran Papers; Institutional Self-Study, 1991–92: Reaffirmation (Visiting) Committee report, 1993, pp. 59–60.

74. Greensboro *News & Record*, 17 May, 30 Aug. 1981; *Campus Calendar*, 30 May–14 June 1983.

75. UNCG *Bulletin*, Dec. 1987, p. 5; Greensboro *News & Record*, 29 Oct. 2000.

76. I have seen no written directive to this effect, but see the remarks of nursing Dean Eloise Lewis on the subject, in 1985 Self-Study: Nursing, Dean's Report, p. 26, Provost Records.

77. Arthur Tollefson, New UNCG School of Music Building, w/James Clotfelter, 3 March 1992, to John C. Hamil, B. of T., Moran Papers; Art Tollefson, in *Alumni News*, 75 (Spring 1987), pp. 8, 19; Frederick A. Beck, Jazz Studies, in 1985 Self-Study: Music, Instrumental Division, Provost Records.

78. John R. Locke, 3 Sept. 1985, to Arthur R. Tollefson, Music, Moran Papers; UNCG Summer Music Camp …., 21 June 1990, 14 June 1991, 15 July 1992, 18 July 1994, OIS New Releases; Greensboro *News & Record*, 21 June 1995.

79. Elisabeth A. Zinser, 17 Aug. 1987, to Moran; Walter W. Heid, 2 Sept. 1988, to Moran; Bernard B. Keele, 14 Oct. 1988, to Moran, Eastern Music Festival, Moran Papers.

80. Arthur Tollefson, New UNCG School of Music Building, w/James Clotfelter, 3 March 1992, to John C. Hamil, B. of T., Moran Papers. For the physical space deficiencies, see also Robert L. Blocker, 16 Dec. 1982, to Larry Fincher, Music School, General, VCAA Records; Institutional Self-Study, 1991–92, Reaffirmation (Visiting) Committee report, 1993, pp. 57–58; Jackson Library, *Library Columns*, April 2000.

81. Richard A. Swanson, 8 Dec. 1982, to Moran et al., HPERD, Moran Papers; *Alumni News*, 71 (Spring 1983), p. 10; Raymond H. Dawson, 7 July 1987, to Moran, Grad School, Moran Papers.

82. 1985 Self-Study: HPERD, Physical Education, and Campus Recreation, Provost Records.

83. See the correspondence concerning these name changes in HPERD, 1989 and 1990, Moran Papers.

84. Richard A. Swanson, 21 Dec. 1983, to Moran, HPERD, Moran Papers.

85. Keith Howell, 29 May 1987, to Richard A. Swanson; Swanson, 23 July 1987, to Elisabeth Zinser; Department of Public Health Education, 3 Aug. 1987, to Swanson; Jacqueline Voss, 24 Nov. 1987, to Zinser; Zinser, 18 April, 12 Sept. 1988, to Moran; Moran, 15 Sept. 1988, to Zinser et al., HPERD; Swanson, 13 Feb. 1989, to Zinser, HPERD: Dean's Review, Moran Papers.

86. E.D. McKinney, 27 Feb. 1980, to Stanley L. Jones; Gay E. Cheney, 21 March 1980, to Jones; Elizabeth C. Umstead, 24 March 1980, to Moran; Jones, 3 April 1980, to Moran, w/enclosure, HPER, Moran Papers.

87. Elisabeth A. Zinser, 9 Jan. 1989, to Moran; Richard A. Swanson, 9 May 1989, to Moran; Moran, 12 May 1989, to HPERD Faculty, HPERD: Dean's Review, Moran Papers. For the transition to departments, see Richard A. Swanson, 9 May 1983, to Stanley L. Jones, VCAA Records: HPERD, Organization & Governance.

88. New York Educator Named Dean . . . , 12 June 1992, OIS News Releases.

89. American Home Economics Association, Site Visit Report, 21–24 March 1982; Stanley L. Jones, Notes: Exit Interview with Visiting Team for Accreditation, 24 March 1982; Jacqueline H. Voss, 18 Dec. 1985, to Moran; Moran, 21 May 1987, to Raymond H. Dawson; Voss, 4 Dec. 1987, to Moran, Home Ec; Voss, 29 Feb. 1988, to Elisabeth A. Zinser; Zinser, 27 Sept. 1988, to Mary Y. Morgan et al.; Donald V. DeRosa, 13 Sept. 1991, to Moran, HES, Moran Papers; Trustees' Minutes, 19 April 1984; Greensboro *News & Record*, 9 Sept. 1985, 18 Nov. 1987; Canaday et al., *History of the School of Human Environmental Sciences*, pp. 49–53. For national background, see Vincenti, "Home Economics Moves," pp. 305–19.

90. For the cafeteria closure, see correspondence accompanying Trustees' Minutes, 9 Sept. 1982.

91. Jacqueline H. Voss, 17 Sept. 1982, to Kinsey Green; Green, 21 Nov. 1983, to Moran; Voss, 17 Feb. 1986, to Moran; Home Economics Foundation, Annual Meeting minutes, 15 Sept. 1987, Home Ec, Moran Papers; *Greensboro Daily News*, 6 Sept. 1983; OH: Stanley L. Jones, 27 Dec. 1990. For the reasons behind the cafeteria closing, see Home Economics Foundation, Directors' Minutes, 25 Jan. 1983, Home Ec, Moran Papers.

92. Moran, 10 Sept. 1987, to Sheron Sumner, Home Ec/HES, Moran Papers.

93. American Home Economics Association, Site Visit Report, 21–24 March 1982, pp. 10–11; Jacqueline H. Voss, 17 Feb. 1986, to Moran, Home Ec, Moran Papers; *Greensboro Daily News*, 6 Sept. 1983.

94. Roi C. Nevaril, 3 May 1991, and Robert M. Ledingham, 20 Aug. 1993, to Moran, HES, Moran Papers; Institutional Self-Study, 1991–92: Reaffirmation (Visiting) Committee report, 1993, pp. 53–56.

95. Chamberlain, *Women in Academe*, pp. 239–41; Ravitch, *Schools We Deserve*, pp. 95–96; Lucas, *Crisis in the Academy*, pp. 230–31.

96. Educational Administration Doctoral Program, UNCG, w/Brad Bartel, 8 April 1993, to Donald V. DeRosa, Education, Moran Papers.

97. 1985 Self-Study: Education, Teacher Education, pp. 18, 21, 39, with Report on Teacher Education at UNCG by the Teacher Education Coordinator's Cabinet, [1986], Provost Records. See also ibid., Education, Dean's Report, and Elisabeth A. Zinser, 20 Feb. 1987, to Academic Deans et al., Education, Moran Papers.

98. 1985 Self-Study: Pedagogical Studies & Supervision, Provost Records; *Campus Calendar*, 27 May–16 June 1985.

99. David H. Reilly, Self-Evaluation, Fall 1985, Education, Moran Papers; 1985 Self-Study: Education, Dean's Report, pp. 55–58; ibid., Department of Curriculum & Educational Foundations, with addendum and dean's response, Provost Records.

100. For the controversy, see Amy M. Charles, 15 Oct. 1981, to Moran, Arts & Sciences, Dean Review; and correspondence in Education, 1981–83, 1985, and in Salary Study, 1981, Moran Papers.

101. A. Edward Uprichard, 5 June 1991, to Moran, w/enclosures, Education, Moran Papers; OH: Elisabeth Bowles, 11 Sept. 1990; Jane Mitchell, 29 Nov. 1990.

102. Correspondence, 1989, in Education: Collegium; NCATE Report on UNCG, [Jan. 1992], in Education, Moran Papers.

103. Wilson Davis, 12 June 1992, to Trish Wilson, Inf, Moran Papers.

104. *Carolinian*, 27 Aug. 1992; External Grants and Contracts . . . , 20 July 1994, OIS News Releases.

105. Donald V. DeRosa. 3 Sept. 1993, to University Faculty, Education, Moran Papers.

106. Moran, 22 April 1993, to Donald V. DeRosa, Education, Moran Papers; UNCG School of Education Creates New Departments . . . , 20 Aug. 1993, OIS News Releases.

107. UNCG Counselor Education Program Gets Top National Honor ..., 4 April 1991, and 31 May 1994, OIS News Releases.

108. UNCG Professor Serving as '90–'91 President for 57,000-Member Counseling Association, 23 Aug. 1990; National Group Gives Bardon Special Award ..., 28 March 1991; UNCG Professor Marilyn L. Miller Receives Top School Librarians Award, 19 May 1993, OIS News Releases; Cora Paul Bomar, 16 Feb. 1987, to Jack I. Bardon, Education, Moran Papers; *Carolinian*, 3 Dec. 1992.

109. See Dale L. Brubaker, 12 Oct. 1984, to David H. Reilly; Harold R. Snyder, 15 Oct. 1984, to Reilly; William Friday, 18 Oct. 1984, to Liston B. Ramsey, Education; Donald W. Russell, 8 June 1988, to Elisabeth Zinser; Zinser, 13 June 1988, to Moran, VCAA; Donald V. DeRosa, 23 April 1993, to Moran; Moran, 16 July 1993, to James T. Rogers, Grad School, Moran Papers.

Chapter 32 Notes

1. *Statistical Abstract of Higher Education in North Carolina*, 1994–95, p. 170.

2. Robert T. Tomlinson, 27 Feb. 1985, to James H. Allen; Moran, 6 March 1985, to William C. Friday, R, Moran Papers; *Carolinian*, 29 Oct. 1987; Tomlinson, in *Alumni News*, 82 (Winter 1993), pp. 8–9.

3. Correspondence, 1993, in Resi, Moran Papers; *Carolinian*, 16 Sept., 2 Dec. 1993, 27 Jan. 1994.

4. Student Senate minutes, 11 Nov. 1975, SGA Records; Robert T. Tomlinson, 21 Oct. 1982, to Janet Yates; Tomlinson, 16 Dec. 1982, to Kim A. Morgan, R, Moran Papers.

5. Barbara Parrish, 18 March 1983, to Anne Snyder Foltz, A, Moran Papers; *Carolinian*, 7 Feb. 1984; UNCG *Fact Book*, 1994–95, p. VI-11.

6. Robert T. Tomlinson, 21 Oct. 1982, to Janet Yates, R, Moran Papers.

7. *Carolinian*, 25 Jan. 1983, 14 Nov. 1991; Dewey Whitaker, CSA President, [Sept. 1988], to Fellow Commuters, Vertical File: Commuting Students Association.

8. *Carolinian*, 26 April 1990; *Student Handbook*, 1993–94, P. 42.

9. Parking space study, 1990, T; Fred L. Drake, 24 March 1994, to Michael Pearson, Student, Moran Papers; Wilson Davis, Interview with Fred Drake, 28 Feb. 1994, transcript in author's possession.

10. Ruth W. Alexander, 12 Jan. 1981, to Stanley Jones, Adult Students; Office for Adult Students...Self-Study and Plan, May 1985, Self Study & Plans, Assistant VCAA Records; UNCG Establishing New ACES Program ...., News release, 7 Feb. 1992, in Vertical File: ACES Program; Remarks by Donald V. DeRosa, w/Faculty Senate Minutes, 26 April 1995.

11. Judith S. White, 28 Jan. 1982, to Thomas W. Lambeth, U–W; Mary K. Wakeman, 18 April 1983, to Moran, W; Elisabeth J. Natalle, The Status of Women's Programs, 31 July 1987, Women's Programs; Diane L. Cooper, 3 Oct. 1988, to James H. Allen, Women's Services, Moran Papers; Ad Hoc Advisory Committee on Women's Programs, March 1988, Vertical File: Women's Programs.

12. *Carolinian*, 7 Nov. 1974; James H. Allen, 18 Dec. 1974, to Richard H. Robinson, Stu Aff; David N. Edwards, 30 Jan. 1975, to James Allen, Stu–Stu Gov, Ferguson Papers; James H. Allen, 26 Nov. 1979, to Mrs. John M. Parker, Students; William Friday, 11 April 1984, to Jimmy Green, Student Affairs; Friday, 28 May 1985, to Michael P. Decker, Sp–St, Moran Papers; *Greensboro Daily News*, letters to the editor, 24 Feb. 1980; *Carolinian*, 24 March 1981; OH: Meredith Carle, 19 May 1991; Astrid Terry, 20 May 1991.

13. Student Senate minutes, 27 Sept. 1983; Student Legislative Assembly minutes, 22 Sept. 1987, 15 Nov. 1988, SGA Records, and 1 Oct. 1991, M, Moran Papers; *Carolinian*, 18 Feb. 1988.

14. Student Senate resolution, 6 Dec. 1983, S; Legislative Assembly resolution, 1 Oct. 1991, M, Moran Papers.

15. Moran, 2 Feb. 1984, to Charles Murph, Se–St, Moran Papers; Greensboro *News & Record*, 6 Oct., 7 Nov. 1996.

16. Human Relations Committee minutes, 25 March 1983, Student Affairs; Charles Johnson et al., 22 June 1986, to Moran; Moran, 8 July 1986, to Johnson, Arts & Sciences: Communications & Theatre; Student Satisfaction Survey, Nov. 1986, Institutional Research, 1987, Moran Papers; James H. Allen, 30 March 1983, to Moran, Black Studies, VCAA Records; Deans' Council Minutes, 30 March 1983; Academic Cabinet Minutes, 6 April 1983; *Greensboro Daily News*, 25, 27 March, 29 June 1983; *Carolinian*, 26 Feb. 1980, 29 Sept. 1983; Barry Beckham, ed., *The Black Student's Guide to Colleges* (N.Y., Dutton, 1982), pp. 219–20, in U, Moran Papers; *Chronicle of Higher Education*, 26 April 1989; OH: Astrid Terry, 20 May 1991.

17. *UNC-G Bulletin*, Dec. 1983, p. 12; *Carolinian*, 1 Nov. 1984; OH: Meredith Carle, 19 May 1991.

18. Draft of a minority recruitment brochure, 10 Aug. 1981, Deans' Council Records; Human Relations Committee minutes, 25 March 1983, Student Affairs, Moran Papers; Assistant Dean of Minority Affairs, annual report, 1982–83, Minority Affairs, VC Student Affairs Records.

19. See folders on Student Affairs, 1982–86, and Minority Affairs, 1987–89, Moran Papers.

20. James Allen, Notes on Student Affairs, 1 April 1980, to Moran, Alumni/Alumni Assn.; 1981–83 Change Budget Requests, pp. 69–70, Budget, Moran Papers.

21. College Administrative Council Minutes, 7 Nov. 1983, Arts & Sciences, VCAA Records; *Carolinian*, 29 Oct. 1987.

22. Minority Affairs, 1988–89, Moran Papers; Greensboro *News & Record*, 18, 19 Feb. 1988; Moran, Campus Response to Minority Concerns, 19 Jan. 1989, w/Faculty Council Minutes, 25 Jan. 1989 (also appearing in *Campus*, Feb. 1989); Trustees' Minutes, 8 Feb. 1990; OH: Robert Eason, 13 March 1996. The Eason committee report accompanies the Academic Cabinet Minutes of 6 Sept. 1989.

23. Correspondence, 1989, in Minority Affairs, Moran Papers.

24. Walter N. Pritchett, 27 March 1991, to Moran; Moran, 10 April 1991, to Pritchett, Alumni Affairs, Moran Papers. See also statement of Sonya Nichole Green, ca. 3 March 1992, and Jerry D. Williamson, 4 March 1992, to James Lancaster, Po–Pu; Moran, 23 March 1993, w/flyer, Things Black Students Need to Know About The Real UNCG, in Minority Affairs; Pam Wilson, 21 April 1994, to James Allen, M, Moran Papers.

25. *Carolinian*, 31 Jan., 7 Feb. 1991, 16 April 1992.

26. Table 31: Student Ratings of Food Service, UNCG Planning Process, 1980–83: Student Life, p. 189.

27. OH: James Allen, 11 Sept. 1990; *Carolinian*, 1 Nov. 1984; Greensboro *News & Record*, 15 Nov. 1988; Wilson Davis, "One of Finest in the Country," OIS Press Release, 7 Nov. 1988; *Student Handbook*, 1993–94, p. 23.

28. *Catalog*, 1986–87, pp. 355–56; *Student Handbook*, 1987–88, p. 23; *Carolinian*, 29 Oct. 1987; Institutional Self-Study Report, 1992, Chap. V, pp. 186–87, 189.

29. James H. Allen, 7 Dec. 1981, to Lawrence Fincher, Budget; Student Health Center Task Force, Reports and Recommendations, Aug. 1989, St–Su; History of Proposed Consolidation of Services for Student Health and Counseling and Testing Centers, and related documents, 1 Feb. 1994, Student, Moran Papers.

30. Moran, 12 Dec. 1991, to Mr. & Mrs. Tom Carlton, Student Health Center; Changes in Student Health Services, 1994–95, Student, Moran Papers; *Carolinian*, 26 April, 6 Sept. 1990, 7 Feb., 22 Aug. 1991, 10 Feb., 17, 31 March 1994.

31. Greensboro *News & Record*, 30 July 1987.

32. *Carolinian*, 30 Sept. 1980; Student Senate minutes, 7 April 1981, SGA Records; Alcoholic beverage regulations, with Chancellor's Cabinet Minutes, 10, 31 Aug. 1981; Trustee Minutes, 17 Sept. 1981, 11 Feb. 1982; Pepper Burns, 3 Aug. 1981, to J. Howard Coble, and Moran, 17, 27 Aug. 1981, to Coble, A; Moran, 6 March 1985, to William C. Friday, R, Moran Papers.

33. *Carolinian*, 20 March 1983, 5 Dec. 1985, 10 April 1986; *Catalog*, 1986–87, p. 354; OH: Meredith Carle, 19 May 1991. For the national trend, see Greensboro *News & Record*, 5 Feb. 1995.

34. *Carolinian*, 14 April 1981; James H. Allen, 2 Oct. 1987, to Moran, Drugs; Moran, 29 April 1988, to All University Employees, Drugs, Illegal, Moran Papers; Greensboro *News & Record* editorial, 11 Dec. 1987.

35. Bob Tomlinson, 8 Sept. 1989, to Vice Chancellors Allen and Drake, Drug Policy; UNC Annual Report on Drugs, 12 Jan. 1990, p. 9: Summary of Violations and Sanctions . . . , in D; Report on Activities Related to Policy on Illegal Drugs, Sept. 1991, B. of T.; Ibid., 6 Sept. 1992, B. of T. (Sept–Oct), Moran Papers; *Carolinian*, 27 Jan. 1994.

36. Greensboro *News & Record*, 21, 29 March 1997; *Chronicle of Higher Education*, 21 March 1997, p. A46.

37. Matthew Millward, 13 Feb. 1989, to Moran, VC Student Affairs; Correspondence, 1990, in Student Affairs: Condoms, Moran Papers; *Carolinian*, 23 Feb. (three articles), 31 Aug., 5 Oct., 2 Nov., 7 Dec. 1989; 1 Feb., 5 April 1990; Student Legislative Assembly minutes, 28 Feb., 14, 21, 28 Nov. 1989; 30 Jan., 13 Feb., 3 April 1990, SGA Records; UNCG Chancellor Authorizes Installation of Condom Vending Machines in Dormitories, OIS News Release, 30 March 1990.

38. *Campus*, 11–24 Aug. 1986.

39. Greensboro *News & Record*, 3 Oct. 1989; *Carolinian*, 12 Oct., 16 Nov. 1989; Melinda F. Hohn, 25 Oct. 1989, to Moran, and other correspondence in VC Business Affairs, 1989, Moran Papers.

40. *Carolinian*, 13 Oct. 1981, 19 March, 12 Nov. 1987, 25 Feb., 17 March 1988, 12 Oct., 7 Dec. 1989; Fred L. Drake, 15 Sept. 1989, to Richard L. Moore, VC Business Affairs; Drake, 29 July 1993, to Don DeRosa, Budget, Moran Papers.

41. Greensboro *News & Record*, 16 Feb. 1998.

42. UNCG *Fact Book*, 1979–80, p. 24; *Catalog*, 1993–94, p. 379; Attachment 1: UNCG General Fees, [1994], Tuition & Fees, Moran Papers.

43. Levine, "How the Academic Profession is Changing," pp. 9–10; Loeb, *Generation at the Crossroads*, pp. 44–46.

44. *Carolinian*, 27 Aug. 1981, 28 Jan., 9 Sept. 1982; *UNCG Bulletin*, Dec. 1982.

45. See Moran, 18 April 1980, to Thomas W. Lambeth; Lambeth, 22 May, 26 June 1980, to Moran, Scholarships/Loans, Moran Papers.

46. Institutional Self-Study Report, 1992, p. 364.

47. Altbach, "Students," pp. 206, 212–13; Boyer, *College*, pp. 245–46; Loeb, *Generation at the Crossroads*, pp. 2–5.

48. *Carolinian*, 17 March 1994.

49. *Carolinian*, 31 March 1981, 2 Feb. 1982.

50. Annual Review of Committees, p. 3, w/Academic Cabinet Minutes, 2 Nov. 1988.

51. Correspondence, 1981, in Student Affairs, Moran Papers; SGA Minutes, 18 Nov. 1981; *Alumni News*, 70 (Winter 1982), pp. 1–2, 18–19; *Carolinian*, 11, 29 Sept., 1, 27 Oct., 3, 5, 19, 24 Nov., 3 Dec. 1981.

52. *Carolinian*, 23, 27, 29 March, 30 Aug., 11 Sept., 6 Nov. 1979, 20, 27 March, 14, 30 Oct. 1980, 19 March 1981, 8 April 1982, 8 Feb. 1983, 8 Feb. 1983, 23 Feb., 6 Dec. 1984, 28 Feb. 1985, 10, 17 April 1986, 9 April 1987, 31 March 1988, 22 March, 25 Oct. 1990, 14, 21 March 1991, 26 March 1992, 1 April 1993; Sybil Mann, The Realities of Student Government, 1 Aug. 1982, Vertical File: Student Government Association; OH: Emily Whitney Ross, 12 May 1991.

53. See Michael Stewart, Report on the Student Government Constitutional Task Force, Fall 1985, w/Chancellor's Cabinet Records, 25 Nov. 1985; Stewart, 31 Jan. 1986, to Moran, Student Government, Moran Papers. For a thumbnail sketch of the system in 1993, see *Student Handbook*, 1993–94, p. 34.

54. OIS News Release, 15 April 1983, in Vertical File: Student Government Association; *Alumni News*, 71 (Summer 1983), p. 20.

55. *Carolinian*, 27 March 1980, 3 Dec. 1987; Jim Lancaster, 27 March 1985, to Jessie Mann and Hoyt Price, Commencement; Margaret A. Healy, 24 Sept. 1990, to Deans, Directors, and Department Heads, Student Affairs, Moran Papers; *Student Handbook*, 1980–81, p. 120; 1981–82, p. 120; 1993–94, p. 50.

56. *Carolinian*, 22 April, 31 Aug. 1982.

57. *Alumni News*, 74 (Spring 1986), pp. 2–3, 5; *Carolinian*, 18 Sept. 1986; Requests for Discretionary Funds... Vice Chancellor for Student Affairs... Class Council Program Funds, [1986 and 1987], Discretionary Funds, Moran Papers.

58. *Carolinian*, 25 Jan. 1990.

59. *Carolinian*, 20 Sept., 4 Dec. 1980, 26 Oct. 1982, 1 Dec. 1983, 5 March 1987; Ginnie Gardiner, ca. 11 Dec. 1981, to Lawrence Fincher, Budget, Moran Papers.

60. *Carolinian*, 25 April 1991; Jennifer L. Miller, 30 April 1991, to UNCG Students, Faculty, Staff and Alumni, Vertical File: *Carolinian*.

61. *Carolinian*, 27 Oct. 1981; So You Want To Know About the Media, [Oct. 1985}, Vertical File: *Carolinian*.

62. *Carolinian*, 24 April, 4 Sept. 1980, 27, 29 Oct. 1981, 31 Jan. 1984; 22 March 1983, 15 April 1993; *Alumni News*, 70 (Winter 1982), p. 17; Charles W. Jones, 9 April 1984, to James H. Allen, M, Moran Papers; Greensboro *News & Record*, 18 April 1993.

63. Chancellor's Cabinet Minutes, 27 Aug., 26 Nov., 10, 17 Dec. 1979, 7 Jan., 4, 11 Feb., 7 July, 14 Sept. 1981, 22 Feb. 1982, 29 April 1985; *Carolinian*, 18 Sept., 25 Oct. 1979, 4 Sept. 1980, 3 Sept. 1981, 20 Sept. 1983, 5 April 1984, 15 Sept. 1988; Ginnie Gardiner, ca. 11 Dec. 1981, to Lawrence Fincher, Budget; Moran, 29 March 1982, to James H. Allen et al., R; Joseph Welling, Television Utilization: A Report, 30 Nov. 1980, p. 6, Television; Woodrow McDougald, Status Report ..., 18 Oct. 1982, R; Status Report, Spring 1983, R; Moran, 26 Aug. 1985, to James H. Allen et al., R; Richard L. Moore, 20 April 1993, to Moran, Budget; Moore, 8 Oct. 1993, to Moran, Ra–Re, Moran Papers; Vertical File: WUAG; *Student Handbook*, 1993–94, pp. 29, 51 (incl. quotation).

64. Joseph Welling, Television Utilization: A Report, 30 Nov. 1980, Television; John W. Dunlop, 27 May 1981, to Moran; Moran, 9 June 1981, to William C. Friday, and other 1981 correspondence in T, Moran Papers; A. Lawrence Fincher and John W. Dunlop, agreement 19 Oct.1981, w/Minutes, 26 Oct. 1981, Chancellor's Cabinet Records; Greensboro *News & Record*, 6, 8 Nov. 1991.

65. *Carolinian*, 15 April 1982.

66. Correspondence in Environment, 1990, and E, 1993, Moran Papers.

67. Robert W. Hites et al., 24 March 1981, to Jack I. Bardon and Gail Hennis, Campus Planning, Moran Papers; Planning Process, 1980–83: Student Life, pp. 54, 292–95; OH: Meredith Carle, 19 May 1991.

68. Report to the Chancellor: The Class of 1988, Admissions, 1991, Moran Papers; Greensboro *News & Record*, 24 Feb. 1996.

69. James H. Allen, 20 May 1988, to Moran; Moran, 23 June, to Allen and Bernard B. Keele, Student Affairs, Moran Papers.

70. Student Government Homecoming Queen Resolution, 6 Oct. 1982; James H. Allen, 19 Oct. 1982, to Sybil Mann, Student Affairs, Moran Papers; *Carolinian*, 26 Oct., 2 Nov. 1982.

71. UNCG Spring Fling Activities . . . , OIS News Release, 29 March 1993.

72. *Carolinian*, 6 Sept. 1984, 29 Aug. 1985, 8 Sept. 1988, 9 April, 27 Aug. 1992, 2 Sept. 1993; Greensboro *News & Record*, 22 Aug. 1997; OH: Emily Whitney Ross, 12 May 1991.

73. Student Fee Study Report, 9 Sept. 1985, pp. 7–8, Deans' Council Records; Committee on the University Performing Arts Program report, 15 April 1988, pp. 2–4, Deans' Council Records, 25 Jan. 1989.

74. James H. Allen, 22 May 1980, to Clifford Lowery; Allen, 22 May 1980, to Fraternity/Sorority Screening and Review Committee; Bruce Harshbarger, 10 Nov. 1980, to Allen, F; [Allen], UNC-G Fraternities and Sororities, Update, Jan. 1981, B. of T.; Greek Update, 22 Sept. 1981, Student Affairs, Moran Papers; *Greensboro Daily News*, 27 April 1980; *Greensboro Record*, 14 Jan. 1981; *Carolinian*, 16, 18 Sept. 1980, 27 Jan., 11 Feb. 1981; Greek Advisors' Meeting, 29 Feb. 1984; James H. Allen, 6 March 1984, to Moran; Allen, 3 April 1984, to William T. Bringham, F, Moran Papers.

75. *Greensboro Daily News*, 14, 16 Nov. 1979.

76. Minutes, Advisory Committee on Student Life, 11 Feb. 1993, B. of T.: Committees on Academic Programs and Student Life, Moran Papers; *Carolinian*, 18, 25 Feb. 1993.

77. Greensboro *News & Record*, 21 Aug. 1987.

78. Trustee Minutes, 8 April, 9 Sept., 18 Nov. 1982. For the friction, see C. Thomas Martin, 27 Feb. 1991, to Moran, and Bruce J. Michaels, 7 March 1991, to Martin, Fr, Moran Papers; *Carolinian*, 9 April 1992; Faculty Senate Minutes, 7 Oct. 1992.

79. Moran, "Observations on Catholic Campus Ministry," *Journal of the CCMA*, [1987], pp. 6–7, in Personal; James H. Allen, 27 Aug. 1990, to Moran, G, Moran Papers; Greensboro *News & Record*, 19 Feb. 1989, pp. C1–2.

80. Fisher and Sloan, *Campus Crime*, pp. 6–15, 35, 83, 230–42.

81. University Police Patrol Twenty Four Hours a Day, in UNCG Development Office brochure: "UNCG Parents' Association," [Dec. 1992], Vertical File: Development Office.

82. Table: Campus Police Forces in N.C., 1979, S; Jerry D. Williamson, Feb. 1986 [no day], to All Faculty and Staff, Se–So, Moran Papers; *Carolinian*, 27 Sept., 2 Oct., 4 Dec. 1979, 11 Feb., 19, 26 March 1981; 2 March 1982, 4 Oct. 1984, 19 March 1987, 24 Aug. 1989, 22 April 1993; Chancellor's Cabinet Minutes, 1 Oct. 1979; 15, 22 Sept., 27 Oct. 1980; 30 March, 27 April, 12 Oct. 1981; 26 April 1982; 17 Jan. 1983; Trustees' Minutes, 10 Feb. 1983; Campus Police Step Up, 6 Sept. 1988, Vertical File: University Police Dept. For comprehensive accounts of campus security measures and staff in 1989 and 1993, see Jerry D. Williamson, 29 Nov. 1989, to Fred Drake, A; and Drake, 3 May 1993, to Moran, VC Bus. Aff., Moran Papers.

83. *Carolinian*, 5 Feb. 1981; *Alumni News*, 69 (Spring 1981), pp. 6–7; Jerry Williamson, "Students Make Caring Cops," *NACAS*, July 1984, pp. 18–21, in Vertical File: Campus Safety & Security.

84. *Carolinian*, 14 Sept., 2 Nov. 1982, 25 Jan., 8 Feb., 20 Sept., 1, 3 Nov. 1983, 17, 24 Jan. 1985, 25 Jan. 1990.

85. Student Legislative Assembly minutes, 13 Sept. 1988, SGA Records; *Carolinian*, 24 Aug. 1989, 10 Oct. 1991, 21 Jan. 1993.

86. William W. McIver, 17 July 1984, to Moran; Elisabeth A. Zinser, 18 July 1984, to Richard Cox et al.; Fred L. Drake, 24 July 1984, to Moran, Music School, General; Jerry D. Williamson, 5 Oct. 1988, to Moran, Police, Moran Papers. For major crimes on all UNC campuses, see N.C. State Universities, Crime Statistics, 1988–91, Po–Pu, 1992, Moran Papers.

Chapter 33 Notes

1. The author was a member of that committee.

2. Robert W. Hites et al., 24 March 1981, to Jack I. Bardon and Gail Hennis, Campus Planning, Moran Papers.

3. OH: James Allen, 11 Sept. 1990; Jean Buchert, 22 Feb. 1990; Rosemary McGee, 21 May 1990; Ellen Greaves, in *Carolinian*, 4 Sept. 1980.

4. Intercollegiate Athletics, Report to the Trustees, 11 Feb. 1982, pp. 227–34, UNCG Planning Process, 1980–83: Student Life; Stategic Planning Issue: Intercollegiate Athletics, [1985], Ca–Ce, Moran Papers; *Carolinian*, 6 Nov. 1979, 23 March, 4 May, 21 Sept., 9 Dec. 1982, 20 Sept. 1983.

5. Moran, in *Alumni News*, 67 (Summer 1979), p. 3; correspondence in Intercoll. Athletics, 1979, Moran Papers; Moran remarks to HPER faculty, 5 Feb. 1980, HPER, Moran Papers.

6. Walter H. Puterbaugh, 6 April 1981, to Moran; Moran, 13 April, 1981, to John R. McCarthy, ICA, Moran Papers.

7. Minutes, Called HPERD Faculty Meeting, 26 Feb. 1981, ICA, Moran Papers.

8. Tony Ladd, 3 Feb., 4 Dec. 1981, to Moran; Moran, 30 April 1981, to Richard A. Swanson, ICA, Moran Papers; Walter H. Puterbaugh, 27 March 1981, to Moran, Committee on Intercollegiate Athletics Records; Trustee Minutes, 9 April 1981; Report on Intercollegiate Athletics, 11 Feb. 1982, B. of T., Moran Papers; *Greensboro Daily News*, 11, 14 Nov. 1979; *Alumni News*, 70 (Spring 1982), p. 17; 73 (Winter 1985), p. 15; *Carolinian*, 23 March, 4 May 1982; Bar graph: UNCG Athletics: Overall Winning Rate, 1980–90, UNCG *Fact Book*, 1989–90, p. XII-[2].

9. UNCG Planning Process, 1980–83: Plan for the Development of the University, pp. 32–33; Greensboro *News & Record*, 27 March 1983.

10. *Greensboro Daily News*, 12 Aug. 1983; *Alumni News*, 72 (Fall 1983), p 16; *Greensboro Record*, 1 Dec. 1983; OH: Nelson Bobb, 25 April 1990; Nelson Bobb, presentation to trustees, 26 July 1984, B. of T., Moran Papers. Moran, 1 Nov. 1985 and 6 July 1990, to David Knight, ICA, Moran Papers. For Ladd's resignation, see *Greensboro Daily News*, 27 May 1983.

11. Academic Cabinet Minutes, 5 Feb. 1986; Moran, 27 Feb. 1986, to Terry Seaks, and 8 May 1986, to Valerie Putney, ICA, Moran Papers.

12. Richard Swanson and Nelson Bobb, Strategic Planning Issue: Intercollegiate Athletics, 12 March 1985, Vertical File: Intercollegiate Athletic Division; Academic Cabinet Minutes, 2 April, 10 Sept. 1986; Donald J. Reichard, 1 April 1986, to James H. Allen, ICA; William M. Snedden, 18 Nov. 1986, to Moran et al., Student Govt., Moran Papers.

13. Faculty Council Minutes, 21 Jan. 1986; UNCG Excellence Foundation, Board of Directors, Executive Committee minutes, 20 Jan., 18 Aug. 1986, Excellence Foundation, Moran Papers; Moran, 5 Aug. 1986, to the File; H. Michael Weaver, 19 Sept. 1986, to Alan Cone, B. of T.; A Proposal for Upgrading Intercollegiate Athletics . . . , 12 Aug. 1986, ICA, Moran Papers; Trustees' Minutes, 19 Feb. 1987; Greensboro *News & Record*, 25 May 1986.

14. For this expectation and for a variety of faculty, student, and other opinion on the matter, together with Moran's views, see Academic Cabinet Minutes, 5 March 1986, and the correspondence in ICA, 1986, Moran Papers.

15. Faculty Council Minutes, 18 Nov. 1986; OH: Jean Buchert, 22 Feb. 1990.

16. Trustees' Minutes, 19 Feb. 1987; Greensboro *News & Record*,20 Feb. 1987. For the two abstentions, see Student Legislative Assembly minutes, 24 Feb. 1987, SGA Records.

17. Maria J.M. Griffin, 1 May 1986, to Charles A. Hayes et al., ICA, Moran Papers.

18. UNCG *Fact Book*, 1994–95, pp. VI 7–9; Wilson Davis, draft annual report for Moran, 21 July 1994, Ca–Co, Moran Papers. For the affiliation with the Big South Conference, see the correspondence in ICA, 1992, and minutes of the Advisory Committee on Intercollegiate Ath-

letics, 31 March 1992, in ACIA, Moran Papers; and *Carolinian*, 27 Aug. 1992. For the male/female budgetary division, see Moran, 15 Oct. 1992, to C.D. Spangler, Jr., Tuition/Fees, Moran Papers.

19. James H. Allen, 13 Aug. 1986, to Moran, G; Jim Clotfelter, 9 Oct. 1992, to Chancellor's Cabinet, Tuition/Fees, Moran Papers; Minutes, Advisory Council on Intercollegiate Athletics, 28 March, 11 April 1994, Intercollegiate Athletics—Advisory Council, Moran Papers; *Carolinian*, 24 Aug. 1989; OH: Nelson Bobb, 25 April 1990. A good statement of the athletic program as it stood in 1992 appears in the Institutional Self-Study Report, 1992, pp. 206–11. For the decision to fund athletic scholarships from gifts rather than student fees, see Academic Cabinet Minutes, 10 Sept. 1986. For athletes' academic progress, see Excellence Foundation, Board of Directors' minutes, 14 Oct. 1992, Excellence Fdn., 1993, Moran Papers; Fred L. Drake, 28 July 1993, to Moran, ICA: NCAA, Moran Papers.; Nelson Bobb interview in *Carolinian*, 8 April 1993.

20. For a detailed look at collegiate athletics nationally, see Shulman and Bowen, *Game of Life*.

21. For the attitudes of non-traditional students nationally, see Levine, "How the Academic Profession is Changing," pp. 6–7.

22. UNCG Responses to Request for Information from Fiscal Research Division, [Jan.–July 1991], ICA, Moran Papers; *Carolinian*, 25 Oct. 1990 (Mark Schumacher interview), 12, 19 Nov. 1992.

23. *Carolinian*, 4, 11, 25 Feb., 28 Oct. 1993, 10 Feb., 17 March 1994; Greensboro *News & Record*, 10 March 1997.

24. Table: UNC, Fees Applicable to All Regularly Enrolled Students . . . , [1992], Tuition/Fees, Moran Papers.

25. Chuck Brewer, 26 Jan. 1993, to Board of Trustees, B. of T., Moran Papers; *Carolinian*, 5, 19 Nov. 1992; Trustee Minutes, 8 Feb. 1996.

26. Moran, 12 July 1994, to H. Michael Weaver, Development-Benefactors, Moran Papers. See remarks of Chancellor Patricia Sullivan in General Faculty Minutes, 23 April 1997.

27. Trustees' Minutes, 8 Feb. 1996; Greensboro *News & Record*, 8, 14 Feb., 2, 10 March 1997.

28. *Alumni News*, 74 (Fall 1985), pp. 30–31; *Carolinian*, 24 Aug. 1989; *Catalog*, 1993–94, pp. 375–76.

29. Grobman, *Urban State Universities*, pp. 40, 42.

30. Black Alumni News, March/April 1981, Alumni, Moran Papers; Barbara Parrish, annual report for 1981–82, Alumni Association Records, 1899–1988.

31. Moran, 16 Sept. 1982, to Charles W. Patterson, G; Bernard B. Keele, 28 Nov. 1988, to Moran, VC Development, Moran Papers; UNCG *Fact Book*, 1994–95, p. VII-6; Planning Process, 1980–83: Plan for the Development of the University, pp. 54–56.

32. For a rare mention of the financial cause of controversy, see Moran, "Status Report on the Working Relationship of the University and the Alumni Association," Aug. 1989, p. 19.

33. Moran, installation speech, 14 March 1980, Chancellor's Installation, Moran Papers; Fisher, *Power of the Presidency*, pp. xvi, 173–77.

34. Moran, 29 Oct. 1979, to Gladys S. Bullard, B. of T./B. of G., Moran Papers; Moran, "Status Report on the Working Relationship of the University and the Alumni Association," Aug. 1989, pp. 14–16; OH: Brenda Cooper, 25 April 1991.

35. Moran, 2 Feb. 1984, to Elisabeth A. Zinser, Grad School; Moran, 8 March 1984, to the File, A, Moran Papers; Bronna, 20 April [1985], to Marilib [Sink], Lois and Barbara [Parrish], in Correspondence, Alumni Association Records, 1899–1988. For Moran's views, see Moran, 17 July 1981, to Charles W. Patterson, G, Moran Papers; and Moran, "Status Report on the Working Relationship of the University and the Alumni Association," Aug. 1989, pp. 4, 10, 13, 17.

36. Bernard B. Keele, 13, 19 Dec. 1985, to Barbara Parrish, in Correspondence, Alumni Association Records, 1899–1988; Keele, 27 Feb. 1986, to Cathy Vaughn, and other correspondence in Alumni, 1986, Moran Papers.

37. Cathy Vaughn, 9 March 1987, to Moran and Alumni AssociationAnnual Giving Council minutes, 28 March 1987, Alum. Assn.; Bernard B. Keele, 14 July 1988, to Moran, Alumni; Keele, 28 Nov. 1988, to Moran, VC Development, Moran Papers; "Alumni Records," [11 Feb. 1988], in Correspondence, Alumni Association Records, 1899–1988; Moran, "Status Report on the Working Relationship of the University and the Alumni Association," Aug. 1989; Moran, 5 Jan. 1990, to Members of the Alumni Association, Academic Cabinet Minutes, 7 Feb. 1990; Greensboro *News & Record*, 7 Jan. 1990. For former Vice Chancellor Charles Patterson's useful retrospective view of these matters, see Patterson, 19 July 1988, to Moran, Alumni, Moran Papers.

38. Catherine S. Vaughn, 27 April 1988, to Moran; [Alumni Association], draft report, 3 March 1988, pp. 35–39, 67–68, 82–86, 89–90, and final report, 27 April 1988; [Chancellor's Office], An Assessment of the Working Relationship of the University and the Alumni Association, [1988], Alumni Reports, Moran Papers; Barbara Parrish, 6 Aug. 1988, to Moran w/enclosure, Alumni, Moran Papers; *Alumni News*, 76 (Summer 1978), pp. 30–31. Most of the voluminous record of the controversy is found in the Alumni, Alumni Association, and Alumni Reports folders in the Moran Papers, 1986–91, and in the Alumni Association Records.

39. Betty Ervin, 3 Nov. 1988, to Moran, Alumni, Moran Papers.

40. George Hamer, 29 June 1988, to Moran, Alumni, Moran Papers. For accounts of the controversy, see *Alumni News*, 78 (Fall 1989), pp. 20–36; (Spring 1990), pp. 14–15.

41. Moran, "Status Report on the Working Relationship of the University and the Alumni Association," Aug. 1989, pp. 4, 10, 13, 17.

42. For the opinion of the state attorney general's office, see Andrew A. Vanore, Jr., 29 Jan. 1990, to Moran, Alum. Assn., Moran Papers. For articulate examples of alumni opinion, see John J. Butler, '79, 5 Jan. 1990, to Moran, Alum. Assn., Moran Papers; OH: Louise Falk, 20 March 1990; Adelaide Holderness, 26 April 1990; Betty Brown Jester, 22 March 1990; Henrietta Huffines, 20 May 1991.

43. Alumni Association Board of Trustees, 10 Oct. 1989, with Addendum, 17 Nov. 1989, to Members of the UNCG Alumni Association, AASA-Alum. Assn., Moran Papers; Greensboro *News & Record*, 7 Feb. 1990.

44. Agreement between the Alumni Association... and the University..., 26 Nov. 1990, Alum. Assn. Agreement; Alumni Association Mediation Team..., 31 Jan. 1991, to Members of the UNCG Alumni Association; Alumni Board of Trustees, 1 Oct. 1991, to UNCG Alumni, Alum. Affairs, Moran Papers; Greensboro *News & Record*, 31 Dec. 1990; OH: Brenda Cooper, 25 April 1991; *Alumni News*, 79 (Fall 1990), pp. 18–19; (Summer 1991), p. 32; 82 (Spring 1993), pp. 5, 10.

45. UNCG *Fact Book*, 1994–95, p. VII-4.

46. Agreement between the Alumni Association... and the University, 1996–98, 2000–02, in possession of the author.

47. Betty Ervin, 11 Oct. 1989, to Moran; Barbara Parrish, 17 Oct. 1989, to Moran and Ervin, AASA–Alum. Assn., Moran Papers; Greensboro *News & Record*, 7 Jan. 1990, 28 May 1991; OH: Louise Falk, 20 March 1990.

48. Richard L. Moore, 15 June, 22 Nov. 1993, 21 Feb., 11 March 1994, to Moran; Moore, 16 May 1994, to Anne Tate et al.; Anne H. Tate, 20 May 1994, to Moran, Alumni, Moran Papers; *Alumni News*, 82 (Winter 1993), pp. 24–25; (Summer 1994), p. 22; 83 (Fall 1994), pp. 20–21; (Summer 1995), p. 11.

49. Boyer, *College*, p. 238; Bowen and Schuster, *American Professors*, pp. 49, 156.

50. J. Gary Hoover, 7 Feb. 1984, to Moran, Education; Aubrey S. Garlington, 13 May 1988, to Moran, Music, Moran Papers; Institutional Self-Study Report, 1992, pp. 154–57, 243; Enrollment Management Committee report, w/Faculty Senate Minutes, 28 April 1993; Enrollment Management Committee report, 1993–94, Enrollment Management Committee Records; OH: Jean Buchert, 22 Feb. 1990; Joanne Creighton, 9 April 1990; M. Elaine Burgess, 8 Nov. 1990. For concerns of the budget committee, see Faculty Senate Minutes, 7 Oct. 1992, 3, 17 Feb. 1993; Joseph E. Johnson, 4 Feb. 1993, to Moran, Faculty Senate, Moran Papers. For other committees, see Traffic Committee report, 3 March 1987, w/Academic Cabinet Minutes, 1 April 1987; Admissions Policies Committee, w/Faculty Senate Minutes, 19 Aug. 1991 and 1 Aug. 1992.

51. John Lee Jellicorse, 18 Feb. 1985, to Moran, Arts/Sciences; Aubrey S. Garlington, 23 April 1986, to Moran; Moran, 23 July 1986, to Garlington, Music; Clifton Bob Clark, 1 Nov. 1986, to Kathleen Kowal, F, Moran Papers; Institutional Self Study Report, 1992, pp. 259–61.

52. *Carolinian*, 5 April 1990.

53. Daniel O. Price, 22 March 1988, to Moran, and other correspondence in VCAA-*Quo Vadimus*; Aubrey S. Garlington, 13 May 1988, to Moran, Music; Robert F. Gaines, 20 June 1988, to Moran, Library, Moran Papers; *Carolinian*, 17 March, 14 April 1988.

54. Bob Clark, 6 Jan. 1992, to Bob Gatten; Gatten, 7 Jan. 1992, to Clark and Henry Levinson, Engineering-Science Research Center, Moran Papers.

55. Faculty Senate Minutes, 15 Jan., 1 April 1992.

56. Institutional Self-Study Report, 1992, pp. 259–61.

57. Report of the Consultants to the Science Planning Committee, pp. 2–3, 15–16, w/R.C. Lewontin, 7 Dec. 1992, to Walter Beale, Eng.-Science Center, Moran Papers.

58. Topics of Discussion in Senate Roundtables, 1992; Faculty Senate Minutes, 7 Oct. 1992, 22 Feb., 3 March, 1 Sept. 1993; Joseph E. Johnson, Status of Faculty, w/Johnson, 21 Oct. 1992, to Members of the Senate; Eleanor F. McCrickard, 15 March 1993, to Moran, Faculty Senate, Moran Papers; Johnson, 11 May 1993, to Members of the University Faculty, w/Faculty Senate Minutes.

59. Faculty Senate, 12 Jan. 1994, to Moran et al., Faculty Senate Minutes, 12 Jan. 1994; Greensboro *News & Record*, 1, 3 Feb. 1994; *Carolinian*, 3 Feb. 1994.

60. Institutional Self-Study Report, 1992, p. 205.

61. Marleen Ingle, in Deans' Council Records, 13 Aug. 1986; *Carolinian*, 17 March 1988.

62. Anne Steele remarks, Faculty Senate Minutes, 1 Sept. 1993; Deans' Council Records, 25 Aug., 17 Nov. 1993; Financial Aid Office, Inc., Financial Aid Operational Review, 23 Nov. 1993, and correspondence, Sept.–Dec. 1993, in Financial Aid, Moran Papers; Donald DeRosa, Remarks to Faculty Senate, 12 Jan. 1994, Enrollment Management Committee Records; *Carolinian*, 9, 23, 30 Sept. 1993, 17 Feb. 1994.

63. Financial Aid Office, Inc., Financial Aid Operational Review, 23 Nov. 1993, and correspondence in Financial Aid, 1993; Philip H. Richman, 4 Aug. 1994, to J. Arthur Leaston, Financial Aid, Moran Papers.

64. Leonard L. Haynes, 12 July 1990, to Marleen B. Ingle, Financial Aid; N.C. State Education Assistance Authority, 2 Feb. 1993, Financial Aid; Moran Papers; OIS News Releases, 24 Oct. 1990, 30 Jan. 1992; Institutional Self-Study Report, 1992, pp. 199–201.

65. George Dehne, Analysis of the [UNCG] Admissions Program . . . , w/Anne C. Steele, 28 Oct. 1992, to Donald V. DeRosa, Admissions, Moran Papers. For Rickard's response to the Dehne report, describing improvements during his tenure, see *Alumni News*, 82 (Winter 1993), p. 17.

66. Moran, 23 March 1982, to Floyd E. Mattheis, Recommendations; Charles E. Rickard, 24 June 1985, to Moran, Admissions, Moran Papers.

67. Elisabeth Zinser, 13 Aug. 1987, to Moran, Salaries; Zinser, 14 July 1987, to Charles E. Rickard; Moran, 16 Aug. 1991, to Rickard; T. Joseph Watts, 14 June 1993, to Moran, Admissions, Moran Papers.

68. Expanded Deans' Council Records, 11 Nov. 1992; Rickard, 7 June 1993, to the Faculty and Staff, Admissions, Moran Papers.

69. Chancellor's Cabinet Records, 3 May 1993; Donald V. DeRosa, 16 Dec. 1993, to University Faculty and Staff, Admissions, Moran Papers; Faculty Senate Minutes, 1 Sept. 1993; Trustee minutes, 23 Sept. 1993.

70. Faculty Senate Minutes, 12 Jan. 1994, 26 April 1995; Deans' Council Records, 19 Jan., 17 Aug. 1994; Financial Aid Office, Inc., Financial Aid Operational Review, 23 Nov. 1993, Financial Aid; Correspondence in Financial Aid, 1994, Moran Papers.

71. Letters of Ruth K. Beesch, 14 May 1993, Fred L. Drake, 14 Oct. 1993, and other correspondence in Music, Moran Papers.

72. Betty Ervin, 7 Jan. 1994, to F. James Becher; Hugh Humphrey, 17 Jan. 1994, to Becher; Moran, Action Item: Site Selection for New Music Building, 18 Jan. 1994, B. of T.: 18 Jan. 1994 folder, Moran Papers; E.S. Melvin, 13 Jan. 1994, to Becher, School: Music, Moran Papers; Trustees' Committee on University Resource Planning (CURP) minutes, 5 Jan., 8, 10 Feb. 1994; Kate Bell, 17 Jan. 1994, to CURP members; James Becher, 26 Jan. 1994, to CURP members, B of T: CURP, Moran Papers; Trustee Minutes, 10 Feb. 1994; Greensboro *News & Record*, 9, 10, 11 Feb. 1994; *Carolinian*, 10 Feb. 1994. For the relationship to Peabody Park, see Fred L. Drake, 14 June 1994, to Moran; Moran, 1 July 1994, to C.D. Spangler, School: Music, Moran Papers; Trustees Minutes, 17 Nov. 1994, 9 Feb. 1995; Kate G. Bell, Statement Regarding the Location and Planning for the School of Music Building, 5 Dec. 1994, Vertical File: Music Bldg.: New.

73. Jencks and Riesman, *Academic Revolution*, p. 16.

74. Greensboro *News & Record*, 11 Feb. 1994; *Campus* newsletter, 21 Feb. 1994; *Carolinian*, 17 Feb. 1994, pp. 1, 4.

75. Greensboro *News & Record*, 11, 14, Feb., 3, 7 March, 15 Aug. 1994; *Alumni News*, 82, (Summer 1994), p. 16; 83 (Fall 1994), p. 15.

76. Trustees Minutes, 9 Feb. 1995; OIS News Release, 10 Jan. 1997; Greensboro *News & Record*, 9 Jan. 1995, 22 Jan., 17 Sept. 1997.

Epilogue Notes

1. UNCG *Fact Book*, 2002–03 (online): Enrollments, Admissions/Retention.

2. Greensboro *News & Record*, 12 Feb. 1994.

3. *Campus Weekly*, 30 April 2003; Greensboro *News & Record*, 25 May 2003.

4. *Campus Weekly*, 15 Jan. 1997; Greensboro *News & Record*, 23 May 1998.

5. Greensboro *News & Record*, 28 April 1997.

6. Greensboro *News & Record*, 10, 23 April, 10 June 1999; Patricia Sullivan, in *UNCG Magazine*, 1 (Fall 1999), p. 2.

7. Greensboro *News & Record*, 25 May 2003.

8. Cross, "The Run to Division I," pp. 86, 98–112.

9. For a 1996 discussion of faculty morale in this vein, see Charles P.R. Tisdale, Faculty Senate News, in *Campus* newsletter, 22 Jan. 1996. See also Greensboro *News & Record*, 18 May 1997.

Bibliography

Manuscripts

Greensboro, N.C.

UNCG Archives, Special Collections Department, Jackson Library
- Directors'/Trustees' Records
  - Board of Directors, 1892–1932
    - Executive Committee, 1906–28
  - Board of Trustees, 1974–96
- Presidents'/Chancellors' Records, including their private papers (in chronological order)
  - Charles Duncan McIver, 1891–1906
  - Julius I. Foust, 1906–34. Including Clora Foust Papers
  - Walter Clinton Jackson, 1934–50
  - Edward Kidder Graham, Jr. 1950–56
  - William Whatley Pierson, 1956–57, 1960–61
  - Gordon W. Blackwell, 1957–60
  - Otis A. Singletary, 1961–66
  - James S. Ferguson, 1964–79
  - William E. Moran, 1979–94
  - Debra W. Stewart, 1994
  - Patricia A. Sullivan, 1995–
- Chancellor's Cabinet Records
- College Scrapbooks (newspaper clippings), 1891–1959
- Dean of Administration Reports, 1934–36
- Institutional Self Studies, 1962–
- Vice Chancellors' Records (abbreviated VC)
  - Academic Affairs (VCAA; after 1988, Provost)
    - Records, 1941–84, 1988–93
    - Assistant Vice Chancellor
    - Deans' Council
  - Administration and Planning
  - Development and University Relations
    - Information Services: News Releases

- Provost. See Vice Chancellor for Academic Affairs
- Student Affairs
  - Records, 1969–87
  - Class Records
  - Dean of Students for Student Services
  - Dean of Women

Library, School, and College of Arts and Sciences Records
- Arts and Sciences
- Business and Economics (B&E)
- Education
  - Curry School
- Health, Physical Education, Recreation, and Dance (HPERD). Later Health and Human Performance (HHP)
- Home Economics. Later Human Environmental Sciences (HES)
- Librarian, Office of
- Music
- Nursing

Department Records
- Commercial Department
- English Department

Faculty Government Records, Minutes
- Academic Cabinet
- Academic Policies Committee
- Ad Hoc Committees: Faculty Governance
- Advisory Committee
- Curriculum Committee
- Enrollment Management Committee
- Faculty Cabinet
- Faculty Council. After 1991, General Faculty
- Faculty Senate
- Faculty-Student Joint Advisory Committee
- Faculty Welfare Committee
- General Education Steering Committee
- Intercollegiate Athletics Committee (in Vice Chancellor for Student Affairs Records)
- Planning Process, 1980–83: Reports of Task Forces and the resulting Plan for the Development of the University
- Study and Planning Committee, 1957–58

Student Records
- Adelphian Society
- Cornelian Society
- Student Government Association

Alumni Records
- Alumnae/Alumni Association

Annual Reports
Minutes of the association and its board of trustees
Records, 1899–1988
Office of Alumni Affairs (in Vice Chancellor for Development Records)
Private Collections
Special Collections Department, Jackson Library
Ashby, Warren
Byrd, Clara Booth
Craig, Marjorie
Elliott, Harriet W.
Gove, Anna M.
Griffin, Ellen
Jarrell, Randall
Lathrop, Virginia Terrell
Satterfield, Frances Gibson
Shaw, Anna Howard
Faculty File
Vertical File

Chapel Hill, N.C.

University of North Carolina: Wilson Library
University Records
Papers of Presidents and Other Administrators
Carmichael, William D.
Friday, William C.
Graham, Frank Porter
Gray, Gordon
Other University Records
Trustees
Minutes
Executive Committee, Minutes
Visiting Committee, Reports
Private Papers: Southern Historical Collection
McLendon, Lennox Polk
Thomas, Howard Wilbur
Tillett, Gladys Avery
Whitaker, Eloise
Wiley, Calvin

Raleigh, N.C.

North Carolina Division of Archives and History
Public Records
Public Instruction, Superintendent
Private Papers

Gash Family
Joyner, James Yadkin
Weil, Gertrude
Williams and Dameron Papers

Primary Published Works

Daniels, Josephus. *Editor in Politics*. Chapel Hill: University of North Carolina Press, 1941.

———, *Tar Heel Editor*. Chapel Hill: University of North Carolina Press, 1939.

Forney, Edward J. et al. *Leaves from the Stenographers' Note Books: Side Lights on Dr. McIver at Work*. Greensboro: Harrison Publishing Co., [1917?].

Goolsby, Elaine L. *Letters Lost and Found*. Durham, N.C.: Carolina Wren Press, 1999.

Harris, Seymour. *A Statistical Portrait of Higher Education*. N.Y.: McGraw-Hill, 1972.

Hicks, John D. *My Life With History: An Autobiography*. Lincoln: University of Nebraska Press, 1968.

Jarrell, Randall. *Randall Jarrell's Letters*. Mary Jarrell, ed. Boston: Houghton Mifflin, 1985.

McIver, Charles D. "Our Next Educational Advance." *State Normal Magazine*, 1 (March 1897): 1–5.

———, "Two Open Fields for Investment in the South." Ibid., 6 (Oct. 1901).

[North Carolina Budget Bureau]. *The Budget*, 1927–. Raleigh: Various publishers, 1926–.

North Carolina Normal and Industrial School/College, and North Carolina College for Women, Board of Directors, *Reports*, 1892–1930.

North Carolina, State Treasurer. *Biennial Reports.*

North Carolina, *Statutes*, 1891–.

Page, Walter Hines. "The Forgotten Man." *State Normal Magazine* 1 (June 1897). (Also in Page. *The Rebuilding of Old Commonwealths*. N.Y.: Doubleday, Page & Co., 1902.)

Pearson, Thomas Gilbert. *Adventures in Bird Protection*. N.Y.: D. Appleton-Century, 1937.

Statistical Abstract of Higher Education in North Carolina, 1969–. [Chapel Hill]: University of North Carolina, 1969–.

United States Commissioner of Education. Report for 1890–1891. *House Executive Documents*, 52 Congress, 1 session, #1, Part 5, Vol. 5, part 1 (Serials set #2938), pp. 1–31.

University of North Carolina at Greensboro. *Fact Book: A Statistical Abstract of Significant Characteristics of the University of North Carolina at Greensboro*, 1979–. Greensboro: UNCG Office of Institutional Research, 1980–.

———. *Program and Mission, 1991–2000*. [Greensboro, N.C.: UNCG], 1991.

Oral History Transcripts

UNC-Chapel Hill. Southern Oral History Program. Southern Historical Collection, Wilson Library
Tillett, Gladys Avery. Interview, 20 March 1974.
UNC-Greensboro. Special Collections Department, Jackson Library
Bardolph, Richard. Oral History Interviews with Alumnae.
Civil Rights Oral History Interviews, 1987–88.
Drake, Fred. Interview, 28 Feb. 1994. Faculty File.
UNCG Centennial Oral History Interviews, 1989–97. (Cited as OH in notes.)

Newspapers and Other Periodicals

State Normal/NCCW/Woman's College/UNCG Publications
Alumnae/Alumni News, 1912–98.
Campus (or *Campus Weekly)* (Newsletter), 1985–.
Carolinian (Yearbook), 1909–17.
Carolinian (Student newspaper), 1919–.
Catalog/Undergraduate Bulletin, annual (title varies), 1892–.
Coraddi (Student literary magazine), 1919–.
Decennial (Yearbook for first decade), 1902.
Pine Needles (Yearbook), 1920–93.
State Normal Magazine, 1897–1919.
Student Handbook, 1897–.
UNCG Magazine, 1998–
Greensboro Daily News
Greensboro *News & Record*
Greensboro Record

Secondary Works

Adams, Charles M. "Library First on Building Program." *Library Journal* 73 (Dec. 15, 1948): 1772–77.

———. "Woman's College Library, the University of North Carolina." *College & Research Libraries* 14 (April 1953): 135–39.

Albright, James W. *Greensboro, 1808–1904*. Greensboro: J.J. Stone, 1904.

Alderman, Edwin A. "Charles D. McIver of North Carolina." *Suwanee Review* 15 (Jan. 1907): 100–10.

Allardyce, Gilbert. "The Rise and Fall of the Western Civilization Course." *American Historical Review* 87 (June 1982): 695–725.

Altbach, Philip G., and Patti Peterson. "Before Berkeley: Historical Perspectives on American Student Activism." *Annals of the American Academy of Political and Social Science* 395 (May 1971): 1–14.

Altbach, Philip G. *Student Politics in America: A Historical Analysis.* N.Y.: McGraw-Hill, 1974.

———. "Students: Interests, Culture, and Activism," in Arthur Levine, ed., *Higher Learning in America, 1980–2000.* Baltimore: Johns Hopkins University Press, 1993.

Altenbaugh, Richard J., and Kathleen Underwood. "The Evolution of Normal Schools," in John I. Goodlad et al., eds., *Places Where Teachers Are Taught.* San Francisco: Jossey-Bass, 1990.

Armstrong, W. Earle. *The College and Teacher Education.* Washington: American Council on Education, 1944.

Arnett, Ethel Stephens. *Greensboro, North Carolina: The County Seat of Guilford.* Chapel Hill: University of North Carolina Press, 1955.

Ashby, Warren. *Frank Porter Graham: A Southern Liberal.* Winston-Salem: John Blair, 1980.

Astin, Helen S. "Educating Women: A Promise and a Vision for the Future." *American Journal of Education* 98 (Aug. 1990): 479–93.

———, and Alan E. Bayer. "Sex Discrimination in Academe," in Alice S. Rossi and Ann Calderwood, eds., *Academic Women on the Move.* N.Y.: Russell Sage Foundation, 1973.

Ayers, Edward L. *The Promise of the New South: Life After Reconstruction.* N.Y.: Oxford University Press, 1992.

Bailey, Hugh C. *Liberalism in the New South: Southern Social Reformers and the Progressive Movement.* Coral Gables, FL: University of Miami Press, 1969.

Bardolph, Richard. A long series of articles on the institution's history, appearing in the *Alumni News*, Fall 1980 to Summer 1993.

Barzun, Jacques. *The American University: How It Runs, Where It Is Going.* 2d ed. Chicago: University of Chicago Press, 1993.

Battle, Kemp P. *History of the University of North Carolina.* 2 vols., 1907–12. Reprint ed., Spartanburg, S.C.: The Reprint Co., 1974.

Bell, Daniel. "*Quo Warranto?*—Notes on the Governance of Universities in the 1970's." *Public Interest* 19 (Spring 1970): 53–68.

Bellas, Marcia L. "Faculty Salaries: Still a Cost of Being Female?" *Social Science Quarterly* 74 (March 1993): 62–75.

Berelson, Bernard. *Graduate Education in the United States.* N.Y.: McGraw-Hill, 1960.

Bernard, Jessie. *Academic Women.* University Park: Pennsylvania State University Press, 1964.

Berube, Maurice R. *The Urban University in America.* Westport, CT: Greenwood Press, 1978.

Biklen, Sari K. "The Progressive Education Movement and the Question of Women." *Teachers College Record* 80 (Dec. 1978): 316–35.

Billingsley, William J. *Communists on Campus: Race, Politics, and the Public University in Sixties North Carolina.* Athens: University of Georgia Press, 1999.

Blackwell, Thomas E. *College and University Administration.* N.Y.: Center for Applied Research in Education, 1966.

Blau, Peter M., and Ellen L. Slaughter. "Institutional Conditions and Student Demonstrations." *Social Problems* 18 (Spring 1971): 475–87.

Boerner, Trilby, and Norma Cofer. *Oh College Dear, To You.* [Greensboro: Privately printed, 1953].

Boroff, David. *Campus USA: Portraits of American Colleges in Action.* N.Y.: Harper, 1961.

Borrowman, Merle L. *The Liberal and Technical in Teacher Education: A Historical Survey of American Thought.* N.Y.: Teachers College, Columbia University, 1956.

Bowen, Howard R., and Jack H. Schuster. *American Professors: A National Resource Imperiled.* N.Y.: Oxford University Press, 1986.

Bowen, Howard R. "Faculty Salaries: Past and Future." *Educational Record* 49 (Winter 1968): 9–21.

Bowen, William G., and Derek Bok. *Shape of the River: Long-Term Consequences of Considering Race in College and University Admissions.* Princeton: Princeton University Press, 1998.

———, and Neil L. Rudenstine. *In Pursuit of the PhD.* Princeton: Princeton University Press, 1992.

———, and Harold T. Shapiro, eds. *Universities and Their Leadership.* Princeton: Princeton University Press, 1998.

Bowles, Elisabeth Ann. *A Good Beginning: The First Four Decades Of The University of North Carolina at Greensboro.* Chapel Hill: University of North Carolina Press, 1967.

Boyer, Ernest L. "Campus Climate in the 1980s and 1990s: Decades of Apathy and Renewal," in Arthur Levine, ed. *Higher Learning in America, 1980–2000.* Baltimore: Johns Hopkins University Press, 1993. Pp. 322–32.

———. *College: The Undergraduate Experience in America.* N.Y.: Harper & Row, 1987.

Boynton, Ruth Evelyn. "The Development of Student Health Services." *Student Medicine* 1 (Oct. 1952): 4–8.

Bradley, Bert E. "Educational Reformers in North Carolina, 1885–1905," in Waldo W. Braden, ed. *Oratory in the New South.* Baton Rouge: Louisiana State University Press, 1979. Pp. 237–75.

Bratton, Mary Jo. "Cradled in Conflict: Origins of East Carolina University." *North Carolina Historical Review* 63 (Jan. 1986): 74–103.

———. *East Carolina University: The Formative Years, 1907–1982.* Greenville, NC: East Carolina Alumni Association, 1986.

Brown, Wade R. *The North Carolina State High School Music Contest-Festival: A History.* Greensboro: Woman's College, 1946.

Brubacher, John Seiler, and Willis Rudy. *Higher Education in Transition: An American History, 1636–1956.* N.Y.: Harper, 1958.

Bryant, Joseph A., Jr. *Twentieth Century Southern Literature.* Lexington: University Press of Kentucky, 1997.

———. *Understanding Randall Jarrell.* Columbia: University of South Carolina Press, 1986.

Butts, R. Freeman. *The College Charts Its Course: Historical Conceptions and Current Proposals.* N.Y.: McGraw-Hill, 1939.

Byrd, Clara. "History of the Alumnae Association." [1943]. Clara Byrd Papers. UNCG Archives.

Cahn, Susan K. *Coming On Strong: Gender and Sexuality in Twentieth-Century Women's Sport.* Cambridge: Harvard University Press, 1994.

Callan, Patrick M. "Government and Higher Education," in Arthur Levine, ed. *Higher Learning in America, 1980–2000.* Baltimore: Johns Hopkins University Press, 1993. Pp. 3–19.

Camp, Cordelia et al., eds. *Some Pioneer Women Teachers of North Carolina.* N.p.: Delta Kappa Gamma Society, North Carolina State Organization, 1955.

Canaday, M. Helen, Rebecca McCulloch Smith, and Sarah Moore Shoffner. *The History of the School of Human Environmental Sciences, 1892–1992.* Greensboro: UNCG, [1992].

Carnegie Commission on Higher Education. *Reform on Campus: Changing Students, Changing Academic Programs.* N.Y.: McGraw-Hill, 1972.

Carter, Susan B. "Academic Women Revisited: An Empirical Study of Changing Patterns in Women's Employment as College and University Faculty, 1890–1963." *Journal of Social History* 14 (Summer 1981): 675–700.

Chafe, William H. *Civilities and Civil Rights: The Black Struggle for Freedom in Greensboro, North Carolina.* N.Y.: Oxford University Press, 1980.

———. *The Paradox of Change: American Women in the 20th Century.* N.Y.: Oxford University Press, 1991.

Chamberlain, Hope. *A Minority of Members: Women in the U.S. Congress.* N.Y.: Praeger, 1973.

Chamberlain, Mariam K., ed. *Women in Academe: Progress and Prospects.* N.Y.: Russell Sage Foundation, 1988.

Chickering, Arthur. *Commuting Versus Resident Students.* San Francisco: Jossey-Bass, 1974.

Cimbala, Diane J. "Greetings From Your Alma Mater: College and University Alumni Publications." *Serials Review* 10 (Fall 1984): 7–17.

Clark, Burton R. *The Distinctive College.* Chicago: Aldine, 1970.

———. "Faculty Organization and Authority," in Gary L. Riley and J. Victor Baldridge, eds. *Governing Academic Organizations.* Berkeley, CA: McCutchan, 1977. Pp. 64–78.

———. "The Organizational Saga in Higher Education." *Administrative Science Quarterly* 17, no. 2 (1972): 178–84.

———. "Small Worlds, Different Worlds: The Uniquenesses and Troubles of American Academic Professions." *Daedalus* 126 (Fall 1997): 21–42.

Clifford, Geraldine Joncich. "'Marry, Stitch, Die, or Do Worse': Educating Women for Work," in David B. Tyack, ed. *Work, Youth, and Schooling: Historical Perspectives on Vocationalism in American Education*. Stanford, CA: Stanford University Press, 1982. Pp. 223–68.

Cline, Ned. *Adding Value: The Joseph M. Bryan Story from Poverty to Philanthropy*. Greensboro, NC: Joseph M. Bryan Foundation, 2001.

Cohen, Michael D., and James G. March. *Leadership and Ambiguity: The American College President*. 2d ed. Cambridge: Harvard Business School Press, 1986.

Cohen, Sol. "The Industrial Education Movement, 1906–17." *American Quarterly* 20 (Spring 1968): 95–110.

Cole, John Y. "Storehouses and Workshops: American Libraries and the Uses of Knowledge," in Alexandra Oleson and John Voss, eds., *The Organization of Knowledge in Modern America, 1860–1920*. Baltimore: Johns Hopkins University Press, 1979. Pp. 364–85.

Cole, Jonathan R. "Balancing Acts: Dilemmas of Choice Facing Research Universities." *Daedalus* 122 (Fall 1993): 1–36.

Conway, Jill K. "Coeducation and Women's Studies: Two Approaches to the Question of Woman's Place in the Contemporary University." *Daedalus* 103 (Fall 1974): 239–49.

Cookingham, Mary E. "Bluestockings, Spinsters and Pedagogues: Women College Graduates, 1865–1910." *Population Studies* 38 (Nov. 1984): 349–64.

Coon, Charles L. "Charles Duncan McIver and His Educational Services." U.S. Commissioner of Education Report, 1907, *House Documents*, 60 Congress, 1 session (Serials #5297). Pp. 329–39.

Cooper, John M., Jr. *Walter Hines Page: The Southerner as American, 1855–1918*. Chapel Hill: University of North Carolina Press, 1977.

Cott, Nancy F. *The Grounding of Modern Feminism*. New Haven: Yale University Press, 1987.

Covington, Howard E., and Marion A. Ellis. *Terry Sanford: Politics, Progress, and Outrageous Ambitions*. Durham, NC: Duke University Press, 1999.

Cox, Marci, and Alexander W. Astin. "Sex Differentials in Faculty Salaries." *Research in Higher Education* 7(Dec. 1977): 289–98.

Coyner, Ruth E. "The South's First University Summer Normal School." *Peabody Journal of Education* 18 (Nov. 1940): 173–82.

Crane, Theodore R. "The Modern American University and Regional Service." *History of Education Quarterly* 22 (Winter 1983): 479–90.

Crawford, Mary Caroline. *The College Girl of America and the Institutions Which Make Her What She Is*. Boston: L.C. Page, 1905.

Creese, Walter L. "Architecture and Learning: A Collegiate Quandary." American Institute of Architects *Journal* 17 (May–June 1952): 241–44, 268–82.

Cremin, Lawrence A. *American Education: The Metropolitan Experience, 1876–1980*. N.Y.: Harper & Row, 1988.

Cross, K. Patricia. "Improving the Quality of Instruction," in Arthur Levine, ed. *Higher Learning in America, 1980–2000.* Baltimore: Johns Hopkins University Press, 1993. Pp. 287–308.

Cross, Michael Edward. "The Run to Division I: Intercollegiate Athletics and the Broader Interests of Colleges and Universities." Ph.D. dissertation, Princeton University, 1999.

Current, Richard N. *Phi Beta Kappa in American Life: The First Two Hundred Years.* N.Y.: Oxford University Press, 1990.

Curti, Merle E., and Roderick Nash. *Philanthropy in the Shaping of American Higher Education.* New Brunswwick, NJ: Rutgers University Press, 1965.

———. *The Social Ideas of American Educators.* 1935. 2d ed., Paterson, NJ: Littlefield, Adams, 1963.

Dabney, Charles W. *Universal Education in the South.* 2 vols. Chapel Hill, University of North Carolina Press, 1936.

Dash, Roger E., and Gary L. Riley. "The Evolution of an Urban University," in Riley and J. Victor Baldridge, eds. *Governing Academic Organizations.* Berkeley, CA: McCutchan, 1977. Pp. 145–58.

De Almeida, Ava. "Lifting the Veil of Sisterhood: Women's Culture and Student Activism at a Southern College, 1920–1940." Master's thesis, University of North Carolina at Chapel Hill, 1989.

Dean, Pamela. "Covert Curriculum: Class, Gender, and Student Culture at a New South Woman's College, 1892–1910." Ph.D. dissertation, University of North Carolina at Chapel Hill, 1994.

———. "Learning to Be New Women: Campus Culture at the North Carolina Normal and Industrial College." *North Carolina Historical Review* 68 (July 1991): 286–306.

———. *Women on the Hill.* Chapel Hill: University of North Carolina Division of Student Affairs, 1987.

Dill, David. "The Management of Academic Culture." *Higher Education* 11 (May 1982): 303–20.

Dillon, Merton L. *Ulrich Bonnell Phillips: Historian of the Old South.* Baton Rouge: Louisiana State University Press, 1985.

Dodds, Harold Willis. *The Academic President: Educator or Caretaker?* N.Y.: McGraw-Hill, 1962.

Dolan, Eleanor F., and Margaret P. Davis. "Antinepotism Rules in American Colleges and Universities: Their Effect on the Faculty Employment of Women." *Educational Record* 41 (Oct. 1960): 285–95.

Donovan, Herman Lee. "Changing Conceptions of the College Presidency [1795– 1957]." Association of American Colleges *Bulletin* 43 (March 1957): 40–52.

Downs, Robert B. "The Role of the Academic Librarian, 1876–1976," in Richard D. Johnson, ed. *Libraries for Teaching, Libraries for Research: Essays for a Century.* Chicago: American Library Association, 1977. Pp. 115–26.

Dressel, Paul L. et al. *The Confidence Crisis.* San Francisco: Jossey-Bass, 1970.
Dressel, Paul L., and Donald J. Reichard. "The University Department: Retrospect and Prospect." *Journal of Higher Education* 41 (May 1970): 387–402.
Dunlap, Connie R. "Órganizational Patterns in Academic Libraries," in Richard D. Johnson, ed. *Libraries for Teaching, Libraries for Research: Essays for a Century.* Chicago: American Library Association, 1977. Pp. 102–14.
Durden, Robert F. *The Launching of Duke University, 1924–1949.* Durham, NC: Duke University Press, 1993.
Earnest, Ernest. *Academic Procession: An Informal History of the American College, 1636 to 1953.* Indianapolis: Bobbs-Merrill, 1953.
East, Marjorie. *Home Economics: Past, Present, and Future.* Boston: Allyn & Bacon, 1980.
Eaton, Clement. "Edwin A. Alderman—Liberal of the New South." *North Carolina Historical Review* 23 (April 1946): 206–21.
Eells, Walter Crosby. *Degrees in Higher Education.* Washington: Center for Applied Research in Education, 1963.
———. "Earned Doctorates for Women in the Nineteenth Century." *AAUP Bulletin* 42 (Winter 1956): 645–51.
———. "Norms for Honorary Degrees in American Colleges and Universities." *Educational Record* 38 (Oct. 1957): 371–81.
———, and Ernest V. Hollis. *Sabbatical Leave in American Higher Education: Origin, Early History, and Current Practices.* [Washington]: U.S. Department of Health, Education and Welfare, Office of Education, 1962.
Elliott, Peggy Gordon. *The Urban Campus: Educating the New Majority for the New Century.* Phoenix, AZ: Oryx Press, for the American Council on Education, 1994.
Fass, Paula S. *The Damned and the Beautiful: American Youth in the 1920s.* N.Y.: Oxford University Press, 1979.
———. *Outside In: Minorities and the Transformation of American Education.* N.Y.: Oxford University Press, 1989.
Fellman, David. "Religion, the State, and the Public University." *Journal of Church and State* 26 (Winter 1984): 73–90.
Ferguson, James S. "An Era of Educational Change." *North Carolina Historical Review* 46 (Spring 1969): 130–41.
Finkelstein, Barbara. "Conveying Messages to Women: Higher Education and the Teaching Profession in Historical Perspective." *American Behavioral Scientist* 32 (July–Aug. 1989): 680–96.
Finkelstein, Martin J. *The American Academic Profession: A Synthesis of Social Scientific Inquiry since World War II.* Columbis: Ohio State University Press, 1984.
Finley, William. "A Noble Tradition: Creative Writing at UNCG." *North Carolina Libraries* 57 (Summer 1999): 53–56.

Fisher, Bonnie S., and John J. Sloan III, eds. *Campus Crime: Legal, Social, and Policy Perspectives*. Springfield, IL: Charles C. Thomas, 1995.

Fisher, James L. *Power of the Presidency*. N.Y.: American Council on Education, 1984.

Flexner, Eleanor. *Century of Struggle: The Woman's Rights Movement in the United States*. Rev. ed. Cambridge: Harvard University Press, 1959.

Flora, Katie Bray. "Schooldays After 1890." College History File. UNCG Archives.

Folger, John K., and Charles B. Nam. *Education of the American Population*. Washington: Government Printing Office, 1967.

Fosdick, Raymond Blaine. *Adventure in Giving: The Story of the General Education Board*. N.Y.: Harper & Row, 1962.

Foust, Julius I. "History of the College." Julius Foust Papers, UNCG Archives.

Freeland, Richard M. *Academia's Golden Age: Universities in Massachusetts, 1945–1970*. N.Y.: Oxford University Press, 1992.

Friedlander, Amy. "A More Perfect Christian Womanhood: Higher Learning for a New South," in Ronald K. Goodnow and Arthur O. White, eds. *Education and the Rise of the New South*. Boston, G.K. Hall, 1981. Pp. 72–91.

Gallien, Louis Bertrand. "The Coeducational Transition of the Woman's College of the University of North Carolina: A Case Study in Organizational Change." Ed.D. dissertation, UNCG, 1987.

Gappa, Judith M., and David W. Leslie. *The Invisible Faculty: Improving the Status of Part-Timers in Higher Education*. San Francisco: Jossey-Bass, 1993.

Garvin, David A. *Economics of University Behavior*. N.Y.: Academic Press, 1980.

Gatewood, Willard B., Jr. *Eugene Clyde Brooks, Educator and Public Servant*. Durham, NC: Duke University Press, 1960.

———. *Preachers, Pedagogues and Politicians: The Evolution Controversy in North Carolina, 1920–1927*. Chapel Hill: University of North Carolina Press, 1966.

Geiger, Roger L. *Research and Relevant Knowledge: American Research Universities Since World War II*. N.Y.: Oxford University Press, 1993.

———. "Research Universities in a New Era: From the 1980s to the 1990s," in Arthur Levine, ed. *Higher Learning in America, 1980–2000*. Baltimore, Johns Hopkins University Press, 1993. Pp. 67–85.

———. *To Advance Knowledge: The Growth of American Research Universities, 1900–1940*. N.Y.: Oxford University Press, 1986.

Gerber, Ellen W. et al. *The American Woman in Sport*. Reading, MA: Addison-Wesley, 1974.

———. *Innovators and Institutions in Physical Education*. Philadelphia: Lea & Febiger, 1971.

Giamatti, A. Bartlett. *A Free and Ordered Space: The Real World of the University*. N.Y.: W.W. Norton, 1988.

Gibbs, Warmoth T. *History of the North Carolina Agricultural and Technical College, Greensboro, North Carolina*. Dubuque, IA: W.C. Brown, 1966.

Gilbert, Dorothy Lloyd. *Guilford: A Quaker College*. Greensboro: J.J. Stone, 1937.

Gilmore, Glenda. *Gender and Jim Crow: Women and the Politics of White Supremacy, 1896–1920*. Chapel Hill: University of North Carolina Press, 1996.

Glassberg, David. *American Historical Pageantry: The Use of Tradition in the Early Twentieth Century*. Chapel Hill: University of North Carolina Press, 1990.

Glazer-Raymo, Judith. *Shattering the Myths: Women in Academe*. Baltimore: Johns Hopkins University Press, 1999.

Gobbel, Luther L. *Church-State Relationships in Education in North Carolina Since 1776*. Durham, NC: Duke University Press, 1938.

Godwin, Winfred L. "Southern State Governments and Higher Education for Negroes." *Daedalus* 100 (Summer 1971): 783–97.

Gordon, Lynn D. *Gender and Higher Education in the Progressive Era*. New Haven: Yale University Press, 1990.

Gordon, Margaret. "The Economy and Higher Education," in Arthur Levine, ed. *Higher Learning in America, 1980–2000*. Baltimore: Johns Hopkins University Press, 1993. Pp. 20–35.

Graham, Patricia Albjerg. "Expansion and Exclusion: A History of Women in American Higher Education." *Signs* 3, no. 4 (1978): 759–73.

Grobman, Arnold B. *Urban State Universities: An Unfinished National Agenda*. N.Y.: Praeger, 1988.

Gruber, Carol S. *Mars and Minerva: World War I and the Uses of Higher Learning in America*. Baton Rouge: Louisiana State University Press, 1975.

Guttmann, Allen. *Women's Sports: A History*. N.Y.: Columbia University Press, 1991.

Hackensmith, Charles William. *History of Physical Education*. N.Y.: Harper & Row, 1966.

Halpern, Stephen C. *On the Limits of the Law: The Ironic Legacy of Title VI of the 1964 Civil Rights Act*. Baltimore: Johns Hopkins University Press, 1995.

Hamlin, Arthur T. *The University Library in the United States: Its Origins and Development*. Philadelphia: University of Pennsylvania Press, 1981.

Hammond, Phillip E., John W. Meyer, and David Miller. "Teaching Versus Research: Sources of Misperceptions." *Journal of Higher Education* 40 (Dec. 1969): 682–90.

Harlan, Louis R. *Separate and Unequal: Public School Campaigns and Racism in the Southern Seaboard States, 1901–1915*. Chapel Hill: University of North Carolina Press, 1958.

Harper, Charles A. *A Century of Public Teacher Education: The Story of the State Teachers Colleges as They Evolved from the Normal Schools*. Washington: National Education Association, 1939.

Harris, Nelson H. "Publicly-Supported Negro Institutions in North Carolina." *Journal of Negro Education* 31 (Summer 1962): 284–92.

Hart, D.G. *The University Gets Religion: Religious Studies in American Higher Education*. Baltimore: Johns Hopkins University Press, 1999.

Hastings, Philip K., and Dean R. Hoge. "Religious and Moral Attitude Trends Among College Students, 1948–84." *Social Forces* 65 (Dec. 1986): 370–77.
Hefferlin, J.B. Lon. *Dynamics of Academic Reform*. San Francisco: Jossey-Bass, 1969.
Heilbron, Louis H. *The College and University Trustee: A View from the Board Room*. San Francisco: Jossey-Bass, 1973.
Heineman, Kenneth J. *Campus Wars: The Peace Movement at American State Universities in the Vietnam Era*. N.Y.: New York University Press, 1993.
Hendrick, Irving G. "Teacher Education and Leadership in Major Universities," in John I. Goodlad et al., eds. *Places Where Teachers are Taught*. San Francisco: Jossey-Bass, 1990.
Herbst, Jurgen. *And Sadly Teach: Teacher Education and Professionalization in American Culture*. Madison: University of Wisconsin Press, 1989.
———. "Liberal Education and the Graduate Schools: An Historical View of College Reform." *History of Education Quarterly* 2 (Dec. 1962): 244–58.
———. "Nineteenth-Century Normal Schools in the United States: A Fresh Look." *History of Education* (London) 9 (Sept. 1980): 219–27.
———. "Teacher Preparation in the Nineteenth Century: Institutions and Purposes," in Donald Warren, ed. *American Teachers: Histories of a Profession at Work*. N.Y.: Macmillan, 1989. Pp. 213–36.
Hexter, J.H. "Publish or Perish—A Defense." *Public Interest* 17 (Fall 1969), 60–77.
Hodgkinson, Harold. *Institutions in Transition: A Profile of Change in Higher Education*. N.Y.: McGraw-Hill, 1971.
Hoffschwelle, Mary S. "The Science of Domesticity: Home Economics at George Peabody College for Teachers, 1914–1939." *Journal of Southern History* 57 (Nov. 1991), 659–80.
Hofstadter, Richard, and Walter P. Metzger. *The Development of Academic Freedom in the United States*. N.Y.: Columbia University Press, 1955.
Holder, Elizabeth Jerome. "History of the Library of the Woman's College of the University of North Carolina, 1892–1945." Master's thesis, University of North Carolina at Chapel Hill, 1955.
Holder, Rose Howell. *McIver of North Carolina*. Chapel Hill: University of North Carolina Press, 1957.
Hollinger, David A. *Science, Jews, and Secular Culture: Studies in Mid-Twentieth-Century American Intellectual History*. Princeton: Princeton University Press, 1996.
Horowitz, Helen Lefkowitz. *Alma Mater: Design and Experience in the Women's Colleges from their 19th Century Beginnings to the 1930s*. N.Y.: Knopf, 1984.
———. *Campus Life: Undergraduate Cultures from the End of the Eighteenth Century to the Present*. N.Y.: Knopf, 1987.
———. "Designing for the Genders: Curricula and Architecture at Scripps College and the California Institute of Technology." *Pacific Historical Review* 54 (Nov. 1985): 439–61.

———. "Smith College and Changing Conceptions of Educated Women," in Ronald Storey, ed. *Five Colleges: Five Histories*. Amherst: University of Massachusetts Press, 1992. Pp. 79–102.

Hull, W. Frank, IV. "The Public University Trustee." *Teachers College Record* 75 (May 1974): 527–39.

Jamison, Minnie L. Diary. Faculty File. UNCG Archives.

Jeffreys-Jones, Rhodri. *Changing Differences: Women and the Shaping of American Foreign Policy, 1917–1994*. New Brunswick, NJ: Rutgers University Press, 1995.

Jencks, Christopher, and David Riesman. *The Academic Revolution*. N.Y.: Doubleday, 1968.

Johnson, Daniel M., and David A. Bell, eds. *Metropolitan Universities: An Emerging Model in American Higher Education*. Denton, TX: University of North Texas Press, 1995.

Johnson, Elmer. "James Yadkin Joyner, Educational Statesman." *North Carolina Historical Review* 33 (July 1956): 359–83.

Johnson, George E., and Frank P. Stafford. "The Earnings and Promotion of Women Faculty." *American Economic Review* 64 Dec. 1974): 888–903.

Johnson, Gerald W. "The Cadets of New Market." *Harpers Magazine* 160 (Dec. 1929): 111–19.

Johnson, Henry C., Jr., and Erwin V. Johanningmeier. *Teachers for the Prairie: The University of Illinois and the Schools, 1868–1945*. Urbana: University of Illinois Press, 1972.

Johnson, William R. "Teachers and Teacher Training in the Twentieth Century," in Donald Warren, ed. *American Teachers: Histories of a Profession at Work*. N.Y.: Macmillan, 1989. Pp. 237–56.

Jones, Deborah Elaine. "A History of Women's Intercollegiate Athletics at the University of North Carolina at Greensboro." Master's thesis, UNCG, 1982.

Jordan, Paula S. *Women of Guilford County, North Carolina: A Study of Women's Contributions, 1740–1979*. Greensboro: Women of Guilford, 1979.

Junk, Cheryl Fradette. "The Waiting Task: The Concept of Service at Woman's College, 1919–1941." *Inquiry* (UNCG Honors Program publication) 1 (Spring 1992): 1–13.

Karabell, Zachary. *What's College For? The Struggle to Define American Higher Education*. N.Y.: Basic Books, 1998.

Kaser, David. Á Century of Academic Librarianship, As Reflected in its Literature," in Richard D. Johnson, ed. *Libraries for Teaching, Libraries for Research: Essays for a Century*. Chicago: American Library Association, 1977. Pp. 219–36.

———. "Collection Building in American Universities," in James Thompson, ed. *University Library History: An International Review*. N.Y.: K.G. Saur, 1980. Pp. 33–55.

———. "Twenty-Five Years of Academic Library Building Planning." *College and Research Libraries* 45 (July 1984): 268–81.

Kearney, Deirdre S. "All Out For Victory: Woman's College and the Impact of the War, 1937–1947. Seminar paper, 1992. UNCG Archives.

Keast, William R., and John W. Macy, Jr., eds. *Faculty Tenure.* San Francisco: Jossey-Bass, 1973.

Keeton, Morris. "The Constituencies and Their Claims," in Gary L. Riley and J. Victor Baldridge, eds. *Governing Academic Organizations.* Berkeley, CA: McCutchan, 1977. Pp. 194–210.

Keller, George. *Academic Strategy: The Management Revolution in American Higher Education.* Baltimore: Johns Hopkins University Press, 1983.

Kelly, Robert L. *The American Colleges and the Social Order.* N.Y.: Macmillan, 1940.

Kennedy, Donald. "Making Choices in the Research University." *Daedalus* 122 (Fall 1993): 127–56.

Keohane, Nannerl O. "Educating Women Students for the Future," in Joyce Antler and Sari K. Biklen, eds. *Changing Education: Women as Radicals and Conservatives.* Albany: State University of New York Press, 1990. Pp. 3–11.

Kerr, Clark. *The Uses of the University.* 2d ed. Cambridge: Harvard University Press, 1972.

Kimmel, Herbert. "A Catalogue Study of the Faculty of the Woman's College of the University of North Carolina, 1892–1940." *Peabody Journal of Education* 20 (Sept. 1942).

King, Arnold K. *The Multicampus University of North Carolina Comes of Age, 1956–1986.* Chapel Hill: University of North Carolina Press, 1986.

King, William E. "Charles McIver Fights for the Tarheel Negro's Right to an Education." *North Carolina Historical Review* 41 July 1964): 360–69.

Kipp, Samuel M. "Old Notables and Newcomers: The Economic and Political Elite of Greensboro, North Carolina, 1890–1920." *Journal of Southern History* 43 (Aug. 1977): 373–94.

Kleinbaum, David G., and Anna Kleinbaum. "The Minority Experience at a Predominantly White University—A Report of a 1972 Survey at the University of North Carolina at Chapel Hill." *Journal of Negro Education* 45 (Summer 1976): 312–28.

Knight, Edgar Wallace. *Public School Education in North Carolina.* Boston, N.Y.: Houghton Mifflin, 1916.

Kousser, J. Morgan. "Progressivism—For Middle-Class Whites Only: North Carolina Education, 1880–1910." *Journal of Southern History* 46 (May 1980): 169–94.

Ladd, Everett C., Jr., et al. *Professors, Unions, and American Higher Education.* [Berkeley, CA: Carnegie Commission on Higher Education, 1973].

Lagemann, Ellen Condliffe. *The Politics of Knowledge: The Carnegie Corporation, Philanthropy, and Public Policy.* Middletown, CT: Wesleyan University Press, 1989.

Lamont, Lansing. *Campus Shock: A First-Hand Report on College Life Today.* N.Y.: Dutton, 1979.

Largent, Vera. "Harriet Wiseman Elliott," in Edward T. James and Janet James, eds. *Notable American Women, 1607–1950: A Biographical Dictionary.* Cambridge: Harvard University Press, 1971. Vol. I, pp. 572–74.

Lathrop, Virginia Terrell. *Educate a Woman: Fifty Years of Life at Woman's College.* Chapel Hill: University of North Carolina Press, 1942.

Le Blanc, M. Elizabeth. "The Concept of General Education in Colleges and Universities, 1945–1979." Ed.D. dissertation, Rutgers University, 1980.

Le Duc, Thomas. *Piety and Intellect at Amherst College, 1865–1912.* N.Y.: Columbia University Press, 1946.

Lee, Calvin B.T. *Campus Scene, 1900–1970: Changing Styles in Undergraduate Life.* N.Y.: David McKay, 1970.

Lee, Mabel, "The Case For and Against Intercollegiate Athletics for Women," in Arthur Weston, ed. *The Making of American Physical Education.* N.Y.: Appleton-Century-Crofts, 1962.

Leloudis, James L. "School Reform in the New South: The Woman's Association for the Betterment of Public School Houses in North Carolina, 1902–1919." *Journal of American History* 69 (March 1983): 886–909.

———. *Schooling the New South: Pedagogy, Self, and Society in North Carolina, 1880–1920.* Chapel Hill: University of North Carolina Press, 1996.

Leslie, David W. et al. *Part-Time Faculty in American Higher Education.* N.Y.: Praeger, 1982.

Leslie, W. Bruce. *Gentlemen and Scholars: College and Community in the "Age of the University."* University Park, PA: Pennsylvania State University Press, 1992.

Levine, Arthur. "Diversity on Campus," in Levine, ed. *Higher Learning in America.* Baltimore, Johns Hopkins University Press, 1993. Pp. 333–43.

———. "How the Academic Profession is Changing." *Daedalus* 126 (Fall 1997): 1–20.

———, and John Weingart. *Reform of Undergraduate Education.* San Francisco: Jossey-Bass, 1973.

Levine, David O. *The American College and the Culture of Aspiration, 1915–1940.* Ithaca, NY: Cornell University Press, 1986.

Lewis, Charles Lee. *Philander Priestley Claxton: Crusader for Public Education.* Knoxville: University of Tennessee Press, 1948.

Lewis, Lionel S. *Marginal Worth: Teaching and the Academic Labor Market.* New Brunswick, NJ: Transaction Publishers, 1996.

Link, Susannah J. *Harriet Elliott: A Brief Appreciation.* [Greensboro: University of North Carolina at Greensboro], 1998.

Link, William A. *A Hard Country and a Lonely Place: Schooling, Society, and Reform in Rural Virginia, 1870–1920.* Chapel Hill: University of North Carolina Press, 1986.

———. *The Paradox of Southern Progressivism, 1880–1930.* Chapel Hill: University of North Carolina Press, 1992.

———. "William Friday and the North Carolina Speaker Ban Crisis, 1963–1968." *North Carolina Historical Review* 72 (April 1995): 198–228.

———. *William Friday: Power, Purpose, and American Higher Education.* Chapel Hill: University of North Carolina Press, 1995.

Lipset, Seymour Martin, "The Activists: A Profile," in Daniel Bell and Irving Kristol, eds. *Confrontation: The Student Rebellion and the Universities.* N.Y.: Basic Books, 1969.

Lockmiller, David A. *The Consolidation of the University of North Carolina.* Chapel Hill: University of North Carolina Press, 1942.

Loeb, Paul Rogat. *Generation at the Crossroads: Apathy and Action on the American Campus.* New Brunswick, NJ: Rutgers University Press, 1994.

Logan, Frenise. "The Movement in North Carolina to Establish a State Supported College for Negroes." *North Carolina Historical Review* 35 (April 1958): 167–80.

Lojko, Gloria Jean. "The Effects of Societal and Cultural Changes on the Historical Development of the Athletic Association at the State Normal and Industrial College." Master's thesis, Appalachian State University, 1983.

Lowell, Robert, Peter Taylor, and Robert Penn Warren, eds. *Randall Jarrell, 1914–1965.* N.Y.: Farrar, Straus & Giroux, 1967.

Lucas, Christopher J. *Crisis in the Academy: Rethinking Higher Education in America.* N.Y.: St. Martin's Press, 1996.

Lyon, E. Wilson. "The University in the South." *Virginia Quarterly Review* 44 (summer 1968): 458–69.

Lyons, James E. "The Adjustment of Black Students to Predominantly White Campuses." *Journal of Negro Education* 42 (Fall 1973): 462–66.

Malone, Dumas. *Edwin A. Alderman.* N.Y.: Doubleday, Doran, 1940.

Marsden, George M. *The Soul of the American University: From Protestant Establishment to Established Nonbelief.* N.Y.: Oxford University Press, 1994.

Matthews, Glenna. *"Just a Housewife": The Rise and Fall of Domesticity in America.* N.Y.: Oxford University Press, 1987.

Maxcy, Spencer J. "Progressivism and Rural Education in the Deep South, 1900–1950," in Ronald K. Goodenow and Arthur O. White, eds. *Education and the Rise of the New South.* Boston: G.K. Hall, 1981. Pp. 47–71.

Mayhew, Lewis B. "Neighboring Black and White Colleges: A Study in Waste." *Educational Record* 52 (Spring 1971): 159–64.

McCandless, Amy Thompson. *The Past in the Present: Women's Higher Education in the Twentieth-Century American South.* Tuscaloosa: University of Alabama Press, 1999.

———. "Preserving the Pedestal: Restrictions on Social Life at Southern Colleges for Women, 1920–1940." *History of Higher Education Annual* 7 (1987): 45–67.

———. Progressivism and the Higher Education of Southern Women." *North Carolina Historical Review* 70 (July 1993): 302–25.

McGrath, Earl J. *Are Liberal Arts Colleges Becoming Professional Schools?* N.Y.: Teachers College, Columbia University, 1958.

McIver, Charles D. "Current Problems in North Carolina." *Annals of the American Academy of Political and Social Science* 22 (June–Dec. 1903): 293–303.

McLaughlin, Judith Block, and David Riesman. "The President: A Precarious Perch," in Arthur Levine, ed. *Higher Learning in America, 1980–2000*. Baltimore: Johns Hopkins University Press, 1993. Pp. 179–202.

Means, Richard K. *A History of Health Education in the United States*. Philadelphia: Lea & Febiger, 1962.

Metzger, Walter P. "Academic Tenure in America: A Historical Essay," in Commission on Academic Tenure in Higher Education. *Faculty Tenure*. San Francisco: Jossey-Bass, 1973. Pp. 93–159.

Meyer, J.W. et al. "Public Education as Nation-Building in America: Enrollments and Bureaucratization in the American States, 1870–1930." *American Journal of Sociology* 85 (Nov. 1979): 591–613.

Meyers, Jeffrey. "The Death of Randall Jarrell." *Virginia Quarterly Review* 58 (Summer 1982): 450–67.

Miller, Gary E. *The Meaning of General Education: The Emergence of a Curriculum Paradigm*. N.Y.: Teachers College Press, 1988.

Millett, John D. *The Academic Community: An Essay on Organization*. N.Y.: McGraw-Hill, 1962.

Mitchell, Theodore R. "From Black to White: The Transformation of Educational Reform in the New South, 1890–1910." *Educational Theory* 39 (Fall 1989): 337–50.

Moran, William E. "The Study of University Organizations." *Journal of Higher Education* 39 (March 1968): 144–51.

Morehead, James T. "DeWitt Clinton Benbow," in Bettie D. Caldwell, ed. *Founders and Builders of Greensboro, 1808–1908*. Greensboro: J.J. Stone, 1925.

Morrison, Jack. *The Rise of the Arts on the American Campus*. N.Y.: McGraw-Hill, 1973.

Morrison, Joseph L. *Governor O. Max Gardner: A Power in North Carolina and New Deal Washington*. Chapel Hill: University of North Carolina Press, 1971.

Newby, Idus A. *Plain Folk in the New South: Social Change and Cultural Persistence, 1880–1915*. Baton Rouge: Louisiana State University Press, 1989.

Newcomer, Mabel. *A Century of Higher Education for American Women*. N.Y.: Harper, 1959.

Nichols, Rodney W. "Federal Science Policy and Universities: Consequences of Success." *Daedalus* 122 (Fall 1993): 197–224.

Nowak, Marion. "'How to Be a Woman': Theories of Female Education in the 1950's." *Journal of Popular Culture* 9 (Summer 1975): 77–83.

Oates, Mary J., and Susan Williamson. "Women's Colleges and Women Achievers." *Signs* 3 (Summer 1978): 795–806.

O'Neill, Marion. "A History of the Physical Education Department at the Woman's College of the University of North Carolina." Master's thesis, Woman's College, 1955.

Orr, Oliver Hamilton, Jr. *Charles Brantley Aycock.* Chapel Hill: University of North Carolina Press, 1961.

———. *Saving American Birds: T. Gilbert Pearson and the Founding of the Audubon Movement.* Gainesville: University of Florida Press, 1992.

Page, Walter Hines. "Charles D. McIver." *South Atlantic Quarterly* 5 (Oct. 1906): 389–92.

———. "McIver, a Leader of the People." *World's Work* 13 (Dec. 1906): 8265–67.

———. *The Rebuilding of Old Commonwealths, Being Essays towards the Training of the Forgotten Man in the Southern States.* N.Y.: Doubleday, Page, 1902.

Palamountain, Joseph C. "Power Structures in the University." *Antioch Review* 26 (Fall 1966): 299–306.

Palmieri, Patricia Ann. *In Adamless Eden: The Community of Women Faculty at Wellesley.* New Haven: Yale University Press, 1995.

Pangburn, Jessie M. *The Evolution of the American Teachers College.* N.Y.: Teachers College, Columbia University, 1932.

Partridge, Arthur R. "The Rise of the University School of Education as a Professional Institution." Ed.D. dissertation, Stanford University, 1958.

Powell, Benjamin E. "Collection Development in Southeastern Libraries since 1948." *Southeastern Librarian* 24 (Winter 1975): 59–67.

Prather, A. Leon, Sr. *Resurgent Politics and Educational Progressivism in the New South: North Carolina, 1890–1913.* Rutherford, NJ: Fairleigh Dickinson University Press, 1979.

Pritchard, William H. *Randall Jarrell: A Literary Life.* N.Y.: Farrar, Straus & Giroux, 1990.

Quinn, Sister M. Bernetta. *Randall Jarrell.* Boston: Twayne, 1981.

Ravitch, Diane. *The Schools We Deserve: Reflections on the Educational Crisis of our Times.* N.Y.: Basic Books, 1985.

———. *The Troubled Crusade: American Education, 1945–1980.* N.Y.: Basic Books, 1983.

Record, Wilson. "Some Implications of the Black Studies Movement for Higher Education in the 1970s." *Journal of Higher Education* 44 (March 1973): 191–216.

Requardt, Cynthia Horsburgh. "Alternative Professions for Goucher College Graduates, 1892–1910." *Maryland Historical Magazine* 74 (Fall 1979): 274–81.

Reynolds, Helen Margaret. "University Library Buildings in the United States, 1890–1939." *College and Research Libraries* 14 (April 1953): 149–57, 166.

Rice, Emmett Ainsworth et al., *A Brief History of Physical Education*. 5th ed. N.Y.: Ronald Press, 1969.
Riesman, David. *On Higher Education: The Academic Enterprise in an Era of Rising Student Consumerism*. San Francisco, Jossey-Bass, 1980.
Riley, Gary L. "Student Participation in Governance: A Review of the Literature," in Riley and J. Victor Baldridge, eds. *Governing Academic Organizations*. Berkeley, CA: McCutchan, 1977. Pp. 239–50.
Roberts, Roy W. *Vocational and Practical Arts Education: History, Development, and Principles*. 3d ed. N.Y.: Harper & Row, 1971.
Robinson, Richard H., Jr. "Betty Brown Jester." *Alumni News* 82 (Summer 1994): 41.
Roper, John Herbert. *U.B. Phillips: A Southern Mind*. Macon, GA: Mercer University Press, 1984.
Rosovsky, Henry. *The University: An Owner's Manual*. N.Y.: W.W. Norton, 1990.
Rossiter, Margaret W. *Women Scientists in America: Before Affirmative Action, 1940–1972*. Baltimore: Johns Hopkins University Press, 1995.
———. *Women Scientists in America: Struggles and Strategies to 1940*. Baltimore: Johns Hopkins University Press, 1982.
Rothstein, Samuel. "Service to Academia," in Sidney L. Jackson, ed. *A Century of Service: Librarianship in the United States and Canada*. Chicago: American Library Association, 1976. Pp. 79–109.
Rourke, Francis Edward, and Glenn E. Brooks. *The Managerial Revolution in Higher Education*. Baltimore: Johns Hopkins University Press, 1966.
Rudolph, Frederick. *The American College and University: A History*. 1962. Reprint ed. Athens: University of Georgia Press, 1990.
———. *Curriculum: A History of the American Undergraduate Course of Study Since 1636*. San Francisco: Jossey-Bass, 1977.
Rugg, Harold Ordway. *The Teacher of Teachers: Frontiers of Theory and Practice in Teacher Education*. N.Y.: Harper, 1952.
Rury, John L. *Education and Women's Work: Female Schooling and the Division of Labor in Urban America, 1870–1930*. Albany: State University of New York Press, 1991.
———. "Vocationalism for Home and Work: Women's Education in the United States, 1880–1930." *History of Education Quarterly* 24 (Spring 1984): 21–44.
———. "Who Became Teachers?: The Social Characteristics of Teachers in American History," in Donald Warren, ed. *American Teachers: Histories of a Profession at Work*. N.Y.: Macmillan, 1989. Pp. 9–48.
Sampson, Elizabeth. "After the Fire: Rebuilding the Catalog of the Woman's College Library." *Wilson Library Bulletin* 21 (Feb. 1947): 434–35.
Satterfield, Frances Gibson. *Charles Duncan McIver, 1860–1906*. Atlanta: Ruralist Press, 1942.
Schmidt, George P. *The Liberal Arts College: A Chapter in American Cultural History*. New Brunswick, NJ: Rutgers University Press, 1957.

Schrag, Peter. "End of the Second Chance?, The Crusade Against Remedial Education." *American Prospect* 11 (May–June 1999): 68–74.
Scott, Anne Firor. *The Southern Lady from Pedestal to Politics, 1880–1930.* Chicago: University of Chicago Press, 1970.
Selden, William K. *Accreditation: A Struggle Over Standards in Higher Education.* N.Y.: Harper, 1960.
Sellers, Charles Grier, Jr. "Walter Hines Page and the Spirit of the New South." *North Carolina Historical Review* 29 (Oct. 1952): 481–99.
Shiflett, Orvin L. *The Origins of American Academic Librarianship.* Norwood, NJ: Ablex, 1981.
Shulman, James L., and William G. Bowen, *The Game of Life: College Sports and Educational Values* Princeton: Princeton University Press, 2001.
Smith, Page. *Killing the Spirit: Higher Education in America.* N.Y.: Penguin, 1990.
[Smith, William Cunningham, ed.] *Charles Duncan McIver, Born September 27, 1860, Died September 17, 1906.* Greensboro: J.J. Stone, [1907].
———. "Charles Duncan McIver." *State Normal Magazine* 11 (Nov. 1906): 67–81.
———. *Mary Settle Sharpe: The Story of a Useful and Beautiful Life.* [Philadelphia: Stackhouse, 192?]. In UNCG Archives.
———. "The North Carolina State Normal and Industrial College." North Carolina Historical Commission *Publications* 1 (1907): 150–67.
Solberg, Winton U. *The University of Illinois, 1867–1894: An Institutional and Cultural History.* Urbana: University of Illinois Press, 1968.
Solomon, Barbara M. *In the Company of Educated Women: A History of Women and Higher Education in America.* New Haven: Yale University Press, 1985.
"Statement from the Conference on the Growing Use of Part-Time and Adjunct Faculty." *Academe* 84 (Jan.–Feb. 1998): 54–60.
Stigler, Stephen M. "Competition and the Research Universities." *Daedalus* 122 (Fall 1993): 157–77.
Stricker, Frank. "American Professors in the Progressive Era: Incomes, Aspirations, and Professionalism." *Journal of Interdisciplinary History* 19 (Autumn 1988): 231–57.
———. "Economic Success and Academic Professionalization: Questions from Two Decades of U.S. History (1908–1929)." *Social Science History* 12 (Summer 1988): 143–70.
Strobel, Marion Elizabeth. "Ideology and Women's Higher Education, 1945–1960." Ph.D. dissertation, Duke University, 1975.
Strober, Myra H., and Audri Gordon Lanford. "The Feminization of Public School Teaching: Cross-Sectional Analysis, 1850–1880." *Signs* 11 (Winter 1986): 212–35.
Sunderman, Lloyd Frederick. *Historical Foundations of Music Education in the United States.* Metuchen, NJ: Scarecrow Press, 1971.
Swain, Martha H. *Ellen S. Woodward: New Deal Advocate for Women.* Jackson: University Press of Mississippi, 1995.

Taylor, A. Elizabeth. "The Woman Suffrage Movement in North Carolina." *North Carolina Historical Review* 38 (Jan., April 1961): 45–62, 173–89.

Taylor, Frances S. "'On the Edge of Tomorrow': Southern Women, the Student YWCA, and Race, 1920–1944." Ph.D. dissertation, Stanford University, 1984.

Tellstrom, A. Theodore. *Music in American Education, Past and Present.* N.Y.: Holt, Rinehart & Winston, 1971.

Thomas, Russell Brown. *The Search for a Common Learning: General Education, 1800–1960.* N.Y.: McGraw-Hill, 1962.

Tindall, George Brown. *The Emergence of the New South, 1913–1945.* Baton Rouge: Louisiana State University Press, 1967.

Trelease, Allen W. *Changing Assignments: A Pictorial History of The University of North Carolina at Greensboro.* Greensboro: UNCG, 1991.

Turner, Paul Venable. *Campus: An American Planning Tradition.* Rev. ed. Cambridge, MA: Massachusetts Institute of Technology Press, 1990.

Turrentine, Samuel Bryant. *A Romance of Education.* Greensboro: Piedmont Press, 1946.

Tyack, David B., ed. *Turning Points in American Education History.* Waltham, MA: Blaisdell, 1967.

———, ed. *Work, Youth, and Schooling: Historical Perspectives on Vocationalism in American Education.* Stanford, CA: Stanford University Press, 1982.

Umstead, Elizabeth Claire. "Mary Channing Coleman: Her Life and Contributions to Health, Physical Education and Recreation." Ph.D. dissertation, University of North Carolina at Chapel Hill, 1967.

Veysey, Laurence R. *The Emergence of the American University.* Chicago: University of Chicago Press, 1965.

Vincenti, Virginia B. "Home Economics Moves Into the Twenty-First Century," in Sarah Stage and Virginia B. Vincenti, eds. *Rethinking Home Economics: Women and the History of a Profession.* Ithaca, NY: Cornell University Press, 1997. Pp. 301–20.

Waldron, Ann. *Close Connections: Caroline Gordon and the Southern Renaissance.* N.Y.: Putnam, 1987.

Walters, Everett. "The Rise of Graduate Education," in Lewis B. Mayhew, ed. *Higher Education in the Revolutionary Decades.* Berkeley, CA: McCutchan, 1967. Pp. 127–37.

Ware, Susan. *Beyond Suffrage: Women in the New Deal.* Cambridge: Harvard University Press, 1981.

———. *Holding Their Own: American Women in the 1930s.* Boston: Twayne, 1982.

———. *Partner and I: Molly Dewson, Feminism, and New Deal Politics.* New Haven: Yale University Press, 1987.

Watson, Jan Carole. "Ethel Loroline Martus Lawther: Her Contributions to Physical Education." Ed.D. dissertation, UNCG, 1980.

Webb, Hanor A. "To Train a Teacher." *Peabody Journal of Education* 37 (Nov. 1959): 132–44.

Wechsler, Harold S. *The Qualified Student: A History of Selective College Admission in America.* N.Y.: Wiley, 1977.

Wells, Herbert. "Undergraduate Admissions to the University of North Carolina at Greensboro: A Review of Recent Policies and Data." 1975. In possession of Herbert Wells, Greensboro, N.C.

West, Martha S. "Women Faculty, Frozen in Time." *Academe* 81 (July/Aug. 1995): 26–29.

Wilson, Louis Round. *The University of North Carolina, 1900–1930: The Making of a Modern University.* Chapel Hill: University of North Carolina Press, 1957.

———. *The University of North Carolina under Consolidation, 1931–1963: History and Appraisal.* Chapel Hill: University of North Carolina Consolidated Office, 1964.

Wolff, Miles. *Lunch at the 5 & 10.* Rev. ed. Chicago: Ivan R. Dee, 1990.

Wolff, Robert Paul. *The Ideal of the University.* Boston: Beacon Press, 1969.

Woodward, C. Vann. *Origins of the New South, 1877–1913.* Baton Rouge: Louisiana State University Press, 1951.

Woody, Thomas. *A History of Women's Education in the United States.* 2v. N.Y.: Science Press, 1929.

Wyche, Mary L. *The History of Nursing in North Carolina.* Chapel Hill: University of North Carolina Press, 1938.

Young, Elizabeth B. *A Study of the Curricula of Seven Selected Women's Colleges of the Southern States.* N.Y.: Teachers College, Columbia University, 1932.

Ziegler, Jerome M. "Continuing Education in the University." *Daedalus* 93 (Fall 1964): 1162–83.

Zilversmit, Arthur. *Changing Schools: Progressive Education Theory and Practice, 1930–1960.* Chicago: University of Chicago Press, 1993.

Zschoche, Sue. "Preserving Eden: Higher Education, Woman's Sphere, and the First Generation of College Women, 1870–1910." Ph.D. dissertation, University of Kansas, 1984.

Index